LIBRARY OF HEBREW BIBLE/
OLD TESTAMENT STUDIES

270

Formerly Journal for the Study of the Old Testament Supplement Series

Editors
David J. A. Clines
Philip R. Davies

Executive Editor
John Jarick

Editorial Board

KING AND MESSIAH IN ISRAEL
AND THE ANCIENT NEAR EAST

edited by

John Day

B L O O M S B U R Y

LONDON · NEW DELHI · NEW YORK · SYDNEY

I am grateful to the following publishers for permission to reproduce illustrations on pp. 139-41: to Vandenhoeck & Ruprecht of Göttingen for Figures 1 and 4 (From B.I. Reicke and L. Rost [eds.], *Biblisch-Historisches Handwörterbuch*, II [1964], cols. 999-1000, and III [1966], cols. 1977-78); to Verlag Dietrich Reimer, Berlin, for Figures 2 and 3 (from *Archaeologische Mitteilungen aus Iran* NS 7 [1974], p. 149, Abb. 1 and p.155, Abb. 2).

Bloomsbury T&T Clark

An imprint of Bloomsbury Publishing Plc

50 Bedford Square
London
WC1B 3DP
UK

175 Fifth Avenue
New York
NY 10010
USA

www.bloomsbury.com

First published by Sheffield Academic Press 1998
Paperback edition first published 2013

British Library Cataloguing-in-Publication Data
A catalogue record for this book is available from the British Library.

ISBN: HB: 978-1-850-75946-1
PB: 978-0-567-57434-3

Library of Congress Cataloging-in-Publication Data
A catalog record for this book is available from the Library of Congress

CONTENTS

Part III
THE MESSIAH IN POSTBIBLICAL JUDAISM
AND THE NEW TESTAMENT

PREFACE

The Oxford Old Testament Seminar has been meeting regularly every fortnight in term time for many years, with papers presented on a wide range of subjects by scholars working within Oxford, as well as by research students and visiting scholars from elsewhere in Britain and abroad. The programme is generally arranged by the Oriel Professor (currently John Barton). Never before, however, has the Seminar produced a collective volume for publication. For three whole academic years, from October 1994 till June 1997, John Barton generously allowed me to take over half the time of the Seminar's programme with papers that I had arranged on the theme of 'King and Messiah', most of which are included in this volume. This particular theme was chosen because of its capacity to draw in a large number of Old Testament scholars, as well as ancient Near Eastern experts and scholars in post-biblical Judaism and the New Testament. This project has therefore been a useful exercise in interdisciplinary cooperation. About half of the contributors are currently in Oxford, but most of them were at Oxford when the idea for the volume was conceived (some having moved on elsewhere), and a few were invited from outside (see the List of Contributors).

I am most grateful to all who have participated in this project and helped to make it so worthwhile. I am particularly grateful to Carol Smith, one of the contributors, who has provided me with valuable assistance prior to the work's submission to the Press, and during the process of publication. To her and all at Sheffield Academic Press who have been involved in the production of this work I express my sincere thanks.

John Day

ABBREVIATIONS

AB	Anchor Bible
ABD	David Noel Freedman (ed.), *The Anchor Bible Dictionary* (New York: Doubleday, 1992)
AcOr	*Acta orientalia*
AfO	Archiv für Orientforschung
AGJU	Arbeiten zur Geschichte des Antiken Judentums und des Urchrisentums
AH	Ancient Hebrew
AJSL	American Journal of Semitic Languages and Literatures
AnBib	Analecta biblica
ANEP	James B. Pritchard (ed.), *The Ancient Near East in Pictures Relating to the Old Testament* (Princeton: Princeton University Press, 1954)
ANET	James B. Pritchard (ed.), *Ancient Near Eastern Texts Relating to the Old Testament* (Princeton: Princeton University Press, 3rd edn, with supplement, 1969)
AnOr	Analecta orientalia
AOAT	Alter Orient und Altes Testament
AOS	American Oriental Series
ATANT	Abhandlungen zur Theologie des Alten und Neuen Testaments
ATD	Das Alte Testament Deutsch
AusBR	*Australian Biblical Review*
AUSS	*Andrews University Seminary Studies*
AV	Authorized Version
BASOR	*Bulletin of the American Schools of Oriental Research*
BDB	Francis Brown, S.R. Driver and Charles A. Briggs, *A Hebrew and English Lexicon of the Old Testament* (Oxford: Clarendon Press, 1907)
BBB	Bonner biblische Beiträge
BETL	Bibliotheca ephemeridum theologicarum lovaniensium
BEvT	Beiträge zur evangelischen Theologie
Bib	*Biblica*
BibInt	*Biblical Interpretation: A Journal of Contemporary Approaches*
BibOr	Biblica et orientalia

BKAT	Biblischer Kommentar: Altes Testament
BN	*Biblische Notizen*
BNTC	Black's New Testament Commentaries
BO	*Bibliotheca orientalis*
BSOAS	*Bulletin of the School of Oriental and African Studies*
BWANT	Beiträge zur Wissenschaft vom Alten und Neuen Testament
BZ	*Biblische Zeitschrift*
BZAW	Beihefte zur *ZAW*
CAT	Commentaire de l'Ancien Testament
CBQ	*Catholic Biblical Quarterly*
CBQMS	Catholic Biblical Quarterly Monograph Series
ConBOT	Coniectanea biblica, Old Testament
DJD	Discoveries in the Judaean Desert
DNEB	Die neue Echter Bibel
DSD	Dead Sea Discoveries
DtrH	Deuteronomistic History
ÉBib	Études bibliques
EncJud	*Encyclopaedia Judaica*
EstBíb	*Estudios bíblicos*
ET	English translation
FzB	Forschung zur Bibel
FOTL	The Forms of the Old Testament Literature
FRLANT	Forschungen zur Religion und Literatur des Alten und Neuen Testaments
GKC	*Gesenius' Hebrew Grammar* (ed. E. Kautzsch, revised and trans. A.E. Cowley; Oxford: Clarendon Press, 1910)
HAR	*Hebrew Annual Review*
HAT	Handbuch zum Alten Testament
HKAT	Handkommentar zum Alten Testament
HSM	Harvard Semitic Monographs
HSS	Harvard Semitic Studies
HTR	*Harvard Theological Review*
IB	*Interpreter's Bible*
ICC	International Critical Commentary
IEJ	*Israel Exploration Journal*
Int	*Interpretation*
JANESCU	*Journal of the Ancient Near Eastern Society of Columbia University*
JAOS	*Journal of the American Oriental Society*
JBL	*Journal of Biblical Literature*
JCS	*Journal of Cuneiform Studies*
JEA	*Journal of Egyptian Archaeology*
JJS	*Journal of Jewish Studies*
JNES	*Journal of Near Eastern Studies*
JNSL	*Journal of Northwest Semitic Languages*

JPSV	Jewish Publication Society Version
JSJ	*Journal for the Study of Judaism in the Persian, Hellenistic and Roman Period*
JSNTSup	*Journal for the Study of the New Testament*, Supplement Series
JSOT	*Journal for the Study of the Old Testament*
JSOTSup	*Journal for the Study of the Old Testament*, Supplement Series
JSPSup	*Journal for the Study of the Pseudepigrapha*, Supplement Series
JSS	*Journal of Semitic Studies*
JTS	*Journal of Theological Studies*
KAI	H. Donner and W. Röllig, *Kanaanäische und aramäische Inschriften* (3 vols.; Wiesbaden: Otto Harrassowitz, 1962–64)
KAT	Kommentar zum Alten Testament
KEH	Kurzgefasstes exegetisches Handbuch zum Alten Testament
KTU²	M. Dietrich, O. Loretz, J. Sanmartín, *The Cuneiform Alphabetic Texts from Ugarit, Ras Ibn Hani and Other Places* (KTU) (Münster: Ugarit-Verlag, 2nd enlarged edn, 1995)
MT	Masoretic Text
MVAG	Mitteilungen der vorderasiatisch-ägyptischen Gesellschaft
NA	E. Nestle and K. Aland (eds.), *Novum Testamentum Graece*
NCB	New Century Bible
n.d.	no date
NICNT	New International Commentary on the New Testament
NICOT	New International Commentary on the Old Testament
NIV	New International Version
n.p.	no publisher
NRSV	New Revised Standard Version
NS	New Series
NTS	*New Testament Studies*
OBO	Orbis biblicus et orientalis
OLZ	*Orientalistische Literaturzeitung*
Or	*Orientalia*
OrAnt	*Oriens antiquus*
OTG	Old Testament Guides
OTL	Old Testament Library
OTP	James Charlesworth (ed.), *Old Testament Pseudepigrapha*
OTS	*Oudtestamentische Studiën*
PAM	Palestine Archaeological Museum
RA	*Revue d'Assyriologie et d'archéologie orientale*
RB	*Revue biblique*
REB	Revised English Bible
RÉg	*Revue d'Égyptologie*
RevQ	*Revue de Qumran*

RHPR	*Revue d'histoire et de philosophie religieuses*
RIH	Ras Ibn Hani
RS	Ras Shamra
RSV	Revised Standard Version
RTP	*Revue de théologie et de philosophie*
RV	Revised Version
SBL	Society of Biblical Literature
SBLDS	SBL Dissertation Series
SBLEJL	SBL Early Judaism and its Literature
SBLMS	SBL Monograph Series
SBLRBS	SBL Resources for Biblical Study
SBS	Stuttgarter Bibelstudien
SBT	Studies in Biblical Theology
Sem	*Semitica*
SHANE	Studies in the History of the Ancient Near East
STDJ	Studies on the Texts of the Desert of Judah
TBü	Theologische Bücherei
TDOT	G.J. Botterweck and H. Ringgren (eds.), *Theological Dictionary of the Old Testament*
ThWAT	G.J. Botterweck and H. Ringgren (eds.), *Theologisches Handwörterbuch zum Alten Testament* (Stuttgart: W. Kohlhammer, 1970–)
TLZ	*Theologische Literaturzeitung*
TOTC	Tyndale Old Testament Commentaries
TRE	*Theologische Realenzyklopädie*
TynBul	*Tyndale Bulletin*
TZ	*Theologische Zeitschrift*
UBL	Ugaritisch–Biblische Literatur
UBSGNT	*United Bible Societies' Greek New Testament*
UCOP	University of Cambridge Oriental Publications
UF	*Ugarit-Forschungen*
VT	*Vetus Testamentum*
VTSup	*Vetus Testamentum*, Supplements
WBC	Word Biblical Commentary
WKAS	*Wörterbuch der klassischen arabischen Sprache*
WMANT	Wissenschaftliche Monographien zum Alten und Neuen Testament
WUNT	Wissenschaftliche Untersuchungen zum Neuen Testament
ZA	*Zeitschrift für Assyriologie*
ZAW	*Zeitschrift für die alttestamentliche Wissenschaft*
ZDPV	*Zeitschrift des deutschen Palästina-Vereins*
ZPE	*Zeitschrift für Papyrologie und Epigraphik*
ZTK	*Zeitschrift für Theologie und Kirche*

LIST OF CONTRIBUTORS

PHILIP S. ALEXANDER
Professor of Post-Biblical Jewish Literature, University of Manchester. (Formerly President of the Oxford Centre for Hebrew and Jewish Studies.)

JOHN BAINES
Professor of Egyptology in the University of Oxford, and Fellow of the Queen's College, Oxford.

JOHN BARTON
Oriel and Laing Professor of the Interpretation of Holy Scripture in the University of Oxford, and Fellow of Oriel College, Oxford.

GEORGE J. BROOKE
Professor of Biblical Studies in the University of Manchester.

JOHN DAY
Reader in Biblical Studies in the University of Oxford, and Fellow and Tutor of Lady Margaret Hall, Oxford.

KATHARINE J. DELL
Lecturer in Divinity (Old Testament) in the University of Cambridge, and Fellow and Tutor of St Catharine's College, Cambridge. (Formerly Tutor in Old Testament, Ripon College, Cuddesdon, Oxford.)

S.E. GILLINGHAM
Lecturer in Theology (Old Testament) in the University of Oxford, and Fellow and Tutor of Worcester College, Oxford.

KNUT M. HEIM
Student Minister, Wesley House, Cambridge.

WILLIAM HORBURY
Reader in Jewish and Early Christian Studies in the University of Cambridge, and Fellow of Corpus Christi College, Cambridge.

PAUL M. JOYCE
Lecturer in Theology (Old Testament) in the University of Oxford, and Fellow and Tutor of St Peter's College, Oxford.

GARY N. KNOPPERS
Head of the Department of Classics and Ancient Mediterranean Civilizations, The Pennsylvania State University, USA. (Formerly Visiting Scholar at the Oxford Centre for Hebrew and Jewish Studies.)

W.G. LAMBERT
Emeritus Professor of Assyriology in the University of Birmingham.

REX MASON
Emeritus Fellow of Regent's Park College, Oxford, and formerly Lecturer in Theology (Old Testament) in the University of Oxford.

J.G. MCCONVILLE
Research Fellow and Senior Lecturer in Old Testament, Cheltenham and Gloucester College of Higher Education, Cheltenham, Gloucestershire. (Formerly Lecturer in Old Testament, Wycliffe Hall, Oxford.)

DAVID J. REIMER
Lecturer in Hebrew and Old Testament Studies, University of Edinburgh. (Formerly Fellow and Tutor in Hebrew and Old Testament, Regent's Park College, Oxford.)

DEBORAH W. ROOKE
Lecturer in Old Testament Studies, King's College, University of London. (Formerly research student in Old Testament, Regent's Park College, Oxford.)

CHRISTOPHER ROWLAND
Dean Ireland Professor of the Exegesis of Holy Scripture in the University of Oxford, and Fellow of the Queen's College, Oxford.

ALISON SALVESEN
Leverhulme Researcher in the Semantics of Ancient Hebrew, University of Oxford, and Fellow of the Oxford Centre for Hebrew and Jewish Studies.

CAROL SMITH
Freelance scholar, writer, and editor, Abingdon, near Oxford. (Formerly research student in Old Testament, Linacre College, Oxford.)

H.G.M. WILLIAMSON
Regius Professor of Hebrew in the University of Oxford, and Student of Christ Church, Oxford.

Part I

THE KING IN THE ANCIENT NEAR EAST

ANCIENT EGYPTIAN KINGSHIP:
OFFICIAL FORMS, RHETORIC, CONTEXT[1]

John Baines

Introduction

Although they were situated geographically near each other and over-lapped temporally, ancient Egypt and the world of the Hebrew Bible were far removed in scale and social institutions. It would therefore be difficult to offer a close comparison between forms of kingship in the two societies. Instead, I present some salient features of the all-encompassing phenomenon of Egyptian kingship. My chief focus is on varieties of presentation of the king in elite sources, most of which date from hundreds of years after the formation of the state. Some points about the early history and background of the institution should be made at the outset.

There were kings in Egypt from prehistory, before the state had come into being.[2] The king was the pivot of cosmos and state. Kingship was the central institution of society and civilization, even if there were periods and contexts where society maintained itself with rather little reference to the institution, or when the lines of kings proliferated in the country, contrary to the principle that the office-holder was single. In

1. I am very grateful to Richard Parkinson and Peter Machinist for commenting on drafts of this chapter. I should also like to thank John Day very much for his invitation to participate in the seminar on which this volume is based, and for his meticulous editing. I study here one principal domain of Egyptian kingship, rather than reconstructing my original seminar.

For reasons of space, I give only limited references, normally citing translations that cite editions of Egyptian texts rather than the editions themselves. For general bibliography, see Bibliographical Note. For dates, see Chronological Outline.

2. J. Baines, 'Origins of Egyptian Kingship', in D. O'Connor and D.P. Silverman (eds.), *Ancient Egyptian Kingship* (Probleme der Ägyptologie, 9; Leiden: E.J. Brill, 1995), pp. 95-156.

all periods a unified Egypt was unthinkable without a single king, even if the incumbent was an absentee Persian or Roman emperor. From the state perspective, the ideological alternative to kingship was not some other form of rule but chaos. If the king or kingship was criticized, this could only be done implicitly; it was necessary to work through the institution and not to attempt to supplant or bypass it. It was difficult in principle to conceive of a social order without a king, although in practice this was not a problem for local leaders in decentralized periods.

The king existed in relation to the gods in a polytheistic belief system in which he was dependent upon them. The absolute status of kingship is relativized in this cosmic perspective, although it may be questioned how far these concerns spread effectively beyond the ruling group. What is absolute about the king of centralized periods is that he was single, whereas both gods and people were many. This unique status between two whole categories gave kingship great prominence and strength.

I study how the king related to his subjects and acted, among other things, as a token of the divine in this world. Although relations between king and subject were fundamental, Egyptian sources on these matters are limited, because any public inscription tends to give a straightforwardly supportive rather than a nuanced presentation; inscriptions were also almost all produced by the small central elite. Separated from their original context in society, formal modes of action, and genre of record, the sources can too easily be seen as claiming factually for the king capacities that were anciently envisaged in metaphorical terms.

The context of public social forms and of kingship in Egypt is strongly affected by conventions that I characterize with the term 'decorum'.[3] Such conventions probably affected the life of ruler and elite significantly, as indeed they do in most societies. What is distinctive in the Egyptian presentation of institutions, which partly reflected and partly constituted the system, is the strong demarcation of spheres of existence. For example, during much of Egyptian history non-royal individuals could not be depicted interacting with the gods even though they might bear theophoric names that evoked such interaction, and

3.   J. Baines, *Fecundity Figures: Egyptian Personification and the Iconology of a Genre* (Warminster: Aris & Phillips, 1985), pp. 277-305; *idem*, 'Restricted Knowledge, Hierarchy, and Decorum: Modern Perceptions and Ancient Institutions', *Journal of the American Research Center in Egypt* 27 (1990), pp. 1-23.

could not represent the king on their own monuments, or even display his original primary title, the Horus Name. These demarcations will have paralleled distinctions of role and style of action among king and elite, as well as embodying a rather profound separation of them from the rest of society. The conventions of decorum focus around figures of the gods and the king. Because most pictorial representation of deities was originally restricted to protected contexts within temples where non-royal people could not be shown, the religious role of the king became highly salient, much more so than it would have been in everyday life. A consequence of decorum is that, in addition to the universal tendency to ascribe actions of subordinates to leaders, practice and belief might be presented in terms of the king when its ultimate referent was different. An instance I discuss below is the representation of the king performing ritual actions in temples, which in part translates the fact that priests performed these duties and in part creates a parallel and distinct universe of discourse; quite separate textual compositions known from inscriptions of the Graeco-Roman period expounded priestly duty and comportment.[4]

Kingship in its Official Manifestations

Titularies and their Extensions

The minimal presentation of the king was in terms of titularies; these were in a certain sense a visual counterpart to his iconographic presence, which became increasingly pervasive during the historical period. A king's titulary was promulgated through the country at his accession.[5] Titularies introduced both royal inscriptions and any official communication issued by government. Material such as contracts came to be dated with relatively full titularies whose changing forms kept pace with political developments, so that the titularies of the Ptolemies and Roman emperors, for example, are different from those of earlier times. The content of particular royal titles was always meaningful and also developed from period to period, often adopting legitimizing

---

4. A. Gutbub, *Textes fondamentaux de la théologie de Kom Ombo*, I (Bibliothèque d'Étude, 47; Cairo: Institut Français d'Archéologie Orientale, 1973), pp. 144-84, with references to parallels.

5. Decree of Thutmose I, known in three copies: K. Sethe, *Urkunden der 18. Dynastie*, I (Urkunden des Ägyptischen Altertums, IV; Leipzig: J.C. Hinrichs, 2nd edn, 1930), pp. 79-81.

strategies that evoked usages of earlier times. Titularies are therefore worth studying both for their structure and for their changing content.

The titulary built up gradually to crystallize into five elements, which give a standard framework from the early Middle Kingdom on. The elements are as follows (some themes in the examples are taken up in the discussion below):[6]

> Horus: the king as a specific manifestation of the principal deity of early times;
>
> Two Ladies: manifestation of, and protected by, the tutelary goddesses of the two halves of the country;
>
> Golden Horus: meaning uncertain, in late times related to Horus defeating his enemy Seth;
>
> Dual King (*nyswt byty*[7]): the 'throne name' and first cartouche name adopted at accession, expressing the king's relation with the sun god Re;
>
> Son of Re: second cartouche name, which is the incumbent's birth name, placed after a title that expresses the king's dependence on and tutelage by the sun god; in two periods followed by the 'dynastic' name Ramesses or Ptolemy.

A typical, relatively simple New Kingdom titulary is that of Thutmose IV:

> Horus: Mighty Bull, Perfect of Appearings (*ḫ'w*, a term also applied to sunrise); Two Ladies: Enduring of Kingship like Atum; Golden Horus: Powerful of Strength of Arm, Who Subdues the Nine Bows (Egypt's traditional enemies); Dual King: Menkheprure (= The Enduring One of the Manifestations of Re); Son of Re: Thutmose, The Appearing One of Appearances (optional extra epithet); beloved of Amon-Re, given life like Re.[8]

This can be compared with the founder of the Twenty-second Dynasty, Shoshenq I. His titulary, largely derived from late New Kingdom tradition, reads:

---

6. For evidence, see J. von Beckerath, *Handbuch der ägyptischen Königsnamen* (Münchner Ägyptologische Studien, 20; Berlin: Deutscher Kunstverlag, 1984). Discussions are very scattered and cannot be listed here; for some points, see material discussed in J. Baines, 'Kingship, Definition of Culture, and Legitimation' in O'Connor and Silverman (eds.), *Ancient Egyptian Kingship*, pp. 3-47.

7. Frequently rendered 'King of Upper and Lower Egypt', but encompassing distinct aspects of kingship in addition to the geographical division of the country.

8. Rock stela at Konosso, near Aswan: C.R. Lepsius, *Denkmaeler aus Aegypten und Aethiopien, Abtheilung* III (Berlin: Nicolai, n.d.), Pl. 69e.

Horus: Mighty Bull, Beloved of Re, whom he caused to appear in order
to unite the Two Lands; Two Ladies: Who Appears with the Double
Crown like Horus Son of Isis, who propitiates the gods with *ma'at*
(order); Golden Horus: Powerful of Strength, who smites the Nine
Bows, great of victories in all lands; Dual King, Lord of the Two Lands,
possessor of strength of arm: Hedjkheperre-satepnare (= The White One
of the coming into being of Re, whom Re chose); Son of Re, of his
body: Shoshenq, beloved of Amun.[9]

From the reign of Ptolemy VIII Euergetes II comes the following
titulary, characteristic of the later Ptolemaic period. It lacks the more
elaborate extensions relating to the cult of the Ptolemaic royal ancestors
occurring in many documents,[10] but includes the full five-name form—
the first three of these being much restricted in use by this date:

Horus: The Youth in Whose Life there is Rejoicing, who is on the throne
of his father, sweet of occasions, sacred in his dazzling, together with the
living Apis Bull;[11] Two Ladies: Who Makes Content the Heart of the
Two Lands; Golden Horus: Great of Strength, Possessor of *sed*-festivals
like his father Ptah-Tanen, the father of the gods; Dual King: Heir of the
Gods Who Go Forth,[12] whom Ptah chose, who performs the *ma'at* of Re,
living image of Amun; Son of Re: Ptolemy, may he live for ever,

9.   The Epigraphic Survey, *The Bubastite Portal* (Reliefs and Inscriptions at
Karnak, 3; Oriental Institute Publication, 74; Chicago: University of Chicago Press,
1954), Pl. 12 (composite from lines 1-3); see M.-A. Bonhême, *Les noms royaux
dans l'Égypte de la Troisième Période Intermédiaire* (Bibliothèque d'Étude, 98;
Cairo: Institut Français d'Archéologie Orientale, 1987), pp. 95-106. The significance of the first cartouche name, shared with Smendes of the Twenty-first
Dynasty, is uncertain; 'whiteness' could refer to solar luminosity as incorporated in
the White Crown.
10.   E.g. K.-T. Zauzich, *Die ägyptische Schreibertradition in Aufbau: Sprache
und Schrift der demotischen Kaufverträge aus ptolemäischer Zeit* (Ägyptologische
Abhandlungen, 19; Wiesbaden: Otto Harrassowitz, 1968).
11.   The Apis Bull of Memphis was a major divine manifestation or hypostasis,
whose relation to a deity—Ptah or Osiris—is analogous to the king's manifesting
various gods (see in general J. Vercoutter, 'Apis, Apis-Bestattung', in W. Helck
and E. Otto [eds.], *Lexikon der Ägyptologie*, I [Wiesbaden: Otto Harrassowitz,
1975], cols. 338-50). The title displays the joyful response of deities and people at
the king's appearance, like that of the Bull.
12.   Translation of the Greek *theoi epiphanes*, the epithet assumed by Ptolemy
VIII's father Ptolemy V and the latter's consort Cleopatra I. This usage of 'gods' in
these epithets is probably of Greek origin and has no close parallel in Egyptian.

beloved of Ptah; together with his wife, the Female Ruler, Lady of the Two Lands: Cleopatra; the Two Efficacious Gods (Greek Euergetes).[13]

The cartouche is a heraldic device going back to the First Dynasty and first used to enclose a king's name in the Second or the Third. Part of its meaning is probably as a protective talisman, but it also symbolizes a perpetual cycle through the 'endless knot' of detailed visual forms.[14] The first cartouche name is the most important element adopted by kings at accession and the form of name by which a king was generally known during his reign, at least in the Middle and New Kingdoms. The more complex forms of the end of the New Kingdom and later were probably not used in this way.

Two important titles that derive from normal language, rather than being items of vocabulary like words for 'king', were frequently placed before the cartouche names. These are 'Lord of the Two Lands' (that is, Egypt), and 'Perfect God' (*ntr nfr*, often rendered 'Good God'), a designation that probably contrasted the king, as what might be termed a 'minor' god although the Egyptians did not do so,[15] with male deities termed 'Major God (*ntr ꜥ3*)', that is, the principal gods of the pantheon.[16] These optional titles focus on the king's political rule, as is evident for the former, and his status as a limited kind of deity, pointing to these as core aspects of kingship.

Other elements in the titulary are dominated by complex conceptions of divine 'manifestation'. A deity can have multiple manifestations, for example in phenomena of nature, and can animate cult images or take on animate forms such as those of cult animals, although in the present

13. H. Junker and E. Winter, *Das Geburtshaus des Tempels der Isis in Philä* (Philä, II; Österreichische Akademie der Wissenschaften, phil.-hist. Klasse, Denkschriften, Sonderband; Vienna: Böhlau, 1965), p. 5. For 'gods', see previous note.

14. W. Barta, 'Der Königsring als Symbol zyklischer Wiederkehr', *Zeitschrift für Ägyptische Sprache und Altertumskunde* 98 (1972), pp. 5-16.

15. See O. Berlev, 'The Eleventh Dynasty in the Dynastic History of Egypt', in D. W. Young (ed.), *Studies Presented to Hans Jakob Polotsky* (East Gloucester, MA: Pirtle & Polson, 1981), pp. 361-77 (362).

16. See J. Baines, '"Greatest God" or Category of Gods?', *Göttinger Miszellen* 67 (1983), pp. 13-28. 'Major God' occurs very rarely with kings and may mark a deification or a specific contextual usage. The usage occurs in the eulogy of the *Tale of Sinuhe* (see p. 31) and in a Second Intermediate Period royal stela: P. Vernus, 'La stèle du pharaon *Mntw-htpi* à Karnak', *RÉg* 40 (1989), pp. 145-61.

case these are those of the king.[17] No single manifestation encompasses
the full extent of a deity, who continues to have a separate existence. A
single manifestation, again such as the king, can be 'inhabited'[18] by
more than one deity; it would be beside the point to ask whether such
multiple inhabitings are contemporaneous or successive. The king is
not himself identical with any one deity. Unlike deities in the full sense,
he does not have an ultimate being in the domain of the gods, of which
his earthly being might be a limited manifestation; rather, for the rest of
humanity he is a limited manifestation of the world of the gods. There
exists a concept of kingship (*nswyt*) that can be set against any incumbent holder of the office; this concept relates strongly to the passage
between generations and to the world of the dead. Individual kings
aspired to become deities in the full sense in the next world. In this
world they were not gods in the same sense as the major gods of the
pantheon.

The final important constituent of most longer titularies and many
short ones is a concluding statement, 'given life'. This is very often
linked to a heraldic usage of the word 'beloved', which asserts that the
king is 'beloved of' a specific deity or deities. Typically the formula
reads 'beloved of DN, given life like Re for ever', where the 'like Re'
probably means 'life like that of Re'. The 'given life' conception is
attested in part-visual part-verbal form from the end of the predynastic
period, in one of the earliest fully formed examples of Egyptian
iconography,[19] and thus is constitutive for how relations of deity and
king were conceived. The king depends upon the gods for the conditions of life. Other material shows that through him humanity—that is,
in the first instance Egyptians—receive 'life'; foreigners, who stand
outside the ordered cosmos, are defeated by him and must beseech him
for the 'breath of life'. The preconditions of existence both depend
upon the gods and are integrated with the cosmic and political establishment of order, mediated by the king. The king is quite often

17. Crucial study: E. Hornung, 'Der Mensch als "Bild Gottes" in Ägypten', in
O. Loretz, *Die Gottebenbildlichkeit des Menschen* (Schriften des Deutschen
Instituts für Wissenschaftliche Pedagogik; Munich: Kösel, 1967), pp. 123-56.

18. Term of Hans Bonnet; see discussion of E. Hornung, *Der Eine und die
Vielen* (Darmstadt: Wissenschaftliche Buchgesellschaft, 1971), pp. 82-90 (ET *Con-
ceptions of God in Ancient Egypt: The One and the Many* [rev. and trans. J. Baines;
Ithaca, NY: Cornell University Press, 1982; London: Routledge, 1983], pp. 91-99).

19. Discussed in Baines, 'Origins of Kingship', pp. 117-18 with Fig. 3.6.

depicted holding the hieroglyph for life in contexts that are specialized, typically but not only in that he faces toward an implied humanity rather than toward the gods.

'Beloved-ness' has similar hierarchical implications: love generally proceeds from superior to dependant. For much of Egyptian history only the king was 'beloved' of the gods.[20] He depended upon them and was comparably treated by all of them. Although some deities had a closer relationship with kingship than others and patronized particular aspects of his being—for example, Mont oversaw his activities as a warrior—he was the 'son' of all of them and could refer to all the gods as his 'fathers'.

The notion of the 'life' the gods give to the king and the king gives to humanity focuses around air, in Egyptian identical with the word for 'breath'. In elaborate eulogies this concept is made more encompassing, and the king is responsible, like a creator god, for the destiny and nourishment of all, so that progeny increases during his reign;[21] but the narrower association of air remains primary.

The usages of titularies are anchored in complex ideological and religious conceptions. Their formal character and constant development, including changes during the course of individual reigns, display their importance for defining who the king is and how he relates to the divine; in a few cases they also incorporate historical information. They are not simply stereotyped. In themselves, titularies do not say much about relations between the king and his subjects, a reticence that is characteristic of core Egyptian ideology, in which humanity plays rather little part. Enemies and the world outside Egypt are more

20. See Hornung, *Der Eine und die Vielen*, pp. 196-98 (ET *Conceptions of God*, pp. 201-203); W.K. Simpson, 'Amor Dei: *ntr mrr rmt m t3 w3* (Sh. Sai. 147–148) and the Embrace', in J. Assmann, E. Feucht, and R. Grieshammer (eds.), *Fragen an die altägyptische Literatur: Studien zum Gedenken an Eberhard Otto* (Wiesbaden: Reichert, 1977), pp. 493-98. This issue is complex and reciprocal expressions between deities and human beings become increasingly common in the New Kingdom, but the point of departure that deities direct their love toward the king seems clear. Further research is desirable, for example on relevant implications of patterns in proper names.

21. E.g. G. Posener, *L'Enseignement Loyaliste: Sagesse égyptienne du Moyen Empire* (Hautes Études Orientales, 5; Geneva: Droz, 1977), §§5.2, 9; P. Grandet, *Le Papyrus Harris I (BM 9999)*, I (Bibliothèque d'Étude, 109; Cairo: Institut Français d'Archéologie Orientale, 1994), p. 339 (18, 13).

strongly present in titularies, appearing as the domain of disorder that has to be mastered.[22]

Titularies cannot demonstrate whether the king 'was' a god; moreover, the Egyptian category 'god' (*ntr*) is too broad to indicate much more than that the king was a special order of being who was unlike other human beings.

Reflections of the Social and Divine Context

Formal titularies can be interspersed with epithets. The epithets cannot be demarcated sharply from rhetorical statements that often form major sections of royal inscriptions following on the initial titulary and preceding narrative or descriptive sections. This overlap in content confirms the vitality of titularies and emphasizes the significance of introductions as a whole. What is difficult to assess is how far the usages are rhetorical or metaphorical rather than incorporating specific beliefs. In the nature of things, it is unlikely that sharp distinctions can be drawn here: the notion that the king is the 'son' of any god is metaphorical, but his dependence upon the gods expressed in the 'beloved' formula is not. The eulogies just referred to, in which characteristics similar to those of major deities and creators are attributed to him, may be primarily rhetorical, because they appear to travesty another semantic domain, in a transgression that would be recognized by an informed audience (I return to this point below). In the carefully formulated and endlessly varied phraseology of Graeco-Roman temple inscriptions, clear distinctions are made between the king's 'being' an exemplar of the gods or, for example, a 'perfect youth', and his being 'like' a god (the deity varies with what is said), in a usage contrasting directly with what is said about gods 'being' other gods.[23] Thus, throughout the life of the institution of kingship, distinctions were maintained between what could be predicated of a god and of a king.

While titularies are an official validation and dissemination of the king's status, epithets that extend into lengthy compositions may relate to the rhetorical and ceremonial practice of public life. Written formulations are no doubt far from their spoken or performed counterparts,

22. See in general Hornung, *Der Eine und die Vielen* (ET *Conceptions of God*); Baines, *Fecundity Figures*, pp. 30-33, 216-17.

23. M.T. Derchain-Urtel, 'Gott oder Mensch?', *Studien zur Altägyptischen Kultur* 3 (1975), pp. 25-41.

but they should still convey something of the latter's flavour. If a plausible context can be modelled for their performance and varying treatments can be identified, it may be possible to improve understanding and to differentiate them according to the purposes for which they were intended. The principal evidence for the general context of performance of royal and elite roles consists of highly formalized texts recording exchanges between kings and members of the elite. For the Old Kingdom these are in non-royal biographical inscriptions, with suggestive parallels in the decoration of funerary temples.[24] From the Twelfth Dynasty on there are examples of a special genre of royal inscription termed the 'royal tale' (*Königsnovelle*), in which the king typically sits in council with his advisers and presents his decisive response to events and/or his decision to take a particular course of action.[25] The advisers urge caution, whereas the king is in favour of pre-emptive action and is vindicated by subsequent events; or an achievement such as the construction of a temple may simply embody his absolute decision. Essentially the same situation is travestied in literary works, for example where the king is bored and asks for advice on how he can be entertained.[26]

The context of king and advisers is also that of addresses to the king. In general, rather little is stated of how the elite might present themselves to the king, although that situation is powerfully fictionalized in

24. J. Baines, 'Kingship before Literature: The World of the King in the Old Kingdom', in R. Gundlach and C. Raedler (eds.), *Selbstverständnis und Realität: Akten des Symposiums zur ägyptischen Königsideologie, Mainz, 15–17.6, 1995* (Ägypten und Altes Testament, 36; Beiträge zur Ägyptischen Königsideologie, 1; Wiesbaden: Otto Harrassowitz, 1997), pp. 125-75.

25. The genre was identified in the ground-breaking monograph of A. Hermann, *Die ägyptische Königsnovelle* (Leipziger Ägyptologische Studien, 10; Glückstadt: J.J. Augustin, 1938). A. Loprieno is re-evaluating the material; preliminary article: 'The "King's Novel"', in A. Loprieno (ed.), *Ancient Egyptian Literature: History and Forms* (Probleme der Ägyptologie, 10; Leiden: E.J. Brill, 1996), pp. 277-95.

26. The *Words of Neferti* and the *Tale of King Cheops' Court* in R.B. Parkinson, *The Tale of Sinuhe and other Ancient Egyptian Poems, 1940–1640 BC* (Oxford: Clarendon Press, 1997), pp. 102-27, 131-43; M. Lichtheim, *Ancient Egyptian Literature* (3 vols.; Berkeley: University of California Press, 1973–80), I, pp. 139-45, 215-22 (omitting the beginning). Both of these are likely to be second-order travesties of a folklore-style motif. *Neferti* is a 'serious' composition, while *Cheops's Court* probably operated the device on more than one level, in relation to Khufu in the lost beginning and to Snofru in the third story.

the *Tale of Sinuhe*.[27] If a subject requested the gift of funerary provision, this was done modestly so that the emphasis was on the generosity of the king's response, which exceeded what had been requested. There is little evidence from earlier periods for the highest claims for royal divinity—put another way, the grossest forms of flattery—being pronounced directly to the king. This relative reticence may temper absolute claims for the king's status and may also be significant as providing an underlying context for the most extravagant forms of praise. A text like the *Tale of the Eloquent Peasant*, in which the protagonist secures a hearing from a high official with an initial piece of flattery that appears in part to travesty speeches that might be addressed to royalty,[28] could suggest that there was a place for such rhetorical strategies, but could alternatively have been recognized as being remote from real-life situations.

This material exemplifies the formalization of relations between king and elite, who together will have presented themselves to the rest of society almost as a unit. The king lived in his palace and was hardly accessible to the people as a whole. When he went out from the palace, he was accompanied by attendants and symbolic paraphernalia and his actions were cloaked in elaborate ritual; such ceremonies are the subject of the earliest evidence.[29] When he was on campaign, his tent was the palace and he travelled with a portable throne that completed the proper context for his presence.[30] Throughout, as with most of the world's royalty, he was surrounded by the elite, rather than mixing directly with the people. Middle ranking and high officials were said to be members of the 'entourage' (*šnwt*), a term deriving from a root associated with ideas of protection, or 'followers' (*šmsw*), again, people who served the king in person. This privileged group mediated the king's relations with his subjects as a whole.

27. Parkinson, *The Tale of Sinuhe*, pp. 40-41; Lichtheim, *Ancient Egyptian Literature*, I, pp. 231-32.

28. Parkinson, *The Tale of Sinuhe*, p. 61; Lichtheim, *Ancient Egyptian Literature*, I, p. 172.

29. See Baines, 'Origins of Kingship'.

30. Evident, for example, in Thutmose III's narrative of the Battle of Megiddo: e.g. Lichtheim, *Ancient Egyptian Literature*, II, p. 31, before (40), translates wrongly 'speech...of the palace', original has 'in'; for a visual counterpart, see e.g. Lepsius, *Denkmaeler*, III, Pl. 153 (Ramesses II, Battle of Qadesh). See also J. Baines, 'Trône et dieu: Aspects du symbolisme royal et divin des temps archaïques', *Bulletin de la Société Française d'Égyptologie* 118 (1990), pp. 5-37.

This enveloping of the king in social and formal symbolic structures both protected and constrained him. There was an active formalism in ritual. In addition to major royal rituals such as those of accession[31] and of renewal after many years (the *sed* festival), the king's entire life was ritualized, seemingly moving through greater and lesser degrees of ritualization—an overdetermination that characterizes the life of rulers anywhere. In extant sources the greatest development of ritual meanings surrounding the king is in temple relief, where he is represented as the sole officiant interacting with the gods, while such material as the furniture and insignia from the tomb of Tutankhamun suggests that the king's daily life was no less elaborate. Only a minority of sequences of temple reliefs show actions that form the stages of rituals. The reliefs are essentially a symbolic counterpart of ritual action that creates a formal iconographic/verbal language through which relations between the king and the gods can be endlessly explored, covering the walls of temples with appropriate symbolic and celebratory content. This language continued to develop into the Graeco-Roman period.[32] Its presentation was more strongly formalized in the most restricted contexts at the centre of temples. Formalization had an intrinsic positive value, and the material that may seem most uninformative to us because it is stereotyped was probably among the most highly regarded in antiquity.

The basic content of temple reliefs can be summarized as the king's making offerings, principally material in character, to the gods, who have created the precondition for his doing this. In response to his rededication to them of the fruits of order, they re-endow him with life and power, the latter including victory over the forces of chaos.[33] There is thus a generalized asymmetry between his more mundane gifts to them and their quintessential and superior ones to him. This is the counterpart of his junior status in relation to the gods, which is

31. The issue of coronation is controversial; it is uncertain whether there was a major coronation ritual as part of a king's installation before Ptolemaic times. The throne and titulary seem to have been more essential to royal legitimacy than crowns; from the Middle Kingdom on the uraeus, the cobra diadem worn on the forehead, was more distinctive than any other headdress.

32. Classic study: E. Winter, *Untersuchungen zu den ägyptischen Tempelreliefs der griechisch-römischen Zeit* (Österreichische Akademie der Wissenschaften, phil.-hist. Klasse, Denkschriften, 98; Vienna: Böhlau, 1968), esp. Part 1.

33. See especially, Hornung, *Der Eine und die Vielen*, pp. 192-200 (ET *Conceptions of God*, pp. 197-205).

expressed in the epithet 'beloved' and indicated in many features of
design and iconography. The exchange between the two spheres
emphasizes especially the close integration of divine and royal worlds,
which is realized most fully within temples, where only the king and
the priests had access, and in more indirect forms on more public
structures, notably gateways.[34] The dependent relation of the king to the
gods parallels the assertion that human beings are similarly dependent
on him, so that he is the fulcrum of the whole cosmic and societal
edifice. As indicated, his uniqueness, which contrasted with the multiplicity of the other two groups, reinforced this position.

Only the king was depicted performing the temple cult. This convention, which was deeply significant for the articulation of belief, did not
mean that priests were mere substitutes for the king. Indeed, in the
Graeco-Roman period the opposite came to be the case and some of the
king's status was as a priestly functionary.[35] Other material makes clear
that priests saw themselves as acting in their own right. Nonetheless,
because the presentation of the king seems to make him the only route
for access to the gods and he was one and they were many, he had an
ideologically overpowering position. This vision may contain something of rhetoric and legitimation: the king was both uniquely responsible and, in an ideal case, uniquely caring for humanity.

Rhetorical Developments and their Contexts
The contexts reviewed above tend to keep the pretensions of kings or
claims on their behalf within bounds and to set them in appropriate
contexts. Even the formal statements of titularies are not extravagantly
hyperbolic in their presentation of the king's status. Moreover, some
kings joined local pantheons after death or deified themselves during
life,[36] something they could only do if their status was below that of a

---

34. Principally for earlier periods; Graeco-Roman gateways are closer in design
to other areas of temple relief.

35. E. Otto, *Gott und Mensch nach den ägyptischen Tempelinschriften der
griechisch-römischen Zeit* (Abhandlungen der Heidelberger Akademie der
Wissenschaften, philosophisch-historische Klasse, 1964.1; Heidelberg: Winter,
1964), pp. 67-74.

36. E.g. B.M. Bryan, in A.P. Kozloff, B.M. Bryan, and L.M. Berman (eds.),
Egypt's Dazzling Sun: Amenhotep III and His World (exhibition catalogue,
Cleveland Museum of Art; Bloomington, IN: Indiana University Press, 1992), pp.
73-111; L. Habachi, *Features of the Deification of Ramses II* (Abhandlungen des
Deutschen Archäologischen Instituts, Abteilung Kairo, Ägyptologische Reihe, 5;

god. Yet in the New Kingdom some royal statuary was set up with the more or less explicit aim of acting as the focus of a royal cult. A few literary texts, mainly of the Middle Kingdom, incorporate very strong eulogistic claims that give the king a role essentially like a creator god; these have often been called 'propaganda', although the term can be problematic because of uncertainty over the audience addressed.[37] Similar claims of royal status are almost uniquely placed in the king's own mouth in the 'Berlin Leather Roll', an Eighteenth Dynasty manuscript with a text announcing a building programme that is cast in the form of a royal tale ascribed to Senwosret I of the Twelfth Dynasty.[38] If genuine, this rare example may be framed in some way to make the self-praise into a royal 'performance'; if it is a later composition, the fictionalizing context would distance the self-praise appropriately. The text is a very highly wrought work of verbal art and seems to be at the limit of verbally formulated royal pretension.

Sources like these are the ones used by scholars who have argued for a cross-culturally exceptional level of royal divinity in Egypt. Against them, others have long argued that the king was not a god in any straightforward sense.[39] There is little point in searching for a rigorous

Glückstadt: J.J. Augustin, 1969); D. Wildung, 'Göttlichkeitsstufen des Pharao', *OLZ* 69 (1973), cols. 549-65.

37. On Middle Kingdom royal ideology, see D. Franke, '"Schöpfer, Schützer, Guter Hirte": Zum Königsbild des Mittleren Reiches', in Gundlach and Raedler (eds.), *Selbstverständnis und Realität*, pp. 175-210. On propaganda, see J. Baines, 'Contextualizing Egyptian Representations of Society and Ethnicity', in J.S. Cooper and G. Schwartz (eds.), *The Study of the Ancient Near East in the 21st Century: The William Foxwell Albright Centennial Conference* (Winona Lake, IN: Eisenbrauns, 1996), pp. 339-84 (339-60).

38. R.B. Parkinson, *Voices from Ancient Egypt: An Anthology of Middle Kingdom Writings* (London: British Museum Press, 1991), pp. 40-43, no. 5; Lichtheim, *Ancient Egyptian Literature*, I, pp. 115-18; dating and comment: Loprieno, 'The "King's Novel"', in Loprieno (ed.), *Ancient Egyptian Literature*, pp. 286-87 with n. 49.

39. E.g. Hornung, *Der Eine und die Vielen*, pp. 131-32 (ET *Conceptions of God*, pp. 141-42). G. Posener's *De la divinité du pharaon* (Cahiers de la Société Asiatique, 15; Paris: Imprimerie Nationale, 1960) is adversely affected here by specifically seeking evidence for the king's being treated as less than a god, rather than exploring the issue more neutrally; this was, however, a valuable corrective to the over-emphasis on royal divinity in such works as H. Frankfort's *Kingship and the Gods: A Study of Ancient Near Eastern Religion as the Integration of Society and Nature* (Chicago: University of Chicago Press, 1948).

consistency of formulation in texts that were intended to be laudatory, and the variation in claims for the king's status might be taken simply as exemplifying a lack of dogmatism and a colourful range of expression. But it would be wrong to adopt this easy approach, because these materials are central products of Egyptian high culture; they should be given due weight as having a deliberate purpose within their highly rhetorical forms. Two interrelated factors are important here: the selection of audience; and the literary character of some sources, notably the Middle Kingdom 'loyalist' instructions. It is difficult to separate the two because a high proportion of Egyptian discursive writing has a strongly literary formulation. What is most relevant is not so much the highly wrought writing as the question of whether the context or the genre influences the reception of statements about royalty.

These issues are exemplified in the oldest surviving extensive source, the early Fifth Dynasty false door of Niankhsakhmet, which bears two complementary texts. In the first, Niankhsakhmet approaches the king and requests the gift of a false door—evidently the one bearing the inscriptions. The second consists principally of a poem in praise of the king, probably occasioned by the completion of the false door and the king's final donation of it:

> Speech by His Person
> to the Chief Physician Niankhsakhmet:
>
> 'As this my nose, beloved of the gods, is healthy,
> may you go forth to the West (die)
> having become greatly old, as a well provided one.'
>
> Give praise to the King greatly,
> thank every god for Sahure;
>
> for he knows me
> as well as the entire retinue.
>
> If anything goes forth from his Person's mouth,
> it happens at once;
>
> for the god gave him
> percipience in the womb
> inasmuch as he is more splendid than any god.
>
> If Re loves you (or, 'If you love Re'?)
> thank every god for Sahure
> who did this for me (i.e. donated this false door).[40]

---

40. Discussion and references: Baines, 'Kingship before Literature'.

The king's dependence on the gods through love is invoked, in this case reportedly in his own words, as well as the statement that 'the god' (probably the sun god Re) gave him his essential qualities. Yet this is also where the king is stated, apparently without irony, to be at least in one way superior to the gods. The poem's quite grandiose claims are addressed to people at large—essentially to the elite—and not directly to the king. In practice, the poem might have been declaimed in the king's presence and so addressed to him after all, but the composition and the context are elaborately framed. The subject's prestation in response to receiving the gift of the work of art of the false door is another work of art, which takes the form of this poem extolling the king. This is not a composition that reports any 'literal' truth.

A still more strongly framed composition is the poem in praise of Senwosret I included in the *Tale of Sinuhe*, the best known literary work of the Twelfth Dynasty. This is pronounced by the protagonist in response to a question from his host, a local ruler, near the beginning of his Palestinian exile. The ruler asks:

> ...How is that land
> without him, that efficacious god (Amenemhat I)
> whose fearfulness pervaded foreign lands
> like Sakhmet in a year of pestilence?[41]

The reference to 'that efficacious god' is very Egyptian, as is the evocation of the violent goddess Sakhmet, so that the Palestinian ruler is hardly characterized here as a foreigner. His question elicits a highly structured panegyric 47 verses long that evokes the delicate issue of the common rule or coregency of a king and his successor, dwells upon the new king's military prowess at length, and rather briefly evokes his qualities as a beneficent and well loved ruler.[42] The underwhelmed host responds:

---

41. Translation mine. Text: R. Koch, *Die Erzählung des Sinuhe* (Bibliotheca Aegyptiaca, 17; Brussels: Fondation Égyptologique Reine Elisabeth, 1990), pp. 30-31, at B 43–45; p. 40, at B 75–76 (passage cited below). For the context, see Parkinson, *The Tale of Sinuhe*, pp. 30-31.

42. Valuable remarks by J. Assmann, 'Verkünden und Verklären: Grundformen hymnischer Rede im alten Ägypten', in Loprieno (ed.), *Ancient Egyptian Literature*, pp. 313-34 (313-14), who does not, however, comment on the relativizing fictional context of the eulogy.

Egypt is indeed fortunate in the knowledge that (Senwosret I) is
   flourishing.
(But) you are here.
You will be with me. What I do for you is good.

The panegyric is evidently suited to its fictional and historical context;
more significantly, however, the Palestinian's response radically com-
promises its ostensible effect. He can gently mock Sinuhe's pretension
and his lack of a sense of when such a recital is appropriate; this one
is not appropriate for those who are not subject to Egypt.[43] The result
is that an important genre is incorporated into *Sinuhe*, along with
several similar travesties, but is identifiable as literary, both internally
and through its placing in the tale. The text nonetheless shares with
Niankhsakhmet's poem the characteristic that extreme praise is osten-
sibly not addressed to the king himself. *Sinuhe* is also likely to have
been written after the reign of Senwosret I, so that it did not extol the
current king.

Other examples of extreme claims for the king's status have less
clear distancing frames than these two texts. The best known group is
in fictional and instructional texts of the same period as *Sinuhe*. The
Instruction of Amenemhat I, a discourse addressed by the deceased king
to his successor Senwosret I, contains a brief passage in which he
claims:

I was a maker of grain, beloved of Nepri (the grain god),
   and the inundation of the Nile honoured me on every expanse of land.[44]

The formulation of this is significant because in religion it was not the
king but the god Osiris who was the 'maker of grain'.[45] The first of

43. The treatment may also comment at once both ironically and positively on
the Palestinian, who would presumably know little of conditions in Egypt. For the
treatment of the foreigner here, see A. Loprieno, *Topos und Mimesis: Zum Bild des
Ausländers in der ägyptischen Literatur* (Ägyptologische Abhandlungen, 48;
Wiesbaden: Otto Harrassowitz, 1988), pp. 41-59.

44. W. Helck, *Der Text der 'Lehre Amenemhets I. für seinen Sohn'* (Kleine
Ägyptische Texte; Wiesbaden: Otto Harrassowitz, 1969), pp. 72-73 (XI, a–b); see
Parkinson, *The Tale of Sinuhe*, pp. 203-11 (207). Parkinson points out (personal
communication) that different readings of this passage from the one proposed here
are possible.

45. Known from the New Kingdom on, but probably much more ancient; see
e.g. A.M. Blackman, 'Osiris as the Maker of Corn in a Text of the Ptolemaic
Period', in *Studia Aegyptiaca*, I (AnOr, 17; Rome: Pontificio Istituto Biblico,
1938), pp. 1-3, with references.

these verses is therefore almost an oxymoron, the first half of it assimilating the king to one of the highest possible beings, while the second makes him dependent on a minor personification who did not receive a cult of his own. A text of the First Intermediate Period shows the king as dependent upon the leading local deity for the control of the inundation;[46] in the second verse Amenemhat therefore claims more than normal, since the inundation, here personified as a deity, aids him directly and the word for 'honour' (*try*) suggests that it defers to him. Thus, the context of the claim of a divine role for the king within the couplet reveals its metaphorical character. While this heightened claim may throw appropriately into relief the qualities of a king who restores prosperity after troubles, as Amenemhat I was said to have done, both the broad literary context and the structure of the couplet temper its impact. The phrase that brings him back to his dependent role in relation to the gods must carry the greater overall weight because it is more widely paralleled.

Two works of the same period, the *Loyalist Instruction*[47] and the *Instruction of a Man for His Son*,[48] include similar phraseology in relation to the king. These have the appearance of didactic texts composed for the education of officials at different levels, but they are also works of fictional literature. An indirect demonstration of this point is that a late Twelfth Dynasty high official inscribed much of the first part of the *Loyalist Instruction* on his funerary stela,[49] changing the object of praise from a generic king to his sovereign Amenemhat III. The biographical texts on stelae and other monuments, which form the largest extant genre of Egyptian fine writing, drew upon narrowly literary formulations as well as influencing literary instructions profoundly.[50]

---

46. J. Vandier, *Moʿalla: La tombe d'Ankhtifi et la tombe de Sébekhotep* (Bibliothèque d'Étude, 18; Cairo: Institut Français d'Archéologie Orientale, 1950), p. 263, text 18.

47. Posener, *L'Enseignement Loyaliste*; Parkinson, *The Tale of Sinuhe*, pp. 235-45.

48. Not completely reconstructed; edition in press by H.-W. Fischer-Elfert collects a multiple of the material known hitherto; see briefly Parkinson, *The Tale of Sinuhe*, pp. 292-93.

49. H.O. Lange and H. Schäfer, *Grab- und Denksteine des Mittleren Reiches im Museum von Kairo*, II (Catalogue Général des Antiquités Egyptiennes du Musée du Caire; Berlin: Reichsdruckerei, 1908), pp. 145-50; IV (1902), Pl. 40.

50. Strong statement: J. Assmann, 'Schrift, Tod und Identität: Das Grab als Vorschule der Literatur', reprinted in his *Stein und Zeit: Mensch und Gesellschaft*

This intertextuality, which would have little meaning if the loyalist declarations were read literally rather than literarily, relativizes the extreme statements of the panegyric. Despite the specific attribution of the passage, the well educated reader of the stela would have recognized the quotation, as do the audiences of praise speeches in many cultures. The passage will have heightened the cultural pretensions of the stela, which is one of the premier non-royal stelae of its period, as well as proclaiming the owner's loyalism. Moreover, those who used the *Loyalist Instruction* itself in antiquity would have been aware of its framing of what it said. But if the instruction itself, or the text of the stela, were 'performed' orally, as is likely to have happened, the claims for the king might have acquired extra, almost non-fictional character, as the symbolic can always be taken literally, in part contrary to the original intention.

These two instructions present a complex interplay of concerns about the king and others in a discourse about the position and responsibilities of members of the elite.[51] In this context, the praise of the king, which is relativized by being one side of the equation, is nonetheless striking. The *Loyalist Instruction* identifies him with Re, making him more beneficial than the inundation of the Nile, and stating that he is a creator (in succession Atum and Khnum), the beneficent goddess Bastet, and the aggressive Sakhmet (stanzas 2, 3, 5). Comparable usages are known from songs in praise of Senwosret III that have refrains and thus were designed for ceremonial performance.[52] These songs are among the texts that emphasize most the king's provision for and care of his subjects, in the context of his successful defence of the country's frontiers and conquests abroad.

Related themes are mobilized in the same king's Semna and Uronarti stelae, which contain an exhortatory text for those manning the Nubian frontier. Like the other sources cited, this has strong literary qualities, and its concluding passage is a variation on themes found in the

im alten Ägypten (Munich: Fink, 1991), pp. 169-99.

51. A. Loprieno, 'Loyalty to the King, to God, to Oneself', in P. der Manuelian (ed.), *Studies in Honor of William Kelly Simpson*, II (Boston: Museum of Fine Arts, 1996), pp. 533-52; short version: 'Loyalistic Instructions', in Loprieno (ed.), *Ancient Egyptian Literature*, pp. 403-14.

52. Lichtheim, *Ancient Egyptian Literature*, I, pp. 198–201; one song: Parkinson, *Voices from Ancient Egypt*, pp. 46–47 no. 7.

Instruction of Ptahhotep.[53] The king's short self-presentation after a brief statement of his establishing the frontier is at the opposite extreme from the Berlin Leather Roll (see n. 38):

> I am a king who (both) speaks and acts:
> what comes to pass through me is what I plan;
>
> one who rages to conquer,
> who is swift to succeed;
>
> who does not sleep with a matter on his mind;
> who takes thought for the poor and stands up for the meek,
> (but) who is not mild to the enemy who attacks him;
>
> who attacks when he is attacked,
> who desists when (the attacker) desists,
> who responds to a matter according to its content.

This text, which is at least as much 'propaganda' as my royal composition, is at the extreme of 'realism' and offers no grounds for claims of royal divinity. Its modesty is likely to belong in the context of a strategy for addressing a group that might have experienced royal participation in actual events and so have a tempered image of the king's capacities.

A cluster of material from the much later reign of the Eighteenth Dynasty king Amenhotep II illustrates a range of treatments of the king's role and person. Perhaps more than other kings, Amenhotep emphasized his own physical prowess and personal activism. Apart from the narratives of his military campaigns, which contrast with those of his predecessor Thutmose III in their greater and possibly artificial dynamism, his 'athletic' achievements were celebrated in textual and pictorial form.[54] His Great Sphinx Stela recounts achievements in rowing and with bow and arrow, the two being treated as successive

---

53. Parkinson, *Voices from Ancient Egypt*, pp. 43-46, no. 6; C.J. Eyre, 'The Semna Stelae: Quotation, Genre, and Functions of Literature', in S. Israelit-Groll (ed.), *Studies in Egyptology Presented to Miriam Lichtheim*, I (Jerusalem: Magnes Press, 1990), pp. 134-65, with references to primary publications. The translation here is mine.

54. See W. Decker and M. Herb, *Bilderatlas zum Sport im alten Ägypten* (Handbuch der Orientalistik, 1.14; Leiden: E.J. Brill, 1994), pp. 147-48, Pls. A, 70, with later parallels pp. 148-50, Pls. 71–72. See discussion of P. der Manuelian, *Studies in the Reign of Amenophis II* (Hildesheimer Ägyptologische Beiträge, 26; Hildesheim: Gerstenberg, 1987), pp. 189-213.

episodes in a narrative.[55] The text has the form of a conventional royal inscription rather than a 'royal tale', as is demonstrated by its long eulogy following after the initial titulary. Nonetheless, the narrative, part of the raison d'être of which is to highlight the regular transition from Thutmose III to Amenhotep II, has strong fictive features including a brief clause in the voice of the narrator, and tells a legitimizing story of youth and early maturity. In athletics, Amenhotep is said to have rowed as the 'stroke' who set the rhythm for 200 oarsmen, continuing to propel the ship single-handed for another 15 km after they had all flagged. He then mounted his chariot and rode past a number of close-set bronze targets 7.5 cm thick, shooting arrows through them and out the other side so that they fell to the ground. Contemporaries will have known that this could not be done and accepted either that their ruler had superhuman powers or that the matter was one of hyperbole where literal accuracy was irrelevant. What was important was that the king was beyond comparison with anyone else.[56]

This material comes from a specialized area of royal attainment, but it can hardly be doubted that it was significant for the presentation of the king to his world. The related, ancient and symbolically laden domain of hunting was celebrated in New Kingdom inscriptions and, for example, on a box of Tutankhamun that has one composition of the king triumphing against his enemies and another of him slaying game in the hunt.[57] A literary parallel in the fragmentary, probably earlier text *The Sporting King*[58] shows that this facet of the king's role spread throughout high culture.

55. Lichtheim, *Ancient Egyptian Literature*, II, pp. 39-43; Manuelian, *Studies in the reign of Amenophis II*, pp. 181-88; commentary on the feats described: E. Edel, 'Bemerkungen zu den Schießsporttexten der Könige der 18. Dynastie', *Studien zur Altägyptischen Kultur* 7 (1979), pp. 23-39 (38-39).

56. See J. Baines, 'The Stela of Emhab: Innovation, Tradition, Hierarchy', *JEA* 72 (1986), pp. 41-53 (44-50). Manuelian, *Studies in the reign of Amenophis II* (see n. 54) points out that some element of competition is visible in the Amenhotep II texts, but this is very slight.

57. N.M. Davies and A.H. Gardiner, *Tutʿankhamūn's Painted Box* (Oxford: Griffith Institute, 1962).

58. R.A. Caminos, *Literary Fragments in the Hieratic Script* (Oxford: Griffith Institute, 1956), pp. 22-39; Parkinson, *The Tale of Sinuhe*, pp. 293-94. This motif, which would repay further investigation, has iconographic parallels from the beginning of Egyptian iconography and is paralleled for the Twelfth Dynasty in an 'annal' inscription of Amenemhat II: H. Altenmüller and A.M. Moussa, 'Die

What is most distinctive for Amenhotep II is the survival of two testimonies to his role from his viceroy of Nubia, Usersatet. One is a relatively conventional composition in a personal rock shrine Usersatet built at Qasr Ibrim in Lower Nubia.[59] Like other shrines at the site, this one is dedicated to local deities and perhaps the king. It includes a scene of tribute to the king of a type known in non-royal tombs.[60] This incorporates an inscription couched in unusual terms enumerating the tribute and giving a flattering speech that is pronounced by officials; unlike other examples, this is followed by a separate eulogy of the king pronounced by Usersatet. The very fragmentary text includes some hyperbolistic phraseology:

> You are (a) Re, chief of the Ennead, (a) Khnum, who created the gods
> ... lord of provisions, rich in food, who enters into knowledge like
> Thoth (the god of wisdom) ...

The unusual composition of this scene and its texts points to its being an original work; it provides another piece of flattery that might be performed before the king, as well as constituting a declaration of loyalism significant in its setting, in the southern colony far from the royal court. The eulogy may never have been performed in the king's presence, or even known by him.

The shrine, which is generally conventional, contrasts with the unique small stela that Usersatet seems to have set up in the fortress at Semna; this celebrated his relationship with Amenhotep II.[61] The scene at the top shows Usersatet presenting gold tribute to the king, who is enthroned under a baldachin, while the text beneath consists of a copy of a letter written by the king to his viceroy, purportedly in his own hand. The damaged text states that the king, who was sitting and drinking and enjoying himself, thought of his former companion

Inschrift Amenemhets II. aus dem Ptah-Tempel von Memphis: Ein Vorbericht', *Studien zur Altägyptischen Kultur* 18 (1991), pp. 1-48 (17-18). The prenomen of Amenemhat II occurs, perhaps coincidentally, on one of the fragments of the *Sporting King*: Caminos, *Literary Fragments*, p. 26.

59. R.A. Caminos, *The Shrines and Rock Inscriptions of Ibrim* (Archaeological Survey of Egypt, 32; London: Egypt Exploration Society, 1968), pp. 65-72, Pls. 28-32.

60. A. Radwan, *Die Darstellungen des regierenden Königs und seiner Familienangehörigen in den Privatgräbern der 18. Dynastie* (Münchner Ägyptologische Studien, 21; Berlin: Bruno Hessling, 1969).

61. W. Helck, 'Eine Stele des Vizekönigs *Wśr-Śt.t*', *JNES* 14 (1955), pp. 22-31.

Usersatet, who had made a notable kill in battle and had acquired several women in different places in the Near East. There follows advice not to be inattentive in dealing with Nubians, as well as a rather obscure mild reproach over a minor official about whom Usersatet had not informed the king (a detail that is also very exceptional in a public inscription). In these two monuments Usersatet seems to have wished to bring the presence of his king to regions outside the traditional frontiers of Egypt and to celebrate him both through the conventional but exaggerated performance inscribed in the shrine and through implicit praise of his closeness to his officials, as exemplified in the letter on the stela; this was, of course, also good for his own status. The contrast between the two treatments tends to relativize the claims in the shrine text. Here as elsewhere, the king's status is bracketed by context, but the individual character that Amenhotep II projected is also discernible.[62]

The phraseology occurring in the *Instruction of Amenemhat* and the loyalist texts—and no doubt in other lost works—was taken up around half a century after Amenhotep II under Akhenaten. As the founder of the monolatric cult of the solar disk (*aten*) and its light,[63] Akhenaten necessarily had a new position in the articulation of cosmos and religion: with a single deity his mediation between human and deity had a different character from what went before. He both emphasized his own status and attributed kingly character to his god, in a merging of divine and royal characteristics that has parallels in later periods, especially the Graeco-Roman.[64] He also seems to have propounded his beliefs in a lost teaching that is echoed in non-royal biographies.[65] He adopted the same phraseology that makes of the king a Shu (the god of air and life, and for Akhenaten of light), as well as a personified 'inundation', 'destiny', and 'fortune'. Like a few predecessors, Akhenaten appears to have claimed some of the qualities of a creator. His solar creator, the

62. Compare Manuelian, *Studies*, Chapter 4, 'A Closer Look at the Person of Amenophis II'.

63. Among the enormous literature, see e.g. J. Assmann, 'Akhanyati's Theology of Light and Time', *Proceedings of the Israel Academy of Sciences and Humanities* 7.4 (1992), pp. 143-76.

64. See P. Derchain, 'La différence abolie: Dieu et Pharaon dans les scènes rituelles ptolémaïques', in Gundlach and Raedler (eds.), *Selbstverständnis und Realität*, pp. 225-32.

65. J. Assmann, 'Die "Loyalistische Lehre" Echnatons', *Studien zur Altägyptischen Kultur* 8 (1980), pp. 1-32.

Aten, was hardly credited with these particular concerns, but Akhenaten did not take them up them by default. Rather, his retention of them shows that they were accepted as metaphorical and that he could therefore assume an almost literary role of creator in accordance with tradition. An adoration text of the official Panehsy addressed to the Aten and invoking the king as intermediary—as is made clear by the iconography—gives the fullest version of this phraseology.[66] Its most striking feature is that it calls the king a 'god' (*nṯr*), the traditional word that was otherwise rare in this period. This usage therefore points rather paradoxically to the metaphorical character of the whole, while the composition of which the passage forms part makes the Aten the focus of the cult, and Panehsy addresses his flattery to him rather than to the king.

Thus, many claims of royal capabilities and divinity, which can appear together on the same monument, are metaphorically framed or incorporated in a role-playing context. Even with Akhenaten's exceptional position, there is no elevation of his status to make it equivalent to that of his god. Nineteenth and Twentieth Dynasty developments tend, if anything, in the opposite direction. Ramesses II's most dramatic composition, the record of the Battle of Qadesh, projects the king as the quintessentially pious worshipper of Amon-Re, who thus elicited an exceptional response from the deity in the form of help in a crisis.[67] This treatment co-existed with a measure of self-deification, in which the king's person was almost split into a living office-holder who performed the cult and a divine recipient of cult from his worshippers (see n. 36). In the Twentieth Dynasty, Ramesses IV spelled out how he achieved his status through moral worth as well as deeds.[68] Although he

66. W.J. Murnane, *Texts from the Amarna Period in Egypt* (SBL Writings from the Ancient World, 5; Atlanta: Scholars Press, 1996), p. 171. The text is also distinctive in not writing the name Akhenaten in a cartouche; this may tend to make his status comparable with that of a god. 'Fortune' is absent from this particular version. See also J. Quaegebeur, *Le dieu égyptien Shaï dans la religion et l'onomastique* (Orientalia Lovaniensia Analecta, 2; Louvain: Leuven University Press, 1975), pp. 109-11.

67. See e.g. J. Assmann, *Ägypten: Eine Sinngeschichte* (Munich: Hanser, 1996), pp. 285-93; Assmann does not cite B.G. Ockinga, 'On the Interpretation of the Kadesh Record', *Chronique d'Égypte* 62 (1987), pp. 38-48, which offers an interesting reconsideration of Assmann's interpretation on the basis of an earlier article.

68. Stela from Abydos: K.A. Kitchen, *Ramesside Inscriptions, Historical and*

too emphasized his deeds—optimistically as it turned out—he did not claim deification in the same way as Ramesses II. This style of self-presentation, which was widespread among the non-royal of the period, was more significant than deification for the developments of subsequent periods.

The cases I have discussed come from periods of centralized rule. When kingship was weak and incumbency generally brief, or there were several dynasties in different parts of the country, kings naturally still wished to project their status. While the record of some periods is very fragmentary, complex projections are just as evident from the Second Intermediate Period as from centralized ones. Several of these texts exploit role-playing models, notably that of the 'royal tale'.[69] They exhibit great literary skill, a quality especially evident altogether later in the very long eighth-century victory stela of the Kushite King Piye, which almost constitutes a single-handed revival of classical Egyptian culture, evoking Middle Kingdom models in particular.[70]

The intermediate periods have not produced non-royal compositions that would be counterparts for the type, attested notably in Middle Kingdom biographies and literary texts, that attributes quasi-cosmic responsibility to its protagonist. Many biographies of all periods are concerned with matters other than royalty and this applies in greater measure to intermediate periods, when some people, especially in the First Intermediate Period, had independent pretensions as local rulers, while others who served royalty might display high aspirations while

Biographical, VI (Oxford: Basil Blackwell, 1983); see P. Derchain, 'Comment les Égyptiens écrivaient un traité de royauté', *Bulletin de la Société Française d'Égyptologie* 87–88 (1980), pp. 14-17. On another stela from the same site Ramesses IV claimed to have done more for his god in four years than Ramesses II had done in his 67: Kitchen, *Ramesside Inscriptions*, VI, p. 19, lines 10-16.

69. Thirteenth–Seventeenth Dynasty royal stelae: Neferhotep: W. Helck, *Historisch-biographische Texte der 2. Zwischenzeit und neue Texte der 18. Dynastie* (Kleine Ägyptische Texte; Wiesbaden: Otto Harrassowitz, 1975), pp. 21-29 no. 32 (Egyptian text only); J. Baines, 'The Inundation Stela of Sebekhotpe VIII', *AcOr* 36 (1974), pp. 39-54 and 37 (1976), pp. 11-20; P. Vernus, 'La stèle du roi Sekhemsankhtaouyrê Neferhotep Iykhernofret et la domination Hyksôs', *Annales du Service des Antiquités de l'Égypte* 68 (1982), pp. 129-35; *idem*, 'La stèle du pharaon *Mntw-htpi* à Karnak' (see above, n. 16).

70. Lichtheim, *Ancient Egyptian Literature*, III, pp. 66-84; see Assmann, *Ägypten: Eine Sinngeschichte*, pp. 356-70.

not naming the kings they served.[71] This absence of an echo of royalty is a significant sign of current weakness of the king, but it does not follow that the institution itself was being questioned. Until late times there was hardly any discourse that did question kingship or attempted to present matters that had been proper to it in terms of other social institutions.

The Maintenance of Order in a Bounded Cosmos

In contrast with eulogies and royal inscriptions, descriptive and discursive materials tend to formulate ideas about kingship not so much in terms of political power as in relation to the order of the cosmos and to the mission of king and elite to maintain, interpret, transmit, and enhance the civilization that embodied that order.[72] In a move that is characteristic of kingship almost everywhere, they appropriated the mundane political side and set it on a different symbolic plane.

The essential symbol that embodied the cosmic mission of king and elite was the temple, the outside of which was decorated with reliefs and inscriptions that displayed how order was maintained; this display consisted either of icons of the king ritually slaughtering enemies or of presentations of royal campaigns (see works cited in n. 91 below). Even this core discourse was hardly addressed as 'propaganda' to people as a whole, because temples were typically set within enclosures and could only be approached by a limited range of people.[73] Major temple complexes with their enclosures were, however, the largest and most enduring structures in most regions and spoke, simply through their presence, to the people as a whole. At festivals gods went out from their temples. They represented a royal as well as a divine presence to people at large, because the convention that the king was the sole person on a par with the gods and hence sole officiant will have been generally known, even though there was no pretence that ritual performers were anyone other than the priests. This broader social embedding of temples will have helped to sustain the cosmic mission of king and elite.

One of the few explicit statements about the overall constitution of

71. E.g. Baines, 'The Stela of Emhab' (see n. 56).

72. J. Baines and N. Yoffee, 'Order, Legitimacy, and Wealth in Ancient Egypt and Mesopotamia', in G. Feinman and J. Marcus (eds.), *Archaic States* (Santa Fe: School of American Research, 1998), pp. 199-260.

73. Baines, 'Contextualizing Egyptian Representations' (n. 10).

the ordered cosmos is that it consists of the gods, the king, the deceased, and humanity—omitting some categories that were dispensable in a condensed statement. The passage is in one of a pair of texts, probably composed in the Middle Kingdom, that seems to have elucidated the temple cult's meaning for a small initiated group and was subsequently inscribed in remote parts of some New Kingdom temples. The composition is therefore not a work of 'propaganda', but it naturally exalts the king's role. After a number of other statements, especially describing the king's knowledge of the solar cult and its meaning, it concludes that the sun god:

> Re has placed King N
> on the earth of the living
> for ever and ever
>
> judging humanity and propitiating the gods,
> realizing order (*ma'at*) and destroying disorder (*izfet*).
>
> He gives offerings to the gods
> and mortuary offerings to the spirits.
>
> The name of King N
> is in the sky like Re.
>
> He lives in joy
> like Re–Harakhte.
>
> The elite rejoice when they see him,
> and the subjects perform a dance of celebration,
> in his form as a youth (late versions: Re, the child).[74]

The king is the pivotal figure in this fourfold articulation of beings, performing religious actions toward the gods and the deceased, as well as relatively secular ones toward humanity. As we have seen, the king's presentation of offerings dominates temple decoration. The notion that he is responsible for offerings to the spirits is articulated elsewhere in

---

74. Daytime text: J. Assmann, *Der König als Sonnenpriester: Ein kosmographischer Begleittext zur liturgischen Sonnenhymnik in thebanischen Tempeln und Gräbern* (Abhandlungen des Deutschen Archäologischen Instituts, Abteilung Kairo, 7; Glückstadt: J.J. Augustin, 1970); English translation: Parkinson, *Voices from Ancient Egypt*, pp. 38-40, no. 4. Nighttime text: M.C. Betrò, *I testi solari del portale di Pascerientaisu (BN2)* (Università degli Studi di Pisa, Missioni Archeologiche in Egitto, Saqqara, 3; Pisa: Giardini, 1990); J. Assmann, *Egyptian Solar Religion in the New Kingdom: Re, Amun and the Crisis of Polytheism* (trans. A. Alcock; London and New York: KPI, 1995), pp. 20-22.

the most widespread of all textual formulas, the funerary recitation in which he gives offerings to the varying gods named so that they may in turn give offerings to the deceased.[75] This does not imply that the gods might depend upon the king for their sustenance, but rather that he stimulates a gracious response from them that will be directed toward the deceased who are the beneficiaries of the recitation.

The deceased constitute a morally ambivalent cosmic domain. A blessed afterlife is the ideal human aspiration, but the dead may in reality be malevolent, while a funerary text states that the creator instituted the prospect of the next world in order to sustain humanity's reverence for the gods.[76] The dead belong more to the night than to the day and they greet the sun god in his nightly passage through the underworld, which is also the context in which he must struggle to maintain the cosmos. Despite the king's provision of offerings for the dead, and in early periods his creation of a mortuary landscape for the elite with his own tomb at its centre, he has little control over the night and the domain of the dead, as is indicated by his minimal presence in the nighttime counterpart of the text just cited. In some senses, the sun god controls night and ultimately the cosmos, while the king is responsible for the day and for Egypt.

This limitation to the king's capabilities is part of the interdependence of king, gods, and other categories of being. All together participate in sustaining the cosmos. The sun god is just as much threatened in his daily passage through the underworld as is the king in his maintenance of order in this world. The king offers his success in so doing to the gods, but he also depends upon them for the preconditions of success. Like the sun god's defence of and provision for the cosmos, his defence of this world cannot be assured and requires constant vigilance. In his service of the gods, the king is further obligated not just to maintain the boundaries of the ordered realm, but if possible to extend them—an ideal he was often unable to meet.[77]

The text cited above also evokes ambivalence in the attitude of the gods toward the king and humanity. The word *sḥtp*, rendered

---

75. W. Barta, *Aufbau und Bedeutung der altägyptischen Opferformel* (Ägyptologische Forschungen, 24; Glückstadt: J.J. Augustin, 1968).

76. Coffin Texts, spell 1130; e.g. Lichtheim, *Ancient Egyptian Literature*, I, pp. 131-33; Parkinson, *Voices from Ancient Egypt*, pp. 32-34, no. 1.

77. E. Hornung, 'Politische Planung und Realität im alten Ägypten', *Saeculum* 22 (1971), pp. 48-58.

'propitiate' above, implies that the gods should be encouraged to show 'favour' (*ḥtp*, among other possible words) toward the human world. While gods, king, and humanity participate together in the cosmos, the gods may be justly—or as personal beings even capriciously—angry toward those who stand beneath them in the cosmic hierarchy. Ideas of divine volition and caprice are well attested from the New Kingdom on, probably through developments in decorum as much as in belief, and they encompass relations between king and god as well as between individual and god.[78] A text like the one cited above suggests that such ideas may have been intrinsic to religion from an earlier period, a possibility that seems also to be presented in the pessimistic literary *Admonitions*, a text probably of the Middle Kingdom.[79]

The fact that the cosmos is threatened is a powerful legitimation of royal authority: although some texts propound a king who is subject to human morality, his cosmic mission means that he can act in a peremptory way, beyond any normal moral constraints, because so much is at stake.[80] The text cited summarizes order under the central concept of *maʿat*. Within human society, *maʿat* is an essentially positive notion that embodies ideas of sociability, concern for others, and the maintenance of social networks down the generations.[81] In cosmic terms more and different matters are at stake, and are distilled in the opposition between realizing order and destroying disorder: the term *izfet* extends from internal opposition to the unbounded, extra-cosmic but ever-present chaos. Practical workings of this concern are evident in magical provisions against harmful beings, for example in the 'execration texts'.[82] These beings range from foreign peoples through

78. For contrasting interpretations, see J. Baines, 'Society, Morality, and Religious Practice', in B.E. Shafer (ed.), *Religion in Ancient Egypt: Gods, Myths, and Personal Practice* (Ithaca, NY: Cornell University Press; London: Routledge, 1991), pp. 172-86; Assmann, *Egyptian Solar Religion*, pp. 190-92; *idem, Ägypten: Eine Sinngeschichte*, pp. 259-77.

79. Parkinson, *The Tale of Sinuhe*, p. 185 (p. 12 of original); Lichtheim, *Ancient Egyptian Literature*, I, pp. 159-60.

80. Different passages of the *Instruction for Merikare* effectively present both of these alternatives: Parkinson, *The Tale of Sinuhe*, pp. 212-34; Lichtheim, *Ancient Egyptian Literature*, I, pp. 97-109.

81. See especially J. Assmann, *Ma'at: Gerechtigkeit und Unsterblichkeit im alten Ägypten* (Munich: Beck, 1990); preliminary French version: *Maât, l'Egypte pharaonique et l'idée de la justice sociale* (Paris: Julliard, 1989).

82. See Parkinson, *Voices from Ancient Egypt* , pp. 125-26, no. 46.

token Egyptians, who form parts of global listings of humanity, to specific known people who had presumably fallen into disfavour. The king could pursue his internal as well as external enemies because they threatened general cosmic order.

Although legitimations conveyed through the medium of written texts and monuments presumably had a limited impact on Egyptians as a whole, this does not mean that these ideas were unimportant, but that they had the reflexive character of elite ideology common in many societies, serving as much to reinforce the sense of mission of king and elite as to communicate more widely. Indeed, the extravagance of the means exploited in the maintenance of order makes those means almost an end in themselves, a vast apparatus of primarily artistic production that satisfies the requirements of gods, king, and elite (and the dead), becoming institutionalized because of the expertise required to create it and sustain it. This apparatus is reflected also in the concluding verses of the text cited above: the proper response to the reaffirmation of order is elation by all human participants (the only point where the text mentions 'subjects'). Other texts emphasize the joy the gods feel at beholding the king's approach and seeing the works he has wrought for them. This atmosphere of celebration, which culminates in temple compositions of the Graeco-Roman period, embodies the triumph of order and, importantly, the banishment of disorder.

Assmann sees the king's evocation of general order as part of the 'primary religion' character of Egyptian beliefs: Egyptian 'religion' is that of a single society or civilization and cannot be detached from that society's social order.[83] The world of the Hebrew Bible was one of declared faith and commitment to a particular deity and religious system by competing, primarily elite groups in a relatively small polity that set itself off against other surrounding societies but also had universalizing aspirations; its normative beliefs were also the subject of intense internal discussion. Such discussion, the contrast with surrounding societies, and the possibility of drawing some distinction between religion and society are for Assmann characteristics of 'secondary', supra-societal religions—ultimately Buddhism, Judaism, Christianity, and Islam. His perspective, which descends, through S.N. Eisenstadt[84]

---

83. See J. Assmann, *Ägypten: Theologie und Frömmigkeit einer frühen Hochkultur* (Stuttgart: W. Kohlhammer, 1984), pp. 9-23.

84. See S.N. Eisenstadt (ed.), *The Origins and Diversity of Axial Age Civilizations* (SUNY series in Near Eastern Studies; Albany: SUNY Press, 1986); for Egypt,

and Karl Jaspers, from such thinkers as Alfred and Max Weber, may hide some points of comparison between earlier and later civilizations, but the general framework is valuable and throws into relief the different social contexts of kingship in Egypt and in the Hebrew Bible. In the latter, the position of the deity is far more dominant than is any one deity in Egypt, while kingship is an institution that cannot be taken for granted and lacks the automatic authority and cosmic embedding of Egyptian kingship. Although one or two Egyptian private sources are frank about the limitations of particular kings[85] and kings appear compromised in some tales,[86] there is nothing in the stream of tradition to compare with the hostility to kingship of the Deuteronomistic tradition in the Hebrew Bible. The powerful anchoring of rulership in a particular society's cosmic mission is common to Egypt and to many Near Eastern and other polities, and can pay scant regard to the realities of the political landscape;[87] Egypt is one of the cases where state, civilization, and cosmos were most nearly co-extensive.

Questioning and Arguing about Kingship: 'Messiah' and Salvation

In conclusion, instead of vainly attempting to summarize the meaning of Egyptian kingship, I review very briefly how its presentation evolved in periods of the native institution's decline and compare it summarily with the position of kingship in the world of the Hebrew Bible (for which this volume will offer ample evidence).

The first millennium BCE began with a period of several centuries when Egypt was split, continued with foreign invasions and shorter periods of restoration and Egyptian power, and ended with the foreign rule of the Ptolemies and Roman emperors. It was marked by a growing integration of Egypt into the Near East and Mediterranean as well as a

see J. Assmann, 'Große Texte ohne eine Große Tradition: Ägypten als eine vorachsenzeitliche Kultur', in S. N. Eisenstadt (ed.), *Kulturen der Achsenzeit II. Ihre institutionelle und kulturelle Dynamik*, 3 (Frankfurt am Main: Suhrkamp, 1992), pp. 245-80.

85. E.g. E.F. Wente, *Letters from Ancient Egypt* (SBL Writings from the Ancient World, 1; Atlanta: Scholars Press, 1990), 183, no. 301.

86. Posener, *De la divinité du pharaon*, pp. 89-103; *idem*, *Le Papyrus Vandier* (Bibliothèque Générale, 7; Cairo: Institut Français d'Archéologie Orientale, 1985).

87. See esp. M. Liverani, *Prestige and Interest: International Relations in the Near East ca. 1600–1100 B.C.* (History of the Ancient Near East: Studies, 1; Padua: Sargon, 1990), pp. 33-78.

lesser cultural uniformity within the country. For individuals, fewer first-millennium biographies than earlier celebrate their protagonists' closeness to the king.[88] The cultural revival in the Twenty-fifth, Twenty-sixth, and Thirtieth dynasties produced some royal inscriptions in the earlier tradition, while several of the most distinctive nonroyal texts are from exceptional periods, notably the two Persian domina-tions.[89] An unusual case of displayed royal service is the group of biog-raphies of the high priests of Memphis. One of the latest of these, that of Psherenptah (41 BCE), the husband of the better known Taimhotep, describes the close relationship of its protagonist with the king (presumably Ptolemy XII Neos Dionysos Auletes, who died a decade earlier), using striking circumlocutions to refer to Alexandria and fictionalizing the whole.[90] The text is steeped in classical Egyptian cul-ture and shows a heavily qualified assimilation of the foreign dynasty. Since it was composed around the time when Cleopatra VII returned to Egypt with Mark Antony, this is not surprising; what is perhaps more surprising is the extent to which Ptolemaic rule was acknowledged in it.

Overall, the first millennium presentation of the king bifurcated. The temples, especially in the Graeco-Roman period, continued tradition and produced an enormous elaboration of the ideology of the king as the perfect junior partner of the gods and intermediary with humanity,[91]

88. U. Rößler-Köhler, *Individuelle Haltungen zum ägyptischen Königtum der Spätzeit* (Göttinger Orientforschungen, 4.21; Wiesbaden: Otto Harrassowitz, 1991), is a valuable treatment despite the criticisms of some reviewers, offering a nuanced presentation of how people displayed their relationship with royalty. See also Baines, 'Kingship, Definition of Culture, and Legitimation'.

89. J.J. Clère, 'La statue du fils aîné du roi Nectanabô', *RÉg* 6 (1951), pp. 135–56; J. Baines, 'On the Composition and Inscriptions of the Vatican Statue of Udjahorresne', in Manuelian (ed.), *Studies in Honor of William Kelly Simpson* (n. 51), I, pp. 83-92, with refs.; inscription of Petosiris: Lichtheim, *Ancient Egyptian Literature*, III, pp. 44-54.

90. E.A.E. Reymond, *From the Records of a Priestly Family from Memphis*, I (Ägyptologische Abhandlungen, 38; Wiesbaden: Otto Harrassowitz, 1981), no. 19, pp. 136-50 (translation unsatisfactory). See also J. Quaegebeur, 'The Egyptian Clergy and the Cult of the Ptolemaic Dynasty', *Ancient Society* 20 (1989), pp. 93-116, who argued that there was a greater native Egyptian acceptance of the Ptolemaic royal cult than scholars such as Erich Winter would allow.

91. P. Derchain, 'Le rôle du roi d'Égypte dans le maintien de l'ordre cosmique', in L. de Heusch *et al.*, *Le pouvoir et le sacré* (Université Libre de Bruxelles, Institut de Sociologie, Annales du Centre d'Étude des Religions, 1; Brussels: no publ., 1962), pp. 61-73; J. Baines, 'Temples as Symbols, Guarantors, and Participants in

while more critical discussion appeared elsewhere, notably in the *Demotic Chronicle* and in a section in the religious compilation of Papyrus Jumilhac.

These texts partake of wider east Mediterranean movements. The *Demotic Chronicle*, which dates to the earlier Ptolemaic period, is couched as a set of oracles predicting an untimely end for most of the kings of the last Egyptian dynasties and looking to a ruler who will appear from Herakleopolis in Middle Egypt and restore the country's fortunes.[92] The kings who are to fail will mostly do so because of their lack of care for the gods. The casting of the text in the form of a prophecy has an ancient precedent in the *Words of Neferti* (see n. 26) but may also relate to Near Eastern 'prophetic' literature. It is different in character from the older Egyptian text because the ruler from Herakleopolis is an unfulfilled eschatological prospect whereas Neferti's 'prospective' saviour was Amenemhat I of the Twelfth Dynasty. As in Akkadian 'prophetic' texts in particular,[93] the collocation of fulfilled prophecies with the future prospect at the end of the text enhances the latter's persuasiveness. Like other compositions of its period, the *Chronicle* no doubt also had oracular literature in its background.

The section of Papyrus Jumilhac is an assembly of cult and mythological information relating primarily to a northerly nome of Upper Egypt. The relevant section is very close to the *Asclepius* tract preserved in Latin, and both relate to the corpus of 'eschatological' literature, now preserved mainly in Greek, from Graeco-Roman Egypt.[94]

Egyptian Civilization', in S. Quirke (ed.), *The Temple in Ancient Egypt: New Discoveries and Recent Research* (London: British Museum Press, 1997), pp. 216-41. Basic work on temples, with general discussion of their symbolism: D. Arnold, *Die Tempel Ägyptens: Götterwohnungen, Kultstätten, Baudenkmäler* (Zurich: Artemis & Winkler, 1992).

92. J. Johnson, 'The Demotic Chronicle as a Statement of a Theory of Kingship', *Journal of the Society for the Study of Egyptian Antiquities* 13 (1983), pp. 61-72. Translation: E. Bresciani, *Letteratura e poesia dell'antico Egitto* (Turin: Einaudi, 2nd edn, 1994), pp. 803-14.

93. See in general J.C. VanderKam, 'Prophecy and Apocalyptics in the Ancient Near East', in J.M. Sasson *et al.* (eds.), *Civilizations of the Ancient Near East*, III (New York: Charles Scribner's Sons, 1995), pp. 2083-94; *Canadian Society for Mesopotamian Studies Bulletin* 23 (1992): *The Origin of Prophecy*, esp. R.D. Biggs, 'The Babylonian Prophecies', pp. 17-20.

94. See P. Derchain, 'L'auteur du Papyrus Jumilhac', *RÉg* 41 (1990), pp. 9-30 (25-28). General intellectual context: G. Fowden, *The Egyptian Hermes: A Histori-*

These works do not focus much on kingship. Papyrus Jumilhac presents the ruin that will happen in the land if offerings are not made to the gods and the temples are not maintained. These had been essential responsibilities of the king but the text does not mention him at all, setting his pre-emptive, defensive, and supportive activities in the background, so that the gods and the perceived and generalizable values of Egyptian civilization are the focuses of interest. While Papyrus Jumilhac itself probably came from the intellectual milieu of the temple, the compositions it assembles were not subject to the same constraints as were temple reliefs.

These developments highlight how far traditional Egyptian civilization was from producing anything like a 'Messiah' figure. While the king saved the country from threatening chaos, this was a core institutional element in his role; it was integrated into the general vision of the cosmos and oriented to the present, not toward a future goal. Egypt like other civilizations had a sense of loss, in that human society represented a fall from an ideal golden age when the gods ruled on earth, but before late times the only matching notion of 'salvation' was political and related to the arrival of new dynasties or rulers—as in the *Words of Neferti*, which is a fictional and somewhat propagandistic work. The affirmation and restoration of order was a cyclical process that could be envisaged in patterns from a day to a year, reign, dynasty, or historical period. With the exceptions of the *Demotic Chronicle* and some other texts of the Graeco-Roman period that do look to a saviour or a catastrophe, Egyptian ideology did not in general envisage an eschatological redeemer who might restore a perfect state of the world. The idea of personal salvation existed and was evoked in pietistic prayers to various gods and in the personification Shed 'Saviour',[95] but he was a minor deity, not a king or a human being.

Thus, 'messianic' views that envisaged perfecting the current world at some near or distant point in the future were largely absent in Egypt. The ultimate destiny of the cosmos was a dissolution that would affect

cal Approach to the Late Pagan Mind (Cambridge: Cambridge University Press, 1986); Assmann, *Ägypten: Eine Sinngeschichte*, esp. pp. 418-30.

95. E.g. G. Fecht, *Literarische Zeugnisse zur 'persönlichen Frömmigkeit' in Ägypten* (Abhandlungen der Heidelberger Akademie der Wissenschaften, philosophisch-historische Klasse, 1965.1; Heidelberg: Carl Winter, 1965), text 9; H. Brunner, 'Sched', in W. Helck and W. Westendorf (eds.), *Lexikon der Ägyptologie*, V (Wiesbaden: Otto Harrassowitz, 1984), cols. 548–49.

the gods as well as the human world.[96] The Egyptian vision of order was as much spatial as temporal. The sanctified world of the gods existed in heaven and in the sun god's passage though the underworld. Both the king and humanity aspired to join that world after death. Within the present world, there were domains of greater and lesser sanctity and perfection, ranging from the temple sanctuary through the temple complex, and comparably through the royal palace and its complex, into the outside world in general.[97] The gods were enjoined by the cult to inhabit their statues and this world. More broadly, Egypt as a whole was a 'sacred' domain and landscape to be set off against the surrounding disorder. These differential degrees of sanctity encompassed the king and worked through him to some extent, because he and his palace mediated in part between the outside world and the temple.

In these areas, Egyptian beliefs were far from Judaeo-Christian tradition, which springs from a society that existed in opposition to its neighbours and distinguished itself as having a mission to create an ideal world. Egyptian kingship embodied societal values in a preemptive and legitimizing fashion. Egypt asserted that it was the only society rather than one set off against others. Egyptian society was larger in scale and far less communitarian in ethos than that of the Hebrew Bible. It took the conception of the king for granted as central and indispensable and did not marginalize it until very late. Conceptions of kingship in some neighbouring societies were far more negotiable and dispensable.

The centrality of Egyptian kingship, its pivotal role in articulating the cosmos and creating order, and its religious, political, and moral authority pervade the ancient record. The visual and verbal forms in which kingship was incorporated and celebrated display nuanced attitudes that were elaborated both conceptually and artistically and that varied with context and period. This complex record is a measure of the institution's importance and of how it developed and was constantly renegotiated, like central elements in any civilization. The surviving

96. Esp. Hornung, *Der Eine und die Vielen*, pp. 166-79 (ET *Conceptions of God*, pp. 172-85).

97. See D. O'Connor, 'Mirror of the Cosmos: the Palace of Merneptah', in R.E. Freed and E. Bleiberg (eds.), *Fragments of a Shattered Visage: The Proceedings of the International Symposium on Ramesses the Great* (Monographs of the Institute of Egyptian Art and Archaeology, 1; Memphis, TN: Memphis State University, 1993), pp. 167-98.

evidence for these negotiations needs also to be set in the lost living context, which was no doubt as elaborate as the high-cultural materials that do survive. Rather than ask, for example, whether the king 'was' a god, it is desirable to confront these materials more directly in their complexity. The king sought to be most things both to humanity and to the gods.

Ancient Egypt: Chronological Outline

Predynastic Period	c. 5000–3000 BCE
Early Dynastic Period	
1st–3rd dynasties	c. 2950–2575 BCE
Old Kingdom	
4th–8th dynasties	c. 2575–2150 BCE
First Intermediate Period	
9th–11th dynasties	c. 2150–1980 BCE
Middle Kingdom	
11th–13th dynasties	c. 1980–1630 BCE
Second Intermediate Period	
14th–17th dynasties	c. 1630–1520 BCE
New Kingdom	
18th–20th dynasties	c. 1540–1070 BCE
Third Intermediate Period	
21st–25th dynasties	c. 1070–715 BCE
Late Period	
25th–30th dynasties, Second Persian Period	715–332 BCE
Macedonian Period	332–305 BCE
Ptolemaic Period	305–30 BCE
Roman Period	30 BCE–395 CE
Byzantine Period	395–640 CE
Muslim conquest	640 CE

This is a rough guide; for earlier periods dates are deliberately rounded. Overlapping dates and dynasty numbers are intentional. I use the rather controversial scheme of R. Krauss, *Sothis- und Monddaten: Studien zur astronomischen und technischen Chronologie Altägyptens* (Hildesheimer Ägyptologische Beiträge, 20; Hildesheim: Gerstenberg, 1985). No consensus on Egyptian chronology has yet emerged.

Bibliographical Note

There is a vast amount of writing on Egyptian kingship. The most recent book, D. O'Connor and D.P. Silverman (eds.), *Ancient Egyptian Kingship* (Probleme der Ägyptologie, 9; Leiden: E.J. Brill, 1995), has an extensive bibliography (pp. 300-29), as well as notes at the ends of some chapters. A historical presentation of writing on the subject forms the first section of my 'Kingship, Definition of Culture, and Legitimation', while the initial essay of the editors also surveys the literature (pp. xxi–xxvii); valuable review by P. Derchain, in *BO* 53 (1996), cols. 690–92. Among books listed in the book's main bibliography, the most important are: H. Frankfort, *Kingship and the Gods: A Study of Ancient Near Eastern Religion as the Integration of Society and Nature* (Chicago: University of Chicago Press, 1948); G. Posener, *De la divinité du pharaon* (Cahiers de la Société Asiatique, 15; Paris: Imprimerie Nationale, 1960); E. Blumenthal, *Untersuchungen zum ägyptischen Königtum des Mittleren Reiches* I. *Die Phraseologie* (Abhandlungen der Sächsischen Akademie der Wissenschaften, 61.1; Berlin: Akademie Verlag, 1970 [no vol. II published]). M.-A. Bonhême and A. Forgeau, *Pharaon: les secrets du pouvoir* (Paris: Armand Colin, 1988), is a synthesis, valuable mainly for later periods, that does not offer a major advance over the works just cited. Older material is now interesting primarily for historical reasons; see Posener's introductory survey, *De la divinité du pharaon*, pp. vii–xv. An important synthesizing review article, especially for iconography (hardly covered in this chapter), is D. Wildung, 'Göttlichkeitsstufen des Pharao', *OLZ* 69 (1973), cols. 549–65. The book Wildung reviewed, L. Habachi, *Features of the Deification of Ramses II* (Abhandlungen des Deutschen Archäologischen Instituts, Abteilung Kairo, Ägyptologische Reihe, 5: Glückstadt: J.J. Augustin, 1969), is important in its own right. E. Hornung, *Der Eine und die Vielen* (Darmstadt: Wissenschaftliche Buchgesellschaft, 1971) (ET *Conceptions of God in Ancient Egypt: The One and the Many* [rev. and trans. J. Baines; Ithaca: Cornell University Press, 1982; London: Routledge, 1983]) has a valuable short section on kingship, pp. 135-42, in a discussion of 'images' and manifestations of gods.

N.-C. Grimal, *Les termes de la propagande royale de la XIXe dynastie à la conquête d'Alexandre* (Mémoires de l'Académie des Inscriptions et Belles-lettres, NS 6; Paris: Boccard, 1986), is a valuable collection of material, but almost without connected discussion or synthesis.

A more penetrating counterpart for an earlier period is E. Hornung, 'Zur geschichtlichen Rolle des Königs in der 18. Dynastie', *Mitteilungen des Deutschen Archäologischen Instituts Abteilung Kairo* 15 (1957), pp. 120-33.

A conference volume on kingship is intended as the start of a series: R. Gundlach and C. Raedler (eds.), *Selbstverständnis und Realität: Akten des Symposiums zur ägyptischen Königsideologie, Mainz 15–17.6.1995* (Ägypten und Altes Testament, 36: Beiträge zur Ägyptischen Königsideologie, 1; Wiesbaden: Otto Harrassowitz, 1997).

Many relevant texts are presented in translation by M. Lichtheim, *Ancient Egyptian Literature* (3 vols.; Berkeley: University of California Press, 1973–80). For the classical literary texts, see R.B. Parkinson, *The Tale of Sinuhe and other Ancient Egyptian Poems, 1940–1640 BC* (Oxford: Clarendon Press, 1997).

The present chapter seeks to extend discussion by focusing on how context affects what is said about the king, building upon my articles 'Kingship, Definition of Culture, and Legitimation', and 'Origins of Egyptian Kingship', in O'Connor and Silverman (eds.), *Ancient Egyptian Kingship*, pp. 3-47, 95-156; and 'Kingship before Literature: The World of the King in the Old Kingdom', in Gundlach and Raedler (eds.), *Selbstverständnis und Realität*, pp. 125-74.

KINGSHIP IN ANCIENT MESOPOTAMIA

W.G. Lambert

Depictions of rulers in various art forms are well known from some periods and areas within ancient Mesopotamia, but by themselves they do not provide much enlightenment. In some cases there is even doubt whether a king or god is meant. Written sources are the prerequisite for some understanding of the institutions, and while true writing, that is, a system of recording human speech on some medium, arose in Mesopotamia only c. 3200 BCE, at first it was restricted to administrative documents and scribal lists of signs and words, although by c. 2600 BCE it was developed sufficiently to record material relevant to our subject, namely, royal inscriptions, literary texts and letters. The script was pictographic or symbolic at first, but the writing on clay with a stylus resulted in the degradation of pictograms or symbols into groups of wedge-shaped marks, which were also on occasion copied on other mediums such as stone and metal. This writing system spread from Sumer to Semites upstream, to Elamites in south-west Iran, and elsewhere, and was developed to express a whole variety of languages over the millennia during which it was used. It finally succumbed to the infinitely simpler alphabetic scripts during the second century CE. But after the fall of the Persian Empire it was restricted to parts of Babylonia itself. Everywhere cuneiform writing was the preserve of professional scribes, employed least or not at all by ordinary people, and mostly by the king, high officials and wealthy businessmen. Thus, royalty figures often in the surviving documents, but rarely is criticism of it preserved—for obvious reasons.

Mesopotamia was not a cultural entity in the ancient world, and we can only know things relevant to our subject when sufficient documents of the right sort survive. Generally, the more powerful and prosperous the state, the more documentation it created. But survival of this documentation is less predictable. Clay tablets in Mesopotamia were mostly dried only in the air, and if the buildings housing them were burnt down, they might be better preserved as a result of the unintended firing. But archives and other documents considered out of date and irrelevant could be thrown out and used as building rubble. The sudden and complete destruction of a town or public buildings might well result in the best possible preservation of cuneiform documents. From the sources which have survived from the area and are most relevant to our subject, three main areas stand out as worthy of study: Sumer in the third millennium BCE, the far south of the Tigris–Euphrates plain; then Babylonia c. 2000–539 BCE, which embraced the former Sumer, with further land upstream to a little beyond the modern Baghdad; and Assyria, a small area on the upper Tigris containing the modern Mosul, c. 2000–612 BCE. The history of these areas is complicated, with ups and downs in the relative statuses of the cultures I shall consider.

In one respect all three of these cultures were unanimous. Rulers ruled by the express authority of the gods, and were expected to create a prosperous, well-governed land. Documents of royal origin frequently state that this aim was achieved, but we do not know how far the subjects of these rulers agreed. But in many matters these areas had major differences in both the royal institutions and their particular aims. The modern term 'king' is itself inadequate and potentially misleading, because of the overtones which it brings, also because it is the conventional English translation of two ancient words, the Sumerian *lugal* and the Akkadian *šarru*. Not all Sumerian rulers used *lugal* of themselves. Other terms were in use. While *šarru* as used by Babylonians and Assyrians does more fully correspond to the English 'king', its being the etymological equivalent of the Hebrew *šar* can mislead. As used, the Akkadian *šarru* equates with the Hebrew *melek*, but the Akkadian equivalent of that by etymology, namely, *malku*, is used comparatively rarely of Babylonian or Assyrian kings, more often of (to them) foreign rulers.

Sumer

Sumer was traditionally a land of city states, each with its patron god, who was notionally the supreme power in that state, and who lived in the form of a statue in his 'house', the major temple of the city. In all cities of any size there were several or even many temples, and each owned irrigated land beyond the city walls, also flocks and herds and appropriate buildings. Thus, the temples were major employers and complete economic units, something like large-scale mediaeval manors, but with a theocratic superstructure. The patron god of the city lived in his 'house' with divine family and courtiers and was provided with two meals a day, clothing, and everything else that wealthy humans would then have expected. Under this system the city ruler was conceived of as a kind of farm bailiff, managing the gods' estates. Reality, can, of course, be quite different from theological presuppositions. There were Sumerian rulers who were aggressive imperialists, by no means content to be 'farm managers'. But the presuppositions did modify human thought at the time.

One strange phenomenon is the lack of any generally accepted term for 'city ruler'.[1] The following are the most commonly found:

> *nam-šita*, literally, 'lord of the mace';
> *ensi,* meaning 'lord of the *si*';
> *en*, meaning either 'lord' or 'high priest';
> *lugal*, meaning literally, 'big man'.

The first of these, written ŠITA + GIŠ + NÁM, but to be read *nám-*^{giš}*šita*, occurs as the first item in a list of officials' titles known first c. 3000 BCE from copies from the city of Uruk. Later scribal material, but not royal inscriptions, confirms that it means 'king'.[2] In all the lexical lists from Uruk dating from that time the terms *ensi* and *lugal* do not occur, so *nam-šita* is on present knowledge the earliest term corresponding to our 'king'. But it seems to have gone out of use quite early, since royal inscriptions from their appearance in the second half of the third millennium BCE do not use it. Better known to us is the term *ensi*, written PA.TE.SI, of which three signs the last is clearly a phonetic indicator. The word is a genitive combination: '*en* of the *si*'. The first part, *en*, might be the common noun, 'lord', but the meaning of *si* is problematical. A rebus writing may be suspected. The Sumerian noun, 'shepherd', is *sipa(d)*, but written PA + LU, but the signs if read *ugula udu* would mean 'foreman of the sheep'. Similarly, PA.TE can be read *ugula temen*, 'foreman of the sacred (temple) enclosure'. This is not yet certain, because there is so far no known Sumerian word, *si*, referring to a temple compound, and the whole word *ensi* was borrowed into Akkadian as *išši'akkum*, referring to a farmer of social status, which seems to lay stress on the temple estates rather than the temple

1.   See generally, W.W. Hallo, *Early Mesopotamian Royal Titles* (AOS, 43; New Haven: American Oriental Society, 1957).

2.   W.G. Lambert, 'Studies in UD.GAL.NUN', *OrAnt* 20 (1981), pp. 94-97.

buildings. A further complication is that in the town Adab in particular the term is written with four signs—PA.TE.SI and GAR—which is so far inexplicable. Whatever the problems of the word and the signs used to write it, the contexts in royal inscriptions and its apparent absence in any other meanings support this as the word expressive of the traditional Sumerian concept of government by a man who manages the gods' estates. The term *en*, as already remarked, is a common noun 'lord', but as a title it can be used of a ruler. A succession of four kings of Uruk around the middle of the third millennium, namely, En-šakušanna, Lugal-kiginne-dudu, Lugal-kisal-si and Lugalzaggesi, may use both *en* and *lugal* of themselves in one sentence. The first styles himself '*en* of Kengi (= Sumer), *lugal* of the land', while the others prefer either '*en* of Uruk, *lugal* of Ur', or '*lugal* of Uruk, *lugal* of Ur'.[3] All were properly king of the town Uruk, though ruling over Ur as well. Thus, I do not accept the usual suggestion that *en* here means simply 'lord', but prefer the other meaning, 'high priest'. Under the Sumerian city state system the ruler of a city had a close bond to the patron deity of his city. He might conquer other cities, but his bond to the patron deities of those cities would be much less, so as not to offend his real patron. Over conquered cities his status was one resulting simply from power, and perhaps the English 'boss' would convey this, since *lugal* is not restricted in Sumerian to rulers of towns, but is applied to the owner of a field or a slave: he was the 'big man' of who or what he had power over.

Thus, the Sumerian equivalents of 'king' do not really correspond to the English term. Notionally he was a subordinate in his one city to the chief deity, and was responsible for running the city justly and efficiently for that deity, within a land of such city states. The reality might have been different, but the ideology stuck for a long time. 'Shepherd' was a royal title by metaphor, and which persisted long after Sumerians had ceased to exist.

The Akkadian Interlude

About 2350 BCE Sumer was shaken by a political and cultural revolution. One of the Semites from upstream made himself first king of one

---

3.   H. Behrens and H. Steible, *Die altsumerischen Bau- und Weihinschriften*, II (Freiburger altorientalische Studien, 5; Wiesbaden: Franz Steiner, 1982), pp. 293-337; cf. Hallo, *Titles*, p. 5.

of the Semitic cities, Kish, then proceeded in stages to make himself master of the whole of southern Mesopotamia, to which he added in time the rest of Mesopotamia and areas beyond. His name, Sargon (*Šarru-kīn*), meaning 'the reliable king', was obviously adopted as a throne name at some point in his rise to supremacy, but it also shows a consciousness of the status implied by that term. While his professions of piety to and dependence upon gods Sumerian and Semitic flow freely, the Sumerian concept of the city ruler as a farm bailiff is plainly rejected. He built up a new town, Akkad, as his capital, and boasts in his royal inscriptions: 'He moored the ships of Meluḫḫa, Magan and Tilmun at the quay of Akkad... 5400 men daily eat in the presence of Sargon...'[4] Prior to this, temples had been the biggest economic organizations, but Sargon did his best to set up a palace economy. Trading ships from the three areas named down the Gulf put in at the quay of his newly built capital town, Akkad, no doubt by order, and the 5400 men who ate at his expense were no doubt a standing army. Previously Sumerian troops had been farm labourers at off-season times. It is then no surprise that Sargon uses the title *lugal* of himself in Sumerian inscriptions and *šarru* in Akkadian inscriptions. Might and power were a major part of the royal ethos of this dynasty. Neither *ensi* nor *sipa(d)* is used of Sargon or his successors on the throne of Akkad. Excavations at Ebla in western Syria have exposed a palace roughly contemporary with Sargon that also served both as a royal residence and as a major economic centre. The archives reveal vast quantities of wool and textiles being handled within the palace, perhaps as a royal monopoly. Thus, Sargon's innovation in southern Mesopotamia of developing his new capital as an international emporium was not an original idea of his, but simply the importation of a practice well known among the Semites of upper Mesopotamia and Syria.

Another innovation of the Akkadian dynasty for Sumer was divine kingship. Though Gilgamesh, a king of Uruk c. 2700 BCE, appears in a list of gods' names a century or so later, where he is a minor god,[5] this was no regular happening. Sumerian rulers generally did not experience

4.   D.R. Frayne, *Sargonic and Gutian Periods* (The Royal Inscriptions of Mesopotamia, Early Periods, 2; Toronto: University of Toronto Press, 1993), pp. 28-29.

5.   P. Mander, Il *Pantheon di Abu-Ṣālabīkh* (Istituto Universitario Orientale, Dipartimento di Studi Asiatici, Series Minor, 26; Naples, 1986), p. 86, col. verso iii 25.

apotheosis at death. Belief in an immortal soul resulted in lavish preparations for the next life, as best known from the royal tombs of Ur, but this is not deification. The new concept arose only with Narām-Sîn, the fourth king of the dynasty, and is known from contemporary inscriptions, one of which declares that the town Akkad petitioned eight major gods: 'Ishtar in E'anna, Enlil in Nippur, Dagān in Tuttul, Ninḫursaga in Kesh, Ea in Eridu, Sîn in Ur, Shamash in Sippar and Nergal in Kutha that he [i.e. Narām-Sîn] should be the god of their city Akkad, and so they built a temple for him in Akkad'.[6] The reality of this conception is confirmed in art on the well-known stele relief showing the king wearing the horns of divinity on his head as he defeats his enemies.[7] Also, some of his royal inscriptions use the divine determinative with his name. Narām-Sîn's son and successor, Shar-kāli-sharri, also on occasion, but not always, has the divine determinative with his name in his royal inscriptions. After Shar-kāli-sharri's reign the dynasty collapsed in chaos, and this gave the Guti people from Kurdistan the opportunity to take over Sumer for a period, though after a few generations they were driven out and a local dynasty emerged, the Third Dynasty of Ur, c. 2113–2004 BCE. This gave Sumer a century of peace and prosperity.

The Third Dynasty of Ur

The intervention of the Guti, who were remembered as crude barbarians who desecrated the whole country, raised a theological problem. Why did the gods allow this to happen? The one answer was that Narām-Sîn had offended the chief Sumerian god, Enlil, and for that the Guti were brought in to punish the country. Thus, the new Ur dynasty had both to build up what the Guti had destroyed or neglected, and to avoid the sins of the Akkad dynasty. It was, then, in the proper sense reactionary: an attempt to reinstate the good old Sumerian values. However, there was no simple putting back of the clock. One ruler governed the whole country, from Ur. No attempt was made to reinstate a land of city states. But piety and concern for the gods was marked.

---

6. I.J. Gelb and B. Kienast, *Die altakkadischen Königsinschriften des dritten Jahrtausends v. Chr.* (Freiburger altorientalische Studien, 7; Stuttgart: Franz Steiner, 1990), pp. 81-82, lines 24-56.

7. H. Frankfort, *The Art and Architecture of the Ancient Orient* (Harmondsworth: Penguin Books, 1954), Pl. 44.

Under the second king of the dynasty, Shulgi, a bureaucracy was set up to gather and distribute animals as taxes from twelve major cities, each having responsibility for supplying such needs for one month of the year. The major temples were beneficiaries of this system, though other official needs were also met from this supply. The epithet 'shepherd' was again used of the king, but *ensi* was not the royal title used; *lugal* continued from the Akkad period, no doubt because *ensi* was appropriate to a city governor, not to the ruler over a country. But the ethos of the older Sumerian city states was revived: rulers who concerned themselves with the well-being of the gods and acted piously and benevolently. But the example of the Akkad dynasty also resulted in some imperialism. An empire was built up to the east of the Tigris, and most of the Ur III rulers were deified during their lives and had shrines where offerings were presented.

Babylonia

This well-meant state did not last long in terms of history. There was a movement of Amorites from the Syrian desert into Mesopotamia, and the rulers of the Third Dynasty of Ur either underestimated the scale of the threat (a wall was built to keep them out) or did not have adequate military forces to repel them. There was also treachery among the city governors. While the basic movement was presumably of nomads moving with their flocks, somehow armies with reasonable equipment and effective leadership arose, so that a serious momentum developed, assisted finally by the Elamites, who delivered the *coup de grâce*. But the Elamites promptly withdrew and so left the Amorite chieftains free to settle down, as many of them did, becoming the new rulers of the country. Thus, from the previous 'Sumer and Akkad' (the Sumerians nearest the Gulf, the Semitic Akkadians further upstream) a more homogeneous Semitic civilization arose, ruled over largely by Amorites. As a spoken language Sumerian died out, and a new dialect, which we call 'Babylonian', appeared. The Amorite language of the new rulers and their fellow invaders is not recorded in a single inscription, though thousands of personal names are clearly Amorite, not Babylonian, for example Hammurabi (or Hammurapi: the etymology of the second element is not certain) begins with what in biblical Hebrew is Ammi-, with ʿ*ayin*.

The result of the take-over was, curiously enough, a land of city states again, as various tribal leader and others imposed themselves on the country. Just as in the desert tribes had to observe certain conventions and act with restraint in order to survive, now, in the newly taken over cities a similar give and take was often observed. But there were also the more ambitious city rulers who aspired to empire, and the last and best known of these was Hammurabi, who converted Babylon from a small town to a capital of southern Mesopotamia, a status it only finally lost to the Persian Cyrus.

The kind of kingship that resulted was a modified form of what went immediately before. The divinity of kings did not continue. In the Diyala valley and a few towns in Babylonia it survived a short time after the fall of the Third Dynasty of Ur, but then it finally died out. Presumably, the Amorites did not have any sympathy for the concept. Then the bureaucratically organized, centralized economic system of the Ur III period could not, of course, survive in a land of city states, and even within the individual cities things changed. Temples remained as big economic organizations, but private capitalism flourished, and no doubt the Amorite kings tolerated or encouraged this. In the desert there were no such institutions as temples or temple estates, and shrewd kings would soon appreciate that a fragmentation of the previously centralized economic system would diminish any threats that it would have been to their own power. The duty of the king to reign wisely, justly and effectively under the aegis of certain gods continued as before. The biggest ideological change was the first appearance in Babylonia of the concept of divine right to kingship based on descent from a certain family line. While son often succeeded father in third-millennium Sumer, there is nowhere any hint that a certain family line was divinely endowed with a right to kingship. It was a matter of human nature that fathers often wished their sons to succeed them and groomed them to that end. The Amorite origin of the new concept is clear. There survives from the reign of Ammi-ṣaduqa, great-great-grandson of Hammurabi and king of Babylon c. 1647–1626 BCE, a list of 28 deceased ancestors of this king.[8] The document is cultic, that is, it comes from a rite in which the shades of these ancestors were invited to partake of offerings of food and drink supplied for them by their current descendant, Ammi-ṣaduqa. It was a cult of dead ancestors. The first

8.   J.J. Finkelstein, 'The Genealogy of the Hammurapi Dynasty', *JCS* 20 (1966), pp. 95-118; W.G. Lambert, 'Another Look at Hammurabi's Ancestors', *JCS* 22 (1968), pp. 1-2; D. Charpin and J.-M. Durand, '"Fils de Sim'al": les origines tribales des rois de Mari', *RA* 80 (1986), pp. 141-83, esp. pp. 159-70.

nine in the list, starting from the end, were all kings of Babylon. Some
of the preceding 19 were no doubt real men, but some appear to be
names of tribes rather than of individuals. Genesis 10 is, of course, in
some senses comparable. The cult of dead ancestors of the ruling
family is known also from pre-Amorite Ebla and Ras Shamra/Ugarit, so
it was clearly a Semitic tradition of the period.[9]

Although the Amorite ruling family of Babylon eventually merged
into the Babylonian upper classes, and although the royal line was
stopped when the Cassites from Kurdistan invaded and settled in
Babylonia for some 450 years (c. 1600–1150 BCE), the driving out of
these Cassite rulers and the restoration of a native dynasty, the Second
Isin dynasty, reveals how firmly this once new doctrine of kingly descent had taken root. The most successful king of the Second Isin
dynasty was Nebuchadnezzar I, 1125–1103 BCE, who boasts that he
was descended from Enmeduranki, one of the antediluvian Sumerian
kings according to the Sumerian King List:

> Nebuchadnezzar, king of Babylon, who supervises all cult centres, and
> confirms the offerings,
> distant scion of kingship, seed preserved from before the flood,
> offspring of Enmeduranki, king of Sippar...[10]

No doubt some justification for this obviously false claim was known
and proffered at the time, but so far we do not know it. After the
Second Isin Dynasty a succession of small and little-known dynasties
followed from 1025 to 732 BCE, most of the kings almost certainly
unrelated in lineage to Nebuchadnezzar I. Next came a succession of
rulers of Babylon from 732 to 626 BCE, of whom most were kings of
Assyria ruling as conquerors over Babylon, but a few were natives of
Babylonia. Among these kings of Babylon from 1025 to 626 BCE some

---

9. For Ebla, see, e.g., A. Archi, 'Die ersten zehn Könige von Ebla', *ZA* 76
(1986), pp. 213-17. In the tablet published there the sign for GOD before each
divine name can be taken either as a determinative, or as a common noun, but the
result is the same: they were deified kings. For Ugarit see D.G. Pardee, *Les Textes
paramythologiques de la 24ᵉ campagne (1961)* (Ras Shamra–Ougarit, 4; Paris:
Éditions Recherche sur les Civilisations, 1988), pp. 168 and 169, reverse, where all
the deified rulers have *'il* prefixed to their names, which can only be the common
noun, 'god'.

10. W.G. Lambert, 'The Seed of Kingship', in P. Garelli (ed.), *Le Palais et la
Royauté* (XIXᵉ Rencontre Assyriologique Internationale; Paris: Geuthner, 1974),
pp. 432 and 435.

were of Aramaean extraction, and so certainly unrelated to native kings of Babylon of any period. One of these was Merodach-baladan II (722–710 BCE), well known in the Old Testament for his embassy to Hezekiah. He uses of himself the phrase 'lasting seed of kingship',[11] which to our knowledge was first employed by Hammurabi of all the kings of Babylon. Thus, the concept of legitimacy to the throne by descent from the right family became normal in Babylonia after 2000 BCE with the arrival of the Amorites.

The Cassite dynasty's views are the least known. But one royal inscription, of Agum II (c. 1600 BCE?), not accepted as genuine by everyone, traces the king's descent back to the Cassite god, Shuqamuna, as well as using the phrases 'pure seed, seed of kingship',[12] which suggests that the Cassite kings also subscribed to the usual Babylonian concept of proper kingly descent. Hammurabi's son and successor, Samsu-iluna, uses the phrase 'lasting seed of the gods'[13] to describe himself, suggesting that the Amorites may have had ideas of royal families' ultimate parents having been divine. But the list we know begins with Ḫarḫar or Ara(r), who is not known anywhere as a deity.

Though the Late Babylonian dynasty (626–539 BCE) is particularly well known, its concept of kingship is not clearly explained. The kings flaunted their dependence on the gods and were 'shepherds', with the responsibilities to their subjects which that term implies, but their ancestry is little explained. The founder, Nabopolassar, nowhere in his royal inscriptions names even his father. He came to prominence as a general appointed by the Assyrians, but later he successfully turned against the Assyrians and was half responsible for destroying their empire and power. His son Nebuchadnezzar II (the biblical Nebuchadnezzar) commonly names his father, but no other forebear. His son, Evil-Merodach, is very little known and ruled briefly. Of the last three kings, the first, Nergalsharezer (Neriglissar) names his father as Bēl-shuma-ishkun and gives him the title 'wise noble', which is the most we know of him. The son of Neriglissar, Labāshi-Marduk, ruled only a few months and left no royal inscriptions that have come down to us.

---

11. Lambert, 'Seed', p. 431.

12. For bibliography see J.A. Brinkman, *Materials and Studies for Kassite History*, I (Chicago: The Oriental Institute, 1976), p. 97. There is no adequate translation. The lines are column i 1-4: 'Agum-kakrime, son of Urshigurumash, pure seed of Shuqamuna', and column i 20: 'pure seed, seed of kingship'.

13. Lambert, 'Seed', p. 429.

The last king, Nabonidus, gives his father's name as Nabû-balāṭsu-iqbi with the title 'wise noble', and his kingdom fell to Cyrus the Persian. The famous Cyrus cylinder, a Babylonian document composed to glorify the Persian ruler, gives his Persian ancestry briefly and then adds the phrase 'lasting seed of kingship'.[14] So probably the concept of royal descent from the right family was alive during the Late Babylonian empire, but the actual pedigrees of the rulers were too obviously not in accord with it for the matter to be formulated of them. Curiously, the term *iššakku* (from the Sumerian *ensi*) enjoyed a great revival in the Late Babylonian royal inscriptions, usually in the phrase 'exalted *iššakku*',[15] but we do not know what nuance it bore at the time.

Light on Late Babylonian kingship comes from ritual texts. There was a series of tablets giving the various rituals performed in the temple of Marduk in Babylon, Esagil. Only a few tablets of the whole series survive, some from Late Assyrian libraries (c. 750–650 BCE), others in Babylonian copies from the Seleucid or even Parthian periods.[16] The texts themselves were probably composed after 1000 BCE, and record the rites as enacted from perhaps that date until the fall of Babylon to the Persians in 539 BCE. Since Marduk was the patron god of the town of Babylon, the capital of the country, the king often participated in the rites. In Esagil on the fourth of Nisan, in the course of the New Year festival, the following is prescribed in the ritual text:[17]

> Water is brought for the king's hands and he is taken into [Esag]il. The artisans depart to the gate. [...] When Bel arrives the high priest goes out and picks up the sceptre, circlet, mace [and...] He picks up his (i.e. the king's) royal crown, takes them in [before] Bel and places them on a seat. Next he goes out and slaps the king's cheek. He puts [...] behind him and leads him (i.e. the king) into the presence of Bel. [...] he drags him by the ears and makes him kneel down on the ground [...] the king recites this once:

14. Lambert, 'Seed', p. 431.

15. M.-J. Seux, *Épithètes royales akkadiennes et sumériennes* (Paris: Letouzey & Ané, 1967), p. 111.

16. F. Thureau-Dangin, *Rituels accadiens* (Paris: Leroux, 1921), pp. 127-54; English translation by A.J. Sachs, in *ANET*, pp. 331-34; G. Çağirgan and W.G. Lambert, 'The Late Babylonian Kislīmu Ritual for Esagil', *JCS* 43–45 (1991–93), pp. 89-106; B. Pongratz-Leisten, *Ina šulmi irub* (Mainz: Von Zabern, 1994), pp. 228-32; W.G. Lambert, 'Processions to the Akītu House', *RA* 91 (1997), pp. 49-80.

17. Thureau-Dangin, *Rituels accadiens*, pp. 144-45, lines 413-52.

'I have [not] sinned, lord of the lands, I have not neglected your
   divinity,
[I have not] destroyed Babylon, I have not ordered its dispersal,
I have [not.]...Esagil, I have not forgotten its rites,
[I have not] slapped the face of any citizen, I have [not] humiliated
   them,
[I have attended] to Babylon, I have not destroyed its walls.'

A few lines are missing at this point, but somehow a reply to the king
comes from Bel, probably through the high priest, of which much is
preserved:

'Fear not, [...
What Bel has commanded [...
Bel [has heard] your prayer [...
He has made your lordship great [...
he has exalted your kingship [...
Do [...] on the *ešeš*-festival day.
Wash your hands at the Opening of the Door,
Day and night ...[...
of Babylon, his city . [...]...[...
of Esagil, his temple...[...
of the Babylonians, his citizens . [...]
Then Bel will bless you...for ever,
he will destroy your enemy and throw down your foe.'

When he has spoken this, the king...[.] he will bring out the sceptre,
circlet, mace and crown and [will give them] to the king. He will slap the
cheek of the king, and if, when [he has slapped] his cheek, tears flow,
Bel is favourable. If tears do not flow, Bel is angry: an enemy will arise
and will bring about his downfall.

Thus on this annual occasion the king was deprived of his regalia by
the high priest, who then slapped his face and made him recite a profession of innocence. In reply a message from Bel assured the king of
Bel's support, and ordered him to nurture the town, chief temple and
citizens of his, in return for which prosperity and success against
enemies were assured. Then the regalia were returned to the king, but a
second time his face was slapped, and a resulting flow of tears was a
guarantee of Bel's support, a lack of tears a guarantee of disaster.

The ritual portrays a remarkable annual humiliation of the king of
Babylon before the patron god of the town.[18] There is, of course, no

18. However, in another Esagil ritual, K 3446+ (see Lambert, 'Processions'),
apparently also from the New Year ritual, the high priest asks for a series of

direct evidence of these acts being carried out, but other matter on the same tablets is alluded to in royal inscriptions of Nebuchadnezzar II, so presumably the prescriptions in the ritual tablets are to be taken seriously.

Assyria

I cover the period c. 2000–612 BCE because, while Assyrians certainly existed before 2000, not enough is known to provide material for this inquiry. The Assyrians ceased as a political power and as a cultural group shortly after the fall of Nineveh in 612 BCE. The problems of their state arose from its small size and the lack of any natural borders. It is possible that in the third millennium BCE they had neighbours who were culturally close to them, but in the period c. 2000–612 BCE they were isolated, alone speaking their dialect of Akkadian, which we call 'Assyrian'. In religion, in organization of the state, and in other matters they were distinctive, though often influenced by their neighbours from downstream. They are generally presented as a great military power, but this is only true for the period c. 1300 and onwards when they did indeed have fine armies and generals so that for a short period they dominated the whole of the Near East. Before 1300 BCE they were not exceptional in military affairs. Their most successful king in this respect was Shamshi-Adad I, a senior contemporary of Hammurabi of Babylon, but Shamshi-Adad was an Amorite who had imposed himself on Assyria, and when his scion and successor was deposed, and Puzur-Sîn, a native Assyrian, seized power, the latter speaks scornfully of his victim as 'not of the flesh of the city Ashur'.[19] During the first few centuries of the second millennium BCE the Assyrians excelled in international commerce, trying to build up a free trade area between themselves and various Babylonian states, and succeeding at creating an organization in Anatolia, which was ruled at the time by various native rulers. Colonies of Assyrians were settled outside (or perhaps also inside) major towns, acknowledging the authority of the Anatolian

blessings on the king from a long sequence of gods, perhaps to offset the harsh treatment earlier.

19. A.K. Grayson, *Assyrian Rulers of the Third and Second Millennia BC* (The Royal Inscriptions of Mesopotamia, Assyrian Periods, I; Toronto: University of Toronto Press, 1987), p. 77, lines 1-14.

rulers, but largely governed by their own laws and rules, being regulated by their seniors in Assyria. They exploited trade between Assyria and Anatolia, but also inner-Anatolian trade. It appears that there was a wealthy aristocracy that dominated this trade and thereby held great power in the Assyrian state, even limiting the king's authority. Migrations and political turmoil finally stopped this trade in the seventeenth century BCE, and for a time Assyria was in sharp decline. Then it was swamped by the Mitanni empire, and it appears that this experience turned the Assyrians into a military nation, which remained their characteristic to the end.

A king ruled *de jure*, but it is clear that a military aristocracy existed, from which indeed the king was normally drawn, and which could serve as a counterbalance to the king. So long as the king ruled and acted in accordance with the ethos of the state, his authority was supreme. But should he fail to provide what was expected, then rumblings of discontent would begin and these could even grow and result in the king being removed from office. Two Assyrian kings were murdered by close members of their own families, and both had been guilty of undertaking ideologically questionable enterprises. Succession to the throne was another potentially explosive issue. The king could, and often did, nominate one of his sons to be 'crown prince', and thereby pre-empt the issue, but if the military aristocracy objected, or was divided on the issue, then trouble could arise on that king's death, even civil war. Clearly, the aristocracy considered that it had the right or even the duty to intervene in royal matters when the well-being of the state was at risk. There was no similar aristocracy in Babylon.

Language, as already noted, was one thing which helped to create a sense of Assyrian identity. Religion was another. The religious capital of Assyria was Ashur, a hill on the west bank of the Tigris. The place was numinous and so deified as Ashur, the state god.[20] In the first half of the second millennium BCE the city and god are interchangeable as written, but Ashur the god was moulded to the norm of other more personal gods and so later the city and land 'Ashur' are not confused with the god. Thus the status of the god Ashur was different from that of Babylonian gods, where a plurality of cities, each with its patron god, many of them more venerable than Marduk (Bel) of Babylon, meant that Marduk did not have the same status as Ashur in Assyria

---

20. W.G. Lambert, 'The God Aššur', *Iraq* 45 (1983), pp. 82-86.

even when he was elevated to be 'king of the gods' c. 1100 BCE.

A seal inscription on documents from the Anatolian merchant colonies begins: 'Ashur is king (*šarru*), Ṣilūlu is *iššakku* of Ashur'.[21] In both cases the name Ashur is written with the determinative for places, not that for gods. Ṣilūlu was what we would call king of Assyria. In a Middle Assyrian coronation ritual (composed c. 1200 BCE), the presiding priest says at a certain point, 'Ashur is king! Ashur is king'.[22] Throughout the text the human king is given the same term. The Late Assyrian coronation hymn for Ashurbanipal (669 BCE) states: 'Ashur is king. Ashur is king indeed, Ashurbanipal is [the] . [...] . of Ashur.'[23] The damaged state of the tablet prevents the reading of one key word, but the sense is clear, and the continuity of tradition is remarkable. Theologically, the Assyrian state god was a king, and the human king was his regent. This is in the old Sumerian tradition, and the seal of Ṣilūlu even uses the loan word, *ensi*. It may be noted that the title '*iššakku* of Ashur' is commonly used of Assyrian kings down the centuries.[24] This concept also helps to explain why loyalty to the state could override duty to the human king in the national interest.

While the Assyrians asserted their racial purity when the Amorite ruling family was driven out, they may also have been influenced by it. The Assyrian King List, the existence of which is first attested in an inscription of Tukulti-Ninurta I (1245–1208 BCE),[25] begins with a list of 'total: 17 kings who lived in tents'.[26] Some of these names also appear in the list of ancestors of the Amorite kings of Babylon, and others are of the same type. Detailed study of the early sections of the list reveals that an ancestry list of Shamshi-Adad I has been incorporated into a selection of names of early Assyrian kings. In later centuries, from Tukulti-Ninurta I (1245–1208 BCE) to Ashurbanipal (669–627 BCE), the phrases 'lasting seed [of kingship]', 'seed of Ashur [the

21. Grayson, *Assyrian Rulers*, pp. 12-13.

22. K.F. Müller, *Das assyrische Ritual*, I (MVAG [E.V.], 41.3; Leipzig: J.C. Hinrichs, 1937), pp. 8-9, line 29.

23. A. Livingstone, *Court Poetry and Literary Miscellanea* (State Archives of Assyria, 3; Helsinki: Helsinki University Press, 1989), p. 26, line 15.

24. Seux, *Épithètes royales*, p. 111.

25. W.G. Lambert, 'Tukulti-Ninurta I and the Assyrian King List', *Iraq* 38 (1976), pp. 85-94.

26. *Reallexikon der Assyriologie*, VI (Berlin: W. de Gruyter, 1980–83), art. 'Königslisten und Chroniken', pp. 101-103.

place]' and similar occur in royal inscriptions.[27] They demonstrate that the Assyrians of these centuries shared with the Babylonians the ideal of kings as members of a certain royal family, but we do not know whether the Assyrians already held this view before the Amorites' invasion, or only after it. At least in Assyria, with its aristocracy, it is more likely that kings over the centuries were blood relatives than in the case of Babylonian kings.

Messianism

The biblical concept of messianism, where it goes beyond the simple institution of kingship, has two main features: first, the Messiah has to be descended from the line of David, the first Israelite king divinely approved; secondly, the Messiah is an ideal king. The Mesopotamian concept of legitimacy to the throne by descent from the right family has been dealt with above. And, as briefly commented before, it was a commonplace of ancient Mesopotamian thought that kings were appointed by gods and were expected to be paragons of rulership. Royal inscriptions of any length often state this and claim that the king in question had been precisely that. Royal inscriptions even have a tradition of giving a price list of basic commodities, to show how well the people were provided for by their enlightened and able king. In this sense ancient Mesopotamia was truly messianic, though historians may exercise some scepticism when confronted by such claims. Perhaps the best example of this concept of ideal government is provided by a letter from the scholar and scribe Adad-shumu-uṣur to Ashurbanipal, in which the writer is presenting a petition to the king, and considers that a little flattery will help. After the formal letter introduction he begins:

> Ashur, [king of the gods], nominated [the king] my lord to kingship over Assyria, and Shamash and Adad by their reliable extispicy have confirmed the king my lord as king of the world. There is a fine reign: days of security, years of justice, very heavy rains, massive floods, low prices. The gods are propitious, religion abounds, temples are well provided for, the great gods of heaven and netherworld are exalted in the time of the king my lord. Old men dance, young men sing. Women and girls are happy and rejoice. Women are married and provided with (ear)-rings. Sons and daughters are born, procreation flourishes. The king my lord pardons him whose crimes condemned to death. You have released

27. Lambert, 'Seed', pp. 430-31.

the prisoner sentenced to many years. Those who have been ill for many days have recovered. The hungry have been satisfied, parched ones have been anointed with oil, the naked have been clothed with garments.[28]

Despite the selfish end of this letter, the description of an ideal reign correctly gives a picture of what the good Mesopotamian king was expected to bring about: messianic bliss.

---

28. S. Parpola, *Letters from Assyrian and Babylonian Scholars* (State Archives of Assyria, 10; Helsinki: Helsinki University Press, 1993), pp. 177-78, no. 226.

Part II

KING AND MESSIAH IN THE OLD TESTAMENT

THE CANAANITE INHERITANCE OF THE ISRAELITE MONARCHY

John Day

In terms of the ancient Near East it was quite late that a monarchy arose in Israel, just before 1000 BCE. Prior to this the tribes of Israel are said to have been ruled by judges (*šōpᵉṭîm*), a word which had broader connotations than our word 'judge', since legal judgment seems to have had only a small part in their role, and is referred to only in Judg. 4.5 and 1 Sam. 7.16-17. Rather, 'rulers' is the basic meaning: one may compare other places in the Old Testament where *šōpēṭ* clearly means 'ruler', as in Isa. 16.5; Hos. 7.7; Amos 2.3; Dan. 9.12, and also in the expression 'judges of the earth' (Pss. 2.10, 148.11; Isa. 40.23), as well as *šāpiṭum* used of a governor in Mari Akkadian, and the Punic *suffētes*, magistrates who combined political as well as judicial authority.[1] Although the Philistine threat appears to have been an important contributory cause in the emergence of a stronger, more centralized, form of government, the monarchy, it may not have been the only reason; monarchy started in the Transjordanian states at roughly the same time (the precise dates are disputed), so there is the possibility of some natural sociological evolution. Since this was new to Israel it was inevitably modelled on foreign precedent. In 1 Sam. 8.19-20, the people say to Samuel '…we will have a king over us, *that we may be like all the nations…*' In seeking for the influences on Israel's new monarchy we must most naturally look to Canaan/Syria/Transjordan, since these were the closest to hand, and in any case, Egypt and Mesopotamia were both weak and uninfluential at this time, a weakness that doubtless facilitated the rise of the Davidic–Solomonic empire.[2] We recall from the El-

---

1. See H. Niehr, *Herrschen und Richten: Die Wurzel špṭ im alten Orient und im Alten Testament* (FzB, 54; Würzburg: Echter Verlag, 1986); E. Lipiński, 'Suffète', in E. Lipiński (ed.), *Dictionnaire de la Civilisation phénicienne et punique* (Turnhout: Brepols, 1992), p. 429.

2. I see no reason to doubt the existence of David and Solomon after the fash-

Amarna letters of the fourteenth century BCE that Canaan was divided into many city states with their own kings—and those included Jerusalem (Urusalim), which David was to make his capital.

The King as Priest after the Order of Melchizedek

The clearest evidence of Canaanite, indeed Jebusite Jerusalemite, influence on Israel's monarchy is indicated by the coronation Psalm 110. In v. 4 the king is addressed in the words, 'You are a priest for ever after the order of Melchizedek'. Melchizedek was, of course, the pre-Israelite Jebusite priest–king of Jerusalem who is said to have encountered Abraham in Genesis 14. There is therefore here explicit evidence of the fusion of Israel's royal ideology with that of the Jebusites. In saying this, we are presupposing (1) that Ps. 110.4 is addressed to the king, (2) that Melchizedek's city of Salem was Jerusalem, and (3) that the fusion of ideologies took place early. Each of these points has been questioned by scholars.

(1)   The view that Ps. 110.4 was not addressed to the Davidic king was argued by H.H. Rowley,[3] who claimed that its words rather relate to Zadok, David's priest in Jerusalem. But, as has been frequently observed, two points speak against this: first, every other verse of the psalm relates to the Davidic king, so it would be odd if this verse were the one exception. Secondly, Melchizedek in Genesis 14 is spoken of as both priest and *king*, so one after his order ought to be not simply a priest, but also a king.

(2)   The view has occasionally been put forward that the Salem where Melchizedek was priest–king in Gen. 14.18 was not Jerusalem, but some other place called Salem.[4] This view has

---

ion of some recent radical scholars. See G.N. Knoppers, 'The Vanishing Monarchy: The Disappearance of the United Monarchy from Recent Histories of Ancient Israel', *JBL* 116 (1997), pp. 19-44, though Knoppers concedes that currently evidence for the existence of David and Solomon is greater than for their empire.

3.   H.H. Rowley, 'Zadok and Nehushtan', *JBL* 58 (1939), pp. 113-41 (124-25); *idem*, 'Melchizedek and Zadok', in W. Baumgartner *et al.* (eds.), *Festschrift Alfred Bertholet* (Tübingen: J.C.B. Mohr [Paul Siebeck], 1950), pp. 461-72 (468-72); *idem*, 'Melchizedek and David', *VT* 17 (1967), p. 485.

4.   E.g. J.G. Gammie, 'Loci of the Melchizedek Tradition of Genesis 14:18-20', *JBL* 90 (19710, pp. 365-96; J.R. Kirkland, 'The Incident at Salem: A Re-exam-

been critically reviewed by J.A. Emerton,[5] who shows how groundless it is. In Ps. 76.3 (ET 2) Salem is clearly equated with Zion—note the parallelism, 'His abode has been established in Salem, his dwelling place in Zion'—and Ps. 110.2 makes it clear that the priest–king rules from Zion. In any case, it is hardly likely that the Davidic monarch would be linked to some other place called Salem of little significance.

(3)   The most natural time for the Israelite royal ideology to have been fused with that of the Canaanite Melchizedek is soon after David's conquest of Jerusalem.[6] John Van Seters,[7] however, has argued that the fusion was rather a case of syncretism in the postexilic period. He notes that the expression 'High Priest of God Most High' (i.e. El-Elyon) was adopted by the Hasmonaean kings in the Maccabaean period (cf. Josephus, *Ant.* 16.163; *Ass. Mos.* 6.1) and believes that it only originated late with the postexilic Jerusalem priesthood. This is most implausible, however, for it was important for the postexilic priesthood to be Aaronite (i.e. descended from Aaron), which Melchizedek could not claim to be. Furthermore, the postexilic high priests were not kings, even if they appropriated royal symbolism, which is debatable.[8] Contra Van Seters, it was entirely natural that the Hasmonaeans should have taken over the title 'High Priest of God Most High' from Genesis 14, since, taken with Ps. 110.4, this could be used to justify their non-Aaronite status.

In Genesis 14 Melchizedek is said to have been both king and priest. That Canaanite kings could also be priests is supported by various

ination of Genesis 14:18-20', *Studia Biblica et Theologica* 7.1 (1977), pp. 3-23.

5.   J.A. Emerton, 'The Site of Salem', in J.A. Emerton (ed.), *Studies in the Pentateuch* (VTSup, 41; Leiden: E.J. Brill, 1990), pp. 45-71. M.D. Goulder, *The Psalms of Asaph and the Pentateuch* (JSOTSup, 233; Sheffield: Sheffield Academic Press, 1996), attempts unsuccessfully to circumvent Emerton's arguments. His own view that Psalm 76 was originally a northern psalm is highly speculative.

6.   Cf. J.A. Emerton, 'The Riddle of Genesis xiv', *VT* 21 (1971), pp. 403-39, for arguments in favour of this and against alternative views.

7.   J. Van Seters, *Abraham in History and Tradition* (New Haven: Yale University Press, 1975), pp. 306-308.

8.   See the contribution by Deborah W. Rooke in this volume and her forthcoming monograph, *Zadok's Heirs: The Role and Development of the High Priesthood in Ancient Israel* (Oxford: Clarendon Press).

pieces of evidence. Menander of Ephesus, as reported by Josephus (*Apion* 1.18) says that Ithobalus, king of Tyre (= Ittobaal, father of Jezebel) was also priest of Astarte. Similarly, Phoenician inscriptions speak of Tabnit, king of Sidon, as 'priest of Astarte', and his father, King Eshmun'azar I is also 'priest of Astarte'.[9] In inheriting the role of Melchizedek, David and the Israelite kings in Jerusalem therefore took over the role of priest; Ps. 110.4 is conclusive evidence that the Israelite kings did indeed function as priests. This is consistent with the fact that David wore a linen ephod, a priestly garment, when taking the Ark up into Jerusalem (2 Sam. 6.14), and with various references to the kings offering sacrifice—Saul at Gilgal (1 Sam. 13.9-10), David at Jerusalem (2 Sam. 6.13, 17-18; 24.25), Solomon at Gibeon (1 Kgs 3.4, 15), at Jerusalem for the dedication of the Temple (1 Kgs 8.5, 62-64), and then at the three great feasts of the year (1 Kgs 9.25). Although in some instances it might be argued that this means that the king 'had sacrifice offered', this will not fit 2 Kgs 16.12-15, where Ahaz goes up to the new altar he has made and offers the first sacrifice, and then commands the priest to continue the liturgy there; further, in 1 Kgs 12.33 it is said that Jeroboam 'went up to the altar to offer sacrifice' (cf. 13.1-2), which is interesting in shedding light on the sacral nature of kingship in the Northern Kingdom, a subject on which we understandably have less information. Again, David and Solomon bless the people in the sanctuary (2 Sam. 6.18; 1 Kgs 8.14), a rite which is reserved to the priests by Num. 6.22-27 and 1 Chron. 23.13.

Clearly the king's priesthood was not a full-time occupation, but a special priesthood, since the general upkeep of the cult would have been the job of the professional priests.

Was Zadok really a Jebusite Priest?

It appears that the Davidic monarchy inherited the Jebusite priesthood. What, then, of the view that Zadok was also a Jebusite priest, whom David appropriated on conquering Jerusalem?[10] The reasons commonly given for this view are as follows.

---

9. See *KAI*, 13.1, 2.

10. The view that Zadok was a Jebusite priest was first proposed by S. Mowinckel, *Ezra den Skriftlærde* (Kristiania: O. Norlis, 1916), p. 109 n. 2, and has been much followed subsequently, and defended most fully by Rowley, 'Zadok and Nehushtan', pp. 113-32. C.E. Hauer, 'Who Was Zadok?', *JBL* 82 (1963), pp. 89-

(1)   It is claimed that Zadok suddenly appears in the biblical text from nowhere in Jerusalem under David. The first reference is in 2 Sam. 8.17 in the list of David's cabinet ministers. However, it may be noted that several of David's other ministers there alluded to have not been mentioned previously either (Jehoshaphat, Seraiah and Benaiah, 2 Sam. 8.17-18), and since the list relates to David's early period in Jerusalem, it would be compatible with this to suppose that Zadok (and the others) had already been with David in Hebron.

(2)   It is claimed that Zadok has no genuine genealogy. The Chronicler's ascription to him of an Aaronite (Levitical-Eleazar) ancestry (1 Chron. 6.3-8) is said to be fictitious, and the genealogy in 2 Sam. 8.17 is claimed to be corrupt. 2 Sam. 8.17 speaks of David's priests as 'Zadok the son of Ahitub and Ahimelech the son of Abiathar'. It is generally agreed that we should read 'Abiathar the son of Ahimelech', rather than 'Ahimelech the son of Abiathar', since this is the name of David's priest elsewhere. But the assumption, common since Wellhausen, that Zadok originally lacked a patronymic and that the reference to him was followed by 'Abiathar, the son of Ahimelech, the son of Ahitub' can be criticized on the grounds that in no other case in the three cabinet lists that we have (2 Sam. 8.16-18; 20.23-26; and 1 Kgs 4.2-19) do we find the grandfather cited in addition to the father. It is therefore preferable to read 'Zadok the son of Ahitub' with MT and all the Versions—in which case Zadok is not left without a patronymic.[11]

(3)   Zadok's Jebusite origin is said to be supported by the occurrence of the same root, ṣdq, in the names of the earlier Jebusite kings Melchizedek (Gen. 14.18) and Adonizedek (Josh. 10.1, 3). But the element ṣdq is, in fact, quite common in West Semitic personal names, as Cross has noted,[12] so need not necessarily point to a Jebusite background for Zadok.

94, put an original gloss on the theory by supposing that Zadok fled to David prior to David's conquest of Jerusalem.

11. Cf. F.M. Cross, *Canaanite Myth and Hebrew Epic* (Cambridge, MA: Harvard University Press, 1973), pp. 211-14.

12. Cf. Cross, *Canaanite Myth and Hebrew Epic*, p. 209.

There are, moreover, problems with the idea that Zadok was a Jebusite priest. It is unlikely that Zadok had previously been the priest–*king* in Jerusalem, since it would have been a dangerous policy for David to have kept an ex-king as his chief priest. This particular problem would be avoided on the assumption that Zadok had previously been a Jebusite priest, but not king, though not on Rowley's version of it, according to which Ps. 110.4's allusion to the priest after the order of Melchizedek refers to Zadok, since, as we have already seen, Melchizedek was both king and priest, and Ps. 110.4 must rather refer to the Davidic king, like the rest of the psalm. What, then, of the view that Zadok had been a previous non-royal Jebusite priest, without linking him with Ps. 110.4? This is the least objectionable form of the thesis, but it still has this fundamental problem: David, we know, had two priests, Abiathar and Zadok, and of these Abiathar came from the north (1 Kgs 2.27, a descendant of Eli of Shiloh). Zadok we should most naturally expect to have come from the south. This would be in keeping with David's intention to unite north and south, as attested by his choice of Jerusalem as his capital on neutral territory. It would be rather odd for one of David's two chief priests to be a northerner, and the other a Jebusite, with no representative at all from the south, especially as this was David's own place of origin. David had been anointed king at Hebron in the south and ruled there for seven and a half years before conquering Jerusalem, so we should naturally expect him to have had a priest there, whom he would have kept on.[13] For what it is worth, 1 Chron. 12.29 (ET 28) mentions Zadok as one of David's supporters already when he was king in Hebron,[14] but it would certainly be wrong to press this verse from the late Chronicler. In conclusion,

13. Cf. Cross, *Canaanite Myth and Hebrew Epic*, pp. 208-15. M. Haran, 'Studies in the Account of the Levitical Cities', *JBL* 80 (1961), pp. 156-65 (161), had earlier connected Zadok with Hebron.

14. S. Olyan, 'Zadok's Origins and the Tribal Politics of David', *JBL* 101 (1982), pp. 177-93, also rejects the Jebusite origin of Zadok and sees him as a native Judahite, but places him rather in the far south of Judah. He attaches a lot of importance to 1 Chron. 12.29 (ET 28), and relates Zadok closely to the Aaronite Jehoiada mentioned in the previous verse (1 Chron. 12.28 [ET 27]), whom he identifies with Jehoiada (called a priest in 1 Chron. 27.5), the father of Benaiah, the latter of whom is said to come from Kabzeel in S. Judah (2 Sam. 23.20). However, there is no evidence that Zadok's place of origin in Judah has to be identical with that of Jehoiada.

therefore, it seems that Zadok was a Judahite priest, probably from Hebron, and not a Jebusite.[15]

The Jebusite Cult of Elyon

Whether or not Zadok was a Jebusite priest, it is clear from the allusion in Psalm 110 to Melchizedek that David's conquest of Jerusalem led to syncretism with the Jebusite cult of Elyon. Outside the Old Testament, the only references to the god Elyon are in the Aramaic Sefire treaty dating from the eighth century BCE and in the account of Phoenician mythology preserved by Philo of Byblos. In the Sefire treaty[16] 'El and Elyān' appear as a pair in a list of deities by whom the treaty was witnessed. In Philo of Byblos[17] Elioun (as he is called) is said to be the father of Ouranos (Heaven) and Ge (Earth). This last point is extremely interesting, since it provides a remarkable parallel to Gen. 14.19 and 22, where El-Elyon is described as 'creator of heaven and earth'. Since Philo of Byblos is certainly not dependent on the Bible, and in any case, Philo's description of Elioun is more mythical (he is called 'father' of the deified heaven and earth), there can be no doubt that Gen. 14.19 and 22 are reflecting genuinely Canaanite conceptions about the god Elyon. The reference to him as creator of heaven and earth suggests that he is similar to El, even though in both the Aramaic Sefire treaty and Philo of Byblos he is distinguished from El.

Granted that David's conquest of Jerusalem resulted in syncretism with the Jebusite cult of Elyon or El-Elyon, two questions naturally arise: (1) Do other places in the Old Testament which mention the name Elyon still retain overtones of the Jebusite god? (2) What, apart from the priesthood of Melchizedek, was actually appropriated from the cult of El-Elyon?

With regard to (1) there does seem good reason to believe that references to Elyon in the Old Testament, sometimes at least, carry with

---

15. G.H. Jones, *The Nathan Narratives* (JSOTSup, 80; Sheffield: JSOT Press, 1990), has claimed that Nathan also was a Jebusite. However, the arguments are very speculative (far more so, indeed, than in the case of Zadok), and it seems natural to see him as a native Israelite traditional Yahwist.

16. See *KAI*, 222 A.11.

17. Philo of Byblos, in Eusebius, *Praeparatio evangelica*, 1.10.15. See conveniently H.W. Attridge and R.A. Oden, *Philo of Byblos: The Phoenician History* (CBQMS, 9; Washington, DC: Catholic Biblical Association, 1981), p. 47.

them allusions deriving from the god in question. I have already mentioned the allusion to him in Gen. 14.19 and 22 as creator of heaven and earth and the parallel references in Philo of Byblos reminiscent of the god El. When we also find the name Elyon associated with El-like characteristics elsewhere in the Old Testament, we are presumably therefore dealing with genuine Canaanite appropriations. One example of this comes in Ps. 46.5 (ET 4), which, speaking of Jerusalem, says, 'There is a river whose streams make glad the city of God, the holy habitation of the Most High (Elyon)'. There is, of course, no literal river in Jerusalem, and this must be mythical imagery applied to the Gihon spring there. Since Elyon was El-like, it immediately strikes us that in the Ugaritic texts El is spoken of as dwelling at the source of the rivers, and this presumably ultimately lies behind the imagery of Ps. 46.5 (ET 4) mediated through the cult of Elyon. Again, Ps. 82.6 refers to the gods as 'the sons of Elyon', which reminds us of the gods as sons of El in Ugaritic. Furthermore, Isa. 14.13-14 associates Elyon with the Mount of Assembly, just as El is associated with the Mount of Assembly in Ugaritic. But Elyon also seems to have had some Baalistic characteristics as well. In Isa. 14.13-14 Elyon's dwelling is also spoken of as Zaphon, which in the Ugaritic texts is the name of Baal's dwelling place, and this name Zaphon is applied to Jerusalem in Ps. 48.3 (ET 2). Now, Psalm 48 has the same theme as Psalm 46, namely the conflict with the nations and the inviolability of Zion, and Elyon has already been mentioned in Ps. 46.6 (ET 5), as was noted above. The conflict with the nations also appears in Psalm 110, a psalm which, with its reference to Melchizedek, is suggestive of Jebusite influence. A good case can therefore be made for the view that the theme of Yahweh's protection of Zion from attack and the conflict with the nations was a theme appropriated by the Israelites from the Jebusite cult of Elyon. Presumably the Jebusite cult of El-Elyon was practised in a Jebusite temple in Jerusalem, but we do not hear of it. We read that when the Ark was brought up into Jerusalem by David he put it in a tent (2 Sam. 6.17), not into an already existing sanctuary. Solomon's temple, in which the Ark was eventually housed, clearly was based on Canaanite precedents, but this is not surprising, since it was built by Phoenician (Tyrian) workmen. The Canaanite parallels have been well rehearsed, for example the threefold structure of the temple (compare Hazor, Tell Tainat), and the two pillars before it—compare the two pillars at the temple of Melqart (Herakles) at Tyre, which Herodotus (2.44) mentions.

One German scholar, K. Rupprecht,[18] has argued that Solomon simply renovated an already existing Jebusite sanctuary, but although this is perfectly feasible, there is no positive evidence to support it.

Royal Anointing

As is well known, the term *māšîaḥ* 'Anointed' (whence the word 'Messiah') is applied in the Old Testament to the current Israelite king, not the future eschatological one. This term clearly relates to the act of anointing at the time of the king's coronation. Whence was this rite derived? It has often been supposed that it was derived either from the Hittites or the Egyptians,[19] the former of whom anointed their kings, while the latter anointed high officials and Syrian vassals. (For the latter, see El-Amarna letter 51, where Addu-nirari writes to the Pharaoh that 'Manaḫpiya [= Thutmose III], the king of Egypt, your ancestor, made [T]a[ku], my ancestor, a king in Nuḫašše, he put oil on his head and [s]poke as follows: "Whom the king of Egypt has made a king, [and on whose head] he has put [oil], [no] one [shall...]".'[20]

However, it seems to me most unlikely that the Israelites derived anointing directly from either the Hittites or the Egyptians. The Hittite empire had long ceased to exist; Egypt was weak at the time of the founding of the monarchy—one reason why David was able to expand his empire—and neither he, nor Saul, of whom anointing is first reported, had any particular relationship with Egypt. Rather, Saul's

18. K. Rupprecht, *Der Tempel von Jerusalem* (BZAW, 144; Berlin: W. de Gruyter, 1976).

19. A Hittite origin is supported by M. Noth, 'Amt und Berufung im Alten Testament', in *Gesammelte Studien*, I (TBü, 6; Munich: Chr. Kaiser Verlag, 2nd edn, 1960), p. 321 (ET 'Office and Vocation in the Old Testament', in *The Laws in the Pentateuch and Other Essays* [trans. D.R. Ap-Thomas; Edinburgh: Oliver & Boyd, 1966], p. 239), and an Egyptian origin is argued by R. de Vaux, 'Le roi d'Is-räel, vassal de Yahvé', in *Bible et Orient* (Cogitatio dei, 24; Paris: Cerf, 1967), pp. 299-300 (ET 'The King of Israel, Vassal of Yahweh', in *The Bible and the Ancient Near East* [trans. D. McHugh; London: Darton, Longman & Todd, 1972], p. 165). E. Kutsch, *Salbung als Rechtsakt im Alten Testament und im alten Orient* (BZAW, 87; Berlin: Alfred Töpelmann, 1963), pp. 52-63, on the other hand, divides Israelite royal anointing into anointing by the people and anointing by Yahweh, and sees the former as reflecting Hittite influence and the latter as Egyptian in character.

20. Cf. W.L. Moran, *Les Lettres d'El-Amarna* (Paris: Cerf, 1987), p. 221 (ET *The Amarna Letters* [Baltimore: The Johns Hopkins University Press, 1992], p. 122).

stamping ground (like David's) was Canaan. We should most naturally expect that the anointing of kings was borrowed from the Canaanites. But what evidence is there that the Canaanites did anoint their kings? One could point to Jotham's fable in Judges 9, vv. 8 and 15 of which imply anointing of Canaanite kings. But, of course, the age of this passage is uncertain and it could be reading back Israelite conceptions into Canaan. Two pieces of Ugaritic evidence might seem to offer support to the notion that the Canaanites anointed their kings. One is the Ugaritic Rephaim text (*KTU*[2] 1.22.II.15-18):

šmn. prst [	]	Oil...
ydr. hm. ym [	]	He vowed, If
'ṣ.[21] *'amr. y'u ḫ[d.ks'a. mlkh]*		At (my?) command, he shall tak[e the throne of his kingship],
nzt.[22] *kḫṯ.dr[kth.]*		the resting place of the seat of [his] domi[nion].

In this passage oil is mentioned in connection with someone's enthronement as king. There could be another Ugaritic text implying royal anointing if we accept J.A. Emerton's translation of a passage concerning the god Athtar's enthronement as king (*KTU*[2] 1.6.I.50-52): *dq. 'anm. lyrẓ 'm. b'l. ly'db.mrḥ 'm. bn. dgn. ktmsm* , 'Let the finest of pigments be ground; Let the people of Baal prepare unguents; (Let) the people of the son of Dagon (prepare) crushed herbs'.[23] Unfortunately, however, the translation of this passage is uncertain.

The King as 'Son of God' and 'God'

As is well known, in ancient Egypt the Pharaoh was regarded as both a god and as the son of a god: he was the son of Re, the incarnation of Horus, and after death he was assimilated to Osiris. In Mesopotamia,

---

21. *KTU*[2] suggests reading *'l* (i.e. 'on') for *'ṣ* ('tree'), which indeed makes more sense.

22. It is generally agreed that one should read *nḫt* 'resting place' for *nzt* because of parallel passages where this occurs.

23. J.A. Emerton, 'Ugaritic Notes', *JTS* N S 16 (1965), pp. 438-43 (441-43). This rendering involves connecting *'anm* with Egyptian *'wn* 'colour, pigment', *yrẓ* with Hebrew *rṣṣ* 'to crush', *mrḥ* with Egyptian *mrḥt* 'ointment', and *ktmsm* as the construct form of a noun *kt* from the same root as Hebrew *ktt* 'to beat, crush by beating', followed by enclitic mem and a noun, *sm*, cognate with biblical Hebrew *sammîm* 'spices', etc. (*KTU*[2] reads *lyrq* where scholars have generally read *lyrẓ*.)

the king was deified only in the earliest times—the Sumerian period—subsequently the kings were regarded rather as representatives of the god. In the Canaanite world, which is the part of the ancient Near East most likely to have influenced the Israelites in matters of kingship, because of its geographical proximity, we do have some evidence of the king's both being a god and the son of the god El. Thus, in the Ugaritic king list, each of the names of dead kings is preceded by the word *'il*, 'god' (*KTU*² 1.113).[24]

That the king's divinity was not simply a post mortem affair—as among the Hittites—is revealed by the Ugaritic Keret text. When King Keret is ill, his son Yaṣṣib says (*KTU*² 1.16.I.10-23), 'Is then Keret the son of El, the progeny of Laṭipan and the Holy One?... We rejoiced in your life, our father, we exulted (in) your immortality... Shall you then die, father, as men... How can it be said (that) Keret is the son of El, the progeny of Laṭipan and the Holy One. Or shall gods die? Shall the progeny of Laṭipan not live?' Subsequently, Keret's daughter, Thitmanat, laments her father in largely identical words (*KTU*² 1.16.II.36-49).

Can we detect any influence from this Canaanite concept on the Israelite notion of the king? In general, contrary to the old Myth and Ritual School, it seems that the Israelites did not regard the king as divine. We note the absence of criticism of divine pretensions of Israel's kings on the part of the prophets (contrast Isa. 14.12-15; Ezek. 28.2-10) and likewise the absence of evidence for ruler worship in Israel. The king was the son of God by adoption, not a literal son of God from birth (Ps. 2.7, 'You are my son, today I have begotten you'). Nevertheless, the king was still called a son of God and it seems likely that this was appropriated from the Canaanites (like the plural expression, 'sons of God' for angels, originally gods, and ultimately derived from the Canaanite 'sons of El' attested at Ugarit). The specifically Canaanite

24. On the Ugaritic king list, cf. K.A. Kitchen 'The King List of Ugarit', *UF* 9 (1977), pp. 131-42. B.B. Schmidt, *Israel's Beneficent Dead* (Forschungen zum Alten Testament, 11; Tübingen: J.C.B. Mohr [Paul Siebeck], 1994), pp. 67-71, and 'A Re-evaluation of the Ugaritic King-list (*KTU* 1.113)', in N. Wyatt, W.G.E. Watson and J.B. Lloyd (eds.), *Ugarit, Religion and Culture. Proceedings of the International Colloquium on Ugarit, Religion and Culture, Edinburgh, July 1994: Essays Presented in Honour of Professor John C.L. Gibson* (UBL; Münster: Ugarit-Verlag, 1996), pp. 289-304, attempts to show that *'il* in each case refers to the deity of the royal dynasty, rather than indicating divinization of the king, but this view seems like special pleading and has little following.

origin might gain support from the obscure verse Ps. 110.3—one verse before the Melchizedek reference—which may read, 'From the womb of the dawn you have the dew wherewith I have begotten you'.[25] Compare Shaḥar and Shalem, 'Dawn' and 'Dusk', the Ugaritic deities, and Shalem in the name Jerusalem, 'foundation of (the god) Shalem'.

It would seem that the Canaanite notion of the divinity of the king has left faint traces in the Israelite royal ideology, for in Ps. 45.7 (ET 6), a royal marriage psalm, it appears that the Israelite king is addressed as *'ᵉlōhîm* in the vocative, 'O God'. How are we to make sense of this? There are two broad categories of interpretation of this verse, the first of which holds that the king is indeed here called 'god' (whether literally or hyperbolically), while the second gets round the problem by attempting to render the verse in some different way.

In favour of the latter type of interpretation it is claimed that the passage would be unique in the Old Testament if the king is here addressed as 'God'. It is pointed out that we could render the Hebrew as 'Your throne is like God's for ever and ever', on the understanding that the word for 'like' (*kᵉ*) has been omitted,[26] perhaps for reasons of euphony, as the word translated 'your throne' (*kis'ᵃkā*) already contains two kaphs. A number of scholars, including C.R. North,[27] have compared the Song of Songs, where in 1.15 the man says to the woman, 'your eyes are doves' (*'ênayik yônîm*, in contrast to 5.12, where the woman says of the man, 'his eyes are *like* doves' (or 'dove's eyes') (*'ênāyw kᵉyônîm*). Alternatively, it has been suggested that one could render the passage in Ps. 45.7 (ET 6) as 'Your throne is God's for ever and ever',[28] which would likewise avoid calling the king a god. Either

---

25. This rendering follows A.R. Johnson, *Sacral Kingship in Ancient Israel* (Cardiff: University of Wales Press, 2nd edn, 1967), p. 131. It involves reading *yᵉlidtîkā* 'I have begotten you' for MT *yalᵉdūtêkā* 'your youth', which is supported by many Hebrew manuscripts, Origen's Hebrew text, LXX and the Peshiṭta. Further, it coheres with the reference to 'from the womb', brings the psalm into line with Ps. 2.7 (part of another coronation psalm), and involves no emendation of the consonantal text. Scholars generally emend the hapax *mišḥār* to *šaḥar* 'dawn', the *m* perhaps being a dittography from the last letter of the previous word *mēreḥem*.

26. C.R. North, 'The Religious Aspect of Kingship', *ZAW* 50 (1932), pp. 8-38 (29-31); J.A. Emerton, 'The Syntactical Problem of Psalm XLV.7', *JSS* 13 (1968), pp. 58-63.

27. North, 'Religious Aspects', p. 30.

28. J.S.M. Mulder, *Studies on Psalm 45* (Nijmegen: Offsetdrukkerij Witsiers, 1972), pp. 33-80.

of these renderings would correspond to the idea that is found in 1 Chron. 28.5, where Solomon is said 'to sit upon the throne of the kingdom of the Lord' (cf. 1 Chron. 29.23).

Though all this is possible, it must be admitted that the more natural way of taking *'elōhîm* in Ps. 45.7 (ET 6) is as a vocative, hence 'Your throne, O God, is for ever and ever',[29] as in all the ancient Versions. What further inclines me to this is the fact that in Isa. 9.7 (ET 6) the ideal future king is similarly referred to as 'mighty god' (*'ēl gibbôr*). Some scholars, such as A.R. Johnson,[30] avoid this conclusion by supposing that *'ēl gibbôr* might be rendered 'god of a hero', 'god' being understood as a superlative, hence 'mighty hero'. However, against this it must be noted that in all the other instances of *'ēl gibbôr* or *hā'ēl haggibbôr* in the Old Testament the meaning is clearly '(the) mighty God' (Isa. 10.21; Deut. 10.17; Neh. 9.32; Jer. 32.18). (Compare *'abî 'ad*, 'father of eternity', also in Isa. 9.7 [ET 6], another term suggestive of God; compare also 'father of years', used of El at Ugarit, and 'Ancient of Days' in Dan. 7.9.) Nevertheless, neither Ps. 45.7 (ET 6) nor Isa. 9.7 (ET 6) need be taken as implying that the king was literally thought of as a god, which would appear to be contrary to the Old Testament view of the king. Possibly we have here examples of hyperbole or court style, which derive from Canaanite notions of divine kingship, but were no longer taken literally. We may compare the fact that the word *'elōhîm* is used elsewhere in the Old Testament of beings who were not literally gods, but had been regarded as such at an earlier stage, namely ghosts (1 Sam. 28.13; Isa. 8.19). (Compare the Ugaritic texts, where the dead are 'gods', *KTU*[2] 1.6.VI.46-48.) Similarly, with the growth of absolute monotheism, when gods were demoted to the status of angels, they continued to be called *'elōhîm* or *benê hā' 'elōhîm*. The word used in both Psalm 45 and Isaiah 9 may therefore have come to mean something like 'superhuman'. Interestingly, in both Psalm 45 and Isaiah 9 the context is that of the king as warrior, which further suggests

---

29. Those who follow this view have sometimes taken the language literally, e.g. J.R. Porter, 'Psalm xlv.7', *JTS* 12 NS (1961), pp. 51-53, though others have seen it simply as hyperbolical language, e.g. H.-J. Kraus, *Psalmen 1–59* (BKAT, 15.1; Neukirchen–Vluyn: Neukirchener Verlag, 5th edn, 1978), pp. 490-91 (ET *Psalms 1–59* [trans. H.C. Oswald; Minneapolis: Augsburg, 1988], p. 455). I shall argue for the latter view below.

30. Johnson, *Sacral Kingship*, pp. 30-31 n. 1.

connecting these verses, and perhaps suggests that it is the king's superhuman power as a warrior that is specifically in mind.

The King's Alleged Immortality

The Canaanite belief that the king was a god naturally led to the belief that he was also immortal. Thus, the passage about King Keret's being a god, to which I have earlier alluded, also speaks of his alleged immortality: 'In your life, our father, we rejoiced; in your immortality (*blmt*) we exulted.' Are there any traces of this conception in the Old Testament? According to John Healey, there are, and he has argued this in an article in the Dahood *Festschrift*.[31] Healey's article appeals to various psalms in an attempt to provide a more moderate alternative to Dahood's view[32] that references to immortality are widespread throughout the Psalter, by claiming that there are a number of instances where it is found of the king, whence, it is claimed, it was later in the postexilic period extended to people generally. However, Healey's argument is weak, because the passages to which he appeals tend either to be only dubiously associated with the king (he tends to follow Eaton's maximalist approach, envisaging scores of royal psalms[33]), or only dubiously speak of immortality, and in some cases both the alleged reference to the king and to immortality are dubious. Thus, Ps. 73.24 very likely does speak of post mortem vindication for the psalmist, but there is nothing to suggest that its subject is a king. It is generally thought to be a postexilic Wisdom psalm. Again, Psalm 21 is undoubtedly royal, but there is no good reason to take v. 5 (ET 4) as alluding to immortality ('He asked life of thee; thou gavest it to him, length of days for ever and ever'). And with regard to Psalm 91, to which Healey also appeals, it is very uncertain whether it is royal, but most unlikely that it alludes to immortality. Psalm 91.15 says, 'With long life I will satisfy him', which falls short of immortality. Psalm 61.7 (ET 6), it is true, declares, 'Prolong the life of the king; may his

---

31. J. Healey, 'The Immortality of the King: Ugarit and the Psalms', *Or* 53 (1984), pp. 245-54.

32. M.J. Dahood, *Psalms*, I (AB, 16; Garden City, NY: Doubleday, 1965–66), p. xxxvi; *Psalms*, II (AB, 17; Garden City, NY: Doubleday, 2nd edn, 1973), pp. xxvi-xxvii; *Psalms*, III (AB, 17a; Garden City, NY: Doubleday, 1970), pp. xli-lii.

33. J.H. Eaton, *Kingship and the Psalms* (The Biblical Seminar, 3; Sheffield: JSOT Press, 2nd edn, 1986).

years endure to all generations!', but this appears to be a hyperbolical pious wish such as there is at British coronation services ('May the king live forever!'), rather than a confident expectation.

Royal Ethics: The Ideal and the Reality

The Old Testament clearly regards it as the task of the king to ensure that justice and righteousness prevail in the land and sees it as his role to protect the interests of widow and orphan, the poor and needy. One finds this, for example, in the royal Psalm 72 and it reappears in eschatologized form in various messianic oracles, such as the one in Isaiah 11.

It is therefore interesting to note that the same ideal of kingship is expressed in two of the Ugaritic epic texts,[34] those about Keret and Daniel. Thus, we read of Daniel that he 'raised himself up (and) sat at the entrance of the gate, among the mighty men who were by the threshing-floor; he judged the cause of the widow, he tried the case of the orphan' $(KTU^2 1.17.V.6-8)$.[35] Again, when King Keret is ill, his son Yaṣṣib upbraids him with the words:

---

34. There are also some Akkadian texts from Ugarit that speak of the king's role as supreme judge in disputes. See J. Aboud, *Die Rolle des Königs und seiner Familie nach den Texten von Ugarit* (Forschungen zur Anthropologie und Religionsgeschichte, 27; Münster: Ugarit-Verlag, 1994), pp. 108-11.

35. It is widely accepted that Daniel is referred to as king in KTU^2 1.19.III.46. Lines 45-46 read *qr.my[m] mlk. yṣm. ylkm. qr. mym*, 'The king cursed Qor-may[im], "Woe to you, Qor-mayim"'. From the context this can refer only to Daniel. Attempts to avoid a reference to Daniel as king are unsuccessful. Thus, H. Dressler, 'The Identification of the Ugaritic Dnil with the Daniel of Ezekiel', *VT* 29 (1979), pp. 152-61 (152-53) and 'Reading and Interpreting the Aqht Text', *VT* 34 (1984), pp. 78-82 (81), holds that *mlk* should be divided into two words, *m* being the final letter of *qr. mym*, the rest of the latter word being on the previous line, and *lk* being 'against you', hence '"Qor-mayim, against you", he reviled, 'Woe against you, O Qor-mayim"'. But it seems highly unlikely that the word *mym* would be spread over two lines without a word divider to separate it from *lk*. B. Margalit, in 'Studia Ugaritica II', *UF* 8 (1976), pp. 137-92 (175-76) and 'Interpreting the Story of Aqht', *VT* 30 (1980), pp. 361-65 (364), also avoids rendering *mlk* as 'king' by translating the passage as '"May thy course be damned, woe-to-thee water-body"'. But this involves the dubious procedure of finding a hapax legomenon *ml* here, cognate with Arabic *mayl* 'inclination, slope', and 2nd p.s. masc. pronominal suffix.

While bandits raid you turn (your) back,
and you entertain feuding rivals.
You have been brought down by your failing power.
You do not judge the cause of the widow,
 you do not try the case of the importunate.
You do not banish the extortioners of the poor,
you do not feed the orphan before your face
(nor) the widow behind your back.
(*KTU²* 1.16.VI.43-50; cf. 1.16.VI.30-34.)

As a consequence, Yaṣṣib declares that Keret should step down from the throne. E. Hammershaimb,[36] the scholar who first drew attention to these references, was struck by the nobility of the conception here, which contrasted with the bad press that the Canaanites receive in the pages of the Old Testament.

A further indication of the importance of justice and righteousness as a Canaanite royal ideal may come from part of a letter from a Ugaritic king to the Egyptian Pharaoh, discovered only a few years ago at Ras Ibn Hani (RIH 78/3 + 30 = *KTU²* 2.81):[37]

[To the Sun], the great king, the king of Egypt, [the goo]d [king], the righteous king, [the king of ki]ngs, the lord of all the land [of Egyp]t, say: Message of [Ammištam]ru, your servant: 'At the feet of [my lord] I [fall]. With my lord may it be well; [may it be well?] with your personnel, with your land, [with] your [horses], with your chariots, [with your X], with all that belongs [to the Sun], the great [ki]ng, the king of Egyp[t, the good king,] the ri[ghteous] king, [the king of kings...].'

The terminology 'just king' and 'righteous king' is more suggestive of a Semitic rather than an Egyptian background and therefore tells us something of the ideals of the Canaanite royal ideology.

But the reality of Canaanite monarchy was not all justice and righteousness, any more than the Israelite monarchy was. In 1 Samuel 8 there is a speech put on the lips of Samuel—part of the so-called 'anti-

---

36. E. Hammershaimb, *Some Aspects of Old Testament Prophecy from Isaiah to Malachi* (Copenhagen: Rosenkilde & Bagger, 1966), pp. 68, 81.

37. The part quoted here is from the obverse, lines 1-12. See P. Bordreuil and A. Caquot, 'Les textes en cunéiformes alphabétiques découverts en 1978 à Ibn Hani', *Syria* 57 (1980), pp. 343-73 (356-58); L. Milano, 'Gli epiteti del Faraone in una lettera ugaritica da Ras Ibn Hani', in O. Carruba (ed.), *Studi Orientalistici in ricordo di Franco Pintore* (Studia Mediterranea, 3; Pavia: GJES Edizioni, 1983), pp. 141-58.

monarchical' version of the foundation of the monarchy—that sets out
the harsh and tyrannical side of monarchy:

> These will be the ways of the king who will reign over you: he will take
> your sons and appoint them to his chariots and to be his horsemen, and
> to run before his chariots; and he will appoint for himself commanders
> of thousands and commanders of fifties, and some to plough his ground
> and to reap his harvest, and to make his implements of war and the
> equipment of his chariots. He will take your daughters to be perfumers
> and cooks and bakers. He will take the best of your fields and vineyards
> and olive orchards and give them to his servants. He will take the tenth
> of your grain and of your vineyards and give it to his officers and to his
> servants. He will take your menservants and maidservants, and the best
> of your cattle[38] and your asses, and put them to his work. He will take
> the tenth of your flocks, and you shall be his slaves (1 Sam. 8.11-17).

I. Mendelsohn[39] has pointed out how on point after point the picture
presented here reflects that in Akkadian texts from Ugarit. There the
king appointed chariot riders, the *maryannu* (cf. vv. 11b-12a), expro-
priated land for the crown, which he gave to his family, high state
officials and others (cf. v. 14), imposed tithes on the products of the
field and on cattle (cf. vv. 15, 17a), and used enforced labour (vv. 12b-
13, 16).

Court Officials

A king naturally has a royal court with officials, and since these too
would have been an innovation with the rise of the monarchy, they also
would have been based on foreign models. A widespread view over the
last half century is that they were based on Egyptian models—this has
been argued by scholars such as Begrich and de Vaux, and more
recently by Mettinger.[40] But of late powerful arguments have been put
forward by scholars such as U. Rüterswörden, B. Mazar, S.C. Layton

---

38. Reading *biqrêkem* 'your cattle' with LXX for *baḥûrêkem* 'your young men',
as this fits the context better.

39. I. Mendelsohn, 'Samuel's Denunciation of Kingship in the Light of the
Akkadian Documents from Ugarit', *BASOR* 143 (1956), pp. 17-22.

40. R. de Vaux, 'Titres et fonctionnaires égyptiens à la cour de David et de Sa-
lomon', *RB* 48 (1939), pp. 394-405; J. Begrich, 'Sōfēr und Mazkīr', *ZAW* 58
(1940), pp. 1-29; T.N.D. Mettinger, *Solomonic State Officials* (ConBOT, 5; Lund:
C.W.K. Gleerup, 1971).

and Stuart Weeks[41] that Israel's court officials were rather modelled on Canaanite precedents.

This seems altogether likely. Scholars have sometimes spoken of 'Solomonic state officials', and it has been supposed that Solomon, with his Egyptian contacts, would have appropriated the officials directly from Egypt. But against this it should be noted that most of Israel's court officials were already in place under David—see the lists in 2 Sam. 8.16-18 and 20.20-23—and David seems to have had no special relationship with Egypt, which was, in any case, weak at this time. Rather, David's stamping ground was Canaan and Transjordan, which is therefore more likely to be the source. In any case, if, as we have seen, Israel's monarchy was influenced by Canaan, the same is likely to have been true of the royal officials.

Detailed arguments about specific cases also seem to support this. For example, the steward in charge of the royal palace was called *'ašer 'al-habbayit*, 'the one over the palace', or *sōkēn*, 'steward'—the two titles are clearly equated in Isa. 22.15, when speaking of Shebna. Now, interestingly, the term *skn* is employed of a Ugaritic official, *Baal-ṣaduq*, in *KTU*^{2} 7.63 (RS 15.117),[42] where he is also called a door-keeper (lines 4-7), which agrees with the imagery in Isa. 22.22, where the *sōkēn*, Shebna, has the key of the house of David.[43] Again, the *mazkîr* or recorder has been compared with the Egyptian official *whmw*, 'reporter, herald', but this Egyptian title is extremely rare after 1100 BCE, well before Israel's monarchy started, and non-existent by the time of David and Solomon.[44] It is, of course, arguable that although Israel's

---

41. U. Rütersworden, *Die Beamten der israelitischen Königszeit* (BWANT, 117; Stuttgart: W. Kohlhammer, 1985), pp. 77-91, 120-21; B. Mazar, 'King David's Scribe and the High Officialdom of the United Monarchy of Israel', in *The Early Biblical Period* (Jerusalem: Israel Exploration Society, 1986), pp. 126-38; S.C. Layton, 'The Steward in the Ancient Near East: A Study of Hebrew (*'ăšer*) *'al-habbayit* in its Near Eastern Setting', *JBL* 109 (1990), pp. 633-49; S. Weeks, *Early Israelite Wisdom* (Oxford: Clarendon Press, 1994), pp. 115-29.

42. Wrongly cited by Layton, 'Steward', p. 647, as RS 15.177.

43. See Layton, 'Steward'.

44. D.B. Redford, 'Studies in Relations between Palestine and Egypt during the First Millennium B.C.', in J.W. Wevers and D.B. Redford (eds.), *Studies on the Ancient Palestinian World Presented to F.V. Winnett* (Toronto: University of Toronto Press, 1972), pp. 141-56 (144 n. 7); K.A. Kitchen, 'Egypt and Israel during the First Millennium B.C.', in J.A. Emerton (ed.), *Congress Volume Jerusalem 1986* (Leiden: E.J. Brill, 1988), pp. 107-23 (113).

court officials were borrowed from the Canaanites, the Canaanites themselves might have appropriated them from the Egyptians. However, this does not seem very likely, since etymologically the names do not generally seem like translations of Egyptian titles.

Conclusion

Although much of the evidence is circumstantial, the conclusion of this essay is that Canaanite influence was a significant factor in the origins of Israel's monarchy. Canaan was the closest model to hand, and in any case Egypt and Mesopotamia were weak at the time. Specifically Jebusite influence is suggested by Ps. 110.4, with its reference to the Davidic royal priesthood after the order of Melchizedek, the Jebusite priest–king, though the idea that Zadok was a Jebusite seems unlikely. Canaanite influence is also likely in the concept of the king as 'son of God', though this was no longer taken to indicate divinity, but rather filial adoption by God, and in the occasional reference to the king as 'god' (Ps. 45.7, ET 6; Isa. 9.5, ET 6), though this again was no longer literal but hyperbolical. Healey's idea that the Canaanite idea of royal immortality is reflected in some psalms does not commend itself, however. The custom of anointing kings may have been adopted from Canaan, though the evidence is not as strong as one might wish. Further, the ethical ideal of the king as one responsible for justice and righteousness towards the poor and needy was appropriated from the Canaanites, as well as certain more oppressive aspects of kingship. Finally, it seems likely that Israel's court officials were appropriated from Canaanite models, rather than the Egyptian ones that have often been supposed in the past.

In addition to Ps. 110.4, a general argument in favour of specifically Jebusite influence on David's kingship is the contrast with his predecessor Saul. Saul's kingship was much simpler and rustic, like that of a permanent judge, whereas David had the full trappings of a court and harem and so on. Since David had meanwhile conquered Jerusalem and made it his capital, it would make sense if David had been influenced by Jerusalemite traditions, though David also integrated other Canaanite city states into his kingdom, so other sources of Canaanite influence were also available.

DAVID'S RELATION TO MOSES: THE CONTEXTS, CONTENT AND CONDITIONS OF THE DAVIDIC PROMISES

Gary N. Knoppers

In an insightful survey of modern scholarship on the Davidic promises, Jon Levenson distinguishes between two fundamentally different approaches to the relationship between the Sinaitic (or Mosaic) covenant and the Davidic covenant.[1] Those scholars pursuing an 'integrationist' approach posit common traits between the Sinaitic and Davidic covenants and draw links between the two.[2] Some even see the latter—the Davidic covenant—as a modification of or codicil to the former— the Sinaitic covenant. Those scholars advocating a 'segregationist' approach stress differences between the two covenants and see few, if any, similarities between them. While the Mosaic pact structures God's relationship with Israel through the instrument of law, the Davidic covenant announces God's grace to a particular dynasty.[3] The former is expressly obligatory and conditional, while the latter is promissory and unconditional. Given this way of understanding the issue, many segregationists view the two covenants as antithetical to one another.[4]

---

1. J.D. Levenson, 'The Davidic Covenant and its Modern Interpreters', *CBQ* 41 (1979), pp. 205-19.

2. E.g. G. Widengren, 'King and Covenant', *JSS* 2 (1957), pp. 1-32; A.H.J. Gunneweg, 'Sinaibund und Davidsbund', *VT* 10 (1960), pp. 335-61; K. Seybold, *Das davidische Königtum im Zeugnis der Propheten* (FRLANT, 107; Göttingen: Vandenhoeck & Ruprecht, 1972), p. 44.

3. E.g. L. Rost, 'Sinaibund und Davidsbund', *TLZ* 72 (1947), cols. 129-34; G.E. Mendenhall, *The Tenth Generation: The Origins of the Biblical Tradition* (Baltimore: The Johns Hopkins University Press, 1973); M. Weinfeld, *Deuteronomy and the Deuteronomic School* (Oxford: Clarendon Press, 1972), pp. 77-81; M. Weinfeld, 'Berît—Covenant vs. Obligation', *Bib* 56 (1975), pp. 120-28; J. Bright, *Covenant and Promise* (Philadelphia: Westminster Press, 1976), pp. 56-77.

4. J. Bright, *A History of Israel* (Philadelphia: Westminster Press, 3rd edn, 1981), pp. 224-27, 294-98; G.E. Mendenhall, 'The Monarchy', *Int* 29 (1975),

One can press Levenson's point about the contrast between segregationists and integrationists a step further. The long-standing differences
between these two approaches have not been eased by the publication
and discussion of thousands of diplomatic texts stemming from various
lands in the ancient Near East. Indeed, proponents of both the integrationist and the segregationist approaches appeal to ancient Near Eastern,
mainly Hittite and Neo-Assyrian, evidence to buttress their positions.[5]
Integrationists have proposed analogies of ancient Near Eastern vassal
treaties with both the covenant (*bᵉrît*) between Yhwh and Israel at Mt
Sinai (Exod. 19–24), renewed in Deuteronomy, and the covenant
between Yhwh and David (2 Sam. 7.1-17; Pss. 89 and 132; 1 Chron.
17.1-15).[6] Some integrationists have viewed the absolute divine pledge
to continue David's dynasty as analogous to a suzerain's pledge to
support his client's dynasty in Hittite vassal treaties.[7]

Segregationists disagree. While conceding that the Hittite and Neo-
Assyrian treaties may form some sort of parallel to the Sinaitic covenant, segregationists have been most hesitant to employ Hittite or
Assyrian treaties as any sort of parallel to the Davidic promises. These
scholars view the Davidic promises as distinctly different from any
ancient Near Eastern treaties.[8] Some segregationists have proposed,
however, a different ancient Near Eastern model for the Davidic
promises: royal land grants.[9] Like royal grants in the ancient Near East,

pp. 155-70; M. Weinfeld, 'The Covenant of Grant in the Old Testament and in the
Ancient Near East', *JAOS* 90 (1970), pp. 184-203.

5.   D.J. McCarthy, *Treaty and Covenant* (AnBib, 21A; Rome: Pontifical
Biblical Institute, 2nd edn, 1978), pp. 29-153, provides a helpful overview.

6.   See the surveys of D.J. McCarthy, *Old Testament Covenant: A Survey of
Current Opinions* (Oxford: Basil Blackwell, 1972); R.A. Oden, 'The Place of
Covenant in the Religion of Israel', in P.D. Miller, P.D. Hanson, and S.D. McBride
(eds.), *Ancient Israelite Religion: Essays in Honor of Frank Moore Cross*
(Philadelphia: Fortress Press, 1987), pp. 429-47; and K.A. Kitchen, 'Rise and Fall
of Covenant, Law and Treaty', *TynBul* 40 (1989), pp. 118-35.

7.   P.J. Calderone, *Dynastic Oracle and Suzerainty Treaty* (Logos, 1; Manila:
Ateneo University Publications, 1966), pp. 41-71; R. de Vaux, 'Le Roi d'Israël,
vassal de Yahvé', in *Mélanges Eugène Tisserant. I. Écriture sainte: Ancien Orient*
(Studi e testi, 231; Vatican: Biblioteca Apostolica Vaticana, 1964), pp. 119-33.

8.   D.R. Hillers, *Covenant: The History of a Biblical Idea* (Baltimore: The
Johns Hopkins University Press, 1969), pp. 98-119; R.E. Clements, *Abraham and
David* (SBT, 5; Naperville, IL: Allenson, 1967), pp. 47-60; H. Kruse, 'David's
Covenant', *VT* 35 (1985), pp. 139-64 (148-49).

9.   First and foremost, Weinfeld, 'Covenant of Grant', p. 185; M. Weinfeld,

the covenants with Abraham and David are purportedly gifts bestowed upon individuals who distinguished themselves by serving their masters loyally. As with the Davidic covenant, such land grants allegedly represent pledges from superiors to clients that are not subject to any conditions.

My purpose in this essay is not to revisit the ancient Near Eastern evidence for either the integrationist or the segregationist positions.[10] Nor is it my intention to try to settle the fundamental differences in scholarly definitions of covenant.[11] Rather, this essay will focus on the principal references to the Davidic promises—2 Samuel 7, Psalms 89 and 132, and 1 Chronicles 17. Specifically, I wish to contest a number of assumptions underlying the integrationist and isolationist positions. In so doing, I hope to call attention to some neglected features of the royal Davidic charter, such as the significant differences between the four versions and the various ways in which these disparate texts link the Davidic promises to traditional institutions and events in Israelite life.

First, there is a common assumption that the Davidic promises are unconditional.[12] Yhwh informs David that his descendants will continue to reign, even though these descendants may sin (2 Sam. 7.14-16; Ps. 89.30-38, ET 29–37). Commentators recognize, of course, that some

---

'Addenda to *JAOS* 90 (1970), pp. 184ff.', *JAOS* 92 (1972), pp. 468-69.

10. In a recently published essay, 'Ancient Near Eastern Royal Grants and the Davidic Covenant: A Parallel?', *JAOS* 116 (1996), pp. 670-97, I take issue with the land grant analogy to the Davidic promises. The structure, form, and content of royal grants are much more complicated than the proposed typology allows. The evidence for language parallels between the Davidic covenant and ancient Near Eastern land grants is misconstrued. Some of the best parallels to the dynastic promises stem from treaties. There is, moreover, significant evidence that ancient Near Eastern land grants were predominantly conditional in nature and function. All of these considerations render doubtful the proposition that land grants are the best analogy for the royal Davidic charter.

11. Some scholars conceive of covenant as an obligation validated by an oath, while others conceive of covenant as an agreement. I incline toward a bilateral understanding of covenant, but recognize that biblical authors employ *b'rît* in various ways. See further, J. Barr, 'Some Semantic Notes on the Covenant', in H. Donner, R. Hanhart, and R. Smend (eds.), *Beiträge zur alttestamentliche Theologie: Festschrift für Walther Zimmerli zum 70. Geburtstag* (Göttingen: Vandenhoeck & Ruprecht, 1977), pp. 25-34.

12. This 'was a kind of covenant which was simply a promise of God and was valid despite anything Israel might do', McCarthy, *Survey*, p. 47.

of the texts dealing with the Davidic promises (e.g. Ps. 132) are clearly
conditional, but these texts are deemed to be later revisions of an earlier
(and normative) unconditional decree.[13]

Secondly, there is a common assumption that the issue of unconditionality is intimately related to the Davidic covenant's ongoing importance in the life of ancient Israel. If biblical authors present Yhwh's
provisions for David as conditional, those authors are considered to be
weakening the force of the Davidic covenant. Moreover, by predicating
the continuance of Davidic rule upon the fidelity of David, Solomon, or
their descendants, biblical authors allegedly mitigated the political
ramifications of the Davidic promises beyond the end of Davidic rule in
the Babylonian exile of 586 BCE. In other words, there is a tacit linkage
between conditionality, the termination of the Davidic kingdom, and
the (future) irrelevance of the Davidic promises. So, for example, those
passages in the postexilic book of Chronicles predicating the future of
the Davidic dynasty upon the obedience of Solomon (1 Chron. 22.12-
13, 28.7-10; 2 Chron. 7.17-18) are construed as limiting David's
enduring social and political significance. The Davidic dynasty may
have had a proper role to play in the conquest of Jerusalem, the
appointment of Levites and priests, and the construction of the long-
awaited Temple, but the Davidic promises have neither present
(programmatic, royalist) nor future (messianic, eschatological) import
for the residents of Yehud.[14]

Finally, some scholars presume that the Davidic promises deal essentially with succession. The issue of continuity in Davidic rule is thought
to lie at the heart of the divine commitments to David. For this very
reason, Levenson can argue that the whole debate about the Davidic
promises is overdrawn.[15] As to which covenant—Sinaitic or Davidic—

---

13. In this, the position of T. Veijola is exceptional, because he situates the
origin of the unconditional dynastic promises in the Babylonian exile, *Verheißung
in der Krise: Studien zur Literatur und Theologie der Exilszeit anhand des 89.
Psalms* (Annales Academiae Scientiarum Fennicae, series B, 220; Helsinki:
Suomalainen Tiedeakatemia, 1982); *idem*, 'Davidverheißung und Staatsvertrag:
Beobachtungen zum Einfluß altorientalischer Staatsverträge auf die biblische
Sprache am Beispiel von Psalm 89', *ZAW* 95 (1983), pp. 9-31.

14. Most recently, W. Riley, *King and Cultus in Chronicles: Worship and the
Reinterpretation of History* (JSOTSup, 160; Sheffield: JSOT Press, 1993), and K.E.
Pomykala, *The Davidic Dynasty Tradition in Early Judaism* (Atlanta, GA: Scholars
Press, 1995), pp. 69-111.

15. Levenson, 'Davidic Covenant', pp. 216-17.

is more important, the answer seems relatively simple. One deals with the divine administration of the Israelite people, 'the basis for law and morality in a whole society', while the other deals only with succession within one lineage, 'the question of what family is to retain the throne'.[16]

Close study of the contexts and content of the four major passages dealing with the Davidic promises will complicate each of these assumptions. Beginning with the issue of unconditionality, this essay argues that the very definition of the divine commitments made to David was a matter of dispute within ancient Israel. Some of the very authors who champion David's importance also make reference to Yhwh's commandments. What the references to Sinaitic law or Mosaic covenant indicate, among other things, is that the issue of integration—the relation of the Davidic promises to the Mosaic covenant—is not simply a modern preoccupation. A variety of ancient Israelite authors sought to relate one to the other. By the same token, the significance of whether the Davidic promises are unconditional or conditional has been overplayed. One can make the case that authors of both types of passages promote the importance of the Davidic dynasty.

The attention modern scholars have devoted to the issue of royal succession is also somewhat misplaced, evincing an essentialist approach to the Davidic promises—the attempt to get at the core of Yhwh's commitments to David. Such a concern is understandable, but inherently problematic. Close study of the principal passages dealing with the Davidic promises will reveal that these promises do not exhibit a consistent structure, form, and content but vary according to how different biblical authors configure them. While it is true that the subject of succession appears in all four passages, each of these texts contextualizes succession in a distinctive way. Moreover, each text manifests a concern with much more than royal rotation, tying the deity's pledges to David to other important subjects in Israelite life. One should not cite, therefore, the issue of succession to marginalize the importance of the Davidic promises. On the contrary, the links ancient Israelite authors draw between the fate of the Davidic dynasty and the fate of other institutions demonstrate the relevance of the Davidic promises for national life.

16. Levenson, 'Davidic Covenant', pp. 215, 217.

1. *Temple, Dynasty, and People in 2 Samuel 7*

The Deuteronomistic History gives extensive coverage to the inauguration of the Davidic promises and to how these promises affect the history of the united monarchy, the rise of the northern monarchy, and the
independent history of Judah. That the Deuteronomist's concern lies
with much more than just royal succession is clear at the beginning of 2
Samuel 7. There a dynasty is nowhere in view. Having been successful
at war, David, like any good ancient Near Eastern monarch, wishes to
build his patron deity a temple.[17] Nathan's response (2 Sam. 7.2-16)
greatly complicates David's plan, but the issue of a temple continues to
drive the plot. Nathan's oracle has Yhwh initially question David's plan
to build a stationary sanctuary (2 Sam. 7.5-7). The following historical
retrospect, in which Yhwh stresses his provisions for David (2 Sam.
7.8), introduces the deity's promises pertaining to the future of Israel,
the construction of the Temple, and the establishment of an enduring
dynasty (2 Sam. 7.9-16). Nathan's oracle assures David of the defeat of
his enemies (v. 9), the establishment of rest for Israel (vv. 10-11), and
the construction of the Temple by one of David's seed (vv. 12-13).
Whereas Psalm 89 never mentions the Jerusalem Temple, 2 Sam. 7.1-
16 plays on the various connotations of 'house' (*bayit*) to link the successful construction of the Temple by one of David's seed to the divine
establishment of an enduring dynasty. In short, Nathan's promises
address a variety of interrelated themes—the defeat of David's enemies,
the succession of one of his sons, the inauguration of an era of national
peace, the construction of a central shrine, and the establishment of an
enduring throne.

David, for his part, is not passive. The very acceptance by one party
of a solemn pledge from another party normally entails a degree of
involvement in the life of the recipient, his family, or his realm by the
other party. David welcomes such divine involvement. In his prayer,
David responds to Nathan's oracle by repeatedly petitioning Yhwh to
effect his promises in the life of Israel and David's house (2 Sam. 7.18-
29).

Nathan's promises and David's petitions find continuity in Solomon's

---

17. V. Hurowitz, *I Have Built You an Exalted House: Temple Building in Light
of Mesopotamian and Northwest Semitic Writings* (JSOTSup, 115; Sheffield: JSOT
Press, 1992), pp. 171-223.

reign. Indeed, as many scholars have recognized, 2 Samuel 7 plays a formative role in the Deuteronomistic History.[18] Solomon's accession, the establishment of secure borders, and a prosperous economy fulfil some of Nathan's pledges and create the requisite conditions for consummating David's hope of a royal shrine. Solomon's missive to Hiram, which redefines Nathan's objections to the Temple, elucidates this Deuteronomistic interpretation of history (1 Kgs 5.17-19, ET 3–5).[19] Nathan had initially rejected David's bid to build the Temple because Yhwh had been perfectly content to 'have gone about in a tent' (2 Sam. 7.3-7), but in the Deuteronomistic version of events David's plan was simply premature. Construction had to await the divinely promised time of peace, the occasion of his son's succession (1 Kgs 5.17, ET 3). The attainment of such rest in the time of Solomon provides impetus toward Temple construction. As Solomon explains to Hiram, he can hardly ignore such propitious conditions for the building of a central shrine.[20] The successful construction and dedication of this sanctuary in Jerusalem inaugurate an age in which the Temple plays a central role in Israelite life. Kings are judged positively or negatively on the basis of their exclusive fidelity to this particular shrine.[21] The Davidic promises engage, therefore, much more than the issue of royal

18. D.J. McCarthy, 'II Samuel 7 and the Structure of the Deuteronomic History', *JBL* 84 (1965), pp. 131-38; F.M. Cross, *Canaanite Myth and Hebrew Epic* (Cambridge, MA: Harvard University Press, 1973), pp. 249-60; T. Veijola, *Die ewige Dynastie: David und die Entstehung seiner Dynastie nach der deuteronomistischen Darstellung* (Annales Academiae Scientiarum Fennicae, series B, 193; Helsinki: Suomalainen Tiedeakatemia, 1975), pp. 32-48; T.N.D. Mettinger, *King and Messiah: The Civil and Sacral Legitimation of the Israelite Kings* (ConBOT, 8; Lund: C.W.K. Gleerup, 1976), pp. 48-63; B. Halpern, *The Constitution of the Monarchy in Israel* (HSM, 25; Chico, CA: Scholars Press, 1981), pp. 19-20; P.K. McCarter, *II Samuel* (AB, 9; Garden City, NY: Doubleday, 1984), pp. 217-31; Kruse, 'David's Covenant', pp. 148-55; G.H. Jones, *The Nathan Narratives* (JSOTSup, 80; Sheffield: JSOT Press, 1990), pp. 59-92.

19. M. Fishbane, *Biblical Interpretation in Ancient Israel* (Oxford: Clarendon Press, 1985), pp. 394-96.

20. Indeed, given the Deuteronomic mandate to construct a central sanctuary when Israel finds rest in its promised land (Deut. 12.10), it is incumbent upon Solomon to begin building the Temple.

21. See G.N. Knoppers, 'Aaron's Calf and Jeroboam's Calves', in A.H. Bartelt, A.B. Beck, C.A. Franke, and P.R. Raabe (eds.), *Fortunate the Eyes That See: Essays in Honor of David Noel Freedman in Celebration of His Seventieth Birthday* (Grand Rapids: Eerdmans, 1995), pp. 92-104, and the references listed there.

succession. In the united monarchy they have much to do with Israel's fate and national well-being.

Given the multifaceted nature of the Davidic promises in the Deuteronomistic History, are these promises unconditional? A quick glance at the cardinal passage portraying these divine assurances—2 Samuel 7—would seem to justify such an assumption. Nathan's oracle emphasizes the close relationship between God and David's successor and underscores the indefeasibility of the dynastic promises.

> I will become his father and he shall become my son. When he commits evil, I will chastise him with the rod of men and with the stripes of the sons of man, but I will not withdraw my loyalty from him as I withdrew it from Saul before you. Your house and your kingship are sure before me forever and your throne shall be established forever (2 Sam. 7.14-16).[22]

As ancient Near Eastern parallels make clear, the use of father–son terminology is significant.[23] The employment of the adoption formula, 'I will become his father and he shall become my son', to depict Yhwh's relationship to David's successor is remarkable, because it expresses a high royal theology.[24] Moreover, the adoption of David's heir is linked to the granting of an enduring dynasty.[25] Through the

22. In 2 Sam. 7.14, I read *ûbᵉhaⁱᵃwôtô* (see the Syriac). The MT reads *ⁱᵃšer bᵉhaⁱᵃwôtô*. In 2 Sam. 7.15, I follow a few Hebrew manuscripts, the LXX, the Syriac, and the Vulgate, reading *'āsûr*. The MT has *yāsûr*. In 2 Sam. 7.16, the MT has *bêᵗkā* ('your house'), while the LXX reads ὁ οἶκος αὐτοῦ ('his house'). I follow the MT (maximum variation). Later in this verse, I follow the argument of McCarter (*II Samuel*, p. 195) for reading *lᵉpānay wᵉkisʾᵃkā* (cf. the LXX, Cyprian, and the Syriac) instead of the MT's *lᵉpānêkā kisʾᵃkā*.

23. F.C. Fensham, 'Father and Son as Teriminology for Treaty and Covenant', in H. Goedicke (ed.), *Near Eastern Studies in Honor of William Foxwell Albright* (Baltimore: The Johns Hopkins University Press, 1971), pp. 121-28; P. Kalluveettil, *Declaration and Covenant* (AnBib, 88; Rome: Pontifical Biblical Institute, 1982), pp. 98-99; J. Day, *Psalms* (OTG; Sheffield: JSOT Press, 1990), pp. 99-100.

24. On the Akkadian expressions for adoption (e.g. *ana māri epēšu*, 'to make as a son', *ana mārūti epēšu*, 'to make into the status of sonship', and *ana mārūti leqû*, 'to take into the status of sonship'), see the survey of S.M. Paul, 'Adoption Formulae: A Study of Cuneiform and Biblical Legal Clauses', *MAARAV* 2 (1979–80), pp. 176-85; and E.C. Stone and D.I. Owen, *Adoption in Old Babylonian Nippur and the Archive of Mannum-mešu-liṣṣur* (Winona Lake, IN: Eisenbrauns, 1991), pp. 1-92. Similar language appears in *KTU* 1.15.II.25-29, Isa. 9.5 (ET 6) and Ps. 2.7-8.

25. In Weinfeld's view, the 'house' (= dynasty), land, and people given to David could only be legitimized by adoption, 'Covenant of Grant', p. 191; 'Addenda', p. 469.

prophet Nathan, Yhwh assures David that his throne will be confirmed forever ('*ad-'ôlām*).

The absolute promise of succession within a particular dynasty is a striking feature of the presentation of the Davidic promises in both Nathan's oracle and in Psalm 89. In neither case, however, are the recipients of the promises devoid of obligations. 2 Samuel 7 and Psalm 89 also contain a bilateral element. In both texts David's descendants have a responsibility to obey Yhwh (2 Sam. 7.14; Ps. 89.31-33, ET 30-32). The disobedience of David's heirs will bring divine chastisement.[26] To be sure, the guarantee of succession is not predicated upon the loyalty of the sons. But these sons will be held accountable for 'commiting evil'. Hence, the Davidic promises are not without conditions.

Nor do the Davidic promises exempt David from personal accountability before Yhwh. The omission of any direct reference to David's own conduct in Nathan's oracle is striking. Nathan's oracle provides assurances pertaining to victory, peace, succession, dynasty, and temple, but it does not assure David himself of peace, success, or prosperity.[27] Nor does it immunize him from the effects of any future perfidy that he might commit. Indeed, as the account of David's sin with Bathsheba demonstrates, David's own responsibility before Yhwh is all too apparent (2 Sam. 11.1–12.12).

The issue of accountability also plays a prominent role in the Deuteronomistic presentation of disunion. There the author blames Israel's decline on Solomon's flouting of divine commands—his sexual relations with foreign women, his building high places for his wives, and his worshipping of their gods (1 Kgs 11.1-8).[28] Solomon's misconduct infuriates Yhwh, the deity who 'appeared to him twice' (1 Kgs 11.9; cf. 1 Kgs 3.4-14, 9.1-9). The resulting punishment affects both foreign and domestic affairs. The revolts of foreign monarchs formerly under the hegemony of David and Solomon end the *Pax Solomonica* (1 Kgs 11.14-25), while the revolt of Solomon's servant, Jeroboam, ends the united monarchy (1 Kgs 11.26–12.20). The author is able to

---

26. Levenson, 'Davidic Covenant', pp. 211-12; Halpern, *Constitution*, pp. 45-50.

27. Unless exemptions from such responsibility are expressly stated, we should not suppose that the prophet intends to bestow them.

28. The actual legal citation in 1 Kgs 11.1-2 draws on both the *traditum* of Deut. 7.3-4 and the *traditio* of Josh. 23.12; G.N. Knoppers, 'Sex, Religion, and Politics: The Deuteronomist on Intermarriage', *HAR* 14 (1994), pp. 121-41.

present this dramatic turn of events as divinely sanctioned because of an ambiguity inherent within the dynastic promises. Nathan mentions the establishment of the heir's kingdom (2 Sam. 7.12), but the promise itself is directed at his kingship (*mamlākâ*) and throne (*kissē'*, 2 Sam. 7.14-16).[29] Because he interprets Nathan's oracle as addressing David's lineage, and not the Israelite kingdom as a whole, the Deuteronomist can present Judah's survival under Davidic leadership as confirming Nathan's promises.[30] One tribe remains under the domain of Solomon's son, not for the sake of Solomon, but for the sake of the divine assurances given to David (1 Kgs 11.13, 32, 34-36, 12.15).

The same understanding of Nathan's oracle allows the Deuteronomist to present a hopeful beginning to the Northern Kingdom. Consistent with his blaming the united monarchy's demise on Solomon's miscreancy, the Deuteronomist has the prophet Ahijah offer the future king of the ten northern tribes the opportunity to secure 'an enduring dynasty' (*bayit ne'emān*) like that of David, should he prove obedient to God's commands (1 Kgs 11.31-38).[31] Clearly, the Deuteronomist understands the Davidic promises as having conditions and limits. Even though continuity in the dynasty is assured, individual monarchs are subject to the rule of (divinely administered) law and the extent of their domain is not vouchsafed by the basic dynastic promise.

There is one further aspect of the Deuteronomist's coverage of the monarchy that pertains to his understanding of David's legacy. The Deuteronomist promotes David as a model of obedience to Yhwh. It is true that the many references to David's merit[32] do not all speak directly to the Davidic promises themselves.[33] But they are relevant in at least two respects. First, the Deuteronomist's introduction to the rise of the Northern monarchy associates the divine bequest of an everlasting

---

29. The omission of border delineations is probably deliberate in 2 Samuel 7; see B. Halpern, *The First Historians: The Hebrew Bible and History* (San Francisco: Harper & Row, 1988), pp. 157-67; G.N. Knoppers, *Two Nations Under God: The Deuteronomistic History of Solomon and the Dual Monarchies. I. The Reign of Solomon and the Rise of Jeroboam* (HSM, 52; Atlanta, GA: Scholars Press, 1993), pp. 151-60.

30. 1 Kgs 11.11–13.34, 12.15; Knoppers, *Two Nations Under God*, I, pp. 167-223.

31. The use of 'enduring dynasty' (*bayit ne'emān*) alludes to 2 Sam. 7.16.

32. 1 Kgs 3.6, 11.4, 6, 33, 34, 38, 14.8, 15.3, 11; 2 Kgs 14.3, 16.2, 18.3, 22.2.

33. Levenson, 'Davidic Covenant', pp. 216-17.

dynasty to David with David's loyalty to the deity.[34] Hence, the Deuteronomist posits a relationship between the comparative and promissory aspects of David's patrimony.[35] Secondly, David's function as a paradigmatic king addresses the relationship between David and Moses. By upholding both the Davidic promises and David as a paradigm of loyal conduct, the Deuteronomist balances two concerns— legitimating the Davidic monarchy and exhorting his audience to observe Yhwh's commands.[36]

The citation, reapplication, and structural use of the Davidic promises in the Deuteronomistic History speak to the gravity of the Davidic legacy.[37] What this history of inner-biblical interpretation shows is that the authors and editors of this lengthy work did not view the commands of Yhwh and the promises made to David as somehow antithetical to one another. Integration was very much an ancient issue and not simply a modern preoccupation. The pertinent question for most writers or editors seems to have been not whether the Sinaitic covenant was relevant to the Davidic covenant, but how.

2. Unconditional and Conditional:
The Davidic Promises in Chronicles

The Chronicler, like the Deuteronomist, devotes significant coverage to the inauguration of the Davidic promises, their redefinition in Solomon's reign, and their role in structuring the history of the early divided monarchy. The Chronicler's development of the Davidic promises differs, however, from that of the Deuteronomist. Especially in its presentation of the united monarchy and the division, the Chronicler's History reinterprets and reapplies Nathan's dynastic oracle in a distinctive way. His additions to and recontextualization of the

34. 1 Kgs 11.37-38, 14.8-11; Knoppers, *Two Nations Under God*, I, pp. 199-206.

35. On the distinction between the comparative and promissory uses of David in Kings, see I. Provan, *Hezekiah and the Book of Kings* (BZAW, 172; Berlin: W. de Gruyter, 1988), pp. 93-99.

36. G.N. Knoppers, *Two Nations Under God: The Deuteronomistic History of Solomon and The Dual Monarchies.* II. *The Reign of Jeroboam, the Fall of Israel, and the Reign of Josiah* (HSM, 53; Atlanta, GA: Scholars Press, 1994), pp. 101-20.

37. Fishbane, *Biblical Interpretation*, pp. 465-67; J.D. Levenson, *Sinai and Zion: An Entry into the Jewish Bible* (San Francisco: Harper & Row, 1985), pp. 209-16.

material he draws from his *Vorlage* provide a unique perspective on Yhwh's provisions for David. As in Samuel–Kings, the negotiation of the Davidic promises within Israelite and Judahite history has major ramifications for understanding the configuration of the larger work.

The Chronicler's versions of Nathan's oracle (1 Chron. 17.1-15) and David's prayer (1 Chron. 17.16-27) are largely drawn from the Chronicler's *Vorlage* of 2 Samuel 7.[38] The relevant differences between the two may be summarized as follows. There is a strong link between David and the work of his son (1 Chron. 17.11-14). Yhwh declares, 'I shall establish your seed after you, one of your own sons, and I shall establish his kingship' (1 Chron. 17.11). Unlike 2 Samuel 7, there is no codicil concerning the behaviour of David's seed. There is no mention of the possibility of the son(s) committing misdeeds. Nathan has Yhwh simply announce, 'I will establish his throne forever...I will not withdraw my loyalty from him as I withdrew it from your predecessor' (1 Chron. 17.12-13). Hence, if one wishes to speak of an absolute and unconditional form of the Davidic promises, 1 Chronicles 17 is a better candidate than 2 Samuel 7.

Like the Deuteronomist, the Chronicler posits a father–son analogy between Yhwh and David's heir (1 Chron. 17.13, 22.10, 28.6). But the Chronicler goes a step further in positing Yhwh's direct election (*bhr*) of Solomon (1 Chron. 28.5,6). Much of David's latter reign is spent, in fact, preparing his divinely chosen son for his duties as David's successor (1 Chron. 22–29). Through his unstinting efforts, David ensures a smooth and seamless transition to the reign of his son (1 Chron. 29.1-25). All of Israel's leaders, warriors, and officials pledge their loyalty to David's designated heir (1 Chron. 29.22-24). Even David's other sons pledge their fidelity to chosen Solomon (1 Chron. 29.24).

The kingdom Solomon is to inherit from David is, however, not simply the kingdom of Israel. In the Chronicler's version of Nathan's oracle, Yhwh declares, 'I shall appoint him in my house and in my kingship forever' (1 Chron. 17.14). The reference to a connection between the Davidic–Solomonic kingdom and Yhwh's kingdom is not accidental. On three other occasions the Chronicler associates the

---

38. The precise nature of the Chronicler's *Vorlage* for 2 Sam. 7.1-16 is disputed. Given the evidence provided by the various textual witnesses to Samuel and Chronicles, one should not assume that the Chronicler's *Vorlage* was identical to that of MT Samuel; cf. S.L. McKenzie, *The Chronicler's Use of the Deuteronomistic History* (HSM, 33; Atlanta: Scholars Press, 1985), pp. 63-64.

Davidic kingdom with God's kingdom (1 Chron. 28.5, 29.11; 2 Chron. 13.8). Similarly, on three occasions he associates the throne of Yhwh with that of David and Solomon (1 Chron. 28.5, 29.23; 2 Chron. 9.8). Given that the Chronicler writes during the postexilic age, such declarations are remarkable.

The Chronicler's own contributions to David's reign underscore the importance of the dynastic promises (1 Chron. 22.6-10, 28.6, 10, 20, 29.1, 19). Consistent with his highly positive portrayal of David and the link between David and his heir in Nathan's oracle (1 Chron. 17.1-15), the Chronicler ties the reigns of David and Solomon together as a unique era of Israelite consolidation, prosperity, and accomplishment.[39] In this respect, the Chronicler's appropriation and reworking of the Davidic promises is relevant to the issue of (un)conditionality. He includes, as we have seen, a version of the dynastic promises of 2 Sam. 7.11-16 that is unconditional in nature (1 Chron. 17.10-14), but he also includes, reworks, and recontextualizes a number of passages found in the final edition of Kings (1 Kgs 2.3-4, 8.25-26, 9.4-9)[40] that render the realization of the Davidic promises dependent upon either the obedience of Solomon (1 Chron. 22.12-13, 28.7-10; 2 Chron. 7.17-18) or the obedience of David's descendants (2 Chron. 6.16-17). The Chronicler accords these texts a prominent position in his own narrative by placing these conditional reformulations into the mouths of both David (1 Chron. 22.10-13, 28.7-10) and Solomon (2 Chron. 6.16-17, 7.17-18).[41]

The Chronicler's record presents, therefore, a paradox: the dynastic promises are both unconditional and conditional. There is some scholarly disagreement as to what to make of this. Since the Chronicler's conditional reformulations make repeated mention of the Temple, some commentators believe that the Davidic promises are fulfilled when Solomon completes this edifice.[42] Others argue that the promises are

---

39. R.L. Braun, 'Solomonic Apologetic in Chronicles', *JBL* 92 (1973), pp. 503-16; *idem*, 'Solomon, the Chosen Temple Builder: The Significance of 1 Chronicles 22, 28 and 29 for the Theology of Chronicles', *JBL* 95 (1976), pp. 581-90; H.G.M. Williamson, 'The Accession of Solomon in the Books of Chronicles', *VT* 26 (1976), pp. 351-61; cf. R. Mosis, *Untersuchungen zur Theologie des chronistischen Geschichtswerkes* (Freiburger Theologische Studien, 92; Frieburg: Herder, 1973), pp. 82-163.

40. Knoppers, *Two Nations Under God*, I, pp. 64-65, 99-103, 109-12.

41. In the Deuteronomistic History, these texts appears only in Solomon's reign.

42. E.g. R.L. Braun, *1 Chronicles* (WBC, 14; Waco, TX: Word Books, 1986).

reaffirmed (or even ratified) precisely because Solomon successfully completes the Temple.[43] Of the two views, the latter is more compelling for a variety of reasons. First, the Chronicler, unlike the Deuteronomist, portrays Solomon as consistently faithful throughout his reign.[44] As directed by his father, Solomon stays the course, happily building and dedicating the long-awaited Temple. Both the beginning and the end of Solomon's tenure are smooth and without incident (1 Chron. 28.1–29.25; 2 Chron. 1.1-2, 9.1-28). Unlike the situation in Kings, in which Solomon's reign is divided into two periods—one good (1 Kgs 1–10), the other bad (1 Kgs 11)—Solomon does not lapse in Chronicles. His reign represents an unprecedented age of peace and international prestige (1 Chron. 17.8-9, 22.9, 18, 29.25; 2 Chron. 1.7-18). Because Solomon, in accordance with his father's admonitions (1 Chron. 28.9), never abandons Yhwh, there are no grounds whereby the conditions of these texts (referring to Solomon) would take effect.

Secondly, the Chronicler employs the (still valid) Davidic promises to structure his history of the early divided monarchy. In Chronicles Solomon is not blamed for the division.[45] As we have seen, Solomon ends his reign in glory (2 Chron. 8.1–9.31). Rehoboam, Jeroboam, and 'the riffraff and scoundrels who surrounded him', together bear responsibility for Israel's defection.[46] The Chronicler explicitly cites the royal Davidic charter to denounce northern secession as seditious. In the speech of King Abijah to 'King Jeroboam and all Israel' (2 Chron. 13.4-12), widely believed to be the Chronicler's own composition, the Judahite monarch plays on the different senses of Israel by asking, 'Do you not know that Yhwh the God of Israel gave the kingship over Israel to David and to his sons (as) a covenant of salt?' (*hᵃlōʾ lākem lādaʿat kî yhwh ʾᵉlōhê yiśrāʾēl nātan mamlākâ lᵉdāwîd ʿal-yiśrāʾēl lᵉʿôlām lô ûlᵉbānāyw bᵉrît melaḥ*, 2 Chron. 13.5).[47] Abijah reaffirms the eternal

---

43. See the foundational treatment of H.G.M. Williamson, 'Eschatology in Chronicles', *TynBul* 28 (1977), pp. 115-54.

44. H.G.M. Williamson, *1 and 2 Chronicles* (NCB; Grand Rapids: Eerdmans, 1982), pp. 132-37, 192-237.

45. G. von Rad, *Das Geschichtsbild des chronistischen Werkes* (BWANT, 40.3; Stuttgart: W. Kohlhammer, 1930), pp. 125-32.

46. 2 Chron. 13.6-7. See further, G.N. Knoppers, 'Rehoboam in Chronicles: Villain or Victim?', *JBL* 109 (1990), pp. 429-32.

47. S.R. Driver, 'The Speeches in Chronicles', *The Expositor*, 1 (1895), pp. 241-56; 2 (1895), pp. 286-308; W. Rudolph, *Chronikbücher* (HAT, 21; Tübingen: J.C.B. Mohr [Paul Siebeck], 1955), pp. 236-37; S. Japhet, *The Ideology of the Book*

validity of the Davidic promises for all who would go by the name of Israel (2 Chron. 13.4-8). The Chronicler, unlike the Deuteronomist, admits of no territorial qualification of the Davidic promises. If one takes the position that the Chronicler considers the Davidic promises to be realized in the building of the Temple, one is unable to make any coherent sense out of his depiction of disunion.[48] The Chronicler's insistence that the Davidic promises remain valid for all elements of Israel explains why he, unlike the Deuteronomist, does not narrate the independent history of the Northern Kingdom.

One final point should be made about the Chronicler's handling of the royal Davidic charter. Like the Deuteronomist, the Chronicler explains Yhwh's patience with errant Davidides by recourse to the promissory aspect of the Davidic promises. So, for instance, in 2 Chron. 21.7 the Chronicler declares that 'Yhwh was unwilling to destroy the house of David because of the covenant, which he cut with David (*habbᵉrît ᵃšer kārat lᵉdāwîd*), and in accordance with his pledge to give a dominion (*nîr*) to him and to his sons in perpetuity'.[49] But the Chronicler, unlike the Deuteronomist, employs both David and Solomon in a comparative sense as setting a standard for others to follow (2 Chron. 30.26, 33.7, 35.3, 4). Such usage is, of course, consistent with the author's complimentary depiction of the united kingdom.

Even though the Chronicler contextualizes and interprets the Davidic promises differently from the Deuteronomist, both authors accord a prominent role to these promises within their histories. In each case, Yhwh's provisions for David have to do with much more than succession. The Chronicler employs the Davidic promises to engage a variety of national interests—the humbling of Israel's enemies, the accession of David's divinely elected son, the achievement of rest for all of Israel,

---

of Chronicles and Its Place in Biblical Thought (ET Beiträge zur Erforschung des Alten Testaments und des Antiken Judentums, 9; Frankfurt: Lang, 1989), pp. 453-55; S. Japhet, *I & II Chronicles* (OTL; Louisville, KY: Westminster/John Knox, 1993), p. 691.

48. G.N. Knoppers, '"Battling against Yahweh": Israel's War against Judah in 2 Chron. 13.2-20', *RB* 100 (1993), pp. 516-18.

49. On the translation of *nîr* as '(territorial) dominion' or 'fief' (instead of 'light' or 'lamp'), see P.D. Hanson, 'The Song of Heshbon and David's *Nîr*', *HTR* 61 (1968), pp. 297-320 and E. Ben Zvi, 'Once the Lamp Has Been Kindled... A Reconsideration of the Meaning of the MT *Nîr* in 1 Kgs 11:36, 15:4; 2 Kgs 8:19 and 2 Chr 21:7', *AusBR* 39 (1991), pp. 19-30.

the construction of the Temple by David's heir, and the establishment of his kingdom.

The Davidic promises in Chronicles are embedded within the context of a continuing narrative, which reinterprets and redefines the terms of the relationship established by Nathan's oracle. That this record contains conditional reformulations of the unconditional dynastic promises matters little in appreciating that the Davidic promises play a formative role in the Chronicler's presentation of the united monarchy, the division, and the independent history of Judah.[50] Like the Deuteronomist, the Chronicler is very much concerned with the issue of integration—how Sinai relates to Zion—but the Chronicler co-ordinates the two somewhat differently. The history of the Judahite kingdom becomes not so much a commentary on Yhwh's relationship to David, as in Samuel–Kings, as a commentary on Yhwh's relationship to both David and Solomon.

3. *Conditional and Promissory: The Davidic Promises in Psalm 132*

After 2 Samuel 7 and the Chronicler's work, Psalm 132 presents a third distinct perspective on the Davidic promises. The author of Psalm 132 commemorates the connections between the ascent of the Ark, the participation of the priests, the provisions for David, and Yhwh's selection of Zion.[51] Comparison between 2 Samuel 7, 1 Chronicles 17, and Psalm 132 reveals the extent to which Israelite authors contextualized and defined the Davidic promises differently. Unlike the Chronicler, who ties the dynastic promises to the accession and activities of Solomon, the psalmist ties the dynastic promises to the ritual procession of the Ark (vv. 6-8) and Yhwh's election of Zion (vv. 13-16).[52]

---

50. The conditions of 2 Chron. 6.16-17, drawn from 1 Kgs 8.24-26, are another matter, because they address the conduct of both Solomon and his sons. How much weight should be placed on this one passage is unclear, because later texts in Chronicles affirm the ongoing validity of the Davidic promises. I am following the principle that clear texts should interpret unclear texts, not vice versa.

51. This combination of features has given rise to a form-critical debate: is Psalm 132 a pilgrimage song, a song of Zion, a royal psalm, or some combination of the above? See H.-J. Kraus, *Psalmen 60–150* (BKAT, 15.2; Neukirchen–Vluyn: Neukirchener Verlag, 5th edn, 1978), p. 1061 (ET *Psalms 60–150* [trans. H.C. Oswald; Minneapolis: Augsburg, 1993], p. 478).

52. T.E. Fretheim, 'Psalm 132: A Form-Critical Study', *JBL* 86 (1967), pp. 289-300; D.R. Hillers, 'The Ritual Procession of the Ark and Psalm 132', *CBQ* 30

Whereas the authors of 2 Samuel 7 have Yhwh promise David an everlasting throne regardless of the behaviour of David's descendants, the author of Psalm 132 has Yhwh predicate a dynasty upon the loyalty of these descendants. The author of Chronicles has Yhwh directly choose (*bḥr*) Solomon, but the author of Psalm 132 has Yhwh choose (*bḥr*) Zion as his resting place in perpetuity (*"dê-'ad*, vv. 13-14). Whereas in the introduction to the divided monarchy in Kings, the Deuteronomist associates David's loyalty with the divine award of a dynasty to David's offspring (1 Kgs 11.37-38, 14.7-9), Psalm 132 associates the divine bequest of a dynasty (vv. 11-12) with Yhwh's choice of Zion (vv. 13-16). In spite of these and other differences, the psalmist shares with the Deuteronomist and the Chronicler a concern with Yhwh's provisions for David, succession in the Davidic ranks, and integration between the Davidic promises and Yhwh's commandments.

The psalm begins and ends with David, but much of the attention is focused on the Ark and Zion's status. The psalm starts with a supplication: 'Remember, O Yhwh, to David all of his self-denial' (*z^ekôr-Yhwh l^edāwîd 'ēt-kol-'unnôtô*),[53] followed by David's oath to Yhwh that he would find him an appropriate sanctuary. David avoids his house and abstains from sleep until he finds a domicile for 'the Mighty One of Jacob' (vv. 3-5). After quoting a summons to worship, 'We have heard it in Ephrathah...let us worship at the footstool of his feet' (v. 7), the psalmist implores Yhwh and the Ark to go to his resting place (v. 8). The priests are clothed in righteousness and his loyal ones shout for joy (v. 9).

Having alluded to the ritual procession of the Ark to Jerusalem, the psalmist returns to David, the man responsible for finding a 'place (*māqôm*) for Yhwh'. On account of David, the psalmist appeals to Yhwh not to turn from the face of his anointed (*māšîaḥ*, v. 10).[54] Just as

---

(1968), pp. 48-55; L. Perlitt, *Bundestheologie im Alten Testament* (WMANT, 36; Neukirchen–Vluyn: Neukirchener Verlag, 1969), pp. 51-52; Cross, *Canaanite Myth*, pp. 256-57; Halpern, *Constitution*, pp. 32-33; Veijola, *Verheißung*, pp. 161-62; H. Kruse, 'Psalm CXXXII and the Royal Zion Festival', *VT* 33 (1983), pp. 279-97; C.L. Seow, *Myth, Drama, and the Politics of David's Dance* (HSM, 44; Atlanta: Scholars Press, 1989), pp. 145-203; Kraus, *Psalmen 60–150*, pp. 1053-66 (ET *Psalms 60–150*, pp. 472-83); C.L. Patton, 'Psalm 132: A Methodological Inquiry', *CBQ* 457 (1995), pp. 643-54.

53. On the translation of the pual of *'nh* in v. 1 as referring to humility or self-denial, see my 'Ancient Near Eastern Grants', p. 680.

54. Psalm 132.8-10 is quoted by the Chronicler in conjunction with Solomon's

the psalmist earlier recalls David swearing (*šb'*) an oath to Yhwh (vv. 2-5), he now recounts Yhwh swearing (*šb'*) an oath to David. The dynastic promises, the truth which Yhwh 'will not revoke' (v. 11), are, however, explicitly conditional. Psalm 132 predicates the enthronement of David's descendants upon their fidelity to Yhwh. God declares to David that he will place the fruit of David's womb upon his throne 'if your sons observe my covenant and my testimonies which I teach them' (v. 12). The promise extends to their sons as well, 'in perpetuity (*'ªdê-'ad*) they will sit on your throne' (v. 12).

Two points are relevant here. The first concerns integration. The psalmist links two monarchical institutions—Davidic kingship and Zion—to two earlier institutions—Yhwh's covenant and the Ark.[55] The mention of 'my covenant' in v. 12 (*bᵉrîtî*) refers not to the Davidic charter, but to a divinely instituted covenant that the Davidides are to observe. The psalmist does not identify the covenant; but, given the parallel reference to 'my testimonies' (*'ēdōtî*), the Sinaitic covenant would seem to be the most likely referent. In any case, there is neither a stated nor a suggested opposition between the covenant the Davidides are to keep and the Davidic promises themselves. Continuity and co-ordination characterize David's oath to Yhwh, the movement of the Ark (and Yhwh) to Zion, Yhwh's oath to David, and the election of Zion. The content of Psalm 132 plays havoc with simplistic or one-sided definitions of the Davidic promises. The dynastic promises structure God's relationship with David and his descendants through the instrument of law, yet these promises announce God's grace to a particular dynasty. The arrangement is both promissory and conditional.

The second point concerns the issue of conditionality. That the per-durability of the dynastic pledge is contingent upon the fidelity of David's descendants is of little consequence in assessing the import-ance of the promises in this particular psalm. The contingent nature of the dynastic pledge is not presented as a devaluation. The mood of Psalm 132 is celebratory and commemorative. Not only does the psalmist proclaim Yhwh's election (*bḥr*) of Zion (vv. 13-16), but he

dedication of the Temple (2 Chron. 6.41-42).

55. H. Gese, 'Der Davidsbund und die Zionserwählung', *ZTK* 61 (1964), pp. 10-26 (reprinted in H. Gese, *Vom Sinai zum Zion* [Munich: Chr. Kaiser Verlag, 1974], pp. 113-29); Mettinger, *King and Messiah*, pp. 256-57; A. Laato, 'Psalm 132 and the Development of the Jerusalemite/Israelite Royal Ideology', *CBQ* 54 (1992), pp. 49-66.

also presents this divine commitment to Zion as the basis for Yhwh's commitments to David. It was David who vowed to find a place for the Ark (vv. 2-5) and David is the basis for divine consideration of Yhwh's 'anointed' (v. 10), yet the psalm associates Yhwh's promises to David with Yhwh's election of Zion.[56] Zion is Yhwh's resting place 'in perpetuity' (*ʿadê-ʿad*); 'there I will dwell, because I have chosen it' (*ʾiwwitîhā*, v. 14). The poem ends, in fact, with Yhwh making a favourable announcement about Zion that centres on David.

> There I shall make a horn sprout (*ʾaṣmîaḥ*) for David,
> I will arrange a dominion for my anointed (*limᵉšîḥî*).
> His enemies I will clothe in shame,
> And his crown shall sparkle upon him (Ps. 132.17-18).

In this version of the Davidic promises, Zion has become the setting for royal dynastic hopes. The compositional history, setting, and form of Psalm 132 continue to be the subject of considerable debate.[57] But there is no clear evidence by which to assume that the conditional formulation of the dynastic promises detracts from their significance.

Against this interpretation, it could be countered that the very conditionality of the Davidic promises has negative implications for their political application beyond the end of Davidic rule in 586 BCE. Assuming that the psalm is pre-exilic and that the Babylonian exile was understood as a judgment against Davidic kingship, it could be argued that the termination of the Davidic kingdom *ipso facto* ends the conditional arrangement propounded in Psalm 132. Two points may be raised in response to such an objection. First, the Sinaitic covenant is expressly conditional, but few scholars speak of the Sinaitic covenant as having been decisively terminated in the Babylonian exile.[58] Biblical writers uniformly blame the Babylonian deportations on assorted Israelite sins, but they do not construe this catastrophe as signalling the definitive end of the Mosaic covenant.

Secondly, on the basis of ancient Near Eastern evidence, one may question whether the connection between disloyalty and covenant dismissal necessarily holds. That a liege failed to honour the terms of a

56. In this regard, the use of the conjunction *kî* at the beginning of v. 13 is telling. See T.E. Fretheim, 'The Ark in Deuteronomy', *CBQ* 30 (1968), pp. 1-14 and Patton, 'Psalm 132', pp. 652-53.

57. Kraus provides an overview, *Psalmen 60–150*, pp. 1055-62 (ET *Psalms 60–150*, pp. 474-79).

58. A point also raised by Levenson, 'Davidic Covenant', p. 212.

treaty does not mean that the pact itself would be nullified completely
or terminated forever. To be sure, a breach could annul an agreement,
but other scenarios are also possible. A suzerain could choose to ignore
the infraction.[59] Or, if a pact had been abrogated by a vassal, that vassal
could move toward or petition for renewal.[60] The overlord could elect
to amend the treaty or to impose a penalty.[61] Another option, not
mutually exclusive with the previous options, would be for the suzerian
to honour the dynastic principle by replacing one monarch with another
from the same lineage.[62] Alternatively, the suzerain could simply
choose to renew the pact itself.[63]

For these and other reasons, it seems plausible that at least some
people in the Babylonian exile and the postexilic period could hear or
read Psalm 132 and ponder the restoration of the Davidic monarchy.
Such a scenario becomes even more likely upon consideration of the
literary movement within the psalm. David's efforts may have led to
the retrieval of the Ark and its ascent to Zion, but Zion becomes the

---

59. For example, in his treaty with Kupanta-Inara of Mirā-Kuwaliya, Muršili II
reinforces the right of Kupanta-Inara to his (adopted) father's house and land despite his father's transgressions; cf. J. Friedrich, *Staatsverträge des Ḫatti-Reiches in
hethitischer Sprache*, I (MVAG, 31; Leipzig: J.C. Hinrichs, 1926), 3.7.12-22; 24.8-
21; G.A. Barton, *The "Treaty" of Mursilis with Kupanta-KAL* (Hittite Studies, 1.2;
Paris: Geuthner, 1928), pp. 37, 61 (§7.55-65; 24.63-70).

60. With respect to the Sinaitic pact, see Exod. 32.11-14, 33.4-6, 34.1-28; Deut.
7.6–10.5; 2 Kgs 23.1-3. Cf. 2 Kgs 11.17-20.

61. So Šuppiluliuma elects to replace Šuttarna III (of Mittanni) with Šattiwaza,
even though Šattiwaza was the son of Šuppiluliuma's former foe Tušratta; cf. E.F.
Weidner, *Politische Dokumente aus Kleinasien: Die Staatsverträge in akkadischer
Sprache aus dem Archiv von Boghazköi* (Boghazköi-Studien, 8; Leipzig: J.C.
Hinrichs, 1923), §2.32. Within biblical literature, see the formulation of the new
covenant in Jer. 31.31-34, which announces the deity's aid in enabling Israelites to
observe 'my torah', that is, the same torah as that of the old covenant.

62. McCarthy, (*Treaty and Covenant*, pp. 131-32) calls attention to the
Assyrian treatment of Ashdod. Sargon replaces Azuri, king of Ashdod (after he
revolted against Assyria) with his full brother Ahimitu; cf. D.D. Luckenbill,
Ancient Records of Assyria and Babylonia. II. *Historical Records of Assyria from
Sargon to the End* (Chicago: Chicago University Press, 1927), pp. 13-14 (§1.30). In
the same manner, Nebuchadnezzar replaces the exiled Jehoiachin with Zedekiah
(2 Kgs 24.8-17).

63. See further, McCarthy, *Treaty and Covenant*, pp. 259-61, 297-98; K. Balt-
zer, *The Covenant Formulary in Old Testament, Jewish, and Early Christian Writings* (Philadelphia: Fortress Press, 1971).

basis for Yhwh's oath to David. It is 'there', after all, that Yhwh 'will make a horn sprout for David' (v. 17). To be sure, the normal context for the psalm's use in the postexilic period would be the cultus. But the recitation of Psalm 132 within the Temple courts does not entail that its hearers understood the poem in purely cultic terms. On the contrary, the use of the psalm may have given rise to certain political aspirations. Given the return(s) from exile and the rebuilding of the Temple in Zion, there may well have been Jews who desired that Yhwh would take the next step and renew his oath to David.[64]

4. *Unconditional yet Renounced: The Davidic Promises in Psalm 89*

As with the three other major presentations of the Davidic promises, Psalm 89 exhibits its own particular structure, form, and content. The psalm contains an acclamation of Yhwh's fidelity (vv. 2-3, ET 1–2), a declaration of Yhwh's granting of an everlasting throne to David (vv. 4-5, ET 3–4), a celebration of Yhwh's incomparable status among the gods (vv. 6-8, ET 5–7), a summation of his creative activity (vv. 9-15, ET 8–14), a reflection on Israel's privileged position (vv. 16-19, ET 15–18), a lengthy description of the Davidic promises (vv. 20-38, ET 19–37), and a lament that bemoans Yhwh's rejection of his covenant with David (vv. 39-52, ET 38–51). Of the four principal passages dealing with the Davidic promises, Psalm 89 is the most elaborate and presents the most exalted picture of David's position.

The context of the Davidic charter in Psalm 89 differs from that of the three other texts. The prophecy of Nathan in 2 Samuel 7 and 1 Chronicles 17 addresses David's request for a Temple by tying the construction of the Temple by one of David's seed to the establishment of his dynasty. But the Jerusalem Temple is never mentioned in Psalm 89. The divine pledge to David in Psalm 132 is associated with the elevation of the Ark and Yhwh's election of Zion, while the Chronicler

---

64. To this last point it could be objected that vv. 17-18 may be a later addition to the text, so C.A. Briggs, and E.G. Briggs, *The Book of Psalms*, II (ICC; New York: Charles Scribner's Sons, 1907), pp. 472-73. Assuming, for the sake of argument, the validity of this objection, the remaining psalm (vv. 1-16) would still be a positive and celebratory acclamation of the relationship between Yhwh, Zion, and David. Even as a gloss these verses are important for the history of interpretation. Since vv. 17-18 speak of a fief for Yhwh's anointed and the humiliation of David's enemies, this addition would be expressing a hope for the return of Davidic rule.

speaks of Yhwh's election of David's successor, Solomon. Nevertheless, the Ark, Zion, and David's immediate successor do not appear in Psalm 89. The blessings bestowed upon David are set against the background of Yhwh's peerless status and omnipotence. Psalm 89 associates Yhwh's promises to David with Yhwh's incomparability in the heavenly council (vv. 6-8, ET 5–7), Yhwh's creative achievements (vv. 9-15, ET 8–14), and the security he provides for his people (vv. 16-19, ET 15–18). Instead of Yhwh's election of Zion or of Solomon, the poem speaks of Yhwh's election of David (vv. 4, 20, ET 3, 19).

To be sure, the description of the Davidic promises (vv. 20-38, ET 19-37) recalls that of 2 Samuel 7. Like 2 Samuel 7, Psalm 89 combines the depiction of divine adoption with the granting of a sure inheritance (vv. 27, 29-30, ET 26, 28-29). Along with 2 Samuel 7, and over against Psalm 132, the overlord's promise of dynastic succession is not contingent upon continuing client loyalty (vv. 31-33, ET 30–32). Yhwh declares that David's descendants are subject to 'my torah' (*tôrātî*) and to 'my judgments' (*mišpāṭay*, v. 31, ET 30). Nevertheless, as in 2 Samuel 7, the basic dynastic pledge is not contingent upon the good behaviour of said descendants (vv. 34-37, ET 33–36).

In spite of these parallels with 2 Samuel 7, there are also important differences. The authors of Psalm 89 blend various formulae into their portrayal of Davidic kingship. Divine adoption and the granting of a sure inheritance do not exhaust Yhwh's provision for his anointed. Yhwh anoints David with holy oil and confers first-born status upon him, 'highest among the kings of the earth' (Ps. 89.21, 28, ET 20, 27)[65]. The psalmist upholds Yhwh's extraordinary status in the heavens to highlight the status of his anointed on earth. The same deity who 'confirms' (*kwn*) his loyalty in the heavens (v. 3, ET 2) also 'confirms' (*kwn*) David's 'throne for all generations' (v. 5, ET 4). God both establishes his faithfulness in the heavens (v. 3, ET 2) and declares that 'I will establish his seed in perpetuity, his throne as the days of the heavens' (v. 30, ET 29). Israel enjoys a privileged position before Yhwh (vv. 16-19, ET 15–18), but the author singles out David for special treatment: 'chosen from the people I have exalted (one)' (v. 20, ET 19).

---

65. H. Gunkel, *Die Psalmen* (HAT; Göttingen: Vandenhoeck & Ruprecht, 1926), pp. 384-96; N.M. Sarna, 'Psalm 89: A Study in Inner Biblical Exgesis', in A. Altmann (ed.), *Biblical and Other Studies* (Cambridge, MA: Harvard University Press, 1963), pp. 29-46, esp. p. 38.

The God whose 'hand is strong', whose 'right hand is exalted' (v. 14, ET 13), pledges that:

> (22, ET 21) My hand shall abide with him,
> my arm shall strengthen him.
> (23, ET 22) The enemy shall not lay claim to him,
> and the wicked shall not humble him.
> (24, ET 23) I will crush his foes before him,
> and strike down those who hate him.
> (25, ET 24) My faithfulness and loyalty shall be with him,
> and in my name shall his horn be exalted.[66]

Images of military victory are also present in 2 Samuel 7 and 1 Chronicles 17, but the power conferred upon David in Psalm 89 goes beyond the human variety. The God who tames the sea and crushes the sea monster Rahab (vv. 10-11, ET 9–10), declares concerning David, 'I will set his hand upon the sea, and his right hand upon the rivers' (v. 26, ET 25). As for David's throne, Yhwh declares that it shall endure 'like the sun before me' (v. 37, ET 36). Hence, the psalm speaks of David's position in mythical terms.[67] In this respect, the royal ideology expressed in Psalm 89 is similar to ideologies of Canaanite kingship, in which the king enjoys a degree of kinship with the divine realm.[68] The king, although human and vulnerable, is mythologically paired with the gods.[69] Like the king of Ḫubur in the Kirta legend, the David of Psalm 89 enjoys a critical position in divine–human affairs.[70] Associating Yhwh's handiwork in the heavens and earth with the

---

66. In Ps. 89.23 (ET 22) the MT reads *lōʾ yᵉʿannennû*, while the lemma of the LXX, προσθήσει τοῦ κακῶσαι αὐτόν (= *yōsîp lᵉʿannôtô*), assimilates toward 2 Sam. 7.10 (cf. 1 Chron. 17.9). I follow the MT (*lectio difficilior*).

67. J. Day, *God's Conflict with the Dragon and the Sea: Echoes of a Canaanite Myth in the Old Testament* (UCOP, 35; Cambridge: Cambridge University Press, 1985), pp. 25-28.

68. K.-H. Bernhardt, *Das Problem der altorientalischen Königsideologie im Alten Testament* (VTSup, 8; Leiden: E.J. Brill, 1961), pp. 67-90; J. Gray, 'Sacral Kingship in Ugarit', *Ugaritica* 6 (1969), pp. 289-302; G.W. Ahlström, *Royal Administration and National Religion in Ancient Palestine* (SHANE, 1; Leiden: E.J. Brill, 1982), pp. 1-25.

69. H. Frankfort, *Kingship and the Gods: A Study of Ancient Near Eastern Kingship as the Integration of Society and Nature* (Chicago: University of Chicago Press, 1948), pp. 251-74.

70. *KTU*² 1.16.II.40-44. See further my, 'Dissonance and Disaster in the Legend of Kirta', *JAOS* 114 (1994), pp. 572-82.

establishment of David's sons accentuates the dynastic pledge in Ps. 89.20-38 (ET 19–37).[71]

Precisely because the psalm applies such a high royal theology to David, the conclusion to the psalm, a lament that Yhwh has repudiated his covenant with David (vv. 39-46, ET 38-45), is all the more poignant. After recounting the Davidic promises at considerable length (vv. 20-38, ET 19–37), the poet complains that Yhwh has spurned, rejected, and become furious with his anointed (v. 39, ET 38). 'You have renounced [piel of *n'd*] the covenant of your servant, and have profaned [piel of *hll*] his crown in the dust' (v. 40, ET 39). Psalm 89 speaks of the Davidic promises in the most exalted terms, yet it is this psalm, and not the conditional formulation of Psalm 132, that speaks of Yhwh 'casting his throne to the ground' (v. 45, ET 44). Apparently, even a covenant in which the dynastic pledge is perpetual could be broken. The same God who earlier declared that 'I will not abrogate my covenant, nor change what comes forth from my lips' (v. 35, ET 34) stands accused of doing just that. Whereas the psalm earlier spoke of 'the enemy not laying claim to him and and the wicked not humbling him' (v. 23, ET 22), the lament speaks of Yhwh 'exalting the right hand of his enemies and causing all of his foes to rejoice' (v. 43, ET 42).

In spite of depicting God's rejection of his covenant with David in such strong and unambiguous terms, the psalm does not end with the termination of the Davidic covenant. The series of questions (vv. 47–50, ET 46-49), which follow the author's complaint (vv. 38-46, ET 37–45), implore God to consider the plight of his servant. Implicit in such questions about the duration of Yhwh's hiding himself and the status of 'your former loyalties, which in your truth you swore to David' (vv. 47, 50, ET 46, 49) is the possibility that the period of divine wrath might end and that Yhwh might look again upon his anointed with favour. Hence, the author reminds God of the abuse that his anointed has endured and that the number of days left before his servant's death are limited (vv. 48-49, 51, ET 47–48, 50).

---

71. E. Lipiński, *Le Poème royal du Psaume lxxxix 1-5. 20-38* (Cahiers de la Revue Biblique, 6; Paris: J. Gabalda, 1967), pp. 21-81; Mettinger, *King and Messiah*, pp. 51-55; Halpern, *Constitution*, pp. 33-38; Veijola, *Verheißung*, pp. 32-46; Kraus, *Psalmen 60–150*, pp. 777-94 (ET *Psalms 60–150*, pp. 197-211).

Conclusions

It has become customary in biblical criticism to refer to the Davidic promises as a covenant and to draw comparisons between this covenant and the Mosaic covenant. In some cases, the two covenants are presented as stark opposites—one obligatory and conditional, the other promissory and unconditional. But this neat typology breaks down upon close scrutiny. In dealing with the Davidic covenant one is confronted with four principal passages and many ancillary references.[72] If the Davidic covenant ever existed as a legal document, it is no longer extant. None of the principal passages is strictly juridical in nature. The different versions of the royal Davidic charter occur in the setting of historical narratives and poems and do not manifest a consistent, much less a uniform, structure. Each of the biblical writers draws upon a repertoire of traditional imagery and sources—mythological, legal, diplomatic, and, in the case of the Chronicler, biblical. Each author has contextualized, shaped, and defined the Davidic promises in his own distinctive way. That two of the principal passages—2 Samuel 7 and 1 Chronicles 17—are embedded within larger narrative frameworks, which redefine and reapply Nathan's promises in new historical contexts, further complicates any attempt to speak simply of the Davidic covenant. Given the wide range of evidence, it may be more accurate to speak of Davidic covenants than to speak of a single pact.

A fairly common response to this diversity is to regard two of the principal texts—Psalm 132 and 1 Chronicles 17—as later revisions and conditionalizations of an earlier unconditional decree. There are at least two major problems with this approach. First, scholars have been unable to agree on the dating of the four texts in question. In the case of Psalm 132, for example, proposed dates of composition range from the tenth century to the Maccabaean age.[73] Given the sharp disagreement, a

---

72. Indeed, whether all of the biblical authors who depicted the Davidic promises viewed them as constituting a covenant is doubtful. Of the four extended references to the Davidic promises—2 Samuel 7, Psalms 89 and 132, and 1 Chronicles 17—only Psalm 89 explicitly refers to these promises as a *bᵉrît* (vv. 4, 29, 35, 40, ET 3, 28, 34, 39). In his history of Judah, the Chronicler twice uses the term *bᵉrît* in referring to Nathan's dynastic oracle (2 Chron. 13.5; 21.7). See further my 'Battling against Yahweh', pp. 515-22.

73. M. Dahood dates the psalm to the tenth century, *Psalms*. III. *101–150* (AB, 16A; Garden City, NY: Doubleday, 1970), p. 241. Fretheim also posits an early

neat chronological typology becomes more difficult to maintain. One could just as well argue that there were disparate, even competing, notions of the Davidic promises within ancient Israel.

Secondly, the unconditional/conditional typology of the Davidic covenant cannot adequately account for the range of evidence. Despite the Chronicler's late date and his obvious dependence on Samuel–Kings, his history contains both unconditional and conditional versions of the Davidic promises.[74] His primary version of the royal Davidic charter (1 Chron. 17) is, in fact, more unconditional than that of 2 Samuel 7. Unlike 2 Samuel 7 and Psalm 89, which subject David's descendants to Yhwh's statutes, 1 Chronicles 17 does not contain any such condition. To confound the typology further, Psalm 132 is both promissory and conditional, while Psalm 89 speaks of Yhwh repudiating the (unconditional) Davidic covenant. The point is not that each of these passages places the same emphasis on human commitment and divine obligation. They clearly do not. Rather, these considerations suggest that the sharp contrast between unconditional and conditional versions of the Davidic covenant has been overdrawn.

To this it could be objected that the lament in Psalm 89 and the material in Kings represent later reworkings of a more original version of the Davidic promises found in Nathan's oracle. There may be some validity to this argument. There is legitimate disagreement about the composition of 2 Samuel 7[75] and the Deuteronomistic History, as there is about the redaction of Psalm 89 itself.[76] But, as we have seen, Nathan's oracle is not without conditions. Individual kings face divine

---

date, 'Ark in Deuteronomy', pp. 1-14. Kraus (*Psalmen 60–150*, p. 1057 [ET *Psalms 60–150*, p. 475]) and Gese ('Der Davidsbund', pp. 113-29) opt for a pre-exilic date, while Patton ('Psalm 132', pp. 653-54) contends for postexilic composition. Briggs and Briggs date the completion of the psalm to the late Maccabaean age, *Psalms, II*, pp. 468-69.

74. This dependence has been questioned recently by A.G. Auld, who speaks of the Deuteronomist(s) and the Chronicler as drawing upon a common source. Auld commendably raises a series of important questions about the relationship between Samuel–Kings and Chronicles; cf. A. G. Auld, *Kings Without Privilege: David and Moses in the Story of the Bible's Kings* (Edinburgh: T. & T. Clark, 1994). Nevertheless, I do not believe that his central thesis can be sustained. See my review in *Ashland Theological Review* 27 (1995), pp. 118-21.

75. See the recent survey of A. Caquot, and P. de Robert, *Les Livres de Samuel* (CAT, 6; Geneva: Labor et Fides, 1994), pp. 421-33.

76. See the references in nn. 65 and 71.

chastisement, should they prove disloyal to Yhwh (2 Sam. 7.14; Ps. 89.31-33, ET 30–32). To be sure, one could take the objection a step further and contend that the codicils of 2 Sam. 7.14 and Ps. 89.31-33 (ET 30–32) are themselves later additions to the text. One might then be left with a pure unconditional promise, untainted by complication or allusion to divine rules.[77] But what would be the rationale and thrust of such a source-critical or redaction-critical analysis? There are no compelling literary or historical reasons for dissociating the dynastic pledge from the legal qualification. Both the dynastic promise and the accompanying codicil, for example, are attested together in the vassal treaty between Tudhaliya IV of Ḫatti and Ulmi-Tešup of Tarḫuntašša.[78]

Even assuming, for the sake of argument, the plausibility of a source-critical strategy that would recover a purely unconditional pledge, how much weight should be placed on such a speculation? It would be a mistake, of course, to confuse the earliest reconstructed layer with the most significant and formative rendering of the text.[79] Most of the passages dealing with the Davidic promises relate these promises in some fashion to Yhwh's commandments. Integration was an ancient concern, not simply a modern approach. If one wishes to discuss the place of the Davidic covenant within the Hebrew scriptures, as well as its relationship to the Sinaitic covenant, it seems illogical to skirt most of the evidence pertaining to the issue.

The question of integration raises a larger issue, that of the relative importance of the Mosaic and Davidic covenants. While it would be ill-advised to trivialize the Sinaitic covenant, it is also ill-advised to marginalize the Davidic promises as engaging only the matter of succession. The modern preoccupation with issues of (un)conditionality

---

77. So L. Rost, for instance, isolates 2 Sam. 7.11b, 16 as representing the oldest layer within the Davidic promises; cf. *Die Überlieferung von der Thronachfolge Davids* (BWANT, 3; Stuttgart: W. Kohlhammer, 1926), pp. 106-107 (ET *The Succession to the Throne of David* [trans. M.D. Rutter and D.M. Gunn, with an introduction by E. Ball; Sheffield: Almond Press, 1982], pp. 86-87).

78. *Keilschrifttexte aus Boghazköi* 4.10. See de Vaux, 'Le Roi d'Israël', pp. 119-33; Calderone, *Dynastic Oracle*, pp. 56-57; G.M. Beckman, 'Inheritance and Royal Succession Among the Hittites', in H.A. Hoffner and G.M. Beckman (eds.), *Kaniššuwar: A Tribute to Hans G. Güterbock on his Seventy-fifth Birthday* (Assyriological Studies, 23; Chicago: Oriental Institute, 1986), pp. 19-20.

79. Such a reconstruction could also mislead scholars into placing undue weight upon a hypothetical oracle as empirical evidence by which to rewrite the history of Israelite religion.

and royal continuity obscures the extent to which biblical writers tie the Davidic promises to other major aspects of Israelite life. The issue in each of the four principal passages is not simply succession within the Davidic line, but its relation to other national interests. It is precisely because the Deuteronomist and the Chronicler are interested in more than royal lineage that they employ the Davidic promises as a cipher to structure and evaluate the united kingdom, the division, and the Judahite monarchy.

For the same reason, the considerable modern interest in the Davidic promises cannot be wholly explained by recourse to the messianic concerns of early Jewish and Christian interpreters.[80] Rather, the attention given to the Davidic promises is best explained by the connections between these promises and broader themes in Israelite life—the election of Zion, the achievement of rest for Israel, the ritual procession of the Ark, divine incomparability, Yhwh's handiwork in the heavens, victory in war, power over nature, the establishment of the Temple, the survival of the Southern Kingdom, and so forth. The rich associations between the royal Davidic charter and Israelite life lend a certain gravity to the Davidic legacy. Indeed, these associations may actually shed some light on why early interpreters took such an interest in the figure of David. The diversity of messianic expectations in early Judaism and Christianity may be attributed, at least in part, to the diversity of associations within the Hebrew Bible itself.[81]

80. *Pace* Levenson, 'Davidic Covenant', pp. 217-19.

81. I would like to thank the members of the Oxford Old Testament Seminar for graciously inviting me to present an earlier (and partial) version of this paper during my sabbatical year at the Oxford Centre for Hebrew and Jewish Studies.

The Trappings of Royalty in Ancient Hebrew

Alison Salvesen

This essay represents work in progress for the Semantics of Ancient Hebrew Database, which covers the whole corpus of Ancient Hebrew (AH) literature, namely the Hebrew Bible, inscriptions, Ben Sira, and non-biblical documents in Hebrew from Qumran.[1] The field assigned to me to cover is that of 'kingship', which is appropriate for the theme of this Oxford Seminar volume, *King and Messiah*. Since the Database is primarily a lexicographical tool, I will not be examining here the institutions of royalty in ancient Israel, but a specific set of 'royal' terms as they are used in this corpus of Ancient Hebrew, whether in an Israelite or foreign or divine context. The words discussed are items that occur at least sometimes in association with the king or other royal figures: *nēzer*, *'ăṭārâ*, and *keter*, which are loosely translated as 'crown'; *'eṣ'ādâ*, 'armlet'; *kissē'*, 'throne', and *hᵃdōm*, 'footstool'; *šēbeṭ* and *šarbîṭ*, 'sceptre'.

Most of what follows could be found by looking at a good dictionary or the articles in the recently completed *Theologisches Wörterbuch zum Alten Testament*.[2] But as in the Database itself, my aim is to provide a discussion of the lines of debate that have led to a particular definition of certain words. This involves surveys of the terms' semantic realms, that is, what fields of meaning are associated with them; their syntagmatic context, meaning what sort of verbs and subjects are used with them; their possible etymology and their relationship to words in other ancient Semitic languages; the textual or theological problems associ-

---

1.   I would like to acknowledge the generous support of the Leverhulme Trust for this research.

2.   G.J. Botterweck and H. Ringgren (eds.), *Theologisches Wörterbuch zum Alten Testament* (10 vols.; Stuttgart: W. Kohlhammer, 1970–96) (ET J.T. Willis, D. Green *et al*. [eds.], *Theological Dictionary of the Old Testament* [Grand Rapids: Eerdmans, 1974–]).

ated with them; and, finally, some general definition of meaning. Where appropriate I have made a tentative comparison with known artefacts or art from the ancient Near East.

The main limitation of semantic studies of a written corpus in a 'dead' language is that we are hindered in our knowledge by the type and range of writings in which a term is found, and by the frequency of that term. Moreover, the precise date of many parts of the Hebrew Bible is uncertain, and that creates further difficulties in charting possible changes in the meaning of a word over time. Overall syntheses are therefore dangerous, but not to attempt them would be somewhat cowardly and certainly unhelpful. It must be borne in mind that we can only describe the evidence as we find it, and our findings are only true for our corpus, which is no doubt a very patchy representation of ancient literary Hebrew. So perhaps it is best to take any attempted definition as a rough guide to steer us in the general direction of the meaning of each biblical writer.

There is a problem of how far a particular text represents historical reality. For example, is there any value in attempting to recover the actual form of the *ʿᵃṭārâ* in Ezek. 21.31 (ET 26), which Zedekiah is described as wearing? The problem is even more acute in the case of *keter* in Esther, where the historical content of the book is debatable. Yet the writers had a clear image in their minds of these forms and their symbolic value, and this is what we are trying to reach, rather than a historical reality that may well be a chimera. If that seems unduly pessimistic, it should be noted that royal accoutrements are by nature very conservative because they represent legitimacy and therefore frequently incorporate traditional details. This can be seen in the coins of the Persian emperors, from the Achaemenids to the Sassanids, a period of a millennium. Certain details of the royal headdress continue for generations, or resurface in a new dynasty: for instance, the Persian headband that goes back to Assyrian times becomes much more prominent and significant in the Seleucid period under Hellenistic influence, where it has become the primary symbol of monarchy, and it continues to be represented under the newer-style Sassanid crown up to the Islamic conquests.[3] We may assume that biblical writers had some

---

3. As can be seen in B. Hrouda, *Die Kulturgeschichte des assyrischen Flach-bildes* (Bonn: Habelt, 1965), Taf. 5, 6; R.D. Sellwood, 'Parthian Coins', in *Cambridge History of Iran*, III.1 (Cambridge: Cambridge University Press, 1983), pp. 279-98, and Pls. 1–8; R. Göbl, 'Sasanian Coins', in *Cambridge History of Iran*,

access to royal symbols, if not directly via the court, then through artistic representations available at the time, the second commandment (Exod. 20.4) notwithstanding.

Another problem is the relationship between an individual word and the general theological or historical context of the passage. Ideally, the meaning of the word should have an impact on the general critical analysis of the passage, instead of the criticism of the passage deciding the meaning of the word. But in practice, it is both sensible and necessary to take into account higher criticism: for instance, some knowledge of the work of the Deuteronomist and of 'C' sheds light on the high occurrence of the expression 'sit upon the throne' (*yāšab 'al-kissē'*) in 1 Kings and Jeremiah.

The Crown and Royal Headgear ('*aṭārâ, nēzer and keter*)

The fact that there are several different terms for royal headgear in AH, including the words normally translated as 'crown', *nēzer*, '*aṭārâ*, and *keter*, ought to make us question whether a crown is a fundamental symbol of kingship at all. It is also clear from the contexts in which these words are used that they are far from synonymous. '*aṭārâ* is the commonest term, occurring 23 times in the Hebrew Bible, three times in Ben Sira and three times in Qumran Hebrew.[4] The root is '*ṭr*, 'to surround'. It is used in non-royal contexts more frequently than royal, and metaphorically of glory or rejoicing. Wearers include Mordecai, Joshua the high priest in Zechariah 6, the drunkards of Ephraim in Isaiah 28, the king and *gᵉbîrâ* in Jeremiah 13, and the *nāśî'*, that is, Zedekiah, in Ezekiel 21. The only undoubted royal figures with an '*aṭārâ* are in Jer. 13.18 (king and *gᵉbîrâ*), Ezek. 21.31 (ET 26) (*nāśî'*), and in Song 3.11 (Solomon). In 2 Sam. 12.30 (= 1 Chron. 20.2) the heavy gold crown may be on the head of Milcom rather than on 'their king', and it may be only the jewel from it that David has on his own head.

An '*aṭārâ* can be made of gold, as in 2 Sam. 12.30//1 Chron. 20.2; Zech. 6.11; Ps. 21.4 (ET 3); and Est. 8.15. Silver is also mentioned in

III.1, pp. 322-42, and Pls. 25–30.

4.   2 Sam. 12.30//1 Chron. 20.2; Isa. 28.1, 3, 5, 62.3; Jer. 13.18; Ezek. 16.12, 21.31 (ET 26), 23.42; Zech. 6.11, 14; Ps. 21.4 (ET 3); Prov. 4.9, 12.4, 14.24, 16.31, 17.6; Job 19.9, 31.36; Lam. 5.16; Song 3.11; Est. 8.15; Sir. 6.31 (A), 45.12 (B), 50.12 (B); 1QSb 4.3; Temple Scroll 17.1, 40.11.

Zech. 6.11. But the context of the word in Isa. 28.1, 3, 5 points to a floral wreath as a sign of revelry and celebration, even though the passage may be a deliberate allusion to the king's loss of control, according to Kraus: he believes that the use of the word *ṣîṣ* with *ʿaṭārâ* hints at the king's *nēzer*—of which more later.[5] In Ezek. 16.12 and 23.42 the *ʿaṭeret tiperet* is evidently headgear given to a woman by her husband or lover, an item of personal adornment for a private individual. Solomon is certainly described as having been crowned with an *ʿaṭārâ* by his mother in Song 3.11, but given the context—'on the day of his wedding, when his heart rejoiced'—it seems far more likely that this was a wreath or crown for his marriage celebrations, not a symbol of kingship.

ʿaṭārâ is used in a metaphorical sense in Proverbs: wealth is the *ʿaṭārâ* of the wise, grandchildren are the *ʿaṭārâ* of the old, a capable wife is the *ʿaṭārâ* of her husband, and so on (Prov. 14.24, 17.6, 12.4). In Job 19.9 and 31.36 it is a symbol of glory and dignity. The Scroll of Blessing from Qumran also takes *ʿaṭārâ* in the metaphorical sense: 'eternal blessings are the *ʿaṭārâ* of your head' (1 QSb 4.3), and so does Sirach in two of its three occurrences: wisdom is an *ʿaṭeret tiperet* (6.31 [A]) and Simon son of Onias the high priest is surrounded by his sons: *ʿaṭeret bānîm* (50.12 [B]).

Therefore the primary connotations of *ʿaṭārâ* in the Hebrew Bible are of honour, rejoicing, and ceremonial, but not of ritual or the cult of Yahweh. The word can be associated with royalty, though it is not an especial symbol of kingship: even a gold *ʿaṭārâ* is not restricted to the king or even to the royal family. It has many similarities with the Greek word στέφανος, which also means a crown or a wreath, and is associated with victory and celebration. Ezekiel 21.31 (ET 26), where it is coupled with *miṣnepet*, does seem to point to *ʿaṭārâ* being a sign of kingship, but even that passage seems to have more to do with humiliation and loss of high office than loss of kingship *per se*. This understanding may help to resolve some of the problems of Zechariah 6, where it has perturbed scholars that Joshua the high priest seems to be granted quasi-royal status by being given a crown and possibly also a throne. But if an *ʿaṭārâ* is not confined to the king alone, there is not quite the same problem with Joshua the high priest wearing one. 'Crown' is such a powerful symbol of the monarchy in Britain, even at

5.   H-J. Kraus, 'hôj als profetische Leichenklage über das eigene Volk im 8. Jahrhundert', *ZAW* 85 (1973), pp. 15-46.

the end of the twentieth century, that it is easy to read too much into *ʿᵃṭārâ* as an equivalent symbol in AH.

In rabbinic Hebrew the meanings 'wreath; honour; bridal crown' continue for *ʿᵃṭārâ*, but there are few royal nuances. Architectural references, such as 'crenellations', show up in the Temple Scroll and rabbinic literature, and also some anatomical ones.[6]

Nēzer

Nēzer is the term used of something worn by the high priest, and by the kings Saul and Joash, but it occurs much more commonly for the dedicated hair of the Nazirite, and in the latter case it is not an artefact at all.[7] It is unclear whether the two uses, for headgear and hair, are from a single root, or from two homonymous roots, and also whether there is a connection at the level of Proto-Semitic between the root *nēzer* and the root *ndr*, 'to vow': this is such a vexed question that it cannot be discussed here.[8] Görg, followed by Milgrom, suggests that the etymology is from Egyptian *nzr.t*, 'snake goddess', or Egyptian *nśr.t*, 'flame', both used for the Uraeus serpent projecting from Pharaoh's crown, which was an apotropaic device.[9] An Egyptian etymology is very unlikely, given that the word is used in Egyptian only in a metaphorical sense and that Egyptian *z* disappeared around 2500 BCE.[10] So at present it is safer to assume a North-West Semitic etymology for *nēzer*.

When *nēzer* occurs in the Bible in the sense of headgear, it is only mentioned as an item of royal attire for Saul and Joash, and in Ps. 89.40 (ET 39), but is worn by the high priest. This provides one of the arguments for saying that the high priest took over royal attributes and

6. Architectural: Temple Scroll 17.1, *m. Ohol.* 14.1, *m. Mid.* 2.8. Anatomical: *b. Yeb.* 55b, *b. Nid.* 47a, *t. Nid.* 6.4.

7. Exod. 29.6, 39.30; Lev. 8.9, 21.12; 2 Sam. 1.10; 2 Kgs 11.12//2 Chron. 23.11; Zech. 9.16; Prov. 27.24; Pss. 89.40 (ET 39), 132.18. Nazirite *nzr*: Num. 6 (× 13); Jer. 7.29.

8. For recent treatments, see J. Berlinerblau, *The Vow and the 'Popular Religious Groups' of Ancient Israel: A Philological and Sociological Inquiry* (JSOTSup, 210; Sheffield: Sheffield Academic Press, 1996), Appendix 4; J.L. Boyd, 'The Etymological Relationship Between NDR and NZR Reconsidered', *UF* 117 (1986), pp. 61-75.

9. M. Görg, 'Die Kopfbedeckung des Hohenpriesters', *BN* 3 (1977), pp. 24-26; *idem*, 'Weiteres zu nzr ("Diadem")', *BN* 4 (1977), pp. 7-8; J. Milgrom, *Leviticus 1–16* (AB, 3; New York: Doubleday, 1991), pp. 511-13.

10. Personal communication, Professor John Baines, Griffith Institute, Oxford.

functions in the postexilic period. Without wishing to comment on that
theory, the *nēzer* worn on the head certainly has a good many cultic
associations: we find in the same context the words *qōdeš*, 'holiness'
(Exod. 29.6, 39.30; Lev. 8.9); *ḥillēl*, 'to profane' (Lev. 21.12; Ps. 89.40,
ET 39); *miṣnepet*, 'turban'; *ṣîṣ*, 'flower'; *rō'š*, 'head'; *māšaḥ*, 'to anoint'
(Lev. 21.12; 2 Kgs 11.12//2 Chron. 23.11). In Psalms 89 and 132 the
word *bᵉrît*, 'covenant', appears in synonymous parallelism to *nēzer*, and
to *bōšet* in antithetical parallelism. All this indicates that *nēzer* belongs
in the realm of the cult and ritual, in cultic and royal adornment. One
should also note that the Nazirite *nēzer* also occurs in the company
of words with similar nuances: *rō'š*, *qōdeš*, *ṭāhᵒrâ*, 'purity'; *ṭāmē'*,
'unclean'; *ṭimmē'*, 'to defile'. So there may be a semantic overlap
between the two forms of *nēzer*, even if they are eventually not found
to share the same etymology: one type of *nēzer* refers to something
sacred to the Lord placed on the head, the other *nēzer* is the hair growth
of the head dedicated to God.

At Qumran, however, none of the three occurrences of *nēzer* refers to
the Nazirite vow, though this sense is frequent in rabbinic Hebrew. One
occurrence seems to refer to the priestly *nēzer*,[11] the second is a royal
nēzer for the scion of David at a ceremony involving embroidered
robes and a throne of honour,[12] and the third is very fragmentary, but
occurs below the words *keter ṣedeq*.[13]

It seems very unlikely indeed that *nēzer* was a crown in the modern
sense of the word, rigid, golden and cylindrical, with crenellations and
jewels. In the case of the high priest, the *nēzer* was attached to the
miṣnepet, the turban, by means of a blue cord, and was engraved with
the words 'Holy to the Lord' (Exod. 28.36, 39.30). The word *nēzer* is
juxtaposed with *ṣîṣ* (Lev. 8.9; Exod. 28.36, 39.30), which usually
means 'flower' or 'blossom', but the LXX and Vulgate render *nēzer* as
'metal plate'. The rabbis said that the priestly *nēzer* was a golden plate
two fingers' breadth, running from ear to ear,[14] and Josephus describes
it as a gold band, τελαμὼν χρύσεος, over the forehead.[15] Mayer suggests that a priestly or royal *nēzer* was a metal fillet with holes for ties,

---

11. 1QSb 4.28.
12. 4QpIsaᵃ 8–10.19.
13. *Festival Prayers* (4Q509) 97–98. ii.3.
14. *b. Šab.* 63b.
15. *Ant.* 3.178; cf. *War* 5.235, and *Letter of Aristeas* 98. See Thackeray's remarks on pp. 398-401 of the Loeb edition of the *Antiquities*.

and some decoration, such as rosettes, imitation flowers or precious stones, presumably to explain the association with the word *ṣîṣ*.[16] Such a form would be appropriate for active wear, since the *nēzer* is described as being worn by the high priest for performing sacrifices and by King Saul in battle, perhaps over a helmet as the priest wore his on the *miṣnepet*. It could not take a form that was too heavy, uncomfortable or unwieldy. From the point of view of archaeological artefacts, possible examples of this type of headgear would be the figured gold strips and the circular floral emblem found in sites to the south of Gaza, the former resembling the royal *nēzer* and the latter the priestly *ṣîṣ*.[17] The phrase in Zech. 9.16, *'abnê nēzer mitnôsᵉsôt*, may suggest the existence of a form of *nēzer* with jewels in the later biblical period.[18]

No one who is not a high priest or a king—for instance, a woman—is described as wearing a *nēzer*. In this it differs from the *ᵃṭārâ*, which does seem to have been worn by women and non-royal men. The associations are strongly cultic, especially through the use of terms for defilement and purity. The two types of *nēzer*, headgear and dedicated hair growth, certainly have elements in common in AH: they are both visible signs of the wearer's consecration to the Lord, they are both connected with the head, and they are both vulnerable to defilement. The influence of the Priestly source on some passages should, however, be borne in mind: both Numbers 6 (Nazirites) and Leviticus 21 (high priestly *nēzer*) come from priestly circles, and even the parallel passages 2 Kgs 11.12//2 Chron. 23.11 involve the placing of the *nēzer* on the king by a priest. The *nēzer* may even have been a token that the wearer had been anointed, like a bishop's ring. This would fit with Exod. 29.7; Lev. 21.12; 2 Kgs 11.12//2 Chron. 23.11, and may also be implied in 2 Sam. 1.10 and 16, where David receives Saul's *nēzer* from the Amalekite and then accuses him of killing 'the Lord's anointed'.

16. G. Mayer, 'NZR', *ThWAT*, V, pp. 329-34.

17. See K. Galling, *Biblische Reallexikon* (Tübingen: J.C.B. Mohr [Paul Siebeck], 2nd edn, 1977), p. 288, Abb. 75 (22–24). The figured strips date from the fourteenth/thirteenth centuries and the floral emblem from the tenth/ninth centuries BCE. The strips and other similar headbands can be found in K. Maxwell-Hyslop, *Western Asiatic Jewellery* c. 3,000–612 BC (London: Methuen, 1971), p. 226 and Pls. 202, 203. See Figure 1 below for two possible examples of the *nēzer* crown from Palestine.

18. Cf. the gold diadem of the third century CE, decorated with glass, stone and mother-of-pearl (*Takšîṭîm mēhā'ôlām he'āṭîq* [Jerusalem: Israel Museum, 1969], Fig. 25).

It is clear that in the earlier period of AH *nēzer* was not synonymous with *ʿᵃṭārâ*. However, Sirach refers to the high priest wearing an *ʿᵃṭeret paz* on his turban, and he does not use the term *nēzer*, so perhaps by the second century BCE the two words had become more or less synonymous when used of headgear.[19]

Keter

Keter is used only in Esther, and occurs three times there: of something worn by Vashti (1.11), something placed on Esther's head by the king when she becomes queen (2.17), and something placed on the head of either the king's horse or Mordecai, in a famously disputed passage (6.8).[20] The Persian king himself is not described as wearing it or any other crown, though other royal accoutrements of his are mentioned, such as the golden sceptre (*šarbîṭ hazzāhāb*, 4.11; 5.2; 8.4), his throne (*kissē' malᵉkûtô*, 1.2, 5.1) and signet ring (*ṭabba'at hammelek*, 3.10, 12; 8.2, 8, 10), as well as his royal robes and horse. Mordecai wears a great golden *ʿᵃṭārâ* in 8.15, but his apparel in this chapter seems to be unrelated to the occasion in ch. 6, where he rides the horse that the king has ridden and wears robes the king has worn, so that it is unlikely that a *keter malkût* is to be identified with the *ʿᵃṭārâ*.

It used to be said that *keter* was a Persian loanword, but no one has either offered or reconstructed a suitable Persian term.[21] According to

---

19. Sir. 45.12 (B).

20. E.g. E. Bertheau, *Die Bücher Esra, Nechemia und Ester* (rev. V. Ryssel; KEH, 17; Leipzig: Hirzel, 2nd edn, 1887), pp. 427-28; P. Haupt, 'Critical Notes on Esther', *AJSL* 24 (1907–1908); reprinted in C.A. Moore, *Studies in the Book of Esther* (New York: Ktav, 1982), p. 48; H. Bardtke, *Das Buch Esther* (KAT, 17.4–5; Gütersloh: Mohn, 1963), p. 348 n. 13; G. Gerleman, *Esther* (BKAT, 21; Neukirchen–Vluyn: Neukirchener Verlag, 1973), pp. 116-18; P. Wernberg-Møller, review of *Esther*, by G. Gerleman, in *JSS* 20 (1975), p. 242; S.B. Berg, *The Book of Esther: Motifs, Themes and Structure* (SBLDS, 44; Missoula, MT: Scholars Press, 1979), p. 61; C.A. Moore, *Esther* (AB, 7B; Garden City, NY: Doubleday, 1971), p. 65.

21. See, for example, P. de Lagarde, *Gesammelte Abhandlungen* (Wuppertal: Brockhaus, 1866), p. 207; G. Rawlinson, cited in Bertheau, *Ester*, p. 390; G.R. Driver, *Aramaic Documents of the Fifth Century BC* (Oxford: Clarendon Press, 1st edn, 1951), p. 55 n.3, refuted by W. Eilers, 'Neue aramäische Urkunden aus Ägypten', *AfO* 17 (1954–56), p. 331, and corrected in Driver's second edition in 1957, p. 98. Eilers surveys words for crowns in Persia and the ancient Near East, but gives nothing that corresponds to *keter* ('Vom Reisehut zur Kaiserkrone. A. Das Wortfeld', *Archaeologische Mitteilungen aus Iran* NS 10 [1977], pp. 153-68).

the third edition of Köhler–Baumgartner, there is a possible Arabic cognate, *katara*, which means 'to have a big hump', and, as often seems to be the case in dictionaries of classical Arabic, is something to do with a camel. However, the most up-to-date lexicon of classical Arabic, the *Wörterbuch der klassischen arabischen Sprache*, gives only a noun, *ka/itrun*, 'hump', which can be used metaphorically, but only of a pile of stones or dates or heaped up foam.[22] Could a Proto-Semitic root, *KTR, yield both a camel's hump and royal headgear? Perhaps it could, if it conveyed the idea of elevation. However, the most plausible etymology is connected with Hebrew *ktr*, 'to surround', which lies behind Hebrew *kōteret*, 'capital of a pillar'.

What complicates both the etymological question and the historical situation is the existence of the Greek word *kidaris*, or *kitaris*, which occurs frequently in classical literature for Persian royal headgear,[23] and which most philologists agree is related to AH *keter* and has a Semitic basis (the corresponding Aramaic word is *kitra*). Because the classical sources are unanimous that only the Persian king was allowed to wear a piece of headgear called the upright *tiara*, which was not a semicircle of diamonds worn by a princess or duchess, but was probably some kind of fabric hat, many ancient and modern writers have tended to identify the *kidaris* with the upright *tiara*.[24] But other ancient sources refer to the two as separate items, worn together.[25] If *kidaris* is the upright *tiara*, and *keter*, *tiara* and *kidaris* all refer to the same item (and of course they may not), why were Esther and Vashti and the horse/Mordecai wearing it? The authors and editors of Esther have enough details of the Persian court authentically represented that it is unlikely that they would have portrayed queens as wearing headgear reserved for the king alone. If *keter* and *kidaris* refer to the same item, it must have been something other than the upright *tiara*: possibly the

22. *WKAS*, I, pp. 46, 544.

23. E.g. Curtius Rufus, *Historia Alexandri* 3.3.19, *cidarim Persae vocabant regium capitis insigne*; Plutarch, *Themistocles* 2.9.7, and *Alexander* 326d–345b; Arrian, *Anabasis* 4.7; Ctesias, Fragment 15.29.

24. Arrian, *Anabasis* 6.29; Plutarch, *Alexander* 326d-45b, Plutarch, *Antonius* 54.8.3, Plutarch, *Artaxerxes* 26.4.5; Hesychius s.v. κίδαρις; Scholia in Platonem, Dial R. Of modern authors to take this approach, A. von Gall is the most prominent: 'Die Kopfbedeckung des persischen Ornats bei den Achämeniden', *Archaeologische Mitteilungen aus Iran* NS 7 (1974) pp. 145-61 and Pls. 31-36. (See below, Figures 2 and 3.)

25. Plutarch, *Antonius* 54.8; Strabo, *Geographia* 11.13.

high metal crowns portrayed in the Persepolis reliefs, which are not confined to the king. However, *keter* is each time defined as 'royal', *keter malkût*, and this suggests that an ordinary type of *keter* existed, as with 'royal robes' (*lᵉbûš malkût*, 6.8; 8.15), 'palace' (*bêt hammalkût*, 5.1), and 'royal throne' (*kissē' malkût*, 5.1).

Xenophon describes Cyrus as wearing a special *diadema* or fabric fillet around the upright *tiara*, and he says that it was also worn by the king's relations.[26] Since headbands of various types were an extremely popular item of dress in the Near East (useful for keeping long hair out of the face), and were worn in various fancy forms and colours by dignitaries, this may be what a *keter malkût* was, a royal headband of fine fabric treated with costly dyes. Furthermore, Curtius Rufus says that the *cidaris* was blue with white spots.[27] Other authors identify the *kidaris* with a *diadema*,[28] and the Greek versions of Esther render *keter* as *diadema*, though this could be a Hellenistic trait, since Hellenistic and Parthian kings wore a *diadema*.

To recapitulate, then:

(a) The upright *tiara* was probably some kind of fabric hat or headdress worn by the Persian king alone. Other dignitaries such as satraps could wear a floppy form of the *tiara*, but it seems to have been an item of Median military attire, and therefore confined to men.

(b) The Greek *diadema* consisted of fine fabric tied around the head and knotted at the back to form streamers.

(c) The Persian attire known as *kidaris* in Greek seems to have resembled the Greek *diadema* in form and significance. The king wore it tied around his upright *tiara*. His relations wore it too, but not the upright *tiara*.

(d) The Hebrew *keter* would be most plausibly identified with the fine fabric Persian *diadema*, the *kidaris*, as a symbol of royalty but not confined to the king alone. We have no explicit information that queens wore it, and none that they did not: there are very few representations of Persian queens in art, or descriptions of their attire in literature.[29]

26. *Cyropaedia* 8.3.13.
27. *Historia Alexandri* 3.3; cf. also 6.6.
28. Philo, *Vit. Mos.* 2.116.2; cf. Diodorus Siculus 17.77.
29. For Persian headbands that may tentatively be identified with different types of *ktr*, see von Gall, 'Die Kopfbedeckung,' Fig. 1, p. 149, Fig. 2, p. 155 for kings

As for AH outside the Bible, the Qumran fragment that mentions a *nēzer* has the words *keter ṣedeq* just above it, and as with the *ʿᵃṭārâ* in Ben Sira that functions as a priestly *nēzer*, mentioned above, it is possible that later Hebrew tended to conflate the types of royal headdress.[30] Certainly rabbinic Hebrew seems to regard *ʿᵃṭārâ* and *keter* as more or less synonymous.[31] However, a reminiscence of *keter*'s original function of a *diadema* may be found when it occurs as a technical term for the 'crownlets' on letter forms: the verb used with it is *qāšar*, 'to tie'.

When it comes to depictions of Israelite kings in crowns, the material is very sparse and unhelpful. On Shalmaneser III's stele, Jehu (or his representative) performs an act of obeisance to the Assyrian king, but he is not wearing distinctive headdress, and in fact he resembles both Sua the Gilzanite and the Israelite porters transporting the tribute, who all have conical caps with the point flopping down.[32] But since Jehu is bowing down before Shalmaneser III as his superior, it is unlikely that he would be wearing something that symbolized his own regal power.

There are only two coronation ceremonies in the Hebrew Bible, that is, ceremonies that mention the placing of a headdress on the king or queen. The first is when Jehoiada places the *nēzer* on Joash (2 Kgs 11.12//2 Chron. 23.11), and the second when the Persian king puts the *keter malkût* on Esther's head and makes her queen (Est. 2.17). This may mean either that inaugural ceremonies involving a crowning were not normally worthy of report, except in the case of the dramatic events of the boy Joash's coronation as king of Judah and of Vashti's replacement by Esther, or that a special headdress was not a central symbol of kingship. In Zech. 6.11 there appears to be a 'coronation' ceremony, in that one or more crowns are placed on the head of Joshua the high priest. But since there is no connection elsewhere between the inauguration of a monarch and an *ʿᵃṭārâ*, Wolter Rose is surely right in saying that an *ʿᵃṭārâ* is not a coronation crown, and whatever is happening to Joshua in Zechariah 6 involving an *ʿᵃṭārâ* is not the coronation

---

(see below, Figures 2 and 3), and Pl. 36.1, 2 for satraps; and D. Head, *The Achaemenid Persian Army* (Stockport: Montvert Publications, 1992), p. 8, Figs. c–e for satraps. Parthian and Sassanid coins frequently depict kings wearing the *diadema*: see *Cambridge History of Iran*, III.1, Pls. 1-8, 25-30.

30. *Festival Prayers* (4Q 509) 97–98.ii.3.

31. L.I. Rabinowitz, 'Crowns, Decorative Headdresses, and Wreaths', *EncJud*, V, cols. 1130–33.

32. *ANEP*, Fig. 355.

ceremony of a king.[33] When other monarchs are inaugurated in the Bible, features of the ceremony can include anointing, enthronement, covenant and public declaration; there is no coronation as such, in that a crown or headdress is not mentioned in these other places.[34]

Marc Brettler notes that nowhere in AH is the Lord described as wearing a crown, whereas there are numerous depictions elsewhere in the ancient Near East of deities in various sorts of headgear. He suggests that this is due to the desire either to avoid plastic representations of the Lord, in keeping with the second commandment, or to prevent God resembling a human king too closely.[35] I will return to this problem later.

The Armlet (*'eṣ'ādâ*)

Another item cited as a royal ornament is the *'eṣ'ādâ*. This is something that the Amalekite removes from the arm of the fallen Saul along with his *nēzer*; he then takes them both to David (2 Sam. 1.10). The other occurrence of this form is in Num. 31.50, where it appears as one of the golden articles (*kᵉlî zāhāb*) plundered from the Midianites and offered to the Lord. A form without the prefixed 'aleph appears in Isa. 3.20, where again it is in a list of items of jewellery. A second royal use would be yielded by accepting Wellhausen's emendation of 2 Kgs 11.12 (and its parallel in Chronicles), so that instead of the priest Jehoiada giving Joash the *'ēdût*, the 'testimony', after placing the *nēzer* on Joash's head, he gives him the *'eṣ'ādâ* instead. Wellhausen objected to *'ēdût* on the ground that it was a Deuteronomistic addition, but most scholars follow von Rad in preserving the text of MT at that point.[36]

33. W. Rose, 'Zerubbabel and צמח' (DPhil. thesis, University of Oxford, 1997), Chapter 5.

34. E.g. Saul (1 Sam. 10.1 [anointing], 10.24 [acclamation and 'rights and duties']), David (1 Sam. 16.13 [anointing], 2 Sam. 5.3//1 Chron. 11.3 [anointing and covenant]), Solomon (1 Kgs 1.34-35, 39-46 [anointing, acclamation, enthronement], 1 Chron. 29.22-23 [anointing, enthronement]). The 'testimony', the anointing and the acclamation are also described in 2 Kgs. 11.12//2 Chron. 23.11. See T.N.D. Mettinger, *King and Messiah: The Civil and Sacral Legitimation of the Israelite Kings* (ConBOT, 8; Lund: C.W.K. Gleerup, 1976), pp. 131-50, 185-232.

35. M.Z. Brettler, *God is King: Understanding an Israelite Metaphor* (JSOTSup, 76; Sheffield: JSOT Press, 1989), p. 78.

36. J. Wellhausen, *Die Composition des Hexateuchs und der historischen Bücher des Alten Testaments* (Berlin: G. Reimer, 3rd edn, 1899), pp. 292-93 and

The root of the word *'eṣ'ādâ* appears to be *ṣ'd*, and of course there is a verb, *ṣā'ad*, meaning 'to step, march'. A plural noun, *ṣe'ādôt*, appears in Isa. 3.20 as part of the catalogue of ornaments, and is taken as meaning 'anklet' by the ancient Versions: perhaps they connected it with *ṣā'ad*, 'to step'. However, it is less clear how Saul's *'eṣ'ādâ*, worn on his arm, could be related to *ṣā'ad*, 'to step'. The Arabic words *'aḍud*, 'upper arm', *'iḍād*, 'bracelet', and, *'aḍād*, 'armlet', may be cognates and would explain better the origin of *'eṣ'ādâ*. Armlets and anklets are known from Egypt and many other places, but they are far from being confined to royalty.[37]

On the biblical evidence, an *'eṣ'ādâ*, 'armlet', was not a significant item of apparel in terms of royal symbolism: once Wellhausen's emendation of 2 Kgs 11.12 is rejected, that leaves us with just 2 Sam. 1.10 to connect *'eṣ'ādâ* with royalty. It is quite possible that Saul's *'eṣ'ādâ* could have been a more personal item, by which he could be identified by his troops, and therefore by which David knew for certain that he was dead. The word hardly appears in rabbinic Hebrew, and then only as a non-royal ornament.[38]

The Throne and Footstool (*kissē'* and *h*ᵃ*dōm*)

A far more important symbol, both from the point of view of the number of occurrences and its connection with kingship in AH, is *kissē'*, a word ultimately derived from the Sumerian *gu.za*, 'chair'.[39] *Kissē'* is

n. 2; G. von Rad, *Gesammelte Studien zum Alten Testament* (Munich: Chr. Kaiser Verlag, 1958) pp. 207-11 (ET *The Problem of the Hexateuch and other Essays* [trans. E.W. Trueman Dicken; Edinburgh: Oliver & Boyd, 1966], pp. 225-29).

37. For Egyptian examples of armlets, see C. Andrews, *Ancient Egyptian Jewellery* (London: British Museum Publications, 1990), pp. 144-63. For Assyrian armlets, see Maxwell-Hyslop, *Western Asiatic Jewellery*, pp. 246-47 and Figs. 139, 142, 143.

38. E.g. *y. Šab.* 36b, *b. Šab.* 63b.

39. 135 times Hebrew Bible; Sir. 10.14A, 11.5A, 40.3B, 47.11B; 17 times Qumran: 4QDibrHaMeoroth 4.7; 4QFlor(4Q174) 1.10; 4QpIsaᵃ 8–10.19; 11QPsᵃCreat (11Q5) 26.11; 4QShirShabb; 4Q405 20 ii 21-22 2, 20 ii 21-22 8, 23 i 3; 11QShirShabb 3-1-9 5–6, 3-4 1, f 5, k 5; 4QSongs of the Sage (4QShirᵇ/4Q511) 2 i 10; 4QWarScroll 11 i 12. For the etymology, see M. Ellenbogen, *Foreign Words in the Old Testament: Their Origin and Etymology* (London: Luzac, 1962), p. 89; A. Murtonen, *Hebrew in its West Semitic Setting: A Comparative Survey of Non-Masoretic Hebrew Dialects and Traditions. I. A Comparative Lexicon. Section Ba. Root System: Hebrew Material* (Studies in Semitic Languages and Linguistics, 13;

usually rendered 'throne' in royal contexts, but the same word can also
refer to an ordinary chair. This common usage is found especially in
later Hebrew, so that the sense 'throne' has to be made clear by adding
a *nomen rectum*, such as *kissē' malkût* for a king's throne, and *kissē'
hakkābôd* for God's throne. *Kissē'* in later Hebrew can also mean
'privy', and *bêt hakkissē'*, literally and euphemistically, 'house of the
chair', does not mean 'throne room'!

Kissē' in royal contexts is used more often metaphorically than
literally, especially in the phrase 'sit on the throne', *yāšab 'al kissē'*.
This expression is more or less synonymous with *mālak*, 'to reign', and
māšal, 'to rule', and occurs very frequently in Deuteronomistic passages. So *kissē'* functions as a symbol of the legitimate monarchy rather
as 'the Crown' does in English.

How did *kissē'* become so central to the idea of monarchy in AH? It
may have been derived from the practice of rulers and judges sitting on
a chair in order to hear cases and give judgment, and in the ancient
Near East both kings and gods are frequently portrayed as enthroned.
The expression 'sit on the throne' indicating kingship is found widely
in Akkadian and Ugaritic as well as Hebrew, so the idea is common to
most ancient Near Eastern societies.[40]

There are plenty of pictures of all types of chairs in art, and they are
mostly of thrones or chairs of state. There is great variety all over the
ancient Near East, and there is a full description of Solomon's throne in
1 Kgs 10.18-20: 'King Solomon made a great ivory throne and overlaid
it with refined gold. The throne had six steps and a rounded top behind
it. On each side of the seat were armrests and two lions stood by the
armrests, and twelve lions stood on each side of the steps.' In spite of
the following words, 'Nothing like it has even been made in any other
kingdom', the description largely tallies with elements found in Egypt
of the New Kingdom, as well as in Mesopotamia. The throne depicted
on Ahiram's sarcophagus is also very similar.[41]

There is a well-known emendation of one element, however: the
rounded backrest of MT's 1 Kgs. 10.19, *rō'š 'āgōl*, seems very likely to
have been a calf's head, *rō'š 'ēgel* in the original, as the Septuagint
rendering προτομαὶ μόσχων suggests. This would have been censored

---

Leiden: E.J. Brill, 1988), p. 189, and *Section Bb. Root System: Comparative
Material and Discussion* (Leiden: E.J. Brill, 1989), p. 235.

40. H-J. Fabry, '*kissē'*', *ThWAT*, IV, pp. 247-72 (ET, *TDOT*, VII, pp. 232-59).

41. *ANEP*, Fig. 458.

out later in the Hebrew to remove any suspicion that Solomon was involved in bull worship.[42] (The parallel verse in 2 Chron. 9.18 appears to have been changed to *kebeś*, 'lamb', later read as *kebeš*, 'footstool'.) However, the emended text of 1 Kings does not correspond to ancient Near Eastern art, where round-backed chairs are common (for instance that of Ahiram), but calves' heads on the backs do not occur.[43] So textual criticism and art are at variance here.

One drawback of a sitting posture when interviewing suppliants and emissaries is that the seated person has to look up at them, which would put the seated person at a psychological disadvantage.[44] This is one reason for petitioners bowing down or kneeling, so that the king or judge can look down on them. Another solution is to raise the throne. This can be done in two ways. The first method is to put it on a dais with a ramp or steps in front to enable the king to reach it, and perhaps to keep people at a distance. The second is more common, and is to make the throne higher, in which case a footstool is needed so that the sitter can get up and down, and also to prevent the sitter's legs from dangling inelegantly. The dais with steps is indicated in the account of Solomon's throne, but footstools are also mentioned in connection with thrones in AH.

Though God in AH does not have a crown, he does have a throne, symbolizing his kingship. The throne is a feature shared with the god El of Ugarit, whereas Baal and Reshef tend to be portrayed standing or striding.[45] The clearest royal depiction of the Lord is in 1 Kgs 22.19, where Micaiah describes his vision of the Lord seated on his throne,

---

42. Cf. Josephus, *Ant.* 8.140, ἀνακέκλιτο δ'εἰς μόσχου πρωτοτομὴν τὰ κατόπιν αὐτοῦ βλέποντος. For a survey of the problem, see F. Canciani and G. Pettinato, 'Salomos Thron, philologische und archäologische Erwägungen', *ZDPV* 81 (1965), pp. 88-108.

43. M. Metzger, *Königsthron und Gottesthron: Thronformen und Throndarstellungen in Ägypten und im vorderen Orient im dritten und zweiten Jahrtausend vor Christus und deren Bedeutung für das Verständnis von Aussagen über den Thron im Alten Testament* (AOAT, 15; 2 vols.; Neukirchen–Vluyn: Neukirchener Verlag, 1985), I, pp. 299-300.

44. W. Krebs, 'Der sitzende Gott', *TZ* 30 (1974), pp. 1-10.

45. I. Cornelius, *The Iconography of the Canaanite Gods Reshef and Ba'al: Late Bronze Age and Iron Age Periods (c. 1500–1000 BCE)* (OBO, 140; Göttingen: Vandenhoeck & Ruprecht, 1994), p. 245: A. Caquot and M. Sznycer, *Ugaritic Religion* (Iconography of Religions, 15.8; Leiden: E.J. Brill, 1980), Pl. 7, shows El seated on a throne.

with the whole host of heaven standing around him. But in Ezekiel 1,
God's actual throne is only described very vaguely, in contrast to the
living creatures and the wheels. It is either made of, or set on, a base of
lapis lazuli, which probably represented the night sky sprinkled with
golden stars. In mystical developments of this theme from Qumran the
throne was identified with the complete *ensemble* of wheels and creatures, and referred to by the term *ks' mrkbh*, 'throne chariot',[46] or by a
masculine plural of majesty, *ks'y kbwd, ksy pl'*, and so on.[47]

God has a footstool as well as a throne. In fact, though footstools
certainly existed throughout the ancient Near East, being portrayed in
art and mentioned in ancient texts, the only occurrences in AH are
metaphorical.[48] *H^adōm* is a symbol of God's worshippers' submission
to him, and the subjection of his king's enemies. (See below, Figure 4,
for a footstool depicting the king's enemies.) The etymology of the
word is difficult: since *hadmu* occurs in Ugaritic and Egyptian at
approximately the same time (eighteenth dynasty, c. 1550–1300), some
say that it is an Egyptian loanword, others that the Egyptians borrowed
it from Semitic. If it is a Semitic word, the root could either be *hdm*,
and related to Arabic *hadama*, 'overthrow', or *dwm*, 'be still, silent',
with a hiphil prefix, hence a place to rest the feet.[49]

One question that arises indirectly with *kissē'* and *h^adōm* is connected with the Ark of the Covenant: was the Ark ever considered to be
God's throne or footstool, as Ps. 132.7-8, Isa. 66.1, Jer. 3.16-17 and
Lam. 2.1 may suggest?[50] *Kissē'* and *h^adōm* may also be implicit in the
epithet applied to the Lord, *yōšēb hakk^erubîm*.[51] In Isa. 6.1, the prophet
may be perceiving the normally invisible divine figure seated on the
cherubim. So were the cherubim in the Temple considered to be the
throne of God, and the Ark his footstool, or did the cherubim flank an
unseen throne, as sphinxes hold up or flank Egyptian thrones? Noth
rejects such notions completely, saying that the position of the Ark in
the sanctuary, with its short ends and poles projecting towards the

46. 4QShirShabb 20 ii-21-22 8.

47. 11QShirShabb 3-1-9, lines 5-6, and f 5.

48. Isa. 66.1; Pss. 99.5; 110.1; 132.7; Lam. 2.1; 1 Chron. 28.2.

49. H.-J. Fabry, '*h^adōm*', *ThWAT*, II, col. 348.

50. For bibliography on the discussion, see G. Fohrer, *Geschichte der israeli-
tschen Religion* (Berlin: W. de Gruyter, 1969) p. 100, and V. Fritz, *Tempel und
Zelt: Studien zum Tempelbau in Israel und zu dem Zeltheiligtum der Priesterschrift*
(WMANT, 47; Neukirchen–Vluyn: Neukirchener Verlag, 1977), p. 135 n. 8.

51. 1 Sam. 4.4; 2 Sam. 6.2 = 1 Chron. 13.6.

beholder, made it impossible that it was ever conceived of as either throne or footstool.[52] Moreover, no box-like thrones are attested in the ancient Near East.[53] On the other hand, box-shaped footstools did exist, and it is possible that the Ark was considered to be the footstool beneath the cherubim throne. Such an understanding would explain the allusions in Ps. 132.7-8 and Jer. 3.16-17.[54]

Since the equation *kissē'* = Ark is never made explicitly, it is questionable whether the idea is relevant to the *semantics* of *kissē'* and *hᵃdōm* at all: rather, the meaning of *kissē'* as established elsewhere should be pertinent to the debate on whether the Ark acts as a throne or footstool.

Yāšab, used of a mortal or divinity, can indicate enthronement, but since the verb also has the sense 'to dwell', expressions such as *mākôn lᵉšibtᵉkā*[55] do not necessarily mean 'place of your throne', as Mettinger assumes, but could mean 'your dwelling place'.[56] The Hebrew is ambiguous, and only the context can decide: sometimes it remains unclear. Without *kissē'* or a preposition, it is hard to determine whether 'sit enthroned' or 'dwell' is intended by *yāšab*.

A different problem is how to tell when a *kissē'* is just an ordinary chair. In the past Eli's seat in 1 Samuel 1 and 4 has been taken as a normal chair, but recently Polzin and Spina have suggested that it is symbolic of either royal or judicial rule.[57] Even the chair provided for Elisha by the Shunammite woman in the room she builds for him (2 Kgs 4.10) has been invested with significance by recent interpreters, since he is a prophet who has a semi-judicial function. But since the other items in the list are hard to understand symbolically, this seems

52. M. Noth, *Könige* (BKAT, 9.1; Neukirchen–Vluyn: Neukirchener Verlag, 1964), p. 179.

53. R.E. Clements, *God and Temple* (Oxford: Basil Blackwell, 1965), pp. 28–36; Metzger, *Königsthron*, p. 354.

54. H-J. Fabry, '*hᵃdōm*', ThWAT, II, col. 355 (ET *TDOT*, III, p. 332). I am grateful to Dr John Day for his helpful comments on this section.

55. Exod. 15.17; 1 Kgs 8.13; cf. 1 Kgs 8.39, 43, 49 = 2 Chron. 6.30, 33, 39, and Ps. 33.14.

56. T.N.D. Mettinger, *The Dethronement of Sabaoth: Studies in the Shem and Kabod Theologies* (ConBOT, 18; Lund: C.W.K. Gleerup, 1982), pp. 26-27.

57. R. Polzin, *Samuel and the Deuteronomist: A Literary Study of the Deuteronomic History. II. 1 Samuel* (San Francisco: Harper & Row, 1989), pp. 23, 31, 44; F.A. Spina, 'Eli's Seat: The Transition from Priest to Prophet in 1 Sam. 1–4', *JSOT* 62 (1994), pp. 67-75.

rather questionable. Another occurrence of *kissē'* that may signify rank is that in 1 Kgs 2.19, where Bathsheba comes to Solomon, he does obeisance to her and gives the king's mother a *kissē'* to sit on at his right hand. *Kissē'* is used for his own throne in this passage, and the question of whether Bathsheba's seat can be considered a throne is relevant to the debate over the role and status of the *gᵉbîrâ* (though the word *gᵉbîrâ* does not in fact occur in the passage).[58]

So there are a number of questions remaining, not so much about the meaning of *kissē'*, but its precise significance for the sense of the passages in which it occurs. All in all, however, it is clear that it is the key symbol of monarchy in AH, not just of God's rule and Israelite kingship, but of Pharaoh in Egypt (in the Pentateuch) and Ahasuerus in Persia (book of Esther), spanning the biblical world and its literature.

The Sceptre (*šēbeṭ* and *šarbîṭ*)

Finally, a few words about *šēbeṭ*. This is just one of a group of words in Hebrew that have the basic, concrete sense of 'stick': *maṭṭeh* and *maqqēl* are two others whose fields overlap with *šēbeṭ*, to the extent that *maṭṭeh* too can mean 'tribe'. Opinion is divided over whether the meaning 'tribe' is derived from the baton symbolizing the leader's authority over the group[59] or from the club as a symbol of the group's autonomy in self-defence.[60]

Šēbeṭ in the sense of 'sceptre', that is, a baton of authority rather than a weapon or rod for punishing or disciplining, occurs between nine and fourteen times in AH, depending on the interpretation of the passages

---

58. See, for example, J. Gray, *I and II Kings* (OTL; London: SCM Press, 3rd edn, 1977) p. 106; Noth, *Könige*, pp. 33-34; Z. Ben-Barak, 'The Status and Right of the *gᵉbîrâ*', in *A Feminist Companion to Samuel and Kings* (ed. A. Brenner; The Feminist Companion to the Bible, 5; Sheffield: Sheffield Academic Press, 1994), pp. 170-85.

59. H.J. Stoebe, 'Zepter', *Biblisch-Historisches Handwörterbuch* (eds. B. Reicke and L. Rost; 3 vols.; Göttingen: Vandenhoeck & Ruprecht, 1962), III, col. 2234.; G. Fohrer, 'Keule', in *Biblisch-Historisches Handwörterbuch*, II, p. 946; G.E. Mendenhall, *The Tenth Generation* (Baltimore: The Johns Hopkins University Press, 1973), pp. 184-88.

60. N.K. Gottwald, *The Tribes of Yahweh* (Maryknoll, NY: Orbis Books, 1979), esp. pp. 245-56; A. Lemaire, '"Avec un Sceptre de Fer": Ps II,9 et l'archéologie', *BN* 32 (1986), pp. 25-30.

concerned and the definition of the word 'sceptre'.[61] But very few of these verses are definitely connected with royal authority, perhaps only Ps. 45.7 (ET 6), *šēbeṭ mîšōr šēbeṭ malkûtekā*, where the clearest and commonest parallels are found in Akkadian rather than in AH.[62] *Šēbeṭ* is found with the root *māšal*, 'to rule', three times (Isa. 14.5; Ezek. 19.11, 14), and is used with *tāmak*, 'to wield', in Amos 1.5, 8. In Gen. 49.10 it is a symbol of authority parallel to *meḥōqēq*, but hardly royal, and also in Judg. 5.14, where it belongs to the *sōpēr*. But in other places it is not so much a static symbol as a weapon or means of chastisement used with verbs of smiting, smashing and so on, for instance the iron rod of Ps. 2.9.

Apart from Ps. 45.7 (ET 6), the static rod, the sceptre of royal iconography, is confined to the four occurrences of *šarbîṭ* in the book of Esther. The king holds a golden sceptre as he sits on his royal throne, and stretches it forth to grant the life of unsummoned suppliants (4.11, 5.2 [twice]; 8.4). It is usually assumed that *šarbîṭ* is the Aramaic, lengthened form of *šēbeṭ* (GKC, §85k), rather as *kûrsyâ* is the Aramaic equivalent of *kissē'*. But Sasson regards the root as related to Arabic *rabaṭa*, 'tie, bind', with a causative shin prefix, the idea being that the Persian sceptre was a bundle of rods, like the Roman *fasces*, which is supposed to have had Persian origins.[63] However, the relief portrait of Darius shows a long single rod rather than a bundle,[64] and in Targum Aramaic and Rabbinic Hebrew *šarbîṭ* is used as the equivalent of *šēbeṭ* in the sense of 'sceptre' and 'rod'.

Conclusions

The foregoing has been an overview of the significance of some key items of royal regalia in AH. It seems fairly clear that *kissē'*, in the sense of a throne, is much more central to the concept of kingship in AH than a particular type of headgear. Even so, headdress is an important component of royal regalia: there is the highly specialized *nēzer*,

61. BDB puts the following occurrences into the category of 'sceptre': Gen. 49.10; Num. 24.17; Judg. 5.14; Isa. 14.5; Ezek. 19.11, 14; Amos 1.5, 8; Zech. 10.11; Pss. 2.9, 45.7 (ET 6), 125.3; Prov. 22.8. The obscurity of Ezek. 21.15, 18 (ET 10, 13) prevents clear categorization.

62. J.P.J. Olivier, 'The Sceptre of Justice and Ps 45:7b', *JNSL* 7 (1979), pp. 45-54.

63. J.M. Sasson, 'A Note on *šarbîṭ*', *VT* 22 (1972), p. 111.

64. *ANEP*, Fig. 463.

worn by the high priest as well as Saul and Joash, so having cultic overtones. There is the more general term *ʿᵃṭārâ*, not confined to royalty but certainly worn by them as a mark of honour and more secular ceremonial. Kellermann believes *ʿᵃṭārâ* to be a superordinate term, *Überbegriff*, for the field, including *nēzer, ṣānîp, miṣnepet, ṣᵉpîrâ, liwyâ*.[65] It certainly overlaps with some of these, yet *ṣānîp* or *miṣnepet*, which were both fabric turbans, could hardly be covered by *ʿᵃṭārâ*, which is made of flowers or of precious metal. As for *keter malkût* in AH, it is used only of the Persian court, and if identified with what the classical authors call the *kidaris*, was some type of fabric fillet. An armlet, *ʾeṣʿādâ*, is not at all significant as a royal symbol, and is probably a personal item. *Hᵃdōm* represents absolute dominion, and the handful of occurrences in AH provide only a metaphorical sense. *Šēbeṭ* also tends to be a poetic image or symbol of authority, particularly for punishment, but the royal sceptre of ceremonial appears in only a very small proportion of the total number of occurrences. God has a throne and a footstool, and a rod for inflicting defeat or punishment, but no crown.

---

65. D. Kellermann, ʿ*ᵃṭara*', *ThWAT*, VI, cols. 24–26.

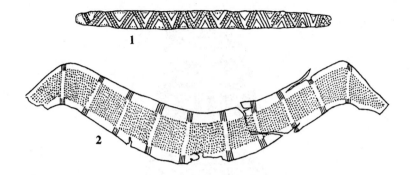

Figure 1. *Examples of the* nēzer *crown from Palestine? (1) Diadem from Tell el-ʿAjjul (gold, 28 cm, 14th–13th century* BCE*) (2); Diadem from Tell Jemmeh (gold, 28 cm, 10th–9th century* BCE*).*

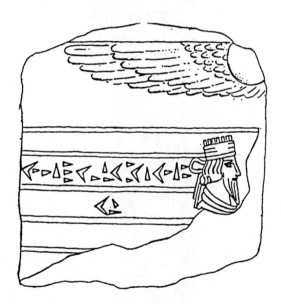

Figure 2. *A possible* keter *headdress on the head of Darius I, from a fragmentary stele from the Suez Canal.*

Figure 3. *Another possible* keter *headdress on the head of a king. Silver statuette from the Oxus treasure.*

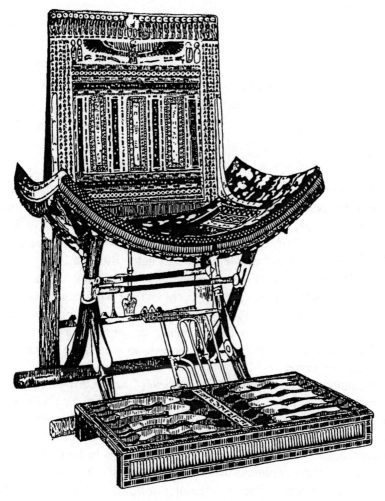

Figure 4. *Throne and footstool from the tomb of Tutankhamun (c. 1330 BCE)*

'QUEENSHIP' IN ISRAEL? THE CASES OF BATHSHEBA, JEZEBEL AND ATHALIAH

Carol Smith

Did the concept of 'queenship' exist in Israel and Judah? Scholars have disagreed about the answer to this question. It can be approached from several directions. Here, I shall consider whether it is possible to begin with a 'definition' of 'queenship' or 'queen' and then ask whether the attributes of any of the women mentioned in the Bible can be said to fit such a definition. I shall then consider two of the words used to describe royal women in the Old Testament and ask what conclusions can be drawn from their use. Finally, I shall examine some biblical narratives about royal women and ask whether any insights about 'queenship' in Israel and Judah can be derived from what they contain and how they are written.

Beginning with a 'definition' of 'queenship' can be difficult, since its interpretation so often depends on the context in which the word is used. If one is looking for a 'queen' who is the equivalent of a male king, then it has to be said that, at least as far as the biblical writer is concerned, Israel and Judah cannot be said to have had a queen at any time. (It is my own opinion that Athaliah did fulfil that role and should be regarded as having been a reigning queen, even though it was the view of the Deuteronomist that she was merely a usurper.) Indeed, even within the United Kingdom, where women can and do rule as monarchs, a woman who is 'queen' is not the exact equivalent of a man who is 'king'. The term 'queen' has at least two different meanings. A king's wife can be queen (as was the case with the current Queen Mother, who was the wife of King George VI). A woman can also be queen by virtue of inheriting the throne (as is the case with Queen Elizabeth II), although in this case, her husband does not become king. While Elizabeth, wife of George VI, and Elizabeth II are both given the title 'queen', Elizabeth II is ruler, while her mother had no claim to the throne on the death of her husband. According to Athalya Brenner, neither of these possible interpretations of queenship was possible in ancient Israel. She states[1] that 'Israelite society did not admit—or did not want to admit—that a monarch's wife could either be a queen in her own right or her royal spouse's deputy'. She concludes:[2] 'the institution of queenship, although recognized in the Old Testament as valid for foreign lands, was considered unacceptable both in Israel and in Judah'. However, against Brenner, it has to be said that certain women associated with royal houses not only wielded power of various kinds—to some effect —but also exhibited some of the characteristics of kingship. Here, I shall consider biblical narratives about three such women—Bathsheba, Jezebel and Athaliah—and ask what can be learned from them.

The Vocabulary

Two important words are associated with royal women, *malkâ* and *gᵉbîrâ*. *Malkâ* is used on only a few occasions in the Hebrew Bible and appears only in Esther (Esther and Vashti), 1 Kings 10 and 1 Chronicles 9 (Queen of Sheba), and Song of Songs 6 (plural). In the book of Esther it is clearly a title given because the women concerned are the wives of a king. The monarch concerned is a foreign king. Further, as Esther is a late text, the use of *malkâ* in the book of Esther cannot be of help to the matters under consideration here.[3] While *malkâ* as a title for the Queen of Sheba may well indicate that she was a ruler in her own right,[4] she was also foreign, which is the reason for her inclusion in the Bible in the first place. The verb *mlk*, 'to rule', is used with a feminine subject only with reference to Athaliah.

The other, and perhaps more significant, word that is used about royal women is *gᵉbîrâ*, and it needs careful consideration, not least because so much discussion is devoted to its use. Ktziah Spanier comments in a note[5] that 'the term *gᵉbîrâ* is most often used to describe the

1. A. Brenner, *The Israelite Woman: Social Role and Literary Type in Biblical Narrative* (The Biblical Seminar, 2; Sheffield: JSOT Press, 1985), p. 17.

2. Brenner, *Israelite Woman*, p. 32.

3. A parallel to the use of *malkâ* in Esther is probably to be found in the use of the Aramaic equivalent in Dan. 5.10.

4. It appears from Assyrian texts (see *ANET*, pp. 283-86) that queens (Samsi and Zabibe are specifically mentioned) ruled in their own right in the Arabian peninsula during the eighth century BCE.

5. K. Spanier, 'The Queen Mother in the Judaean Royal Court: Maacah—A Case Study', in A. Brenner (ed.), *A Feminist Companion to Samuel and Kings* (The

mother of the king rather than his wife'. Ben-Barak, like many others, speaks throughout her article[6] of the *gᵉbîrâ* as if this term means 'queen mother'. Although it is widely accepted that it does, and 'queen mother' is one of the definitions of *gᵉbîrâ* in both BDB and the new Sheffield Dictionary, I am not sure that this is the case. The term in the form *gᵉbîrâ* is used six times: with reference to Pharaoh's wife, Tahpenes (1 Kgs 11.19); Asa's mother, Maacah (1 Kgs 15.13; 2 Chron. 15.16); the mother of 'the royal princes', sons of Ahaziah (2 Kgs 10.13); 'the king [Jehoiachin] and *gᵉbîrâ* of Judah' (Jer. 13.18; note that although *gᵉbîrâ* is translated 'queen mother' in this verse in NRSV, it does not have to mean this); and the *gᵉbîrâ* associated with King Jeconiah (Jer. 29.2; again, not necessarily his mother, although possibly the mother of his sons). Taken literally, the word means something like 'great lady' or 'mighty lady' and is the female equivalent of the male *geber*, which can mean 'male person' (as in Deut. 22.5), and is also used in the form *gibbôr*, with the meaning 'mighty man' (as in Josh. 10.2). In the Hebrew Bible, a similar term, *gᵉberet*, is applied to other powerful women than the mothers of kings, and in these cases it is translated differently. In Genesis 16 it is applied to Sarah as an indication of her position as a mistress of servants. In 2 Kgs 5.3 (where it is applied to Naaman's wife) and elsewhere it is also used of women who are in charge of large households. Generally, the uses of *gᵉbîrâ*, and related terms in the Hebrew Bible seem to indicate that this was a term of respect that was applied to powerful women and served as an acknowledgment of their authority. As such, it is not surprising that it was applied to royal women. However, the fact that the term was applied to women who were queen mothers does not necessarily mean that it *means* 'queen mother'. It could simply be a recognition of the positions of power and authority that they held. The term *gᵉbîrâ*, when applied to a woman, could mean that she was the most significant woman in the kingdom at that time: in which case, she could well be the queen mother, although she might well not be.

The above does not rule out the possibility that when *gᵉbîrâ* was used as a title it indicated a particular status. This is suggested by the account in 1 Kings 15, which tells how Asa 'removed his mother from being

Feminist Companion to the Bible, 5; Sheffield: Sheffield Academic Press, 1994), pp. 186-95 (186 n. 1).

6.   Z. Ben-Barak, 'The Status and Right of the *gᵉbîrâ*', in Brenner (ed.), *A Feminist Companion to Samuel and Kings*, pp. 170-85.

$g^e b\hat{\imath}r\hat{a}$, because she had an abominable image made for Asherah' (1 Kgs 15.13a). In this instance the removal of the title appears to be an indication of denial of status and Asa achieves qualified approval from the biblical writer for his action in thus 'demoting' Maacah. However, the question remains: did the woman's power and influence arise as a consequence of her being the $g^e b\hat{\imath}r\hat{a}$, or was she given the title because she was already influential and powerful? My own view is that the latter is the case: that a woman who was seen to be powerful was granted the title as a recognition of that power. This would mean that a woman could be a $g^e b\hat{\imath}r\hat{a}$ without being the mother of a king or even a member of the royal court, or could also be a 'queen mother' without being designated $g^e b\hat{\imath}r\hat{a}$. One problem with such speculation is that there is often no way of knowing whether the fact that a particular term is used or not used is a matter of chance, of fashion, or of deliberate intent.

Queen Consort or Queen Mother: Where Does the Power Lie?

Whether or not $g^e b\hat{\imath}r\hat{a}$, means 'queen mother', many scholars have used the word as a starting point for discussion of the role of the queen mother in Israel and Judah, often reaching conflicting conclusions. Niels-Erik Andreasen argues that 'it soon becomes obvious from the text that the queen mother was not merely treated with deference by the monarch, but that she held a significant official political position superseded only by that of the king himself'.[7] In this he is supported by Ktziah Spanier, who states[8] that 'An examination of the biblical records indicates that the queen mother was the most important female in the Judaean royal court' and appears 'as an important personage within the inner circle of the king's entourage'. This is echoed by Tomoo Ishida, when he is discussing the role of queen mothers in ensuring the succession of their sons. He suggests that '[t]he queen-mother's authority in this matter stemmed from her official rank at the court'.[9]

---

7.   N.-E.A. Andreasen, 'The Role of the Queen Mother in Israelite Society', *CBQ* 45 (1983), pp. 179-94 (180).

8.   K. Spanier, 'The Queen Mother in the Judaean Royal Court', p. 186.

9.   T. Ishida, *The Royal Dynasties in Ancient Israel: A Study on the Formation and Development of Royal-Dynastic Ideology* (BZAW, 142; Berlin: W. de Gruyter, 1977), p. 156.

This view is contested by Zafrira Ben-Barak,[10] who says of the queen mother's role that 'as a rule, the *geḇîrâ* or queen mother had no official political status in the kingdom', and adds that there is no 'known law or other direct evidence furnished by either the OT or extrabiblical sources' to support the assumptions made by scholars. She argues that evidence given in the examples most commonly cited—Bathsheba, Maacah, Hamutal and Nehushta—tell us less about the supposed 'official' role of the queen mother than about the fact that since each of the women concerned 'was the mother of a younger son who was without right to the succession, which legitimately belonged to an older brother',[11] it would be more appropriate to say that 'these were ambitious and strong women who were prepared to use every available means in order to obtain royal succession for their offspring'.[12]

My own view is that a correct assessment lies somewhere between these two extremes. However powerful and ambitious a woman might be, the fact that she was able to wield power effectively must reflect a position in the court that enabled her to do so. In other words, her power may well have derived originally from her position in the court, even though it was her own qualities that enabled her to wield it effectively. Thus, it might be expected that the mothers of kings had the potential to be women who wielded power in the kingdom. My own difficulty with the widely held view that many of the women who held powerful positions did so by virtue of being the mothers of kings, is that I am by no means sure that in many of the instances cited the woman's power derives from being a mother rather than a consort, even though, on the basis of comparisons between ancient Near Eastern material and the biblical evidence, Ishida argues that 'there was no official rank of queen–consort at the court of Judah'.[13] For example, while attention has been focused on Bathsheba as the mother of Solomon (with some justification), she also appears to have a role as the wife of David. Although Bathsheba is instrumental in bringing about Solomon's taking the throne, she wields her influence *while David is still alive*. Indeed, it is difficult to see how she could have played any role at all in the succession of Solomon if she had not already been in a position of some strength. Jezebel is certainly

10. Ben-Barak, 'Status and Right', p. 185.
11. Ben-Barak, 'Status and Right', p. 181.
12. Ben-Barak, 'Status and Right', p. 182.
13. Ishida, *Royal Dynasties*, p. 157.

influential as the wife of Ahab, although Ishida circumvents this difficulty by suggesting that she took on the role that would normally have been reserved for the queen mother. It does not seem to me that it was necessarily the case that royal women became powerful when their sons became kings. Rather, they used the positions they already possessed by virtue of being the most prominent consorts—whether because of the king's preference, personal ability or charisma, or official position—to ensure that *their* sons, rather than those of other wives took over the throne. In this way they were able to retain at least some of the status they already had and even had the possibility of building on it. For these reasons, I believe it is more important to focus on the role of 'royal women' rather than 'queen mothers'.

Queens in Context

The biblical narratives about royal women, like all narratives, cannot be considered without reference to the contexts in which they appear. This context has three aspects. The first is the context of the ancient Near East and what light that might shed on the narratives. The second is the context of the biblical writers: the kind of society in which they were working and their presuppositions and cultural assumptions. The third is any specific agenda being addressed: in the case of the narratives about Bathsheba, Athaliah and Jezebel, this means the Deuteronomistic agenda.

The Ancient Near Eastern Context

The task of making comparisons with other ancient Near Eastern cultures has been undertaken by some scholars, notably Ishida.[14] He argues, when discussing Jezebel, that 'in the light of the cited instances of the prominence of the queen-mother in western countries, it is unlikely that it was only in the Northern Kingdom that she held aloof from politics'.[15] Nonetheless, it could be argued that comparisons cannot be made with other ancient Near Eastern cultures in order to clarify the situation found in the biblical narratives. My own belief is that some comparisons might be possible, on the assumption that it would be unlikely that Israel and Judah were completely unlike their neighbours with regard to queenship when they were clearly very like

14. Ishida, *Royal Dynasties*, pp. 155-60.
15. Ishida, *Royal Dynasties*, p. 157.

them in other respects. Indeed, a recurring complaint of the biblical writers is that they were *too* like their neighbours! In fact, according to 1 Sam. 8.5, the institution of kingship was introduced in the first place because 'all the elders of Israel' came to Samuel and asked him to 'appoint a king for us, then, a king to govern us, *like other nations*'. On the other hand, caution is needed when making such comparisons; first, because there is relatively little relevant material available either from the Bible or from other ancient Near Eastern sources, and secondly, because it is clear from the biblical narratives that in some respects (at least officially), Israel, and more particularly Judah, *were* different from their neighbours. It is perhaps difficult for us, at this distance, to assess accurately to what degree they were different.

The World of the Biblical Writers

Feminist biblical scholars have discussed at length the ways in which women were regarded in biblical times and the attitudes towards them displayed in the biblical narratives. Athalya Brenner says this:[16] 'Outside motherhood and family politics, women appear to have had almost no role open to them in ancient Israel's and Judah's political and religious life'. However, some women did indeed achieve positions of power and influence and for feminists the question then becomes whether such power can be considered to have any real value. Some would argue that it does. Others would say that it does not, because it is, by definition, derived from males—the woman would not even have potential power, let alone actual power, if she was not the wife of a husband or the mother of a son.

The Context of the Deuteronomistic History

The narratives about the monarchies in Israel and Judah not only reflect the prevailing climate with regard to women, they also show evidence of the specific concerns of the Deuteronomistic school. Their concern about the dangers posed to the nation by foreign women has been much discussed, as have the formulae defining 'good' rulers as those who (supposedly) conformed to the biblical historian's idea of what constituted a good worshipper of Yahweh. But when considering narratives about royal women, these concerns become magnified. For example, if the king is to be closely identified with Yahweh, who (officially, at

16. Introduction to Brenner (ed.), *A Feminist Companion to Samuel and Kings*, pp. 13-24 (15).

least) has no consort, then it should be expected that the consort of the king will not have the kind of high profile she might have in other ancient Near Eastern cultures that have female deities and powerful female consorts of male gods. It appears that many royal women were not only worshippers of foreign deities, including female ones, but were actively involved in their cults. Susan Ackerman speculates on the nature of the involvement of royal women in the cult and goes so far as to suggest that 'the queen mother did have an official responsibility in Israelite religion: it was to devote herself to the cult of the mother goddess Asherah within the king's court'. She adds that 'this cultic role was primary among [her] other obligations'.[17] While Ackerman admits that the evidence for her thesis is not extensive, she gives convincing arguments for the involvement of royal women in cultic matters. Since, according to the Bible itself, this involvement cannot have been in the orthodox Yahwistic cult, it must have been elsewhere. This must have been a significant factor in determining the attitude of the Deuteronomist towards the royal women about whom he was writing.

An awareness of the context in which the biblical narratives about royal women were written can assist interpreters of those narratives. So, while the purposes, presuppositions and prejudices of the biblical writer might permeate the lines of the text, this does not make it impossible for the discriminating reader to read between them. For example, there can be no question that the biblical writer disliked Athaliah and Jezebel. Burke Long speaks of Jezebel as someone who 'epitomizes evil for the [Deuteronomistic] writer'.[18] However, even in spite of an obvious desire to portray her in a bad light, hints remain of Jezebel's positive qualities, which is perhaps an indication of their significance. It must not be forgotten that the Deuteronomistic historian was not only concerned to pour out his prejudices, he also intended to paint some kind of credible picture of events. He was attempting to write not just a stream of polemic, but a 'history' of sorts, whatever his motives and however polemical it might become. This creates a kind of tension between real events and perceptions of events and it is at this point of tension that the door is opened to other possible interpretations and nuances. In this way, other readings than the most superficial become possible for the discerning reader. It may well be that it is in the stories about women

17. S. Ackerman, 'The Queen Mother and the Cult in Ancient Israel', *JBL* 112 (1993), pp. 385-401 (388).

18. B.O. Long, *2 Kings* (FOTL, 10; Grand Rapids: Eerdmans, 1991), p. 130.

that the significance of this point of tension becomes most acute. For it is in these stories that the prejudices of the biblical writer may well coincide most effectively with those of traditional interpreters, which would explain why such narratives have often been so problematic for interpreters and also why they are such a target for feminist scholars.

Three Royal Women: Bathsheba, Jezebel and Athaliah

The Deuteronomist's agenda of depicting (and maybe helping to create?) a monarchy that could only be deemed to be effective insofar as it espoused monolatrous Yahwism and eschewed all things foreign, most particularly foreign women, is particularly pertinent to discussion of the stories of Bathsheba, Jezebel and Athaliah. It is not only important to see their histories against this background, it is probably impossible to see them without it. Bathsheba, Jezebel and Athaliah are three remarkable women. Their stories continue to fascinate—to such an extent that even for those who have never read the biblical account of her activities, the name Jezebel remains evocative to this day. These three women cannot be seen in isolation from each other. Their stories are part of a larger story—that of the monarchy in Israel and Judah, which is depicted in the Bible itself as a continuous whole. As the narrative proceeds, the text constantly moves between the Northern and Southern Kingdoms and reference is constantly being made back to David, even though the whole 'history' reaches its final form with an underlying awareness of the fall of Jerusalem and the exile.

Bathsheba

Bathsheba plays a major part in two significant narratives: 2 Samuel 11–12, which tells of the beginning of her relationship with David, and 1 Kings 1–2, when the succession to the throne is under discussion. According to the Bible, Bathsheba's importance arises out of first, her beauty, and secondly, the fact that she is the mother of Solomon, and these are emphasized in each of these narratives. In 2 Sam. 11.2, Bathsheba's beauty is highlighted. The Hebrew phrase applied to Bathsheba is *hā'iššâ ṭôbat mar'eh mᵉ'ōd*. It is almost as if the biblical writer is attempting to explain David's passion for Bathsheba, even though he cannot condone it. This impression is given, even though, as will be discussed below, it is at least possible that David had motives other than lust for his actions.

If Bathsheba's first appearance were her only one in the Old Testament, it might be felt that she indeed has no more power than that of a 'passive object'.[19] However, her second appearance is very different and, in my view, represents more than the 'ironic parody of her first appearance in "David's story"' described by Cheryl Exum.[20] In 1 Kings 1, when it becomes evident that David's power is waning, he calls for Bathsheba. Far from being simply a nameless member of the harem, or even the foremost member of it, Bathsheba is someone who is consulted by David when the succession is in question. Only after Bathsheba has been told that David wishes Solomon to be the heir are Zadok the priest, Nathan the prophet and Benaiah called in to act on his decision and anoint Solomon as king. In fact, the impression that Bathsheba is an important part of this process has already been given in 1 Kgs 1.11-14, since it is to her that Nathan turns after Adonijah has claimed the throne. Nathan, powerful figure though he is, tells Bathsheba that he 'will come in after [her] and confirm [her] words' (1 Kgs 1.14). Even if the view is taken that the so-called 'Succession Narrative' was written after the event, as a justification for Solomon's succession, the question still remains as to why such stress is laid on the involvement of Bathsheba. If the biblical writer were attempting to make as strong a case as possible, it is only reasonable to assume that he would have included those factors most supportive of his cause. It may well be that 'David's *giving* of the kingdom is in fact illusory',[21] and Bathsheba may well be colluding with Nathan in 'an act of deliberate deception',[22] but nevertheless, plotting or not, it is deemed important that Bathsheba be seen to be present. Gunn points out that there is a 'strong possibility' that 'where David in his senility imagines that he is bestowing the kingdom, in actuality it is being taken from him', even though the taking is not violent. He goes on: 'Thus ironically it is the son of Bathsheba who brings to final expression the theme of seizure established originally by David's taking of Bathsheba'.[23] To take Gunn's point further,

19. J.C. Exum, *Fragmented Women: Feminist (Sub)versions of Biblical Narratives* (JSOTSup, 163; Sheffield: JSOT Press, 1993), p. 173.

20. Exum, *Fragmented Women*, p. 198.

21. D.M. Gunn, *The Story of King David: Genre and Interpretation* (JSOTSup, 6; Sheffield: JSOT Press, 1978), p. 105.

22. Gunn, *The Story of King David*, p. 106. Gunn remarks: 'Certainly it is remarkable that any other reference to this crucial promise is missing from the story' (p. 105).

23. Gunn, *The Story of King David*, p. 106.

Bathsheba is involved in both events—while powerless at the first event, she is powerful at the second, although at least some, and maybe most, of her power derives from her position as the mother of Solomon and the consort of David. (Andreasen suggests the possibility that 'as queen mother Bathsheba functioned as a counsellor in the political and judiciary affairs at court and perhaps as mediator between the political factions in the nation'.[24]) Just as she is used to initiate the proclamation of Solomon as the heir, so she is used by Adonijah in an attempt to secure his power base (or, perhaps, merely his survival). It is to Bathsheba that Adonijah turns in his attempt to secure Abishag the Shunammite as his wife. Her approach to Solomon, who is now king, initiates the elimination of Adonijah and those who have supported him. Thus, in the narrative structure of 1–2 Kings, Bathsheba is used by the biblical writer to initiate both the proclamation of Solomon as king and the securing of that kingship by the elimination of Adonijah.

Two ways of interpreting the change in mood between Bathsheba's first appearance and her second immediately spring to mind. One is to suggest that the contrast is a literary device designed to demonstrate a move from lack of power to the wielding of power by a female character.[25] This is not an unknown motif within the Bible, although it is more commonly found in narratives about males, such as the stories of Joseph, Jacob, and even David himself. Another possibility is that the account in 2 Samuel 11–12 contains indications that Bathsheba was not simply a powerless victim and that David's motives in taking her first as his mistress and then as his wife were about more than simple lust. This suggestion has been explored by Randall Bailey[26] and becomes more plausible in the light of Gunn's observation that the account of the initial encounter between David and Bathsheba is rather passionless. Gunn comments, 'David's dealings with Bathsheba have a

---

24. Andreasen, 'The Role of the Queen Mother', p. 189.

25. I have suggested that an interpretation along these lines can also be applied to the story of Lot's daughters in Gen. 19. See C. Smith, 'Challenged by the Text: Interpreting Two Stories of Incest in the Hebrew Bible', in A. Brenner and C. Fontaine (eds.), *A Feminist Companion to Biblical Methodologies, Approaches and Strategies* (The Feminist Companion to the Bible, 11; Sheffield: Sheffield Academic Press, 1997), pp. 124-48.

26. R.C. Bailey, *David in Love and War: The Pursuit of Power in 2 Samuel 10–12* (JSOTSup, 75: Sheffield: JSOT Press, 1990), pp. 83-101.

curiously matter of fact character'.[27] It also seems to be the case that David not only married Bathsheba, but elevated her to a position of some prominence. If this was a marriage based merely on physical lust, there is no reason why Bathsheba should not simply have become one more nameless (or almost nameless) member of the harem. In fact, if this were a union based on transient lust, one might have expected that as she aged, Bathsheba would have lost her power over David. Bailey notes that Bathsheba's first designation is not as the wife of Uriah, but as 'the daughter of Eliam'. He points to the appearance of an Eliam as a 'son of Ahithophel of Giloh' in 2 Sam. 23.34 and suggests that 'if these two references are to the same person, this would mean that Bathsheba came from a politically influential family, since Ahithophel is noted as one of David's key advisors' (2 Sam. 16.23), who then defected to Absalom.[28] If Bailey is correct in this suggestion, then the use of Bathsheba by Nathan becomes even more understandable. Bailey goes so far as to suggest that it is the view of the biblical writer that David is more concerned about the woman's political connections than her marital status.[29]

Whether the text is viewed as a literary construction and Bathsheba as a device within it, or as an accurate record of events, or as a formulation created by Solomon's supporters to justify his kingship, Bathsheba appears as a powerful and significant figure within it. Since it is widely assumed that this is not to be expected within the patterns of the Israelite and Judaean monarchies, such a portrayal is worthy of remark.

Jezebel

There are two significant points to remember about Jezebel: first, she was active in Israel at a time of considerable stability, and secondly, she is portrayed almost exclusively as an opponent of Elijah. The latter point is perhaps more significant than the former.

1 Kgs 16.21-23 tells how Omri instigated a period of stability in Israel by quelling his opponents and building a capital. Omri's son Ahab, husband of Jezebel, reigned for twenty-two years (1 Kgs 16.29). According to the book of Kings, the manifold sins of Ahab were compounded by his marriage to Jezebel ('And as if it had been a light thing

27. Gunn, *The Story of King David*, p. 99.
28. Bailey, *David in Love and War*, p. 87.
29. Bailey, *David in Love and War*, p. 87.

for him to walk in the sins of Jeroboam the son of Nebat, he took for wife Jezebel the daughter of Ethbaal king of the Sidonians', 1 Kgs 16.31). Jezebel is blamed for Ahab's turning to Baal worship and for his construction of an Asherah (1 Kgs 16.31-33). Although it seems to have been the fashion for the biblical writers to blame foreign wives for causing their husbands to turn to the worship of foreign gods, this particular accusation may well have been true. An analysis of the biblical account of the reign of Ahab seems to indicate that Jezebel was not only the more powerful in the relationship, but seems to have been more politically aware than Ahab[30] and probably realized that such a move would reinforce Ahab's power base. Her strategy appears to have succeeded, given the length of Ahab's reign, and the hold over the people they appeared to be able to maintain. Jezebel's obvious gifts in the area of governing may have derived from the fact that she came from a royal house and was brought up in an atmosphere of ruling. Leah Bronner says of Jezebel[31] that 'Everything we know about her shows her to have been a woman born to rule'. Brenner comments:[32] 'Unlike any other king's wife or mother in the Old Testament, Jezebel was a real queen, assistant and partner in government to her husband... she actually participated in the business of government with her husband's consent'. What is interesting is that even though the biblical writers and redactors disapproved of Jezebel, they acknowledge both her importance and her power. (Phyllis Trible has said of Jezebel that 'No woman [or man] in the Hebrew Scriptures endures a more hostile press than Jezebel', and she is probably right.[33]) Her importance is registered in the introduction to the reign of Ahaziah, son of Ahab (1 Kgs 22.51), which says of him that 'He did what was evil in the sight of the Lord, and walked in the way of his father, and in the way of his mother, and in the way of Jeroboam the son of Nebat, who made Israel to sin'. This addition of a 'mother' to the usual Deuteronomistic formula

30. Alexander Rofé makes the following comment on the relationship: 'They seem to be different from each other both in nature and in their conception of kingship. Jezebel is firm, self-confident, master in the art of ruling a nation. Not so Ahab' (A. Rofé, 'The Vineyard of Naboth: The Origin and Message of the Story', *VT* 38 [1988], pp. 89-104 [91]).

31. L. Bronner, *The Stories of Elijah and Elisha as Polemics Against Baal Worship* (Pretoria Oriental Series, 6; Leiden: E.J. Brill, 1968), p. 9.

32. Brenner, *Israelite Woman*, p. 20.

33. P. Trible, 'Exegesis for Storytellers and Other Strangers', *JBL* 114 (1995), pp. 3-19 (4).

must be a reference to Jezebel, and must also be an indication of her significance for the biblical writers/redactors.

This brings me to the second point—the biblical writer's portrayal of Jezebel as being diametrically opposed to the prophet Elijah. Elijah first appears in 1 Kings 17, informing Ahab that there will be a drought. Jezebel appears first as a protagonist in Israelite matters in 1 Kgs 18.4, where it is said that she 'cut off the prophets of the Lord', causing Obadiah to flee with a hundred colleagues and hide in a cave. Obadiah tells Elijah of Jezebel's action, initiating the power struggle between the two, which is in itself a power struggle between Yahweh and other gods, the most memorable episode of which is the confrontation on Mount Carmel (1 Kgs 18).

Phyllis Trible has written of the account of the encounters between the two[34] that the biblical writers have 'shaped a narrative in which Elijah and Jezebel (among other characters) emerged as quintessential opposites: he the epitome of good; she of evil'. Trible points to the similarities in the narratives of Elijah and Jezebel and says:[35] 'In behavior and mode of being Elijah and Jezebel become mirror images that haunt the ages'. Trible makes an important point by drawing these parallels: if Jezebel had not been such a powerful figure, she would not have been a worthy opponent for such a giant as Elijah. Nowhere else in the Old Testament is there a confrontation of this magnitude between a ruler and a supporter of Yahweh—and this leads to questions about the significance of the opponent's being a woman.

What becomes clear as the narrative proceeds is that not only is Ahab dependent on the leadership of his wife, but Elijah is afraid of her. In 1 Kgs 19.1, after the events at Mount Carmel, it is to Jezebel that Ahab turns and it is she who then confronts Elijah. What is more, Elijah is afraid of her and flees to Beersheba in Judah to escape her.

Although the biblical narrative portrays a conflict between Yahwism and the religions of other gods, there are also hints that it is about more than this. Ahab addresses Elijah as 'you troubler of Israel' (1 Kgs 18.17), and it would seem that Elijah is creating unrest in a nation which has only comparatively recently found stability. We notice in 1 Kgs 19.16, after Elijah has fled from Jezebel, that he is told by Yahweh to anoint another king, Jehu, to replace Ahab. If the politically acute Jezebel is seeking to remove Elijah in order to be rid of disruptive

34. Trible, 'Exegesis for Storytellers', p. 3.
35. Trible, 'Exegesis for Storytellers', p. 18.

factions in the kingdom, she is probably right to do so. Tomoo Ishida[36] has spoken of the 'Yahwist revolution in the Northern Kingdom' in the context of its effects on Judah. The incident of Naboth's vineyard is revealing, not only because it reveals Ahab's dependence on Jezebel's judgment and his own weakness (he sulks when he cannot have his own way and waits for her to come and ask him what is wrong), but also because it tells the reader something about Jezebel's motivation. What is more, Jezebel's power is recognized by Ahab's subjects. Jezebel writes in Ahab's name to proclaim a fast (1 Kgs 21.9-10), but 'the men of his city, the elders and the nobles who dwelt in his city, did as Jezebel had sent word to them' (1 Kgs 21.11). They knew where the real power lay! It is Elijah who will not recognize Jezebel's authority— *he* confronts Ahab (1 Kgs 21.20-22). That the matter of Naboth's vineyard is a matter of retaining power for Jezebel is clear from her words to Ahab: 'Do you now govern Israel?' (1 Kgs 21.7). However unfair and unreasonable Ahab's request, Jezebel knows that if it is not followed through, Ahab will have lost some of his authority—a situation that would open the door to further dissent.

Athaliah

Athaliah took power after a coup following the death of her son Ahaziah, in which she killed all the royal family except Joash, who was hidden away by her opponents.[37] Athaliah appears to have been the only woman who can be said to have 'reigned over the land' (even though Jezebel can be said to have done so, despite the fact that her husband was nominally the ruler), and it is clear that the biblical writer struggled with the fact that she did so. Cogan and Tadmor point out[38] that 'From the point of view of the Deuteronomistic editor of Kings, Athaliah's reign is not granted full legitimacy, for neither an opening nor a closing formula is given for her six years'. Nevertheless, they insist[39] that 'the narrative acknowledges Athaliah as queen, even though it is highly critical of her usurpation of the throne'.

---

36. Ishida, *Royal Dynasties*, p. 160.

37. For a redaction critical study of the Athaliah narrative in 2 Kings 11, see C. Levin, *Der Sturz der Königen Atalja* (SBS, 105; Stuttgart: Katholisches Bibel-werk, 1982). I am grateful to Dr John Day for pointing out this reference.

38. M. Cogan and H. Tadmor, *II Kings* (AB, 11; Garden City, NY: Doubleday, 1988), p. 133.

39. Cogan and Tadmor, *II Kings*, p. 134.

Athaliah is linked to Jezebel by the biblical writers. She also forms a link between the Northern and Southern Kingdoms at a crucial time in their history. She is described as the daughter of Omri and the mother of Ahaziah, son of Jehoram, king of Judah (2 Kgs 8.25-27), but she is also referred to as Ahab's daughter (2 Kgs 8.18). (Whether Omri or Ahab was her father is still a matter for debate.) The opponent of Athaliah after she has taken the throne is a supporter of Yahweh, Jehoiada the priest. Ahaziah's reign, according to the biblical writer, is characterized by its similarity to that of Ahab (2 Kgs 8.27). Since Athaliah is clearly mentioned in connection with it, the implication is clear: Athaliah encouraged the worship of Baal. Nevertheless, it is noticeable that Athaliah appears not to have been charged with suppressing Yahwism. It would seem that although there was worship of Baal, this took place in a separate shrine.[40]

However, there is another possible interpretation of the events recorded in 2 Kings. When Athaliah discovers that Jehoiada has declared Joash king in Yahweh's house, her first reaction is, 'Treason!' (2 Kgs 11.14). Ishida has suggested[41] that it was the aim of Jehoram and Athaliah to 'establish the regime in full co-operation with the House of Omri', but they were opposed in this by the 'nationalists', whose agenda stood in opposition to the ruling party, based in Jerusalem, who were seen as opponents of Yahwistic religion. Ishida[42] sees the references to 'the people of the land' which appear in accounts of events in Judah as evidence of a group not bound up with the royal administration and evidencing an opposition between those of 'the city' and those of 'the land'. He suggests that the young Joash was, in fact, taken by representatives of this group and then crowned by them, which would mean that Athaliah's assumption of the throne had more to do with a desire to maintain stability and the *status quo* than to oppose Yahwism. Such an interpretation is an interesting one, because it indicates a degree of disillusionment with the idea that Jerusalem and the Temple represented the centres of true Yahwism. It accords well with what we know of Elijah's ministry in the Northern Kingdom, but not with a Temple-centred Deuteronomistic theology. Thus, if the Yahwistic agenda of the Deuteronomists is put aside, it is possible to see in the actions of Jezebel and Athaliah evidence of strong and

40. Cogan and Tadmor, *II Kings*, p. 134.
41. Ishida, *Royal Dynasties*, p. 159.
42. Ishida, *Royal Dynasties*, pp. 160-61.

sensible leadership and a desire for stability. From another point of view, they both could be seen as good rulers. The fact that the biblical writer takes such pains to depict them otherwise is perhaps an indication of the potential strength of such a counter-tradition. Patricia Dutcher-Walls suggests that the contempt in which Athaliah is held has several aspects:[43] 'Regardless of the "historical" Athaliah's actions or motives, she is cast by the worldview of the Deuteronomist to fit ideas of evil, danger and illegitimate power—all of which are inherent in her status as foreign, female and apostate.'

I do wonder, however, how right Dutcher-Walls is to suggest that condemnation of Athaliah had as one of its primary motivations the fact that she was female. Bathsheba, also female, and possibly foreign (she was the wife of a Hittite, 2 Sam. 11.3), apparently suffered no such condemnation. This may well have been because she was regarded as a supporter of Yahweh. If this was the case, then the threat posed by Athaliah could have arisen from her worship of foreign gods. The same would apply to Jezebel. This interpretation has the advantage that it conforms with what the text actually says. Whatever the hidden or sub-conscious agenda, this was seen as the real threat by the Deuteronomistic redactors. The fact that the association of foreign women with foreign cults might well have led to their condemnation does not militate against this view. All that happens is that the debate moves to whichever was the primary consideration: the fact that a woman was a woman or the fact that, as a woman, she worshipped foreign (and quite possibly female) deities.

The biblical writer is right to emphasize the links between Jezebel and Athaliah (with Jezebel being 'Athaliah's kinswoman and closest northern analogue'[44]). As Dutcher-Walls has put it, for the biblical writer, 'Athaliah represents an evil Omride intruder who interrupts the dynastic succession in Judah and can only be seen as a violent, illegitimate influence'.[45] There are indeed parallels between them. Rainer Albertz has suggested[46] (in connection with the Omri dynasty) that

43. P. Dutcher-Walls, *Narrative Art, Political Rhetoric: The Case of Athaliah and Joash* (JSOTSup, 209; Sheffield: Sheffield Academic Press, 1996), p. 112.

44. Dutcher-Walls, *Narrative Art, Political Rhetoric*, p. 112.

45. Dutcher-Walls, *Narrative Art, Political Rhetoric*, p. 100.

46. R. Albertz, *Religionsgeschichte Israels in alttestamentlicher Zeit* (Göttingen: Vandenhoeck & Ruprecht, 1992), I, p. 232 (ET *A History of Israelite Religion in the Old Testament Period* [trans. J. Bowden; London: SCM Press, 1994], I, p. 150).

It is relatively improbable that the royal house practised an aggressive religious policy against Yahweh religion, as the texts accuse Jezebel in particular of doing, but it very probably allowed, if not encouraged, the juxtaposition of Yahweh and Baal worship, and at all events did not prevent the revitalization of Baal religion.

He also sees the prophets as part of a movement that was certainly religious, but also focused on social matters. Prophets, he suggests,[47] were 'recruited above all from a lower class which was either without means or had been impoverished'. Being landless and without other means of support, the prophets earned their living as 'itinerant miraculous healers, exorcists or oracle-givers'. Albertz continues,[48] 'It was only from such economic independence and the position of social outsider that part of Israelite prophecy took on the function of criticizing the system'. He would class Elijah and Elisha as being of this group, which would certainly make them comparable with 'the people of the land' referred to above and whose popular leaders appear to have been vociferous and active in Judah. Albertz suggests[49] that 'the later tradition certainly exaggerates in saying that Jezebel systematically had the prophets of Yahweh persecuted and killed... but the royal house will not have accepted the attacks on its religious policy completely without counter-measures'. This leaves us with the very real possibility that Jezebel and Athaliah were opposing dissident elements within their nations in order to avoid a serious threat to stability and to maintain order in their respective kingdoms.

Comparing and Contrasting

There are some interesting questions about the ways in which the three women—Bathsheba, Jezebel and Athaliah—are portrayed. Bathsheba and Athaliah have in common that they appear to derive their power primarily from being the mothers of sons, whereas Jezebel is a queen–consort. Jezebel and Athaliah have in common that they are apparently opposing similar kinds of threats within their respective kingdoms. All three women have in common that they are portrayed as being on the side of the ruling party, and, in the cases of Athaliah and Bathsheba, ruling parties centred on Jerusalem as the seat of power. This is inter-

---

47. Albertz, *Religionsgeschichte*, p. 235 (ET *History*, p. 151).
48. Albertz, *Religionsgeschichte*, p. 234 (ET *History*, p. 151).
49. Albertz, *Religionsgeschichte*, p. 241 (ET *History*, p. 154).

esting, because in Bathsheba's case the support for the ruling powers in Jerusalem is perceived positively by the biblical writers and in Athaliah's negatively. This could well reflect a change in attitude brought about by the experience of living under such regimes. In fact, the biblical text itself expresses disillusionment with such rule and places that disillusionment as far back as the reign of Solomon.

There are both points of comparison and points of contrast between these three women. Jezebel and Athaliah are both 'royal' women, coming from royal houses and used to court ways, even though those courts were foreign ones. (That the foreignness of these women was an issue for the biblical writer cannot be doubted. Long speaks of the Deuteronomistic writer pursuing the theme of 'outright war between the forces of Yahweh and Baal' and suggests that for this writer 'the disease enters the body politic through marriage'.[50]) Bathsheba, however, was a commoner. Both Jezebel and Athaliah—one in the Northern Kingdom and one in the South—were seen as threats to Yahwistic religion and opponents of those who supported it. Bathsheba, on the other hand, is not a threat. She is seen as aligned with orthodox religion in the persons of Nathan and Zadok, and, of course, her son Solomon.

All the women appear to have in common that their power derives, at least in part, from the men with whom they were associated. Further, they seem to be able to exercise their own power most effectively when there is some sort of male power vacuum. Ahab and David have in common that they appear to be besotted with their wives. This point is not made in the case of Athaliah. Nevertheless, she, like the other two, appears to exercise most power when male power is absent or negligible. In Athaliah's case it is absent; in the case of Bathsheba it is when David is old and weak and his lack of sexual virility appears to be a major concern of those around him in the court. Jezebel's power seems to come from Ahab's weakness, to which the text makes reference when the incident of Naboth's vineyard is described.

Is there, then, anything in the stories of Bathsheba, Jezebel and Athaliah that can tell us something about 'queenship' in ancient Israel? If it is assumed that one cannot really speak of a 'queen' unless she is specifically named as such, then it cannot be said that the stories contribute much to ideas about queenship. Neither Bathsheba, Jezebel, nor

---

50. Long, *2 Kings*, p. 155. This became even more of an issue later, as can be seen from, for example, the events recorded in Ezra 9–10; Solomon's taking of foreign wives is cited as the cause of the break-up of the kingdom in 1 Kgs 11.1-13.

Athaliah is specifically called a 'queen', even though we are told that Athaliah 'ruled' (*mōleket*) the land (2 Kgs 11.3). However, if one looks at the stories and what they tell us, a pattern does seem to emerge. All three women had parts to play in affairs of state. Bathsheba was consulted on the matter of the succession to the throne and regarded by significant national figures as a person of influence and authority. Jezebel, product of a royal house, and used to the machinery of ruling, was clearly the stronger and more able partner in the marriage between herself and Ahab. She takes over the situation that arises over Naboth's vineyard, and challenges the powerful Elijah on the matter of religion. Elijah's fear of Jezebel is in itself a testimony to the extent of her power. Athaliah rules after engineering a coup and it takes six years for her to be overthrown. The Deuteronomist's accounts of the reigns of Athaliah and Jezebel indicate that even though in orthodox terms they were unfit rulers for Judah and Israel, they had considerable skills in statecraft and could wield power effectively. It is interesting to speculate on how their capabilities as rulers would have been assessed had the biblical writer not been committed exclusively to a particular understanding of kingship.

It is simply not sensible to argue that because the only power these women had derived from their connection with males then it cannot be counted as 'real' power. It certainly was real power, whatever its provenance. Obviously, if women derive their power from men, then the more powerful the man, the more the potential power of the woman with whom he is associated. The words 'potential power' are important in this context, because it is here where distinctions can be made between women: some realized this potential power, while others did not. The point that even though a woman's power derives from a man it is still real needs to be made since it seems to be frequently overlooked, both by traditional and feminist scholars. The power of royal women has been discounted for patriarchal reasons—the assumption either that it is not possible for women to have or wield power, or that any power they have is valueless—or for feminist reasons—that women's power in biblical times could only derive from men and was therefore meaningless. However, it is the prevailing view of the biblical writers that the power of the great men of the Bible derives from Yahweh, and yet it is not suggested that it therefore has no worth or meaning.

In Conclusion

I began with a question: 'Was there such a thing as "queenship" in Israel and Judah?' The answer to that question has to be that although royal women were rarely, if ever, given the specific title 'queen', there can be no doubt that they exercised power and authority by virtue of their association with royal courts. Although, given the nature of the society in which they lived, their power derived originally from the males with whom they were associated, there can be no doubt that it was real power and that it was wielded very effectively indeed by some royal women. Inevitably, the concerns of the biblical writers have led to royal women being portrayed in specific ways, pertinent to the biblical agenda, that do not necessarily reflect the extent of their power and how they used it. Bathsheba, Jezebel and Athaliah in particular can be seen, even through the distorting lens of the Deuteronomistic overlays on their narratives, to have been women who were forces to be reckoned with in their respective kingdoms and women who, if not specifically designated as 'queens', were certainly such in all but name.

THE KING IN THE WISDOM LITERATURE

Katharine J. Dell

The wisdom literature would probably not be the first part of the Old Testament to which one would turn for information on kingship in general or on the kings of Israel in particular. Whilst one might turn to it for general maxims regarding expectations of kingly behaviour and attitudes one might adopt towards one's ruler, one certainly would not turn to it for specific information on individual Israelite kings, the only two mentioned being Solomon and Hezekiah (in addition to the foreign king Lemuel of Massa in Prov. 31.1). These are the two categories into which the material naturally falls. The first category contains the proverbial material concerned with the king and his position in relation both to his subjects and to God. The second concerns the mention of certain kings mainly in connection with attribution of the wisdom books. A prior question is raised about the extent of the wisdom literature. It is interesting that in the book of Job there are only three references to a king: in 12.18 as part of a description by Job of God's arbitrariness, 'He looses the bonds of kings, and binds a waistcloth on their loins', in 29.25 simply as a simile, 'I dwelt like a king among his troops', and in 36.7 in the speech of Elihu as part of a description of God's just dealings, 'He (God) does not withdraw his eyes from the righteous, but with kings upon the throne he sets them for ever, and they are exalted'. Furthermore, there is no attribution to any king, actual or implicit, in the book of Job,[1] a factor which I find of significance

---

1. Contrast A. Caquot in 'Traits royaux dans le personnage de Job', in *Maqqél Shâqédh: La Branche d'Amandier. Hommage à Wilhelm Vischer* (Montpellier: Causse, Graille & Castlenau, 1960), pp. 32-45. Caquot argued that Job is depicted as a king in ch. 29; however perhaps we should see Job as a chief or sheikh rather than a king there. Interestingly, Job is said to be a king in the appendix at the end of the book in the LXX version.

when considering the classification of Job as a wisdom text.[2] The fact
that both general references to the activities of kings and the use of king
imagery are also minimal in Job could be seen to add weight to my
argument, depending on how crucial this factor is perceived to be in the
characterization of a text as wisdom. Given this, I shall exclude Job
from my debate here and focus on the wisdom books of Proverbs and
Ecclesiastes. In fact my main focus will be on the book of Proverbs as
it is here that most wisdom regarding the king is to be found.

The second category of attribution can be dealt with quite quickly
and so I shall begin with this. We read at the beginning of Proverbs,
'The proverbs of Solomon, son of David, king of Israel' (1.1). This
may be the title of the whole book, which it is most commonly taken to
be, although it may well refer to the first section only. Proverbs 10.1
denotes the following section 'The proverbs of Solomon' and 25.1
begins a collection of additional 'proverbs of Solomon, which the men
of Hezekiah, king of Judah, transcribed'. It is widely held that these
Solomonic attributions are not to be taken literally or historically but
that they are traditional ascriptions imposed on the material to give it
greater authority. The description of the 'men of Hezekiah' as editors is
perceived as more likely to be historical, but does not in itself constitute
enough evidence on which to build a 'royal court' hypothesis for the
whole book, which, as we shall see, some scholars have been inclined
to do. For this, the proverbs themselves need to be examined. It is possible that the transcribing of proverbs into a collection was started by
the men of Hezekiah or some such group.[3] It may be that popular
sayings were collected and then gathered together in more literary
circles at this time as they were recontextualized at a time of national

2.   K.J. Dell, *The Book of Job as Sceptical Literature* (BZAW, 197; Berlin:
W. de Gruyter, 1991), pp. 57-88.

3.   The reference to the 'men of Hezekiah' in Prov. 25.1 leads R.B.Y. Scott,
'Solomon and the Beginnings of Wisdom in Israel', in M. Noth and D. Winton
Thomas (eds.), *Wisdom in Israel and in the Ancient Near East* (Festschrift H.H.
Rowley; VTSup, 3; Leiden: E.J. Brill, 1955), pp. 262-79, to argue that his reign
was a time of significant literary activity. Recently, however, M. Carasik, 'The Men
of Hezekiah', *VT* 44 (1994), pp. 289-300, has argued that this cannot be maintained
with any certainty. He concludes, 'the citation of the "men of Hezekiah" in Prov.
xxv 1 could just as well be exegetical as it could historical...the court of Hezekiah
can no longer be considered the first, fixed point in the transmission of wisdom
literature' (p. 300).

resurgence.[4] However, much of this remains speculative.

The superscription in Ecclesiastes is equally puzzling. It is interesting that the author of Ecclesiastes does not use the name Solomon directly in 1.1. Attribution to a famous personage would have given authority to the book, to ease the book's progress into the canon, if for no other reason.[5] However, we have to deal with the fact that this is not a straightforward attribution. If Qoheleth had wanted to state specifically that Solomon was the author, why retain the name Qoheleth? Why did he include the reference to 'son of David' or describe himself as 'king in Jerusalem' unless he wanted to be identified with Solomon? Of course, it is possible by means of translation to assert that Qoheleth is calling himself 'property owner in Jerusalem' rather than 'king' here and that it is mistranslation that has led to misinterpretation.[6] However, this view has not been widely espoused by scholars. Another possibility is that Qoheleth is not meant to be read as a proper name. Alternatively, the concealed reference to Solomon may be an editorial gloss by those

4.   M.V. Fox in 'The Social Location of the Book of Proverbs', in M.V. Fox *et al.* (eds.), *Texts, Temples, and Traditions: A Tribute to Menahem Haran* (Winona Lake, IN: Eisenbrauns, 1996), pp. 227-39, argues for the transmission of proverbs in royal circles such as those mentioned in Prov. 25.1, 'or at least to men who know how to act when near the king' (p. 235). He thus places such proverbs in a possible context later than the Solomonic period. He sees the attribution of proverbs to 'simple folk' as strained. My response to this, however, is to see the limitation of proverbs to a royal context as strained in that it does not allow for a development from a broader oral base to a more educated and literary context.

5.   See discussion in K.J. Dell, 'Ecclesiastes as Wisdom: Consulting Early Interpreters', *VT* 44 (1994), pp. 301-29.

6.   H.L. Ginsberg, 'The Structure and Contents of the Book of Koheleth', in Noth and Winton Thomas (eds.), *Wisdom in Israel and in the Ancient near East*, pp. 138-49, argues that *mlk* should be vocalized as *mōlēk*, meaning 'property-holder'. He writes, '*mlk* quite certainly means not "to be king" but "to own" in ii 12b ("for of what sort will be the man who will come after me, who will own all that I have already acquired"—reading *'aharai...hammolek...'asiti*), whose proper position is immediately after ii 11... We therefore conclude that all Koheleth asserted in the original form of i 12 was "I, Koheleth, was a property owner in Jerusalem"' (pp. 148-49). In a footnote Ginsberg notes that 'where Koheleth boasts that he surpassed "all that were before me in Jerusalem" he does not speak of kings (i 16; ii 7, 9), and when he does relate that he amassed "treasures (as) of kings" (ii 8) he does not say "*other* kings" or "*the other* kings" nor claim that he outdid kings' (p. 149 n. 1). See also H.L. Ginsberg, *Studies in Koheleth* (New York: Jewish Theological Seminary of America, 1950) pp. 12-15.

promoting Solomonic authorship after the period in which Qoheleth was writing. Along these lines B.S. Childs[7] suggests that the identification of Qoheleth with Solomon was a deliberate canonical technique. He sees Qoheleth as a teacher whose role was sufficiently significant to have prevented the exclusion of his name when, nevertheless, those who shaped the book wished to give it the authority of Solomonic attribution. So they settled for a veiled identification of Qoheleth with Solomon. The Solomonic fiction is of course continued in the section Eccl. 1.12–2.26 in which the persona of Solomon is again suggested. However, this may have started life as an example story and then been incorporated into this wider concern for attribution. The king is held up as an example of the wider wisdom maxim that happiness cannot be found, however hard one seeks it, for 'all was vanity and a striving after wind' (2.11).

So what are we to conclude from the presence of these attributions, whatever the motivation for including them? Their primary role seems to be to give the literature authority, maybe even orthodoxy. It is a question of the status of the texts and their role as authoritative wisdom, since Solomon was the king who had wisdom in great abundance. Maybe it even spills over into a question of the divinely authorized status of the material as it comes to form the authoritative word for succeeding generations. We will bear these thoughts in mind as we come on to the second, more fruitful area of the sayings themselves.

My main concern is with the first category I mentioned, the sayings about the king, his role and his relationships. Contextual questions tend to be at the forefront as we consider these texts, as this is the area that has primarily occupied scholars in recent years as they have sought to understand the social framework(s) that generated the wisdom texts. In fact, these questions have tended to dominate over an evaluation of the content and the place of these maxims within wisdom thought as a

7. B.S. Childs, *Introduction to the Old Testament as Scripture* (Philadelphia: Fortress Press, 1979), p. 584. Childs writes of the function of such an attribution, 'In its canonical form the identification assures the reader that the attack on wisdom which Ecclesiastes contains is not to be regarded as the personal idiosyncracy of a nameless teacher. Rather, by his speaking in the guise of Solomon, whose own history now formed part of the community's common memory, his attack on wisdom was assigned an authoritative role as the final reflections of Solomon. As the source of Israel's wisdom, his words serve as an official corrective from within the wisdom tradition itself. Once this point was made, the literary fiction of Solomon was dropped' (p. 584).

whole, an imbalance that I shall seek to rectify in my own reading of these texts. In the context of a review of recent scholarly work on the maxims concerning kings in Proverbs, I shall look afresh at the king-sayings, at their possible context and at their themes, considering their place in the wider wisdom enterprise and their overall theological significance.

The King in the Book of Proverbs

Let us turn first to the book of Proverbs. The main point at issue amongst scholars is the following: Do the proverbs concerning the king presuppose a court circle intimately acquainted with kingly ways and vices or is there a broader context for such sayings? Until recently a court context for early wisdom was assumed, building on the views of older scholars.[8] I shall outline the arguments of W.L. Humphreys[9] to illustrate this. However, more recently, the work of Weeks,[10] Golka,[11] and Whybray[12] has cast varying amounts of doubt on this supposition.[13]

---

8. E.g. H.-J. Hermisson, *Studien zur israelitischen Spruchweisheit* (WMANT, 28; Neukirchen–Vluyn: Neukirchener Verlag, 1968), who held that mention of the king indicated a court origin for a saying. Hermisson wrote, 'Bei den Königs-sprüchen können wir uns kurz fassen, denn als Volksgut kommen sie durchweg nicht in Betracht. Theoretisch ist es zwar denkbar, daß sich die Phantasie des Volkes mit dem König beschäftigt hat und daraus Sprüche hervorgegangen sind, aber solcher Art sind die Königssprüche in den Proverbien nicht' (p. 71).

9. W.L. Humphreys, 'The Motif of the Wise Courtier in the Book of Proverbs', in J. Gammie (ed.), *Israelite Wisdom: Theological and Literary Studies in Honor of Samuel Terrien* (Missoula, MT: Scholars Press, 1978), pp. 177-90.

10. S. Weeks, *Early Israelite Wisdom* (Oxford: Clarendon Press, 1994).

11. F. Golka, *The Leopard's Spots: Biblical and African Wisdom in Proverbs* (Edinburgh: T.& T. Clark, 1993).

12. R.N. Whybray, *Wealth and Poverty in the Book of Proverbs* (JSOTSup, 99; Sheffield: JSOT Press, 1990).

13. Golka has recently been supported by C. Westermann, *Wurzeln der Weisheit* (Göttingen: Vandenhoeck & Ruprecht, 1990) (ET *Roots of Wisdom* [trans. J.D. Charles, Edinburgh: T. & T. Clark, 1995]). Westermann argues that the king-sayings are popular folk material that did not originate in court or school. He compares the language of these sayings to that of Ps. 45, which he argues could not have been produced anywhere but in the royal court or its environs. He writes, 'In the royal sayings in Proverbs, there is no mention of splendour and might, which would be unfurled in the royal court and which would be a sign of a portrait or evidence of merit' (p. 35). In turn, Golka has been attacked in a recent article by

I shall first outline the position taken by each of these scholars in turn and then go on to consider each of the sayings in the light of this ongoing debate.

On the basis of comparison with Egyptian motifs of the wise courtier, W.L. Humphreys argues that there were educational establishments in the royal courts of Israel and Judah providing training for officials in the royal service in which maxims such as the king-sayings would serve an important educational role. He acknowledges that there is little in the way of biblical references or archaeological evidence to draw upon. Nevertheless, using material from the Egyptian Instructions of Ptahhotep and Kagemni from the Old Kingdom and Ani and Amenemope from the New Kingdom, his aim is to characterize the figure of the wise courtier as the typical wise man in Israelite terms. Humphreys argues that the Egyptian Instructions are primarily directed to a person in the service of the king, as evidenced by the authorship of all the Instructions, except that of Ani, by courtiers. He then goes on to analyse Proverbs 10–29, noting that there is little evidence from context that courtiers handled this material and so focusing on the content of the sayings as proof of this context. He first considers king-sayings that, he argues, appear to address the situation of the courtier directly—this category relates to our concern. He then treats other sayings on rulers, for example, which he interprets as referring often, although not exclusively, to the courtier's situation[14] especially noting where themes occur that are matched in the Egyptian Instructions.

S. Weeks in *Early Israelite Wisdom* provides some modification of these views, without wanting to go as far as Golka and Whybray, and hence I shall treat him next. He notes that sayings consistent with a

Fox, 'Social Location', who leans towards Humphreys' viewpoint.

14. Humphreys sees Prov. 24.5-6, for example, as also referring to the situation of the courtier: 'A wise man is mightier than a strong man, and a man of knowledge than he who has strength; for by wise guidance you can wage your war, and in abundance of counsellors there is victory'. Again this could be interpreted as a general observation on the triumph of brains over brawn! Whybray sees this as a general observation rather than as advice to royal counsellors. Humphreys places emphasis also on Prov. 23.1-3, which speaks of wariness in the presence of a ruler who might be enticing one with good foods in order to deceive one. Humphreys remarks that this saying presents the court as 'a place of danger, a complex and slippery setting where appearances can be deceptive' ('Motif', p. 184). Its range of application could, however, be seen to be broader—anyone with power might well seek to influence others by providing a good meal.

court setting did not necessarily originate there. He cites von Rad,[15] who acknowledged that the proportion of court-oriented sayings in Proverbs was low and so suggested that the wise men of the court also collected material that had not actually originated there. Weeks raises the possibility, in contrast, that instead of a lot of non-courtly material being collected at court, 'rather...a little courtly material was collected outside the court'.[16] Weeks notes that scholars have usually assumed a court context for those proverbs showing favour to the king but not for those critical of the king. He argues for the favourable material having a wider context and writes, 'we can hardly assume that everyone except courtiers hated the king'.[17] Conversely, I would add that it seems to me more likely that courtiers would hate the king—backbiting by those in close proximity is a common enough occurrence! Weeks suggests that the sayings, even if they originated in a royal court, may not have originated in an Israelite context but may have been an inherited convention from elsewhere, Egypt for example,[18] which was simply imitated. He maintains this on the grounds that there is little sign of innovation in the Israelite proverbs about the king. Furthermore, he holds that they may have been of interest to redactors or to a broader Israelite population rather than to courtiers themselves. He notes the close connection of king-sayings with Yahweh sayings in chs. 16 and 22 but assumes that the sayings refer literally to the king or rulers and wishes to play down the divine aspect. So, whilst noting that in the sayings about the king he is often portrayed as 'an inerrant instrument of the divine will',[19] Weeks puts more emphasis on the distancing between a ruler and God in 29.26 (a text that is not in fact a king-saying), an emphasis I feel is misplaced. I will go on to discuss this issue in relation to the king-sayings.

F. Golka, in an article first published in 1986,[20] argues strongly

15. G. von Rad, *Weisheit in Israel* (Neukirchen–Vluyn: Neukirchener Verlag, 1970), p. 30 (ET *Wisdom in Israel* [London: SCM Press, 1972], p. 17).

16. Weeks, *Early Israelite Wisdom*, p. 47.

17. Weeks, *Early Israelite Wisdom*, p. 48.

18. Weeks's view on Egyptian parallels can be seen to be slightly ambivalent, as he holds elsewhere that whilst interaction of ideas between Egyptian and Israelite cultures is probably undeniable, this can be assumed without also holding that the institutions were the same.

19. Weeks, *Early Israelite Wisdom*, p. 47.

20. First published as F. Golka, 'Die Königs- und Hofsprüche und der Ursprung der israelitischen Weisheit', *VT* 36 (1986), pp. 130-36; republished as Chapter 2 of *The Leopard's Spots*, from which I cite.

against a court context for most of the sayings. Using evidence from African parallels Golka argues that proverbs concerning a chief, king or ruler often arose amongst those who were far from the court as regards social location. He therefore argues strongly in favour of a common origin for many such proverbs. A note of caution should be sounded about using extra-biblical parallels in this way, and this comment is equally applicable to Humphreys' work on Egyptian parallels. The danger is of taking a model from elsewhere and then interpreting this material solely in that light, and of course with African parallels we are on very different cultural ground from the Egyptian parallels, the possibility of dependence being that much more remote. Golka is not, however, claiming any kind of dependence; rather, he is showing that sayings of a certain type can arise in certain situations and he does find some striking parallels to the material we have in Proverbs. His African proverbs fall broadly into the following categories, although not all his examples are explicitly about the king and many are veiled in metaphor and so their meaning is not precisely clear. He finds proverbs critical of the chief or king, he quotes sayings that describe the dependence of chief upon people, and he looks at proverbs that put the people above the chief and some that describe the transitoriness of power. He sees fear of the chief by the common man as a theme, and he finds sayings that express the dependence of the people on their chief and ones which express hatred of him and threats against him, for example, 'The mist rests in the valleys/ the crocodiles lie in the streams/ the lowly hate the lofty' (Malagasy proverb 1428). Some proverbs criticize submissiveness in the presence of the chief, others counsel the chief to be persuasive rather than authoritarian. Some treat the chief critically—for example rulers think they can get away with not paying their debts—whilst others point out the limits of the chief's authority within geographical boundaries. The list continues, but the point is made that people generally are concerned with their relationship with their leaders and with their ideas on how that ruler should behave; it is not merely a courtly privilege, although, of course, courtiers may have more opportunity to watch the king's behaviour at first hand.

Not only does the chief or king himself come under scrutiny, Golka also finds many popular sayings critical of the court, demonstrating the unpopularity of those who are close to the king. It is often felt best to by-pass such people when wishing to raise a matter with the chief. The people enjoy the fall from grace of a courtier, especially a conceited favourite. The envy of courtiers towards the king is also described, for example, 'The leopard envies the lion's resting place', and this often leads the people to have a certain amount of sympathy for the chief. Problems for people in relating to the chief include themes of serving two masters, perhaps where there are rival claims for leadership or more than one leader, and themes of how to evaluate his glory, his claim to exercise justice and the blessing he can endow. Golka convincingly maintains against Hermisson that 'the methodological principle applies that among all peoples popular origin of proverbs has to be assumed until there is proof to the contrary'.[21] He argues strongly against the assumption that mention of the king or court means that proverbs originated there and he goes on to evaluate Proverbs 10–29 in this light.

Whybray's 1990 book, *Wealth and Poverty in the Book of Proverbs*, contributes significantly to this debate. His study involves a broader evaluation of the context in which the book of Proverbs was born. He finds no precise arrangement of the proverbs about kings[22] and no evidence that they have been collected for the use of courtiers. He finds no common attitude expressed towards kings and notes the small place such sayings hold in the context of Proverbs as a whole. He writes, 'that such a large and wide-ranging collection of proverbs should contain a fair number of proverbs about kings is not at all surprising: comments and reflections by ordinary citizens on the supreme authority by which they are ruled and by whom their lives are in some measure affected are to be expected'.[23] He notes a few English parallels such as 'A cat may look at a king'. He holds, like Golka, that the majority of royal proverbs do not imply that the speaker was closely associated with the king and finds it quite plausible that ordinary people should give expression in their proverbs to their views of their leaders and their own relationship to them. He sees the 'royal court' theory as too dependent upon presuppositions derived from non-biblical sources and not supported by the internal evidence itself. Interestingly, he notes that not even all Egyptian proverbs concerning kings have court connections, in particular the late Demotic instructions.

Whybray does a thorough survey of the proverbs about kings under the following thematic classifications: first, 'proverbs that attribute

---

21. Golka, *The Leopard's Spots*, p. 27.
22. Against Humphreys, who argues that the king-sayings shaped the sections in which they are found. Weeks also expresses caution about this method.
23. Whybray, *Wealth and Poverty*, p. 47.

absolute power to kings or rulers', secondly, 'proverbs that uncritically attribute righteousness and justice to kings', and thirdly, 'proverbs that regard the power or success of rulers as limited in various ways and/or condemn those rulers who do not recognize or who exceed these limits'.[24] This is unusual amongst the scholars I have been considering who have been more concerned with context than with themes. I wish to reiterate this as an area of concern which I believe cannot be divorced from contextual questions but bears on them in a significant way. I suggest that we need to ask three questions. The first is how far these sayings are specific to a royal context or whether they are simply reflections on wider wisdom principles, the king being used in an exemplary role. Secondly, how specifically do these maxims treat the role of the king? Are they rather about issues such as justice and power on a broader scale? Whybray draws out justice and power themes in his categories but restricts them to the 'kingship' role. Are they to be seen as more far-reaching than that? Thirdly, what is the relationship between the human institution of kingship and God as ultimate authority?

I shall now run through those maxims in which a king is specifically mentioned. In the section Proverbs 10–15 there are only two references to a king. The first is 14.28, 'In a multitude of people is the glory of a king, but without people a prince is ruined'. Humphreys classes this as a general observation that can be seen to be making a comment about societal structures rather than belonging to a court setting.[25] Golka remarks that the people are probably the speakers here and detects a note of criticism. My own reading, based on the questions I have formulated, sees this as a reflection on the two-way nature of relationships such as we find elsewhere in wisdom. I am thinking in particular of the human need for God and the divine need of God to reveal himself to humans found in the motif of the figure of Wisdom in Proverbs. Kings therefore need many subjects as much as those subjects need a king, whether the reason be economic, political or religious. There is an issue of power here, too—the king is nobody without subjects. In the same way, it can be inferred, God needs his people. This maxim thus illustrates a wider principle than just reflecting on the king's role, although it does state a truth in reference to that.

24. Whybray, *Wealth and Poverty*, p. 48.

25. See also C.H. Toy, *A Critical and Exegetical Commentary on the Book of Proverbs* (ICC; Edinburgh: T. & T. Clark, 1899), who suggested it was a political observation referring to industrial activity and international wars.

Humphreys puts more emphasis on 14.35, 'A servant who deals wisely has the king's favour, but his wrath falls on one who acts shamefully', observing that this seems to speak of the courtier, and Weeks also sees this saying as consistent with a court origin. However, Golka argues that it is quite possible for an ordinary person to have experienced this. Whybray supports this indirectly in noting that most scholars take this saying (along with 16.14, 15, 19.12, 20.2) as a warning to courtiers to avoid angering the king on the assumption that the word *'ebed* in association with *melek* denotes a royal official or minister of state. He writes, 'However, *'ebed* has a very wide range of meanings, and in fact any or all of the king's subjects can be described as his "servants"'.[26] A more general context is not therefore out of the question for this proverb. On a thematic level this proverb could be read as simply advocating the benefits of wise behaviour in general— the king as the highest arbiter of justice is the model for such a maxim. The king could very easily be replaced with God here.

Proverbs 16.10–22.16 provides more scope. Humphreys writes of the king-sayings in chs. 16 and 20–21: 'These reflect the situation of one who might experience the wrath or favor of a ruler, one whose life is devoted to royal service and whose existence is bound intimately to royal favor'.[27] Golka, on the other hand, sees this section as showing the perspective of ordinary people who call upon God for protection from royal arbitrariness. He finds the originators of these sayings to be farmers and petty bourgeois rather than diplomats or civil servants. So we find in 16.10: 'Inspired decisions are on the lips of a king; his mouth does not sin in judgment'.[28] Humphreys considers this a judgment from those 'in the know'. Golka finds African parallels which suggest that this kind of comment represents the opinion of 'little people'. Fox attacks Golka's view, maintaining that this verse represents pure courtly flattery.[29] Whybray, more convincingly, classifies this as a proverb showing 'simple faith in royal justice'.[30] It is interesting that the divine

26. Whybray, *Wealth and Poverty*, p. 49.
27. Humphreys, 'Motif', p. 180.
28. Debate centres on the meaning of *qesem*, literally 'divination', possibly 'an oracle'. Whybray finds a similar pronouncement by the wise woman of Tekoa in 2 Sam. 14.20, in which the king's wisdom is likened to the wisdom of divine beings, and at the end of Solomon's judgment in I Kgs 3.16-28, in which the wisdom of God gives the king the ability to judge justly.
29. Fox, 'Social Location', p. 235.
30. Whybray, *Wealth and Poverty*, p. 51. He also finds the same view of the

dimension is contained in the word *qesem*; it is not merely a matter of having faith in the justice of the king, but rather the king is uttering the divine word, acting as the upholder of God's justice on earth. There is an interesting juxtaposition too with a Yahweh proverb in 16.11, which is the only proverb in this small section 16.10-15 that does not mention a human king. A deliberate divine emphasis is perhaps to be inferred.

In 16.12 we find the comment that 'It is an abomination to kings to do evil, for the throne is established by righteousness'. Commentators are divided on the question of whether this verse speaks of the evil of others that the king should abominate, or whether it is in fact a reference to evil done by the king. Whybray takes it as the latter, as does Golka on the basis of African parallels that see the king as the fountainhead of the health of the people. Humphreys presupposes the former. Whichever is chosen, the proverb can still be taken as a general maxim and a court setting need not be presupposed. According to the principles of wisdom it is up to all to avoid evil. For kings, however, it is that much more difficult because they are taking on the divine role of upholders of justice.

In 16.13 we read, 'Righteous lips are the delight of a king, and he loves him who speaks what is right'. This saying is for Whybray another proverb expressing simple faith in royal justice, and for Golka it reflects the experience of the 'little people' dealing with those 'up there', thus reiterating the motif of the king as upholder of rightness. For Fox it 'is relevant only to someone who might experience the king's anger firsthand and attempt to assuage it'.[31] Whybray sees 16.14 as a proverb that envisages the king as absolute monarch in its concern with the wrath or favour of the king: 'A king's wrath is a messenger of death, and a wise man will appease it'. He argues that this seeming attribution of arbitrary powers to the king might suggest an origin in 'the rather naive minds of persons who had no first-hand knowledge of the reality of Israelite kingship',[32] for there is nothing elsewhere in the

king's justice elsewhere in the Old Testament, notably in some Psalms and in Isaiah, and writes, 'No doubt few of his subjects had access to the king when he sat as judge or at any other time; the rest had no opportunity to assess his personal qualities at first hand. Such personal acquaintance is not what lies behind these proverbs. Rather, they express the confidence of ordinary people in the king as the supreme guarantor under God of the soundness of the judicial system' (pp. 51-52).

31. Fox, 'Social Location', p. 235.
32. Whybray, *Wealth and Poverty*, p. 50.

Old Testament to indicate that the king's power was unlimited and in fact the king is often kept in his place. However, I do not find this meaning inherent here. Rather, I believe it is simply expressing the fact that because the king has power, when he is angry he has the means to punish in any way he sees fit. This is not necessarily out of step with the rather ideal portrayal of the king's role that is found elsewhere, nor is it without more general application to all with power over others. The 'wise man' here may be the courtier who would have more experience of his anger than others, but it could simply apply to anybody in contact with an angry person with power—try to steer clear of him until the anger cools down. Golka again finds African parallels which suggest that such observations can and were made by ordinary people of the king. Whilst this may be so, there is also a wider principle to be gleaned here.[33] In 16.15 we have the converse of v. 14, 'In the light of a king's face there is life, and his favour is like the clouds that bring the spring rain'. Whybray notes that '16.15 does not necessarily imply a face-to-face acquaintance with the king: it is a general statement about the king as the source of the prosperity of his subjects'[34] He places the maxim in his 'king as absolute monarch' section and notes that this is about the king being an arbiter of fate rather than about any moral qualities of the king being discussed. In my view this maxim is about power: the favour of the king is in another league from that of ordinary humans, but for a theological reason—he represents the meeting place of the human with the divine. The language of metaphor is used, typical of the wisdom literature, to express the high status of the king. This proverb can almost be seen as a personification of the king in terms usually referred to the figure of Wisdom and choosing the path to life through her.

I now move on to 20.8, 'A king who sits on the throne of judgment winnows all evil with his eyes', and to 20.26, 'A wise king winnows the wicked, and drives the wheel over them'.[35] These are both in

---

33. The same comments that were made on 16.14 about the king's wrath are relevant to 19.12, 'A king's wrath is like the growling of a lion, but his favour is like dew upon the grass', and to 20.2, 'The dread wrath of a king is like the growling of a lion; he who provokes him to anger forfeits his life'.

34. Whybray, *Wealth and Poverty*, p. 49.

35. Either a wheel of fortune or more likely an agricultural wheel (so D. Winton Thomas, 'Proverbs 20:26', *JJS* 15 [1964], pp. 155-56)—maybe even some kind of punishment.

Whybray's category of proverbs that express simple faith in royal justice in their reference to the king's function as judge (cf. on 16.10). Clearly it is up to the wisdom of the king to ensure that the wicked are punished. It is again a picture of an ideal king, as found, for example, in Isa. 16.5. In such an ideal is contained the wider principle of justice and the moral character that is essential to wisdom so that from the king down this is the behaviour that wisdom advocates. Whybray also puts into this same category Prov. 20.28, 'Loyalty and faithfulness preserve the king, and his throne is upheld by righteousness' (cf. on 16.13). Golka finds a popular origin for both, seeing in 20.28 overtones of a warning to the king by the people, but I do not myself find this overtone here. Clearly the justice issue is predominant, and once again the king's role on behalf of the divine as upholder of righteousness is at the centre of concern.

Humphreys airs the suggestion made by Gese[36] that in the king-sayings in this section the term *melek* could be replaced with Yahweh, since there is a good deal of mixing of king-sayings with Yahweh, especially in the sayings in chs. 16 and 20–21. But he is concerned, following Skladny,[37] to stress the difference between the level of divinity of the king and God. Whilst these sayings show the divine aspect of the king's role and its God-given authority, he argues that proverbs such as those found in 21.1 and 21.30-31 keep the king in his place. These proverbs, it seems to me, do stress Yahweh's ultimate control but they are very general, only the first being a king-saying, and they do not put the king down at all: 'The king's heart is a stream of water in the hand of the Lord; he turns it wherever he will' (Prov. 21.1), and 'No wisdom, no understanding, no counsel, can avail against the Lord. The horse is made ready for the day of battle, but the victory belongs to the Lord' (Prov. 21.30-31). In my view this section demonstrates the closeness of role between the king and God, as 16.10-15 did, and I find myself attracted by Gese's view. Humphreys, however, leaps from this observation to the conclusion that the real angle being given here on the presentation of the ruler is that of the courtier who would praise the king to the skies and not view him critically. He writes of the structuring of this section: 'the significant placement of the combined

36. H. Gese, *Lehre und Wirklichkeit in der alten Weisheit* (Tübingen: J.C.B. Mohr [Paul Siebeck], 1958).

37. U. Skladny, *Die ältesten Spruchsammlungen in Israel* (Göttingen: Vandenhoeck & Ruprecht, 1961).

Yahweh- and king-sayings at the head and toward the end of the collection suggests that it received its shape from the hands of those concerned with the training of future courtiers'.[38] I myself do not see how he reaches this conclusion from the evidence he has presented.

This brings us on to consider 21.1, which refers to the dependence of the king on divine control. Whybray includes it in his 'royal justice' section, but as a proverb that goes beyond simple affirmation of the king's justice to confirm such affirmation by stressing the God-given nature of it. He reads it very much in conjunction with the following verses in Prov. 21.2-3, which contrast evaluation of human behaviour with what is acceptable to God. Golka cites McKane, who saw this proverb as critical of the civil service, that is to say, the king does not depend on his courtiers for guidance, he depends on Yahweh. Golka sees this as strengthening his case that the speakers are the people rather than courtiers. Whybray too sees no reason to suppose that such a proverb arose at the royal court. Weeks notes the variety of interpretations of this verse, citing McKane and also Skladny, who saw it as an assertion of the distance between even the mightiest of men and God. My view is that it expresses the closeness of the two rather than the distance. Finally in this section there is Prov. 22.11, 'He who loves purity of heart, and whose speech is gracious, will have the king as his friend', a proverb that Whybray considers so corrupt that its evidence cannot really be used to prove anything about the milieu in which the proverb originated. It is clearly a general maxim, the example of the king being used to stress the ultimate sanction for goodness, similar to 16.13.

The third section to consider is Prov. 22.17–24.34. Humphreys airs afresh the links of this section with the Instruction of Amenemope. He likens Prov. 22.29 in particular to Amenemope ch. 30. Proverbs reads, 'Do you see a man skilful in his work? He will stand before kings; he will not stand before obscure men', whilst Amenemope states, 'As to a scribe who is experienced in his position, he will find himself worthy of being a courtier'. Whybray expresses reservations about this parallel. He interprets *māhîr* as referring not to a scribe or official but rather takes it in a general sense to mean a man who is efficient in his business, and he notes that 'kings' in the plural is an indication of a general proposition. He thinks it possible that the author had the scribal profession in mind but that this does not mean that the author himself was a

---

38. Humphreys, 'Motif', p. 183.

scribe. There could be a contextual link with scribes, but it might simply be a general comment on the value of skilled work—it could mean simply that it is enjoyed in high places or it might suggest that skilful workmanship will be acknowledged by rulers and reward given. Alternatively it could simply be a statement of the possibilities of human achievement. In my view, the stress on the Amenemope parallel has led to overcontextualization of this verse.[39]

The next king-saying is in Prov. 24.21-22, 'My son, fear the Lord and the king, and do not disobey either of them; for disaster from them will rise suddenly, and who knows the ruin that will come from them both?'[40] Whichever translation one follows, the gist of the maxim seems to stress obedience to those in power—to God as supreme authority and to the king as temporal authority. Here there is a striking parallel use of God and king in which the two terms virtually perform the same role. Again Humphreys states, 'the perspective here seems to be that of the courtier', and when he goes on to characterize the structure of the section he argues that these sayings that were influenced by the Instruction of Amenemope show traces of the wise courtier motif but 'have here been extended in application to apply to a broader group than those who might actually stand before kings'.[41] In his final proviso Humphreys shows, I think, that he himself is not entirely convinced by his own conclusions. Whybray sees these verses as obscure but argues that given the uncertainty of the meaning of *śônîm*, no conclusions about the social status of the author can be drawn from these verses. He puts more emphasis on 23.1, which he sees as reflecting the social status of the author of this section, whom he takes to be a literate person but not necessarily a scribe, a city-dweller of good rank in society but not one of the upper class.

In Proverbs 25–27 there are two sayings aligning the king and God; in fact 25.2-6 forms another section comparable to 16.10-15. At 25.2, 'It is the glory of God to conceal things, but the glory of kings is to

---

39. R.N. Whybray, 'The Structure and Composition of Proverbs 22:17–24:22', in S.E. Porter, P.M. Joyce and D.E. Orton (eds.), *Crossing the Boundaries: Essays in Biblical Interpretation in Honour of Michael D. Goulder* (Leiden: E.J. Brill, 1994), pp. 83-96.

40. Debate centres on the reference of *śônîm* (usually 'noblemen'). AV and RV translate 'meddle not with them that are given to change'; NIV, 'do not join with the rebellious'.

41. Humphreys, 'Motif', p. 184.

search things out'. Again, we find the king and God mentioned in the same verse, but here a comparison is being made. Toy[42] finds a difference between the role of God in nature and history, which is inscrutable, and the function of kings which is to be straightforward in government. However, the reference may well be less specific: we could well liken this comparison to divine and human wisdom and their respective roles. The king embodies that tension in his person since he is a manifestation of the divine to humans and yet he has human limitations. This tension lies at the heart of the wisdom literature. Skladny saw this verse as relating to the king's role as judge, which Golka comments would be a role in which ordinary people would relate to him. Proverbs 25.3 reads, 'As the heavens for height, and the earth for depth, so the mind of kings is unsearchable'. According to Skladny this proverb gives the reason for respect before the king, and Golka again sees this as having a popular origin. This verse very explicitly links the king with the divine creative order and is an indication of the link between human and divine made in v. 2. This is followed by two sayings on the position of the king: 'Take away the dross from the silver, and the smith has material for a vessel; take away the wicked from the presence of the king, and his throne will be established in righteousness. Do not put yourself forward in the king's presence or stand in the place of the great; for it is better to be told, "Come up here", than to be put lower in the presence of the prince' (Prov. 25.6-7). A situation of a royal feast seems to provide the immediate context but again there is a wider principle. Humphreys concludes that the primary addressee is the courtier here and he finds other themes reminiscent of Egyptian courtiers in the section. G.E. Bryce[43] has suggested that in 25.2-7 we have a set of instructions addressed to future courtiers for educational purposes and, not surprisingly, Humphreys finds this argument attractive. This section would then have been incorporated into a larger and more varied collection, perhaps by the men of Hezekiah (25.1). Whybray raises strong doubt about the theory that 25.6-7 in particular is addressed to the ambitious courtier. As Plöger[44] has

42. Toy, *Proverbs*.

43. G.E. Bryce, 'Another Wisdom-"Book" in Proverbs', *JBL* 9 (1972), pp. 145-57.

44. O. Plöger, 'Zur Auslegung der Sentenzensammlungen des Proverbienbuches', in H.W. Wolff (ed.), *Probleme Biblischer Theologie: Gerhard von Rad zum 70 Geburtstag* (Munich: Chr. Kaiser Verlag, 1971), pp. 402-16.

pointed out, this advice has a broader application to anyone with social pretensions. Whybray does not believe that $g^e dōlîm$ and $nādîb$ denote particular ranks at court. He writes, 'There is, then, nothing improbable in the view that Prov. 25.6-7 is a general admonition which does not necessarily imply a connection with a royal court'.[45] Golka agrees, again citing Skladny, who wrote, 'In Collection C (Prov. 25-27) the king is regarded with great respect, but from the perspective of someone who does not belong to his company'.[46] However, Skladny maintains that this is an adaptation of court wisdom to the world of ordinary people and Fox argues for a context for this in administrative hierarchy on the grounds that it resembles the numerous counsels of etiquette found in Egyptian wisdom.[47] However, it may be that it is just as plausibly an adaptation of an ordinary saying to a court setting rather than having its origins in administration.

The final section in Proverbs 10–29 is in chs. 28–29, in which there are a number of king-sayings (28.15, 16, 29.4, 14). These sayings are concerned about justice and the lack of it from a wicked ruler. Humphreys admits that the motif of the wise courtier is not explicitly found in this section. Proverbs 29.4 reads, 'By justice a king gives stability to the land, but one who exacts gifts ruins it'. Golka remarks, 'A deeply felt sigh of the ordinary people, perhaps against Solomon's taxation?'[48] Whybray comments that the meaning of this verse is disputed but 'it is probably an attack on ruinous taxation or, possibly, on the acceptance of bribes by the king',[49] and so it comes under his 'sayings critical towards kings' category. It could, however, be a wider comment on the centrality of justice and of the possible abuse of power. Again in 29.14, 'If a king judges the poor with equity his throne will be established for ever', the ideal of justice is expressed—the king has a moral responsibility, backed by divine blessing. Whybray sees this maxim as laying down conditions for the stability of the throne: it has to be based on justice.

45. Whybray, *Wealth and Poverty*, p. 55.

46. Skladny, *Die ältesten Spruchsammlungen*, p. 54 (Golka's translation).

47. Fox, 'Social Location', p. 235. This is perhaps Fox's strongest example and, in my view, not enough evidence on which to construct a demolition of the folk wisdom hypothesis. Fox sees the court as the decisive locus of creativity. He writes, 'Everything we have was channelled to the court and through it; the flow cannot be supposed to move in the other direction' (p. 236).

48. Golka, *The Leopard's Spots*, p. 33.

49. Whybray, *Wealth and Poverty*, p. 53.

Humphreys reaches the end of his analysis of king-sayings at ch. 29 but Whybray goes on to consider an extra category of king-sayings in Proverbs 30. In 30.27-28, 31 we find animal imagery brought into relation with the activities of kings, 'The locusts have no king, yet all of them march in rank; the lizard you can take in your hands, yet it is in kings' palaces...the strutting cock, the he-goat, and a king striding before his people'. Whybray writes,

> These proverbs show how the idea of kings and their characteristics was so prominent in the Israelite mind that it sprang easily to mind when comparisons between ordinary phenomena were made... These proverbs reflect a picture of kings and their surroundings in the minds of ordinary people who really knew little or nothing of royal courts. A similar process of thought may easily have given rise to such sayings as Prov. 25.6-7.[50]

The pride, dignity and authority of the king all come across in these images.

In Prov. 31.1-9 there is an instruction addressed to a young and inexperienced king, Lemuel of Massa. Its origin is unknown but it may be from outside Israel. The instruction is from the queen mother teaching her son the behaviour expected from kings and the duties performed by them. This is very different from the Egyptian instructions in which the father of the pupil is the teacher. There is a strong concern in this section with the poor and with the role of the king in upholding justice. There are warnings against women and against drunkenness. This section would seem to me to provide the strongest argument for a court setting for a part of the book of Proverbs and yet this evidence is rarely discussed. Why is the material here in Proverbs? Is it to increase the fiction that this wisdom was from a royal context after all? If so, why choose such an obscure character to whom to attribute the material? Is it an appendix or later addition to be discounted? Or is it the expression of an ideal in which all can participate, whether they are kings or not? Has it emerged after the exile as part of the recontextualization of Proverbs? An older view was that after the exile kings were more accessible to people and therefore of more interest. The questions are manifold and answers scarce, but it is an intriguing passage.

In his conclusions on Proverbs 10–29 Humphreys notes that the motif of the wise courtier plays a limited role in these chapters, with it dominating only in Prov. 16.1–22.16 and 25.2-37. The hints he has

---

50. Whybray, *Wealth and Poverty* , p. 56.

found in some sections, such as 22.17–24.22, he regards as a residue in materials now addressed to a more general audience. From this he argues that originally the motif was more important, but little has survived.

> There may have been specific centers for training of courtiers—and possibly royal sons as well (2 Kgs 10:1-11)—and probably Proverbs 16:1–22:16 and 25:2-27 were shaped for them. But the probability must be considered that circles other than a court educational center played formative roles in the middle stages of the development of the book.[51]

He also argues that the motif was of necessity less prominent in Israelite culture because the king and God were not so closely identified as in Egypt and hence there was a potential clash of allegiance for the courtier who was a Yahwist. He sees the freedom of Yahweh motif as a stumbling-block to the idea of the king as upholder of the divine order and hence to a theological understanding of the relationship between God and human beings. He writes, 'In this setting the theological and ethical potential of the motif of the wise courtier was decidedly restricted'.[52] I wish to take issue with this point on the limited extent of the relationship between God and king; on the contrary, I have attempted to show how synonymous the roles of God and king often are and do not see the God-given nature of the kingly role as clashing with other elements of divine activity. I suggest that the wise courtier motif has its limitations precisely because not enough notice is being taken in scholarly analysis of the broader ethical and theological contexts. The use of the king motif to illustrate wider wisdom maxims and the centrality of God in the picture of the ideal king militate against such a narrow context.

The King in Ecclesiastes

Before reaching my own conclusions, however, I wish very briefly to treat the book of Ecclesiastes, in which sayings that include reference to the king are few and are generally of the same kind as we found in Proverbs. We find our first mention, after the attribution, in 2.12, 'So I turned to consider wisdom and madness and folly; for what can the man do who comes after the king? Only what he has already done. Then I saw that wisdom excels folly as light excels darkness.' This

51. Humphreys, 'Motif', p. 187.
52. Humphreys, 'Motif', p. 188.

forms part of the Solomonic fiction and yet it appears to be a more general reference. The wider context is a discussion of the benefit of wisdom over folly but there is an overtone of 'nothing new under the sun' in the thought that there is a limit to what a man can achieve. The king is here mentioned again as a kind of figurehead or pinnacle of achievement: 'when you have been a successful king, what more is there to achieve?' is the sense that I get from this verse, although its meaning is somewhat obscure. The second king-saying is in 4.13-14, 'Better is a poor and wise youth than an old and foolish king, who will no longer take advice, even though he had gone from prison to the throne or in his own kingdom had been born poor'. Even if it once had a historical reference to the Ptolemies,[53] it is clearly being used in this context as an example story, a moral tale with universal application. It represents a reversal of traditional values in which old age and wisdom tend to be synonymous and in which the old are venerated in society. However, it is consistent with Qoheleth's own thoughts on old age as these become apparent at the end of the book in 12.1-8 in the poem on old age. It does, however, make the more general point that is found in other wisdom that the hardening of ideas is a bad thing and that wisdom is to be valued above all else.

The third maxim is in 5.8-9, 'If you see in a province the poor oppressed and justice and right violently taken away, do not be amazed at the matter; for the high official is watched by a higher, and there are yet higher ones over them. But, in all, a king is an advantage to a land with cultivated fields.'[54] This represents a clear airing of the justice issue: there is often apparent injustice, sometimes even perpetuated from the top, but on balance having a king who at least pertains to some form of justice is better than not having a final court of appeal at all. Another maxim regarding the king is found in 8.2-4:

> Keep the king's command, and because of your sacred oath be not dismayed; go from his presence, do not delay when the matter is unpleasant, for he does whatever he pleases. For the word of the king is supreme, and who may say to him, 'What are you doing?'

53. G.A. Barton, *A Critical and Exegetical Commentary on the Book of Ecclesiastes* (ICC; Edinburgh: T. & T. Clark, 1912).

54. Verse 9 presents translational difficulties; cf. NIV translation, 'The increase from the land is taken by all; the king himself profits from the fields', which changes the sense completely.

It has been suggested that 'king' here may mean no more than provincial governor or that such sayings about the king may be simply following a literary convention, rather than expressing deeply held truths. I find both these views unconvincing; for a start the sacred oath referred to could well be a coronation oath. The issue here is power and there is a strong overtone of the absoluteness of the king's power, maybe because he gets his authority from Yahweh. Again, the two-sided nature of power is presented: power corrupts as well as upholds and it is the duty of the king as the leader of his people and representative of God to use his power wisely.

In 9.14-16 there is another moral tale:

> There was a little city with few men in it; and a great king came against it and besieged it, building great siegeworks against it. But there was found in it a poor wise man, and he by his wisdom delivered the city. Yet no one remembered that poor man. But I say that wisdom is better than might, though the poor man's wisdom is despised, and his words are not heeded.

Again, wisdom is upheld above everything, even above the apparent might of kings. Any powerful monarch could be meant here and suggestions have been made from King David to Persian kings, but the reference need not be seen as specific. Finally, in 10.16-17, 20, 'Woe to you, O land, when your king is a child, and your princes feast in the morning! Happy are you, O land, when your king is the son of free men, and your princes feast at the proper time, for strength, and not for drunkenness!... Even in your thought, do not curse the king....' There have been suggestions of a particular historical reference intended here, perhaps to the Ptolemies.[55] However, it is usually taken in a more general sense. The maxim appears to speak out against hereditary kingship, according to which system a child-king may well be installed as king with no real power of his own. Over that is to be preferred a strong king, freely chosen. It seems to be a question of power being a necessity for an effective king. It suggests that the life of those around the king is affected by the quality of behaviour coming from the centre—here the warning is against the drunkenness of princes rather than of the king (as found in Prov. 31.5-7). There could be a hint of a court setting here in that it would be likely to be those near the king who would be

---

55. For example, Ptolemy V Epiphanes, who came to the throne of Egypt in 205 BCE aged five years.

fraternizing with him in this way. The power of the king comes across in the idea that one should never curse him, even in one's thoughts; again a divine element to his authority might be posited here. The underlying agenda here seems to be prudent, wise behaviour over imprudence and foolishness, namely, that which characterizes the wisdom quest overall.

Conclusion

So where does this survey leave us? Let us look back at Whybray's three thematic categories: the king as absolute monarch, uncritical attribution of righteousness and justice to kings, and criticisms of rulers. My proviso on the first category would be that there is no absolute power to monarchs, since all are subject to God and to the principles of justice and righteousness on which their leadership is founded. The uncritical attribution of righteousness and justice to kings is part of an ideal picture that serves to stress the close link between human and divine authority. However, there is also the issue of power: many proverbs concern the wise use of power and in reference to the monarch this is even more important. This motif is not so much criticism of the king as realization of the importance of the maintenance of the ideal. Contrasts are made in usual wisdom style to show that kings are not infallible and often fail to satisfy the ideal. I have tried in my own comments to draw out the relationship of these maxims to the wisdom quest in general and find myself leaning towards the view that in contextual terms a court setting need not be posited. I have also, however, tried to show the essential theological connections of these sayings— the king is primarily in the role of maintainer of justice, the ultimate human court of appeal before God himself. He has God-given power to effect good, power which can, if used wrongly, corrupt himself and others. He is the ultimate human authority and yet his power is divinely legitimated. He is in fact upholding the divine order and his role is God-given. He is therefore part of the manifestation of God to humanity, standing at the crossroads of the human and the divine much as, elsewhere in the wisdom literature, divine Wisdom herself mediates between the human and the divine. I see this theological tension as characterizing the wisdom quest, even in its seemingly more secular concerns, and find evidence of it in these sayings about the king. As for the context, I see no reason why the picture of an ideal king and the use of kings as examples of wise behaviour might not be one of wisdom's earliest concerns, from the time of the kings themselves perhaps. However, there has clearly been an important theological context given to these sayings, maybe later as part of a recontextualization process at the time of Hezekiah, maybe as part of their original formulation. Certainly in their latest context when the attributions were added there was an attempt to give the books the highest human authority and to secure their authority within the canon of Scripture as part of the divine revelation to humankind.

KINGSHIP AS PRIESTHOOD: THE RELATIONSHIP BETWEEN THE HIGH PRIESTHOOD AND THE MONARCHY

Deborah W. Rooke

The idea of the Israelite monarchy as an example of sacral kingship has become an accepted piece of received scholarly wisdom; and of course one of the characteristics of sacral kingship is that it bestows upon its office-holders a priestly role. That this was as true of the Israelite monarchy as it was of other ancient Near Eastern dynasties is evidenced in a number of biblical sources, and not even the proverbial Deuteronomistic ambivalence about the institution of monarchy disguises the unmistakably cultic duties undertaken by the kings themselves (2 Sam. 6; 1 Kgs 8, 12; 2 Kgs 16). However, this raises the question of the relationship between the role of the monarch and that of the high priest, indeed, that of the priesthood in general. Was there something distinctive about the royal priesthood which set it apart from 'ordinary' priesthood, and if so, what? This paper is by way of a comment on the relationship between monarchy and priesthood which, it is hoped, will offer some elucidation of their respective roles. The paper contains three sections: 1. The Monarch and the Chief Priest in the Pre-exilic Period; 2. The High Priest in the Post-exilic Period; 3. Kingship and Priesthood in the Hasmonaean Period.

1. *The Monarch and the Chief Priest in the Pre-exilic Period*

It is probably fair to say that the most explicit reference to the monarch's priestly prerogatives is that of Ps. 110:4:

> The Lord has sworn and will not change his mind,
> 'You are a priest for ever, after the order of Melchizedek'.[1]

Of course, the psalm has not always been viewed as referring unequivocally to the monarch. It is well known that scholarship in the early

---

1.   See the discussion below on the translation of this phrase.

years of this century applied the whole psalm to Simon the Maccabee
on the basis of both its content and the acrostic 'Simon' or 'Simon is
terrible', which was supposedly identifiable in the two stanzas of the
psalm.[2] However, largely since the acceptance of a theory of sacral
kingship for Israel, the concept of Maccabaean dating for the psalm has
fallen widely into disfavour, and the overwhelming majority of scholars
now accept that Psalm 110 is a royal psalm, specifically a coronation
psalm, dating most probably from the early monarchic period.[3] In support of the royal interpretation, it may be noted that the psalm clearly
addresses a royal figure to whom priestly prerogatives are subsequently
granted by divine oath, and not a priestly figure who is being granted
some kind of kingly rule. In addition, it uses as an analogy the figure
of Melchizedek, who in his only other appearance in the Hebrew
Scriptures (Gen. 14.18-20) is introduced as a king who is also a priest.
This implies that for the addressee of the psalm, as for Melchizedek, the
priesthood is a function of the kingship rather than the ruling power
being a function of the priesthood, so that the one to whom the psalm is
addressed is first and foremost a king.[4]

On the assumption, then, that the psalm does address a king and confirms or bestows upon him priestly prerogatives, the question is whether
his priesthood differs essentially from that of the non-royal priests who
surround him. In order to answer that question, it is necessary to
examine the basis on which both royal and non-royal figures claim the
right to priesthood, and indeed what the nature of priesthood itself is
conceived to be. Priesthood is the responsibility of acting as a mediator
between the human and the divine within a given context of ritual, and

---

2.   For a more recent example of this approach, see M. Treves, 'Two Acrostic
Psalms', *VT* 15 (1965), pp. 81-90 (86), and *The Dates of the Psalms: History and
Poetry in Ancient Israel* (Pisa: Giardini Editori E Stampatori, 1988), pp. 84-85.

3.   Exceptions to this general pattern include Treves; S. Schreiner, 'Psalm cx
und die Investitur des Hohenpriesters', *VT* 27 (1977), pp. 216-22; G. Gerleman,
'Psalm cx', *VT* 31 (1981), pp. 1-19; and M.C. Astour, 'Melchizedek', in *ABD*, IV,
pp. 684-86. Of these scholars, Schreiner regards the psalm as applying to Joshua
the high priest of the Restoration period, while the other three all consider it to
apply to Simon Maccabee. Treves's view of Psalm 110 is part of his general conviction that all the psalms except for two or three are to be dated to the period 170–
103 BCE (*Dates of the Psalms*, p. 9).

4.   Cf. F.M. Cross, *Canaanite Myth and Hebrew Epic* (Cambridge, MA:
Harvard University Press, 1973), p. 211 n. 60: 'Both Genesis 14 and Psalm 110 are
rooted in the royal ideology not in the priestly'.

it appears in the biblical records with two main characteristics. The first is its functional nature: priesthood is primarily about *doing* things, about carrying out rituals and procedures, rather than about *being* a particular kind of person or having a particular genealogical descent. This seems to be supported by the very form of the word *kōhēn*; although the corresponding verb meaning 'to serve as a priest' is only attested in the piel, *kihēn*, and is classified in BDB as a denominative formation from *kōhēn*,[5] the noun *kōhēn* itself has the form of a qal participle, thereby implying that the *kōhēn* is the one who carries out the action of the verbal root behind the participial noun. Noth remarks,

> The more ancient Old Testament tradition never once recognizes a special act in the conferring of the priestly office, for the traditional expression used [in the Old Testament]...as a technical term for the appointment of a priest obviously does not signify a consecrating act.[6]

In this way, Noth argues, the priest is to be distinguished from both the prophet and the king, for whom divine election and endowment with the Spirit are necessary prerequisites for the performance of their tasks.[7] Something of the functional nature of priesthood can also be gleaned from the description of the eighty-five priests of Nob slain by Doeg the Edomite at Saul's command (1 Sam. 22.18). The priests are described as *nōśē' 'ēpôd bād*, a phrase rendered by a number of Versions, such as the RSV and NRSV, as 'who wore the linen ephod'. However, if the phrase is treated in line with the LXX so that the term *bād* is dropped as a gloss and the verb *nāśā'* is rendered not as 'wear', but as 'bear', which is its usual translation when used of the ephod,[8] the emphasis is

---

5. BDB, p. 464 col. 2.

6. M. Noth, 'Amt und Berufung im Alten Testament (Rektoratsrede an der Rheinischen Friedrich-Wilhelms-Universität zu Bonn 1958)', in *Gesammelte Studien zum Alten Testament* (Munich: Chr. Kaiser Verlag, 3rd enlarged edn, 1966), pp. 309-33 (311) (ET 'Office and Vocation in the Old Testament', in *The Laws in the Pentateuch and Other Studies* [trans. D.R. Ap-Thomas; Edinburgh: Oliver & Boyd, 1966; repr. London: SCM Press, 1984], pp. 229-49 [231]). So also R. de Vaux, *Les Institutions de l'Ancien Testament*, II (Paris: Cerf, 1960), pp. 196-98 (ET *Ancient Israel: Its Life and Institutions* [trans. by John McHugh; New York: McGraw–Hill, 1961], pp. 346-47); A. Cody, *A History of Old Testament Priesthood* (AnBib, 35; Rome: Pontifical Biblical Institute, 1969), p. 59. The expression in question is *millē' yad*, literally, 'fill the hand'.

7. Noth, 'Amt', pp. 322-31 (ET 'Office', pp. 240-47).

8. See G.B. Caird, 'The First and Second Books of Samuel', in *IB*, II, pp. 853-

shifted from a descriptive to a functional definition of the priests as 'bearing the ephod'—in other words, they are defined by what they do, which is ephod-bearing and presumably consulting, not by what they look like.

An additional indicator of the priesthood's fundamentally functional nature is that it initially appears as something which can be undertaken by anyone,[9] although there always seem to have been preferred specialists in the shape of the Levites. Thus, Micah the Ephraimite employs one of his own sons as a priest for the personal shrine that he constructs in his house (Judg. 17.1-5), although he is very happy to replace his son with a passing Levite and considers it in his interest to have done so (Judg. 17.7-13). Other examples of non-Levitical priests are David's sons (2 Sam. 8.18) and Ira the Jairite (2 Sam. 20.26);[10] and of course as part of his sin Jeroboam is said to have appointed non-Levitical priests to serve both at the 'houses on high places' which he built (1 Kgs 12.31; cf. 2 Chron. 13.9) and at the royal shrine of Bethel (1 Kgs 12.32). Bearing in mind the obviously polemical nature of the whole Jeroboam episode as it is related in 1 Kings, the rather scathing

---

1176 (890); Cody, *Priesthood*, p. 75; P.R. Davies, 'Ark or Ephod in I Sam XIV.18?', *JTS* NS 26 (1975), pp. 82-87 (85-86).

9. Noth, 'Amt', p. 310 (ET 'Office', p. 230).

10. The question as to whether these individuals were strictly speaking priests has given rise to much discussion. See Cody, *Priesthood*, pp. 103-105; C.E. Armerding, 'Were David's Sons Really Priests?', in Gerald F. Hawthorne (ed.), *Current Issues in Biblical and Patristic Interpretation: Essays in Honor of Merrill C. Tenney* (Grand Rapids, MI: Eerdmans, 1975), pp. 75-86; G.J. Wenham, 'Were David's Sons Priests?', *ZAW* 87 (1975), pp. 79-82; and M. Haran, *Temples and Temple-Service in Ancient Israel* (repr. with corrections; Winona Lake, IN: Eisenbrauns, 1985 [1978]), pp. 80-81. The suggestion rehearsed by Wenham that in 2 Sam. 8.18 *sōkᵉnîm* ('stewards') was very early on corrupted to *kōhᵃnîm* is unconvincing, not least because it is difficult to see why such a controversial reading should be adopted instead of one which may have been unfamiliar but which would certainly be less provocative theologically speaking. Equally, Haran's suggestion that David's sons and Ira acted as sacrificial priests who dealt with the king's offerings only at the high places and solitary altars contradicts his own definition of 'priest' as one who serves specifically at a temple and not at a solitary altar (pp. 16, 64). The very fact that these individuals are designated priests in a work which elsewhere shows preference for the Levitical priesthood, particularly when the later more strongly Levitical orthodoxy of the Chronicler was unable to tolerate the idea of David's sons as priests (cf. 1 Chron. 18.17), seems to be a good indication that they were indeed priests.

tone of the remark about non-Levitical priests should perhaps not be taken too seriously. Rather, it should be interpreted as Deuteronomistic disapproval of what would have been a perfectly legitimate practice at the time, in the same vein as the Deuteronomist's recurrent disapproval of the high places.[11] The absolute limitation of legitimate priestly rights to particular groups is a later development, very probably politically motivated. Doubtless, rivalries over precisely who was entitled to serve in the Jerusalemite Temple with its exalted status as national and royal shrine, and later sole legitimate site of worship, required a distinct theological justification and claim to be put forward by the appropriate parties.

This leads on to the second major characteristic of the priesthood which appears throughout the records from the earliest periods, namely, its involvement with sanctuaries.[12] Thus, the priest appointed by Micah the Ephraimite is appointed to serve in Micah's sanctuary (Judg. 17.5-12); Eli and his sons are priests at the shrine of Shiloh (1 Sam. 1.3, 9); Ahimelech is priest of Nob where there is evidently a sanctuary in which shewbread is laid out (1 Sam. 21.2-7, ET 1–6). Admittedly, not every single priest appears in direct connection with a sanctuary: Abiathar is of the priestly family at Nob, but flees from the massacre there and joins David's travelling band (1 Sam. 22.20-23; 1 Kgs 2.26). He then seems to function as a kind of roving ephod consultant for the group (1 Sam. 23.6-14). However, once David becomes established in Jerusalem Abiathar is listed as a priest along with Zadok (2 Sam. 8.17), and is shown in charge of the Ark (2 Sam. 15.24). Similarly, Ahijah son of Ahitub, son of Phinehas, son of Eli the priest at Shiloh, is a part of Saul's band in Gibeah (1 Sam. 14.3), but all that he is shown doing is consulting the oracle for Saul, and he carries out no sanctuary service. However, the comment is also made that the Ark was present with the group (1 Sam. 14.18). Hence both these 'non-sanctuary' priests function in the context of the symbol of Yahweh's presence, which is after all what a sanctuary is.

It seems, then, that the normal priesthood at its root is basically a function performed by certain members of the population on behalf of

11. Haran's argument that Levitical descent is the only legitimate priesthood recognized in any of the sources seems to arise mainly from a desire to combat Wellhausenian interpretations challenging the antiquity and purity of the Israelite tradition. See Haran, *Temples*, pp. 58-71, 76-83.

12. Cody, *Priesthood*, p. 13; Haran, *Temples*, pp. 16, 64.

the rest of the population—it is an office as opposed to a vocation.[13]
Even though the criteria of ritual purity and specific descent in time
came to limit the numbers of those who were entitled to exercise the
priestly function, and even though the precise elements involved in that
function changed over time, it was doing the job that made individuals
priests, not their descent or nature as such (cf. Lev. 21.17-23). This can
be seen from the provisions of Deuteronomy concerning the Levites. In
Deut. 18.6-7 any Levite from the provinces has the right to come to the
central shrine and minister in the name of the Lord (*w^ešērēt b^ešēm yhwh*,
18.7) like the other Levites who are (already) standing there before the
Lord (*hā'ōm^edîm šām lipnê yhwh*, 18.7). The verbs used here, *šērēt* and
'āmad, are used in 17.12 of the one specifically designated as a priest,
who is said to 'stand to minister' (*'āmad l^ešāret*), and similarly 18.5
speaks of the priests as having been chosen 'to stand to minister
(*la^{'a}mōd*) in the name of the Lord'. The use of the same two verbs in
18.7 to refer to the Levites at the central shrine implies that the Levites
already 'standing there' as well as those who 'come to minister' are
likewise thought of as being engaged in priestly duties, and are therefore effectively priests, whereas those who are not described as standing
or ministering are not priests. In addition, the inclusion of Levites with
the widows, the fatherless and the sojourner (Deut. 14.28-29, 16.11, 14,
26.12, 13) and the repeated exhortations not to neglect the Levites
(12.12, 18-19, 14.27) indicates their tenuous economic position in the
community and their usual dependence on charity rather than on the
regular income that would accrue to them from sacrificial portions if
they were actually priests.[14] Hence there is an evident distinction
between those who are in theory entitled to exercise a priestly ministry
and those who are actually exercising it, and the transition from non-
priest to priest is brought about not by any pressing divine summons
but by the desire of a person's heart (*b^ekol 'awwat napšô*, Deut. 18.6), a

---

13. L. Sabourin, *Priesthood: A Comparative Study* (Studies in the History of
Religions, 25; Leiden: E.J. Brill, 1973), p. 136. This certainly makes sense if, as is
implied by the Blessing of Moses in Deut. 33.8, the most ancient function of the
priesthood was as oracle-givers rather than altar-servers, and priestly participation
in sacrificial rituals was at one stage considerably less important than it later
became. The skill of manipulating the oracle could easily be viewed as a craft
which was then passed down through the generations, practised and learnt by those
who had no particular 'holy status' but who simply specialized in it for whatever
reason. See Cody, *Priesthood*, pp. 59-60, 114-20.

14. See Haran, *Temples*, pp. 62, 68-69, 71, 72.

phrase which Haran interprets most prosaically to mean dire economic need.[15]

By comparison, however, the priesthood of the monarch arises from quite a different basis. He is certainly shown as a priest, that is, as undertaking a role of mediation between the human and the divine within ritual and specifically sanctuary contexts, but this is not because he has sought employment in a sanctuary as a religious functionary. Rather, it is because of his unique position before Yahweh that he has what might be called an *ex officio* priestly status, arising out of the sacral nature of his kingship. A key characteristic of sacral kingship is the understanding of the monarch as in some way either the embodiment of the god or as having been brought into a particularly close relationship with the deity by being chosen and imbued with divine power. The Israelite version of this understanding was that from the day of his enthronement the monarch became the adopted son of God. As with the declaration of the monarch's priesthood, the prime examples of this concept appear in the psalms:

> You are my son, today I have begotten you (Ps. 2.7).

> He shall cry to me, 'Thou art my Father, my God and the Rock of my
>   Salvation'.
> And I will make him the first-born, the highest of the kings of the earth.
> (Ps. 89.27-28, ET 26–27)

Anointing, which is connected with the endowment of power from above for the new king (cf. 1 Sam. 10.1-10, 16.13), can be seen as the outward symbol of this adoption, since the Lord's anointed is set apart and inviolable, regarded as the embodiment of light and life among his people (Lam. 4.20). As Yahweh's adopted son, the monarch was effectively the deity's delegated surrogate on earth, ruling at Yahweh's behest over Yahweh's people (cf. 1 Sam. 10.1; 2 Sam. 7.8; Ps. 2); and as such it was only natural that he should be answerable to Yahweh for the nation and should fulfil the function of national mediator between people and deity (Ps. 20.7-10, ET 6–9, 84.9-10, ET 8–9). When the king's priestly function is seen in this context, it is evident that it is qualitatively different from what might be called a 'normal priestly role', a comment which has been made by several scholars. De Vaux, for example, speaks of the king as 'a sacred person with a special relationship to Yahweh' and argues that although 'he could, in solemn

---

15. Haran, *Temples*, p. 62.

circumstances, act as the religious head of the people, he was not a priest in the strict sense'.[16] Similarly, Cody considers that 'In a certain sense [kings] were priests',[17] but he argues that 'the Hebrew mentality shrank from considering and calling the king a *kōhēn*'[18] on the grounds that a *kōhēn* was involved with sanctuary functions and was always in the service of another person rather than primarily the deity, both of which elements would sit uneasily with the concept of kingship. The point is that the king would not have been a priest in the sense of having as his primary function the carrying out of all the minutiae of sanctuary duties, because his primary task was to govern the country. But it would nevertheless have been legitimate and even necessary for him to undertake the mediating, priestly role when national interests were at stake, because he was responsible under Yahweh for the nation's well-being, and was the channel through which Yahweh's sovereignty of the nation was exercised,[19] as is clear from the eulogy of Psalm 72.

In the light of this analysis of the royal priesthood, it is perhaps possible to suggest an interpretation of the term *kōhēn hārō'š*, which appears as a designation for the senior priest at the Jerusalem Temple during the period of the monarchy.[20] If, despite his right to act as a mediator between deity and people, the king did not function as a priest in the sense of participating regularly in the daily ritual of the Temple, the question is how to interpret his occasional participation in the ceremonial. Was he effectively taking the place which would normally go

16. De Vaux, *Les Institutions de l'Ancien Testament*, I (Paris: Cerf, 1958), p. 175 (ET *Ancient Israel*, p. 114).

17. Cody, *Priesthood*, p. 100.

18. Cody, *Priesthood*, p. 101.

19. See de Vaux, 'Le Roi d'Israël, Vassal de Yahvé', in *Bible et Orient* (Paris: Cerf, 1967), pp. 287-301 (ET 'The King of Israel, Vassal of Yahweh', in *The Bible and the Ancient Near East* [trans. D. McHugh; London: Darton, Longman & Todd, 1972], pp. 152-62).

20. Although the main witness to this title is the Chronicler, and there are only two occurrences of it in earlier literature (2 Kgs 25.18; Jer. 52.24), neither of which date from before the exile, it seems reasonable to take the title as pre-exilic for two reasons. First, the title is always used in the context of pre-exilic subject matter, and secondly and perhaps more importantly, the title found in literature which both dates from and refers to the postexilic period is *hakkōhēn haggādôl*, whereas *kōhēn hārō'š* does not appear in this kind of context. The reference to Ezra *hakkōhēn hārō'š* in Ezra 7.5 is no exception to this; it is not in the construct format which is being discussed here, nor does it refer to a senior priest but to Aaron, whom it designates as the fount or originator of priesthood (LXX *ho hiereus ho prōtos*).

to the senior priest of the Temple, thereby acting *in loco sacerdotis*, or
was it normally the job of the senior priest to function *in loco regis* and
carry out what were technically delegated royal duties on a daily basis,
so that when the king participated in the cult he was effectively reclaiming from the senior priest his rightful position? In the light of the king's
undoubted supremacy in cultic matters and the repeated depictions
of monarchs initiating cultic practice and reforms (1 Kgs 12.26–13.1;
2 Kgs 16.10-14, 18.1-4, 22.1–23.24), it seems reasonable to conclude
that the king would have had the right, if not the duty, to perform quite
a number of ritual observances, but that his responsibilities were largely
delegated to the senior priest. Such a scenario offers a way of explaining
the construct formation of the title *kōhēn hārō'š* for the senior priest,
which at first sight is rather perplexing. It could be interpreted as an
appositional construction, 'the priest who is the chief/head', and indeed
this is how it is somewhat tentatively classified in Gesenius-Kautzsch.[21]
But the classification does not seem very satisfactory, not least because
there also occurs a more straightforwardly appositional format of
the title, namely *hakkōhēn hārō'š*. This appears in 2 Chron. 31.10 of
Azariah II, where the point of its use is evidently that Azariah is
replying in his capacity as *head of the priesthood* to Hezekiah's query,
which is aimed at all the priests and Levites: 'Azariah the priest, the
head, of the house of Zadok, said to him'. Support for this as the
correct, or at least a credible, interpretation comes from the earlier 2
Chron. 24.6, where king Joash summons the priest Jehoiada to ask why
the Temple taxation measures required by the king have not been
implemented by the Levites. Jehoiada is simply referred to as *hārō'š*,
because he is acting here in his capacity as head of the priesthood; the
designation *rō'š* is not therefore titular but appositional ('Jehoiada the
head'). The similarity between Jehoiada's position in 2 Chron. 24.6 and
Azariah's in 2 Chron. 31.10 is such that it seems entirely reasonable to
interpret Azariah's designation *hakkōhēn hārō'š* as an appositional construction rather than as an alternative form of the title *kōhēn hārō'š*.
However, by the same token, it seems unwarranted to interpret the
grammatically more obscure construction of *kōhēn hārō'š* as an appositional formulation, since the normal rules of apposition clearly can
and do apply in the juxtaposition of the nouns *kōhēn* and *rō'š*.

  However, if *kōhēn hārō'š* is taken as a subjective genitive and translated not as 'the head priest' but as 'the *head's* priest', that is, the

21. GKC, §131 *b* (p. 423).

king's priest (cf. Isa. 7.8, 9), it can then be interpreted as referring to the priest who is entitled to represent the king on the cultic occasions where the king does not, for whatever reason, exercise his right to serve in a priestly capacity, or indeed, on other occasions where such representation would be appropriate. The Hebrew Scriptures contain several examples of a chief priest representing the monarch in both cultic and non-cultic contexts. When Ahaz has consecrated a new altar of Damascene design for the house of the Lord by making offerings upon it himself, he tells Uriah, who is evidently the chief priest at the time, to offer upon it among other things the king's burnt offering and his cereal offering (2 Kgs 16.12-15). That Ahaz is perfectly entitled to make his own offerings is evidenced by the fact that he does so for the first use of the altar; but then he delegates the responsibility for his offerings to Uriah the chief priest, who thereby acts in his place (2 Kgs 16.16). In a non-cultic context Amariah *kōhēn hārō'š* is appointed by king Jehoshaphat to fulfil a judicial responsibility alongside Zebadiah the governor of the house of Judah; Amariah is to have responsibility for all matters of the Lord and Zebadiah for all the king's matters (2 Chron. 19.11). It seems unquestionable that if this episode has any historical basis and such appointments were in fact made, the officers fulfilling them would effectively be acting in the name of the king; and if that is the case, then despite the non-cultic context, the title *kōhēn hārō'š* is here being used in the context of a priestly substitution for royalty.[22] A little later Azariah *kōhēn hārō'š* is involved in a confrontation with King Uzziah, who wants to burn incense but who is told that that is the priests' job (2 Chron. 26.16-20). It is perhaps to be speculated that behind this episode lies some tension between the monarch and the senior priest, maybe a growing jealousy among the priesthood or on the part of the *kōhªnê hārō'š* to retain the privilege of acting as the king's representative or to protect their professional autonomy, to the extent that the monarch's attempts to reassert his own sacral rights met with some discontent.[23]

22. J.R. Bartlett, 'The Use of the Word ראש as a Title in the Old Testament', *VT* 19 (1969), pp. 1-10 (5-6), argues from the same incident that the title was applied to the senior priest because of his judicial function per se rather than because of any substitution for the monarch that such a function would imply.

23. See S. Japhet, *The Ideology of the Book of Chronicles and its Place in Biblical Thought* (ET; Frankfurt am Main: Peter Lang, 1989), pp. 425-27; *I & II Chronicles* (OTL; London: SCM Press, 1993), p. 885.

Of course, it goes without saying that the priest who was designated
as the king's representative would also be the chief priest in the sense
of being the most senior among the priests in the Temple. Hence in Jer.
52.24 Seraiah *kōhēn hārō'š* is followed by Zephaniah *kōhēn hammišneh*
in an evidently hierarchical arrangement.[24]

It appears, then, that the priest for ever whose model is Melchizedek
is a different kind of priest from the normal priests, and in fact the
difference is summed up in Ps. 110.4:

> The Lord has sworn, and will not change his mind;
> 'You are a priest for ever after the order of Melchizedek'.

The important part of the verse for illuminating the royal priesthood is
not, however, the reference to Melchizedek, which would make defining
the nature of the king's priesthood dependent upon defining priesthood
'after the order of Melchizedek'. Indeed, the translation 'after the order
of Melchizedek' is based on the LXX's *kata tēn taxin Melchisedek*,
whereas the Hebrew *'al-dibrātî malkî-ṣedeq* signifies 'because of' or
'for the sake of Melchizedek' rather than 'after the order of
Melchizedek'. If the Hebrew is followed and the rendition 'because of'
or 'for the sake of Melchizedek' is preferred, Melchizedek does not in
fact appear as the founder or the defining element of a succession of
priests into which the present Hebrew monarch is incorporated—it is
not a question of the king becoming a 'priest after the order of
Melchizedek'. Rather, the two distinctive features of the royal priesthood are its bestowal by divine oath (The Lord has sworn and will
not change his mind) and its eternity (You are a priest for ever).
Melchizedek is then cited as a paradigm or precedent for such priesthood (because of Melchizedek), but he is an adjunct to the main message rather than a part of its substance. The point of such an interpretation is this: if priesthood is usually defined on a functional basis so
that it is those who are actually doing the job who are the priests, and
not simply those who are eligible to do the job, then the king's
occasional participation in cultic ceremonial is no real basis on which
to call him a priest, because he is not doing the kind of job which a
priest would normally be expected to do in order to earn the designation 'priest'. However, the oath has been sworn to him that he *is a*

---

24. The majority reading of the parallel passage in 2 Kgs 25.18 refers to
Zephaniah as *kōhēn mišneh*, without the definite article, but the hierarchical sense
of the terms *rō'š* and *mišneh* remains unchanged.

priest, and a priest *for ever*, so that even though he is not a priest in the sense of one who carries out the regular functions of a sanctuary attendant, because of his vocation and his relationship to Yahweh he is nonetheless an *ex officio* priest, a mediator between his God and his people, and will remain such as long as he lives; no-one can deprive him of his mediating, priestly status. Indeed, it could also be taken as a kind of warning, that for the king there is no evading the responsibility of mediation, no choice not to be a priest or carry out priestly duties, unlike others who were permitted by their lineage but who were perhaps unable or unwilling to serve as priests.

2. *The High Priest in the Postexilic Period*

So far, the discussion has focused on the relationship between the monarchy and the priesthood in the period when they co-existed, namely, the pre-exilic period, and has offered a way of interpreting the relationship between the monarch and the chief priest, as well as the royal priesthood itself. However, it is also necessary to consider the relationship between the postexilic high priesthood and the monarchy, a question made all the more pressing by the tendency to equate the priestly functions of the monarch with those of the high priest. The most comprehensive picture of the high priesthood is that which is found in the Priestly writer, and when this picture is compared with the picture of the monarchy it cannot be denied that there are important correspondences between the two. First, both monarch and high priest appear in their respective contexts as representatives of the whole community before Yahweh. The Deuteronomist shows Solomon at the dedication of the new Temple (1 Kgs 8.1-66), offering sacrifices and praying on behalf of the whole gathering, while P's high priest has the duty of officiating on behalf of the people when they are regarded as having being collectively contaminated by an unwitting sin of the whole community (Lev. 4.13-20). Whatever may have been the origins of the ceremonial for the Day of Atonement, the understanding of it as preserved in Leviticus 16 is that, as in Leviticus 4, the high priest represents the community in carrying out rites for their purification as well as for the cleansing of the sanctuary (Lev. 16.17, 21, 24, 32-33). Secondly, as well as representing the community before Yahweh in a ceremonial context, both king and high priest are regarded as being liable to pollute the whole community by their personal sin. Thus,

plague is brought upon the whole of the Israelite nation because of
David's sin (2 Sam. 24), and likewise the high priest's sin is said to
bring 'guilt on the people' (Lev. 4.3). Thirdly, a more physical area of
resemblance between the two is in their garments: the high priest's
headdress and breastpiece are apparently borrowed from the royal
costume, thereby giving the impression that the high priest became the
equivalent of the monarch in the postexilic society after the demise of
the Davidic line. Finally, both king and high priest are shown as
anointed figures who are chosen specifically by Yahweh for his service,
thereby apparently blurring the boundary between the office of priesthood and the vocation of kingship. Indeed, of P's seven references to
the high priest as 'anointed', four of them come in the context of his
officiation on behalf of the community as a whole (Lev. 4.3, 5, 16;
16.32), thereby apparently underlining the correspondence of the high
priesthood with the monarchy as a vocational position that is vital for
the well-being of the whole sacral community.

However, the apparent formal similarities between the priesthood
exercised by the monarch and that exercised by the high priest are only
part of the picture. In determining precisely how the two relate to each
other, and therefore whether the high priest in the form in which
he appears in P can truly be regarded as a substitute king or even a
messiah-figure, it is necessary to ascertain more exactly the nature of
the high priesthood. It has already been pointed out that the monarch is
portrayed as the adopted son of Yahweh, and that his right, indeed, his
duty, to be called a priest was dependent upon his functioning as a
surrogate for the divine king, which gave him a special relationship to
the deity above and beyond that of the usual priesthood. However,
when P's portrayal of the high priesthood is examined it becomes clear
that there the high priest is shown as a priest like any other; that is, his
priesthood displays the same functional characteristics as that of the
ordinary priests, and there is no indication of any divine charisma being
necessary to fit him for carrying out his particular tasks of mediation,
nor of any particularly close relationship between the high priest and
the deity. Instead, his exalted position is defined in terms of an inten-
sifying of the normal priestly characteristics, and this can be seen in
two ways.

The first indication is in the high priest's relation to the sanctuary. It
was pointed out earlier that priesthood was connected with sanctuaries,
and this is also true of the high priest, whom P shows as being con-

nected with the Tabernacle. Indeed, the setting aside of Aaron as high priest and his sons as priests (Exod. 28.1–29.37) follows hard on the heels of the description of the Tabernacle and its appurtenances (Exod. 25.1–27.21). However, the high priest's connection with the shrine is much closer than that of the ordinary priests. This can be seen from the ephod and breastpiece of his ceremonial garments, which are made out of the same material as the veil of the Tabernacle (*ḥōšēb*, Exod. 26.31, 28.6, 15), whereas the ordinary priests officiate in white linen; it is also apparent in the duties reserved to the high priest alone, which all require him as the officiant to enter the Tabernacle. The duties in question are burning incense on the incense altar and trimming the Tabernacle lamps (Exod. 30.1-10); arranging the shewbread each Sabbath (Lev. 24.5-9); atoning for his own sin or for that of the whole community where necessary (Lev. 4.1-21); and officiating on the Day of Atonement (Lev. 16). The other priests serve the altar outside in the courtyard, but do not enter the Tabernacle itself. However, although the ordinary priests do not share the Tabernacle duties with the high priest, he apparently shares the everyday priestly responsibilities outside the Tabernacle with them, since on two occasions in P's wilderness scenario Aaron is addressed by Yahweh and given instructions for the whole priesthood which are framed in the second person plural, thereby including Aaron himself in their remit (Lev. 10.9-11; Num. 18.1, 5). Especially noteworthy are Num. 18.5, 'You (pl.) shall attend to the duties of the sanctuary and the duties of the altar', and Num. 18.7, 'You and your sons with you shall attend to your priesthood for all that concerns the altar and that is within the veil'. Neither passage makes any distinction between service of the altar in the Tabernacle courtyard and service within the Tabernacle itself. The high priest's priesthood therefore seems to include all the sanctuary duties that pertain to the ordinary priesthood as well as the additional duties reserved for him alone.

A second typically priestly characteristic which applies to the high priest is the possession of the sacred lots, the Urim and Thummim. Indeed, according to P it is the high priest alone who possesses the lots; they rest in the 'breastpiece of judgment' (*ḥōšen mišpāṭ*, Exod. 28.15), a part of the high priest's festal garments which is probably adapted from a neck-pouch once used by ordinary priests to contain the lots. However, P never shows the high priest actually using the lots, so that even though he is supposedly marked out from the other priests by having them, the practical difference they make in terms of his status is negligible. In fact, in P's wilderness scenario the lots are redundant, because all enquiries of the Almighty are dealt with via Moses, who speaks with the Lord face to face. Hence, to see the lots as indicative of a particular type of intimacy between high priest and deity which is not available to other priests, and therefore as indicative of a qualitative difference between high priesthood and ordinary priesthood, is unwarranted. The high priest is the epitome of *priesthood*, as evidenced by his functions in the sanctuary and his possession of the lots, but he is the epitome of priesthood and of nothing more or less than that. His priesthood is quantitatively but not qualitatively different from that of the other priests; he does everything that they do and more besides rather than doing something completely different from them, so that the difference between the high priesthood and the ordinary priesthood is a difference of degree, not of kind. The high priest is therefore effectively a sacred functionary like all the other priests.

That this is indeed P's view of the high priesthood is evidenced by the titles that P uses for the office. In Lev. 21.10 the designation *hakkōhēn haggādôl mē'eḥāyw* is used of the high priest, a designation which in the truncated form *hakkōhēn haggādôl* is the most commonly used postexilic title for the high priest.[25] In the format found in Lev. 21.10 it seems to be a comparative or relative description, referring maybe to the eldest or the senior priest, and as such is ontological rather than functional—that is, it describes the high priest in terms of his relation to his fellow priests rather than actually defining what he does by virtue of being high priest. Hence, although the high priest is exalted in his holiness compared with the other priests, the title implies that it is more of the same kind of holiness rather than something quite

---

25. Hag. 1.1, 12, 14, 2.2, 4; Zech. 3.1, 8, 6.11; Neh. 3.1, 20, 13.28. The title also comes in P in Num. 35.25, 28, and as a textual variant for *hakkōhēn* in Num. 35.32. By contrast, Jacob Milgrom, *Leviticus 1–16* (AB, 3; New York: Doubleday, 1991), p. 231, argues that *kōhēn hārō'š* is the postexilic title, whereas *hakkōhēn haggādôl* is pre-exilic, but there seems little or no evidence to this effect. Certainly Milgrom's claim that *kōhēn hārō'š* is used 'thirteen times in Ezra, fourteen times in Nehemiah, and ninety-one times in Chronicles', a claim in support of which he cites no references, is quite incredible. The construct form *kōhēn hārō'š* signifying 'chief or high priest' occurs in neither Ezra nor Nehemiah, and occurs unequivocally only twice in Chronicles (2 Chron. 19.11, 26.20). For further discussion of terminology for the high priest, see my forthcoming monograph on the high priesthood, *Zadok's Heirs: The Role and Development of the High Priesthood in Ancient Israel* (Oxford: Clarendon Press).

different. However, it should be noted that Aaron, who is presented in Exodus 28 as the epitome of high priesthood, is only ever referred to either by name alone or as Aaron *hakkōhēn* (Exod. 31.10, 39.41; Lev. 7.34, 13.2, 21.21; Num. 3.6, 18.28, 26.64, 33.38).[26] This means that it is not always clear whether Aaron is acting in a specifically high priestly capacity, whether *hakkōhēn* should be taken to mean 'priest' or 'high priest' (cf. Lev. 4), or even whether on occasion the name 'Aaron' should be understood as a reference to priests in general (cf. Num. 16.11, 18.28). This blurring of the boundary between Aaron/the high priest and the rest of the priesthood is also evidenced in P's practice of referring to Aaron and his sons as a group with no apparent distinction between them (e.g. Exod. 28.40-43, 29.44; Lev. 7.31, 35-36; Num. 6.22-27). Such an approach is consistent with the interpretation of *hakkōhēn haggādôl* as effectively a relative designation, since both portray the high priest as fundamentally a priest like any other.

It would therefore seem that the origin of priesthood and the foundations of high priesthood are the same to the extent that they share a common concept of the nature of their priesthood as the role of a sacred functionary, and that the high priest is effectively primus inter pares who, despite having particular responsibilities close to the inner sanctum and representative functions on behalf of the community as a whole, also has the same kind of mundane responsibilities as the other priests. Hence, the high priest is a priest in the true sense of the word, unlike the monarch, who did not share the more mundane priestly responsibilities.

In the light of this it is questionable whether, when the high priest appears as a mediator on behalf of the whole community, his action has the same significance as the mediation of the monarch would have in similar circumstances. Indeed, it is arguable that when the high priest officiates on behalf of the community as a whole, he does so not primarily as the one responsible for the people before Yahweh, but as a kind of 'sanctuary warden' whose job it is to keep the sanctuary free from the contamination caused by sin. This interpretation arises from a theology which Milgrom describes as 'the Priestly *Picture of Dorian*

---

26. This does not include the potentially ambiguous references in Exod. 38.21; Num. 3.32, 4.16, 28, 33, 7.8, 17.2, ET 16.37, 25.7, 11, 26.1, which contain the phrase 'PN the son of Aaron the priest'. In these cases either Aaron or his son could be 'the priest'—'PN the son of Aaron the priest', or 'PN, son of Aaron, the priest'.

Gray',[27] that is, the concept of both ritual and moral impurity as powerful pollutants that defile the sanctuary, and which must therefore be cleansed from it in order to maintain the holiness of the place. The degree of pollution depends upon the severity of the offence committed; individual, inadvertent sin contaminates the altar of burnt offering in the courtyard, but the sin of the whole community (or the high priest) results in pollution of the inner altar of incense in the Tabernacle, and more serious, wanton sin pollutes the Ark itself inside the veil. This is why the high priest has to officiate inside the tent when atonement is required for such sin—he is effectively purifying those inner areas from the defilement wrought upon them by the sin.[28] In this way he still guards the interests of the community in relation to the deity by ensuring that the contamination of the sanctuary does not accumulate to a point where it drives away the holy presence, but this is not achieved by means of any particular relationship between high priest and deity on behalf of the community. On the contrary, it is the high priest's supreme connection with the sanctuary, and in that sense his epitomizing of the functional, non-vocational style of priesthood, which enables him to achieve the same for the community as would the monarch's mediation from a position of intimacy with Yahweh.

It might be argued that the command to Moses to bring Aaron and make him and his sons the only legitimate priests (Exod. 28.1) is an expression of the kind of vocational priesthood that was suggested for the monarchy, but this cannot be sustained. Despite Yahweh's apparent nomination of Aaron to be his priest, as already noted there is no indication of any charisma accompanying the appointment, a state of affairs which is all the more pointed when the craftsman Bezalel ben Uri who is to construct the Tabernacle is given a personal divine calling and filled with the Spirit of God (Exod. 31.1-3). There is little warmth in the Yahweh–Aaron relationship; it is true that Aaron as the high priest is allowed to come into the holiest place, but only when Yahweh specifies, and then only with the blood of sacrifices (Lev. 16.1). In addition, out of all the legislation given in P, including that which concerns the priesthood and the high priesthood, only two portions are addressed to Aaron himself, with the rest being given to Moses. In fact, the presence of Moses alongside Aaron underlines the paucity of the

---

27. Milgrom, *Leviticus*, p. 260.

28. See the fuller discussion of this and other aspects of the purification offering in Milgrom, *Leviticus*, pp. 253-61.

Yahweh–Aaron relationship by its contrast with the Yahweh–Moses relationship. Moses seems to come and go quite freely into and out of the holy of holies (Num. 17.19, 22, 23, 25-26, ET 17.4, 7, 8, 10-11), and it is he, not Aaron, who speaks face to face with the Lord, as well as receiving the vast majority of the legislation. Indeed, it would be fair to say that of the Yahweh–Moses relationship and the Yahweh–Aaron relationship, the Yahweh–Moses relationship, with its sense of one divinely chosen and commissioned to lead the people of Yahweh and therefore entitled to act as a mediator on their behalf, is certainly the closer of the two to the Yahweh–monarch relationship.

The question of the royal elements in the high priest's ceremonial garments is also less straightforward than it appears at first sight. The elements concerned are the breastpiece, the turban and the diadem, all of which seem to parallel items identified elsewhere as parts of a royal costume, and which therefore seem to imply some kind of equivalence of status between the high priest and the monarch. The breastpiece, with its rows of semi-precious stones (Exod. 28.15-29), resembles the design of a royal pectoral found at Byblos.[29] The turban (*miṣnepet*, 28.37, 39) appears in Ezek. 21.31 (ET 21.26) in parallelism with the term 'crown' ('*ʿaṭārâ*') in an oracle addressed to the prince of Israel,[30] thereby implying that the turban, like the crown, was an item of royal headdress. The diadem (*nēzer*, Exod. 29.6) appears once as an alternative to and twice as a supplementary description of the inscribed gold plate (literally 'blossom', *ṣîṣ*, Exod. 28.36) which is fastened to the turban,[31] and if the item in question was indeed a diadem or crown, the implication would certainly seem to be that its wearer enjoyed the status of royalty.[32] However, upon closer examination it becomes clear that the items are not the unequivocal indicators of royal status that they appear to be. This is most evident in the case of the diadem. It is indisputable that the term *nēzer* is used in royal contexts (e.g. Ps.

---

29. Noth, *Das zweite Buch Mose: Exodus* (ATD, 5; Göttingen: Vandenhoeck & Ruprecht, 1959), pp. 181-82 (ET *Exodus* [trans. J.S. Bowden; OTL; London: SCM Press, 1962], pp. 222-23).

30. In line with the usage elsewhere in Ezekiel, the designation 'prince' (*nāśîʾ*) in 21.30 (ET 21.25) is certainly to be understood as a royal title.

31. Exod. 28.36 simply speaks of *ṣîṣ zāhāb*, and Exod. 29.6 of *nēzer haqqōdeš*, whereas Exod. 39.30 refers to the *ṣîṣ nēzer haqqōdeš*, and Lev. 8.9 uses the phrase *ṣîṣ hazzāhāb nēzer haqqōdeš*.

32. M. Haran, 'Priesthood, Temple, Divine Service: Some Observations on Institutions and Practices of Worship', *HAR* 7 (1983), pp. 121-35 (123).

132.18); however, the root *nzr* signifies separation and consecration, as in the designation Nazirite for one who takes a vow of separation and consecration (Num. 6.1-21). Hence, the *nēzer* as part of the high priest's attire may well indicate separation and consecration to the Lord rather than royal status. In fact, given the sacral nature of the Israelite monarchy, the use of the root *nzr* in *royal* contexts may similarly be due to its connotations of consecration; in that case, the reason for its use in respect of both the monarch and the high priest would be because of the priestly aspects of the monarchy rather than because of supposed royal aspects of the priesthood. The breastpiece, too, is an ambiguous item; although its appearance resembles that of a royal pectoral, in its construction and function it is definitely priestly. As noted above, it is made from the same kind of material as the ephod (Exod. 28.15), so that it shares with the ephod the priestly connotations of holiness and links with the Tabernacle. It also functions as a pouch for the Urim and Thummim (Exod. 28.30), which were always a priestly responsibility, never a royal one (cf. Deut. 33.8; 1 Sam. 14.3, 18-19). Finally, although the turban is mentioned once as an item worn by the prince of Israel, as with the diadem it is conceivable that this is due to the priestly overtones of the monarchy rather than to monarchic aspects of the high priesthood, especially since of the twelve occurrences of *miṣnepet* in the Hebrew Bible eleven are in P and are used of the high priest's headdress. Such weight of evidence points overwhelmingly to the turban as a priestly item rather than a royal one. It must be concluded, then, that the high priest's ceremonial garments cannot be used to argue convincingly for the high priest as a quasi-monarch; what they do seem to support, however, is the quasi-priesthood of the monarchy.

Another characteristic of the high priesthood which is often taken to indicate its monarchic nature is the oil of anointing. However, once again initial impressions are misleading. Milgrom points out that the high priest was anointed not in order to bestow on him divine attributes, which was the case in royal anointing,[33] but to bring about a change in his status so that he could function in the sacred realm;[34] in other words,

---

33. See Noth, 'Amt', pp. 321-22 (ET 'Office', pp. 239-40); A.R. Johnson, *Sacral Kingship in Ancient Israel* (Cardiff: University of Wales Press, 2nd edn, 1967), pp. 14-16.

34. Milgrom, *Leviticus*, pp. 553-55; see also P. Budd, *Leviticus* (NCB; Grand Rapids: Eerdmans; London: Marshall Pickering, 1996), p. 137. C. Houtman, 'On the Function of the Holy Incense (Exodus xxx 34-38) and the Sacred Anointing Oil

royal anointing was intended to empower, whereas high priestly anointing was intended to sanctify (cf. Exod. 28.41, 30.30; Lev. 8.12). Certainly in the accounts of the early monarchy, anointing with oil and bestowal of the divine spirit follow on from each other (1 Sam. 10.1-10, 16.13), whereas the high priest is never shown as having been endowed with the Spirit of Yahweh even after having been anointed (cf. Lev. 8.12). Also, both Saul and David follow their anointing with success in battle—in other words, they are anointed to enable them to go out into the non-sacral realm and perform the duties of kingship. By contrast, Aaron's anointing results in his being closeted more closely than ever in the sacred realm of the Tabernacle (Lev. 10.7, 21.10-12), cut off from the profane realm rather than being immersed in it as the kings were. The admittedly late evidence of the Babylonian Talmud distinguishes between the anointing of a king, which was done in the shape of a wreath, and the anointing of a priest which was done in the shape of the Greek letter chi,[35] a distinction that indicates that the Rabbis too perceived a difference in the anointing of king and high priest. P's picture of the anointed priest should not therefore be interpreted in terms of hierocratic kingship or monarchic equivalence but rather in terms of sanctification for ritual and cultic responsibility.

3. Kingship and Priesthood in the Hasmonaean Period

It seems only right to conclude a paper on the relationship between the monarchy and the high priesthood with a short comment on the Hasmonaeans, since they apparently epitomized the combination of kingship and high priesthood. Yet the records that have survived indicate that their period of ascendancy was viewed with ambivalence by many of their compatriots, and in the light of the foregoing discussion it is perhaps possible to suggest why. Although the resistance leaders Jonathan and Simon the Maccabee were of priestly descent, they rose to prominence among the Jews not because of their priestly ancestry but

(Exodus xxx 22-33)', *VT* 42 (1992), pp. 458-65, argues that just as the unique fragrance of the sacred incense used in the Tabernacle designates the shrine as Yahweh's domain, so too the unique fragrance of the sacred anointing oil designates those who bear it as Yahweh's priests, marking them with his personality and enabling them to serve at the altar without fatal consequences. Hence, the anointing of priests serves to maintain the boundaries between the sacred and the profane.

35. *b. Hor.* 12a.

on the basis of their military prowess and leadership skills, to the extent that the admittedly Deuteronomistic-like apologia of 1 Maccabees could quite happily portray their rise and rule in terms of the rise of the Israelite monarchy. Their acceptance of the high priesthood followed their rise to prominence, and can perhaps be compared with the way in which the king of Psalm 110 is also granted priesthood as a function of his kingship. In 1 Macc. 14.4-15 Simon is given a positively messianic eulogy based on Psalm 72, and the later Hasmonaeans clearly thought of themselves primarily as kings, despite their priestly origins. And yet they were neither true high priests nor true kings. As priests, they were of the Aaronide descent, which by this time was an accepted criterion for the ordinary priesthood, but they were not of Zadokite descent, when Zadokite lineage had been the norm for the high priest. However, an even more serious indictment was that they were not of the Davidic line to which the monarchy was viewed as having been promised irrevocably (cf. 2 Sam. 7.8-16; Ps. 89.36-38, ET 35-37), nor, despite the Deuteronomistic-like apologia, are Jonathan and Simon portrayed as having the vocation and anointing of kingship which might conceivably be regarded as superseding the Davidic promises, and without which true monarchy would have been inconceivable. Although there would doubtless have been those for whom the main stumbling block was the Hasmonaeans' non-Zadokite high priesthood, there were also those for whom the unthinkable was that non-Davidides had usurped the monarchy, as is evidenced by the *Psalms of Solomon*:

> You, Lord, chose David as king over Israel, and you swore to him concerning his descendants for ever that his kingdom should not fail before you. But in our sinfulness, sinners rose up against us, fell upon us and drove us out; those to whom you made no promise deprived us by force. They did not glorify your esteemed name with glory; they preferred a kingdom to what was their true crown; they laid waste the throne of David with arrogant shouts (*Pss. Sol.* 17.5-8).

In fact, based on the analysis presented here it may well be that the perceived usurpation of the monarchy was a far more heinous crime than the illegitimate assumption of the high priesthood. After all, a priest is basically a religious functionary, and at least the Hasmonaeans were of priestly descent; but if monarchy is a vocation, an election by the deity and a raising to be the adopted son of the divine, to claim to be monarchs when the evidence of such an adoption or election is absent is equivalent to blasphemy of the worst kind. This of course is despite the attempts to portray Simon in particular in messianic terms.

The relationship between the monarchy and the high priesthood is therefore an uneven one. The monarch can fulfil priestly duties because of the nature of his kingship, but equally because of the nature of his priesthood the high priest cannot be a king, nor should he ever be confused with a messianic figure. Kingship may well be priesthood in a certain sense, but priesthood, even high priesthood, is certainly not kingship.

THE MESSIAH IN THE PSALMS:
A QUESTION OF RECEPTION HISTORY AND THE PSALTER

S.E. Gillingham

Introduction

Over the last century, one of the besetting issues in psalmic studies has been the extent to which an understanding of the religious background of psalmody has been influenced as much by eisegetical concerns as it has been by exegetical ones. The history of scholarship, with its numerous proposals regarding the date, authorship and provenance of different psalms, would suggest that more often than not it has been a case of reading *into* the psalms cultic activity and theological assertions which might not in fact be there. Given the stereotypical language and the anonymity of the psalmists, both the historical-critical method and theological readings have reflected an agenda that has been brought to the psalms and, to my mind, these tell us more about the interpreters than about the psalms themselves.[1]

Applying these initial observations to the issue before us, I believe that it is difficult to propose that any Messianic interpretation was intended, both in the earliest stages of the composition of individual psalms and in the later stages of the assembling of the Psalter as a whole. In the pre-exilic period, and probably for some time after the

---

1. This is illustrated in the vast difference of approaches used by the History of Religions School and the Biblical Theology Movement. The former, with its 'myth and ritual' concerns, is dependent upon data from comparative religion for its assumptions about sacral kingship, the enthronement of Yahweh, a new year festival, and so on. The other approach presumes a 'prophecy and fulfilment' schema, taking a Christological framework whereby the psalms are seen as prophetic texts that witness to a time of future fulfilment, a condition which has been met through the person and work of Christ. Both approaches thus look at the psalms 'from outside in'. On this issue, see R.E. Clements, 'The Messianic Hope in the Old Testament', *JSOT* 43 (1989), pp. 3-19.

exile, the term *māšîaḥ* seems to have meant, quite simply, an 'anointed one', referring to one who held an office, whether that of a prophet, a priest or a king. Hence in the psalms one would expect the term to refer to a particular person with a particular office in the Israelite cultus. In this socio-religious context, it is difficult to see how the psalmists could use the term to denote a title for an idealized coming figure.[2] The future the psalmists point to, even in postexilic times, appears to be that of the present or the next generation, rather than any great and golden age breaking in from beyond. Like the prophets, the future orientation was short-term, contemporary and immediate, and only became more long-term and idealized on account of the influence of later generations.[3] Large-scale eschatological expectations, let alone particular Messianic hopes, do not appear to have been part of the agenda of those who composed or collected the psalms—even in those psalms which use (or imply) the term *māšîaḥ*.[4] This means that this study will make a careful

2.   On this issue, see R.A. Horsley, 'Messianic Movements in Judaism', in *ABD*, IV, pp. 791-97, noting how the anointing of kings demonstrated a certain revolutionary and conditional element (p. 792). See also J.J.M. Roberts, 'The Old Testament's Contribution to Messianic Expectation', in J.H. Charlesworth (ed.), *The Messiah: Developments in Earliest Judaism and Christianity* (Minneapolis: Fortress Press, 1992), pp. 39-51, who concludes that with the exception of Isa. 45.1 (regarding Cyrus) every occurrence of the term in the biblical material refers to the contemporary Israelite king, to indicate the close relationship between Yahweh and his chosen one (p. 39).

3.   See J. Barton, *Oracles of God* (London: Darton, Longman & Todd, 1986), pp. 96-140.

4.   See Clements, 'The Messianic Hope', pp. 8-14 on this issue. On one side, most history of religion scholars, emphasizing the mythical and ritual elements in early psalmody, would see that this also implied a primitive eschatological worldview. See, for example, W.O.E. Oesterley, *The Evolution of the Messianic Idea: A Study in Comparative Religion* (London: Pitman, 1908); H. Gressmann, *Der Messias* (FRLANT, 40; Göttingen: Vandenhoeck & Ruprecht, 1929); A. Bentzen, *Messias–Moses Redivivus–Menschensohn* (ATANT, 17; Zürich: Zwingli, 1948), (ET *King and Messiah* [London: Lutterworth Press, 1955]). By contrast, S. Mowinckel is more cautious, seeing that in pre-exilic times the national messiah was 'in origin a political figure belonging to this world, who could not easily be accommodated to the transcendental, other-worldly thoughts and longings of the new eschatology': see *Han som kommer* (Copenhagen: G.E.C. Gad, 1951), p. 185 (ET *He That Cometh* [trans. G.W. Anderson; Oxford: Basil Blackwell, 1956]), p. 280; also *Offersang og Sangoffer* (Oslo: H. Aschehoug & Co., 1951), Chapter III, pp. 57-59 (ET *The Psalms in Israel's Worship*, I [trans. D.R. Ap-Thomas; Oxford: Basil Blackwell, 1962]), Chapter 3, pp. 46-48. Mowinckel holds a midway position in

distinction between the function of a messiah (small m), and the title Messiah (capital M). The former denotes the figure of the king and his dynastic rule, and thus refers to many successive figures; the latter, by contrast, presumes a once-for-all figure coming either at the end of time, or heralding it.

This paper will address this issue in three parts. The first stage will be to determine precisely which psalms should be used within the debate. Here three categories might be proposed: (a) psalms which employ the term *māšîaḥ* (some eight psalms in all); (b) psalms which depict a royal figure whose identity corresponds with the *māšîaḥ* in the previous list of psalms, although the term itself is not used (a further five psalms, all of which may be termed 'royal psalms'); and (c) psalms which suggest more implicitly a royal figure and which some commentators would still therefore classify as upholding a royal ideology (another fourteen psalms).[5] The second stage will be to assess how the proposed royal psalms might have been used in the postexilic period, after the demise of the monarchy—to ask whether at this time they would have been adapted for an eschatological purpose, or whether in the process of editing and collecting they were preserved simply to 'sanctify' the memory of the house of David. The third stage, taking seriously the way in which both Jewish and Christian interpreters have nevertheless read the psalms in a Messianic way, will seek to assess how and why this shift in Messianic emphasis took place in their reception history.

this respect, for the other side of the divide is marked by those who take more seriously the conditional role of the king as expressed in the narrative literature; see, for example, M. Noth, 'Gott, König, Volk im Alten Testament', in *Gesammelte Studien* (TBü, 6; Munich: Chr. Kaiser Verlag, 1957), pp. 188-229 (ET 'God, King, and Nation in the Old Testament', in *The Laws in the Pentateuch and Other Studies* [trans. D.R. Ap-Thomas; London: SCM Press, 1966], pp. 145-78, especially pp. 161-78); K.-H. Bernhardt, *Das Problem der altorientalischen Königsideologie im Alten Testament* (VTSup, 8; Leiden: E.J. Brill, 1961), pp. 82-90; and more recently, R. Albertz, *Religionsgeschichte Israels in alttestamentlicher Zeit,* I (Göttingen: Vandenhoeck & Ruprecht, 1992), pp. 174-85 (ET *A History of Israelite Religion in the Old Testament Period,* I [trans. J. Bowden; London: SCM Press, 1994], pp. 116-22), who would see the king's role in the psalms as a political and cultic figurehead only.

5.   See S.J.L. Croft, *The Identity of the Individual in the Psalms* (JSOTSup, 44; Sheffield: JSOT Press, 1987), pp. 73-132 on the individual as the king, offering criteria for an extensive list of royal psalms. For a more cautious approach, see J. Day, *Psalms* (OTG; Sheffield: JSOT Press, 1990), pp. 21-25, 88-90.

King and Messiah

1. The So-Called Messianic Psalms

Psalms which Explicitly Use the Term māšîaḥ

Māšîaḥ (an adjectival noun form with passive connotations from the verbal √ *mšḥ*) is found in eight psalms; seven use the noun form, and an eighth has been included because it uses the term in its verbal form. Of these eight, six may be classified as royal psalms, and two suggest post-exilic compositions.

Psalm 2.2 speaks of hostile peoples plotting against 'the Lord and his anointed':

> The kings of the earth set themselves,
> and the rulers take counsel together,
> against the Lord and his anointed.

The reference to the enemy powers (*mal^{e}kê-'ereṣ w^{e}rôz^{e}nîm*, lines 1 and 2) suggests not so much any idealized Messianic age, but rather the threat of international unrest at the time of the coronation of the Davidic king.[6] The promise of the victorious rule of God over the might of nations (vv. 4-6, 7-8) may explain why the psalm was used eschatologically in later times, but this belief in the kingship of God is sufficiently early (see for example Pss. 24.1-2, 47.3, 9 [ET 2, 8] ; Isa. 6.8) to suggest that a pre-exilic date is more than likely. Similarly the idea of the universal dominion of the king (vv. 7-8) may also explain why the psalm was used later to describe a Messianic age, but this too is a common feature in royal ideology (see for example Pss. 18.44-48 [ET 43-47], 72.8-11, 89.26 [ET 25]) and so again does not preclude a pre-exilic context.[7] The concern in this psalm is with the immediate future of a newly anointed royal figure: it is a coronation psalm, most probably composed for use by any Davidic king, at a typical time of political unrest such as would have followed the death of the previous monarch.[8] The change of speakers may suggest the liturgical use of the

---

6. Cf. P.C. Craigie, *Psalms 1–50* (WBC, 19 ; Waco, TX: Word Books, 1983), p. 66: '...the reference of the term in the context of the psalm's initial use is simply to the *human* king, for whom the coronation was conducted'.

7. Cf. H.-J. Kraus, *Psalmen 1–59* (BKAT, 15.1; Neukirchen–Vluyn: Neukirchener Verlag, 5th edn, 1978), pp. 145-48 (ET *Psalms 1–59* [trans. H.C. Oswald; Minneapolis: Augsburg, 1988], pp. 126-28).

8. Cf. A.A. Anderson, *Psalms,* I (NCB; Grand Rapids: Eerdmans, 1972), pp. 64-65; also A. Weiser, *Die Psalmen* (ATD, 14–15; Göttingen: Vandenhoeck &

psalm, probably at the time of the coronation of the king.[9] All in all, this indicates that the use of $w^{e'}al$-$m^e\check{s}\hat{\imath}h\hat{o}$ in v. 2 refers to the newly anointed king. Those who presume this psalm was Messianic from the start appear to do so on account of eisegetical concerns.[10]

Psalm 18.51 (ET 50) speaks of the Lord showing steadfast love to his anointed:

> Great triumphs he gives to his king,
> and shows steadfast love to his anointed,
> to David and his descendants for ever.

The parallelism in this verse ('to his king' [*malkô*] in line 1; 'to his anointed' [*lim^e\check{s}îhô*] in line 2; 'to David and his descendants' [*l^edāwid ûl^ezar'ô*] in line 3) surely places the reference to 'his anointed' in the context of the actual Davidic dynasty. The archaisms in the theophanic language, with recognized correspondences with other ancient Near Eastern poetry,[11] and the theme of thanksgiving for some military victory offer some parallels with ancient battle poems such as in Exodus 15 and Judges 5; the difference in Psalm 18 is that the focus is on a royal figure through whom God's victory has been effected.[12] As in Psalm 2, we may note the same beliefs in the universal dominion of the king and in the victorious rule of God (vv. 14-15, ET 13-14, and vv. 47-51, ET 46-50) and again this does not preclude a pre-exilic setting. Whereas Psalm 2 serves as a coronation psalm, for use by any Judahite

Ruprecht, 5th edn, 1959), pp. 341-42 (ET *The Psalms* [trans. H. Hartwell; OTL; London: SCM Press, 1962], pp. 109-10).

9. In vv. 1-2, a cultic leader addresses the congregation; in v. 3, the enemy nations speak for themselves; in vv. 4-6, the leader again addresses the congregation and offers an oracle from God; in vv. 7-9, he addresses the king and offers another oracle from God; and in vv. 10-12 the leader (? and congregation) address the enemy nations.

10. See for example W.C. Kaiser, *The Messiah in the Old Testament* (Grand Rapids: Zondervan, 1995), p. 90: 'With such high accolades, there can be little doubt that the anointed is not simply one of God's earthly appointed ones in the Davidic line; he has [sic] God's heavenly appointed one, Jesus Christ.'

11. See Kraus, *Psalmen 1–59*, pp. 291, 294-95 (ET *Psalms 1–59*, pp. 261, 264-65); Anderson, *Psalms*, I, pp. 157-60; Craigie, *Psalms 1–50*, pp. 169-72, 173-74.

12. Cf. W.O.E. Oesterley, *The Psalms* (Guildford: SPCK, 1939), p. 162, who sees the king (possibly Josiah) as the speaker. Kraus, *Psalmen 1–59*, p. 296 (ET *Psalms 1–59*, p. 266), observes: 'Mythical metaphors and formulations are mixed into the narration. But neither the myth nor the cultic drama predominates. The secret of the royal psalms lies in the historical dimension.'

king at the time of his accession to the throne, Psalm 18 is a thanks-giving psalm, for use by any Davidic king after a time of military victory over enemy nations (vv. 44-46, ET 43-45). Like Psalm 2, the anointed figure is the king himself: the future envisaged is that of the continuation of the Davidic dynasty. Whatever use the psalm may have had long after the demise of the monarchy, in its earliest stages it looked back to the figurehead of David as a basis for faith in God's promises; there is no suggestion that the psalmist looked forward to any once-for-all-time coming figure.[13]

Psalm 20.7 (ET 6) speaks of the Lord helping his anointed:

> Now I know that the Lord will help his anointed;
> he will answer him from his holy heaven
> with mighty victories by his right hand.

The military concerns in this psalm correspond with Psalm 18 before it and Psalm 21 following it. Mowinckel views Psalm 20 as a 'national psalm of intercession for the king before he goes to war', used as part of ritual for the day of preparation for battle, along the lines of 1 Sam. 7.9 and 13.9-12.[14] As with Psalm 2, the changes in speaker suggest liturgical use: vv. 2-6 (ET 1–5) form the votive prayer for the king, v. 7 (ET 6, the verse quoted above) is a declaration of victory for the king, probably by a cultic prophet, and vv. 8-10 (ET 7–9) are the praise from the congregation. The psalm may well belong to an annual festival commemorating the various victories of the king, or it could have a more specific use at a service before a critical time of battle.[15] Whether used annually or for specific occasions, it is clear that this is a battle psalm, and the anointed one dependent on the victory promised by God (*bigᵉbūrôt yēša' yᵉmînô*, v. 7 line 2) is the ruling king.

Psalm 89.39 (ET 38) begins a lament concerning the defeat of the king:

---

13. This point is reinforced by the inclusion of the same psalm in 2 Sam. 22, where its narrative context further illustrates a historical rather than eschatological reading. It will be seen later how the reflection on David as a figure of the *past* (rather than on David as an idealized figure for a future age) also influenced those who preserved these royal psalms.

14. *Offersang og Sangoffer*, pp. 221, 228 (ET *The Psalms in Israel's Worship*, I, pp. 219 and 225).

15. On the latter view, see Craigie, *Psalms 1–50*, pp. 185-88, who notes a similar pattern in 2 Chron. 20.5-12 (= vv. 1-5), 13-17 (= v. 6), 18-19 (= vv. 7-9).

> But now thou hast cast off and rejected,
> thou art full of wrath against thy anointed.

The sense of God's wrath (*hit'abbartā*) against his anointed (*'im m'šîhekā*, line 2) is in stark contrast to what we have seen in Psalms 2, 18 and 20. The negative tone is continued in vv. 51-52 (ET 50–51), part of the same lament, as it ends with a prayer for deliverance:

> Remember, O Lord, how thy servant is scorned;
> how I bear in my bosom the insults of the peoples,
> with which thy enemies taunt, O Lord,
> with which they mock the footsteps of thy anointed.

Within the context of the lament, the description of the anointed one being mocked and taunted (*ḥēr'pû...m'šîhekā*, line 4) by God's enemies (*'ôy'bêkā*, line 3) suggests a time of national crisis where the king is severely threatened by enemy nations. The actual crisis is of course impossible to establish: it might refer to the time of the death of Josiah, it could be the time of the exile of Jehoaichin, although the most likely date is 586, at the time of the total demise of the monarchy under Zedekiah. Whoever the actual monarch was, the references to the broken covenant made with God's servant (v. 40a, ET 39a) and the crown defiled in the dust (v. 40b, ET 39b) and the references to the loss of his sceptre and his throne (v. 45, ET 44) together suggest this is a lament that has been composed for a specific historical occasion which threatened the continuation of the Davidic dynasty.[16] This does not necessarily imply the ritual humiliation of the king, from which dramatic symbolism some eschatological hope may have developed; the figure in vv. 39-52 (ET 38–51) appears to be too human to be typical and idealized.[17] In Psalm 89 as a whole, the hymn extolling God's kingship in vv. 2-19 (ET 1–18), along with the adaptation of the covenantal promises concerning David (see 2 Sam. 7) in vv. 20-38 (ET 19–37) both become dramatic means whereby the composer of the lament in vv. 39-52 (ET 38–51) contrasts the present fate of the king with the past

---

16. The fact that this lament on the monarchy in Ps. 89 completes Book Three, and Book Four very quickly moves into the theme of God as King, suggests that this psalm has been placed here with the purpose of witnessing to the demise of the entire monarchy. See n. 46 below.

17. See H.-J. Kraus, *Psalmen 60–150* (BKAT, 15.2; Neukirchen–Vluyn: Neukirchener Verlag, 5th edn, 1978), p. 792 (ET *Psalms 60–150* [trans. H.C. Oswald; Minneapolis: Augsburg, 1989]), p. 210; also Oesterley, *The Psalms*, p. 397.

promises of God.[18] Hence far from looking forward into some great and glorious future, the purpose of the lament in the last part of Psalm 89 is to enable the psalmist to look back to when the Davidic dynasty was more secure. The anointed figure (*māšîaḥ*) is thus part of the same line of David: the continuity with the past is vital. It is difficult to see how the use of *māšîaḥ* in this psalm has any Messianic (note capital) connotations.

In Ps. 132.10, the psalmist asks God to hear the prayer of his anointed one:

> For thy servant David's sake
> do not turn away the face of thine anointed one.

Psalm 132.17 is the quotation of an oracle, and its concern is about Jerusalem as much as it is about the Davidic dynasty. Here the psalmist recalls the promises of God who has 'prepared a lamp for his anointed':

> There I will make a horn to sprout for David;
> I have prepared a lamp for my anointed.

Whether by way of prayer (v. 10) or by way of oracle (v. 17), the parallelism in both these verses indicates that the anointed one is indeed a Davidic king. Like Psalm 89, the poet's attention is on the past, focusing on the founding of the Davidic dynasty through the bringing of the Ark to Jerusalem. The only future orientation in this psalm is in its firm belief that God will not go back on his promises made in the past to David: he will ensure the continuation of the Davidic dynasty (vv. 11-12), that is, the king of the line of David. As with Psalms 2 and 20, some liturgical composition might be detected, in this case suggesting a ritual procession involving the role of the Ark.[19] Verses 1–10 relay the story of the bringing of the Ark to Zion in the form of a poetic prayer, with vv. 1-2, 3-5, and 6-10 suggesting some antiphonal res-

---

18. On the adaptation of 2 Sam. 7 by the poet of Ps. 89, see M. Fishbane, *Biblical Interpretation in Ancient Israel* (Oxford: Clarendon Press, 1985), pp. 466-67, quoted in M.E. Tate, *Psalms 51–100* (WBC, 20; Dallas: Word Books, 1990), pp. 417-18. On the influence of 2 Sam. 7 (or the traditions behind it) within other royal psalms, and the implications this has for a non-eschatological reading of these psalms, see n. 21, on Ps. 132, below.

19. This reference to the Ark in a ritual context further suggests that this is a pre-exilic psalm; the recital of this tradition was also used by the Deuteronomists, and in this psalm it simply serves the immediate needs of the community. See L.C. Allen, *Psalms 101–150* (WBC, 21; Waco, TX: Word Books, 1983), pp. 209-11.

ponses between the cultic leader and the congregation. Verses 11-18 consist of two oracles, the first concerning David (vv. 11-12) and the second, Zion and David's place there (vv. 13-16, 17-18). The references to the horn, lamp and crown in the latter oracle (vv. 17-18: *qeren, nēr, nizrô*) all suggest an actual reigning king, whose reign is ratified by the dynastic promises which God once made to David.[20] Furthermore, even in the postexilic period, this psalm would have served a similar purpose of creating new faith in the past promises of God. 2 Chron. 6.41 uses Ps. 132.8-10 ('Arise, O Lord, and go to thy resting place, thou and the ark of thy might') and its purpose there is to assure the restoration community of the importance of Zion by way of reference to the founding of Zion by David. Far from having an eschatological purpose in preparing the way for a great and glorious future, Psalm 132 served a historical purpose, not only in pre-exilic times, but also in the postexilic community, for its ancient promises assured the people of their origins and election from times of antiquity.[21]

In Ps. 45.8 (ET 7), the king is addressed as one who has been anointed by God. Here the Qal form of the verb is used ($\sqrt{m\check{s}h}$), rather than the noun *māšîaḥ*, as in the previous psalms. The reference to the 'oil of gladness' (*šemen śāśôn*, line 2) indicates the ceremony whereby the king 'becomes' the *māšîaḥ*:

> Therefore God, your God, has anointed you
> with the oil of gladness above your fellows.

Set within the context of the elevated courtly language in v. 7 (ET 6), concerning the king's throne being like the throne of God,[22] the two

20. Here again there is some connection with 2 Sam. 7, as in Ps. 89. See Allen, *Psalms 101–150*, pp. 208-209, and Kraus, *Psalmen 60–150*, pp. 1058-59 (ET *Psalms 60–150*, pp. 476-77), who refers to L. Rost, *Die Überlieferung von der Thronnachfolge Davids* (BWANT, 3.6; Stuttgart: W. Kohlhammer, 1926), suggesting that this was composed for a royal festival occasion. See also nn. 28 and 36 below.

21. The fact that this was used in the latter part of the Songs of Ascents shows further its purpose as a Zion psalm. Without a Davidic heading, it celebrates the founding of Zion as much as the inauguration of the Davidic dynasty. See Roberts, 'The Old Testament's Contribution', pp. 42-43, on the way that Psalm 132 was used to uphold royal Zion theology.

22. Concerning *kis'ăkā 'ĕlōhîm 'ôlām wā'ed šēbeṭ mîšōr šēbeṭ malkûtekā*, Craigie, *Psalms 1–50*, p. 337 prefers 'Your throne, O God, is forever and ever', reading *'ĕlōhîm* as vocative; Kraus, *Psalmen 1–59*, pp. 486-87 (ET *Psalms 1–59*, pp. 451-52) reads 'Your throne, O divine one, (stands) for ever and ever', seeing the

verses together show the intimacy of the king with God in his repre-
sentative office. In its verbal form the expression $m^e \check{s} \bar{a} h^a k \bar{a}$ $^{\prime e} l \bar{o} h \hat{i} m$ indicates the way in which the king is 'set apart' by the ritual of anointing
for his kingly office. The psalm is a wedding song, composed by a
court poet for the king, as v. 1 seems to imply:

> I address my verses to the king;
> my tongue is like the pen of a ready scribe...

The one addressed throughout the psalm is thus a royal bridegroom,
and so the anointed figure in v. 8 (ET v. 7) is the reigning king, probably from Judah.[23] The specificity of the references in vv. 9-10 (ET 8-
9), regarding the king's riches and his royal entourage, further imply
that the setting is the court of the king. Although it is impossible to
ascertain whether any ritual enactment of sacred marriage lay behind
this poem, as some commentators affirm,[24] it is nevertheless clear that
the occasion has everything to do with the present reign of the king and
little to do with any expectations of an idealized figure coming at some
future time.

Two other psalms use the term *māšîaḥ*. These may be contrasted with
the previous six, which are royal psalms, but they nevertheless confirm
my earlier observations. Psalm 28.8 speaks of Yahweh as the saving
refuge of his anointed:

> The Lord is the strength of his people,[25]
> he is the saving refuge of his anointed.

The psalm, which in this case may well be a postexilic composition,
is a combination of individual lament (vv. 1-5) and a thanksgiving for
deliverance (vv. 6-7), to which has been added a prayer of intercession

address is to the king. The preferred translation is taken from J.A. Emerton, 'The
Syntactical Problem of Psalm XLV.7 ', *JSS* 13 (1968), pp. 58-63, 'Thy throne is
like God's throne for ever and ever' (see Kraus, *Psalmen 1–59*, p. 487 [ET *Psalms
1–59*, p. 452]).

23. See Anderson, *Psalms*, I, p. 346; Weiser, *Die Psalmen*, pp. 243-45 (ET *The
Psalms*, pp. 361-63); also Day, *Psalms*, p. 93.

24. For example, A. Bentzen, *Introduction to the Old Testament*, I (Copen-
hagen: G.E.C. Gad, 4th edn, 1952), p. 129; G. Widengren, *Sakrales Königtum im
Alten Testament und im Judentum* (Stuttgart: W. Kohlhammer, 1955), p. 78.
Against this idea, see Day, *Psalms*, p. 105.

25. Here emending *lāmô* ('his strength') to *l^e'ammô* ('of his people') following
some Hebrew MSS, the Septuagint and Peshiṭta.

for the people as a whole. The reference to *mᵉšîḥô* in v. 8 thus has several possible interpretations: if it is pre-exilic, it is possible that it again refers to the king, who (as may be seen in the parallelism) represents the people as a whole. But it is more likely to be postexilic. In this case, a more corporate interpretation is fitting, due to the demise of the monarchy, whereby the people appropriated for themselves the promises once made to David: this is akin to the democratization of the royal promises suggested by Isa. 55.3.[26] Another possibility, also seeing the psalm as a postexilic composition, is that it is a reference to the anointed high priest, but the parallelism in the verse (reading *ʿōz–lᵉʿammô* ['the strength of his people'] and seeing it in parallelism with *ûmāʿōz...mᵉšîḥô* ['the saving refuge of his anointed']) makes the first option more preferable. By taking up a form of designation used previously for the king, the community as a whole can both remember and participate in the ancient (once royal) realm of salvation. Hence again *mᵉšîḥô* is used by way of reference to the past; the term still has no eschatological overtones.[27]

The final explicit use of *māšîaḥ* in the psalms is found in Ps. 84.10 (ET 9), where it occurs in a prayer asking God to look upon the face of his anointed:

> Behold our shield, O God;
> look upon the face of thine anointed!

Like Psalm 132, this psalm celebrates the importance of Zion in God's purpose for his people, and may well be a pilgrimage psalm sung before the gates of the Temple. Like Psalm 28, its more personal reflective tone suggests it is also a postexilic composition. If so, this poses the question of what purpose a prayer for the well-being of 'thine anointed' (*mᵉšîḥekā*, line 2) serves in the heart of such a psalm. Rather than having a communal application, as in Psalm 28, the term here does

---

26. See also the use of the term 'my anointed ones' (Hebrew) in Ps. 105.15, *'al-tiggᵉʿû bimᵉšîḥāy wᵉlinᵉbî'ay 'al-tārēʿû*, where the reference is to the patriarchs and prophets, again in a democratized sense. This has similarities with the way that the servant is used to denote the whole community in Isa. 41.8 and 44.1.

27. See Kraus, *Psalmen 1–59*, p. 375 (ET *Psalms 1–59*, p. 342), who, speaking of those who prefer an eschatological and messianic interpretation of this verse, states: '....."royal ideology"...is not able to see the distinctive relation of "the individual participation in the mystery of the royal realm of salvation"; it broadens the "royal elements" and covers the individual laments with a fictitious ideological interpretive category'.

seem more likely to recall the memory of the king: the parallelism of *māginnēnû* ('our shield') with *mᵉšîḥᵉkā* ('thine anointed') seems to suggest a royal designation. If the psalm is *pre-exilic*, then the explanation could simply be that the psalmist, at the royal shrine, is praying for the well-being of his patron, the Davidic king, upon whose welfare the well-being of the sanctuary in part depends. If the psalm is *postexilic*, as I have suggested, then such a prayer to the king need not be anachronistic: by recalling God's promise made to the king in ancient times the psalmist feels able to enter the same privileged royal realm of salvation.[28] Whichever date of composition one takes, the term *māšîaḥ* in this psalm has nothing to do with any Messianic overtones: it is used to point back to the past, not forward to the future.

To conclude: where *māšîah* is used in the six royal psalms, it concerns the living, reigning monarch and his successors; its meaning is entirely political and immediate.[29] To quote J. Becker, 'A preexilic messianism is almost a contradiction in terms, since the savior king is in fact present'.[30] Even when considering the use of the prayer in the two psalms which may well be postexilic, they look back to ancient days, using the memory of the monarchy as a means of evoking new faith in God's protection in the present. In none of these psalms is the term *māšîah* used with any eschatological orientation.

Psalms which Implicitly Refer to an 'Anointed One'
Five other psalms also speak of the king in an elevated courtly style, although *māšîah* itself is not used. Nevertheless, the royal figure appears to possess the same social and religious standing in the community as

28. This same point was made with reference to the use of Ps. 132.8-10 in 2 Chron. 6.41 in postexilic times. This also fits with the way in which other postexilic prayers about the well-being of the king were used, as in Pss. 61.6 and 63.11. On these two psalms, see below.

29. Cf. Roberts, 'The Old Testament's Contribution', p. 42 (referring to Pss. 2 and 110): 'The divine promises contained in these texts were made to particular kings or their subjects at particular points in the history of the monarchy. They were not prophecies holding out hope for a distant future but oracles that gave expression to political, social, and religious expectations for the reign of a contemporary king just being installed into office. As such, they served a political as well as a religious function...'

30. J. Becker, *Messiaserwartung im Alten Testament* (SBS, 83; Stuttgart: Katholisches Bibelwerk, 1977), p. 33 (ET *Messianic Expectation in the Old Testament* [trans. D.E. Green; Philadelphia: Fortress Press, 1980]), p. 38.

in the six royal psalms noted earlier. In Psalms 21 and 144, he is a leader in battle, along the lines of Psalms 18 and 20; in Psalm 110 he is a sacral figure in the cult, giving authority to the traditions of Zion, and suggesting a celebration of his accession to the throne, along the lines of Psalms 2 and 132. Psalms 72 and 101 stand apart from the earlier categories, implying instead some form of coronation oath, whereby the king promises to uphold the values of justice and wisdom throughout his reign. These so-called 'royal psalms' reflect some use by the monarch himself; as with the previous psalms, their purpose is thus to serve the immediate needs of the royal cult, and to presume any eschatological orientation in the first instance is to miss their original use.

The relevant parts of Psalm 21 are vv. 2 and 8 (ET 1 and 7):

> In thy strength the king rejoices, O Lord;
> and in thy help how greatly he exults! (v. 2, ET 1)

> For the king trusts in the Lord;
> and through the steadfast love of the Most High he shall not be moved.
> (v. 8, ET 7)

These verses, offered to the king by some cultic leader, perhaps a prophet, are prayers petitioning for successful military exploits. Whether this concerns a particular time of national crisis or a regular annual festival is unclear. But, as in previous psalms, the king is seen to be in a close relationship before God, who, by protecting him in battle, will also uphold the welfare of his people (vv. 9-13, ET 8–12), so that the royal victory leads to the exaltation of God himself (v. 14, ET 13). And here again this seems to refer to the reigning monarch himself; there is no suggestion of any once-for-all-time figure who is to come in the future.

Psalm 144, the other battle psalm, is a royal complaint (vv. 1-11) followed by a prayer of blessing (vv. 12-15). As a prayer concerning victory in battle it has a close relationship with Psalm 18, and hence also with 2 Samuel 22. In this case, the king is not explicitly mentioned, although the figure in question appears to have some standing within the community. There are so many associations with other psalms that it suggests a later creation impersonating a royal psalm.[31] Like Psalm 84, it is a means whereby the psalmist (probably, on account of the borrowings, after the exile) picks up older forms as a

---

31. On the borrowing of Ps. 144 from other psalms, see v. 5b//Ps. 104.32b; v. 9//Ps. 33.21-22; v. 15b//Ps. 33.39; v. 4b//Pss. 102.12 (ET 11) and 109.23.

way of giving his words authority by 'entering the royal realm'.[32] The fact that the Septuagint and the Targums give the psalm a particular historical context in the life of David's fight with Goliath, further illustrates this 'historicized' interpretation. The psalmist uses royal categories of thinking to build up the faith of the community: he looks back into the dynastic line of David, rather than looking forward into any eschatological future.

Psalm 110 offers an interesting range of interpretations regarding the relationship between the Davidic and Messianic, or between the historical and eschatological. Kidner, for example, understanding that the psalm has been Messianic from the outset, proposes that in v. 1a ('The Lord says to my Lord...') the king is offering homage to one greater than he; this indicates King David's own subordination to another Coming Figure, and hence it is an implicit prophecy about a future Messianic King.[33] But most commentators, on account of the archaic language and the disputed textual corruptions, assume the psalm to refer obliquely to some ancient sacral rites in the royal cult, although the exact setting of such rites is unclear. Its three oracular utterances (vv. 1, 3, 4) suggest it was part of some liturgy whereby (like Psalm 20) a cultic prophet addressed the reigning king and assured him of the success and prosperity which was his due (v. 4 and vv. 5-6). In this way Psalm 110 is like Psalm 132, in that it recalls the Davidic tradition in order to elevate as well God's protection of Zion. Like Psalm 132, it was used by the reigning king in order to remember the capture of Jerusalem and the accession of David to the Jebusite throne. Within such a religio-political context it could hardly refer to any eschatological ideal in the distant future.[34]

Psalm 72 is an accession or coronation psalm, whereby the people and a cultic leader pray for the king to uphold justice so that peace and prosperity may be the hallmark of his reign. Such a prayer is most likely to be used at the accession of a new king. In this case, of all the so-called Messianic psalms, we see here some merging of a present political reality with an idealized future hope; in this sense, one could argue that the interpretation of this psalm is more open than others to an

32. On this expression, see comments on Pss. 28 and 84 above.

33. Cf. D. Kidner, *Psalms 1–72* (TOTC; Leicester: Inter-Varsity Press, 1973), pp. 391-92.

34. Cf. Kraus, *Psalmen 60–150*, pp. 929-30 (ET *Psalms 60–150*, pp. 346-47); Anderson, *Psalms*, II, pp. 767-72; Allen, *Psalms 101–150*, pp. 83-86.

eschatological interpretation.[35] There are limitations in this view, however. For example, the references to political realities in the portrayal of the king's responsibility to protect the oppressed and the poor (vv. 12-14) hardly conform to the conditions of a great and glorious Messianic age; and furthermore, the people still intercede for the king's well-being (vv. 15-17), which could hardly be anyone other than a human figure—a greater Messiah (capital M) would pray for them. Therefore it could still be quite likely that, on account of the intercessory language, the psalm has been composed for a Davidic monarch, and the hoped-for future concerns the reign of that particular king—or at least, the reigns of his descendants. The Solomonic title indicates further the interest in the *historical* succession of kings after David.

Psalm 101 is similar to Psalm 72 and in many ways confirms the above observations. It was either composed for the time of the king's coronation, or for an annual festival commemorating the king's accession to the throne: like Psalm 72, it suggests a vow or a promise regarding the king's responsibilities throughout his reign. The references to the retinue and household (vv. 2, 7) and to judicial authority over evildoers (vv. 6, 8) indicate that, despite the typical language, the speaker of the vow is most likely to be the reigning king. The psalmist focuses more on the present realities of his vow, and less on any idealized future, as was seen in Psalm 72. No eschatological reading of Psalm 101 in its earlier setting is necessary.

Whether these five psalms are royal psalms or later imitations of royal psalms (possibly the case with Psalm 144), the figure they consistently refer to is the Davidic king, whether as a contemporary ruler, or

---

35. Cf. K. Heim, 'The Perfect King of Psalm 72', in P.E. Satterthwaite, R.S. Hess and G.J. Wenham (eds.), *The Lord's Anointed: Interpretation of Old Testament Messianic Texts* (Carlisle: Baker Books, 1995), pp. 223-48. Speaking of the psalm's original cultic setting, its later literary setting (at the end of Book Two) and its place in later Jewish and Christian reception history, Heim concludes that the prayer is an intercession for the present king, and the answer was expected during his lifetime (p. 231) but that its placing in the Psalter with the concluding doxology demonstrates that its contents began to 'encourage a messianic interpretation' (p. 248) in the way the discrepancy between the non-fulfilment of the Davidic covenant and the promise of God gave way to some future hope. Anderson, *Psalms*, I, p. 519 makes the same point: 'the psalm must have looked not only to the present but also to the future...when the ideals and hopes expressed by this poem would be realised'. See also Weiser, *Die Psalmen*, pp. 341-42 (ET *The Psalms*, p. 502).

as King David himself as the focal point of God's covenant made in earlier days.[36] Whether serving as battle psalms (21, 144), or as psalms recalling the king's accession (110), or as psalms of royal decree (72, 101), they all reflect earthly, historical, political roots. There is no need to give these psalms a Messianic reading when the material and natural meaning will do.[37] It seems safer to assume, with Mowinckel, that '...the substance of the Messianic hope was taken from the royal ideology, and not vice versa'.[38]

Other Psalms which may Refer to a Royal Figure
Scholars have long recognized that the so-called royal psalms might also include a much larger group on the basis that the suppliant seems to have some authority over the people as well as that degree of intimacy with God which would be expected of a king.[39] Furthermore, because some of these psalms (notably Psalms 22 and 69) form the basis of a good deal of Messianic interpretation in New Testament times, and because they are key psalms for those who take seriously a prophecy–fulfilment schema in psalmody, their potential as Messianic psalms is a serious issue.[40]

The clearest examples in this category include Psalms 9–10, 22, 40, 41, 49, 56, 59, 68, 69, 86, 88, 91 and 116. It is impossible in the scope of this paper to look at each of these psalms in any detail; but, on account of the fact they are even more enigmatic about a particular

36. The traditions of the founding of Zion and of the promises made through Nathan to King David (as in 2 Sam. 7) are of paramount importance here; this tradition has undoubtedly influenced Pss. 2, 89 and 132 explicitly, but also Pss. 72 and 110 referred to here.

37. Such a reading corresponds well with the fact that there is very little Messianic awareness in other pre-exilic material, not least in the Deuteronomistic history and in the classical prophets. See Roberts, 'The Old Testament's Contribution', pp. 44-49 ; also K.E. Pomykala, *The Davidic Dynasty Tradition in Early Judaism. Its History and Significance for Messianism* (SBLEJL, 7; Atlanta: Scholars Press, 1995), Chapter 2, 'The Biblical Background', pp. 11-68.

38. Cf. Mowinckel, *Han som kommer*, p. 88 (ET *He That Cometh*, p. 124).

39. For example, see Croft, *The Identity of the Individual*, pp. 179-81, which lists 47 so-called royal psalms.

40. On this issue, particularly that of prophecy and fulfilment in psalmody, see J.G. McConville, 'Messianic Interpretation of the Old Testament in Modern Context', in Satterthwaite, Hess and Wenham (eds.), *The Lord's Anointed*, pp. 1-17, esp. pp. 9-15.

reigning king, let alone about any specific coming figure, to label them as 'Messianic' creates great difficulties of interpretation. The best illustrations are perhaps Psalms 22 and 69. Both are mixed psalms: 22.2-22 (ET 1–21) is a lament, and 22.23-32 (ET 22–31) is a thanksgiving; similarly, 69.2-30 (ET 1–29) is a lament, and 69.31-27 (ET 30–36) is praise. For Christian interpreters, one key reason for assuming them to be royal at all is that the suffering figure may refer to the ritual humiliation and eventual restoration of the king; this then becomes a 'type' for Christological eisegesis. There are problems in this approach, however: for example, they may not be pre-exilic and hence the suffering figure may not be the monarch after all; or again, even if they are pre-exilic, any ritual humiliation cannot be established with any certainty, for the experiences depicted in them may be more actual and personal than typical and ritual.

A more cautious approach is to see that these two psalms, as well as the other psalms in the above list, are significant *not* because of a royal and Messianic ideal written into them at the outset, but because they are good examples of how psalms *become* Messianic on account of what is brought to them (mainly in Christological terms). To study this group of psalms would therefore take us too far into the complexities of the reception history of particular psalms. Thus we must return instead to the question whether any Messianic interpretation was given to the other psalms we have looked at—if not in pre-exilic times, at least in the later stages of their liturgical and literary history.

2. The Question of a 'Messianic' Orientation in Psalmody during the Early Second Temple Period

If Psalms 84 and 144 are postexilic compositions, then these provide a useful starting point for understanding royal orientation in psalmody in the Second Temple period. And even if they are not, other psalms prove the same point. The Davidic prayers added to postexilic psalms such as 61.7-8 (ET 6–7), 'Prolong the life of the king; may his years endure to all generations!' and 63.12 (ET 11), 'But the king shall rejoice in God; all who swear by him shall glory...' each illustrate how prayer forms sought to model themselves on the piety of revered kings—again not suggesting any eschatological sense, but a reflective, exemplary one.

During the process of the growth of the Psalter in the postexilic period, two other significant factors illustrate that psalmody was still understood at this time more in terms of its orientation backwards, into the time of the Davidic dynasty, rather than forwards, in terms of some great and glorious Messianic kingdom. The first concerns the Davidic superscriptions; the second, the three royal collections usually known as the 'Davidic Psalters'.

Although commentators such as Brevard Childs, who were concerned to demonstrate the close theological relationship between the Old and New Testaments, believed the Davidic superscriptions to be Messianic,[41] it is more likely that their purpose was to portray David as the ideal figure of piety. The life and times of King David, as seen in the 13 historical superscriptions to the psalms,[42] become a 'type' for others to follow. A further 59 psalms were given a Davidic heading: whatever one makes of the date and provenance of the recurring superscription 'Psalm of David' (*mizmôr lᵉdāwid*) it cannot be denied that it served to promote the memory of the royal cult, thus giving authority to the antiquity of psalmody by way of reference to its patron.[43] Thus these Davidic superscriptions illustrate the way in which the collectors and editors looked *back* to the ancient figurehead of David as much as they looked *forward* to an ideal Messianic figure to come.[44] This process in psalmody has interesting correspondences with the Chronicler's use of the traditions of David: although some scholars have proposed that the Chronicler does indeed have an eschatological bias, it is equally possible that his appropriation of the many Davidic traditions corresponds with the historical approach of the psalmists.[45] Although

---

41. Cf. B.S. Childs, *Introduction to the Old Testament as Scripture* (London: SCM Press, 1979), pp. 515-17.

42. Pss. 3, 7, 18, 34, 51, 52, 54, 56, 57, 59, 60, 63, 142.

43. See Day, *Psalms*, pp. 114-15; S.E. Gillingham, *The Poems and Psalms of the Hebrew Bible* (Oxford: Oxford University Press, 1994), pp. 246-48.

44. Cf. G.H. Wilson, *The Editing of the Hebrew Psalter* (SBLDS, 76; Chico, CA: Scholars Press, 1985), pp. 171-73, who sees the purpose of the historical superscriptions was to enhance the narrative by way of a poetic commentary, thus reflecting a historically orientated reading of these psalms.

45. For a positive view of eschatology in Chronicles, cf. G. von Rad, *Das Geschichtsbild des chronistischen Werkes* (Stuttgart: W. Kohlhammer, 1930), pp. 119-31, who sees the hope as Messianic. By contrast, see M. Noth, *Überlieferungsgeschichtliche Studien* (Tübingen: Max Niemeyer, 2nd edn, 1957), pp. 179-80 (ET *The Chronicler's History* [trans. H.G.M. Williamson with introduction; JSOTSup, 50; Sheffield: JSOT Press, 1987] pp. 105-106), who sees what future hope there is, lies in the restoration of the Davidic dynasty. On this point, see also H.G.M. Williamson, 'Eschatology in Chronicles', *TynBul* 28 (1979), pp. 115-54. For a more reserved view, that the Chronicler's use of David is to legitimize the present

this is not to negate entirely any future orientation within the books of Chronicles, the Chronicler's concern to legitimize the Second Temple cult, on the basis that its roots lie way back in royal antiquity, has many associations with the ways in which Psalms 110 and 132 would have been used in this period. An appeal to David was an appeal to the founding of Zion, and from this, a justification for the reinstating of Zion theology by the building of the Second Temple. To reflect upon the promises once made through the Davidic covenant made some sense of the present conflict between faith and experience: hence to look back to David was in part a means of evoking a typical figure of piety, but more importantly, in socio-political terms, it was also a means of gaining legitimization for the Second Temple cult. Even when the Davidic traditions do seem to have hints of a future hope (illustrated by a few references, not in Samuel and Kings, to the eternal covenant made with David, for example in 1 Chron. 16.17, taken from Ps. 105.1-15), this may be seen as essentially 'royalist' (that is, a hope for the restoration of the Davidic dynasty itself) rather than particularly 'eschatological': in other words, the Chronicler is still thinking in messianic, not Messianic terms. Throughout the time when the psalms were being edited and collected, the *historical* David seems to have been as important a factor as it had been in the pre-exilic times.

A second indication of this backward look to David is found in the three Davidic collections. McCann's observations are important in this respect. He notes that the placing of strategic royal psalms at the seams of Books One, Two and Three gives the Psalter a sequence of critical events in the life of the monarchy—first, the inauguration of the covenant with David (Psalm 2), then the statement about the responsibilities of the Davidic king (Psalm 72), and finally the account of the downfall of the dynasty (Psalm 89).[46] After Book Three we find a so-called psalm of Moses (Psalm 90), recalling a different covenant from

Temple community by way of reference to royal traditions of antiquity, see D.N. Freedman, 'The Chronicler's Purpose', *CBQ* 23 (1961), pp. 436-42; also S. Japhet, *The Ideology of Chronicles and Its Place in Biblical Thought* (ET Beiträge zur Erforschung des Alten Testaments und des Antiken Judentums, 9; Frankfurt am Main: Peter Lang, 1989), pp. 493-504.

46. See J.C. McCann, 'Books I–III and the Editorial Purpose of the Hebrew Psalter', in J.C. McCann (ed.), *The Shape and Shaping of the Psalter* (JSOTSup, 159; Sheffield: JSOT Press, 1993), pp. 93-107. Also G.H. Wilson, 'Shaping the Psalter: A Consideration of Editorial Linkage in the Book of Psalms' in McCann (ed.), *The Shape and Shaping*, pp. 72-82.

that with David; after this are the many psalms extolling God as King (e.g. Pss. 93, 95–99), which focus instead on the ever-present sovereign rule of God in the absence of the dynastic rule of the king.

Two observations follow from this. First, there *is* an eschatological element in psalmody in Books Four and Five, as expressed in the enthronement psalms and the other hymns of praise which speak of the kingly rule of God.[47] When such a future hope is expressed, it is still by way of reference to the securing of a better future for the Temple community in that or the next generation; although we cannot look at these psalms in detail here, none of them suggests the idealized eschatology depicting a new era, with a Coming Deliverer who will bring about a new and different future at a time known only to God. Consequently, the other fragmentary Davidic collections included in Books Four and Five do not serve any Messianic purpose. Psalms such as 101, 110, 132 and 144, discussed earlier, each with a focus on the historical figure of the Davidic king, at the very most may have pointed to the hope in the restoration of the Davidic dynasty, and so could be seen as messianic in a royalist sense. Through the process of editing the Psalter as a whole, the faith which is expressed in the fifty-seven *ledāwid* psalms is still rooted in the memory of the monarchy, and even though there may be some element of hope in the reiteration of such promises, their main purpose (as seen especially in Psalms 110 and 132, as we saw earlier) is to uphold the legitimacy of the Temple, and with that, the worship of God there.[48]

47. Most of the royal psalms have this same emphasis on the kingly rule of God; this suggests that their key theological appeal during the restoration period was not only their belief in a coming kingly messiah, but also, more fundamentally, their belief in *God* as king. It was this latter emphasis which influenced the apocalyptic writings such as Zech. 14 and Dan. 7: see S.E. Gillingham, 'Psalmody and Apocalyptic in the Hebrew Bible: Common Vision, Shared Experience?', in J. Barton and D.J. Reimer (eds.), *After the Exile: Essays in Honour of Rex Mason* (Macon, GA: Mercer University Press, 1996), pp. 147-69, especially p. 163, on the influence of the Kingship Psalms on apocalyptic ways of thinking.

48. This feature in Books Four and Five may also explain a problem with regard to Pss. 2, 72 and 89, the psalms at the seams of Books One, Two and Three. All these three psalms fail to have a *Davidic* heading: Ps. 2 has no heading, Ps. 72 is ascribed to Solomon, and Ps. 89 to Ethan. It may be that the themes of the Kingship of God and the place of Zion in these three psalms was sufficient; it is certainly odd that, if a royalist and/or eschatological interpretation was intended, they have received no Davidic superscription.

We may therefore conclude that in the earlier and later stages of the growth of the Psalter, the theological concerns of the postexilic editors and collectors was as 'non-Messianic' as were those of the pre-exilic composers. A 'Messianic' reading of the psalms thus occurred at some stage later. So when and why did any Messianic consciousness influence a reading of psalmody?

3. *The Rise of Messianic Expectation and its Impact on Psalmody*

Between the period of the editing and collecting of the psalms, when the royal Messianic interpretation seems to have been peripheral, and the Christian period, when over half of the Psalter appears to have been adapted to some Messianic interpretation,[49] something clearly happened within the Judaeo-Christian tradition to bring about this change of emphasis. For the Christians were not the initiators of such a Messianic orientation: it was a tradition which they popularized, but had inherited from Jewish midrashic practices before them.[50]

Three pieces of evidence give some hints as to how this gradual process of the Messianic reading of the psalms took shape. These are first, the Septuagint translation of the Psalter, secondly, copies of psalmody found at Qumran, and thirdly, the apocalyptic psalms in the *Psalms of*

---

49. See L. Sabourin, *The Psalms: Their Origin and Meaning* (New York: Alba House, 1974), pp. 163-71, who lists 360 quotations from the psalms used in the New Testament, many of which have a Messianic interpretation. See also Kaiser, *The Messiah*, pp. 92-135, who examines eleven psalms which he sees are used in the New Testament in this way.

50. See J.H. Charlesworth, 'From Messianology to Christology: Problems and Prospects', in Charlesworth (ed.), *The Messiah*, pp. 3-35; also Pomykala, *The Davidic Dynasty Tradition*, pp. 270-71, who also makes the important point that there is most certainly not one single unvariable tradition of Davidic Messianism, whether in the Judaic or the Christian tradition. Furthermore, it is important to see that the Christian eisegesis was, more often than not, in radical discontinuity with the Jewish tradition: royal psalms such as Pss. 2, 89, 110 and 132, which previously were used to legitimate the Jews as a nation over and against the foreign nations, whereby the 'Messianic figure' would put down the might of enemy powers, were used to show that this figure would depose even the Jewish people themselves, in favour of the Christian community *over and against* the Jews. See, for example, D.J.A. Clines, *Interested Parties: The Ideology of Writers and Readers of the Hebrew Bible* (JSOTSup, 205; Sheffield: JSOT Press, 1995), especially 'Psalm 2 and the MLF (Moabite Liberation Front)', pp. 244-75, on a typically Christian reading of Psalm 2.

Solomon. None of these offers evidence of a really dramatic change of direction, but the last two examples in particular reveal an interesting relationship between psalmody and apocalyptic, and so offer illustrations of the way in which the language of liturgy became combined with the particular eschatological expectations of the day.[51]

The Septuagint translation of the Psalter is usually dated between the second and first centuries BCE. A comparison between the Greek version and the Hebrew reveals some small but nevertheless interesting differences and adaptations, not only in terms of a general eschatological outlook, but also in terms of some specific examples of Messianism.[52] Schaper's work on the Greek Psalter is seminal in this respect, not least his assertion that the theology of the translators reveals certain anti-Hasmonaean and proto-Pharisaic tendencies.[53]

Two examples of what we might now call 'Messianic *eis*egesis' must suffice. They are important because each occurs in psalms which we looked at earlier (Psalms 72 and 110), and we can see the way in which a previously royal, human figure is now given a transcendent, even pre-existent status, thus transforming a messianic function into a Messianic title.

Psalm 72.17 (Greek 71.17) reads:

> ἔστω τὸ ὄνομα αὐτοῦ εὐλογημένον εἰς τοὺς αἰῶνας,
> πρὸ τοῦ ἡλίου διαμενεῖ τὸ ὄνομα αὐτοῦ·
> καὶ εὐλογηθήσονται ἐν αὐτῷ πᾶσαι αἱ φυλαὶ τῆς γῆς,
> πάντα τὰ ἔθνη μακαριοῦσιν αὐτόν.

We may note briefly the change of emphasis in line 1 of this verse, where the name of the king is blessed (εὐλογημένον); this compares with the Hebrew *yᵉhî šᵉmô lᵉ'ôlām*, which implies that the name of the king is to endure (euphemistically, is to be 'remembered') for ever. This anticipates the importance of the blessing of the king in lines 3 and 4, but line 1 is a change of meaning. A more significant change is found in line 2 of v. 17: the emendation πρὸ τοῦ ἡλίου διαμενεῖ τὸ ὄνομα αὐτοῦ ('before the sun was created, his name will remain') certainly

51. See Gillingham, 'Psalmody and Apocalyptic', pp. 163-69.

52. See J. Schaper, *Eschatology in the Greek Psalter* (WUNT, 2.76; Tübingen: J.C.B. Mohr [Paul Siebeck], 1995), especially pp. 26-30, 'On the Question of Eschatology and Messianism', and pp. 144-64, 'Eschatological and Messianic Expectations'.

53. See Schaper, *Eschatology*, pp. 138-44; also Pomykala, *The Davidic Dynasty Tradition*, pp. 128-31, and more specifically, on the Septuagint, pp. 270-71.

hints at a belief in this figure's pre-existence, and certainly changes the sense of, for example, the Hebrew *lipnê-šemeš yinnôn šᵉmô* and the RSV rendering '[may] his fame continue as long as the sun'. The Hebrew text is admittedly difficult, not least because of its poetic hyperbole, but the fact that in Hebrew the subject is the reigning king is evident from the context of the rest of the psalm as well as from the parallelism in the previous line:

> May his name endure for ever,
> his fame continue as long as the sun!

This certainly seems to be an invocation that the name of the king should be remembered for successive generations after his reign.[54] This also corresponds with a similar idea expressed earlier in the psalm:

> May he live while the sun endures (v. 5).[55]

In the earlier discussion of Psalm 72, I noted how the psalm came close to the idea of an idealized future which was part of a more Messianic interpretation; hence it could be argued that this psalm lends itself well to the way the Greek translators chose to reinterpret the original meaning. The representation of this figure as mysterious and pre-existent corresponds interestingly with the same idea of a pre-existent Messiah in apocalyptic writings such as *1 En.* 48. 2-3: 'Before the sun was created, His name was named before the Lord of Spirits'.

Another example of this same sort of 'Messianic eisegesis' is found in the second half of Ps. 110.3 (Greek 109.3). There are obvious difficulties both in translating and in understanding the meaning of this verse at all. The relevant part of the verse reads:

> From the womb of the morning
> the dew your youth will come to you.

---

54. On Ps. 72, see for example Anderson, *Psalms*, I, p. 256, referring to the way some translations replace *šᵉmô* (his name) with *zarʿô* (his descendants), thus recalling the Abrahamic promises in Genesis about the name, land and descendants, and underscoring the royal and political reading of this verse. See also Tate, *Psalms 51–100*, pp. 224-25; and Kraus, *Psalmen 60–150*, pp. 659, 661 (ET *Psalms 60–150*, pp. 79-80), who both prefer the ordinary, literal reading of v. 17 as well as of v. 5.

55. Note that the Septuagint has similarly changed the meaning of this verse, so that the Hebrew *yîrā'ûkā* ('they will fear you') is translated as συμπαραμενεῖ, reading the Hebrew as *yaʿᵃrîk* ('he will endure'), which corresponds theologically with the same changes made in v. 17.

As was noted earlier for this psalm, its context suggests a cultic setting whereby a prophetic figure offers an oracle concerning the blessings due to the now reigning king.[56] Unlike Psalm 72, there is no way in which the psalm could be read eschatologically as a royal psalm in a pre-exilic context. Certainly there is little to suggest that the psalmist is concerned about the king's status before birth.[57] But the Septuagint reads Ps. 110.3c (Greek 109.3c) in a similar way to the reading of Ps. 72.17 (Greek 71.17), ἐκ γαστρὸς πρὸ ἑωσφόρου ἐξεγέννησά σε, which might be translated: 'From the womb I have begotten you before the morning star'.[58] This again suggests that the figure who is the subject of the psalm is one conceived even before the earth itself; again, he is a pre-existent figure, and, by rereading the Melchizedek blessing in v. 4, a figure whose work could be combined with *priestly* as much as *royal* concerns.[59] Hence again any suggestion of this psalm referring back to the pre-exilic Davidic king, with his sacral role in the Temple cult, is now overlaid with a more superhuman interpretation. To use my earlier terminology, the status of the Messiah in this psalm is no longer a small m, but a capital M.

Two verses from two psalms hardly do justice to the full scope of this argument, but at least they serve to demonstrate in part the shift from the historical to the eschatological mode of interpretation. Those who need to be persuaded further about the eschatological and Messianic bias in the Greek Psalms should consult Joachim Schaper's work, which covers not only the psalms that were discussed earlier but also a number of other 'non-royal' psalms.[60]

A second illustration of this shift in interpretation is found in the writings from Qumran. On the negative side, the lack of *Pᵉšārîm*, or biblical commentaries on the relevant psalms, means that we have very little information about the Messianic use of our canonical psalms at

56. On this psalm, see above.

57. Allen, *Psalms 101–150*, pp. 80-81 translates this 'From the womb of the dawn you will have the dew of your youth'. Kraus, *Psalmen 60–150*, p. 934 (ET *Psalms 60–150*, p. 350) sees the dew as signifying life-giving strength to the king. Both readings illustrate how this can be applied to the actual, reigning king.

58. Cf. Schaper, *Eschatology*, pp. 101-107, 129.

59. See Schaper, *Eschatology*, pp. 140-42, who notes how the translators saw in the psalm an ideal combination of priestly (v. 3) and transcendent (v. 4) Messianic tendencies as a way of dissenting against the ascendency of the Hasmonaean house.

60. Cf. Schaper, *Eschatology*, pp. 26-30, and pp. 138-39 on the development of this theme.

Qumran.[61] In addition, the existence of other psalms such as 151, describing David's fight with Goliath, might suggest that an important way of understanding the figure of David was as an exemplar of piety—again, in historical terms rather than eschatological ones.[62] Nevertheless, the Qumran community does in fact offer some interesting examples of an eschatological reading of psalmody, in their *copies* of psalms which use apocalyptic ideas expressed in liturgical language. The most obvious examples are found in *The Psalms of Thanksgiving* or *Hôdāyôt* (1QH). One illustration is the hymn in col. 11 (formerly numbered 3), where vv. 5-18 speak of the birth of the Messiah and the destruction of the wicked; as well as using the prophetic language from Isa. 9.2-6 (ET 3-7) and 11.1-9, a good deal of psalmic language is also evident throughout the hymn:[63]

> For amid the throes of Death
> she shall bring forth a man-child
> and amid the pains of Hell
> there shall spring from her child-bearing crucible
> A Marvellous Mighty Counsellor;
> and a man shall be delivered from out of the throes.[64]

61. For example, *Commentary on the Psalms* (4Q171; 4Q173) is mainly concerned with Ps. 37, a non-royal psalm, applying it to the present conflicts concerning the Teacher of Righteousness and the Wicked Priest, without any Messianic reorientation.

62. Cf. 11QPs[a], although this of course also could be applied to the Septuagint, which also has a Greek version of Ps. 151.

63. See G. Vermes, *The Complete Dead Sea Scrolls in English* (London: Allen Lane, Penguin Press, 1997), p. 259, from which the translation of this verse is taken. See also L.H. Schiffman, 'Messianic Figures and Ideas in the Qumran Scrolls' in Charlesworth (ed.), *The Messiah*, pp. 116-29, who is cautious about proposing any Messianic figure in the Scrolls (pp. 128-29). See also Pomykala, *The Davidic Dynastic Tradition*, pp. 212-14, who notes that the Qumran documents also speak of a royal messianic figure, but one subordinated to a priestly messianic leader (1QSa 2.11-21).

64. Another example might be *The Melchizedek Scroll* (11QMelch), concerning 'Heavenly Prince Melchizedek'. Although neither a translation nor a commentary on Ps. 110 itself, as a document of some thirteen fragments it depicts Melchizedek (rather than any royal figure) as a heavenly deliverer, proclaiming liberty to the captives at the end of time, and in this sense is a type of midrash on the tradition in Ps. 110. On 11QMelch 2.4-18, see L.L. Grabbe, *An Introduction to First Century Judaism* (Edinburgh: T. & T. Clark, 1996), pp. 88-93, who sees this as the *earliest*

Despite the *Hôdāyôt*, many Qumran scholars are rightly cautious about there being sufficient evidence for a Messianic figure in the Scrolls. Pomykala's position is thus interesting in the context of this paper. Believing that the community's writings often demonstrate an anti-Hasmonaean stance (akin to that proposed by Schaper on the part of the Septuagint translators) he takes five documents (4Q504, 4Q252, 4Q174, 4Q161 and 4Q285) and shows how these depict a figure known as 'the Branch of David' (*ṣemaḥ dāwid*) who was to arise in the last days. This is a coming figure, who fulfils the Davidic covenant (passages such as 2 Samuel 7 and Psalms 89, 132 thus being a critical part of this tradition), whose life reflects typically royal qualities (for example, righteousness, wisdom and might, as seen in Psalm 72), and whose chief purpose is to fight against the sons of darkness. Pomykala concludes that although this figure is by no means as distinctive as in apocalyptic literature, there is nevertheless sufficient evidence to believe that the Qumran community interpreted in a Messianic way the Davidic dynastic tradition which forms the core of the psalms.[65]

The third illustration of the Messianic use of the psalmic traditions is found in *The Psalms of Solomon*, especially *Psalms of Solomon* 17. This psalm is particularly important, because it refers to Pompey's capture of Jerusalem and the exile of Aristobolus II, but is silent about the revolt of Alexander in 57 BCE, and so can be dated between 61 and 57 BCE. It thus gives important specific insights regarding Messianic expectation at this time. Verse 4 is dependent upon the same historical tradition of the Davidic ruler which is found in 2 Samuel 7 and in the royal psalms such as 89 and 132:

> Lord, you chose David to be king over Israel,
> and swore to him about his descendants forever,
> that his kingdom should not fail before you.[66]

The psalm goes on to explain how the Davidic line has been usurped by impostors, how God has punished the sinners by the hand of a foreigner, and how this figure in turn scattered the pious so that the land and

---

text concerning a heavenly Messiah; although it is a development of the psalmic tradition, because of the priestly appropriation, it is not as striking as the example from the *Hôdāyôt*.

65. Cf. Pomykala, *The Davidic Dynasty Tradition*, pp. 232-46; Pomykala however sees that this hope did not really flourish until the Herodian period.

66. The translation is from *OTP*, II, pp. 665-66.

people, now tainted by sin, are in need of deliverance which God alone can give. As thinly veiled references to the rise of the Hasmonaean dynasty, to Pompey's capture of Jerusalem, and to the consequences this had for the Temple community, the prayer in v. 21 has its own historical context:

> See, Lord, and raise up for them their king,
> the son of David, to rule over your servant Israel
> in the time known to you, O God.

The plea to 'raise up a king' demonstrates that the belief in the historical David has been increasingly transformed into an eschatological hope. This coming deliverer will purge Jerusalem—not so much with military might, as in Qumran, but with justice and righteousness. As the royal king in Ps. 2.9 was promised success in his reign by breaking the nations with an iron rod, so the coming 'Son of David' (the first time this title has been used in Jewish writings) will smash with an iron rod *his* opponents—not only the Gentiles, this time, but the sinners of his own people as well (v. 24). Verses 32-43 develop this Messianic interpretation even more explicitly: like David himself, this is a divinely appointed king, but unlike the Davidic dynastic rulers, who were dependent upon successive leaders, the figure here is a once-for-all-time Deliverer. And whereas the royal house of David was to establish continuously peace and order from one generation to another, the figure in *Psalms of Solomon* 17, coming in an age of chaos where all order has broken down (both within and without the Temple community), is appointed by God to bring about an entirely *new* world order.

It is therefore clear that *Psalms of Solomon* 17 offers the first really clear example of a Messianic interpretation of the Davidic psalms. Even the term itself, *māšîaḥ*, is found in *Pss. Sol.* 17.32.[67] We may note Pomykala's observations about the way *Psalms of Solomon* 17 provided a key turning point in the development of Messianic expectation on account of the disappointment with the Hasmonaeans at this time:

> Thus, *Pss. Sol.* 17 is the first evidence for the expression of hope for a davidic messiah in early Jewish literature. The emergence of this interpretation of the davidic dynastic tradition in the mid-first century BCE was based on the utility of the concept of a Son of David for negating

---

67. The term is also found in *Pss. Sol.* 18.5, 7 and in the superscription to this psalm. Space prevents a further analysis of this other psalm.

the legitimacy of the Hasmonean royal house and for envisioning an ideal social and political order, free from oppression and impurity, and characterized by piety, righteousness, and wisdom.[68]

Hence in various stages from the time of the Seleucid rule in the second century onwards, and especially by the time of the Hasmonaeans in the mid-first century BCE, various dissenting Jewish parties enabled the Messianic interpretation of the psalms to gain some credibility. The Hasmonaeans, a priestly party taking upon themselves the titles of Davidic kings whilst having no Davidic descent, created the need on the part of the dissemblers to look forward to the inauguration of a new, genuinely Davidic age—an age which would mark the completion of the old Davidic covenant, yet (on account of the demise of the monarchy and hence the break in the dynasty itself) would also be entirely different from it, in terms of the supernatural origins and once-for-all nature of the Royal Deliverer. A striking illustration of this way of thinking (for it took on many facets) is thus *Psalms of Solomon* 17, for it shows us how this new way of reading psalmody was influenced as much by socio-political factors as by theological ones.[69] This is, of course, also evident in a vast array of other non-liturgical literature from this time onwards: texts such as *1 En.* 45.3, 46.3, 48.2, 6, 49.2, 53.6, 54.4, 55.4 , and also *2 Baruch* 29, *4 Ezra* 7, 12, 13, and Sir. 36.1-13 serve as diverse examples of the same approach. The search for a Messianic figure to bring in a new age, albeit developed in different ways in different traditions, is very much the hallmark of this period. This is important because it shows that what we have seen here to be evident in the interpretation of the Psalms is but a smaller part of a much larger process.[70]

68. Pomykala, *The Davidic Dynastic Tradition*, p. 169. See also Grabbe, *An Introduction*, pp. 66-71, on *Pss. Sol.* 17, who makes a similar point.

69. In addition to Pomykala and Schaper who hold this view of the reception history of psalmody, see Becker, *Messiaserwartung im Alten Testament*, Chapter 14, 'Messianische Erwartung an der Schwelle des Neuen Testaments', pp. 82-87 (ET *Messianic Expectation in the Old Testament*, Chapter 14, 'The Threshold of the New Testament', pp. 87-92); also Mowinckel, *Han som kommer*, Chapter 9, 'Den nasjonale Messias' (ET *He That Cometh*, Chapter 9, 'The National Messiah').

70. On this issue, see for example R.A. Horsley, '"Messianic" Figures and Movements in First-Century Palestine', in Charlesworth (ed.), *The Messiah*, pp. 261-75. This process is not only evident in the Jewish tradition: other peoples in the ancient Near East who had also been deprived of their national identity by the Greeks used their own ideologies of kingship in a similar eschatological way. On

The development of Messianic expectation in the first century BCE also explains how and why the psalms were used in this way by Christians. They simply continued a tradition that had been set before them. Furthermore, it explains why this approach to psalmody continued after the Christian era within the Jewish tradition: the *Christian* Messianic adaptation of the psalms was a small part of a much larger Jewish process which preceded it and continued alongside it.[71]

Conclusions

We may therefore conclude that although the psalms provided the soil for Messianic eisegeis, they were certainly not written as Messianic compositions. In the pre-exilic period, when the royal psalms were first composed and used, their orientation was present, immediate, literal and royal; this focus continued into the postexilic period, with the royal dimension now offering the Jerusalem Temple community a particular sense of their identity in Zion on the basis of God's promises to David in the past. At this stage, the use of the Davidic figure in the psalmic collections was no more than the use of the Solomonic figure in the wisdom writings, or the Moses figure in the legal material: at that time, neither Moses nor Solomon were understood then in any developed, eschatological sense; and nor, so it would seem, was David.

Hence it should be clear that the question of 'The Messiah in the Psalms' cannot be answered positively within canonical psalmody; the answer is only found in the later reception history of the psalmic tradition. The question is not about the nature of the composition, editing and collecting of the psalms in their earliest stages, but about their adaption and usage at the stage after they have been brought into a recognizable liturgical collection. Providing this distinction is made and acknowledged, it is possible to talk about the Messiah in the Psalms— not as a theological agenda arising out of the psalms themselves, but as one which has been imposed upon them.

this issue, see for example J.J. Collins, *The Apocalyptic Vision of the Book of Daniel* (HSM, 16; Missoula, MT: Scholars Press, 1977), pp. 192-93, referring to the Egyptian Demotic chronicle, the Potter's Oracle, and the Persian oracle of Hystaspes.

71. See for example U. Simon, *Four Approaches to the Book of Psalms from Saadiah Gaon to Abraham Ibn Ezra* (trans. L.J. Schramm; New York: State University of New York Press, 1991), on the four uses of the psalms in later Jewish tradition, of which one is the continued use of the psalms as 'Mandatory Prophetic Prayers' (pp. 59-111).

THE MESSIANIC TEXTS IN ISAIAH 1–39

H.G.M. Williamson

The aim of the present essay is to look again at four of the five classical messianic passages in the first part of the book of Isaiah. In the present state of Isaiah research, however, it would be irresponsible to ignore their setting in the wider book as a whole. Before turning to a discussion of the passages themselves, therefore, two introductory matters require attention in the belief that they may help us to make some slight progress on what, it must be admitted, is an otherwise well-worn topic.[1]

Apart from the formulaic headings in Isa. 1.1 and 6.1, the first character in the book of Isaiah to be called king is 'the Lord of hosts' (6.5), who is portrayed as seated in exaltation on a throne in his palace (*hêkāl*), probably in royal garb (6.1),[2] and surrounded by his royal attendants in the heavenly court.

It has sometimes been suggested that this description is intended as a deliberate contrast with the human king, since the chapter starts by noting the death of king Uzziah and is followed by a chapter which most commentators regard as sharply critical of his next significant successor, Ahaz. Whether or not that is so, it points us to the wisdom of examining the themes of divine and human kingship in tandem in the book of Isaiah. When we do so, certain observations arise which establish some fundamental critical and theological guidelines to govern more detailed exegetical study of particular passages.

The first point to observe is that in those parts of the book that are

---

1. On these and the other matters discussed below, see the fuller treatment (with more extensive bibliography than is possible here) in my book *Variations on a Theme: King, Messiah and Servant in the Book of Isaiah* (Carlisle: Paternoster Press, 1998). I have there also attempted to trace the relevant themes through into the later sections of the book, something which limitations of space preclude here.

2. For a cautionary note on this, see M.Z. Brettler, *God is King: Understanding an Israelite Metaphor* (JSOTSup, 76; Sheffield: JSOT Press, 1989), pp. 79-80.

widely agreed to come from the exilic period or later, God's kingship comes strongly to the fore, while conversely human kingship disappears completely from view, at least so far as Israel is concerned.

In Deutero-Isaiah God is called 'king of Jacob' (41.21), 'king of Israel' (44.6) and 'your [i.e. Israel's] king' (43.15). In addition, the phrase *mālak ʾᵉlōhāyik* occurs at one of the major climaxes of the book, in 52.7. In contrast, the only reference to David is at 55.3, where it is made clear that the covenant which God had formerly made with his house is now to be transferred to the people as a whole. Nothing whatsoever is said about a continuing role for the royal dynasty, and indeed, in line with the expectations of 55.3, the most overtly royal language in the so-called servant songs comes precisely at 42.1-4, the servant passage that seems most easily and naturally in its context to refer to Israel as a whole. Finally, as is well known, the title *māšîah* is ascribed to Cyrus in 45.1. Although elaborate theological schemes have sometimes been spun out of this usage, in my opinion not so much should be made of it. When it is remembered that nowhere in the Old Testament does the title have the later technical sense of a future king, that it can be applied to more offices than that of king alone, and that at least one other foreign king was ordered by God to be anointed by a prophet (Hazael of Damascus, 1 Kgs 19.15), it does not seem necessary to conclude further than that Cyrus is here said to be commissioned by God for a specific task. That in itself might be regarded as remarkable enough, of course,[3] and this is borne out by the elaborate justification for his statement with which the prophet felt it necessary to preface his announcement (44.24-28). Furthermore, there is no denying the astonishing way in which Cyrus's relationship with God is here described (45.4-5). None of this, however, amounts to an interpretation of 'Messiah' in the way to which centuries of later usage have programmed us, and indeed the usage here suggests that the word did not yet have such a technical meaning. For our present concern, perhaps the single most important conclusion to be drawn is the negative point that the agent of the anticipated restoration will not be an Israelite or Davidic king. But then in Deutero-Isaiah we should not expect him to be, as we have already seen.

---

3. Especially in view of the fact that his commission is positive towards Israel, unlike the kings of Assyria and Babylon in the pre-exilic period; see, for instance, Isa. 10.5-15; Jer. 25.9, 27.6.

In Trito-Isaiah God is never expressly styled *melek*,[4] but royal language is used in close association with him on a couple of occasions. The most striking such passage is 66.1, where he is said to have a throne and a footstool. The rhetorical use of this language, however, is not to stress his royal attributes as such, but to emphasize that he is not concerned with a physical temple, viewed as a divine throne room; rather, 'this is the one to whom I will look, to the humble and contrite in spirit, who trembles at my word' (66.2). A similar point is made at 57.15, where the title 'the high and lofty one (*rām wᵉniśśā'*)' is an obvious allusion to the divine king in 6.1. Here too, however, this language is only preparatory to the striking contrast that 'I dwell in the high and holy place, and also with those who are contrite and humble in spirit'.[5] It seems, therefore, that the author so takes the notion of divine kingship for granted that he can use it as an agreed basis for his further development in terms of God's surprising condescension. We may note too that he makes no reference to a restoration of the Davidic monarchy or to a future king.

Within Isaiah 1–39 itself, several extended passages are by common consent to be dated to the exilic or postexilic period. One such is the Isaiah Apocalypse in chs. 24–27. Here again we find an explicit reference to the kingship of God in 24.23 (*kî mālak yhwh ṣᵉbā'ôt*), perhaps in association with his divine council,[6] while 25.6-8, often characterized as a 'messianic banquet', has been aptly described by Day as 'the banquet in celebration of Yahweh's enthronement'.[7] A number of other references in these chapters which recall the myth of Baal's victory further suggest that the concept of divine kingship may underlie even more of this material.

Finally, Isaiah 33 contains two striking references to God as king—in v. 17, where again there is a probable allusion to ch. 6, and in v. 22. Here too, as in the case of the Isaiah Apocalypse, the considerable emphasis on the importance of Zion is not matched by any allusion

---

4.   On 57.9 see J. Day, *Molech: A God of Human Sacrifice in the Old Testament* (UCOP, 41; Cambridge: Cambridge University Press, 1989), pp. 50-52.

5.   See more fully my *The Book Called Isaiah: Deutero-Isaiah's Role in Composition and Redaction* (Oxford: Clarendon Press, 1994), pp. 232-33.

6.   As suggested by T.M. Willis, 'Yahweh's Elders (Isa 24,23): Senior Officials of the Divine Court', *ZAW* 103 (1991), pp. 375-85.

7.   J. Day, *God's Conflict with the Dragon and the Sea: Echoes of a Canaanite Myth in the Old Testament* (UCOP, 35; Cambridge: Cambridge University Press, 1985), p. 148.

whatsoever to the restoration or continuing role of the Davidic monarchy. If the argument from silence may be allowed, it would seem that the stress on God's kingship has completely supplanted that of the human king.

This brief survey of the treatment of kingship in the certainly non-Isaianic portions of the book of Isaiah shows a remarkable consistency of approach. Despite the fact that these passages span the exilic and postexilic periods, they show no interest in the Davidic monarchy as an institution. And this, it should be emphasized, is true not only of the second half of the book as a whole but also of later material which has been added in to the first half as well. Unless, therefore, we are to regard the growth of the book as the work of totally separate groups with opposing viewpoints (a view that is becoming increasingly difficult to hold as more and more literary connections across the traditional boundaries are recovered), it would seem that we are forced towards the conclusion that a pre-exilic date is most plausible for those four or five passages that deal in a substantial manner with the issue of the Davidic monarchy and its future. This is not a conclusive argument, of course, nor does it point necessarily to an eighth rather than a seventh or even early sixth-century date. It does, however, indicate a firmly pre-exilic setting as the most plausible context within which to set about the task of interpretation, something which the structure of the book itself suggests. It also draws attention to the fact that some recent attempts to drive every such passage down into the postexilic period[8] go very much against the grain of what we can recover of the ideological development of the Isaianic tradition as a whole. They leave these presumed later writers with no trigger in the work as they would have known it which would have caused them to take this radically different turn in the first place. To postulate such a procedure would run counter to most recent research on Isaiah 1–39, which has tended to show how much the later editors built on what already lay before them.

The second introductory matter requiring attention arises as a direct consequence of the first. If I am right in suggesting that the main passages to be considered should be studied in the context of the pre-exilic Isaianic material, then it is necessary to know something of the fundamental ideology of that material. The reason for this is that the so-called messianic passages have often been thought to be somewhat

---

8.   E.g. W. Werner, *Eschatologische Texte in Jesaja 1–39: Messias, Heiliger Rest, Völker* (FzB, 46; Würzburg: Echter Verlag, 1982), pp. 17-88.

detached from this context. If, by contrast, lines of continuity can be discerned, then that will further help to anchor them where *prima facie* they belong.

The easiest point of access comes once more by way of Isaiah 6. As has been noted before,[9] the vision of God 'high and lofty' and thrice holy seems to have had a profound influence on all of Isaiah's thinking.[10] This comes most obviously to expression in those several passages where Isaiah condemns people or institutions on the ground of their pride and arrogance, since such an attitude is tantamount to challenging God's supreme status. Thus in ch. 2, for instance, in a passage which seems to have been extensively glossed or expanded, God is said to have a day 'against all that is proud and lofty (*rām*), against all that is lifted up (*niśśā'*) and high' (v. 12), and this is then illustrated by a list of features such as hills and mountains, some of which are qualified with the same adjectives. All this is to underline that 'the haughty eyes of people shall be brought low, and the pride of everyone shall be humbled, and the Lord alone will be exalted in that day' (v. 11), a sentiment repeated in v. 17 after the illustrative list.

This well-known feature of Isaianic theology is repeated in varying ways on many occasions, almost verbatim at 5.15-16, and with reference to different sections of the population at, for instance, 3.16-17, 9.7-11, and 28.1-4. It also underlies his attitude towards some of the foreign nations, most famously Assyria in 10.5-15 (another passage which seems to have been the subject of later elaboration). While I cannot enter into detail here, the theme was picked up and developed in various directions by later editors, for instance in the taunt against the unnamed king of Babylon in 14.4-21, in the reversal of the theme at 30.25, and in God's own stated intention at 33.10.

---

9.   See, for instance, T.C. Vriezen, 'Essentials of the Theology of Isaiah', in B.W. Anderson and W. Harrelson (eds.), *Israel's Prophetic Heritage: Essays in Honor of James Muilenburg* (London: SCM Press, 1962), pp. 128-46; W.L. Holladay, *Isaiah: Scroll of a Prophetic Heritage* (Grand Rapids: Eerdmans, 1978), pp. 25-45; J.J.M. Roberts, 'Isaiah in Old Testament Theology', *Int* 36 (1982), pp. 10-43; H.G.M. Williamson, 'Isaiah and the Wise', in J. Day, R.P. Gordon and H.G.M. Williamson (eds.), *Wisdom in Ancient Israel: Essays in Honour of J.A. Emerton* (Cambridge: Cambridge University Press, 1995), pp. 133-41.

10.   Or, if this is not an account of Isaiah's initial call (as I am inclined to believe), to have been phrased in terminology which gave particular expression to that thinking. For the influence of the chapter on the later Isaianic tradition, see Williamson, *The Book Called Isaiah*, pp. 30-56.

From this fundamental tenet of Isaiah's theology we may deduce that the prophet had a strong sense that everything should take its proper place within the divine ordering of things, whether natural, international or social. His understanding of reality was distinctly hierarchical. It is for this reason that he regards with horror, and indeed as an expression of God's judgment, the breakdown of the natural ordering of society as it slips into a state of anarchy, as in 3.1-12 (and note how 3.12b is echoed at 9.15), or civil war, as in 9.18-20. Again, the idea of children who disobey their parents is a violation of the same self-evident principle, and requires no further explanation (1.2-3, 30.8-9). Similarly, leaders should lead, so that a society which either rejects their leadership or where the leaders themselves are corrupt is automatically doomed; see, for instance, 1.23, 3.14-15, 5.18-24, 9.15, 10.1-4, 28.7-15, 30.10-11.

If we now inquire after the foundational qualities of a society which is properly ordered under God, we need have no hesitation in answering that they are righteousness (*ṣedeq/ṣᵉdāqâ*), justice (*mišpāṭ*) and truth or faithfulness (*ᵉmet* and its associated adjective *ne ᵉmān*).[11] These qualities characterize God's own rule and activity (5.16, 28.6, 17), they were distinctive of Zion's golden age and will be so again when God restores her (1.21-26, 28.17, 32.16-17, 33.5), and he looks for them and regularly exhorts the people to that end in the present or condemns their absence or perversion (1.17, 3.10, 5.7, 23, 10.1-2). Although several of

11. Of course, both in Isaiah and beyond, these words, when they occur on their own, have a wide range of meaning. It is their use in combination (especially the first two) which turns them into almost a catch-phrase for Isaiah's understanding of the ideal society. Elsewhere in the Old Testament and in the ancient Near East at large, this word pair is characteristic of ideal royal rule; see, for instance, M. Weinfeld, '"Justice and Righteousness"—וצדקה משפט—The Expression and its Meaning', in H. Graf Reventlow and Y. Hoffman (eds.), *Justice and Righteousness: Biblical Themes and their Influence* (JSOTSup, 137; Sheffield: Sheffield Academic Press, 1992), pp. 228-46. While it is clear that Isaiah was dependent upon this stereotypical phraseology, I have tried to demonstrate in the first chapter of *Variations on a Theme* that his use of it was distinctive in covering a far broader range of issues than 'social justice' (Weinfeld's summarizing conclusion) alone. For the importance of these terms for messianism in Isaiah, see most recently D. Schibler, 'Messianism and Messianic Prophecy in Isaiah 1–12 and 28–33', in P.E. Satterthwaite, R.S. Hess and G.J. Wenham (eds.), *The Lord's Anointed: Interpretation of Old Testament Messianic Texts* (Carlisle: Paternoster Press; Grand Rapids: Baker Book House, 1995), pp. 87-104.

the references just listed come from the hand of later editors, they demonstrate that here again the later tradents were fully in accord with the fundamental tenets of Isaiah's own theology.

It is noteworthy that in all the passages referred to in this brief summary of some of Isaiah's leading themes the person of the king receives little or no mention. As we shall see, some of these concerns, especially the last named, do find expression in the passages about to be considered, but it is perhaps significant that (unlike, for instance, in Jeremiah) the king is not listed among the corrupt leaders, nor is the loss of kingship referred to as part of the breakdown of social order. The passages about kingship thus appear to stand somewhat in isolation from the remainder of Isaiah's work, at first sight supporting the majority impression noted above. On the one hand, this again suggests, however, that there would not have been much of a trigger to cause later writers to add this material if they were responsible for these cardinal passages in their entirety; coupled with my earlier observation about the ideological direction which the development of the book of Isaiah took, it looks increasingly likely that something, at least, about human kingship must have been present in the work of Isaiah from the very first. On the other hand, the challenge which faces us is to see whether (and which of) these passages can be integrated harmoniously into the picture of Isaiah's own theology that has just been sketched. It is with these questions in mind that I shall now examine the four passages in turn. The initial survey will follow the canonical order. I shall return to diachronic concerns in the conclusion.

Isaiah 7.1-17

A significant preliminary question governing the interpretation of this much discussed passage[12] relates to the possibility that it forms part of an original 'Isaiah Memoir' comprising 6.1–8.18 (or 9.6), minus various later additions. This view has been widely adopted in the wake of Budde's monograph of 1928,[13] though in recent years there have been

---

12. The inclusion of full bibliographical references is out of the question here. For a recent relatively comprehensive survey both on this passage and on most of the others discussed below, see P.D. Wegner, *An Examination of Kingship and Messianic Expectation in Isaiah 1–35* (Lewiston, NY: Edwin Mellen Press, 1992).

13. K. Budde, *Jesaja's Erleben: Eine gemeinverständliche Auslegung der Denkschrift des Propheten (Kap. 6,1–9,6)* (Gotha: Leopold Klotz Verlag, 1928).

several significant challenges to it.[14]

As usually understood, the suggestion is that Isaiah himself committed the original form of the passage to writing as a record of his ministry during the Syro-Ephraimite crisis. If that were so, the increasingly popular view that Immanuel was a son of the prophet,[15] and not a royal child, would have a certain amount to commend itself, especially

Budde first outlined the theory in 'Ueber das siebente Capitel des Buches Jesaja', in *Études archéologiques, linguistiques et historiques dédiées à Mr. le Dr. C. Leemans* (Leiden: E.J. Brill, 1885), pp. 121-26, though so far as I can determine he first used the term *Denkschrift* (without further introduction) in 'Zwei Beobachtungen zum alten Eingang des Buches Jesaja', *ZAW* 38 (1919–20), p. 58. The basic notion is also found (though again without use of the word *Denkschrift*) in the classic commentary of B. Duhm, *Das Buch Jesaia* (HAT, 3.1; Göttingen: Vandenhoeck & Ruprecht, 1892).

14. These challenges take two forms. On the one hand, there are those who effectively reject the theory outright, such as H. Graf Reventlow, 'Das Ende der sog. "Denkschrift" Jesajas', *BN* 38–39 (1987), pp. 62-67; S.A. Irvine, 'The Isaianic *Denkschrift*: Reconsidering an Old Hypothesis', *ZAW* 104 (1992), pp. 216-31. On the other hand, some still use the language of the memoir, but effectively undermine its most powerful attraction by arguing that it does not represent an early independent 'book', but is the result of later redactional compilation: e.g. W. Dietrich, *Jesaja und die Politik* (BEvT, 74; Munich: Chr. Kaiser Verlag, 1976), pp. 60-99; W. Werner, 'Vom Prophetenwort zur Prophetentheologie. Ein redaktionskritischer Versuch zu Jes 6,1-8,18', *BZ* NS 29 (1985), pp. 1-30; O. Kaiser, *Das Buch des Propheten Jesaja: Kapitel 1–12* (ATD, 17; Göttingen: Vandenhoeck & Ruprecht, 5th edn, 1981), pp. 117-209 (ET, *Isaiah 1-12: A Commentary* [OTL; London: SCM Press, 2nd edn, 1983], pp. 114-218); R. Kilian, *Jesaja 1-12* (DNEB, 17; Würzburg: Echter Verlag, 1986), pp. 47-69; more subtly, M.A. Sweeney, *Isaiah 1–39, with an Introduction to Prophetic Literature* (FOTL, 16; Grand Rapids: Eerdmans, 1996), pp. 132-88. For a much fuller exposition of my own difficulties with the theory, see ch. 3 of *Variations on a Theme*.

15. This was the view already of Jerome, Rashi and Ibn Ezra. In more recent times it has been held notably by, for instance, J.J. Stamm in a long series of articles beginning with 'La prophétie d'Emmanuel', *RHPR* 23 (1943), pp. 1-26; N.K. Gottwald, 'Immanuel as the Prophet's Son', *VT* 8 (1958), pp. 36-47; J.J.M. Roberts, 'Isaiah and his Children', in A. Kort and S. Morschauser (eds.), *Biblical and Related Studies Presented to Samuel Iwry* (Winona Lake, IN: Eisenbrauns, 1985), pp. 193-203; and R.E. Clements, 'The Immanuel Prophecy of Isa. 7:10-17 and Its Messianic Interpretation', in E. Blum *et al.* (eds.), *Die Hebräische Bibel und ihre zweifache Nachgeschichte: Festschrift für Rolf Rendtorff zum 65. Geburtstag* (Neukirchen-Vluyn: Neukirchener Verlag, 1990), pp. 225-40 (reprinted in *Old Testament Prophecy: From Oracles to Canon* (Louisville, KY: Westminster/John Knox, 1996), pp. 65-77.

in view of 8.16-18.[16] On this view, the passage as a whole would be of much less relevance to our present concern than has traditionally been thought. At best (as argued by Clements) the messianic interpretation would be a secondary, redactional shift due to the inclusion of 8.23–9.6 at the end of the memoir, with Immanuel now identified as Hezekiah.

This approach to the composition of the passage seems to me, however, to ride somewhat roughshod over several noteworthy features. First, whereas chs. 6 and 8 are couched in the first person singular, 7.1-17 is a narrative in the third person. Budde and most of those who have followed him have supposed that it was originally also in the first person and have emended the text to make it so—a clear circular argument. Admittedly, the changes required are not as drastic as might at first be thought, but nonetheless there is no evidence to support such a change. Indeed, in view of the prevailing context it seems most unlikely that the present form of the text would have arisen secondarily. This at once casts serious doubt on the memoir hypothesis as normally conceived.

Secondly, Budde argued that the original connection between the end of ch. 5 and 9.7–10.4 was interrupted by the insertion of the memoir as a pre-existing booklet. In fact, however, the 'original connection' is not clear-cut, and consequently Budde had to argue that there had been additional accidental disorder at the time of the insertion of the memoir—another circular argument. Without usually recognizing the damage which is done to Budde's theory, most scholars nowadays maintain that the arrangement of the text, especially at the end of ch. 5, is the result of deliberate redactional activity,[17] and thus can afford no support to the memoir hypothesis.

Thirdly, Budde argued that since Isaiah 6 describes Isaiah's call it must have originally stood at the start of his work. This in itself is not

---

16. There would remain, however, the difficulty of the designation of the child's mother as an *'almâ*. While it may be agreed that this need not, in its original context, at least, refer to a technical virgin, it is equally agreed that it cannot refer to a woman who has already borne a child some years previously. To avoid the problem that this raises with regard to Shear-jashub, it is necessary to resort to explanations (such as that Isaiah's first wife had died and that he had remarried) which neither arise from the text nor find any support within it.

17. Precise opinions on this vary, of course. For my own proposal, with some further bibliography, see *The Book Called Isaiah*, pp. 125-43, and 'Isaiah xi 11-16 and the Redaction of Isaiah i-xii', in J.A. Emerton (ed.), *Congress Volume, Paris 1992* (VTSup, 61; Leiden: E.J. Brill, 1995), pp. 343-57.

necessarily so, however, as comparison with Amos 7 shows, but in any case it is by no means certain that Isaiah 6 is the description of an initial call. Form-critically it differs significantly from the call narratives of Jeremiah or Amos, for instance, whereas conversely its closest Old Testament analogy is with the vision of Micaiah the son of Imlah in 1 Kings 22.[18] This suggests that, as with Micaiah, the vision relates to a commission for a specific task given during the course of the prophet's ministry, not necessarily at its start.

If Budde's main arguments in favour of the memoir hypothesis are thus found wanting, it is necessary to suggest an alternative way of accounting for the material in Isaiah 6–8, and in ch. 7 in particular. Again, there are several points to be considered.

First, it is well known that 7.1 is more or less the same as 2 Kgs 16.5, where it fits smoothly into the history's account of the reign of Ahaz. Unless we are to indulge in the common but gratuitous speculation that it was added later to an original Isaiah memoir, we may perhaps ask whether this is an indication that the narrative of Isaiah 7 which it introduces has been drawn in its entirety from somewhere else altogether, somewhere much closer to the circles that produced the Deuteronomistic History itself.

The second point reinforces this impression, for in recent years a number of scholars have observed that there are some striking points of connection between this account in ch. 7 and the stories about the later king Hezekiah in chs. 36–39.[19] These points stretch all the way from the

18. Cf. W. Zimmerli, *Ezechiel. I. Ezechiel 1–24* (BKAT, 13.1; Neukirchen–Vluyn: Neukirchener Verlag, 1969), pp. 16-21 (ET *Ezekiel. I. A Commentary on the Book of the Prophet Ezekiel, Chapters 1–24* [trans. R.E. Clements; Hermeneia; Philadelphia: Fortress Press, 1979], pp. 98-100).

19. See, for instance, P.R. Ackroyd, 'Isaiah 36–39: Structure and Function', in W.C. Delsman *et al.* (eds.), *Von Kanaan bis Kerala: Festschrift für Prof. Mag. Dr. Dr. J.P.M. van der Ploeg O.P. zur Vollendung des siebzigsten Lebensjahres am 4. Juli 1979* (AOAT, 211; Kevelaer: Butzon & Bercker; Neukirchen–Vluyn: Neukirchener Verlag, 1982), pp. 3-21 (reprinted in *Studies in the Religious Tradition of the Old Testament* [London: SCM Press, 1987], pp. 105-20); J. Blenkinsopp, *A History of Prophecy in Israel from the Settlement in the Land to the Hellenistic Period* (London: SPCK, 1984), pp. 109-10; K.A.D. Smelik, 'Distortion of Old Testament Prophecy: The Purpose of Isaiah xxxvi and xxxvii', in A.S. van der Woude (ed.), *Crises and Perspectives: Studies in Ancient Near Eastern Polytheism, Biblical Theology, Palestinian Archaeology and Intertestamental Literature* (OTS, 24; Leiden: E.J. Brill, 1986), pp. 70-93; M.A. Sweeney, *Isaiah 1–4 and the*

general and overarching to the specific and particular, and I cannot list
them all here. Just to give a flavour, we may note that in both passages
the king is confronted with an invading army which is threatening
Jerusalem (7.1, 36.2), that he is reduced to near panic (7.2, 37.1), and
that Isaiah offers him a reassuring 'fear not' oracle (7.4-9, 37.6-7),
backed up in each case by the offer of a 'sign' (7.11, 37.30; see too
38.7, 22). Although in both narratives the king and the city are spared,
this is followed by a prediction that a worse disaster will follow in the
future (7.15-25, 39.6-7). A striking point of detail is the reference in
both cases to the otherwise unknown 'conduit of the upper pool on the
highway to the Fuller's Field' (7.3, 36.2), which can hardly be coin-
cidental. Alongside these similarities, however, there are marked contrasts between the ways in which the kings react, with Ahaz rejecting
the way to deliverance offered by the prophet, while Hezekiah follows
the way of faith and is spectacularly delivered. On the basis of these
and other such comparisons, we may agree with those who have concluded that there is a conscious attempt to contrast the responses of the
two kings, one negative and the other positive.

Now, this contributes to our wider consideration when it is recalled
that the longer narrative in chs. 36–39 is also recounted in virtually
identical terms in 2 Kings 18–20. I think myself that there can be little
doubt that it has been taken over from Kings with generally only very
slight changes and inserted in its present setting in the book of Isaiah by
a later editor.[20] At the same time, however, there are a number of features of these chapters which distinguish them from most of the other
material in Kings and which associate them with what we may loosely
call Isaianic circles. Again, a mere sample of the evidence should suffice
to substantiate this claim.[21] These chapters differ from the rest of the

Post-Exilic Understanding of the Isaianic Tradition (BZAW, 171; Berlin: W. de
Gruyter, 1988), pp. 12-13; E.W. Conrad, 'The Royal Narratives and the Structure
of the Book of Isaiah', *JSOT* 41 (1988), pp. 67-81, substantially reproduced in
E.W. Conrad, *Reading Isaiah* (Minneapolis: Fortress Press, 1991), pp. 34-51; C.R.
Seitz, *Zion's Final Destiny: The Development of the Book of Isaiah. A Reassess-
ment of Isaiah 36–39* (Minneapolis: Fortress Press, 1991), pp. 89 and 195-6; *idem,
Isaiah 1–39* (Louisville, KY: John Knox Press, 1993), p. 64.

20. I have sought to defend this common view against some recently proposed
alternatives in *The Book Called Isaiah*, pp. 189-211, and 'Hezekiah and the
Temple', in M.V. Fox *et al.* (eds.), *Texts, Temples, and Traditions: A Tribute to
Menahem Haran* (Winona Lake, IN: Eisenbrauns, 1996), pp. 47-52.

21. For fuller accounts, see the works cited in n. 19 above, together with J.W.

books of Kings in that, for instance, they are the only place in the Deuteronomistic History where a prophet whose sayings are separately recorded in the books of the Latter Prophets is mentioned in the narrative, and, furthermore, in that they include poetic material. On the other hand, there are links with the rest of the Isaianic tradition which go beyond those already noted with ch. 7, for instance (i) Shebna and Eliakim (36.3) are also the subject of 22.15-25; (ii) the use of the divine title 'the Holy One of Israel' (37.23) is peculiarly characteristic of the book of Isaiah; (iii) the emphasis on 'trust' in the Rabshakeh's speeches (36.4, 5, 6, 7, 9, 15) recalls 30.15; (iv) the stress on the impotence of Egypt, for all her chariots and horses (36.6, 9), is strongly reminiscent of Isaiah's anti-Egyptian oracles (30.1-5, 31.1-3); and (v) 37.30-32 has clear links with the Isaianic tradition, especially with regard to the remnant, the structure of the first part of v. 32, which has a close parallel in 2.3b, and most notably of all the ending of v. 32, which is verbally identical with the ending of 9.6, 'The zeal of the Lord of hosts will do this'. In the light of this and other comparable evidence, we need to envisage two stages in the development of this section of the book. Originally composed in a shape about which we can only speculate by these Isaianic circles, it was used as a source along with the many others at his disposal by the author of Kings. It was then further reused at a later date by an editor of the book of Isaiah.

The thematic and stylistic similarities that I have noted between this material and Isaiah 7 lead me to conclude that this latter chapter too was composed as part of the same work sometime between the lifetime of Isaiah and the composition of the books of Kings.[22] It is thus very clearly to be distinguished from a first-person memoir by Isaiah himself, a conclusion which the earlier discussion has already made clear. The next step, therefore, is to consider why it has been placed where it is by some later editor.

We may start by noticing that the general shape of Isaiah 6–8 is not unparalleled in the prophetic literature. Amos 7–8 is closely

Groves, *Actualization and Interpretation in the Old Testament* (SBLDS, 86; Atlanta: Scholars Press, 1987), pp. 191-201.

22. By a different route, R. Bickert, 'König Ahas und der Prophet Jesaja: Ein Beitrag zum Problem des syrisch-ephraimitischen Krieges', *ZAW* 99 (1987), pp. 361-84, arrives at a similar conclusion for what he takes to be the original form of Isa. 7.1-9. His radical literary-critical surgery on these verses, however, raises questions about how secure his results can be.

comparable[23]—a first person account that is interrupted by a third-person narrative. I have argued independently elsewhere[24] that the narrative in Amos 7.9-17 was added by Deuteronomistic circles in order to make their familiar point that it was rejection of the prophetic warning which sealed Israel's fate. The narrative following Amos's first three visions illustrates that rejection in a personal manner, and it is then followed by the fourth vision with its categorical statement that 'the end has come upon my people Israel' (8.2).

The situation in Isaiah 6–8 is similar. In the first-person material in chs. 6 and 8 we find a concern for the nation as a whole, characterized throughout by the title 'this people' (6.9, 10; 8.5, 11, 12). We may naturally assume that Isaiah wrote ch. 8 in part to indicate how, despite the promise contained in the name Maher-shalal-hash-baz at the start of the chapter, 'this people' sealed their own fate (cf. 6.9-10) because they preferred political intrigue to the way of God as indicated by the prophet; they heard, but did not understand.

This relatively straightforward situation has been elaborated at a later stage, however, by the addition of ch. 7. Here the focus is different. There is no reference to 'this people', but rather the king himself is individually confronted by the prophet. The general shape of the events may be similar to what we find in ch. 8, but while the underlying theology is thus comparable, it is here targeted at a different audience. Just as in the case of Amos, so here, the fate of the nation is seen to be bound up much more in the decisions which its leaders take with regard to the prophetic word. Not surprisingly in view of what we have already seen, this too is characteristic of the Deuteronomists. We may thus conclude that by his placement of Isaiah 7 the editor has reflected later concerns in order to add a further dimension to the interpretation of the difficult hardening saying of Isa. 6.9-10.[25]

23. In view of the many links between Amos and Isaiah which have long been noted (see especially R. Fey, *Amos und Jesaja: Abhängigkeit und Eigenständigkeit des Jesaja* [WMANT, 12; Neukirchen–Vluyn: Neukirchener Verlag, 1963]), it is surprising that this connection has been overlooked by the commentators. It no doubt has something to do with the strength of the prevailing memoir hypothesis.

24. H.G.M. Williamson, 'The Prophet and the Plumb-Line: A Redaction-critical Study of Amos vii', in A.S. van der Woude (ed.), *In Quest of the Past: Studies on Israelite Religion, Literature and Prophetism* (OTS, 26; Leiden: E.J. Brill, 1990), pp. 101-21.

25. In order to avoid possible misunderstandings, I should like to emphasize that this conclusion has no necessary bearing on the historical value of Isa. 7, nor

In the light of all these considerations, it is clear that we are free to examine ch. 7 on its own terms in the first instance. When we do so, and in line with our last conclusion, we can hardly fail to be impressed by the particular emphasis which is placed throughout on the present and future of the dynasty.[26] First, both parts of the passage are explicitly addressed to 'the house of David (*bêt dāwid*)' (vv. 2 and 13; see too v. 17). Secondly, in contrast with the account of the same events in 2 Kings 16, the main aim of the hostile coalition is specifically to replace the Davidic Ahaz with an apparently Aramaean puppet (v. 6), while Ahaz's appeal to Assyria for help receives no mention. Thus the focus of the narrative is here restricted to its dynastic implications, in contrast with the different presentation in Kings. Thirdly, the unexpressed, because obvious, conclusion to draw from Isaiah's emphasis on Rezin and the son of Remaliah as the 'head' of Damascus and Samaria respectively in vv. 8a and 9a is that Ahaz is the divinely appointed head of Judah and Jerusalem and that he can therefore face the enemy in battle with confidence.[27] Fourthly, this confidence is reinforced by the recollection of the Nathan oracle in the (possibly proverbial) saying at v. 9b, 'If you do not stand firm in faith, you shall not stand at all' (see 2 Sam. 7.16, and cf. 1 Sam. 25.28; 1 Kgs 11.38; Ps. 89.29, 38, ET 28, 37; Isa. 55.3). The plural form of address in this saying suggests that the whole 'house of David' is in view, not just Ahaz as an individual. And finally, the passage concludes in v. 17 with a reference to the division of the monarchy following the death of

should it be taken to mean that the first part of the book was subjected to systematic Deuteronomistic editing in the way that seems to be true of Amos.

26. See especially E. Würthwein, 'Jesaja 7,1-9: Ein Beitrag zu dem Thema: Prophetie und Politik', in *Theologie als Glaubenswagnis: Festschrift zum 80. Geburtstag von Karl Heim* (Hamburg: Furche-Verlag, 1954), pp. 47-63 (reprinted in *Wort und Existenz: Studien zum Alten Testament* [Göttingen: Vandenhoeck & Ruprecht, 1970], pp. 127-43). Contrast B.C. Ollenburger, *Zion the City of the Great King: A Theological Symbol of the Jerusalem Cult* (JSOTSup, 41; Sheffield: JSOT Press, 1987), pp. 124-27.

27. I take this also to be the purpose of v. 4, though the interpretation of that verse is disputed. It has often been thought to imply that Ahaz should do nothing, but simply trust in God for deliverance. Among 'war oracles', however, the closest in wording to Isa. 7.4 is Deut. 20.3-4, a passage which shows that the promise of divine help is not opposed to human involvement; rather God's help is promised pecisely in the forthcoming battle. The same thought provides a plausible background to Isa. 7, despite the protestations of several commentators.

Solomon, an incident which also recalls the belief that no matter how far an individual Davidic king might stray from God's appointed way, the promise that the dynasty itself would endure remained secure.

This last point, together with the prevailing dynastic context of the passage as a whole, seems to offer the most plausible background for the interpretation of the Immanuel oracle. Ahaz has been both challenged (v. 9b) and encouraged (v. 11) to exercise faith on the basis of the promises to David that his position is secure, but he has rejected the invitation (v. 12). At this point, Isaiah turns his back on the house of David: it is striking that address (*šim'û*), personal suffix (*mikkem*) and main verb (*tal^e'û*) are all plural, indicating clearly that what is to follow reaches beyond the individual Ahaz alone; this seems to link back to the comparable second person plural formulation in v. 9b. Furthermore, as has often been remarked, Isaiah regards God as siding with him in his stance rather than with those who are addressed, as the shift from 'your God' in v. 11 to 'my God' in v. 13 makes clear.

Some commentators have advocated the view that, despite the apparent impatience of Isaiah demonstrated by v. 13, the prophet continued to offer resolute support for Ahaz and his neutral political stance, and that the Immanuel oracle is an indication of such support.[28] The problem with this interpretation is that it fails to take seriously the conditional nature of v. 9b. Since Isaiah continued to stress that the enemy coalition would fail (cf. v. 16), it cannot be the general safety of the land that is made conditional. Rather, it must be the continuity of the Davidic dynasty itself, as the allusion to the Nathan oracle in v. 9b further suggests.[29] It is this which Ahaz has apparently forfeited by his demonstrable lack of faith, and it will have further serious consequences in the form of Assyrian intervention in the affairs of Judah, as later passages indicate. Even within the restricted horizon of 7.1-17 this comes to expression in v. 17. Taken on its own, and without the reference to the king of Assyria, which is usually thought to be a later, his-

---

28. E. Hammershaimb, *Some Aspects of Old Testament Prophecy from Isaiah to Malachi* (Copenhagen: Rosenkilde og Bagger, 1966), pp. 19-20; J. Høgenhaven, *Gott und Volk bei Jesaja: Eine Untersuchung zur biblischen Theologie* (Acta Theologica Danica, 24; Leiden: E.J. Brill, 1988), pp. 87-93; S.A. Irvine, *Isaiah, Ahaz, and the Syro-Ephraimitic Crisis* (SBLDS, 123; Atlanta: Scholars Press, 1990), pp. 164-71.

29. Irvine, *Isaiah*, pp. 158-59, recognizes the force of v. 9b in this sense ('the prophet warns the royal court that this divine promise will be forfeited'), but then fails to draw the obvious consequences.

toricizing gloss, this verse can be, and has been, taken as either a promise or a threat. Naturally, a decision either way depends to a large extent on how each commentator understands the difficult preceding verses, where similar ambiguities can be found. Without going into the problems of vv. 15-16 here, however, it may be stated that in the light of our understanding of the passage as a whole, which is by now becoming clear, v. 17 seems best to be taken as a dire threat not only against Ahaz personally but also against his entire dynasty (*bêt 'ābîkā*), in contrast with the promise to Immanuel in the previous verses. In further support of this approach, it may be noted that *hēbî' + 'al* is usually threatening in nature, and in addition that this interpretation has the advantage that the supposed gloss at the end of the verse (which must be threatening) would not then be standing the intention of the remainder of the verse on its head, as has cavalierly to be assumed by those who find an original promise in this verse.

What, then, shall we say of Immanuel, in the light of this discussion? Two points would seem to follow. First, there is a clear suggestion that he represents a radical discontinuity with the present heirs of the Davidic family, who have collectively failed to live up to the hopes which might reasonably be expected of them. And secondly, since the sign element is predominantly to be sought in his name rather than the circumstances of his birth,[30] he also represents continuity of a different sort, namely a continuity in terms of God's provision of effective leadership for his people. The name itself contains an obvious allusion to the Zion tradition as attested especially in Ps. 46.8, 12 (ET 7, 11) and Mic. 3.11, with which, of course, the royal dynasty was closely associated (see especially 2 Sam. 23.5). It therefore seems that God's commitment to his people overrides a specific concern for any particular historical dynasty.

All this implies that Isa. 7.14 has somewhat more of a 'messianic' flavour than most recent commentators have been prepared to allow.

30. This is not to deny, but only to put into proper perspective, the fact that the birth oracle in 7.14 falls into a standard pattern attested both at Ugarit and elsewhere in the Old Testament. The parallels have been frequently set out by others, e.g. H.-P. Müller, 'Glauben und Bleiben: Zur Denkschrift Jesajas Kapitel vi 1-viii 18', in *Studies on Prophecy: a Collection of Twelve Papers* (VTSup, 26; Leiden: E.J. Brill, 1974), pp. 25-54 (38-40); H. Wildberger, *Jesaja. I. Jesaja 1–12* (BKAT, 10.1; Neukirchen–Vluyn: Neukirchener Verlag, 2nd edn, 1980), p. 289 (ET *Isaiah 1–12: A Commentary* [trans. T.H. Trapp; Minneapolis: Fortress Press, 1991], p. 307); Høgenhaven, *Gott und Volk bei Jesaja*, pp. 88-90.

That is to say, even among those who still accept a broadly royal interpretation of the oracle, the tendency has been to regard the birth of
Immanuel as the birth merely of Ahaz's successor: Ahaz is rejected, but
the future of the dynasty is already secured. That reductionist interpretation does not do justice, however, to the element of discontinuity to
which I have drawn attention. Nothing is said of the biologically
Davidic nature of the child even while he takes the place that the ideal
Davidide should hold. On the other hand, it needs hardly to be said that
in the immediate context the prediction of his birth is securely tied to
the prevailing historical circumstances of the reign of Ahaz, so that a
long-range messianic prediction is ruled out, at least at the primary
level. The passage seems to fall firmly between these two extremes.

The contribution of the passage to our broader theme may now be
evaluated, and as it turns out that contribution is relatively modest.
Since the emphasis of the sign is on the naming of the child, nothing is
said about the character or nature of his rule in the terms which I outlined at the conclusion of my introductory remarks. The sole point that
we learn is that Isaiah was deeply committed to the fact of a divinely
appointed leader of the people within the framework of God's broader
purposes for Zion (Immanuel is not, of course, explicitly designated as
king) and that such a leader will have implicit faith in God. Every
opportunity is given for that role to be fulfilled by a member of the
house of David, but Davidic descent is not the sole or even a necessary
condition. In line with what we saw earlier, Isaiah cannot conceive of
an ideal society without hierarchical leadership, but in the very broadest
terms God is willing to guarantee the quality of that leadership even at
the expense of judging and, by implication, removing the representatives of the present dynastic family. So it is the bare fact of divinely
appointed leadership that emerges most strongly for our purposes.
Where such a conviction fits chronologically is a question which can be
discussed only after other relevant material has been considered.

Isaiah 8.23b–9.6 (ET 9.1-7)

The range and complexity of the exegetical problems raised by this
passage are far too formidable to be treated here in full. I shall therefore
concentrate rather narrowly on what can be reasonably securely established about its understanding of the character and nature of kingship.

In the first place, human kingship comes to expression only in the
last two verses of the passage, where it forms the third reason for the

people's joy introduced in v. 1.[31] This joy is explicitly the result of God's activity in v. 2 (*hirbîtā* and *higdaltā*) and in the first explanatory verse (3, *haḥittōtā*), so that we should doubtless understand his activity to lie behind the impersonally expressed second explanatory verse (4) as well. He is also, therefore, the obvious logical subject of the passive verbs in v. 5, and this is confirmed by the emphatic concluding clause in v. 6.[32] The birth[33] of the king is thus not primarily to be seen as the arrival of a saviour-figure in his own right but rather as part of the deliverance which God will effect for the people. The passive verbs of v. 5a reinforce this impression, and the fact that the figure is not explicitly styled *melek* may be related.[34] The main focus of the passage, therefore, is on God's direct work on behalf of his people, and the provision of the royal figure is regarded as a part of this. He serves as a sign of its gracious nature and he is a primary agent through whom God will work.

Secondly, the purpose behind God's provision of this character comes to expression in v. 6b, vv. 5 and 6a (on which most scholarly attention has been focused) being more in the nature of preparatory description.[35] It is to establish and then to sustain his kingdom with *mišpāṭ* and *ṣᵉdāqâ*, precisely the terms which we saw earlier were central to Isaiah's notions of the proper ordering of society. Since vv. 3-4 speak of God's work of deliverance from foreign oppression without reference to any human agency, it may be suggested that the thought here is that the

31. I shall here use the Hebrew verse numbering throughout. In English translations, they are one figure higher.

32. The suggestion that this final clause is a later addition (e.g. B. Renaud, 'La Forme poétique d'Is 9, 1-6', in A. Caquot, S. Légasse and M. Tardieu [eds.], *Mélanges bibliques et orientaux en l'honneur de M. Mathias Delcor* [AOAT, 215; Kevelaer: Butzon & Bercker; Neukirchen–Vluyn: Neukirchener Verlag, 1985], pp. 331-48) has not found general acceptance.

33. Or, as some think, the accession, following A. Alt, 'Jesaja 8,23–9,6: Befreiungsnacht und Krönungstag', in *Festschrift Alfred Bertholet zum 80. Geburtstag gewidmet* (Tübingen: J.C.B. Mohr [Paul Siebeck], 1950), pp. 29-49 (reprinted in *Kleine Schriften zur Geschichte des Volkes Israel*, II [Munich: Beck, 1953], pp. 206-25). Significant difficulties confront this view, however, on which see P.D. Wegner, 'A Re-examination of Isaiah ix 1-6', *VT* 42 (1992), pp. 103-12, and *idem*, *Examination of Kingship*, pp. 169-76

34. Cf. Harrelson, 'Nonroyal Motifs in the Royal Eschatology', in Anderson and Harrelson (eds.), *Israel's Prophetic Heritage*, pp. 147-65.

35. NRSV is misleading in turning the second half of v. 6 into a separate and free standing sentence. The original RSV ('to establish it...') was preferable.

king's role should relate to the internal ordering of the life of the nation.[36] It thus draws him into the centre of one of Isaiah's major concerns, something which was seen to be lacking in the more generally expressed statements of this theme elsewhere in the book.

Thirdly, v. 6 leaves no doubt that this figure is a member of the Davidic dynasty, and furthermore the use in combination of words like *kissē'*, *mamlākâ*, *l'hākîn* and *'ad-'ôlām* suggests that the wording of the Nathan oracle lies in the background of the formulation of the passage. Although 2 Sam. 7.12-17 provides the closest point of comparison, the use of similar language in many other passages[37] reminds us that this may not be so much an allusion to a specific textual authority as to a tradition which was in wider circulation and which carried its own stereotypical language. In this light, it further becomes attractive to read the wider context with this in mind. In particular, the reference to the 'rod of the oppressor' in v. 3 may be an allusion to the possibility that an individual king may need to be disciplined 'with a rod such as mortals use' (2 Sam. 7.14) even while the promise about the dynasty as a whole is secure *'ad-'ôlām* (v. 6; 2 Sam. 7.13).

If there is, therefore, a strong case for the view that the promises to the Davidic dynasty underlie this passage, it is surely not without significance that that whole tradition is here made subservient to the responsibilities of justice and righteousness. This may, perhaps, be regarded as an Isaianic 'twist' on a familiar theme, for what is prayed for in, for instance, Psalm 72 is here promised. For Isaiah, the right

---

36. It might be objected that the child himself also inaugurates the conditions of *miśrâ* (which comparison with v. 5 suggests is a reference to freedom from external oppression) and *šālôm* (which may refer to the same freedom within which the dynastic oracle was given in the first place), since he is called *śar šālôm* and, as *'ēl gibbôr*, he uses military power to achieve this. In response, attention may be drawn to Wegner's proposal (above, n. 33) that v. 5 should be understood as giving the child two theophoric names: 'a wonderful planner (is) the mighty God' and 'the Father of eternity (is) the prince of peace'. (Note in particular that *'ēl gibbôr* is certainly understood as a reference to God in 10.21.) This proposal, which has yet to be fully evaluated, aligns these names with common Israelite practice, circumvents the necessity to indulge in special pleading to explain how divine titles could be ascribed to a human king (this would be difficult enough in an accession oracle, but would be virtually impossible if this is, in fact, a birth announcement), and fits the predominant thought of the passage as a whole that the establishment of peace is the work of God.

37. See the survey in H. Kruse, 'David's Covenant', *VT* 35 (1985), pp. 139-64.

ordering of society is the very *raison d'être* of the dynasty. Ultimately, God's interest is not in the Davidic dynasty as such, but in his wider purpose of establishing justice and righteousness. It is the task which matters, not the agent.

Finally, in view of the discussion about the 'tenses' of the verbs in this passage, to say nothing of more general uncertainties about this aspect of the verbal system in classical Hebrew, it may be observed that a secure time frame for the writer's perspective is provided by v. 6— *mē'attâ wᵉ'ad-'ôlām*. This indicates that the deliverance and new style of rule are on the point of inauguration and that the outlook is towards the future. Such an understanding seems to be eminently appropriate at the time of a royal birth, perhaps particularly at a time when the previous king has suffered foreign oppression, interpreted theologically as a period of divine discipline. I have argued elsewhere that Isaiah's hopes for the future developed over the course of his long ministry[38] from an expectation of imminent change in his earlier years to a realization in his later years that this change would be delayed into the indefinite future. On the assumption that this passage comes from him, its outlook would seem to fit in at the middle point of this development, closely in line with what we find at 8.16-18, and indeed it is striking in this connection that in 8.18 Isaiah speaks of 'the children whom the Lord has given me', with which the first line of 9.5 is similar.

There are many aspects of the interpretation of these opening verses of Isaiah 9 which we have not been able to explore here. Restricting ourselves to the topics closest to our central concern, we may nevertheless conclude that the passage as a whole seems to announce that its readers are living at a turning point in the dynasty's fortunes and that the long hoped-for rule of justice and righteousness is about to begin. None of this implies a break in dynastic rule or a restoration of the monarchy. The predominant thought of the passage neither demands, nor is even particularly suitable to, a postexilic date.[39] The hopes vested in the early Hezekiah or in the early Josiah would seem to be historically possible, and a case for both has been made out by recent major

38. See Williamson, *The Book Called Isaiah*, pp. 95-106.

39. For some further considerations, see my 'First and Last in Isaiah', in H.A. McKay and D.J.A. Clines (eds.), *Of Prophets' Visions and the Wisdom of Sages: Essays in Honour of R. Norman Whybray on his Seventieth Birthday* (JSOTSup, 162; Sheffield: Sheffield Academic Press, 1993), pp. 95-108.

studies.[40] As was stressed earlier, however, this particular point is not the primary concern of the passage, and that may well be one of the reasons why it has proved so difficult to pin down its date more securely. To suggest an original setting within Isaiah's ministry would be inevitably speculative, but its present redactional setting in the aftermath of the Syro-Ephraimite crisis is by no means unreasonable. Its proximity to 8.18 may be thought to support this. For its possible reinterpretation following the redactional insertion of ch. 7, see further below.

Isaiah 11.1-5

In discussions of this passage, most attention has been focused on the first verse. Before we come to that, however, there are some more straightforward matters in vv. 2-5 which are of direct relevance to the broader study. In order not to allow these to be overshadowed by what, from one point of view, is a secondary matter of 'authenticity', it will be convenient to treat these first.

We are told first that the spirit of the Lord will rest upon the figure who is being described (*weṇāḥâ 'ālāyw rûaḥ yhwh*). The phrase used here is not the usual idiom for the charismatic endowment of kings or of their predecessors in the so-called judges period. The closest parallel is in Num. 11.25-26, where God takes part of the spirit that was on Moses and transfers it to the seventy elders in order that they might help Moses in his administrative duties. Similarly, in 2 Kgs 2.15 the spirit of Elijah is said to rest upon his successor Elisha. In neither case is the spirit in question explicitly termed the spirit of the Lord, though it is probably implied in the first instance. An important element of Isa. 11.2 is thus without parallel. Putting these two points together, a clear

---

40. See, for instance, H. Barth, *Die Jesaja-Worte in der Josiazeit: Israel und Assur als Thema einer produktiven Neuinterpretation der Jesajaüberlieferung* (WMANT, 48; Neukirchen–Vluyn: Neukirchener Verlag, 1977), pp. 141-77; J. Vermeylen, *Du Prophète Isaïe à l'apocalyptique: Isaïe, I–XXXV, miroir d'un demi-millénaire d'expérience religieuse en Israël*, I (Paris: J. Gabalda, 1977), pp. 232-45; R.E. Clements, *Isaiah 1–39* (NCB; Grand Rapids: Eerdmans; London: Marshall, Morgan & Scott, 1980), pp. 103-109; Sweeney, *Isaiah 1–39*, pp. 175-99. Others think rather of an 'ideal king'; cf. M.E.W. Thompson, 'Isaiah's Ideal King', *JSOT* 24 (1982), pp. 79-88; A. Laato, *Who is Immanuel? The Rise and Foundering of Isaiah's Messianic Expectations* (Åbo: Åbo Academy Press, 1988), pp. 173-96; Wegner, *Examination of Kingship*, pp. 139-215. Irvine, *Isaiah, Ahaz, and the Syro-Ephraimitic Crisis*, thinks that the oracle refers to Ahaz, but see above on 7.1-17.

picture emerges. On the one hand, the closest analogies in terms of phraseology indicate that the role in question is one of deputy, assistant or successor, while on the other hand the explicit qualification of the spirit as the spirit of the Lord makes clear that the figure is here said to be endowed in order to act in that role in relation to God. Though expressed in a very different way, this is not far from the conclusions I have reached with regard to the figure in ch. 9, and interestingly enough there is further support for the comparison in that 'the spirit of counsel and might (*'ēṣâ ûgᵉbûrâ*)' may well be a conscious echo of what was interpreted above (n. 36) as the first of the two theophoric names in 9.6.

Secondly, the role for which this figure is so well suited is described in vv. 3-5,[41] and it is without doubt primarily judicial. Such notions are fully in line with the wider Davidic traditions, as attested especially in Psalm 72, and beyond that they are shared to a considerable extent with wider ancient Near Eastern ideas of kingship.[42]

Thirdly, does this all mean, then, that this passage has less to contribute to our overall theme than ch. 9? On the contrary! I should like to suggest that the somewhat conventional description of the king's role in v. 4 has been framed by material which, rather as in the case of ch. 9, gives it a peculiarly Isaianic 'twist'.

On the one hand, v. 3 is strikingly reminiscent of 6.10. The probability that we should associate these two verses is strengthened by the observation that the language of 11.3 is without parallel in the Old Testament.[43] Since the relevant paragraph in Isaiah 6 has exerted a pervasive influence on many parts of the book of Isaiah,[44] it seems probable

41. A strong case can be made out for the view that 3a, 'His delight shall be in the fear of the Lord', should be deleted as a corrupt dittograph of the preceding line.

42. Despite initial appearances, v. 4b does little more than amplify on the judicial role of the previous lines. In the first place, Wildberger (*Jesaja*, p. 454 [ET *Isaiah 1–12*, p. 477]) points to Egyptian and Mesopotamian parallels, and secondly, even if we retain MT's *'ereṣ* against the more probable emendation to *'āriṣ*, it is clear from the previous line that it refers narrowly to the land, not universally to the whole earth (contrast Ps. 2.8-9).

43. *Mišmaᶜ 'ōzen* occurs nowhere else; *mar'ēh 'ênayîm* does occur occasionally elsewhere, but not in legal or judicial contexts, nor in connection with hearing.

44. See R.E. Clements, 'Beyond Tradition-History: Deutero-Isaianic Development of First Isaiah's Themes', *JSOT* 31 (1985), pp. 95-113 (reprinted in *Old Testament Prophecy*, pp. 78-92), and 'Patterns in the Prophetic Canon: Healing the Blind and the Lame', in G.M. Tucker, D.L. Petersen and R.R. Wilson (eds.), *Canon, Theology, and Old Testament Interpretation: Essays in Honor of Brevard S.*

that this is the explanation for the otherwise unparalleled language of
11.3 as well. The purpose, of course, will have been to draw a contrast
between Isaiah's contemporaries as depicted in ch. 6 and the character
of the coming ideal king, but applied now in particular to the judicial
sphere.

The wording of v. 5, the other half of our 'frame', is also suggestive.
The language of righteousness and faithfulness brings us back to the
centre of the vocabulary group which we introduced earlier. *Ṣedeq*
picks up explicitly on the judicial role in v. 4a, but by putting it now in
parallel with the broader 'faithfulness' (*'ᵉmûnâ*; cf. 1.21, 26), it suggests that that role is to be seen as an example, only, of the wider
characteristics which mark the work of the ideal king. Indeed, this concern may explain why we do not find here the commoner 'justice and
righteousness' which was so central to the passage in ch. 9. This king
will 'judge (*šāpaṭ*)' in righteousness; had 'justice (*mišpāṭ*)' then
appeared in v. 5, we should have been tempted to take the verse as
merely a recapitulation of v. 4. As it is, however, the introduction of the
alternative language of 'faithfulness' brings the passage as a whole into
the wider sphere of the king as upholder of the ideal society.

To sum up thus far, we may conclude that there is a close parallel
between the king as depicted here and his role as teased out from ch. 9.
In both cases, though in different ways, his function as (merely) an
agent of God is emphasized,[45] and although the common ancient Near
Eastern ideal of the king as supreme judge of his people is more
marked in ch. 11, both passages ultimately testify to his important part
in establishing the kind of society which God desires for his people.

We may now turn to the first verse of the chapter. It is on this that
most attention has been focused in scholarly discussion. In particular, it
has been thought to provide the main evidence for regarding the passage as a whole as postexilic in date, as well as featuring in analyses of
the passage's redactional setting within its wider context in the book.

We may start most conveniently by expressing agreement with those

---

Childs (Philadelphia: Fortress Press, 1988), pp. 189-200; see too Williamson, *The
Book Called Isaiah*, pp. 46-51.

45. This point is also emphasized by J.J.M. Roberts, 'The Divine King and the
Human Community in Isaiah's Vision of the Future', in H.B. Huffmon, F.A. Spina
and A.R.W. Green (eds.), *The Quest for the Kingdom of God: Studies in Honor of
George E. Mendenhall* (Winona Lake, IN: Eisenbrauns, 1983), pp. 127-36.

who, at least since the time of Herder,[46] have pointed out that the chapter division with which we are familiar is unfortunate at this point. Not only does the verse begin with the conjunction, but the imagery of a tree which has been felled looks like a direct continuation of the last two verses of ch. 10.

Establishing this link does not, however, immediately solve all our problems, because there is then the further dispute whether 10.33-34 refers to judgment on the Assyrians or whether it refers to judgment on the people of Judah. A case can be made out for either interpretation.

In sorting out this ambiguity, I find the discussion by Nielsen to be the most helpful.[47] In brief, she demonstrates that the first interpretation depends upon the passage's present redactional setting. Starting at 10.5, the whole passage is built up into two parallel panels of three sections each. Disregarding minor glosses and additions, we have 10.5-15 and 10.28-32 describing the Assyrian's pride, followed in each case by a judgment oracle (10.16-19 and 10.33-34), and then finally an indication that the fall of Assyria will lead to a positive future for Israel (10.20-27 and 11.1-9). We note further that the judgment oracle in each panel makes use of tree imagery—a forest fire in the first case and forest-felling in the second.

Few would doubt that material of varying origins has been brought together to assemble this tidy arrangement, and it follows, of course, that the earliest date for this interpretation would be the date of whatever is reckoned to be the latest section within the whole. Beyond that, however, it also frees us to inquire after the significance of each constituent section before it was assembled into its present wider context. If, then, we look at 10.33-34 on its own, we are at once struck by its close comparability with 2.9-17. It shares a good deal of common vocabulary as well as similarity of general theme. There is thus a strong probability that it originally represented a comparable threat against all that is proud in the land. If so, 11.1 would not refer so much to a restoration after foreign invasion as to the hope of a fresh beginning after God has purged his people by some unstated means.

46. J.G. von Herder, *Vom Geist der ebräischen Poesie. II. Eine Anleitung für die Liebhaber derselben und der ältesten Geschichte des menschlichen Geistes* (Leipzig: Barth, 3rd edn, 1825), pp. 406-408.

47. K. Nielsen, *There is Hope for a Tree: The Tree as Metaphor in Isaiah* (JSOTSup, 65; Sheffield: JSOT Press, 1989), pp. 123-44.

On this basis, it is possible to mount a reasonable case for the Isaianic authorship of the opening verses of ch. 11.[48] If my understanding of the redactional development of chs. 10–11 as a whole is sound, then this particular passage must predate the emphasis on the promised fall of Assyria. A strong body of current opinion would put that promise some time in the reign of king Josiah,[49] while others still maintain that it is Isaianic. Either way, the passage was first written before that, being originally intended for a different purpose. In further support of that conclusion, we may note with many other commentators that 10.33-34 is thoroughly Isaianic in both theme and wording, and that the role of a Davidic figure in the restoration of society after God's purging is closely parallel to what we have already seen in ch. 9. A further argument, which I have not seen noted elsewhere, derives from a consideration of 11.10. That verse clearly refers back to 11.1, but it interprets 'the root of Jesse' in terms of the 'signal for the nations' which follows in v. 12, where it is associated with the regathering of the dispersed exiles. This looks very much like the kind of development of the understanding of the ideas of kingship which we have seen is typical of the book of Isaiah as a whole, and suggests that 11.1, with its indication of a new individual Davidic ruler, is earlier than the interpretation given it in the exilic–postexilic development which the second half of ch. 11 shares.

48. An additional small argument is advanced by H. Cazelles, 'De l'idéologie royale', *JANESCU* 5 (1973), pp. 59-73, who observes that the parallelism of *ṣedeq* with *mîšôr* in v. 4 is close to early, especially Phoenician, usage, whereas, on the basis of the Psalms, it appears to have dropped out of use by the postexilic period.

49. Indeed, we may note that some scholars have argued that the king in 11.1-5(9) is himself Josiah; cf. Vermeylen, *Du prophète Isaïe à l'apocalyptique*, pp. 269-75; Sweeney, *Isaiah 1–39*, pp. 204-205. The argument from the youth of the Davidic figure is strongest with regard to 11.6, which I take to be later in any case; that 11.1 refers to a young king is pure surmise. Furthermore, in terms of those who argue for a Josianic redaction of Isaiah's words on the ground that it was only then that an Assyrian withdrawal was a realistic possibility, such a situation will not have obtained as early as Josiah's accession; cf. N. Na'aman, 'The Kingdom of Judah under Josiah', *Tel Aviv* 18 (1991), pp. 3-71. Of course, it is more than likely that this passage would have been read with renewed hopes in Josiah's time, but that is not a sufficient argument for dating its composition then. It is noteworthy that neither of the two chief proponents of a Josianic redaction do so: Barth believes that the passage is authentically Isaianic, while Clements dates it to the postexilic period.

The only serious argument against this conclusion is the proposal that 'the stump of Jesse' in 11.1 presupposes the fall of the Davidic monarchy. If this verse be read as the direct continuation of 10.33-34, however, the stump imagery may be seen to derive directly from the picture of judgment there described and so does not necessarily presuppose any specific historical incident.[50] But what of Jesse? Does the fact that the writer goes back behind David imply that the house of David has fallen? If that were the intention, we might suppose rather that he would have referred to the stump of David, just as Amos 9.11 speaks of 'the booth of David that is fallen'.[51] The point of referring to Jesse, rather, seems to be not so much negatively to dwell on the nature of the judgment which has fallen as positively to make the point that the new ruler will be a second David. Though the imagery is completely different, the underlying idea does not seem to be very far removed from that of 28.16-17, where the establishment of a new or renewed Zion speaks of a foundation stone without commentators necessarily drawing the conclusion that the old Zion has been physically razed to the ground. In both cases, the need for such imagery certainly implies strong criticism of the prevailing *status quo*. In neither, however, is there any necessary implication that the institution in question is already a matter of the past. The most which might be deduced (and this is already a matter of some moment) is that Isaiah does not seem to be particularly concerned with a narrowly defined

50. Indeed, there are those who believe that the original anti-Judaean aim of this saying (as opposed to its later anti-Assyrian redactional reuse) included a hidden reference to God's judgment on the currently reigning Davidic king, since 10.33a may refer to a single tree, and Lebanon also has royal overtones in several other contexts. If this is true, '10.33–11.9 forms a consciously created entity that interprets the *fall of the proud king of Judah* as resulting from Yahweh's righteous *punishment*, but then proclaims that the dynasty will nevertheless endure; a new king, a *new David* will appear... The connexion between tree-felling and new sprouting is as organic as it is possible to imagine: from the lineage of the old king is born the new king of Judah' (Nielsen, *There is Hope for a Tree*, p. 136, following a detailed discussion).

51. It is noteworthy in this connection that in the several references to this passage in the Qumran scrolls where a messianic interpretation seems to be advanced, 'the stump of Jesse' is said to be 'the branch of David'; for references and discussion, see conveniently K.E. Pomykala, *The Davidic Dynasty Tradition in Early Judaism: Its History and Significance for Messianism* (Atlanta: Scholars Press, 1995), pp. 171-216.

dynastic succession. His commitment is not so much to the next king in the biological line of descent, but more to the Davidic ideal of leadership as such.

I conclude, therefore, that 11.1-5 originally expressed a comparatively modest hope by Isaiah that the new society which he anticipated being established after the threatened judgment would be led both judicially and more broadly by a righteous Davidide. The shift in emphasis which came about with the redactional reuse of 10.33-34 as referring to the downfall of Assyria entailed an accompanying movement towards a more 'messianic' application of 11.1-5,[52] even though the new David remains, apparently, within the historical continuum, and has not yet been cast as an eschatological figure.

Isaiah 32.1-5[53]

As is only to be expected, there have been many proposed identifications for the king referred to in the first verse of this passage (such as Hezekiah, Josiah, or the Messiah) as well as disagreements over whether it was written by Isaiah himself, by one of his early (pre-exilic) editors, or by a late postexilic redactor.[54]

On this occasion, I believe it is possible to cut through much of the debate by proposing that the nature of this verse has been generally

---

52. If vv. 6-9 are indeed a secondary addition to the passage (as I am inclined to think on other grounds), then they will have greatly contributed to this shift in interpretation.

53. Space limitations preclude attention to the frequently neglected messianic passage in 16.4-5. The problems raised by its setting within the Moab oracle in chs. 15-16 are formidable; for recent surveys, with fresh proposals of their own, see B.C. Jones, *Howling over Moab: Irony and Rhetoric in Isaiah 15–16* (SBLDS, 157; Atlanta: Scholars Press, 1996), and T.G. Smothers, 'Isaiah 15–16', in J.W. Watts and P.R. House (eds.), *Forming Prophetic Literature: Essays on Isaiah and the Twelve in Honor of John D.W. Watts* (JSOTSup, 235; Sheffield: Sheffield Academic Press, 1996), pp. 70-84. In ch. 2 of *Variations on a Theme*, I have sought briefly to defend the view that the Davidic figure is here presented in a scribal and priestly guise, and that the passage derives from the postexilic period. While it is certainly of significance that it draws on some of the major vocabulary stock which has been our concern above and that it is the most overtly messianic passage in the first part of the book of Isaiah, it clearly stands apart from the main line of the argument which is being developed in the present study.

54. Once again, the various opinions are helpfully surveyed most recently by Wegner, *Examination of Kingship*, pp. 275-301.

misunderstood. As we shall see immediately, it has a number of features which distinguish it from those that I have studied so far, features on which some commentators have seized to make the case that this passage cannot come from Isaiah. It would be a mistake, however, to move straight from this observation to a discussion of authenticity. Rather, it should lead us in the first instance to inquire more carefully about the form of this verse. In short, building on the insights of the minority of scholars[55] who regard this verse as hypothetical in form ('If...'), and so link it directly with the next verse ('then...'), I suggest that it takes the form of a proverb.

Among the reasons for this conclusion we may briefly note the following arguments. Unlike any of the passages I have studied so far, this one refers explicitly to a king (*melek*), but it lacks the definite article and it is set in parallel with 'princes'. Taken together, these points suggest that we are not here dealing with one specific king, but with any king—kings in general, even. The point is not to single out one king from others, but to refer to him as a leader of the people, just as princes are. Next, the verbs in this verse are in the imperfect, and in each case the verb and the noun derive from the same root—*yimlok-melek* and *śārîm... yāśōrû*. Both these stylistic features are appropriate, each in its own way, to the proverbial form. Furthermore, the key words 'justice' and 'righteousness' (here *ṣedeq* rather than the usually preferred form *ṣᵉdāqâ*) are given in reverse order. Putting *ṣedeq* first, and so giving it greater prominence, brings the thought of the verse very much into line with the outlook of the wisdom writers. Significantly, when these key words are picked up and developed later on in the chapter (v. 16), they are used in their usual form and order, giving the impression of an Isaianic interpretation of a non-Isaianic saying. And finally, several of the verses in the passage following this one are also proverbial in nature, as most commentators recognize (see certainly vv. 6-8, but probably vv. 4 and 5 as well), so that it would not be surprising to find v. 1 taking the same form too. We might therefore propose as a

---

55. See, for instance, E.J. Kissane, *The Book of Isaiah*, I (Dublin: Browne & Nolan, 1941), pp. 357-63; R.B.Y Scott, *IB*, V, pp. 342-43; O. Kaiser, *Der Prophet Jesaja, Kapitel 13-39* (ATD, 18; Göttingen: Vandenhoeck & Ruprecht, 1973), pp. 254-56 (ET *Isaiah 13–39: A Commentary* [OTL; London: SCM Press, 1974], pp. 320-22); W.H. Irwin, *Isaiah 28–33: Translation with Philological Notes* (BibOr, 30; Rome: Biblical Institute Press, 1977), p. 120; J.D.W. Watts, *Isaiah 1–33* (WBC, 24; Waco, TX: Word Books, 1985), pp. 411-12.

translation: 'Behold, a king should reign so as to bring about[56] righteousness, and princes should rule so as to maintain justice'.

Both the wording and the sentiment of this verse have some close parallels in the wisdom literature.[57] The most striking example of this is Prov. 8.15-16, where in the first half of each verse we find precisely the same subjects and verbs as in our verse, as well as a generally similar outlook:

> By me kings reign (*mᵉlākîm yimlōkû*),
>> and rulers decree what is just (*ṣedeq*);
> by me rulers rule (*śārîm yāśōrû*),
>> and nobles, all who govern rightly (*ṣedeq*).

That a king and rulers should govern in such a way as to establish justice is also a common thought in Proverbs, for example at 16.10, 13; 20.8, 26; 29.4, 14; 31.4-5.

We have in Isa. 32.1, therefore, a general saying about rulership. It is not possible to decide whether Isaiah coined it himself, or whether it was in general circulation for him to cite. The slight differences I have noted from Isaiah's own usual formulations might incline us slightly towards the latter possibility.

In the following verses, consequences are drawn if these guidelines are followed. First, in v. 2, such rulers will be a protection for their people. As Wildberger has shown,[58] the imagery used here was widespread in ancient Near Eastern royal ideology. However, with regard to the Hebrew Bible itself this is not the case; rather, the commonest use of these images by far is in association with the role of God towards his people.[59] From what we have seen previously, however, it would not be surprising if Isaiah had applied this to the consequence of righteous

---

56. The translation of the preposition *l* has been variously discussed. The case for understanding it as an expression of purpose, as well as an exposure of the weaknesses in other views (widespread though they are), is carefully argued by J.W. Olley, 'Notes on Isaiah xxxii 1, xlv 19, 23 and lxiii 1', *VT* 33 (1983), pp. 446-53, and his position is adopted here.

57. There has been a long history of discussion about the connections between Isaiah and the wisdom tradition. I have sought to summarize this, and to offer some guidelines for future work, in Williamson, 'Isaiah and the Wise' (see n. 9).

58. H. Wildberger, *Jesaja. III. Jesaja 28–39: Das Buch, der Prophet und seine Botschaft* (BKAT, 10.3; Neukirchen–Vluyn: Neukirchener Verlag, 1982), pp. 1255-56.

59. See Roberts, 'The Divine King', pp. 133-34.

rule, since for him the rule of God and of his appointed king coincide so closely. Interestingly, the closest parallel to this verse occurs in the so-called Isaiah Apocalypse, at Isa. 25.4-5, where the imagery is again applied to God. The coincidences of vocabulary are so strong here that it seems clear that we have a direct literary allusion. This is a subject that has been carefully analysed by Sweeney, who shows that it is characteristic of the Isaiah Apocalypse to cite from elsewhere in the Isaiah tradition (as well as from elsewhere in the Hebrew Bible) in a consistently 'universalizing' direction, so that we should certainly hold that the same is the case here.[60] This is an important conclusion, because it demonstrates that this part of Isaiah 32 predates the Isaiah Apocalypse. That does not settle its date in an absolute sense, of course, but it is clearly in line with the direction in which I have been moving.

The next verse, 32.3, gives us further evidence to support the case. It is obvious that the anticipated blessing referred to here is a reversal of the 'hardening' passage in 6.9-10. As was noted above in connection with ch. 11, the theme of this passage is one that has exerted a particularly strong influence on the whole of the Isaianic tradition. At this point, however, we need to note in slightly greater detail how that theme was developed in order to be able to locate the present verse within it. In brief, the main points to observe are that in the second half of the book there is something of a shift in that the specific words 'blind' and 'deaf' are introduced into the phraseology, as though there is a movement from the metaphorical to the literal,[61] and that this feature becomes even more marked in passages relating to the theme which, though included within the first half of the book, are without doubt to be regarded as even later additions—notably at 29.18 and 35.5-6. In both cases the healing, as it has now become, is put into the eschatological future. Isaiah 32.3 is different in each respect from this, however. There is no reference to the blind and the deaf as such, and the overall context is not that of the eschatological future. By contrast, the language is very much closer to that of Isaiah himself. In addition to the fact that 'the eyes of those who see' and 'the ears of those who hear' are as similar as the context will allow to 'see with their eyes' and 'hear with their ears'

60. M.A. Sweeney, 'Textual Citations in Isaiah 24–27: Toward an Understanding of the Redactional Function of Chapters 24–27 in the Book of Isaiah', *JBL* 107 (1988), pp. 39-52. I have myself sought to build on Sweeney's insights in *The Book Called Isaiah*, pp. 180-83.

61. This is noted especially by Clements in 'Patterns in the Prophetic Canon'.

in 6.10, we should note in particular that the rare verb *š''* is used in both verses. This verb also occurs twice at 29.9, a verse generally agreed to be by Isaiah himself. Indeed, these references may account for the sum total of uses of this verb in the Old Testament, although it is difficult to be certain because of possible confusion between it and the similar *š'h* elsewhere.[62] At any rate, it is not in doubt that the word is characteristic of Isaiah, and that it does not occur in the later writers who built on this theme elsewhere in the book. Finally, attention may be drawn to a characteristic juxtaposing of words in v. 4, *ûlᵉbab nimhārîm yābîn lāda'at*. Three of these four words also occur together in 6.9-10 in a way which, as I have tried to show elsewhere, was also influential on later tradition.[63]

From all this evidence, I conclude that the formulation of 32.3 is certainly earlier than the major development in the Isaiah tradition that came about during the exile, and that in all probability it should be ascribed to Isaiah himself. *A fortiori*, the same will apply to 32.1, and I suggest that the appreciation that this verse is proverbial answers all the arguments that have been raised in order to suggest that it is postexilic. The verse may have been quoted rather than written by Isaiah, but it should nevertheless be included among the evidence for his view of kingship. Its setting near the end of what was probably the earliest form of his book is thus appropriate. It is not, however, a messianic text in the usual sense of that term.

Conclusions

It is now time to draw the threads of this discussion together. First, if the analysis of 32.1-5 is correct, it demonstrates that Isaiah did after all express himself in a general manner (that is to say, without reference to a specific present or future king) on the subject of kingship in connection with one of the major themes of his work which was introduced at the start. The verse thus ties our main topic into his broader ideological framework in a way that appeared to be lacking in my initial survey. This then forges a strong point of connection between his thought and the focus on justice and righteousness in the royal passages in chs. 9

---

62. Indeed, there is some confusion in the text about this issue in 32.3 itself, though the context leaves no doubt that the line adopted above is the correct one; for discussion, see *The Book Called Isaiah*, p. 254.

63. See Williamson, *The Book Called Isaiah*, pp. 48-50.

and 11. As he looked in hope for a better king in the future, he did so in the expectation that the king would serve as God's agent in the inauguration of a society more in line with what he conceived to be the will of God.

Secondly, although these same two passages show knowledge of the Davidic origins of the monarchy in Jerusalem and specifically some familiarity with the dynastic promise, this feature has not emerged as a central focus. The stress throughout is on the role rather than the person of the king. This was already the case to a limited extent in ch. 9, and it is even more prominent in 11, where the reference to Jesse points back behind the immediate royal family to the hope for a second David—a fresh beginning, in other words. We have not found any evidence that God was somehow inalienably wedded to the Davidic descendant, that God would protect him against his enemies regardless of his conduct.

Thirdly, although the language in which these ideas are couched is often familiar from elsewhere in the Old Testament and beyond, it is given what I have called a peculiar 'twist' by Isaiah. It is easy to overlook this point by moving straight from parallels of language to the assumption that the same ideas are being expressed. In the case of Isaiah, however, this would be misleading, for it is the small but significant variation that he introduces which reveals some of the most distinctive aspects of his thought. This again reinforces the point that his dominant interest was not in kingship as such but in the wider nature of the society over which the king ruled and of its proper ordering under God.

So far, there is nothing in this that we could properly term 'messianic'. We have seen, however, that there was a move in this direction after the time of Isaiah himself in the redactional setting of at least one of his royal sayings in the context of the anticipated fall of Assyria. The possibility of doing this will have been helped both by the fact that by the end of his ministry Isaiah's own hopes for the future had apparently been cast into the longer term future (cf. 30.8) and by the fact of his comparative detachment from a concern for the immediate Davidic line of descent. It was certainly in line with the main direction of Isaiah's own thinking that his hopes could be turned towards a more remote future.

The decisive shift in this direction, however, came, I suggest, with the incorporation of ch. 7, probably around the time of the fall of Jerusalem to the Babylonians with its consequent loss of kingship. The understanding of this passage as set out above suggests that, regardless of its original earlier formulation in the aftermath of the Syro-Ephraimite crisis, which is now probably beyond recall, its present attitude towards the Davidic dynasty is similar to that found in, for instance, Jeremiah 22–23. In this latter passage in its present form, there is an equal openness to the possibility of the end of the dynasty (22.24-30), expressed in categorical terms. At the same time, however, we find shortly afterwards an expectation that God will raise up another ruler 'for David' who will reign according to the ancient ideals of wisdom, justice and righteousness (23.5-6). In the light of this, the placement of Isaiah 7 is most likely a reflection on the fall of the Davidic dynasty to the Babylonians.[64] Its concern was to explain the judgment which had fallen in the light of the hardening passage in ch. 6.

Once this had happened, it was inevitable that the passages in chs. 9 and 11 should equally be read in a similar context. Although it would be anachronistic to speak of a messianic hope (in the strict sense) in connection with the historical Isaiah of Jerusalem, the growth of the book in the light of subsequent events inevitably and, it may be held, justifiably led in that direction. Ultimately, once that general direction in interpretation had been set, the later tendency towards an atomistic reading of scripture opened the way for even 7.14 to be interpreted messianically within the Christian church.

Finally, in view of the emphasis that we have discerned on the role rather than the person of the coming king, it may be seen that even the radical directions in which these themes were developed in later parts of the book are by no means entirely inappropriate. While concern there turns towards the people in place of the Davidic king, there are correspondences that can be easily traced between their task on the universal stage and his on the national. In the book as a whole, the messianic hope concerns the agent of God in the inauguration of a society based upon the principles of justice, broadly understood—a servant of the Lord indeed.

---

64. Without reference to Isa. 7, the case for an exilic redaction elsewhere in Isaiah 1-39 has been argued most forcefully by R.E. Clements, 'The Prophecies of Isaiah and the Fall of Jerusalem in 587 B.C.', *VT* 30 (1980), pp. 421-36.

KING AND MESSIAH IN DEUTERONOMY
AND THE DEUTERONOMISTIC HISTORY

J.G. McConville

Deuteronomy and the historical books that follow it (Joshua, Judges, Samuel and Kings) are of special importance to the topic of kingship in the Old Testament for two reasons. First, Deuteronomy contains the only law concerning kingship in the Old Testament (Deut. 17.14-20), and secondly, the foundational text for the promise of Yahweh to the Davidic dynasty is found in 2 Sam. 7.11b-16. These two texts constitute, as we shall see, the poles of a dialogue about the nature of kingship in Israel that is played out between law and narrative in this large body of literature. The context of the dialogue is the theory and practice of kingship in the ancient Near Eastern culture of which Israel was part. The issue for interpretation is how far our literature offers an alternative, distinctively Israelite understanding of the king's role. And consequently, what is the content and force of the 'messianic' theology of kingship that is found especially in the books of Samuel (where, alone in DtrH, the term *māšîaḥ* is applied to kings)?

The data for our discussion cannot be reduced to the two texts mentioned above, however, as the issues surrounding leadership in Israel are so fundamental to the thematics of the literature. The kingship story line may be briefly given as follows. Deuteronomy permits Israel to appoint a king (Deut. 17.14-20), who would be chosen from his 'brothers' in Israel, and who would be conspicuously less powerful than the common run of oriental kings. Kingship does not feature overtly in Joshua, where Joshua himself is Israel's supreme commander in the war against the nations of Canaan. (As we shall see, however, Joshua has sometimes been seen as a virtual king, a 'mon-arch', and a proto-type of Josiah. Moses too, indeed, has been regarded similarly.) Kingship becomes an issue with new force in Judges, where it appears as a kind of dark alternative to the charismatic leadership of the 'judges'. In the ambiguities of Gideon's disclaimer (Judg. 8.22-23), the misadventure of Abimelech (Judg. 9), the caveat of Jotham (Judg. 9.7-15) and the depicted chaos of kingless Israel (Judg. 17–21) there are foreshadowings of the decision about leadership that will drive a wedge between Samuel and the Israel of his day. This comes to a head in 1 Samuel 8–12, which (in its present form) sees the request for a king 'like all the nations' as a rejection of Yahweh as king (1 Sam. 8.7). If Saul is the ill-starred product of that negotiation, his succession by David, the 'man after God's own heart' (1 Sam. 13.14; 16) seems to hold better things in store. David's establishment of the Ark of the Covenant in Jerusalem (2 Sam. 6), Yahweh's promise to him of a dynastic house 'for ever' (2 Sam. 7.11b-16), and his wise exercise of power (2 Sam. 8.15) bring a certain closure to Deuteronomic expectation (Deut. 12.5; cf. 12.10 and 2 Sam. 7.1).

The apogee of royal splendour is attained only in Solomon, however, the son of David who built the Temple, and who became a byword for wealth and wisdom (1 Kgs 3–10). Unlike David, he is expressly bound over to keep the Torah (1 Kgs 2.2-4). His glory is in the end tarnished by idolatry and foreign wives (1 Kgs 11), and he initiates the chronicle of kings, in divided northern and southern kingdoms, who patently fail, with a few significant exceptions, to match the royal ideal (whether Deuteronomic or Davidic). In this story of covenantal failure, the assurance that the promise remains valid for Solomon's descendants 'for the sake of my servant David and for the sake of Jerusalem' (1 Kgs 11.32) introduces an ambiguous note. Among the kings the greatest accolades are heaped upon Josiah of Judah, peerless before and since (2 Kgs 23.25), and evoking both Davidic and Mosaic echoes. He is so eulogized that he has seemed to many to be the real climax of a story that saw in him the fulfilment of Davidic promise. Yet instead of the glorious epoch thus heralded, the story runs to its bitter end, with the slide of Judah into political annihilation and Babylonian captivity managed by the last successors of Josiah, and of David (2 Kgs 23.31–25.30).

There are enormous tensions in this narrative. Not the least is the disconcerting dissonance between the grandeur of Josiah and the speed of the collapse after him. But the underlying tension is the apparent discrepancy between, on the one hand, the Deuteronomic portrayal of the king as subject to Torah and limited in power, and on the other the permanency attached to the Davidic promise, and indeed the modelling of David, and especially Solomon, on lines that seem to owe much to the ancient world. The contrast between the law and the narrative is nowhere more marked than in the portrayal of Solomon.

We can identify at the outset, therefore, a crucial question for our study, namely whether Deuteronomy and the historical books speak with a single voice on the subject of kingship. When Solomon is approved by Yahweh for his prayer for wisdom to rule his people, Yahweh bestows on him the very wealth that the Deuteronomic law withholds (1 Kgs 3.13; Deut. 17.17), symbolized in both places, apparently, by vast stables (1 Kgs 4.26; Deut. 17.16).[1] Scholars have met this problem in a variety of ways. For some, the law-code and the ensuing narratives are essentially in harmony. The law provides a 'norm' for the history.[2] This usually means that the law is favourably disposed towards the establishment of kingship in Israel, and that it has natural connections with parts of the narrative that can be interpreted in a similar way. Thus H.J. Boecker finds Dtr's attitude in texts that are positive to the monarchy in 1 Samuel 8–12. He cites Yahweh's instruction to make a king in 1 Sam. 8.22, and the development of this in 10.17, 20-21b, where Yahweh himself takes the initiative in the 'lot'. Samuel's 'law of the kingdom' (*mišpaṭ hammᵉlûkâ*, 10.25), belongs here also.[3] Dtr, however, built into his picture some of the old tensions that there had been over the monarchy, and is critical of kingship in its aspect of political machination, as portrayed in 1 Samuel 8, and also insofar as it is demanded for the purposes of warfare, thus sidelining Yahweh in his ancient role as holy warrior.[4] Boecker, therefore, sees the problem for interpretation in terms of elements that are favourable or unfavourable to the concept of monarchy as such. His answer to this problem is to find the true voice of Dtr in the texts that speak positively about kingship, to argue that these are in agreement with Deuteronomy, and to regard other texts as divergent from the main line. In this he is echoed by a number of other scholars.[5] F. Crüsemann, in his study of

---

1.   See Gary N. Knoppers, 'The Deuteronomist and the Deuteronomistic Law of the King', *ZAW* 108 (1996), pp. 337, 339-42.

2.   H.J. Boecker, *Die Beurteilung der Anfänge des Königtums in den deuteronomistischen Abschnitten des 1. Samuelbuches* (WMANT, 31; Neukirchen–Vluyn: Neukirchener Verlag, 1969), pp. 28-29. He distances himself from the view of Noth, and before him Kuenen, who had seen the Deuteronomic law as only negative on kingship; cf. *Beurteilung*, p. 28 n. 3.

3.   Boecker, *Beurteilung*, p. 89.

4.   Boecker, *Beurteilung*, pp. 91-92.

5.   Cf. K. Galling, 'Das Königsgesetz im Deuteronomium', *TLZ* 76 (1951), cols. 133–38. Galling thought the law, though circumscribing kingship in certain

the anti-monarchical strain in DtrH, found that it diverged from Dtr's main line, which was to be heard in the positive texts, such as 1 Sam. 10.17-27.[6] It is not clear, however, that these studies penetrate the more important question, concerning the nature of kingship in Israel.

Other studies, in contrast, emphasize the stark difference between the Deuteronomic law and the dominant voice in the narratives. Jon D. Levenson took up Noth's postulate that Dtr had inserted the code into his history, and attempted to establish this by identifying theological topics on which Dtr diverged seriously from the Deuteronomic code. Chief among these was the concept of covenant. For Levenson the 'unconditional' (or in his terms 'ancestral') Davidic covenant could not be reconciled with the 'conditional' (or 'contemporary') Deuteronomic version.[7] Secondly, the concept of the king in DtrH is wholly unlike that of Deuteronomy. Following Noth, he points out that Josiah, in promulgating the Deuteronomic law, acts in defiance of it, for Deuteronomy would more probably have assigned the role he plays in the reform to a prophet.[8] Dtr's role of the king, in fact, is 'undeuteronomic and an obstacle in the way of any argument that Dtr1 has positioned Dtn as the frontispiece and the keynote to his work'.[9] Levenson also notes differences between the law and the narrative on sacrifice, intermarriage with foreigners, and priesthood.[10]

In similar vein, G.N. Knoppers argues that Dtr 'promotes a much more formative role for the king than the authors of Deuteronomy ever

respects, was more positive than 1 Sam. 8, which was uniformly hostile to kingship; see cols. 134-35, and cf. Boecker, *Beurteilung*, p. 29 n. 1.

6.   F. Crüsemann, *Der Widerstand gegen das Königtum: Die antiköniglichen Texte des Alten Testaments und der Kampf um den frühen israelitischen Staat* (WMANT, 49; Neukirchen–Vluyn: Neukirchener Verlag, 1978).

7.   Jon D. Levenson, 'Who Inserted the Book of the Torah?', *HTR* 68 (1975), pp. 203-33 (224-27).

8.   Levenson, 'Book of the Torah', pp. 227-228; cf. M. Noth, *Überlieferungsgeschichtliche Studien* (Tübingen: Max Niemeyer, 2nd edn, 1957), p. 94 (ET *The Deuteronomistic History* [trans. H.G.M. Williamson; JSOTSup, 15; Sheffield: JSOT Press, 1981], p. 82); G. von Rad, 'Die deuteronomistische Theologie in den Königsbüchern', in *Gesammelte Studien zum Alten Testament* (TBü, 8; Munich: Chr. Kaiser Verlag, 1958), pp. 189-204 (202 n. 13) (ET 'The Deuteronomic Theology of History in I and II Kings', in *The Problem of the Hexateuch and Other Essays* [trans. E. Trueman Dicken, London: SCM Press, 1984], pp. 205-21 [218 n. 14]).

9.   Levenson, 'Book of the Torah', p. 228.

10.   Levenson, 'Book of the Torah', pp. 228-30.

countenanced'.[11] He pursues this thesis in relation to Solomon's wealth, his horses and his wives. While Dtr's treatment of the last two have been seen by some scholars as implying criticism of Solomon according to the Deuteronomic law,[12] Knoppers argues that Dtr means in all these cases to show that Solomon has indeed been blessed in his kingship by Yahweh. Solomon's enormous wealth represents the fulfilment of Yahweh's promise to him at Gibeon (1 Kgs 3.13).[13] His impressive household of chariots and horsemen demonstrates the extent of his administration, and is catalogued among his accomplishments.[14] And his vast harem implies no criticism in itself, since Dtr assumes the legitimacy of royal polygamy in David's case (2 Sam. 12.8); it is only mixed marriage that is criticized.[15]

Knoppers therefore argues that, in making the king the supreme official in cultic matters, Dtr has departed from Deuteronomy and adapted to an ancient Near Eastern view of the monarch's role. While Dtr can draw on Deuteronomy, he can also be independent of it, and even 'subvert the very code he incorporates within his history'.[16] While Knoppers thus has elements in common with Boecker, in finding a positive view of kingship in DtrH, he is quite different in that he no longer sees the law operating as a 'norm', or at least not straightforwardly. DtrH is quite independent here.

Furthermore, in Knoppers's treatment, the main issue for interpretation has rightly been identified as the nature of kingship. My initial observation of tensions between the two blocks has been sharpened: does Deuteronomy have a radical and distinctive view of kingship in relation to the ancient world? And does DtrH promote it, refine it, or reject it? I shall try to answer these questions by turning now to the law itself, to see if its setting and function can be established, and then by comparing and evaluating the relevant texts in DtrH.

11. Knoppers, 'The Deuteronomist', p. 333.
12. E.g. M. Z. Brettler, 'The Structure of 1 Kings 1–11', *JSOT* 49 (1991), pp. 91-93; and see Knoppers, 'The Deuteronomist', pp. 339, 343, for further bibliography.
13. Knoppers, 'The Deuteronomist', p. 339.
14. Knoppers, 'The Deuteronomist', p. 340.
15. Knoppers, 'The Deuteronomist', pp. 343-44.
16. Knoppers, 'The Deuteronomist', pp. 344-45.

A Setting for the Law of the King

Deuteronomy evidently intends somehow to circumscribe or restrict the powers of the king.[17] The king as presented here differs enormously from that of the usual ancient Near Eastern concept of the king as the chief executive in all aspects of the nation's life. The limits on his power are adumbrated by the formulaic introduction of the law, which reaffirms that it is Yahweh who has given the land (17.1); there is no sign here of the king as the one who makes land grants. His kingship, furthermore, is not in the natural order of things; this king must await the request of the people, then appointment by them (17.14-15; cf. 28.36). He is no military figure; the people's qualification of their request in 1 Sam. 8.20c ('...and go out before us and fight our battles') is a significant variation from the letter of this law.[18] The ban on many horses (17.16) may be understood in this connection; the prohibition of an extensive household of chariotry is designed to preclude a private standing army with a permanent officer class.[19] The prohibitions of acquiring wealth and a large harem (17.17) can be understood as opposing a centralized royal administration, which concentrates a nation's wealth by means of a tax system, and which uses royal marriage as a tool of international diplomacy. Most significantly, the king is not the 'son' of God, in the terms of Zion theology (Ps. 2.7). That metaphor is applied rather to Israel (1.31—thus putting Deuteronomy closer to Exod. 4.22-23 and Hos. 11.1 than to passages that reflect the Zion ideology). Indeed, the Zion concept of kingship may be subtly challenged in Deuteronomy's formula of divine choosing, which is applied only to the place of worship (12.5, etc.) and to the king.[20] This pair of

17. U. Rüterswörden, *Von der politischen Gemeinschaft zur Gemeinde: Studien zu Dt 16,18--8,22* (BBB, 65; Frankfurt am Main: Athenäum, 1987), pp. 90-91.

18. Cf. Boecker, *Beurteilung*, pp. 91-92.

19. N. Lohfink, 'Distribution of the Functions of Power: The Laws Concerning Public Offices in Deuteronomy 16:18–18:22', in D.L. Christensen (ed.), *A Song of Power and the Power of Song* (Winona Lake, IN: Eisenbrauns, 1993), pp. 336-52 (345); originally 'Die Sicherung der Wirksamkeit des Gotteswortes durch das Prinzip der Gewaltenteilung nach den Ämtergesetzen des Buches Deuteronomium (Dt 16,18–18,22)' in H. Wolter (ed.), *Testimonium Veritati* (Festschrift Wilhelm Kempf; Frankfurter theologische Studien, 7; Frankfurt am Main: Knecht, 1971), pp. 144-55.

20. The people is also chosen (7.6), as is the priestly tribe of Levi (18.5). But

objects of choice corresponds to those in the Zion theology (Ps. 2.6). But the anonymity of the former in Deuteronomy, and the humble place allowed to the latter, bespeak a different way of thinking about the nature of Israel's organization. Far from being God's son, in a special way, the king is a brother Israelite (17.15b, 20). His subordination to the Torah (vv. 18-19) corresponds to this fundamental equality of standing with his fellows. He will, indeed, be followed on the throne by his sons; but this dynasty does not look like the powerful centralized administration of the Davidic line.

The extent of the restriction of the king's powers emerges more fully when the law is seen in the context of the series of laws in Deuteronomy that prescribe a constitution for Israel (Deut. 16.18-18.22). These provide for the establishment of judges, both in the cities of Israel and at the central sanctuary (16.18-20, 17.9); the Levitical priests, both in their capacity as judges (17.9) and in respect of their cultic duties (18.1-8); and the prophet (18.9-22). Of these offices only that of the king is not actually prescribed by Yahweh. The programme for Israel's political life (its 'polity', to borrow the term used by S. Dean McBride[21]) provides for what Lohfink calls a 'distribution of the functions of power' among the offices.[22] In the context of this distribution of powers, the king occupies a position that can be seen as less influential than either the priest[23] or the prophet.[24] Over all the offices, however, is the entity that is addressed as 'thou' in this section of Deuteronomy. This

only the king and the place of worship are the subjects of promises concerning Yahweh's future choice.

21. S. Dean McBride, 'Polity of the Covenant People: The Book of Deuteronomy', *Int* 41 (1987), pp. 229-44; repr. in Christensen (ed.), *Song of Power*, pp. 62-77.

22. Lohfink, 'Distribution', pp. 339, 347-49.

23. Rüterswörden, *Gemeinschaft*, p. 110, sees the Levitical priests as the 'executive' of the Torah, while the prophet has the function of 'legislative' in relation to it. McBride applies the term 'executive' to the king, and speculates that he may have shared in the activity of administering and interpreting the law with the Levitical priests. Yet he agrees that 'the levitical priests potentially exercise more power than the king over the Israelite nation' ('Polity of the Covenant People', pp. 74-75). Contrast Lohfink, 'Distribution', p. 340, who thinks the royal prerogative of judging is abrogated here; cf. Rüterswörden, *Gemeinschaft*, pp. 90-91: 'Im Deuteronomium ist der König weder an der Legislative, Judikative, noch am Militärwesen beteiligt'.

24. Lohfink, 'Distribution', p. 351; Rüterswörden, *Gemeinschaft*, pp. 92-93, and see last note. Cf. also Knoppers, 'The Deuteronomist', p. 334.

addressee is best regarded simply as Israel itself, as a body,[25] or, with B. Halpern, as the properly constituted assembly.[26] The Deuteronomic covenant is between God and Israel, unmediated by the king. In respect of the exercise of power, indeed, the people has taken on the specifically royal prerogative of presiding over its various aspects.

The immediate question is whether this picture represents a real programme for the exercise of kingship, and other powers, in ancient Israel. While DtrH's portrayal of the monarchy can naturally be attributed to exilic reflections on its demise, the date of the Deuteronomic law of the king is not so easily established, nor indeed whether it is a true part of the Deuteronomic programme, or an addition from a sectional source. The question as normally posed is whether it is a pre-exilic law that was intended to be enforced in the Israelite (or Judaean) state. Or is it a utopian theory, devised in the exile, and never intended for, or capable of, implementation?

This latter view is represented by L. Perlitt.[27] Perlitt believes that Deut. 16.18–18.22 could not be a constitution of Israel for a number of reasons. Deuteronomy 16.18 does not appear to initiate a new section of the book.[28] The king-law in particular is dependent on the Deuteronomistic concept of history, because of its historical preamble ('when you come into the land...').[29] The law, in any case, is not realistic, because it in no way corresponds to the actual political conditions of the Israelite and Judaean monarchies. No king could defend a territory without horses. Deuteronomy actually contains no thinking about a monarchy, and nothing at all about a king. The law, in reality, is no more than a Dtr invention, based on 1 Samuel 8, and intended to

---

25. With G. von Rad, *Das Gottesvolk* (BWANT, 47; Stuttgart: W. Kohlhammer, 1929), p. 17.

26. B. Halpern, *The Constitution of the Monarchy in Israel* (HSM, 25; Chico, CA: Scholars Press, 1981), pp. 188-216. It is less likely to be the *'am hā'āreṣ, pace* H. Cazelles, 'Droit public dans le Deutéronome', in N. Lohfink (ed.), *Das Deuteronomium: Entstehung, Gestalt und Botschaft* (BETL, 68; Leuven: Leuven University Press, 1985), pp. 101-102; cf. Rütersworden, *Gemeinschaft*, pp. 94-95.

27. L. Perlitt, 'Der Staatsgedanke im Deuteronomium', in S.E. Balentine and J. Barton (eds.), *Language, Theology and the Bible: Essays in Honour of James Barr* (Oxford: Oxford University Press, 1994), pp. 182-98.

28. Perlitt, 'Staatsgedanke', p. 186.

29. Perlitt, 'Staatsgedanke', p. 188. Here he follows Lohfink's review of Rütersworden, *Gemeinschaft*, in *TLZ* 113 (1988), cols. 425-30; see further below on Rütersworden.

provide an ideological grounding for prophetic critique of the kings.[30] The Deuteronomic law (Deut. 12–18) does not address the question of a constitution for Israel; it is essentially the document of a cultic and religious reform, and the basis (with P) of the Jewish separation of religion and state.[31]

Perlitt's literary point is important. It is hard to maintain that Deut. 16.18–18.22 is in itself the constitution for ancient Israel, since it is embedded in the paraenesis of Deuteronomy. However, it is not self-evident that the laws in this section have no basis in Israel's early politics. Perlitt's treatment is resolutely orientated towards the exile. If Deuteronomy does not address the issue of kingship it is because its time is past. The king-law's echoes of the debates in 1 Samuel 8 can only mean that the law is late and derivative. Yet there are problems with Perlitt's position. Most seriously, it allows no weight to the likely influence in early Israel of a locus of authority apart from the royal court, as reflected in 1 Samuel 8–12 and other texts.[32] Its vision of Deuteronomy as 'religious', not political, somewhat pre-empts discussion of the point. And the idea that the king-law is a Dtr invention to ground the prophetic critique of the kings faces two problems: (1) Dtr appears to congratulate at least one king (Josiah), who is as centralist (thus against the terms of the king law) as any; and (2) Dtr's criticism of kings focuses on apostasy, not on the arrogation of a centralized royal power in itself.

There is a case, therefore, for exploring the theory that the king-law has a background in the life of ancient Israel. The belief that it has pre-exilic origins is widely held. In literary-critical terms, it is thought to consist essentially of the threefold prohibition of multiplying horses, wives and wealth (17.16-17), an ideal which may have prophetic roots.[33] More significant, however, are those theories which (*pace* Perlitt) see the function of the laws of the officials as a whole as a 'constitution' for pre-exilic Israel. The most ambitious attempt of this sort was made by

30. Perlitt, 'Staatsgedanke', pp. 189-93.
31. Perlitt, 'Staatsgedanke', pp. 194-97.
32. See further below.
33. A.D.H. Mayes, *Deuteronomy* (NCB; London: Marshall, Morgan & Scott, 1979), p. 270. Deut. 17.18-19, however, is often thought to be Dtr, because of the emphasis on the written Torah, which refers to the whole law only here in the code (Mayes, *Deuteronomy*, p. 273). Cf. Rüterswörden, *Gemeinschaft*, p. 108, who thinks the concept of the Levitical priests as executive of the constitution is Dtr (contrast the sole priest in 17.12).

Halpern. His arguments, which seek to establish that the law functioned
in practice as a regulation governing kingship in ancient Israel, may be
summed up or grouped as follows. (1) It is unlikely that a 'utopian' law
should emerge late in Israel, after the demise of the monarchy. Yet
equally, it is scarcely likely that Josiah would accept or promote such a
law, since it would have limited his powers.[34] Therefore, it must already
have been in existence by his time. (2) The law corresponds in important respects to the account of the inception of the kingship in DtrH.
Central to this contention is Halpern's view that it is Israel itself that
takes the initiative in making the king in 1 Samuel. Deuteronomy's idea
of the brotherhood of Israelites corresponds to this ideology of people-
hood, as does the 'distribution of powers' enshrined in Deuteronomy,
and found also in Samuel–Kings, especially between priest and prophet. There are, furthermore, close verbal links between Deut. 17.14-15
and 1 Sam. 8.4, 20. (The relationship between law and narrative must
be taken up again below). (3) The law has not been devised as a protest
against Solomon: it does not address the main concern of DtrH at this
point, which condemns Solomon for apostasy, not for 'big government'.[35] (4) There are connections between the law and other early Old
Testament literature. The idea of a king bound by Torah is known in
Psalm 132, and the prophets appear to know a law like that of Deuteronomy (Hos. 8.4, 10.3-4; Isa. 30.2, 31.1).

Halpern's analysis finds echoes in two other recent works. U. Rüterswörden finds in Deut. 16.18–18.22 a Deuteronomic constitutional
draft, covering the functions of judge, priest, king and prophet, which
sets out their institution, functions, nature of their authority, and succession.[36] S. Dean McBride, opposing what he called the 'reductionist'
view of von Rad and others that the book is merely religious teaching,
also saw Deuteronomy as constitutional law, a 'polity' for pre-exilic
Israel.[37] In his view the intention to enact this polity is declared already
at 1.3, 5, then specified as comprising testimonies, statutes, ordinances

---

34. Halpern, *Constitution*, pp. 228, 226. The points that follow are based on
Halpern's discussion on pp. 226-33.

35. Halpern, *Constitution*, pp. 226-27; cf. Levenson, 'Book of the Torah',
p. 230, who contrasted DtrH's concern with apostasy with Deuteronomy's prohibition of many wives.

36. Rüterswörden, *Gemeinschaft*, pp. 89-90. His Deuteronomic core is Deut.
16.18*, 19, 21-22, 17.8-10, 12-15, 16aa, 17*, 20, 18.1*, 3-4, 6-8, 9-15.

37. McBride, 'Polity', pp. 65-66.

(4.44-45). In this context the role of the king is as 'judge' consulting the 'Torah' in order to fulfil his obligations as president in a council of judges and Levites. 'Torah' in 17.11 is to be understood as the polity, and the king takes the role of the judge specified in 17.9-12.[38] To establish this view, McBride includes 'Torah' passages in his picture, which others (including Rüterswörden) had excluded from the original law (17.11, 18-19).[39]

These interpretations make Deuteronomy a radical document in the ancient world. The picture of the king's responsibilities is not a post-exilic picture of ideal piety, but a powerful concept of the supremacy of Torah, or constitutional law, in the life of the people. This is the distinctive characteristic of Deuteronomy in the ancient Near East, namely to empower and protect the individual in the political community. Deuteronomy is for this reason something 'genuinely new, the charter for a constitutional theocracy'.[40]

While there is debate over the origin and dating of the law, it is plain that it provides for a kind of kingship that is radically different from kingship as it is known from ancient Near Eastern custom and practice. The question is only whether it arises as a real alternative programme to such practice (whether strictly 'Davidic', or simply ancient Near Eastern), or whether it is a critical rejection in retrospect of an institution that had finally failed. On the latter view, Halpern is right, I think, that it is handicapped by its need to postulate an ideal king in a time of much disillusionment with kingship in general (cf. Jer. 22.30).[41] Indeed, it becomes highly speculative about the nature of thinking and debate about kingship in the exile.[42] Specifically, the books of Kings, though they present favourable, arguably 'ideal', accounts of both Hezekiah and Josiah, do not finally hold out hope of a restoration of the monarchy (1 Kgs 8.46-53).

38. McBride, 'Polity', p. 75.

39. See above, n. 36.

40. McBride, 'Polity', pp. 69-71; cf. Halpern, *Constitution*, pp. xx-xxviii.

41. Halpern, *Constitution*, p. 229.

42. See T. Veijola, *Die ewige Dynastie* (Annales Academiae Scientiarum Fennicae, series B, 193; Helsinki: Suomalainen Akatemia, 1975), pp. 130, 139-40, 142; cf. W. Dietrich, *Prophetie und Geschichte* (Göttingen: Vandenhoeck & Ruprecht, 1972), pp. 142-43; and below, n. 55.

The View of Monarchy in DtrH

If Deuteronomy promotes a particular view of kingship, what view is expressed in DtrH? An older generation of scholars, following Well-hausen, found pro- and anti-monarchical sources in the historical books. For him, support of the monarchy represented the natural and universal pre-exilic position, while criticism of the monarchy occurred only at the time of the exile or after.[43] Noth's understanding of Dtr as the exilic chronicler of the well-deserved demise of Judah, king and people, fol-lowed suit. The Davidic dynasty stands condemned for its failure to maintain the covenant consistently: '(Dtr's) censure of the monarchy as an institution and his description of it as a secondary phenomenon in the history of the nation are crucial to his approach to history'.[44]

Since Noth, however, the question how to understand the function of the dynastic promise to David (2 Sam. 7.11b-16) in the context of the history as a whole has returned with new force. Noth, advancing his thesis of a single author writing in the exile, focused on the end of the story, with its implication of final judgment on the people and the dynasty. Yet, as others quickly objected, this hardly did justice to the dynastic promise. Von Rad found evidence in its inclusion in DtrH of messianic expectations surviving into the exile, and claimed that the eternal decree in the dynastic promise is never negated in the subse-quent history.[45] But the decisive counterpoint to Noth was provided by F.M. Cross.

Cross, for whom DtrH is essentially a product of the Josianic heyday of the Judaean monarchy, sees it as the story of an unbreakable prom-ise. In this story his analysis of 2 Samuel 7 plays a key role. In his view, the dynastic promise forms the heart of the Dtr purpose in this chapter. (The first oracle, concerning the building of a temple, runs counter to Dtr's programme, and is here a minor theme. For Dtr, Yahweh's reticence about a temple is only a moratorium.[46]) At the

43. J. Wellhausen, *Prolegomena zur Geschichte Israels* (Berlin: Georg Reimer, 1883), pp. 259-68 (ET *Prolegomena to the History of Israel* [trans. J.S. Black and A. Menzies; Edinburgh: A. & C. Black, 1885], pp. 247-56).

44. Noth, *Überlieferungsgeschichtliche Studien*, p. 110 (ET *Deuteronomistic History*, p. 99).

45. G. von Rad, *Deuteronomium-Studien* (Göttingen: Vandenhoeck & Ruprecht, 1947), pp. 52-64, esp. pp. 59-63 (ET *Studies in Deuteronomy* [trans. D. Stalker; SBT, 9; London: SCM Press, 1953], pp. 74-91, esp. pp. 84-89).

46. F.M. Cross, *Canaanite Myth and Hebrew Epic* (Cambridge, MA: Harvard University Press, 1973), pp. 241-43, 246-47, 255.

centre of the promise, in turn, is v. 14, establishing a relationship of sonship between Yahweh and the king. It is at home in the Judaean coronation liturgy, and behind it stands the Canaanite sonship ideology, which was absorbed by the Jerusalem court, and which was by nature permanent, or 'eternal'.[47] This permanency emerges from a range of Old Testament texts (Pss. 89.28-29, ET 27–28, 2.7; Isa. 9.5-6, ET 6–7). Other texts, however, use a covenantal formulation, and these may be conditional (Ps. 132.11-12), unconditional (Ps. 89.20-38, ET 19–37) or ambiguous (2 Sam. 23.5).[48] Cross concludes that two separate streams of thought about the kingship, the decree and the covenant, both visible in Ps. 89.20-38 ET 19-37, merged in early Israel. Dtr, however, understood the oracle of Nathan to be an eternal divine decree.[49] Covenant language in Dtr is an actual survival from Davidic times, reflecting that king's understanding of his relationship with Yahweh. A transformation occurred within the royal cult of Solomon, however, with the result that the ancient patriarchal covenant was remythologized in terms of the Canaanite royal ideology of the Baal myth.[50]

Cross's reading of the dynastic oracle is closely connected with his setting of the historical work in the time of Josiah, and in the spirit of confident royal expansion. This edition was characterized by two great themes, which resolved the history of the two kingdoms up to that point in relation to the dynastic oracle. These themes were, first, the sin of Jeroboam, which explained the fall of the Northern Kingdom in terms of persistent apostasy, and secondly, the promise of favour to the Davidic line 'for the sake of David my servant and for the sake of Jerusalem which I have chosen' (1 Kgs 11.12, 13, 32, 34, 36, 15.4; 2 Kgs 8.19, 19.34, 20.6). The story line from the dynastic promise to the reform of Josiah is a development of this theme, and can only be explained as an expression of the ideology of the Judaean monarchy in a time of its greatest success. (Dtr's account of the reform is defined as 2 Kgs 22.1–23.25). This is a quite different solution to the problem of the dynastic promise from von Rad's, whose Dtr was exilic like Noth's, and whose theory (in Cross's view) rested on a narrow basis that lacked a convincing setting.[51] Cross regarded the final chapters of 2 Kings

---

47. Cross, *Canaanite Myth*, pp. 256-58.
48. Cross, *Canaanite Myth*, p. 259.
49. Cross, *Canaanite Myth*, p. 260.
50. Cross, *Canaanite Myth*, pp. 262-65.
51. Cross, *Canaanite Myth*, pp. 276-89, esp. pp. 278, 281-83.

(2 Kgs 23.26–25.30) as an exilic addition from a second Deuterono-mist.[52] He thus read the original history as favourable in principle to the Davidic monarchy as an institution. This was a recasting of the Deuter-onomist, who was henceforth not a critic of the monarchy but one of its greatest apologists. It was also to make the dynastic promise, with its 'messianic' associations, the key to the whole history.[53] A corollary of his analysis, however, is that the Deuteronomic law cannot be integrat-ed readily into Dtr's purpose. Cross attributed it in one place to the 'traditional law of the league', though 'it was never reformulated in a state law code'. In another note he says it arose from polemic against Solomon.[54] 'Conditional' elements generally, furthermore, are regarded as non-deuteronomistic. The old 'conditional' view of the kingship is returned to by the second, exilic Deuteronomist, who revised the history as a proclamation of doom.

Cross's work has strongly affected the most recent discussion. It has predominated at length over the other major development from Noth, namely the tendency to identify a number of different exilic hands at work in the composition of DtrH.[55] And its effect may be seen in the work of G.N. Knoppers,[56] S.L. McKenzie[57] and others, who regard the core of DtrH as a Josianic production, with a variety of exilic additions. This is the context in which Knoppers proposed his view that Dtr held out Solomon, portrayed in his wisdom and glory, as the kingly ideal.

52. Cross, *Canaanite Myth*, pp. 285-87.

53. For the centrality of the dynastic oracle in the theology of DtrH see also D.J. McCarthy, 'II Samuel 7 and the Structure of the Deuteronomic History', *JBL* 84 (1965), pp. 131-38.

54. Cross, *Canaanite Myth*, p.221 n. 9; pp. 222-23.

55. This theory originates with R. Smend, 'Das Gesetz und die Völker', in H.W. Wolff (ed.), *Probleme biblischer Theologie: Gerhard von Rad zum 70. Geburtstag* (Munich: Chr. Kaiser Verlag, 1971), pp. 494-509. It is best represented on our present topic by Veijola, who postulated a pro-Davidic basic DtrG, followed by a hostile 'prophetic' redaction (DtrP), and finally by a moderating 'nomistic' voice (DtrN) in *Die ewige Dynastie*. Veijola's analysis of 2 Sam. 7 corresponds with Cross's at certain points: his DtrG thinks the prohibition of the temple-con-struction only temporary, and it extends an older promise of a successor to be 'for ever' (p. 78). See G.N. Knoppers's critique of the Smend school in *Two Nations under God: the Deuteronomistic History of Solomon and the Dual Monarchies* (HSM, 52; 2 vols.; Atlanta: Scholars Press, 1993), pp. 38-42.

56. Most importantly in his *Two Nations*.

57. S.L.McKenzie, *The Trouble with Kings: The Composition of the Book of Kings in the Deuteronomistic History* (VTSup, 42; Leiden: E.J. Brill, 1991).

The search for the provenance of DtrH in the time of Josiah's reform has resulted in a quite different understanding of the meaning of the history from that proposed by Noth. And its tendency is to drive a wedge between the history and the law of Deuteronomy. Is it the case, then, that DtrH is, in contrast to Deuteronomy, an apologia for the principle of dynastic kingship? Some further consideration of aspects of DtrH will suggest that this is too simple a view.

The Pursuit of a Royal Ideology in DtrH. I. *Joshua*

The belief that DtrH is part of the programme of Josiah's reform has lent credence to the interpretation of the characters in the narrative as ideal royal figures. G.E. Gerbrandt's treatment of kingship in DtrH culminates in Josiah, and consequently he confines his account of Hezekiah and Josiah—the key text in his view—to 2 Kings 18–23.[58] For Gerbrandt, Dtr idealized Hezekiah as a model of trust in God, and aimed to show that hope for Judah lay in this kind of kingship.[59] The tendency to find royal figures in DtrH, moreover, is not confined to actual kings. Seen as a story of Israel's leaders from Moses to Josiah,[60] Moses himself becomes a 'quasi-regal' figure, as does Joshua after him. For M. Weinfeld, Moses and Joshua stand at the head of a succession in Israel which passes from them to David and Solomon and thence to other kings (he cites Josh. 1.7-8, 8.30-35, 22.5, 23.6). He writes: '...it seems that the Deuteronomist could not conceive of the implementation of the moral law contained in the "book of the Torah" in the absence of a monarchy or of a quasi-regal figure like Joshua'.[61]

A large number of studies have pressed the similarities between Joshua and kings. First, Joshua carries out what is prescribed for a righteous king in Deut. 17.14-20, by dint of his obedience to the Torah (Josh. 1.7-8, 8.30-35).[62] Secondly, he is portrayed as successor to

58. G.E. Gerbrandt, *Kingship According to the Deuteronomistic History* (SBLDS, 87; Atlanta: Scholars Press, 1986).

59. Gerbrandt, *Kingship*, pp. 78-79, 85-89.

60. M.A. O'Brien, *The Deuteronomistic History Hypothesis Reassessed* (OBO, 92; Göttingen: Vandenhoeck & Ruprecht, 1989), p. 288. O'Brien's thesis owes something to Smend as well as to Cross; nevertheless he sees an important connection between the authorship of DtrH and Josiah, reflecting Cross's influence.

61. M. Weinfeld, *Deuteronomy and the Deuteronomic School* (Oxford: Clarendon Press, 1972), pp. 170-71.

62. This observation apparently goes back to A. Dillmann, *Die Bücher Numeri, Deuteronomium und Josua* (KEH, 13; Leipzig: Hirzel, 2nd edn, 1886), p. 444. See

Moses. The prominence of this in the accounts about Joshua has led some to think that the succession has its origins in enthronement ceremonies. His conquest and distribution of land, and his covenant renewal have also been taken as royal acts.[63] N. Lohfink's analysis of Josh. 1.2-9 as the transfer of an office (or rather Moses' two offices of conquest and distribution) has been used in support of the argument, though Lohfink did not present it as a function of kingship.[64] Particular parallels have also been indicated between Joshua and Josiah. R.D. Nelson, for example, has seen in both leaders examples of ancient royal ideology.[65] And L. Rowlett considers the book of Joshua a Josianic tract.[66]

While there is indeed a kind of succession from Moses through Joshua to David (the promise of Yahweh: 'I will be with you', Exod. 3.12; Josh. 1.5, 17; 1 Sam. 18.12-14, is a scarlet thread running through the narratives), it remains a question whether these first leaders must be called 'kings'. The idea of Joshua as king, in particular, suffers from certain obvious problems, especially in the matter of succession: as O'Brien has rightly said, he succeeds Moses only in respect of the task of possessing the land; furthermore, when he dies, no-one succeeds.[67] As for the general point, leaders in Israel may exercise functions which in other places (or at other times) kings exercise; but that seems only to beg the question whether Israel is therefore 'like the nations' or in fact quite different, in that those functions are performed by people who are precisely not kings. The logic that says that 'royal' functions may only be exercised by kings has received a severe critique from C. Schäfer-Lichtenberger.

Calling Joshua 'Mon-Arch' she addresses the question of the type of his leadership sociologically, noting three types of leadership in which

C. Schäfer-Lichtenberger, *Josua und Salomo: Eine Studie zu Autorität und Legitimität des Nachfolgers im Alten Testament* (VTSup, 58; Leiden: E.J. Brill, 1995), p. 219.

63. J.R. Porter, 'The Succession of Joshua', in J.R. Porter and J.I. Durham (eds.), *Proclamation and Presence* (Festschrift G.H. Davies; London: SCM Press, 1970), pp. 102-32; cf. Gerbrandt, *Kingship*, pp. 116-23.

64. N. Lohfink, 'Die deuteronomistische Darstellung des Übergangs der Führung Israels von Moses auf Josua', *Scholastik* 37 (1962), pp. 32-44.

65. R.D. Nelson, 'Josiah in the Book of Joshua', *JBL* 100 (1981), pp. 531-40.

66. L. Rowlett, 'Inclusion and Marginality in the Book of Joshua', *JSOT* 55 (1992), pp. 15-23.

67. O'Brien, *Deuteronomistic History*, pp. 28-30.

authority is vested in one person, namely kingship, monarchy and monocracy. 'Monocratic' principles, she argues (citing Max Weber), are present in all 'nicht kollegial bestimmten Herrschaftsformen'. Further, 'Nicht jede Mon-Archie folgt den Strukturen dynastisch verfasster Monarchie'.[68] She is particularly critical of the kind of reading which makes of the 'succession' texts (Deut. 17.14-20; Josh. 1.7-8, 8.30-35) direct evidence for Joshua as king, because this requires postulating a 'linear relationship' (*linearen Inbeziehungssetzung*) between them, and furthermore 'an implicit assumption of mono-causal relationships between the king-law in Deuteronomy and the actual leader-figure in the book of Joshua'.[69]

It is truer to the contours of the narrative of DtrH to recognize in it, with O'Brien, 'a sense of continuity within a larger trajectory of change and development' in the transition to kingship in Israel.[70] The theory that DtrH is a product or programme of the Josianic reform can obscure certain historical and theological questions that should be put to the texts.

The Pursuit of a Royal Ideology in DtrH. II. Solomon
The pursuit of a royal ideology in DtrH focuses more importantly, perhaps, on Solomon. We observed at the outset that the portrayal of Solomon, which depicts kingship at its most glorious, has been thought to demonstrate the fundamental difference between the royal ideal in Deuteronomy and that which we find in DtrH.[71] In treatments of DtrH that find a variety of views on kingship in the narrative, it is often held that a tradition has been preserved that is highly sympathetic to Solomon. For Noth, Dtr expressed at best a qualified approval of Solomon as the builder of the Temple.[72] But essentially he included the positive material on him because he found it in his sources, and 'out of a scrupulous respect for historical fact'.[73] Veijola's 'DtrG', on the other

---

68. Schäfer-Lichtenberger, *Josua und Salomo*, p. 220 and n. 555.

69. Schäfer-Lichtenberger, *Josua und Salomo*, p. 220.

70. O'Brien, *Deuteronomistic History*, p. 30.

71. See above, nn. 7-16.

72. Noth, *Überlieferungsgeschichtliche Studien*, p. 105 (ET *Deuteronomistic History*, pp. 94-95).

73. Noth, *Überlieferungsgeschichtliche Studien*, p. 108 (ET *Deuteronomistic History*, p. 98).

hand, is essentially favourable to the king, though he thinks that material hostile to him, such as the portrayal of his ruthless disposal of his enemies (1 Kgs 1) has inevitably been preserved as part of DtrG's debt to his sources.[74]

It is once again proponents of the Josianic edition who provide a thoroughgoing rationale for the portrayal of Solomon's glorious kingship, in terms of the Judaean royal ideology. Both Cross and Nelson included the bulk of Solomon's dedication prayer (1 Kgs 8) in the material that they thought Dtr used to promote that ideology.[75] And Knoppers, as we saw, believes that Dtr took a positive view of Solomon's wisdom, wealth and many wives, as part of his promotion of an essentially Canaanite style of kingship in Josiah's Judah.[76]

Deuteronomy and DtrH: A 'Design for Kingship'?

In this quest for DtrH's theory of kingship, the glories of Solomon and the excellence of Josiah have proved powerful factors. Where Deuteronomy and DtrH are thought to present a coherent view, the story line has been conceived as a story of leadership culminating in Josiah, the greatest fulfilment of the dynastic promise to David. Where the stark difference between the Deuteronomic ideal and the Solomonic royal state have been recognized, DtrH has been thought openly to have rejected the law-code as its norm in this respect. These approaches, though they stand in contrast, agree that DtrH's portrayal of the ideal king is found on the Solomon–Josiah axis. The latter approach, however, has reckoned more realistically with the problem of the law and the narrative: the law could not brook an all-powerful king.

It remains to consider whether the law and the narrative might not after all share a concept of kingship, and whether the portrayal of kings in Israel and Judah should be interpreted in a way that takes more account of notes of criticism in it. We have seen already that a number of scholars have indeed seen the law as providing the norm for the

---

74. Veijola, *Die ewige Dynastie*, pp. 24-26. Cf. G.H. Jones, *The Nathan Narratives* (JSOTSup, 80; Sheffield: Sheffield Academic Press, 1990), pp. 53-57, who thinks the account in 1 Kgs 1 derives from a Jebusite tradition that celebrated Solomon's triumph over the Hebronite Adonijah, and which made no attempt to gloss over Nathan's deceit in bringing this about.

75. Cross, *Canaanite Myth*, pp. 278, 282; R.D. Nelson, *The Double Redaction of the Deuteronomistic History* (JSOTSup, 18; Sheffield: JSOT Press, 1981), p. 70.

76. See above, together with nn. 12-15.

narrative. The most rigorous attempt to establish a link, however, has been made by Halpern. We have already noticed Halpern's argument that the king-law, along with the laws governing other offices in Israel, had an actual function in the constitution of the people. He went further, however, to argue that the account of the inception of the kingship in Israel conformed to the requirements of that constitution. As Deuteronomy provided for a separation of the powers of the sacral authority and the assembly of Israel, with Yahweh himself exercising a sovereign choice, so the author of 1 Samuel depicts the separate roles of Samuel himself (effectively the sacral authority) and the representatives of the people in the making of a king, which happens, here too, as a consequence of Yahweh's choosing. (1 Sam. 10.17-19 deploys the protagonists and sets the scene.)

The story is recounted mostly in what he calls the 'B'-narrative in 1 Samuel 8–12 (1 Sam. 8.4-22, 10.17-25), which shows that there was tension originally between the sacral authority and the assembly.[77] This was resolved, however, when Samuel showed the people that a king would demand rights of taxation (the *mišpaṭ hammelek*, 8.11-18), but agreed with them on a limitation of his powers, by making a covenant with them, in which those powers were governed by the *mišpaṭ hammᵉlūkâ* (10.25). The *mišpaṭ hammelek* and the *mišpaṭ hammᵉlūkâ* Halpern distinguishes as, respectively, the 'rights of the king' and 'the law governing the kingship'.[78] With this agreement in force, Saul's kingship was in fact limited to the power to unify the tribes and secure the people in its land. He attempted no administrative centralization.[79] Furthermore, the tribes continued to have real power in Israel, reflected in the rallying of many in Israel to Absalom and Adonijah, and even in the struggle between Ahab and the social forces appealed to by Naboth.[80] DtrH, then, has a concept of the king 'under Torah', which makes it similar to Psalm 132 and to the law of the king in Deuteronomy.[81] The verbal echoes of the law in the narrative (Deut. 17.14-15; 1 Sam. 8.5, 20) suggest that the author of Samuel had the law in mind.[82] Halpern thinks there is other evidence that the law may inform the

77. Halpern, *Constitution*, p. 185.
78. Halpern, *Constitution*, pp. 216-25.
79. Halpern, *Constitution*, pp. 237, 240.
80. Halpern, *Constitution*, pp. 241-42, 247.
81. Halpern, *Constitution*, p. 230.
82. Halpern, *Constitution*, pp. 227-28.

narrative, and even that David may have known and followed it.[83] His
main contention is, however, that the law and the assumptions in the
narrative are entirely compatible. His treatment is an important advance
on those of Boecker, Crüsemann and others, in that it tries to base
the continuity between Deuteronomy and 1 Samuel in a theory about
Israel's pre-monarchical constitution. Furthermore, the tensions in Israel
reflected in 1 Samuel 8–12 also receive a rationale in terms of that
constitution.

If Halpern's reconstruction is right, then the history of the kings must
be read quite differently from the way proposed by those who think that
DtrH promotes the Judaean royal ideology. On this scenario, Deuteronomy's radical provision for a king, as one who plays a limited role in
the administration alongside other office-bearers, is a demythologization of oriental kingship. The polities of both Babylon and Canaan may
be said to be symbolized in the divine realm,[84] and the king is the
essential figure in this symbolic world. Deuteronomy consigns the king
to an administrative role that, always allowing for the element of
Yahweh's choice, might be called secular. DtrH also rejects the sacral
oriental theories. Here the nostrums of oriental kingship are always in
the background as danger and warning. Joshua, far from being a 'quasi-
royal' figure, is divested of all royal (and sacral) pretensions, even as he
takes the role of human attendant of the heavenly divine warrior in the
act of conquest of territory.[85] And Solomon sounds the note of danger
loudest of all; he 'violates systematically every limitation imposed by
the tribes'.[86] Kings may be constrained in theory by laws and conventions, but if they are powerful enough they can overstep the limits and
stray in practice into the ways of their powerful neighbours. In this
argument, there are echoes of the more literary-critical kind of approach
to the texts of 1 Samuel, which saw that even pro-kingship texts had to
allow that kings could arrogate too much power to themselves. Here

83. Halpern, *Constitution*, pp. 231-33. He finds this in David's hamstringing of
the enemy's horses in the war against Hadadezer (2 Sam. 8.4), in an allusion to the
mišpāṭ of the priests (Deut. 18.3) in 2 Sam. 2.12-13 (along with other verbal
echoes), and in an assumption of the law of the prophet in 1 Kings 22.

84. For Babylon, see Halpern, *Constitution*, pp. 52-60; and for Canaan, see
L. Handy, *Among the Host of Heaven: The Syro-Palestinian Pantheon as
Bureaucracy* (Winona Lake, IN: Eisenbrauns, 1994), for example his treatment of
mlk, pp. 111-13.

85. Halpern, *Constitution*, pp. 88-94, esp. pp. 93-94.

86. Halpern, *Constitution*, p. 245.

again, however, further substance is given to the point by seeing the texts as a confrontation with ancient Near Eastern ideology.

The thesis outlined chimes in with interpretations of Solomon that arise from quite different interests. A number of scholars have argued that the apparently positive portrayal of the king (for example, in 1 Kgs 3) is thoroughly overshadowed by the surrounding negative indications. His ruthlessness in suppressing every potential threat to his sole grip on power (1 Kgs 1–2) is now allowed to emerge with full force (where, as we saw, it was sometimes glossed over as an inevitable debt to sources).[87] 1 Kgs 3.1-3, omitted from H. Kenik's treatment,[88] can be taken to mean that Solomon has been remiss in delaying to build the Temple. The marriage to Pharaoh's daughter is a further hint of false priorities (1 Kgs 3.1; cf. 9.24), and the acceptance of the gift of Gezer from Pharaoh (1 Kgs 9.16) undermines the picture of Solomon as all-powerful in the region. For reasons like this, some think Solomon is portrayed negatively throughout 1 Kings 3–11, and even contrasted unfavourably with Josiah.[89]

An even more radical hermeneutic of suspicion is applied by scholars such as L. Eslinger and A.G. Auld. To Eslinger Solomon in his dedicatory prayer (1 Kgs 8) cleverly adopts the language of piety in order to claim that the promises to David are fulfilled in him. Indeed, 'Solomon's rhetoric aims to compel God by saying that he has done the very things that the narrator and the narrative show that he has not done'.[90]

---

87. See J.T. Walsh, *Berith Olam: 1 Kings* (Collegeville, MI: Liturgical Press, 1996), p. 77.

88. H. Kenik argues that the comment in 3.2-3 is not meant disparagingly, but merely reflects the practice in the time before the Temple, in *Design for Kingship: the Deuteronomistic Narrative Technique in 1 Kings 3:4-15* (SBLDS, 69; Chico, CA: Scholars Press, 1983), p. 204.

89. M.A. Sweeney, 'The Critique of Solomon in the Josianic Edition of the Deuteronomistic History', *JBL* 114 (1995), pp. 607-22, argues that this king functions as a contrast to Josiah. On reading 1 Kings 1–11 with 'suspicion', cf. J.G. McConville, 'Narrative and Meaning in the Books of Kings', *Bib* 70 (1989), pp. 31-49. See also Schäfer-Lichtenberger, *Josua und Salomo*, pp. 264-65, 267-70, 334-35, who argues that the texts that imply something negative (such as 3.1-3; 9.24-25) are counterbalanced by what follows them. Yet in the latter case she admits that it signals that the apostasy is near.

90. L. Eslinger, *Into the Hands of the Living God* (JSOTSup, 84; Sheffield Academic Press: Sheffield, 1989), pp. 174-75.

Auld also thinks that Dtr uses the high theology of the dedicatory prayer to criticize the Davidic monarchy.[91]

If these latter treatments take readerly 'suspicion' to undue lengths, there is nonetheless a strong case for thinking that DtrH wants to show that the history of kingship, even in its heroes, departs from the royal ideal of Deuteronomy. Kenik, who has stressed the divine gift of the king's authority, and thinks that Josiah represented DtrH's ideal for kingship, recognizes that that ideal also comprised submission to Torah, and that Solomon failed to exemplify this.[92] Setting her study in a broader context, she sees DtrH as 'a controversy between prophets and the kings, a dialectic already forecast in the exposition of Moses as prophet par excellence set in balance with Solomon, one of the unfaithful kings'.[93] Knoppers allows for a more qualified criticism of Solomon, as part of a demonstration of the sequence of sin, judgment and renewed promise.[94]

And the point may apply to the story of the kings as a whole. If the portrayal of Solomon in all his glory may not be taken at its face value as a hymn of praise to the Davidic dynasty, may the same reservations have to be entered about the portrayal of Josiah? Was Noth right after all to suppose that the narrative of the fall of Judah was an integral part of the argument of Kings, and not just a late addition that ran counter to its main thrust? This view too has found its more recent advocates, notably H.-D. Hoffmann, who showed with great cogency that the cycle of reform and subsequent decline was essential to the structure and concept of the books of Kings,[95] and J. Van Seters, in the context of his attempt to re-establish the theory of a single exilic Deuteronomist.[96] These writers counsel that the story of the Reform, like that of Solomon, must be read with alertness to the underlying thrust of the

91. A.G. Auld, *Kings Without Privilege* (Edinburgh: T. & T. Clark, 1994), pp. 40-41.

92. Kenik, *Design for Kingship*, pp. 56, 206.

93. Kenik, *Design for Kingship*, p. 173. She does think, however, that Josiah fulfilled the ideal.

94. Knoppers, *Two Nations*, pp. 138-39.

95. H.-D. Hoffmann, *Reform und Reformen: Untersuchungen zu einem Grundthema der deuteronomistischen Geschichtsschreibung* (Zürich: Theologischer Verlag, 1980). Cf. T.R. Hobbs, *2 Kings* (WBC; Waco, TX: Word Books, 1985); and McConville, 'Narrative and Meaning'.

96. J. Van Seters, *In Search of History* (New Haven: Yale University Press, 1983).

narrative. The glories of Josiah, if they issue in Jehoiakim and ultimately Nebuchadnezzar, take on a paler hue.

Messianic Theology in Deuteronomy-DtrH?

This study has shown that there is no easy path from our texts to a messianic theology. The interpretations of the texts differ, and interpretations are in turn supported by rather different literary and historical reconstructions. However, the parameters of a messianic theology are clear. Its first reference point is the law of the king in Deut. 17.14-20. This establishes the radical concept of a king with limited powers, a king whose power is not to be equated with that of the state, but who exercises authority in conjunction with others, and who is, most importantly, 'under Torah'. The same concept can be found in the narrative of the foundation of kingship in Israel (1 Sam. 8–12). The significance of this account is not fully penetrated by literary-critical distinctions between 'pro- and anti-monarchical' sources in these chapters. Rather, the placement of this section at the head of the story of transition to monarchy in Israel sets criteria for the evaluation of the kings who are still to come. The concept of a king who is himself under authority, indeed, who is not even essential to the constitution of Israel (as priests, judges, prophets, and even the assembly of the people apparently are), must be judged one of the special contributions of the Deuteronomic literature, and indeed of the Old Testament. I have taken the view that the concept is ancient in Israel, as it would have been unlikely to have been invented either for Josiah's far more regal programme, or by exilic wisdom after the event. It should be seen as part of the Old Testament's demythologization of oriental ideology. As such, of course, it may not seem to be promising for 'messianic' theology. Deuteronomy's provision for kingship is permissive, not prescriptive, and it is significant that 'messianic' lines have been followed from its law of the prophet, at least in the Samaritan tradition. Even so, the concept of a king under Torah is not lost even in the entrance of Davidic dynastic concepts into the story. And it is instructive to observe connections with the teaching Messiah in Matthew's gospel.[97]

The other inescapable reference point for a theology of kingship in our literature is the dynastic promise to David, and specifically because

97. See the essay of Christopher Rowland in the present volume.

of its permanent, or eternal, character, from which Old Testament messianism chiefly draws its force. Here, it seems, mythological ideas are not far away. The difficult question for interpretation is how to reconcile this theory—with its exalted role for the king, its mythological associations, its apparent guarantee to the house of David, and the absence of clear requirements in terms of Torah from its classic text—with Deuteronomy's revolutionary thought.

Source-critical solutions lie at hand, with their offer of divergent strands of tradition, more or less 'conditional'. Cross's analysis, reviewed above, thought of a confluence of the Canaanite 'eternal decree' with patriarchal Israelite covenantal thought. This may have validity. But his specific analysis—that Dtr advocated the eternal decree, while receiving and transmitting literature that also preserved covenantal ideas—was not cogent. The eternal and the conditional resolved too neatly into his first and second Deuteronomists. The idea of a royal covenantal idea is present also in the Samuel traditions (2 Sam. 23.1-7), as well as other ancient Old Testament texts (Pss. 89, 132).[98]

The idea of a 'trajectory' in the story that runs from Moses to the exile is more fruitful. This allows for the individuality of the various phases of the story and the characters in it, in a way that accords with Schäfer-Lichtenberger's understanding of Joshua, for example.[99] It also permits a genuine dialogue to take place between the fundamental programme of Deuteronomy and actual developments in the monarchy. The dynastic promise arises in a chain of events in which key players play their constitutional roles (1 Samuel 8–12). The result is a synthesis of a Torah-constitutional understanding of kingship with a promise or decree that has permanent or eternal validity. If such a synthesis is couched in strictly theoretical terms it seems impossible. But if the concepts are allowed to be formed by the narration of events in history a resolution may be achieved after all. It is no accident that the history told ends on a note that is at best ambiguous for the future of the dynasty (2 Kgs 25.27-30), and probably inauspicious (cf. 1 Kgs 8.46-53, with its absence of hope for a restoration to the land); yet the classic text for the dynastic promise retains a prominent position, and may be read yet as full of expectation. The modern trend towards reading the books of DtrH as separate works,[100] each with their own tendency and

98. See above, nn. 46-52.
99. For Schäfer-Lichtenberger see above, nn. 69-70.
100. G. von Rad, *Theologie des Alten Testaments*, I (Munich: Chr. Kaiser

theology, supports a reading of DtrH that allows the messianic theology of Samuel to survive, even though the outcome of the particular story is gloomy. One way in which the New Testament signals an end to the story is in Matthew's portrayal of Jesus as both the Davidic king and as 'the prophet Jesus from Nazareth' (Mt. 21.8-11).

Verlag, 1957), p. 344 (ET *Old Testament Theology*, I [trans. D.M.G. Stalker; Edinburgh: Oliver & Boyd, 1962] p. 347). In a distinctive development, C. Westermann, *Die Geschichtsbücher des Alten Testaments: Gab es ein Deuteronomistisches Geschichtswerk?* (TBü, 87; Gütersloh: Chr. Kaiser Verlag, 1994), has argued for the separate growth and development of the books of DtrH. Other modern studies have addressed the books of Samuel as a separate literary entity, e.g. G. Keys, *The Wages of Sin: A Reappraisal of the 'Succession Narrative'* (JSOTSup, 221; Sheffield: Sheffield Academic Press, 1996).

THE (GOD-)FORSAKEN KING OF PSALM 89:
A HISTORICAL AND INTERTEXTUAL ENQUIRY

Knut M. Heim

Psalm 89, which is related to 2 Sam. 7.1-16 on almost any account, is also the basis for Isa. 55.3-5 and Rev. 1.5, both of which echo some of the psalm's most important concerns.[1] Part of the historical meaning and continuing relevance of the passage derives from its relationship with these other texts.[2] In view not only of its original historical setting but also of its setting in the biblical canon, the psalm has acquired messianic implications that an exclusive focus on its original *Sitz im Leben* may fail fully to uncover. The exilic experience of the psalm's first audience forced questions about the relationship between divine promise and political reality that refuse to go away, as the later biblical material testifies.

1. *Structure, Date and Setting of Psalm 89*

Psalm 89 consists of three main parts, vv. 1-19, 20-38 and 39-52, with an editorial note in v. 53 that operates mainly on the level of the whole Psalter, but also influences the reception of the psalm (cf. 2.2.1 below).[3]

1. Verses 1-19 form a hymnic composition which praises the divine constancy and faithfulness as displayed in God's promise to David that his dynasty would last forever. The Lord's omnipotence is emphasized.

---

1. I am grateful to Daniel P. Bailey for reading (and rereading!) the manuscript of this essay and making many helpful suggestions.

2. Cf. J. Goldingay, 'Isaiah 40–55 in the 1990s: Among Other Things, Deconstructing, Mystifying, Intertextual, Socio-Critical, and Hearer-Involving', *BibInt* 5 (1997), pp. 225-46 (234).

3. The versification of Ps. 89 in this article consistently follows the Hebrew. However, in the English Bible the numbering runs one verse behind the Hebrew, e.g. Ps. 89.37 = ET 89.36. The English translations given in this essay generally follow the NRSV.

2. Verses 20-38 are a poetic expansion of Nathan's oracle (2 Sam. 7.1-16), promising the perpetuity of the Davidic dynasty in Israel: 'His line shall continue forever, and his throne endure before me like the sun' (Ps. 89.37). Yahweh's solemn commitment and legal obligation to this promise are particularly emphasized: 'Once and for all I have sworn by my holiness; I will not lie to David' (Ps. 89.36).

3. Verses 39-52 are a lament comprised of a section which accuses Yahweh of breaking this covenant, culminating in a passionate plea to restore the king's fortunes.

There is no consensus on the date of Psalm 89: it is impossible to date precisely (although this has sometimes been attempted).[4] It is also unclear whether the psalm or its constituent parts were created before or after the exile. While a rehearsal of the entire debate is unnecessary, some arguments relevant to the present investigation deserve attention. There are two crucial arguments for a pre-exilic date. (1) The Davidic king appears still alive and speaking in Ps. 89.51-52.[5] (2) The psalm does not mention the destruction of Jerusalem and the Temple or the deportation of a large number of Israelites.[6]

The crucial argument for an exilic or postexilic date is not the report of the king's defeat *per se*, but its note of finality: the Lord has 'renounced the covenant' with his servant (v. 40; cf. vv. 39-46). According to Psalm 89, the covenant stipulations did not exclude military defeat and national catastrophe. As long as the Davidic monarchy persisted, the covenant remained intact. The oracular section in Psalm

---

4. One of the most precise and convincing arguments for a particular pre-exilic date (735–734 BCE) has been provided by N.M. Sarna, 'Psalm 89: A Study in Inner Biblical Exegesis', in A. Altmann (ed.), *Biblical and Other Studies* (Cambridge, MA: Harvard University Press, 1963), pp. 29-46 (42-45).

5. Cf., e.g., J. Day, *God's Conflict with the Dragon and the Sea: Echoes of a Canaanite Myth in the Old Testament* (UCOP, 35; Cambridge: Cambridge University Press, 1985), p. 26; but cf. now his exilic dating in Day, *Psalms* (OTG; Sheffield: JSOT Press, 1990), p. 95; J.M. Ward, 'The Literary Form and Liturgical Background of Psalm LXXXIX', *VT* 11 (1961), pp. 321-39 (337-39); R.J. Clifford, 'A Lament Over the Davidic Ruler's Continued Failure', *HTR* 73 (1980), pp. 35-47 (47). See also K.M. Heim, 'The Perfect King of Psalm 72: An "Intertextual" Approach', in P.E. Satterthwaite, R.S. Hess and G.J. Wenham (eds.), *The Lord's Anointed: Interpretations of Old Testament Messianic Texts* (Grand Rapids: Eerdmans; Carlisle: Paternoster Press, 1995), pp. 223-48 (224-26).

6. Sarna, 'Psalm 89', pp. 39-42 mentions no less than nine arguments.

89 (vv. 20-38) 'does not promise that kings of Judah will never experience defeat. On the contrary, it anticipates that they may well suffer setbacks of various kinds, including military catastrophes, as punishment for covenant infidelity.'[7] However, this catastrophe which prompted the lament in Psalm 89 cannot be just *any* defeat, for this would not have provoked the daring complaint of vv. 39-52, where the Lord is implicitly accused of unfaithfulness to the covenant stipulations (especially in v. 50).[8] Most likely, then, Psalm 89 is a prayerful response to the historical disaster of the exile.[9]

There is also no agreement about the provenance of 2 Sam. 7.1-16 and most of the other Old Testament texts related to the Davidic covenant tradition, including Psalm 132; 2 Sam. 23.5; 1 Kgs 2.3-4, 6.12, 8.25; 1 Chron. 17.1-15 (cf. also 1 Chron. 28.1-10). Each of these texts has been seen as a historically reliable and unified literary composition by some, while others have questioned both aspects. In fact, individual texts have been dated at periods as far as 600 years apart.[10] 'Es fehlt der "Urtext"!'[11] It is impossible to determine the original textual manifestation of the dynastic promise with our current knowledge of the data.[12] Therefore the present study takes a different approach, starting from what we can know historically about the *reading* of biblical texts.

---

7.   M.H. Floyd, 'Psalm LXXXIX: A Prophetic Complaint about the Fulfillment of an Oracle', *VT* 42 (1992), pp. 442-57, esp. pp. 454-55, quotation p. 455; cf. also p. 455 n. 21.

8.   Cf. Floyd, 'Prophetic Complaint', p. 455.

9.   While this reconstruction of the psalm's setting will be assumed for the remainder of this study, the argument does not absolutely depend on it because to a large degree this study concerns the reception of Ps. 89.

10.   E.J. Waschke, 'Das Verhältnis alttestamentlicher Überlieferungen im Schnittpunkt der Dynastiezusage und die Dynastiezusage im Spiegel alttestamentlicher Überlieferungen', *ZAW* 99 (1987), pp. 157-79 (159); cf. the literature cited by Waschke in n. 8.

11.   Waschke, 'Verhältnis', p. 163.

12.   Cf. M. Sæbø, 'Zum Verhältnis von "Messianismus" und "Eschatologie" im Alten Testament: Ein Versuch terminologischer und sachlicher Klärung', in E. Dassmann, G. Stemberger *et al.* (eds.), *Der Messias* (Jahrbuch für Biblische Theologie, 8; Neukirchen–Vluyn: Neukirchener Verlag, 1993), pp. 25-55 (48), and the literature cited in n. 101.

2. *Exposition of Psalm 89 in the Light of 2 Samuel 7*

The oracular section in Psalm 89 is portrayed as quoting a divine speech from the past:[13] 'Then (*'āz*) you spoke in a vision to your faithful one, and said' (Ps. 89.20). For readers and listeners who know 2 Samuel 7 only the speech related there could have been meant. This conclusion is inescapable, for the narrative framework in 2 Sam. 7.4-5 marks these words as the Lord's address to the prophet Nathan the night before David received the promise. On the literary level, then, the *Urtext* of the dynastic promise is 2 Samuel 7.

2.1. *The Psalm's Development of the Dynastic Promise*

A comparison between Psalm 89 and 2 Samuel 7 reveals that the psalmist displayed considerable freedom in changing and adapting Nathan's oracle of old. Accordingly, the faithfulness of the psalm to the original tradition has sometimes been called into question (cf. 2.1.2 below). Although the present essay reaches a more positive conclusion regarding the psalm's continuity with the tradition (cf. 2.1.3 below), it is necessary first to illustrate in detail how the dynastic promise was developed.

2.1.1. *The Development Illustrated.* Some of the psalm's changes to the original oracle are displayed in the following list. We find that:[14]

1. there is no rest for the people (cf. 2 Sam. 7.10-11);
2. the expansion of David's rule to a worldwide scope is spelled out explicitly (Ps. 89.26);
3. the adoption formula (cf. 2 Sam. 7.14) has been changed to highlight God's responsibility to protect David (Ps. 89.27-28);
4. the adoption focuses on David himself, not his successor (Ps. 89.27-28);
5. the divine chastisement has been transferred from David's immediate successor (cf. 2 Sam. 7.14) to the whole dynasty (Ps. 89.31-33);

13. For this and the following, cf. H.-J. Kraus, *Psalmen*, II (BKAT, 15.2; Neukirchen–Vluyn: Neukirchener Verlag, 5th edn, 1978), pp. 788-92 (ET *Psalms 60–150* [trans. H.C. Oswald; Minneapolis: Augsburg, 1989], pp. 207-10).

14. Cf. Sarna, 'Psalm 89', pp. 37-38; M. Fishbane, *Biblical Interpretation in Ancient Israel* (Oxford: Clarendon Press, 1985), p. 467; J.-B. Dumortier, 'Un rituel d'intronisation: Le Ps. lxxxix 2-38', *VT* 22 (1972), pp. 176-96 (193-96).

6. the oracular promise has become a full-blown covenant (Ps. 89.4, 35, 40, 50).

One consequence of this shift away from the promise of rest for the people (above, point 1) is that the survival of the Davidic dynasty has now become the sole guarantor of peace and tranquillity for the whole people. The emphasis on the Davidic king's universal rule (point 2) draws out the poignant contrast with the military humiliation described in the psalm (Ps. 89.39-46) and highlights the theological problems involved in this apparent 'breach of contract'. The more personal expression of the adoption formula (point 3) highlights the close relationship between the Davidic king and the Lord, as well as his frailty and dependence on God for protection. This emphasizes the divine responsibility to protect the Davidic line (cf. vv. 22-26). Security is the most important benefit which the 'first-born' relationship is supposed to bestow. The focus of the adoption on David alone (point 4) is not a limitation of the promise, but treats David as a symbol of his dynasty. The extension of divine chastisement to David's line (point 5) means that David has become the 'dynastic symbol'.[15] In converting the promise into a covenant (point 6) the psalmist has made use of a very early exegetical tradition (cf. the 'last words of David', 2 Sam. 23.5). This puts further stress on the Lord's responsibility and makes him accountable for the dynasty's survival.

These changes appear carefully designed to serve the poet's purposes. The comparison between Psalm 89 and 2 Samuel 7 highlights how the changes in the psalm skilfully and forcefully buttress the inviolable nature of the Lord's commitment to the dynasty. In Psalm 89 the Davidic promise/covenant remains *unconditional*, and it introduces legal covenant terminology to emphasize the *immutable certainty* of this unconditional and perpetual promise:

> If his children forsake my law...then I will punish them with the rod...
> but I will not remove from him my steadfast love...I will not violate my
> covenant (Ps. 89.31-34).

Why Psalm 89 did not actually change the unconditional nature of the promise/covenant, as other texts have done, will be considered below (2.1.3).

---

15. Sarna, 'Psalm 89', p. 38.

2.1.2. *The Psalm's Faithfulness to the Original Oracle Questioned.* In view of the numerous changes and developments observed above, one obvious question concerns whether or not Psalm 89 is faithful to Nathan's oracle as found in 2 Samuel 7. Fishbane, who assumes that Psalm 89 is a conscious exegesis of 2 Samuel 7, is critical of its handling of the tradition, as the following extended quotation illustrates:

> [T]he old royal document of 2 Sam. 7...was clearly reapplied to a new historical situation, and its ambiguities and original foci were reshaped accordingly. What is particularly important here is the degree to which Ps. 89 reflects a reality in which divine oracles were believed to be vital, 'event-begetting' potencies, and the fact that their theological credibility was so basic and indeed so important that subtle adjustments were necessary to ensure oracular validity. So powerful was this cognitive–theological motivation, in fact, that our psalmist does not turn from misquoting YHWH's own oracular words back to him...and even reinforces the old oracle with another exegetical change. Finally, Ps. 89: 4, 35-36, 40, 50 strikingly refers to the prophecy in covenant–legal terms. No such reference is found in the prose version of the dynastic oracle in 2 Sam. 7.[16]

Fishbane concluded that the exegesis of Nathan's oracle in Psalm 89 is 'clearly false' because of the numerous tendentious changes which go well beyond any implicit sense.[17] He assumed that these changes were introduced because the validity of the divine oracle and, by implication, the theological credibility of the God of Israel himself, were threatened by the new historical circumstances of military defeat. The following considerations, however, demonstrate that Psalm 89 is a highly artistic piece of poetry. It may go *beyond* its source text, but it does not go *against* it.

2.1.3. *Affirmation of the Oracle and Appeal for Fulfilment.* As observed above, the psalm's treatment of the tradition appears carefully designed and creatively draws out the consequences implicit in 2 Samuel 7 itself.

Fishbane's notion that the psalm's developments or changes were introduced mainly to protect the validity of the original oracle loses conviction when we note that more effective changes to this effect could have been introduced. Yet Psalm 89 still maintains that the Davidic promise–covenant is *unconditional*, although changing the unconditional

---

16. Fishbane, *Biblical Interpretation*, p. 467.
17. Fishbane, *Biblical Interpretation*, p. 534.

nature of the psalm into a conditional one would have brought the covenant more in line with political reality and resolved the theological problem. Such a transformation would have been part of the psalmist's toolbox, for many other texts employed exactly this type of change (e.g. Ps. 132.12; 1 Kgs 2.3-4, 6.12, 8.25).[18]

The changes in Psalm 89 actually seem to make the contrast between the oracular prediction and the reality of the psalmist's day (vv. 39-46) stand out in sharp contrast, while Fishbane's theory would seem to predict that they should be downplayed. First, through the omission of the rest for the people (point 1) the survival of the Davidic dynasty remains as the only guarantor for peace. Yet the plight of the Davidic king is the main focus of the lament section (vv. 39-46). Secondly, the addition in Ps. 89.26 (point 2) heightens the contrast between the oracular prediction of political superiority and the military defeat inflicted upon the present ruler. Thirdly, the more elaborate adoption formula (point 3) contrasts the frailty and dependence of the inferior party to the covenant, which places more responsibility on the superior partner to keep his covenant obligations. And this leads on to the fourth change. By converting the promise into a covenant the legally binding character of the Lord's agreement to protect the Davidic dynasty is made manifest.[19]

Specific elements of vocabulary and theme point in the same direction. The opening section in Psalm 89 is littered with expressions denoting on the one hand the Lord's trustworthiness (vv. 2, 3, 4, 9, 15, 17) and care for his people (vv. 2, 3, 4, 16, 18, 19), and on the other hand his unlimited power (vv. 7-8, 9, 10, 11, 12, 13, 14, 18) and the perpetual validity of his protection for his people (vv. 3, 4, 5). Divine weakness and inability are not a valid explanation in the psalmist's mind for God's apparent failure. Rather, by means of these expressions, the Lord is made accountable for the Jerusalem throne. On the basis of Ps. 89.2-19 it seems unthinkable that the Lord could possibly forsake

18. K. Seybold, *Die Psalmen* (HAT, 1.15; Tübingen: J.C.B. Mohr [Paul Siebeck], 1996), p. 498.

19. For the alleged affinity between the dynastic promise or Davidic covenant with ancient Near Eastern treaties, see T. Veijola, 'Davidverheißung und Staatsvertrag', *ZAW* 95 (1983), pp. 9-31, and esp. M. Weinfeld, 'The Covenant of Grant in the Old Testament and in the Ancient Near East', *JAOS* 90 (1970), pp. 184-203. For a powerful critique of the alleged analogy, see G.N. Knoppers, 'Ancient Near Eastern Royal Grants and the Davidic Covenant: A Parallel?', *JAOS* 116 (1996), pp. 670-97.

his anointed and his people. Consequently, the emotionally and theologically loaded question, 'Lord, where is your steadfast love of old, which by your faithfulness you swore to David?' (v. 50), virtually accuses the Lord of a breach of contract. Thus the title of this essay may well turn out to be a misnomer. Psalm 89 seems much more concerned with the *God* who apparently broke his covenant than with the failure of the king whom he forsook.

Another subtle but effective twist in the psalm's rendering of the oracle is that, according to v. 36, God has not simply promised dynastic perpetuity to David, but he has actually 'sworn' by his 'holiness', a seemingly innocent detail picked up in the plea for help (v. 50). Thus, in the psalm's version of Nathan's oracle, the Lord's integrity is at stake.

All this suggests that the composer of Psalm 89 did not forge the material contained in 2 Samuel 7 into an apologetic. Rather, the psalm appears to take the discrepancy between the dynastic promise and present political reality seriously. Drawing out the implications of what the dynastic promise had come to mean in its day, it points out that either the Lord *has* betrayed David (v. 36) and broken his covenant (vv. 40, 50), or he must help his anointed. In this sense the psalm is *open-ended*, looking forward to the Lord's action in the defiant hope that the divine promise as expressed in Nathan's oracle is still valid.

2.2. *The Psalm's Development of the Oracle's Eschatological Implications*

It is now generally recognized that the Old Testament does not contain a developed 'Doctrine of the Last Things'.[20] Nevertheless, it contains traditions which envisage radical future developments that constitute a significant break with contemporary realities, and that could therefore be called 'eschatological'.[21] These tradition complexes evolved over time, and the diverse traditions were sometimes in tension with one another.[22] Thus it is not surprising to find that there are almost as many approaches to 'eschatology' in the Old Testament as there are scholars

---

20. Cf. W.H. Schmidt, 'Aspekte der Eschatologie im Alten Testament', in Dassmann, Stemberger *et al.* (eds.), *Der Messias*, pp. 3-23, esp. pp. 5-6; Sæbø, '"Messianismus" und "Eschatologie"', p. 36.

21. R. Smend, 'Eschatologie, II: Altes Testament', in *TRE*, X, pp. 256-64 (257).

22. D.L. Petersen, 'Eschatology (OT)', *ABD*, II, pp. 575-79.

investigating the concept.[23] Particularly contested (besides the issue of definition and terminology) are the questions of how important 'eschatology' really was in the Old Testament, and when certain aspects and traditions arose.[24]

While not every development in the understanding of matters eschatological can safely be plotted in a historical scheme, it nevertheless seems clear that significant historical situations, national and communal crises in particular, provided a fruitful seedbed for future expectations and helped to shape existing eschatological notions.[25] The traumatic events surrounding the fall of Jerusalem in 587 BCE appear to have been the single most influential catalyst in the process of eschatological thought.[26] More elaborate future-oriented perspectives on present realities developed after the exile,[27] culminating in late postexilic times in 'apocalypticism'.[28]

Psalm 89 develops the eschatological implications of the Davidic promise in the light of the circumstances. Admittedly, overt signs of eschatological expectations in Psalm 89 are lacking. This does not, however, mean that there is no room for a future-oriented perspective, as the following points reveal.

2.2.1. *The Psalm's Postscript Anticipates Divine Intervention.* The postscript in v. 53, which is generally regarded as providing the conclusion to book three of the Psalter, praises God despite the unresolved tension in the preceding lament. The addition of v. 53 ('Blessed be the Lord forever. Amen and Amen') right after the emotional lamentations and complaints of vv. 39-52 is inexplicable or cynical, unless one assumes that v. 53 expresses a belief that the Lord would surely answer the requests of vv. 39-52. While it is generally recognized that the

23. Sæbø, '"Messianismus" and "Eschatologie"', pp. 25-30.

24. Cf. the surveys of scholarship in Sæbø, '"Messianismus" und "Eschatologie"', pp. 26-39 and Smend, 'Eschatologie', pp. 257-59, esp. p. 259. See also the articles gathered in H.D. Preuss, *Eschatologie im Alten Testament* (Wege der Forschung, 480; Darmstadt: Wissenschaftliche Buchgesellschaft, 1978).

25. Cf. Petersen, 'Eschatology', pp. 578-79.

26. Cf. Petersen, 'Eschatology', p. 576.

27. Cf. R.E. Clements, 'The Messianic Hope in the Old Testament', *JSOT* 43 (1989), pp. 3-19, esp. p. 13.

28. See Sæbø, '"Messianismus" und "Eschatologie"', pp. 40-43; cf. Smend, 'Eschatologie', p. 257. For the term 'apocalyptic', see J.J. Collins, 'Early Jewish Apocalypticism', *ABD*, I, pp. 282-88 (283-84).

postscript functions on the editorial level of the Psalter as a whole, it nevertheless seems unlikely that those who introduced v. 53 were unaware of or uninterested in the apparent inappropriateness of v. 53 in the context of the preceding verses. More likely is the assumption that they believed that the Lord would surely answer the requests in vv. 39-52.[29] Alternatively, the editors may have believed that the Lord had actually responded in their own lifetime. This, however, would only have been plausible during the short time span when the exiles had just returned to Judah and high hopes were invested in the Davidide Zerubbabel, until those expectations, too, were shattered.[30]

2.2.2. *The Dynastic Promise is Unlimited.* The covenant with David includes his dynastic line, without a final point being identified. The promise is open-ended from the start (vv. 29-30, 34-38), no matter what the actual temporal expressions in the psalm may mean or may have meant. Certainly, until the monarchy's abolition no end-point was perceived either by the psalm's author or its readers. Indeed, even after the monarchy's demise, texts like 2 Samuel 7 and Psalm 89 still could not be read in a way that would envisage a complete end to the Davidic dynasty. It is this circumstance that prompted the righteous indignation that shines through in the rhetorically loaded accusations (vv. 39-40) in the opening lines of the lament section: the Lord has not kept his part of the covenant stipulations.

2.2.3. *The Psalm's Finale Demands a Response.* The lament carries right through to the end of the psalm proper. The tension between the divine promise and its apparent failure finds no resolution. The *Urklage*, 'How long, O Lord...!' (v. 47) hangs as if in mid-air, awaiting the divine response. The two questions in v. 47 are rhetorical, implying a negative answer: No, the Lord will not forever hide himself; his anger may burn, but *not* like fire, not at least to the point that the object set aflame is entirely consumed. Similarly, the question in v. 50, 'Lord, where is your steadfast love of old, which by your faithfulness you swore to David?' puts a legal claim on God to fulfil his covenant obligations. The tension in the psalm will not be alleviated until the

29. Cf. G.H. Wilson, *The Editing of the Hebrew Psalter* (SBLDS, 76; Chico, CA: Scholars Press, 1985).

30. Cf. also Hag. 2.20-23; Zech. 3.8, 4.6-10, 6.11, 12-13.

Lord has answered.[31] In an exilic or postexilic context, without restored national sovereignty and without the restoration of the Davidic line to the throne, the psalm's demand for the Lord to fulfil his covenant obligations continues to sound with urgency.

This leads to the conclusion that the central issue in Psalm 89 is the call for the Lord's intervention to end the exile by restoring the Davidic monarchy—a significant break with contemporary historical realities indeed.

3. *Exposition of Isaiah 55.1-5 in the Light of Psalm 89*

While Psalm 89 attempted to reverse the calamity that had befallen king and country by a prayerful appeal to Yahweh for the restoration of the dynasty in keeping with the Davidic covenant, Isa. 55.1-5 contains Yahweh's appeal to the exiles in Babylon to recognize *him* as the source of their liberation out of that same calamity. This appeal is accompanied by the promise to re-establish the Davidic covenant in the (near) future as well as promises of a grateful international recognition of Israel for her conveyance of the worship of Yahweh to all the world.[32]

The number of features common to Psalm 89 and Isa. 55.3-5 considered in isolation is limited, partly due to the brevity of the passage. Accordingly, a connection between Isa. 55.3-5 and Psalm 89 has occasionally been called into question (cf. 3.2 below), while even scholars who accept a link dispute the precise way in which the psalm was applied in Second Isaiah (cf. 3.3 below). These points can be discussed only after we have established the connection between Isa. 55.3-5 and Psalm 89.

3.1. *The Link Illustrated*
A comparison between Psalm 89 and Isaiah 40–66 reveals a number of common features which suggest that the psalm may have influenced Isa. 55.1-5.

---

31. For a similar response almost certainly conected to the fall of Jerusalem, see Lam. 5.20-22.

32. Cf. O. Eissfeldt, 'The Promises of Grace to David in Isaiah 55:1-5', in B.W. Anderson and W. Harrelson (eds.), *Israel's Prophetic Heritage: Essays in Honor of James Muilenburg* (Philadelphia: Fortress; London: SCM Press, 1962), pp. 196-207 (202-203). Although the conceptual and verbal parallels between Ps. 89 and Isa. 55 are restricted to vv. 3-5, a proper understanding of these verses may only be achieved within the literary context provided by vv. 1-2.

1. Both passages deal with the same theme, the restoration of the Davidic covenant.
2. Both Second Isaiah and Psalm 89 support their petitions for Yahweh's saving intervention or the promise of restoration with a reference to Yahweh's power (cf. Ps. 89.7-14 and Isa. 41.12-31, 51.9-11).[33]
3. Both Second Isaiah and Psalm 89 often employ the same words and expressions, which are rare elsewhere (Eissfeldt's list covers almost a whole page).[34]
4. The 'enduring loyalty promised to David' (Isa. 55.3, JPSV) finds close echoes in Ps. 89.2, 25 and 50, and the concept is central to both passages.[35]
5. Isaiah 55.3 offers 'an everlasting covenant', described as Yahweh's 'enduring loyalty promised to David' (see above, point 4; for parallels with Psalm 89, see further below).

These parallels call for an explanation. The various arguments, both for and against a deliberate use of Psalm 89 by the author of Isa. 55.1-5, serve to highlight the literary and theological problem.

3.2. The Link Challenged and Defended

Fohrer has rejected a dependence of Isa. 55.3-5 on Psalm 89. His arguments, however, remain unconvincing. First, he assumed that the concept of covenant is not important for Second Isaiah, so that his rejection of the Davidic covenant here is a form of circular reasoning. Secondly, Fohrer postulated that the reason why the covenant with David is mentioned in the present context is primarily that he regarded the Davidic covenant as having proved itself as perpetual.[36] Thirdly, Fohrer thought

---

33. Eissefeldt, 'Promises', p. 199.

34. Eissfeldt, 'Promises', pp. 199-200; cf. Day, *Conflict*, p. 92.

35. Eissfeldt, 'Promises', pp. 196-207 (195). For a powerful defence of this rendering (objective genitive) rather than 'David's enduring loyalty' (subjective genitive), see H.G.M. Williamson, '"The Sure Mercies of David": Subjective or Objective Genitive?', *JSS* 23 (1978), pp. 31-49.

36. The German reads: 'An dieser Stelle handelt es sich denn auch um den Bund mit *David*, der näherhin als *andauernde, beständig erwiesene Gemeinschaft* bestimmt wird, so daß der Begriff Bund letztlich die feste unauflösliche Beziehung meint'; G. Fohrer, *Jesaja 40–66: Deuterojasaja/Tritojesaja* (Zürcher Bibelkommentare AT, 19.3; Zürich: Theologischer Verlag, 2nd edn, 1986), p. 177 (his emphasis).

that the only characteristic of the Davidic covenant emphasized in Isa. 55.3-5 is David's function as a witness to the superior divine power. For Fohrer, then, the reference to the Davidic covenant simply is 'illustrative material' (*Anschauungsmaterial*).[37]

All three arguments employed by Fohrer stand on unfirm ground. First, even if the concept of covenant were not important to Second Isaiah, this does not mean that he could not have used it *in this particular context*. The list of parallels between Psalm 89 and Second Isaiah take up a whole page in Eissfeldt (see above). Since any of the other covenants between the Lord and his people might have been used to good effect in the present context, the covenant with David must have been employed for a specific purpose. Yet the reason for its employment has nothing to do with Fohrer's second argument. Far from being considered a perpetual communion ('andauernde, beständig erwiesene Gemeinschaft', in Fohrer's words) between the Lord and David, the author of Isa. 55.1-5 knew quite the opposite: the presumably *everlasting* and *unconditional* covenant with David was *broken*! Thus it is the *restoration* of this broken covenant that is promised, and nowhere else have the three covenantal aspects 'everlasting', 'unconditional' and 'broken' been treated so comprehensively and passionately as in Psalm 89.[38] These parallels between the psalm and the use of the Davidic covenant in Isa 55.3 also answer Fohrer's third argument. David's covenant is not only mentioned with regard to its function as a witness to the divine power, but also points to the Lord's integrity. It is a signal that Israel's fortune is going to be reversed!

It seems impossible to *prove* that either of the two compositions Psalm 89 and Isa. 55.1-5 is directly dependent on the other, although the majority opinion holds that Second Isaiah knew of and used Psalm 89.[39] A decisive proof of their interdependence, however, is not essential to the present argument. Rather, the number of intertextual links is sufficient to establish a reading process that takes account of both texts and combines them with regard to their particular purposes. But how do the two texts interact in such a reading process? In order to answer this

37. Fohrer, *Jesaja*, pp. 177-78 and n. 160.

38. Cf. esp. Eissfeldt, 'Promises', pp. 205-206.

39. E.g., Eissfeldt, 'Promises', p. 199; C. Westermann, *Das Buch Jesaja: Kapitel 40–66* (ATD, 19; Göttingen: Vandenhoeck & Ruprecht, 5th edn, 1986 [1966]), p. 228 (ET *Isaiah 40–66* [trans. D.M.G. Stalker; OTL; London: SCM Press, 1969], pp. 283-84).

question, a closer analysis of some of the concepts in Isa. 55.1-5 is necessary.

3.3. *The Link Interpreted*

Most exegetes detect a significant change in Second Isaiah's version of the Davidic covenant. Isaiah 55.3-5 apparently contains no reference to the divine promise that a Davidic representative should always sit upon the Jerusalem throne and rule over the other nations.[40] Rather, it is claimed, the inviolable divine promises of grace to David are now promised to Israel as a whole—and therefore *not* to David's dynasty any longer.[41] Commentators speak of a *transferral* (*Übertragung*) of the original promise from the Davidides to Israel. It is open to question, however, whether this transferral necessarily involved stripping the royal dynasty of its covenant privileges. Admittedly, this understanding carries a *prima facie* plausibility, since, after the destruction of Jerusalem, the Davidic covenant appeared obsolete. Yet Psalm 89 seems to suggest a keen desire for the restoration of David's monarchy. Thus, the offer of David's original 'everlasting covenant' to the whole people is perhaps not so much a transferral, but an *extension*— *Ausweitung* rather than *Übertragung*, the term used by many German scholars. Thus the dispute whether the verse is 'messianic' or whether it 'democratizes' the Davidic covenant may have created a false dichotomy. Isaiah 55.3 clearly includes the whole people in the promised covenant renewal, and may thus justifiably be called 'democratic',[42] but this by no means excludes the Davidic dynasty (although the inclusion of a Davidic king would not necessarily make the verse messianic). The idea of the extension of legal conceptions from individuals to Israel as a whole is central to the development of Second Isaiah's message of hope. For example, in the so-called fourth servant song (Isa. 52.13–53.12) the servant *represents* the people. This is relevant in the context

40. Cf. Eissfeldt, 'Promises', p. 203.

41. Cf. H.-J. Kraus, *Das Evangelium der unbekannten Propheten: Jesaja 40–66* (Kleine Biblische Bibliothek; Neukirchen–Vluyn: Neukirchener Verlag, 1990), p. 162; Westermann, *Jesaja*, p. 228 (ET *Isaiah 40–66*, pp. 283-84); C.R. North, *The Second Isaiah: Introduction, Translation and Commentary to Chapters XL–LV* (Oxford: Clarendon Press, 1964), p. 258; O. Kaiser, *Der königliche Knecht: Eine traditionsgeschichtlich-exegetische Studie über die Ebed-Jahwe-Lieder bei Deuterojesaja* (FRLANT, 70; Göttingen: Vandenhoeck & Ruprecht, 2nd edn, 1962), esp. pp. 132-34.

42. Williamson, 'Subjective or Objective Genitive?', p. 44 n. 1.

of Isa. 55.3-5, for chs. 54–55 form the joyful response to what has gone before.[43] In other words, the invitation in Isa. 55.1-5 is probably depicted as the direct outcome of the suffering servant's substitutionary suffering (instead of the people, excluding them) and representative vindication (including the people).[44]

43. Few scholars even consider the contextual relationships between chs. 54–55 and the preceding parts of the book, presumably because Isa. 52.13–53.12 has been identified as one of the so-called servant songs which—according to Duhm's theory —are supposed to be completely isolated from their textual environment; cf. B. Duhm, *Das Buch Jesaja* (HKAT, 3.1; Göttingen: Vandenhoeck & Ruprecht, 1892; 4th rev. edn, 1922), p. 407. Motyer has pointed out, however, that chs. 54–55 respond to what the servant has done for the people as described in Isa. 53; cf. J.A. Motyer, *The Prophecy of Isaiah* (Leicester: Inter-Varsity Press, 1993, repr. edn, 1994), p. 444; other studies emphasizing the importance of context in the interpretation of the servant songs include T.N.D. Mettinger, *A Farewell to the Servant Songs: A Critical Examination of an Exegetical Axiom* (Lund: C.W.K. Gleerup, 1983), pp. 23-28, esp. p. 26; Kaiser, *Der königliche Knecht*, p. 10; and E.J. Young, *The Book of Isaiah: The English Text, with Introduction, Exposition, and Notes*, III (NICOT; Grand Rapids, Eerdmans, 1972), pp. 360 and 374.

44. See esp. B. Janowski, 'Er trug unsere Sünden: Jes 53 und die Dramatik der Stellvertretung', in B. Janowski and P. Stuhlmacher (eds.), *Der leidende Gottesknecht: Jesaja 53 und seine Wirkungsgeschichte* (Forschungen zum Alten Testament, 14; Tübingen: J.C.B. Mohr [Paul Siebeck], 1996), pp. 27-48; H.-J. Hermisson, 'Das vierte Gottesknechtslied im deuterojesajanischen Kontext', in Janowski and Stuhlmacher (eds.), *Gottesknecht*, pp. 1-25, esp. p. 18. For a fuller exposition of Janowski's thought, see the final section in D.P. Bailey, 'Concepts of *Stellvertretung* in the Interpretation of Isaiah 53', in W.H. Bellinger and W.R. Farmer (eds.), *Jesus and the Suffering Servant: Isaiah 53 and Christian Origins* (Valley Forge: Trinity Press International, 1998), pp. 225-52 (247-52). See also Bailey's short summary of Hermisson, 'The Suffering Servant: Recent Tübingen Scholarship on Isaiah 53', in Bellinger and Farmer (eds.), *Jesus and the Suffering Servant*, pp. 253-61 (256-57).

Among others, Motyer goes so far as to suggest that 'the covenanting work of the servant is the realization of "the sure mercies of David" (55:3)', concluding that the portraits of the servant and the king in the book of Isaiah are 'facets of the one Messianic person' (Motyer, *Prophecy*, p. 13, cf. also p. 14 for details of his argument). For a thorough investigation of the king in the book of Isaiah, with relevant literature and further arguments for an identification of the servant and the king, see R.L. Schultz, 'The King in the Book of Isaiah', in Satterthwaite, Hess and Wenham (eds.), *The Lord's Anointed*, pp. 141-65, esp. pp. 154-59. For a position that understands the servant as a royal figure without, however, identifying the king of Isa. 1–39 with the servant of chs. 40–66, see Kaiser, *Der königliche Knecht*, esp. pp. 11-12 and 134.

Westermann's contribution, representative of most commentators on Isa. 55.3-5, will be scrutinized in depth. Westermann has highlighted that the conflict between the promise of Nathan's oracle and the historical reality of the exile severely challenged Jewish confidence in Yahweh's integrity. He has detected two distinct responses aimed at dissolving this dilemma: (1) the hope in a new king, from the same line yet entirely different from his predecessors, the Messiah; and (2) the 'modification' found in Isa. 55.3-5, the transferral of the ancient dynastic promise to the whole people. His structural analysis of vv. 3b-5, represented below, is dependent on this.[45] Verse 3b contains the promise of the new covenant with the people:

> I will make with you an everlasting covenant, my steadfast, sure love for David.

Verse 4 elaborates the old Davidic covenant:

> See, I made him a witness to the peoples, a leader and commander for the peoples.

Verse 5a confronts the old promise with the 'new' covenant, the alleged contrast between vv. 4 and 5 being indicated by the repeated *hēn*, 'see', at the beginning of each verse:

> See, you shall call nations that you do not know, and nations that do not know you shall run to you.

Verse 5b introduces the goal for which this 'new' covenant has been made:

> because of the Lord your God, the Holy One of Israel, for he has glorified you.

Unlike the 'old' hope in a new Davidic king, which is attested in other portions of the book of Isaiah, the new promise, the 'modification' of the old hope in Isa. 55.3-5, appears isolated; thus one would expect a *more detailed explanation* of this new hope in the subsequent verses. Yet this is precisely what does not happen, as Westermann himself admits. One would have expected a detailed description of the blessings arising from this new promise, but—*astonishingly* (and not only in Westermann's view)—vv. 4-5 say hardly anything of the kind. Only one isolated consequence of the alleged transferral of the Davidic blessings to the people is explained, characteristic of Deutero-Isaiah but

---

45. See Westerman, *Jesaja*, pp. 226 and 228–30 (ET *Isaiah 40–66*, pp. 283-86).

only remotely corresponding (nur ganz entfernt) to the Davidic blessings in v. 4 (so Westermann). The fulfilment of the alleged new promise is that the people of Israel will become a new kind of witness to
God, not through military prowess, but because other nations volun-
tarily desire to belong to Israel *for the sake of their God.*

While Westermann's explanation of the text is possible, much of it
seems forced. The following critical remarks are therefore integrated
with an alternative and more simple explanation of the data.

First, close attention to the relationship between Isa. 55.1-5 and
Psalm 89, combined with the above considerations about the extension
of David's covenant to all Israel, reveals that detailed explanation of the
promise in v. 3 is unnecessary because the promise remains essentially
the same. The covenant blessings valid for David's dynasty *are* the
blessings expected for all Israel—just as they have been from the
beginning,[46] and so they need not be detailed in the present context.
The text's silence about the expected blessings is thus not astonishing,
but natural.

Secondly, the contrast between vv. 4 and 5 as suggested by Westermann unnecessarily complicates the structural relationships in Isaiah
55. Rather than driving a wedge between vv. 4 and 5, it is essential to
recognize the internal dynamics in the passage. The contrast between
vv. 4 and 5 is not between David and the people, as Westermann presumes, but between then and now, past and future. Yet this temporal
contrast is not a contrast of opposites, but indicates a strong continuity
as well as development. Just as David has been a witness to God's
superior power by way of his military victories of the past (v. 4), so
Israel will now become a witness to God's faithfulness and power,
manifest in the miraculous intervention inaugurating the people's return
from exile. This results in an even more powerful witness to the Lord's
strength and faithfulness that will lead to the desire of the Gentile
nations to come to Israel (v. 5).[47]

Thirdly, the relationship between vv. 4 and 5 is not 'remote', as
Westermann was forced to acknowledge, but logical and clear.
Westermann's explanation fails to explain the function of v. 4. Second
Isaiah does not adduce '*no more* than … a fact of history' in the second
half of the verse, nor is the statement about David's witness in the first

---

46. Cf. the pre-exilic Psalm 72.

47. 'The return from exile in Babylon is both a new creation and a new exodus'
(Day, *Conflict*, p. 92; for references in Second Isaiah, see Day, *Conflict*, p. 92 n. 13).

part 'an interpretation of his own' (*eigene Deutung*).[48] In Westermann's interpretation v. 4a can only mean that David, by means of his military prowess, witnessed to the power of Israel's God, which is simply a historical fact. Yet, from the viewpoint of exilic Israel, this witness would be peculiar indeed. For, in the meantime, the Davidic covenant has collapsed with the monarchy's dissolution, and under present circumstances mention of David's past victories would rather be a serious embarrassment to the divine power and integrity.

Thus the function of v. 4a is to hint at the deeper significance of the return from exile: it amounts to the restoration of the Davidic covenant. Just as it used to be in the past, before the exile, so it will be again in the future, after the exile. The temporary effects of Jerusalem's destruction will be obliterated and God's faithfulness will be manifest again. And as the temporary suspension of the Davidic covenant had national consequences, so its re-establishment will have to occur on a national scale with internationally recognized results (v. 5). Similarly, the pragmatic function of v. 4b is closely related to v. 5. While David's testimonial function in the past was enforced by human military force (v. 4b), the promised restoration of the covenant will be ensured by Israel's God himself. Significantly, however, God's future action on behalf of his people will not heighten international tensions, but peacefully help to resolve them (v. 5b). Thus v. 4b provides more than merely circumstantial historical detail. It is carefully phrased to highlight the *means* by which divine glory is achieved.

To sum up, interpreting Isaiah 55 within its context in Second Isaiah and with particular reference to Psalm 89 leads to the conclusion that Isa. 55.1-5 can be read as the divine answer to the open question of Psalm 89 that is bound to hang in the air until Judah's restoration as a monarchy has been accomplished. Significantly for the thesis of this essay, Second Isaiah has not modified the covenant tradition in the way envisaged by Westermann and others: the divine answer consists not of a transferral of the original promise from the Davidides to Israel, but in the promise of restoration for the Davidic dynasty. This promise was not realized in the immediate or even middle-term future of Second Isaiah's composition. Nevertheless, this delay did not lead to a widespread disillusionment in the extant biblical texts, but to a continually future-oriented expectation based on the divine promise. The challenge to the Lord's integrity prompted by his apparent failure to fulfil his

---

48. Westermann, *Jesaja*, p. 229 (ET *Isaiah 40–66*, p. 285).

covenant obligations may be answered in the light of Second Isaiah's use of Psalm 89.[49]

Has Second Isaiah developed the covenant tradition, and if so, in what way? Could it be that Isa. 55.3-5, like other passages in Isaiah, expresses hope in a new and different king, the Messiah? In order to answer such questions, the perception of David in Psalm 89, and, by implication, the perception of each successive Davidic king, must first be understood. For Second Isaiah the restoration of Israel in Isa 55.3-5 is in effect the reinstatement of the Davidic covenant. The question is why this recalling of the covenant seemed such a natural response to the new prospect of restoration.

4. The Idealization of David in Psalm 89

It would in fact be perfectly natural for Second Isaiah to have recalled the Davidic covenant in the context of his new hope if Psalm 89 had occasioned the attribution of messianic features to David among later readers, including Second Isaiah. If there are indeed strong parallels between David and Yahweh in the original psalm, as J.-B. Dumortier has argued,[50] then the material prerequisites for a later, more messianic reading are already at hand.

Dumortier has shown that there is a close relationship between the opening hymn (vv. 1-19) and the oracular section (vv. 20-38), not only in matters of vocabulary but also in content and theme. He has demonstrated that the heavily expanded section of the oracle (vv. 20-28) displays striking parallels between qualities credited to David and characteristics attributed to the Lord in the preceding hymn (vv. 6-19). Six of these are listed below (after Tate).[51]

1. David possesses power comparable to the Lord's (cf. vv. 6-19 and 22-28).

---

49. Since completing this manuscript I have come across an argument by Christopher R. Seitz, *Word Without End: The Old Testament as Abiding Theological Witness* (Grand Rapids: Eerdmans, 1998), pp. 154-58, 160-61, 163, who makes very similar points to mine about the relationship between Ps. 89 and Isa. 55.1-5, arguing against Westermann in particular (Seitz, *Word Without End*, pp. 155-57, 160).

50. Cf. Dumortier, 'Rituel d'intronisation', pp. 185-89.

51. Cf. M.E. Tate, *Psalms 51–100* (WBC, 20; Dallas: Word Books, 1990), p. 423.

2. The mighty arm and hand of the Lord, with which he has established and maintains his universal rule (v. 14), is used to empower David so that no enemy can defeat him (vv. 22-24).

3. The Lord raises the horn of his faithful people (v. 18) and raises the horn of David through the divine name (v. 25).

4. David will rule over the rivers and the sea (with his 'hand', v. 26), as the Lord rules the chaos waters (with his 'mighty arm', vv. 10-11) and indeed the universe (with his 'mighty arm' and his 'hand', v. 14). (Cf. Ps. 72.8.)

5. Righteousness and justice support the Lord's throne (v. 15), while his steadfast love and faithfulness accompany his presence with David (v. 25; cf. Prov. 16.12).

6. David is given the status of 'Most High' (v. 28), a common epithet for God. Although this epithet does not occur with reference to the Lord in Psalm 89, he is still portrayed as the head of the heavenly assembly (vv. 6-9; cf. Ps. 82.6), just as David towers over the earthly kings.[52]

Dumortier remarked that

> [t]he king, true lieutenant [*sic*] of Yahweh on earth, possesses powers *directly* proportionate to the divine power. It is in this kind of perspective that one can understand the seeming excess of royal claims. We will see in fact that the different promises which concretize the royal 'election' are only a slightly weakened echo of the manifestations of divine power about which the preceding cosmic hymn sings.[53]

Clifford's translation ('lieutenant') of Dumortier's original word 'lieutenant' obscures that Dumortier's expression (lit. 'place-holder') is a theological word-play on the Davidic king as *vicarius dei*.[54] In other words, the characteristics ascribed to David in Psalm 89 are so close to those ascribed to the Lord that it seems impossible to avoid concluding that some degree of idealization of the Israelite king was intended by the author. In the New Testament, certain characteristics of this idealized David were indeed applied to the Messiah.

52. Cf. Tate, *Psalms 51–100*, p. 424.

53. Clifford, 'Lament', p. 45, translating Dumortier, 'Rituel d'intronisation', p. 187; emphasis added.

54. Cf. Dumortier, 'Rituel d'intronisation', p. 193.

5. *Psalm 89 in the Book of Revelation*

One New Testament text which is directly related to Psalm 89 is the opening section of the book of Revelation, another future-oriented work. The following table shows expressions in Rev. 1.5 reminiscent of Ps. 89.28 + 38. There are three instances of verbal parallels, and the closeness of each suggests that the intertextual link between Rev. 1.5 and Psalm 89 is intended.

Revelation 1.5	Psalm 89 (LXX 88).28 and 38
Ἰησοῦ Χριστοῦ, ὁ μάρτυς ὁ πιστός	ὁ μάρτυς ἐν οὐρανῷ πιστός (v. 38)
Jesus Christ, the faithful witness	the faithful witness in the sky
ὁ πρωτότοκος τῶν νεκρῶν	πρωτότοκον θήσομαι αὐτόν (v. 28a)
the first-born of the dead	I will make him the first-born
ὁ ἄρχων τῶν βασιλέων τῆς γῆς	ὑψηλὸν παρὰ τοῖς βασιλεῦσιν τῆς γῆς
the ruler of the kings of the earth	(v. 28b)
	the highest of the kings of the earth

Like the three instances in Rev. 1.5, all Old Testament references in Revelation are allusions rather than direct quotations. With 636 allusions, the entry under Revelation in the 'Index of Allusions and Verbal Parallels' of the *UBSGNT* fourth edition is by far the longest.[55] In the past most studies of the use of the Old Testament in the New Testament have focused on the question whether or not a given New Testament author has 'respected the context' of the Old Testament texts he alluded to. However, the fact that Revelation contains not a single direct quotation, while abounding in allusions and allusive clusters, suggests that such studies may have asked the wrong question. Allusions often do not use their source text as prooftexts, but evoke associations of a different kind. Readers are invited to engage in a search for the larger meaning of the text in its original context. All quotations and allusions take the absorbed material out of its context to a certain degree.[56] Therefore, 'the relevant question concerning the presence of Old Testament quotations or allusions in the New Testament is not, "has the author respected the context", but "in what ways do the two contexts interact?"'[57]

55. A manual counting of the references in *UBSGNT*[4], pp. 900-911, yielded 636 references. This is just one more than the 635 found in NA[26].

56. S. Moyise, *The Old Testament in the Book of Revelation* (JSNTSup, 115; Sheffield: Sheffield Academic Press, 1995), pp. 18-19.

57. Moyise, *Old Testament in Revelation*, p. 19.

Caird claimed that two small adjustments in Rev. 1.5 have given a distinctively Christian character to the Old Testament text alluded to in Rev. 1.5. The addition of τῶν νεκρῶν after ὁ πρωτότοκος changed the reference from earthly royal power to a kingship that must be understood in the light of the cross, and πρωτότοκος must consequently be understood as a statement about Christ's resurrection. 'Christ is king, but it is a kingship won by passing through suffering and death', so that for Caird '**firstborn**, instead of being an honorific title, is the guarantee that others will pass with him through death to kingship'.[58] For Caird, then, the titles for Christ were chosen to express the paraenetic concerns of the Apocalypse, not in order to apply Psalm 89 to Christ. The following extended citation demonstrates how Caird interpreted the pragmatic impact of Rev. 1.5a:

> His friends are called to bear the costly witness of martyrdom, trusting that in his death Christ has been a **faithful witness** to God's way of overcoming evil; to look into the open jaws of death, remembering that he has risen as **the firstborn** of many brothers; to defy the authority of Imperial Rome in the name of a **ruler** to whom Caesar himself must bow.[59]

Not only did Caird neglect the Old Testament allusion, as we can see, but his reconstruction of the occasion or *Sitz im Leben* of the book as a whole unduly influenced his understanding of the section, leading him to ignore the basic form of the text. The following outline demonstrates that vv. 4b-6 are in no way imperative: there is no 'call' to do anything. Rather, Rev. 1.4-6 contains fairly typical elements of the opening to a contemporary letter.[60]

58. G.B. Caird, *The Revelation of St. John the Divine* (BNTC; London: A. & C. Black, 2nd edn, 1984), pp. 16-17 (emphasis original); also cited in Moyise, *Old Testament in Revelation*, p. 117.

59. Caird, *Revelation*, p. 16 (emphases original); cited also in Moyise, *Old Testament in Revelation*, p. 117.

60. Cf. J. Roloff, *Die Offenbarung des Johannes* (Zürcher Bibelkommentare NT, 18; Zürich: Theologischer Verlag, 2nd edn, 1987), p. 31 (ET *The Revelation of John* [trans. J.E. Alsup; Minneapolis: Fortress Press, 1993], pp. 22-23), and G.D. Fee, *Paul's Letter to the Philippians* (NICNT; Grand Rapids: Eerdmans, 1995), pp. 2-7.

sender (v. 4a)	John
addressee(s) (v. 4a)	to the seven churches that are in Asia:
greetings/blessings (v. 4b)	Grace to you and peace
sender (vv. 4b-5)	from him who is and who was and who is to come,
	and from the seven spirits who are before his throne,
	5and from Jesus Christ,
	the faithful witness,
	the firstborn of the dead,
	and the ruler of the kings of the earth.
thanksgiving/doxology (vv. 5b-6)	To him who loves us and freed us from our sins by his blood, 6and made us to be a kingdom, priests serving his God and Father,
	to him be glory and dominion forever and ever. Amen.

This section, including the allusions, is not imperatival, but describes Christ.[61] His blessings are wished upon the seven churches. These blessings have nothing to do with 'martyrdom' or 'defying Imperial Rome', but consist of grace and peace! The descriptions of Christ do not serve as an incentive to act in a certain way, but are meant to encourage the addressees by hinting at some of the characteristics of Christ, from whom this grace and peace are expected to flow on the basis of the greeting/blessing. This statement, however, is not a 'guarantee that others will pass with him through death to kingship' (Caird). Rather, the emphasis is exclusively on the positive thought that those who believe in Christ will rise according to his paradigm as the firstborn, no matter what they may have to suffer in the present age (cf. Col. 1.18, which probably also alludes to Ps. 89.28). Caird has in effect eliminated the allusion to Psalm 89; he gives it no rhetorical function, despite his acknowledgment of it.

Older commentators like Charles and Swete took the allusion to Psalm 89 more seriously. They, however, saw the allusion only as a reference to power. According to Charles, πρωτότοκος should be taken in its secondary sense of 'sovereignty'.[62] The threefold title, according

---

61. But cf. Roloff (*Offenbarung*, p. 32; ET *The Revelation of John*, p. 24), who thinks that the reference is to the seven 'angels of the Presence', who according to Jewish conceptions are mediators of God's will.

62. R.H. Charles, *A Critical and Exegetical Commentary on the Revelation of St John*, I (ICC; Edinburgh: T. & T. Clark, 1920), p. 14; cited also in Moyise, *Old Testament in Revelation*, p. 116.

to Swete, 'answers to the threefold purpose of the Apocalypse, which is at once a Divine testimony, a revelation of the Risen Lord, and a forecast of the issues of history'.[63] But even these statements remain on the surface of the allusion. Moyise, responding to Charles, Swete and Caird, affirmed the significance of the allusion by pointing to the context of Psalm 89 itself. He characterized the correspondences (not allusions) between Psalm 89 and Revelation in general as follows:

> The psalm speaks of God's anointed (v. 20; cf. Rev. 1.1, 2, 4, etc.), whose throne will be established forever (v. 29; cf. Rev. 3.21). It promises that his horn will be exalted (v. 24; cf. Rev. 5.6) and that God's faithfulness and steadfast love (vv. 1, 2, 5, 8, 14, 24, 33, 49) shall be with him (v. 24; cf. Rev. 1.5, 3.14). Finally, the psalm ends with the cry, 'How long, O Lord?' (v. 46; cf. Rev. 6.10).[64]

Moyise concluded that the connotations of royal power and cosmic stability taken from Ps. 89.28 and 38 (Moyise's ET 27 and 37) are relevant to the needs of John's addressees. Furthermore, the psalm has not been 'silenced', as Caird maintained. A closer look at the context of Psalm 89 and its correspondences with Revelation 1 will reveal that the psalm functions as more than a grab-bag for allusions. Similarly, Revelation 1 is more than a dumping-ground for vague references to the Old Testament.

It was observed above that the allusions to Psalm 89 in Rev. 1.5 are part of the formal letter opening. They are titles describing the nature of the one from whom 'grace' and 'peace' are wished upon the letter's recipients. The threefold allusion complemented by the doxology in vv. 5b-6, which refers exclusively to the second person of the Trinity, shows that the emphasis is neither on the 'seven spirits' nor, in fact, on the Lord, but on Christ. All three allusions were taken from the middle section of the psalm, the poetic transformation of Nathan's oracle into a dynastic covenant (vv. 20-38). In Revelation 1 each allusion makes a statement about Jesus the Christ which identifies him as the answer to the question posed in Psalm 89.

---

63. H.B. Swete, *The Apocalypse of St. John* (London: Macmillan, 3rd edn, 1911), p. 7; cited also by Moyise, *Old Testament in Revelation* as 'Swete, *Revelation*, p. 7'.

64. Moyise, *Old Testament in Revelation*, p. 117; his versification follows the English. Psalm 89 ends with v. 53; Moyise probably means that the *Urklage*, 'How long, O Lord?' begins the final section of the psalm.

5.1. *Christ as the Faithful Witness*

In Ps. 89.35-38 the Davidic line (lit. 'his seed') is promised perpetuity, like the sun and the moon, both of which are 'an enduring (or faithful) witness in the sky'.[65] Revelation 1.5 converts the comparison into a simile and makes Christ himself the 'faithful witness'. For those who are aware of the intertextual link between Psalm 89 and Rev. 1.5, this subtle transformation ensures that Christ guarantees the Lord's adherence to his oath (v. 35). Yahweh has not lied to David. His covenant still stands, now renewed, to be consummated in Christ's glorious return as foretold in Revelation.

5.2. *Christ as the First-born from the Dead*

The controversy as to whether 'first-born' primarily or exclusively refers to Christ's death and resurrection or to his sovereignty over mortals may be resolved by paying attention to the context of Ps. 89.28. There the term 'first-born' is in synonymous parallelism with 'the highest of the kings of the earth', which shows that the notion of sovereignty is clearly present in the allusion. The apparent 'change' by means of the addition of 'from the dead' alleged by Caird, however, finds an echo in the wider context of Psalm 89. In vv. 47-51 the lament comes to a powerful climax, culminating in a whole series of urgent questions. Most relevant to the present discussion are those in v. 49: 'Who can live and never see death? Who can escape the power of Sheol?'. Both are rhetorical questions expecting a negative response: No, nobody can live without dying! Nobody can escape Sheol! Yet, in stark contrast to this, the book of Revelation puts forward the one who can. Readers may pick up that there is a Davidic 'king' who did die, yet lived and escaped (from) Sheol. Contra Caird, then, the paradigm for the Asian churches is not Christ's death, but his resurrection. As the Christian addressees of Revelation suffer and face the threat of a violent death they are reassured and encouraged by the one who suffered like them but has conquered death and reigns over all the kings of the earth—even those who threaten their very lives. This second

---

65. With T. Veijola, 'The Witness in the Clouds: Ps 89:38', *JBL* 107 (1988), pp. 413-17, following C. Brockelmann, *Hebräische Syntax* (Neukirchen–Vluyn: Neukirchener Verlag, 1956), §58, against E.T. Mullen, 'The Divine Witness and the Davidic Royal Grant: Ps 89:37-38', *JBL* 102 (1983), pp. 207-18; cf. also P.G. Mosca, 'Once Again the Heavenly Witness of Psalm 89:38', *JBL* 105 (1986), pp. 27-37.

allusion then reassures the readers of Revelation that Christ is in control. But the emphasis is on his resurrection.

5.3. *Christ as Universal Ruler*

This allusion clearly and exclusively refers to Christ's God-given universal sovereignty. In Psalm 89 this statement is partly hyperbolic (cf. Psalm 72). It is this-worldly and speaks of the political sovereignty and international influence of the Israelite king as *vicarius dei*. In Revelation the significance of this statement may be similar. The Asian Christians to whom the book is addressed are encouraged to hope for Christ's direct, powerful intervention on their behalf, saving them from immediate danger. However, this statement takes on a broader significance when viewed against the backdrop of the whole book which it introduces. The rest of Revelation goes on to describe how Christ, in a sequence of eschatological events, eventually gains universal dominion over the dark forces in the universe, and Christians may feel reminded that he can bless their own lives now and in the future, with tangible results in this world. Furthermore, this offers the eschatological answer to the open question of Ps. 89.50: 'Lord, where is your steadfast love of old, which by your faithfulness you swore to David?' For Revelation, the answer lies in Jesus Christ, but current readings of Psalm 89 may also be deepened through an appreciation of its use in Revelation.

6. *Conclusion*

Psalm 89 responded to a situation in which the political survival of the Jewish state and the credibility of Israel's God were at stake. In so doing, it took seriously the tension between the Lord's covenant obligation to protect the Davidic dynasty and his apparent failure to fulfil it. If anything, the psalm has drawn out the contrast even more sharply than necessary—highlighting the problem of theodicy. In this sense the topic of the psalm is not only the survival of the Davidic dynasty, but also the Lord's credibility. The Davidic king stands and falls with the Lord, and vice versa. Not until the monarchy's restoration would this theological problem be solved, and the continual wrestling with this issue is witnessed to in subsequent biblical writings, only a small number of which have been treated here.

The tradition complex surrounding Nathan's oracle is at the centre of a process of rereading that was prompted by a severe political and theological crisis. Studies of a biblical text's *Wirkungsgeschichte* (reception history), such as presented here, have their place among other historical methods of interpretation. The result of this historical process of rereading, which in many cases must have involved searching theological questioning and rethinking (as the biblical texts treated here testify), was the gradual growth of a new theological concept, the anticipation of a Davidic king of a different kind: the Messiah.

KING AND MESSIAH IN EZEKIEL

Paul M. Joyce

The primary task of the prophet Ezekiel (like that of his prophetic contemporary, Jeremiah) was to provide a theological interpretation of the disaster which was engulfing his nation. The first stage of the nation's collapse had indeed taken place in 597 BCE, with the fall of Jerusalem to the Babylonians and the initial deportation, before his call to be a prophet in c. 593 BCE. Standing in the tradition of the eighth-century classical prophets, Ezekiel affirms that the catastrophic events of his own day are not merely chaotic and meaningless, but are rather the powerful and just actions of the God of Israel, who is acting right-eously to punish the present generation of Israelites for their sins. Within the present generation, judgment is falling especially upon the leaders and, among these, more specifically, upon the royal leaders of the nation. Condemnations of kings and princes abound in the book. I shall later consider the usage of Hebrew terms, but for the moment I shall speak of royal leaders as a whole.

Judgment upon Royal Leaders

In the prophet's explanation of the disaster, judgment on the royal rulers of Israel plays a very significant part. There are numerous references, either reporting the discomfiture of these leaders or condemning their sins explicitly. These will be reviewed briefly in biblical order here. The second verse of the book broaches the theme in an indirect way, for it defines the date of the opening vision as being 'the fifth year of the exile of King Jehoiachin' (1.2). The context of the book is thus defined from the start in terms of divine judgment upon the royal house. In 7.27, following references to prophet, priest, and elders, we read, 'The king shall mourn, the prince shall be wrapped in despair... According to their way I will deal with them; according to their own judgments I will judge them'. Chapter 12 contains Ezekiel's strange acted sign of

digging through a wall and carrying baggage through it. This is interpreted in v. 10: 'This oracle concerns the prince in Jerusalem and all the
house of Israel in it'. The 'prince' referred to is probably Zedekiah.
Verse 11 declares, 'They shall go into exile, into captivity', and vv. 12-
13 continue, 'And the prince who is among them shall lift his
baggage ... I will bring him to Babylon ... he shall die there'.

Chapter 17 features the allegory of the two eagles and the vine.
Verses 2-10 present the images and then in vv. 11-21 an interpretation
is offered. The king of Babylon came to Jerusalem and took its king
(presumably Jehoiachin) to Babylonia (v. 12). He took one of the royal
offspring (presumably Zedekiah) and made a covenant with him
(v. 13). However, this vassal rebelled, sending ambassadors to Egypt
(v. 15). And so, we are told in v. 16, 'in the place where the king resides
who made him king ... in Babylon he shall die'. Chapter 19 contains a
lamentation for the princes of Israel. There is first the allegory of the
lioness, representing Judah. One cub, who stands for a royal figure
usually understood to be Jehoahaz, is taken to Egypt (vv. 3-4). A
second cub representing another royal figure, variously understood as
Jehoiachin or Zedekiah, is taken to Babylon (vv. 5-9). A second allegory, in vv. 10-14, tells of a vine, again representing Judah. In v. 11, we
read: 'Its strongest stem became a ruler's sceptre'. It is unclear whether
we should read singulars or plurals here. The Masoretic text has plurals
throughout the sentence, whereas the LXX has singular forms. Singular
subjects follow, even in the Hebrew, and this (together with the fact
that the Hebrew of v. 14 features the singular in a phrase very similar to
that of v. 11) leads most commentators to take v. 11 as singular (and to
interpret the reference as being to Zedekiah). The vine was transplanted
to a dry land, 'so that there remains in it no strong stem, no sceptre for
ruling' (vv. 13-14).

I turn next to part of the sword oracle in ch. 21. Verse 17 (ET 12)
declares that the sword 'is against all Israel's princes; they are thrown
to the sword, together with my people'. Verse 30 (ET 25) has 'As for
you, vile, wicked prince of Israel, you whose day has come, the time of
final punishment...' and the next verse continues, 'Remove the turban,
take off the crown'.[1] Within the same chapter, there arises the disputed

---

1.   The Hebrew word used here for 'crown', *ᵃṭārâ*, is a somewhat low-key one,
used of headgear in many non-royal as well as royal senses and contexts; this is one
of several features here which cohere with disparagement of a royal figure, probably to be taken as Zedekiah.

issue of the 'despised rod' or 'rejected sceptre', in vv. 15b (ET 10b) and 18a (ET 13a), which may bear upon these matters. These obscure verses could simply refer to failure to respect chastisement, as in the NRSV's rendering of v. 15b (ET 10b): 'How can we make merry? You have despised the rod, and all discipline'. On the other hand, Allen has persuasively argued that we are to find, in both v. 15b (ET 10b) and 18a (ET 13a), reference to the doomed Davidic monarchy, described in theological terms as 'the rejected sceptre'.[2]

Chapter 22 focuses on the 'bloody city'. In v. 6 we read: 'The princes of Israel in you, everyone according to his power, have been bent on shedding blood.' There is a reference later in the chapter which could be relevant. Verse 25 declares that 'A conspiracy of its prophets within it are like a roaring lion tearing the prey'. The Masoretic text here refers to prophets, but the LXX has 'princes', and, on this basis, the *BHS* apparatus proposes emending the Hebrew to refer to princes rather than prophets.

Chapter 34 is a particularly important one for our theme. It features a sustained polemic against the 'shepherds' of Israel. Both the context here and usage elsewhere indicates that this is a reference to royal leaders. Verse 2 broaches the theme: 'Prophesy against the shepherds of Israel ... Ah, you shepherds of Israel who have been feeding yourselves!' Verse 4 continues, 'with force and harshness you have ruled them', and v. 5, 'So they were scattered, because there was no shepherd'. In v. 10 we read, 'I am against the shepherds; and I will demand my sheep at their hand'. The punishment of the shepherds is not spelled out explicitly until later in the chapter; in v. 16 we find: 'the fat and the strong I will destroy', and then in vv. 17-22 the theme of judgment is developed to take in divine judgment between sheep and sheep, rams and goats.

Thus we may affirm that in the prophet's explanation of the disaster,

---

2. L.C. Allen, 'The Rejected Sceptre in Ezekiel xxi 15b, 18a', *VT* 39 (1989), pp. 67-71. Allen takes v. 15b (ET 10b) as a transposed marginal gloss on 21.3 (ET 20.47), and offers the translation: 'Every Tree: or the ruler(s) of Israel, the rejected sceptre'. Allen takes 18a (ET 13a) as a transposed marginal gloss on 21.32b (ET 27b), and offers the translation: 'For investigation has been made and what if (it means that) also the rejected sceptre will not continue?'.

Commenting further on the words of 21.3 (ET 20.47), 'I will kindle a fire in you, and it shall devour every green tree in you and every dry tree', Allen suggests the possibility that the 'green tree' may represent Jehoiachin and the 'dry tree' Zedekiah.

judgment on the royal rulers of Israel plays a very significant part.[3] This should be qualified in two respects. First, it is striking that Ezekiel's diagnosis of the nation's ills traces the malaise way back to before the rise of monarchy; indeed, Ezekiel is unique in reviewing Israel's history of sin from as far back as the sojourn in Egypt (20.8; 23.8), with no pre-monarchic 'honeymoon' period as is found, for example, in Hos. 2.16-17 (ET 14-15) and Jer. 2.2. Secondly (and paradoxically), we may note that Ezekiel stresses that, however dreadful the history of the nation's sin (cf. chs. 16, 20, and 23), it is the sins of the present genera-tion alone that are being punished in the exilic crisis (cf. especially ch. 18). For this reason Ezekiel does not share the Deuteronomistic motif of blaming the notoriously wicked King Manasseh (cf. 2 Kgs 23.26).

Notwithstanding these two qualifications, it remains very much the case that in the prophet's explanation of the national disaster judgment on the royal rulers of Israel plays a particularly prominent part. The current rulers exemplify all the worst features of the nation's long his-tory of sin, monarchic and pre-monarchic (as is said in 16.44, 'like mother, like daughter'); for the sins of the nation in Ezekiel's own day, of which the crimes of the royal leaders are in many ways the most scandalous, the nation is undergoing cataclysmic judgment.

Even within chs. 40–48, with their future orientation and positive tone, the polemic against royal leaders continues, for example, in 43.7b, 43.9, 45.8, 9, and 46.18. I shall consider these texts from chs. 40–48 further later, within the theological context of future hope.

Future Hopes Vested in Royal Figures

How much can be found in Ezekiel which vests future hopes in a royal figure and may reasonably be called, at least in that minimal sense, 'messianic'?[4] Again, let us review the potentially relevant material

3.   A.R. Mein has argued that a major part of the divine judgment articulated by Ezekiel relates to sins which only the 'elite' of Judaean society (of whom the royal leaders are paradigmatic) could commit, notably sins in the realms of foreign policy and the ordering of the state cult: *Ezekiel and the Ethics of Exile* (Oxford: Clarendon Press, forthcoming).

4.   Definition of the word 'messianic' is, of course, difficult. It may be helpful to envisage a continuum ranging from *any* future hope vested in a royal figure, however modest or mundane the hope may be, through to the most elevated developments of these ideas found in later Judaism and Christianity. When the words 'messiah' and 'messianic' are used in what follows (always within inverted

briefly in biblical order. First, 17.22-24. This is one of only four sustained passages of hope within chs. 1–24 (the others being 11.14-21, 16.59-63 and 20.40-44). In this respect, this material is untypical of chs. 1–24. An editorial schema may have streamlined the book (in contrast to Jeremiah), but these four passages are the exceptions to that neat pattern. Ezekiel 17.22-24 picks up the language of the allegory of the two eagles and the vine found in vv. 2-10, which are (as we have seen) interpreted in vv. 11-21. This earlier part of the chapter had spoken of a great eagle (representing the king of Babylon) breaking off the topmost shoot of a cedar tree (the king of Judah). This was all, of course, in the context of judgment upon Judah. But now Yahweh says, 'I myself will take a sprig from the lofty top of a cedar... I myself will plant it on a high and lofty mountain' (17.22), and 'Under it every kind of bird will live' (v. 23). Although more explicitly royal language is lacking, a picture of great blessing is thus painted, through the picking up and inversion of the language of an oracle of judgment upon the royal house of Judah.

I now come to Ezek. 21.32b (ET 27b), perhaps the most marginal of the cases to be considered in this review: 'Until he comes whose right it is; to him I will give it'. The context is provided by the judgment on the 'vile, wicked prince of Israel' in 21.30-31 (ET 25-26), discussed earlier. It is difficult to know how to construe the preceding phrase in 21.32 (ET 27), 'Such has never occurred', but it seems to be the culmination of the judgment passage. The next words—those which concern us— certainly appear more positive, but they are difficult and cryptic: 'Until he comes whose right it is; to him I will give it'. There is no overtly royal or 'messianic' language here, but in the context of judgment on the 'prince', these words could imply a future, worthy royal recipient of divine favour and blessing. Such an interpretation is the more likely in view of a possible allusion here to Gen. 49.10.[5] (We may note that in this context the Ezekiel Targum speaks of Gedaliah inheriting Zedekiah's crown, but only temporarily, and does not not develop this

commas) there is no implication that beliefs of the more developed kind are necessarily present. For a helpful discussion of these and related matters, see R.E. Clements, 'The Messianic Hope in the Old Testament', *JSOT* 43 (1989), pp. 3-19; reprinted in R.E. Clements, *Old Testament Prophecy: From Oracles to Canon* (Louisville, KY: Westminster John Knox, 1996), Chapter 3.

5.   It is interesting to observe a particular similarity to the Syriac of Gen. 49.10.

text in a more 'messianic' direction.)[6]

Isolated in the midst of the oracles against Egypt (chs. 29–32), there is a verse which is often taken to have 'messianic' reference, namely 29.21: 'On that day I will cause a horn to sprout up for the house of Israel, and I will open your lips among them. Then they shall know that I am the Lord.' The language of this verse is significant; we may note especially the introductory eschatological formula 'On that day', and also the use of the words 'horn' and 'sprout up' (compare in particular Ps. 132.17: 'I will cause a horn to sprout up for David; I have prepared a lamp for my anointed one').

We are left with the two chapters with particularly overt 'messianic' hope language, namely chs. 34 and 37. First, ch. 34. Following on from the scathing critique of the 'shepherds', the royal leaders who have failed in their duties, we read in v. 23, 'I will set up over them one shepherd, my servant David, and he shall feed them: he shall feed them and be their shepherd'. And again in v. 24: 'And I, the Lord, will be their God, and my servant David shall be prince among them; I the Lord have spoken'. This is certainly a clear and important case (though, as we shall see, *Yahweh* as 'shepherd' is arguably an even more prominent theme in this chapter than that of a new Davidic 'shepherd'). We turn to ch. 37. Following on from the image of the two sticks (representing Judah and Ephraim) joined together as one stick, we read in v. 22: 'I will make them one nation in the land, on the mountains of Israel, and one king shall be king over them all. Never again shall they be two nations, and never again shall they be divided into two kingdoms.' Verse 24 reads: 'My servant David shall be king over them; and they shall all have one shepherd', and then v. 25, 'My servant David shall be their prince forever'. Again, this is clear and important evidence of future hope vested in a royal figure. However, the primary concern here seems to be the renewed unity of the people (we may compare the aspirations to recover the North in Josiah's time), rather than the renewal of monarchy as an end in itself. Moreover, it is at least possible (as we shall see later) that v. 22 refers to *God* as the one king ruling over the reunited nation rather than to any human king.

Such then is the list of passages appearing to vest future hopes in

6. Alexander Sperber (ed.), *The Bible in Aramaic. III. The Latter Prophets according to Targum Jonathan* (Leiden: E.J. Brill, 1992), p. 312; Samson H. Levey, *The Targum of Ezekiel* (The Aramaic Bible, 13; Edinburgh: T. & T. Clark, 1987), p. 68.

royal figures. The issue of primary and secondary (or authentic and inauthentic) is, of course, a recurrent one in the study of the prophetic books: in the present case, how much comes from the prophet Ezekiel himself? Whereas the primary provenance of most of the judgmental material in the book is not often questioned, it is in relation to hopeful passages in Ezekiel that such questions loom largest for most scholars. And indeed, the authenticity of each of the hopeful cases just reviewed has been challenged. Siegfried Herrmann, for example, judged the hopeful material as a whole in Ezekiel to be secondary,[7] but I have argued elsewhere that hope is integrally related to judgment in Ezekiel's theology, both themes being rooted in the prophet's conviction of the holiness of Yahweh.[8] One should not regard hope as, in itself, necessarily constituting evidence of secondary provenance. Nevertheless, some specific doubts must be acknowledged. Ezekiel 17.22-24 forms a hopeful appendix to an otherwise judgmental chapter; moreover, its presence in the first half of book could also point to redactional origin. 21.32b (ET 27b) has perhaps the best claim to authenticity, but—paradoxically—this is the most cryptic of the potentially 'messianic' references. Conversely, 29.21 is one of the clearest 'messianic' references, but the case for its authenticity is relatively weak, isolated as it is, even within its immediate context, and buried among the foreign nation oracles. Scholars are divided over the 'authenticity' of the references in chs. 34 and 37. But throughout this discussion one must remain mindful of the homogeneity of the Ezekiel tradition and the advisability of a proper agnosticism about how much we can know for sure about authorship.[9] With Clements, I think it very likely that the book of Ezekiel was essentially complete by the end of the sixth century BCE;[10] this is the more likely in the case of our present theme,

7. S. Herrmann, *Die prophetischen Heilserwartungen im Alten Testament: Ursprung und Gestaltwandel* (BWANT, 85; Stuttgart: W. Kohlhammer, 1965), pp. 241-91.

8. P.M. Joyce, *Divine Initiative and Human Response in Ezekiel* (JSOTSup, 51; Sheffield: JSOT Press, 1989), pp. 116-17.

9. P.M. Joyce, 'Synchronic and Diachronic Perspectives on Ezekiel', in J.C. de Moor (ed.), *Synchronic or Diachronic? A Debate on Method in Old Testament Exegesis* (OTS, 34; Leiden: E.J. Brill, 1995), pp. 115-28.

10. R.E. Clements, 'The Chronology of Redaction in Ezekiel 1–24', in J. Lust (ed.), *Ezekiel and his Book: Textual and Literary Criticism and their Interrelation* (BETL, 74; Leuven: Leuven University Press and Peeters, 1986), pp. 283-94; reprinted in R.E. Clements, *Old Testament Prophecy: From Oracles to Canon*

for by the end of that century political realities will have taken over from aspirations, and many expectations will have been falsified by historical developments. Perhaps the best we can do with confidence is to speak of the sixth-century witness of the book of Ezekiel on these themes of king and 'messiah'.

Terminology

Up to this point, I have spoken of 'royal rulers', but of course more than one Hebrew term is used. We must now turn to this issue. Apart from expressions which are uncommon (in this context at least), such as 'shepherd' (throughout ch. 34) and 'ruler's sceptre' (19.11-14), the two recurrent terms are *melek*, generally translated 'king', and *nāśî'*, usually rendered 'prince'.

Of these terms, it is *nāśî'* that is particularly problematic. The word is used elsewhere mostly within what has commonly been called 'Priestly' material, with much the greatest concentration coming in the book of Numbers (56 times). It is the technical term for the leader of a clan, and is always used of authorities in subordination to a greater authority (e.g. alongside Moses in Exod. 16.22). In a comparable way, the term *nāśî'* is used in Ezra 1.8 of Sheshbazzar, leader of the returning exiles— clearly a person under Persian authority.

Turning to Ezekiel, *nāśî'* is used more times in this book than in any other in the Hebrew Bible, with the single exception of the book of Numbers. In total, there are 33 cases, of which almost half (16) are in chs. 40–48. In Ezekiel *nāśî'* is certainly sometimes used of subordinate rulers, in accordance with the general usage indicated above (27.21, of Kedar; 32.29, of Edom; 39.18, of Gog's allies). However, somewhat surprisingly, it is also used of powerful kings (e.g. 30.13, of Egypt). Especially odd is the use of the term for Gog as 'chief prince' (38.2-3; 39.1). These cases lead us naturally to the really distinctive feature of Ezekiel's usage. This is the use of *nāśî'* to designate the king of Israel, not only when speaking of the past and present but also when speaking of the future. The word *melek* is sometimes used, as one would expect, but less often than the term *nāśî'*.[11]

(Louisville, KY: Westminster John Knox, 1996), Chapter 10.

11. Duguid has written a valuable study of the leaders of Israel as portrayed in Ezekiel, including a detailed survey of the usage of *melek* and *nāśî'*: I.M. Duguid, *Ezekiel and the Leaders of Israel* (VTSup, 56; Leiden: E.J. Brill, 1994), pp. 10-57.

It seems likely that this move to the word *nāśî'* represents a downgrading of royal language. In some cases this is in the context of judgment on the past, for example in 12.10, 12 and 21.30 (ET 25), both probably referring to Zedekiah, the description of whom as *nāśî'* befits his status as a mere vassal.[12] In other cases it is with reference to the place given to royalty in the future (34.24; 37.25). In the one case outside Ezekiel where a king of Israel is called a *nāśî'* (Solomon in 1 Kgs 11.34), the point seems to be precisely the limitation of kingly authority. Speiser and others have rightly suggested that Ezekiel's use of *nāśî'* of kings of Israel represents a deliberate archaizing, an echo of the leadership patterns of pre-monarchic Israel, as pictured in the book of Numbers.[13] This appears to be so not only in the critique of past and present but also in looking ahead to the future. Moreover, this evocation of early Israel is all the more significant since Ezekiel—unlike some others—by no means idealizes the pre-monarchic period.

An important issue is how the unusual usage of *nāśî'* of the king in chs. 1–39 relates to what we find in chs. 40–48. In chs. 40–48, the *nāśî'* is essentially the chief patron of the liturgy, responsible for supplying the materials required for the sacrificial system of worship. He has relatively little else to do—his is certainly a limited role, albeit one of prestige and influence. Do chs. 40–48 constitute a special case, discontinuous with chs. 1–39? Or is the emphasis rather on continuity? Some, such as Hammershaimb and Caquot, have emphasized continuity between chs. 1–39 and 40–48.[14] Others have highlighted the discontinuity. A distinctive recent example is that of Tuell, who drives a decisive wedge between the *nāśî'* of 34.24 and 37.25 and the *nāśî'* who features in chs. 40–48.[15] For Tuell, consistent with his general thesis involving a very 'realistic' interpretation of chs. 40–48, the *nāśî'* of chs. 40–48 is none other than the Governor of the Persian Province of

12. See also n. 1.

13. E.A. Speiser, 'Background and Function of the Biblical nāśî'', *CBQ* 25 (1963), pp. 111-17.

14. E. Hammershaimb, 'Ezekiel's View of the Monarchy', in F. Hvidberg (ed.), *Studia Orientalia Ioanni Pedersen Septuagenario ... Dicata* (Copenhagen: E. Munksgaard, 1953), pp. 130-40 (repr. in E. Hammershaimb, *Some Aspects of Old Testament Prophecy* [Copenhagen: Rosenkilde og Bagger, 1966], pp. 51-62); A. Caquot, 'Le Messianisme d'Ézéchiel', *Sem* 14 (1964), pp. 5-23.

15. S.S. Tuell, *The Law of the Temple in Ezekiel 40–48* (HSM, 49; Atlanta, GA: Scholars Press, 1992), p. 108.

Yehud.[16] A valuable middle way between continuity and discontinuity is offered by Levenson; he has argued that although in the use of the term *nāśî'*, especially in chs. 40–48, there is a desire to define and restrict the powers of monarchy in order to avoid abuse of power, this does not rule out important elements of continuity or indeed imply a denial of the Davidic nature of future leadership.[17]

The grounds for a sharp distinction between usage in chs. 1–39 and in chs. 40–48 are certainly not strong. The *nāśî'* who appears frequently in chs. 40–48 stands in essential continuity with the figure of chs. 34 and 37, though this is not to deny redactional elaboration in chs. 40–48 or indeed some changes in emphasis. To put it another way, the understanding of *nāśî'* in chs. 40–48 represents an exegesis of the 'messianic' *nāśî'* references of 34.24 and 37.25. Just as the move to *nāśî'* as a title for the future king of Israel in 34.24 and 37.25 represents a downgrading of royal language, so we see this process continued in the limited role assigned to the *nāśî'* in chs. 40–48.[18]

Thus *nāśî'* replaces *melek*, so as to undo the damage done in the past by royal leaders. But more needs to be said now of the theological context of all of this within Ezekiel.

Yahweh as King in Ezekiel

It is not possible to understand the role of king and 'messiah' in Ezekiel without considering the motif of God as king in the book. This theme is a persistent if not pervasive one, and is often implicit even when not explicit. It is to be seen as one manifestation of the radical theocentricity

16. Tuell, *The Law of the Temple*, pp. 115-20.

17. J.D. Levenson, *Theology of the Program of Restoration of Ezekiel 40–48* (HSM, 10; Missoula, MT: Scholars Press, 1976), pp. 55-107. Similarly F. Raurell, when commenting on the Masoretic text in 'The Polemical Role of the ΑΡΧΟΝΤΕΣ and ΑΦΗΓΟΥΜΕΝΟΙ in Ez LXX', in J. Lust (ed.), *Ezekiel and his Book: Textual and Literary Criticism and their Interrelation* (BETL, 74; Leuven: Leuven University Press and Peeters, 1986), pp. 85-89. (Raurell's main purpose is to offer a survey of the Greek usage in this area in the LXX of Ezekiel. He finds in the LXX a sharp antithesis between chs. 1-39, with their use of ἄρχοντες of wicked kings, and chs. 40–48, where ἀφηγούμενοι is employed of idealized kings.)

18. In this context reference may be made to the use of the plural in 45.8-9, where we read, 'And my princes shall no longer oppress my people'. It may well be that this use of the plural represents a further downgrading, undercutting any unique place of honour.

of Ezekiel, which we shall see to be the key to our issue in the book.

The close interrelation of language about human political structures and models of the divine has long been recognized.[19] A broadly-based study of this phenomenon in modern times was presented in two volumes by the late David Nicholls, *Deity and Domination* and *God and Government in an 'Age of Reason'*.[20] Within the study of the Hebrew Bible, Ronald Hendel in his study of the origins of the aniconic tradition in early Israel has traced the prohibition on divine images within the Hebrew tradition to negative attitudes to the human political institution of kingship and its iconography in early Israel.[21] Marc Zvi Brettler has presented a detailed treatment of God as King in the Hebrew Bible, with a particular sensitivity to the function of metaphor.[22] Even those, such as John Eaton, who argue that within the royal ideology and theology of ancient Israel it is divine kingship which is primary and that human rule mediates the divine, have to acknowledge that the social and cultural reality is more complex and reciprocal than this.[23] Human political realities have been projected heavenward and conversely theological discourse can have a profound influence on perceptions of human rule.

Within Ezekiel, we first encounter royal themes of God in the important first chapter, with its throne vision. As the chapter reaches its culmination (the statement in v. 28 that 'This was the appearance of the likeness of the glory of the Lord'), we read in v. 26: 'And above the dome over their heads there was something like a throne, in appearance like sapphire; and seated above the likeness of a throne was something that seemed like a human form'. It is telling to contrast with this vision of Yahweh's reigning actively, even in Babylonia, the reference in the same chapter to the passive deportation of King Jehoiachin (1.2). One is reminded indeed of Isaiah 6, with its contrast between the reported

19. This insight is of course a commonplace within the social sciences in the wake of the influence of, in particular, Marx, Durkheim and Weber.

20. D. Nicholls, *Deity and Domination: Images of God and the State in the Nineteenth and Twentieth Centuries* (London: Routledge, 1989), and *God and Government in an 'Age of Reason'* (London: Routledge, 1995).

21. R.S. Hendel, 'The Social Origins of the Aniconic Tradition in Early Israel', *CBQ* 50 (1988), pp. 365-82.

22. M.Z. Brettler, *God is King: Understanding an Israelite Metaphor* (JSOTSup, 76; Sheffield: JSOT Press, 1989).

23. J.H. Eaton, *Kingship and the Psalms* (The Biblical Seminar, 3; Sheffield: JSOT Press, 2nd edn, 1986).

death of the human King Uzziah and the vision of the King, the Lord of Hosts, reigning in the Temple (Isa. 6.1, 5). Yahweh continues to reign in exile, unlike the human king.

Chapter 1 is, of course, the first example of a feature which is sustained throughout the book—the movement of the divine glory. The departure of the glory from Jerusalem is recounted within the context of the vision of chs. 8–11, where the throne reference is again explicit at 10.1, and conversely the return of the glory to Jerusalem is a feature of the extended Temple vision of chs. 40–48 (see especially 43.1-5). In 43.7 we read 'Mortal, this is the place of my throne and the place for the soles of my feet, where I will reside among the people of Israel forever'. Significantly, the second half of that very verse links this with a denigration of human kings: 'The house of Israel shall no more defile my holy name, neither they nor their kings, by their whoring, and by the corpses of their kings...' (43.7b).

Reverting to biblical order, we turn next to ch. 20, specifically v. 33, which yields the book's only explicit use of the root *mlk* of Yahweh. Having surveyed the history of the nation's sin, the prophet at v. 30 addresses his contemporaries: 'Will you defile yourselves after the manner of your ancestors?' From this we know that the context of v. 33 is the exilic situation. Verse 33 reads: 'As I live, says the Lord God, surely with a mighty hand and an outstretched arm, and with wrath poured out, I will be king over you' (the verb *mlk*, 'to reign' or 'to be king', is used). Verses 34-35 go on to speak of God bringing the exiles out of the lands of their dispersal into the wilderness, where he will enter into judgment with them face to face. Again, it is striking that, back in a wilderness situation, with no human king, it is Yahweh who reigns as divine king and who judges his people.

I move now to ch. 34. After the condemnation of the 'shepherds', the royal leaders of Israel, but before we come to the references in vv. 23 and 24 to David as 'shepherd' and 'prince', Yahweh is presented as declaring in vv. 11 and 12, 'I myself will search for my sheep' and in v. 15, 'I myself will be the shepherd of my sheep'. This motif seems to be given primacy over renewed Davidic 'shepherding', and it is telling to note that after the David references, the chapter culminates in v. 31 with the following formulation: 'You are my sheep,... and I am your God, says the Lord God'.[24] We may draw in here also some words

24. This feature was stressed by W.R. Aytoun, 'The Rise and Fall of the "Messianic" Hope in the Sixth Century', *JBL* 39 (1920), pp. 24-43 (see especially

found at the very end of ch. 36: 'So shall the ruined towns be filled with flocks of people. Then they shall know that I am the Lord' (36.38).

And so on to 37.15-28, which could possibly provide a further relevant case. I have suggested that the primary theme here is the reunification of the nation. I have noted that renewed Davidic rule is explicitly promised in vv. 24-25. However, it is conceivable that in the earlier reference in this passage rule by *God* as king is intended. The verse in question is v. 22: 'I will make them one nation in the land, on the mountains of Israel, and one king shall be king over them all' (such an interpretation is perhaps the more possible in the light of the words of the following verse, 23, 'Then they shall be my people, and I will be their God'). If the divine king is intended here at v. 22, this passage would in this respect resemble the 'two-decker' pattern of ch. 34, presenting divine and human royal figures in parallel, with of course the human figure subordinate to the divine, like a viceroy. However, on balance, the most natural reading of 37.22 is probably as a reference to a human king.

Such then are the cases in which Yahweh is, directly or indirectly, presented as 'king' in the book of Ezekiel.[25] The theme of God's kingship is particularly important because of the discernible pattern whereby the downgrading of human royal rule in the Ezekiel mirrors the upgrading of the royal sway of God. As one decreases, the other increases, and vice versa. This phenomenon fits very naturally within the context of Ezekiel's distinctive radical theocentricity.[26] A good example of this is afforded by the analogy which appears to be drawn in 17.22-24. As in vv. 3-4 the eagle (representing Nebuchadrezzar) had taken a sprig (representing the house of David), so now in v. 22 Yahweh himself takes a sprig, which becomes a great tree. It is reasonable to argue that Yahweh himself is now to the 'messiah' as Nebuchadrezzar had been to

pp. 28-29). Aytoun unnecessarily overstated the case, however, by excising all references to future human rule in ch. 34 as postexilic glosses.

25. A further possible case may be suggested. In 16.12, 13 Israel is presented as queen (albeit disgraced) in relation to Yahweh, and by implication at least this passage could be said to present Yahweh as king.

26. In this context one might ask whether the elevation of Yahweh's sway within Ezekiel, indeed the radically theocentric presentation of the book as a whole, accounts to some degree for a negative feature of this tradition, namely the misogyny which marks especially chs. 16 and 23. Some feminist critics have argued that this may be so and that this aspect of Ezekiel should be viewed with suspicion—but that is a subject for another essay.

the Davidic house. As the Judaean kings had only stayed in place by
the sufferance of their suzerains, so, in Ezekiel's view of the future, the
'messiah' will reign only in so far as his rule remains subject to the
stated will of Yahweh.[27]

The *nāśî'* in Ezekiel's future expectation is at best a 'viceroy' to
Yahweh as king. Such had of course always been so within the royal
ideology of Israel, but now it is to the marked detriment of the human
figure, who does not always have even the honour which the word
'viceroy' suggests. We have noted that even within chs. 40–48, with
their future orientation and positive tone, the polemic against royal
leaders continues. Following straight on from 43.7a, with its reference
to the throne of Yahweh, we read in 43.7b: 'The house of Israel shall
no more defile my holy name, neither they nor their kings, by their
whoring, and by the corpses of their kings...' And again in 43.9: 'Now
let them put away their idolatry and the corpses of their kings far from
me, and I will reside among them forever'. And then we may note several texts which circumscribe the behaviour of the prince or princes and
warn against excess. In 45.8, we read: 'And my princes shall no longer
oppress my people; but they shall let the house of Israel have the land
according to their tribes'. And again in v. 9: 'Enough, O princes of
Israel! Put away violence and oppression, and do what is just and right.
Cease your evictions of my people, says the Lord God.' At 46.18, we
read: 'The prince shall not take any of the inheritance of the people,
thrusting them out of their holding...so that none of my people shall be
dispossessed of their holding'. The protective note conveyed here by
the phrase '*my* people' is particularly striking. These texts remind one
of the tone of the so-called 'Law of the King' of Deuteronomy 17, from
much the same period of Israel's history: they share with that material
what might be described as a dialectical critique of monarchy, allowing
it a place within the divinely ordained polity, but only when radically
subordinated to the will of God and to the real needs and interests of
the community of the people of God. Indeed the *nāśî'* within chs. 40–48
might almost be described as a functionary of the worshipping community as a whole. It may be appropriate to compare this with a feature
of another text from broadly the same period as Ezekiel, namely the
probable 'democratization' of Davidic language in Isa. 55.3, which may
envisage former royal privileges being transformed for the benefit of
the community.

27. Cf. Levenson, *Theology*, pp. 79-81.

The importance within Ezekiel of the recurrent 'Recognition For-mula' ('that they may know that I am Yahweh' and similar) is widely acknowledged and deserves mention here. The formula is very fre-quently appended to judgments upon royal figures (e.g. 7.27 and 12.15). Moreover, it is even added to 'messianic' blessings in a way that ap-pears to 'cap' them (e.g. 17.24 and 29.21). We sense that in these most characteristic formulations of the future hope in Ezekiel, there is no ultimately significant role for royal mediators; the function of kings has melted away, overwhelmed—it would seem—by the emphasis on the holy God.[28] The 'messianic' figure is at best on the fringes of what for Ezekiel is the real focus of future expectation, namely the restored sanc-tuary.[29] At the end of ch. 37, we read: 'My dwelling place shall be with them; and I will be their God, and they shall be my people. Then the nations shall know that I the Lord sanctify Israel, when my sanctuary is among them forevermore' (37.27). And, finally, at the very end of the book: 'And the name of the city from that time on shall be, The Lord is There' (48.35). We look in vain here for a 'messianic' figure, for Ezekiel's radical theocentricity has eclipsed all reference to human leaders.

28. D.I. Block has wisely put it: 'The issue is not the return of David, but the presence of Yahweh', in D.I. Block, 'Bringing David Back: Ezekiel's Messianic Hope', in P.E. Satterthwaite, R.S. Hess and G.J. Wenham (eds.), *The Lord's Anointed: Interpretation of Old Testament Messianic Texts* (Carlisle: Paternoster Press; Grand Rapids: Baker Book House, 1995), pp. 167-88 (187). Cf. Aytoun, 'Rise and Fall' (see especially p. 29, on ch. 34: 'instead of a kingdom of David, a kingdom of God').

29. A point emphasized by W. Zimmerli, *Ezechiel*, II (BKAT, 13.2; Neukirchen–Vluyn: Neukirchener Verlag, 2nd edn, 1979), p. 918 (ET [of German 1st edn] *Ezekiel*, II [Hermeneia; Philadelphia: Fortress Press, 1983], p. 279).

The Messiah in the Postexilic Old Testament Literature

Rex Mason

Whoever is invited to discuss 'The Postexilic ... Anything' is immediately faced with a problem of definition. Just what was 'the postexilic biblical literature'? Is there not a real sense in which the whole Old Testament is postexilic? I refer not merely to any of the latest fads for dating everything late, but to the fact that, even those books whose origin can with some confidence be traced to the pre-exilic period, were undoubtedly finally edited, arranged, and brought to assume their present form after the exile. Not only so, but it was in the postexilic period that they became more widely read, were preserved, commented on and increasingly regarded as authoritative.

I mention this at the outset because something of the problem confronts us now in dealing with the subject 'The Messiah in the Postexilic Old Testament Literature'. Even if we confine ourselves (as I shall) to material whose origin we may with some confidence assign to the postexilic period, we can never forget that it was in this same period that the earlier literature was being read, reread, assembled and collected. How did its readers understand it, especially those passages that made promises about the Davidic dynasty, or held out hopes for its glorious future? How did they read the royal psalms, for instance? We may catch tantalizing glimpses in the way the Chronicler uses psalms, and in the way postexilic books cite from earlier texts with increasing frequency, giving the passages they use new contexts and new applications.[1] We may assume that the exegetical practices we find in the intertestamental Jewish literature, among the Qumran Covenanters and, above all, in the New Testament, did not occur without earlier precedent. But, in the end, we have to confess that there will be a great deal

---

1. For a full and authoritative discussion of such inner-biblical exegesis see M. Fishbane, *Biblical Interpretation in Ancient Israel* (Oxford: Clarendon Press, 1985).

about postexilic messianic belief and expectation we do not know. We may talk about the 'Messiah in the postexilic *literature*'. We must not think that thereby we have gained anything like a full understanding of the different messianic expectations which were held by different groups in the postexilic *period*.

There is a further difficulty of method which faces us. Even if we see that our scope for knowledge is limited to the extant postexilic Old Testament literature, just what are we to include in that? What about passages which have been widely thought to be exilic or postexilic additions to pre-exilic books? Mowinckel cites a number of such passages, which he assigns to the later period: Isa. 4.2, 11.1-9; Mic. 4.8, 5.1-3, ET 2-4; Jer. 23.5-6 = 33.15-16, 30.9, 21; Ezek. 17.22-24, 34.23-24, 37.22-25.[2] The trouble is that the decision about the date of origin of any one passage is notoriously difficult and subjective. One scholar's postexilic gloss is for another a triumph of the advanced thinking of the original author. It would be easy to show that Mowinckel's own judgment is influenced by his belief that we can only speak of any kind of 'messianic hope' *after* the exile. It is, certainly, difficult to deny that there are postexilic glosses in the pre-exilic literature, but it is hazardous to be specific. I shall ignore such passages in this chapter, and in this I am helped by the fact that other chapters deal with the books mainly affected. Again, however, we must note that this further diminishes any claim we might make to be presenting a comprehensive picture of postexilic messianic thought.

One further difficulty needs to be mentioned before we address the particular texts which are left us (and which prove to be mercifully few!). At some point we need to know just what we mean when we speak of 'the Messiah'. Do we mean the hope of a restoration of the historic Davidic dynasty or, indeed, of any royal line after 538 BCE? Or do we narrow our term to imply the intervention of some heavenly deliverer who breaks into the time–space continuum of this world from outside and above it? Do we limit it necessarily to thought of a *royal* figure at all? We can put this problem another way. What possible means were open to postexilic writers and theologians when faced with the problem of the end of the Davidic dynasty which had, according to at least some of their traditions, been promised by God an everlasting continuity? They could announce its restoration after the exile. They

2. S. Mowinckel, *Han som kommer* (Copenhagen: G.E.C. Gad, 1951), p. 21 (ET *He That Cometh* [trans. G.W. Anderson: Oxford: Basil Blackwell, 1956], p. 16).

could reinterpret it to say that the promise was being fulfilled, even if in a different form. They could ignore it, assuming that God had now other plans for his people. They could cast it into an indefinite future and give it an almost transcendental quality, believing that some heavenly deliverer would one day appear to deliver them from all their enemies. We must keep these, and perhaps other, possibilities before us as we examine the literature, and try to differentiate between them, or, again, our picture of the Messiah in the postexilic biblical literature will be a distorted, even muddled one.

Haggai

With all these caveats safely aired I can turn to the first text to engage us, Hag. 2.23:

> On that day, says the Lord of hosts, I will take you,
> O Zerubbabel my servant, the son of Shealtiel,
> says the Lord, and make you like a signet ring;
> for I have chosen you, says the Lord of hosts.

It is important to set this last verse of the book in the context of Haggai's message as a whole. He calls for the rebuilding of the Temple, meeting the complaint of the Judaean population that they cannot afford it, by saying that their poverty is the result of their failure to build it. In the face of their discouragement he assures them that the completed Temple will be the place to which Yahweh returns so that his presence (*kābôd*) will again fill it. From there he will reign as universal king as all nations bring their tribute. The heavens and the earth will be 'shaken', foreign powers with their vast armies will be conquered, and Zerubbabel will rule in God's name. Haggai draws on a number of traditions in formulating this message. Traces may be observed of the Zion tradition expressed in some psalms. Some of the hopes expressed in the so-called 'Psalms of Yahweh's Enthronement' are echoed. There are traces of Second Isaiah and certainly of Ezekiel, especially with the thought of the return of Yahweh's *kābôd*. There are links with Deutero-nomistic covenant language, with its preconditions for the blessing and fertility of the land, but, equally, with the Zion tradition here also.[3]

3. For a brief discussion of the traditions which appear to have influenced Haggai (and Zechariah chs. 1-8), see my 'The Prophets of the Restoration', in R.J. Coggins, A. Phillips and M. Knibb (eds.), *Israel's Prophetic Tradition: Essays*

The name Zerubbabel means 'shoot of Babylon' and there is a considerable degree of confusion in the records about him. All seem to agree that he was a Davidide, the grandson of King Jehoiachin (1 Chron. 3.16-19). Here and in Ezra 3.2 his father's name is said to be Shealtiel, although 1 Chron. 3.19 gives his father's name as Pedaiah (the LXX correcting this discrepancy). There is further the problem that Ezra 3.1–4.4 seems to suggest that he led in an earlier attempt to rebuild the Temple in the time of Cyrus, while in the book of Haggai the implication is that the Temple lies still in ruins in the time of Darius. On the other hand, Ezra 5.7-17 attributes the earlier attempt to build to Sheshbazzar, also a Davidide if he is to be identified with the 'Shenazzar' of 1 Chron. 3.18. Both Sheshbazzar (Ezra 5.14) and Zerubbabel (Hag. 1.1, 2.2, 21) are described as 'governor' (*peḥâ*) and it is interesting both that the Persians placed descendants of Judah's royal house as governors and that these had taken Babylonian names.

What exactly is promised to and of Zerubabbel here? All the terms used could have royal connotations but, equally, none necessarily need be so interpreted. 'My servant' is, of course, a term used repeatedly of David (and almost exclusively of him among the kings of Israel and Judah), but of others as well: Abraham, Moses, Job, and the 'Servant' of Second Isaiah. 'I will take you' is a phrase which can indicate the divine election of a king (e.g. 2 Sam. 7.8, of David) or of a prophet (Amos 7.15), of Moses (Exod. 6.7), or Abraham (Josh. 24.3).[4] God will 'make him (Zerubbabel) like a signet ring' (*kaḥôtām*). This has led many to see a connection with his grandfather Jehoiachin. Jeremiah 22.24 expresses God's determination to judge king and people with the words, 'As I live, says the Lord, though Coniah the son of Jehoiakim, king of Judah, were the signet ring on my right hand, yet I would tear you off...' Yet even this term may have more general connotations. The signet ring can give authority for a certain action, witness 1 Kgs 21.8, much quoted in this connection, where Jezebel sealed letters with Ahab's signet ring, so giving the king's supposed authority to the action which they called for. Yet the same noun occurs in Exodus 28 of stones on Aaron's turban, each bearing the names of six of the tribes of Israel 'like the engraving of a signet ring' for remembrance, while one

in Honour of Peter Ackroyd (Cambridge: Cambridge University Press, 1982), pp. 137-54.

4. See S. Amsler, *Aggée*, in S. Amsler, A. Lacocque, R. Vuilleumier, *Aggée, Zacharie, Malachie* (CAT, 11c; Geneva: Labor et Fides, 2nd edn, 1988), p. 39.

on the high priest's breastplate was inscribed 'Holy to the Lord' and
was connected with his taking upon himself the guilt of the people. So,
while Hag. 2.23 may imply special royal status now being, or shortly to
be, reinstated, it may carry a more general connotation of God's remembrance of and affection for Zerubbabel and the people he represents.
And, of course, the same may be said of the verb 'I have chosen you',
which is used of David, but also by the Chronicler of Solomon and the
Levites, while Deuteronomy and some psalms use it of God's choice of
his people generally, a sense perhaps carried over in its use by Second
Isaiah of the servant.

It is no doubt this open-endedness about these terms which led
Meyers and Meyers to deny any 'messianic' overtones in 2.23.

> The term [i.e. servant] places Zerubbabel, or anyone else so designated,
> in a subservient relationship to Yahweh, who emerges as the sovereign
> ruler. Zerubbabel's role, therefore, as a ruler in and of himself is not
> indicated in this oracle. Both "servant" and "signet"...emphasize his
> instrumentality and not his independence.

Again, they conclude, 'Haggai uses no language that refers directly to
Zerubbabel as king...'[5] As we have seen, this is a perfectly possible
and legitimate reading of Hag. 2.23. However, the balance of probability (it is no more) seems to me to tilt towards a belief that Haggai
thought, that when Yahweh began his universal reign in the completed
Temple, Zerubbabel would succeed to royal status. His Davidic descent, and especially the fact that Jehoiachin was the last Davidic king,
the reversal of whose banishment as expressed by Jeremiah is here
suggested by the use of the rare word 'signet ring', seem more than co-
incidence. The strongly eschatological nature of the promises of
Yahweh's return to his Temple, the destruction of the great powers and
their armies, and Yahweh's universal reign suggest something more
than a merely continuing governorship for Zerubbabel under Persian
domination. Further, we have to note a strong later tendency to deny
any military or royal power to him (Zech. 4.6b-10a, see below).

Even if this is so, however, there is no reason to see in Hag. 2.23
anything other than a belief that the Davidic dynastic line would be
renewed in Jerusalem and would be a feature of the new, postexilic age
of God's rule as it was of the earlier, pre-exilic one.

---

5.   C.L. and E.M. Meyers, *Haggai, Zechariah 1–8* (AB, 25B; Garden City,
NY: Doubleday, 1987), pp. 68, 70.

Zechariah 1–8

If it is difficult to interpret the very brief material in the book of Haggai, Zechariah 1–8 presents us with still greater problems. Indeed, it would be a rash commentator who claimed to be able to explain satisfactorily the varying signals of 'messianic hope' that confront us here. The editorial superscription and the system of dating in which both Haggai and Zechariah 1–8 have been set suggest that Zechariah was a contemporary of Haggai's. Certainly he appears to have been influenced by very much the same traditions to which Haggai gives prominence. He stands in the same Zion tradition, announcing that it is the city of Yahweh's choice, who will shortly be returning to it to live there and defend it. Both land and people will then be cleansed, an act as much a miraculous initiative of Yahweh as the completing of the rebuilding of the Temple. So similar are these aspects of the message of the two prophets that some commentators have argued that the same editors have assembled them as a unified work.[6] This message is expressed in a series of 'visions of the night' with accompanying oracles, a tradition which probably stems from the older idea of a 'true' prophet being one who has been admitted to the 'Council of Heaven' (e.g. Jer. 23.18-22; 1 Kgs 22).[7]

However, there are differences (even if only of emphasis) between Haggai and Zechariah 1–8 as we now have these works. Zechariah appears to have held out a more universalistic note than Haggai in addition to sharing Haggai's belief that Yahweh would overthrow the nations who had oppressed Judah (e.g. 2.15, ET 2.11). There seems to be some difference also in his 'messianic' expectation. In no passage where Zerubbabel is named is he described as ruling in the way Haggai predicts in Hag. 2.21-23. He is named only in 4.6b-10a, widely held to be an insertion into the account of the vision of the lampstand with the two trees beside it in ch. 4. It could be dropped and its omission would not be noticed in a text which would then run from 6a, 'Then he said to me ...' straight on to 10b, 'These seven are the eyes of the Lord ...' The effect of this interpolated passage seems to be that Zerubbabel will

6. E.g. Meyers and Meyers, *Haggai, Zechariah 1–8*, pp. xliv-xlviii.

7. Apart from the commentaries, the most thorough and systematic examination of the oracles which accompany the visions is that of A. Petitjean, *Les Oracles du Proto-Zacharie* (Ebib; Paris: J. Gabalda, 1969). See also W.A.M. Beuken, *Haggai–Sacharja 1–8* (Assen: Van Gorcum, 1967).

complete the building of the Temple (vv. 7-10), but his will be no rule
which will be, or should be, characterized by military power (6b).
There is far too little material here to justify us in weaving complicated
webs of supposed history which sees a reaction to the kind of hopes
raised by Haggai's predictions for Zerubbabel. But this picture of
Zerubbabel does recall the Chronicler's picture of David as mainly a
Temple-builder (see below) and fits exactly the description of
Zerubbabel's activity given in Ezra 3–6.

If we allow, then, that in those verses we have some (later?) recasting
of the role assigned to Zerubbabel away from that associated with
traditional ideas about a Davidic, 'messianic' ruler, can we say anything
about the role he had been expected to play by the prophet himself? If
the vision of the candlestick and the two trees expresses the prophet's
expectations, he has certainly not expressed them all that clearly.
Presumably the lampstand recalls the 'Menorah' in the Second Temple
and was meant to symbolize Yahweh's presence there among his
people. The role and the identity of the two olive trees with branches
are somewhat confusing. One would have thought, naturally, that their
role was to supply the lamp with oil, but that hardly fits the symbolism,
since, presumably, God's servants do not supply him with the source of
light. Further, they are described as 'sons of oil', rendered in most
English Versions by the word 'anointed', although the Hebrew word
for 'oil' here (*yiṣhār*) is not the one usually used in the sense of
'anointing'. Indeed, it is used in such a sense only here in the whole
Hebrew Bible. It is possible that the figure of the olive trees has
influenced the choice of word since it is regularly used of the oil of the
olive. But it is not a very clear way of expressing just what the
significance of 'anointing' is, and their role of 'standing by the Lord of
the whole earth' is also depicted only vaguely. Further, they are not
explicitly named. It is difficult to avoid the conclusion, however, that,
at least in the final form of the book, since only Joshua and Zerubbabel
have been named, they are the two meant. Does the vision suggest
some type of diarchic rule between the priest and the governor? And, if
so, does that go back to Zechariah himself? It is hard, if not impossible,
to say. That appears to be the suggestion of 6.13, but that is a verse
which also bristles with problems of its own.

Twice in these chapters, someone called 'Branch' is mentioned (3.8,
6.12). In each case he is unnamed and his coming seems to be envisaged as an event some way away in the future. In the first instance it

occurs in the context of an explanatory 'oracle' to a vision, here a vision of Joshua's in which Yahweh intervenes to acquit him from the charge of 'the Adversary' (the meaning of the Hebrew term 'Satan' which, occurring with an article denotes an office, as in Job 1–2, not a proper name, as in 1 Chron. 21.1). Whether this is meant to indicate that the priests returning from the 'uncleanness' of exile will be entrusted with their sacred office again, or whether Joshua, as high priest, represents and symbolizes the whole community, whom it is now God's intention to cleanse and forgive (symbolized by the change of clothing), is a matter for (differing) scholarly opinion. The second interpretation would fit with Zechariah's promises of divine cleansing for the whole community to be found in the visions recorded in ch. 5. However, in the oracle which expands Joshua's vision and offers its explanation, conditional promises are made to Joshua and 'the companions who sit before him' (fellow priests?), and Joshua is crowned (the word translated 'turban' in the English Versions, Heb. *ṣānîp*, is usually associated with the headdress of a priest, but it appears capable of having 'royal' associations, as in Isa. 62.3, *ṣᵉnîp mᵉlûkâ*). They are promised that they will 'rule my house'. The verb 'to rule' (*dîn*, 'to give judgment') and its noun is used of judgments given by various officials including priests (e.g. Deut. 17.8-13) but also kings (Jer. 21.12, 22.16; Ps. 72.2; Prov. 31.9). 'My house' might suggest exclusively the Temple, but we have to remember that in the monarchic period palace and Temple formed one complex, the same Hebrew word standing for both. Joshua and his companions will also have charge of 'my courts' for which the same can be said. He is also to have access 'among these who are standing'. Is that an allusion to the heavenly court in which Yahweh is surrounded by his angelic host? If so, this, as indicated above, would give Joshua the same kind of authority as a 'true' prophet. Thus there are priestly, royal and prophetic overtones about Joshua and, presumably, the postexilic line of which he is (re)founder, forerunner and representative. As such, he and his companions are guarantors of the divine promise that ultimately 'my servant', the 'Branch' will come. Literally, they are 'men of portent', or 'omen', that is, their continuing presence and activity are signs of the promise which is to be fulfilled. The word 'branch' (Heb. *ṣemaḥ*) is not that which occurs in the 'messianic' passage of Isa. 11.1, but it does appear to have such connotations in Ps. 132.17 where its verbal form appears (meaning 'to make sprout', or 'branch out'), Jer. 23.5 (the noun) and 33.15 (noun and verb).

It is, therefore, difficult to believe it could have been interpreted in any other way by the readers of Zechariah.

The other passage in which the term occurs, Zech. 6.9-15, raises just as many questions. The prophet is commanded to take silver and gold from certain named returned exiles (it is strange that the list of names here and in v.14 differ but that need not detain us here except to note that it is a slight embarrassment to any who would still claim that this passage, as it stands, is in a state of pristine order and purity) and with it to make either a crown or crowns. The Hebrew both in v. 11 and v. 14 is in the plural and this led some older commentators to argue that an original command to crown both Joshua and Zerubbabel has been changed because, for some reason, Zerubbabel dropped out of the reckoning. That is entirely possible but it is not the inevitable conclusion to be drawn from the plural form of the noun since it is used in the plural elsewhere where it clearly denotes only one object (Job 31.36). Perhaps it gets its plural form because it was made up of a number of bands or circlets and could be used much as, in English, the word 'scissors' is used as a plural. What follows is unexpected because Joshua, the high priest is to be crowned, while the words which accompany the act appear as though they should have been addressed to Zerubbabel: 'See, a man, "Branch" is his name, and he shall "sprout" [the verbal form of the noun "Branch"] in [or "from"] his place and he shall build the Temple of Yahweh. And he will build the Temple of Yahweh and he will bear honour and shall sit and rule upon his throne. And there shall be a priest upon/over/against/by [all are possible renderings of the Hebrew preposition *'al*] his throne and there shall be a peaceful accord between the two of them' (although what I have rendered as 'peaceful accord' could also be translated in various ways, 'a counsel of peace', or even 'a plan for salvation').

We must each make what we can of this. It would be a brave exegete who would claim to know the one, true meaning of it. Most of us lack bravery on such occasions and prefer to cower behind ramparts of judicious footnotes and the objective reporting of the views of others. There could be a simple explanation, one suggested as an alternative long ago by P.R. Ackroyd.[8] That is to assume that this is spoken at a time before Zerubbabel had come to Judah from Babylon. Joshua, as high priest, is crowned proleptically on his behalf. Joshua thus becomes

---

8.   P.R. Ackroyd, *Exile and Restoration* (London: SCM Press, 1968), pp. 196-200.

guarantor that Zerubbabel will come, that both religious and civil heads will share power, and that Zerubbabel will complete the building of the Temple with the help and encouragement of others who have also yet to come to Judah from exile (v. 14). However, there are certain difficulties. It is strange that again Zerubbabel is not named but given a 'messianic' title as in 3.8. What does the strange phrase 'he shall sprout in/from his place' mean? Does it mean that the 'Branch' will take *Joshua's* place? Does it mean he will grow into royal dignity where he is now, or when he comes back from wherever he is? How does this square with 4.6b-10a, which appears to limit the scope of Zerubbabel's royal power? Each of these questions needs to be asked, whatever answers we may claim to have found for them, and whatever degree of authority we may claim for those answers

There is another line of explanation altogether. Both 3.6-10 and 6.9-15 appear to concentrate mainly on the *present* position and authority of Joshua and the priestly line. Zechariah 4.6b-10a appears to warn against the attributing of military power and authority to the role of Zerubbabel. The 'messianic Branch', unnamed, has now become a figure whose appearance can be expected at some, unspecified, time in the future. Such a reading could give rise to the idea that meanwhile it is the priests who bear a divinely given authority and responsibility. The theocracy is God's present arrangement for the governance of his people but, at at the same time, they are guarantors of his future plans for a messianic 'Branch'. However, quite understandably, representatives of the theocracy do not expect to be done out of a job when that great day dawns. They are careful to point out that, even then, priests and kings will share government jointly.

There are problems with this view also. What do we make of the promises that this 'Branch' will 'build the Temple' (6.13, 15)? Does that not suggest a time before the completion of the Temple after the exile? It is this which has led a number of recent commentators to argue that the books of Haggai and Zechariah 1-8 must have assumed their present form early, within (or very soon after) the lifetime of the prophets.[9] Clearly Zerubbabel was involved with the rebuilding of the Temple. But is it possible that this could be seen, in later times, as a kind of paradigm for the activity of all who were truly to follow in his steps?

9. Meyers and Meyers, *Haggai, Zechariah 1-8*, p. xlv; J.E. Tollington, *Tradition and Innovation in Haggai and Zechariah 1-8* (JSOTSup, 150; Sheffield: Sheffield Academic Press, 1993).

The Chronicler shows that it was David who gathered all the building material for the first Temple and received from God the blueprint for its construction, while Solomon actually did the job. But all subsequent kings are judged by how they too 'build' the Temple in terms of 'building up' its worship, the observance of its laws and the upkeep of the theocracy of which it was the focal point. There is plenty of Old Testament evidence for understanding 'building the Temple' in this metaphorical way (e.g. Pss. 51.20, ET 18, 147.2, 13), as Eaton showed.[10]

From such obscure and varied material it is hard to form a final judgment and impossible to be dogmatic about any conclusions we do reach. These have to remain tentative. One possible reading is that Zechariah saw a joint rule of Joshua and Zerubbabel and believed that would come about very soon, when the Temple had been completed. For some reason he tends to avoid mentioning Zerubbabel by name, preferring a title which must have had some 'messianic' connotations for his hearers. He stresses that priest and governor will rule in perfect harmony and accord but can describe Zerubbabel's rule in terms of 'honour' or 'splendour' and speak of his 'throne' (6.13). At the same time, for some reason unknown to us, he seems to find it necessary to warn Zerubbabel (and others?) that his role is primarily that of Temple-builder and does not lie at all along the path of military might (4.6b-10a). If all this is the teaching of the original prophet Zechariah, it appears to suffer some strains of inconsistency, unless it can be said to represent a development of his thought as events unfolded in the course of time.

The other possible reading of the text is to see a more complex redaction process behind it. Possibly, Zechariah himself did envisage a kind of diarchy between Joshua and Zerubbabel (if that is a proper interpretation of the vision of the lampstand and two olive trees with its climax in 4.14). However, as time passed, for some reason unknown to us, Zerubbabel faded from the scene or the hopes attached to him by those such as Haggai appeared to founder on reality. In fact, a theocracy emerged in the postexilic, Temple community of Judah/Jerusalem

10. J.H. Eaton, 'The Psalms and Israel's Worship', in G.W. Anderson (ed.), *Tradition and Interpretation* (Oxford: Clarendon Press, 1979), pp. 268-69: 'It may be that the phraseology about "the building up" of the walls...and city....and restoration of the gate-bars...originates in the festal ideas rather than (as often assumed) in post-exilic circumstances of reconstruction, for the theme is also found in Babylonian festal prayers (*ANET*, pp. 390f.)'.

under the political hegemony of Persia. This was shown to be within the purpose and ordaining of God. The priests now subsume within themselves and their office priestly, prophetic and even royal functions and attributes. However, the 'messianic' hope, which once may have attached to Zerubbabel, was still held out as a distant hope. In due course the promised ruler would come. But the priestly circles, in which the books of Haggai and Zechariah 1–8 developed, saw to it that that if ever a claimant did show up, they would still keep their position and power.

Of these two possibilities, I have just enough exegetical bravery to say that I favour the second, especially as it reflects exactly the kind of theological stance we see in the work of the Chronicler (see below). It was a process divined long ago by Beuken (see n. 7). I still find it more probable than the somewhat more simplistic views of those who argue for a tight-knit unity of view in texts all produced at one time in the lifetime of the eponymous prophets. The text shows too many cracks and fissures to make such a view convincing. But such bravery as I have by no means extends to the foolhardiness of saying we are doing any more than balancing probabilities.

Isaiah 56–66, Malachi, Isaiah 24–27 and Joel

Apart from this hope, if it be such, in Haggai, somewhat moderated in Zechariah 1–8, we search other immediately postexilic prophecy in vain for any mention of the Davidic dynasty or any form of monarchy at all. Isaiah 56–66, much of which is often thought to originate from the period following 538 BCE, is silent on the subject. When God acts he comes among his people himself to effect his aims (e.g. 59.15b-20, 62.11, 63.1-7, 66.15-16). It is true that some speaker (in 61.1-4) claims anointing by the Spirit to fulfil a ministry of proclamation of what God is about to do, and the terms in which he describes his ministry are redolent of the Servant passages and other elements to be found in Second Isaiah. But there are no explicit royal characteristics assigned to this messenger. Malachi, a prophet usually dated between early and mid-fifth century BCE,[11] is equally silent on the subject. He predicts the

---

11. None of the arguments usually advanced to support this dating is unquestionable, yet it remains the most probable. See my *The Books of Haggai, Zechariah and Malachi* (Cambridge Bible Commentary; Cambridge: Cambridge University Press 1977), pp. 137-39.

coming of a 'messenger' of Yahweh, whose role will be to prepare for God's own coming to effect judgment (Mal. 3.1a, 5). Efforts to suggest that a 'royal' figure is intended here have not convinced, especially as Bentzen, who argued for this, had to emend the text to make his point.[12] Although the Chronicler uses the term 'messenger' in a very general way in 2 Chron. 36.15-16, 'The Lord, the God of their fathers, sent persistently to them by his messengers...' and has shown by the words attributed to them that those messengers included kings, the term in Mal. 3.1 is far more likely to have had a prophetic connotation, bearing in mind its echo of the title of the book, and the way the addition in 3.23-24, (ET 4.5-6) links it with Elijah.

The silence of the postexilic prophets other than Haggai and Zechariah, then, is deafening. It is reminiscent of the famous Sherlock Holmes saying about 'The curious incident of the dog that barked in the night'. When Watson objected that it did not bark Holmes replied, 'That is the curious incident'.

The position is little different if we turn to what is often termed the more 'apocalyptic'-type literature. Even if we transgress our self-denying ordinance and include Isaiah 24–27, the 'Isaiah Apocalypse', much of which, while possibly containing earlier material, may well be dated after, though not necessarily long after, the exile, there is not a whisper there of any messianic figure. All that is to happen in the future is to be direct action of God. The same is true of the book of Joel. In response to the penitence of priests and people God will come to live again in Zion as universal king and will subdue his enemies. There is no hint of any human agent or intermediary. Indeed, on the contrary, it is possible to see in 3.1-2 (ET 2.28-29), with its promise that God's spirit will be poured out on everybody so that even servants will be endowed and equipped to carry out the tasks hitherto the prerogative of the 'professionals', an almost Beaumarchais-like anti-clericalism and anti-establishmentarianism.[13] Indeed, when one thinks of the strong denunciation of all economic and political exploitation in such prophets as 'Trito-Isaiah' and Malachi, it is tempting to speculate whether the silence concerning monarchy in these postexilic prophets can be due

---

12. A. Bentzen, 'Priesterschaft und Laien in der jüdischen Gemeinde des fünften Jahrhunderts', *AfO* 6 (1930–31), pp. 280-86.

13. See P.L. Redditt, 'The Book of Joel and Peripheral Prophecy', *CBQ* 48 (1986), pp. 225-40, and also R.A. Mason, *Zephaniah, Habakkuk, Joel* (OTG; Sheffield: JSOT Press, 1994), pp. 125-27.

merely to the brevity and scarcity of the extant literature, its genre or accidental omission. May not some of the 'anti-monarchic' traditions to be found earlier, especially in sections of the Deuteronomistic History, have persisted? In many ways it would be surpising had they not after the exile when historical monarchy, in addition to the memory of all its pre-exilic abuses, could be seen to have 'failed'.[14]

Zechariah 9–14

This needs to be borne in mind when we turn to Zechariah 9–14, which has a number of features in common with Joel. For here the 'messianic silence' is broken, in the famous passage of 9.9-10 and the somewhat enigmatic 12.7–13.1. These chapters notoriously present the commentator with many problems of date, genre, inner cohesion, order, redaction and, above all, meaning. Some of these may mercifully be ignored here but some may not, since judgments about genre and composition in particular will affect how we interpret these passages and relate them to any 'overall' message the chapters may have. I have addressed elsewhere the question of why and how they may have come to be added to Zechariah 1–8 and have been engaged in a little good-natured discussion about this with John Day since.[15] As to chs. 9–14 themselves,

---

14. A recent study by E. Ben Zvi of Obadiah, which he regards as a postexilic text, emphasizes the absence of any hope of a restored monarchy there: *A Historical-Critical Study of the Book of Obadiah* (BZAW, 242; Berlin: W. de Gruyter, 1996), pp. 228, 258. This chimes with an even stronger set of conclusions he draws from the same lack of reference to the monarchy in the book of Zephaniah (which he also sees in its present form as a postexilic text), *A Historical-Critical Study of the Book of Zephaniah* (BZAW, 198; Berlin: W. de Gruyter, 1991). See especially p. 356 of the last-named work: 'Significantly, in this society, not only that the old social-political monarchical elite will have no place, but no other and just social-political elite is mentioned as replacing it. No human (or messianic) just and pious king, officer or judge is referred to; there is no expectation of their coming in the book... The only King in the ideal society will (be) YHWH; the only social group, those humble and poor people who rely on YHWH and speak no lies.' I discuss the prophetic and 'apocalyptic' reaction to the propaganda and power claims of monarchy and priesthood in R.A. Mason, *Propaganda and Subversion in the Old Testament* (London: SPCK, 1997), Chapters 5 and 6.

15. R.A. Mason, 'The Relation of Zechariah 9–14 to Proto-Zechariah', *ZAW*, 88, 1976, pp. 227-39. See J. Day, 'Prophecy', in D.A. Carson and H.G.M. Williamson (eds.), *It is Written: Scripture Citing Scripture. Essays in Honour of Barnabas Lindars* (Cambridge: Cambridge University Press 1988), pp. 39-55 (49).

opinions range all the way from some who have seen a tight chiastic structure throughout, to others who have given up all attempts to find any shape, regarding them as a loose collection of disparate and originally independent pericopae which they have dated all the way from the eighth century BCE to the Greek period.[16] Indeed, so diverse have been the results from attempts to 'date' the material from supposed historical allusions within it that the validity of the method must be questioned. Many commentators have supported the view that a new section begins with the heading *maśśā'* at 12.1 and have spoken of a Deutero- and Trito-Zechariah.

The only thing which can be done with confidence is to identify the main divisions of the text as it now stands. Zechariah 9.1–11.3 (omitting 10.1-3a) comprises a number of eschatological pieces, heavily dependent on earlier prophetic literature, with little apparent order and structure apart from a few editorial linking devices. They express sentiments and beliefs that are often inconsistent with each other, but they share a generally optimistic hope of salvation for Israel/Judah and judgment for their enemies. I have elsewhere referred to this section as forming a kind of 'eschatological hymnbook'. P.D. Hanson's view that ch. 9 is shaped in the form of a 'Divine warrior' hymn answers to a general pattern, which may be observable but requires a lot of fiddling with the details of the text and the ignoring of inner inconsistencies.[17] Two more eschatological sections occur in 12.1–13. 6 and in ch. 14. In

I think Day took it that I was claiming a close and specific literary dependence between the two, while I intended to argue only for a quite general thematic continuity.

16. The most thoroughgoing attempt to establish the first position was that of P. Lamarche, *Zacharie IX–XIV: Structure littéraire et messianisme* (Paris: J. Gabalda, 1961). A much more balanced approach can be found in M. Butterworth, *Structure and the Book of Zechariah* (JSOTSup, 130; Sheffield: Sheffield Academic Press, 1992). For the most recent position, see L. Bauer, *Zeit des Zweiten Tempels–Zeit der Gerechtigkeit* (Beiträge zur Erforschung des Alten Testaments und des Antiken Judentums, 31; Frankfurt am Main: Peter Lang, 1992). For a survey of more 'fragmentary' views see O. Eissfeldt, *Einleitung in das Alte Testament* (Tübingen: J.C.B. Mohr [Paul Siebeck], 3rd edn, 1964), pp. 587-90 (ET *The Old Testament: An Introduction* [trans. by P.R. Ackroyd; Oxford: Basil Blackwell, 1965], pp. 435-37).

17. See P.D. Hanson, 'Zechariah 9 and the Recapitulation of an Ancient Ritual Pattern', *JBL* 92 (1973), pp. 37-59, and *The Dawn of Apocalyptic: The Historical and Sociological Roots of Jewish Apocalyptic Eschatology* (Philadelphia: Fortress Press, 2nd edn, 1979).

each of these there is an increasing degree of anguish to be experienced by the people of God before the promised salvation arrives, and each of them has often been held to evince growingly sharp 'apocalyptic' characteristics, most markedly in ch. 14. Interspersed between these main sections are a number of 'controversy' passages in which 'shepherds' are attacked for their misdirection of the people—10.1-3a, 11.4-17, 13.7-9—these passages occurring across the alleged divide of the chapters at 12.1. Further, all the material is alike characterized by strong dependence on earlier biblical, and especially prophetic literature.[18] It is because of these strong attacks on leaders of the community, who are seen as false and who, as in earlier biblical prophetic books (especially Jeremiah and Ezekiel) are described as 'shepherds', that we find some links with Joel, with its call to priests to perform their proper task in leading the people in penitence and its possible vision of a future which dispenses with such traditional leaders. And it is the overall context in which we have to try to interpret and evaluate the 'messianic' passages.

With these preliminary observations I will now turn to Zech. 9.9-10.

> Daughter of Zion, rejoice with all your heart;
> shout in triumph, daughter of Jerusalem!
> See, your king is coming to you,
> his cause won, his victory gained,
> humble, and mounted on a donkey,
> on a colt, the foal of a donkey.
> He will banish the chariot from Ephraim,
> the war-horse from Jerusalem;
> the warrior's bow will be banished,
> and he will proclaim peace to the nations.
> His rule will extend from sea to sea,
> from the River to the ends of the earth. (REB)

This is marked off as a separate pericope since in 9.1-8, in a mixture of third and first person speech, it is God who will attack Israel's enemies, while bringing the Philistines in as his people, and who then will dwell at the sanctuary guarding his people from all future oppressors. It may be said that, in a general way, this action of God will have prepared the

---

18. See M. Delcor, 'Les Sources du Deutéro-Zacharie et ses procédés d'emprunt', *RB* 59 (1952), pp. 385-411, and R.A. Mason, 'The Use of Earlier Biblical Material in Zechariah 9–14: A Study in Inner-Biblical Exegesis' (unpublished doctoral thesis, University of London, 1973). I hope to return to this aspect of the study of Zech. 9–14 in a future work.

way for the peaceful rule of the king who comes, but the section beginning at v. 11 speaks of further action as God leads his people out against the heathen using his people as his bow, arrow and shield.

Who the king may be is unspecified. It can certainly not allude to Yahweh himself, for Yahweh in his first person divine speech refers to the king in the third person and the picture of Yahweh riding on a donkey is a somewhat strained one. As we have seen, the link between vv. 9-10 and their context in ch. 9 is very general. Indeed, the promise that there will be no more need of weapons of war in conditions of 'peace' in v. 10 appears inconsistent with the promise of v. 13 that God will use Judah as his bow, Ephraim as his arrow and will brandish the male inhabitants of Zion as a warrior's sword. We are, then, thrust back on the description of the king and his mission to afford us any clues as to what is intended here.

The first adjective is *ṣaddîq*, rendered by REB as 'his cause won'. This is a royal attribute, since the prayer is offered in Ps. 72.1 that God will give the king 'your *ṣᵉdāqâ* so that he may judge the people with righteousness. But it is also an attribute of the servant in Second Isaiah, since he claims in Isa. 50.8, 'he who pronounces me *ṣaddîq* is near' (the Hebrew is *maṣdîqî*). Certainly the word in Second Isaiah can almost be taken as the equivalent of 'victory', even if it carries the overtone of 'righteousness vindicated'. The second word is the niphal participle of the verbal root *yš'*, *nôšā'*. This could be rendered 'saved' but is more often translated by some such phrase as 'bearing salvation', or, as in REB, 'his victory gained'—that is, he is the human inter-mediary of God's *yᵉšû'â*, 'salvation/victory'. The same participle is used of the king in Ps. 33.16, which stresses that the king is not *nôšā'* by virtue of his great army or his great strength. Indeed the 'horse' is explicitly repudiated as a means of his experience of victory which, as the context makes clear, belongs to God alone. So it is interesting that in Zech. 9.10 God says, 'I will cut off the horse from Jerusalem'. Equally it is worth noting that in Isa. 49.6 God says to the 'servant', 'I will give you as a light to the nations that my salvation (*yᵉšû'ātî*) may reach to the ends of the earth'. The servant of Second Isaiah is also, then, a bearer of God's 'salvation'.

The next phrase, *'ānî*, raises more questions. It can be legitimately translated either as 'humble' or 'afflicted'. It is not used of the king. We could only therefore apply it to him if we were to accept some form of the idea of a 'ritual humiliation' of the king in a form of the New Year

Festival similar to that of the Babylonian *Akitu* festival.[19] Even if we do not accept that, we may note Johnson's point that it is only a 'humble' people who will experience God's deliverance and, in Ps. 18.28 (ET 27), this is presumably being expressed by the king, 'For thou dost save a humble (*'ānî*) people'.

But a point of further interest arises in the use of forms of the verbal root *'nh* in the final 'servant song' in Second Isaiah. In 53.4 we read, 'yet we esteemed him stricken, smitten by God and *afflicted*' (a pual participle), and again in v. 7, 'He was oppressed and *afflicted*' (niphal participle). It is difficult to avoid rendering this 'afflicted' in either instance, for the parallels of the roots *ng'*, *nkh* make the more active alternative to 'humbled' likely.

The riding on a donkey, of course, does not imply any special humility. On the contrary, the animal was regarded as a suitable royal mount in the ancient Near East.[20] Further, in the often quoted 'Blessing of Jacob', Gen. 49.11 suggests the donkey as a royal mount, a passage which might even have inspired Zech. 9.9. Yet surely significant is the abbreviated quotation from the royal Psalm 72 in the second half of v. 10. For the quotation from Psalm 72 continues, 'May his foes bow down before him, and his enemies lick the dust'. Instead of that we have the striking alternative, 'he will speak (or command) *šālôm* ('peace') to the nations'. Long ago W. Eisenbeis drew attention to the remarkable force of this in his study, *Die Wurzel* שלם *im Alten Testament*.[21]

The possibility that we have here, therefore, some deliberate reinterpretation of traditional messianic and royal ideology in the light of the suffering servant figure is an intriguing one. Meyers and Meyers dismiss the idea somewhat brusquely by saying, '... it would be overburdening the text to see it as a reflection of conflicting ideologies (as

---

19. As argued by A.R. Johnson, *Sacral Kingship in Ancient Israel* (Cardiff: Uniersity of Wales Press, 2nd edn, 1967).

20. See, e.g., S. Feigin, 'Babylonian Parallels to the Hebrew Phrase "Lowly, and Riding Upon an Ass"', in L. Ginzberg and A. Weiss (eds.), *Studies in Memory of Moses Schorr 1874–1941* (New York: The Professor Moses Schorr Memorial Committee, 1944), pp. 227-40 (in Hebrew). Meyers and Meyers mention (but do not cite) terms cognate to the Hebrew *ḥᵃmôr* at Ugarit and Mari used for animals on which a deity rides or that draw a ritual chariot (*Zechariah 9–14* [AB, 25C; Garden City, NY: Doubleday, 1993], p. 130).

21. W. Eisenbeis, *Die Wurzel* שלם *im Alten Testament* (BZAW, 113; Berlin: W. de Gruyter; 1969).

Hanson ... and Mason ...).[22] What does appear is that this figure must surely be intended as a deliberate and ideal contrast to the false 'shepherds' who are attacked so bitterly in the three 'controversy passages' for their abuse, exploitation and misdirection of the flock, much in the way such attacks are found in the books of Jeremiah and Ezekiel. Whether or not the thought that the royal figure of 9.9-10 is intended not only as a foil to them but also to traditional 'royal' and 'messianic' concepts must be left for each to judge. As with so much in these chapters, certainty in interpretation is difficult to arrive at.[23]

However, there is another passage which must bear on this and that is 12.7–13.1, in which there is specific mention of the 'house of David'. Once again the context is of God using his people to overcome the 'nations' who, in this instance, have come to lay siege to Jerusalem. It is a prosaic passage and many of the details of its interpretation remain unclear. The burden is that God will deliver Jerusalem and Judah from the threat. Indeed, the people of Judah will take heart from the way God strengthens the inhabitants of Jerusalem. However, God will give pride of place in delivering first those who dwell outside the capital in Judah 'so that the glory of the house of David and the glory of the inhabitants of Jerusalem may not be exalted over that of Judah' (v. 7). A very natural provincial suspicion of the capital seems to be at work here! But it certainly limits the role of the house of David. It is by no means the agent of deliverance but is every bit as passive as the king who comes in triumph in 9. 9-10. Indeed, there is even a hint they might be inclined to get a bit 'uppity' and so need to be kept in their proper place. It is extremely difficult to know what is meant by v. 8. That, inspired and strengthened by Yahweh's intervention on their behalf, the feeblest inhabitant of Jerusalem shall become 'like David', ready to take on 'lions' and 'giants' is not surprising, especially if they are not actually required to do any fighting! But what is the force of the statement that 'the house of David shall be like God'? That it was startling to inter-

---

22. Meyers and Meyers, *Zechariah 9–14*, p. 130.

23. A. Laato says of this passage, '...the humble and righteous king in 9:9-10 is in fact a programmatic criticism levelled at the members of the House of David because they failed to fulfil the hopes of restoration which prevailed among the Jews', in *Josiah and David Redivivus: The Historical Josiah and the Messianic Expectation of Exilic and Post-Exilic Times* (ConBOT, 33; Stockholm: Almqvist & Wiksell, 1992), p. 275. Like much in this book, this is interesting but goes beyond the evidence.

preters before us appears in the strong likelihood that the phrase 'like the angel of the Lord' was an addition aimed at softening the force of the first sentence. In the same way the Versions (Targum, LXX and Vulgate) have softening renderings. There is a possible parallel which might have been behind this, although it can be offered as a tentative suggestion only. There is a similar phrase in Exod. 4.16, where Moses complains that he cannot speak fittingly. God promises that Aaron shall be his spokesman, 'He shall speak for you to the people; and he shall be a mouth for you, and you shall be to him as God'. Moses, by virtue of his special relationship to God will enable Aaron to speak and act in accordance with Yahweh's mind and purpose. Yet Aaron is a vital link in the working out of that purpose. Is it possible that such a thought is implicit in Zech. 12.8? The house of David will be restored to its right relationship with God and thus will become an intermediary in God's purpose to renew the *whole* community. The house of David will again have a place and role in the renewed community, but it will no longer be the sole mediator of Yahweh's life and blessing. For, it becomes clear immediately afterward, the house of David needs to take its place alongside every other family and group in the community in mourning and repentance for what they have done to God (we may safely leave aside here the difficulties of v. 10 and exactly who it is they 'pierced'). It is because God pours out on the house of David and all the inhabitants of Jerusalem and all sections of the people a new spirit that they will all one day be cleansed by the fountain which God will open for the house of David *and* the inhabitants of Jerusalem (13.1). All need it, and all will experience it because of the divine outpouring of a new spirit. We are not so far from the spirit of Joel 3.1-5 (ET 2.28-32). This sees a place for a Davidic family, therefore, but it is far from the 'messianic deliverer' kind of picture we normally think of. For all its difficulties, this passage may be seen to provide some support for a view of 9.9-10 as offering an alternative royal ideology.[24]

Daniel

As far as the more 'apocalyptic' type of postexilic biblical literature goes, that appears to be it. The last great representative of the genre, in

---

24. Laato, in *Josiah and David Redivivus*, says that these chapters come from a group who blamed the Davidides for failing to live up to their ideal. Yet they still held out hopes for dynasty and Temple and that is why the Davidic house will one day mourn its failures (see esp. pp. 300-301).

the view of some the only true form of the genre in the Old Testament, the book of Daniel, need not detain us long since it does not lay great emphasis on messianism, and lacks any specific reference to the Davidic dynasty. The infinitive of the verb *māšaḥ* occurs in 9.24, in a retrospect of history (in the guise of prophecy) from the fall of Jerusalem to the time of the writer in the second century BCE. What, or whom is to be 'anointed' at the end of that period is a 'holy of holies', or 'a most holy'. Commentators have divided over whether this is a reference to the Temple or to a person. If the reference is to the Temple, then clearly no kind of 'royal' messianism is being envisaged. If to a person, however, there is no clear suggestion that he is seen as a *royal* figure. It would appear rather more naturally to be a priestly one. Lacocque, who is among those who interpret it as a person, finds here a reference to someone who symbolizes the 'saints of the Most High', thus embodying the idea of Israel as 'a kingdom of priests'.[25] The following verse speaks of the coming of an 'anointed one' (*māšîaḥ*), 'seven weeks' (i.e. forty-nine years, see the reinterpretation of Jer. 25.12 and 29.10 as 'seventy weeks of years') into the 'seventy weeks' period which stretches from Jeremiah's prediction of the rebuilding of Jerusalem following the Babylonian exile until the defeat of Antiochus Epiphanes. This 'anointed one' is further described as *nāgîd*, usually translated 'prince', but a term used both of kings and of priests. As such, this might be a reference either to Zerubbabel or to Joshua, who are recorded as being placed in positions of power after the exile. It is difficult to be dogmatic about the exact force of such highly symbolic language and such vague time references. However, the fact that in 11.22, in a clear reference to the overthrow of the priestly Onias III, he can be described as a '*nāgîd* of the covenant' (in Hebrew the word is in the construct) suggests that the reference in 9.25 is more likely to be to one of the priestly line and, if so, the term *nāgîd* would suggest an enhanced role for the priestly line after the exile. We seem to be reckoning with the idea of a renewal of the kind of theocracy envisaged by the Priestly writers and the Chronicler and in the present form of the books of Haggai and Zechariah 1–8. The Chronicler several times uses the term of priests or Levites who had positions of responsibility in oversight of the Temple (e.g. 1 Chron. 9.11; 2 Chron. 35.8). Among such circles, and it appears we have to include the book of Daniel among them, in Lacocque's

---

25. A. Lacocque, *The Book of Daniel* (trans. David Pellauer; London: SPCK, 1979), pp. 193-94.

words, 'we pass from a hope for the Davidic line to a priestly type of eschatology'.[26]

There has been an immense amount of discussion as to the meaning of the term 'one like a son of man' in ch. 7.[27] Whoever is meant, he is no deliverer come down from heaven. On the contrary, he comes *to* the Ancient of Days (v. 13) and is presented before him. He *receives* dominion, glory and rule, presumably in a representative capacity. Even if there are some elements of royal ideology here, particularly reflecting as the chapter does some of the psalms of Yahweh's enthronement, no specific or detailed portrayal of the one like a son of man in terms of a descendant of the Davidic dynasty is even so much as hinted at. There are certainly parallels to the description of other heavenly, angelic figures in the book (8.15, 10.16,18) and, again, as with the 'holy of holies' in 9.24, we may be faced with the understanding of a heavenly counterpart of the people of God in the heavenly realm. There is a close relationship throughout the book between the earthly and heavenly realms, people and events on earth being seen as in some ways projections of figures who are acting, and of events which are taking place, in heaven.[28] Nevertheless, the fact remains that this 'heavenly figure' is not the agent of deliverance. He receives the kingdom on behalf of the people from God. The decisive act of salvation is God's direct accomplishment.

The Chronicler

This brings us finally to the picture of David and his dynasty presented by the Chronicler. It is clear that he gives David and Solomon a central place as he does to the Davidic dynasty as a whole. Hugh Williamson has shown how he structures his history on this theme, first with the ideal period of the united monarchy under David and Solomon, then the period of the divided monarchy when the 'estranged brethren' of the north have been misled from their true allegiance, and finally the period of the reunited monarchy which, for the Chronicler, begins with

---

26. Lacocque, *The Book of Daniel*, p. 195.

27. The matter is fully discussed by John Day, *God's Conflict with the Dragon and the Sea: Echoes of a Canaanite Myth in the Old Testament* (UCOP, 35; Cambridge: Cambridge University Press, 1985), pp. 151-78.

28. A point strongly emphasized by J.J. Collins, *The Apocalyptic Vision of the Book of Daniel* (HSM, 16; Missoula, MT: Scholars Press, 1977). See esp. p. 165.

Hezekiah.[29] It is often pointed out that the Chronicler bypasses the
Exodus in favour of putting all emphasis on David and his line. To an
extent that is true but it must not be overstated. For he does show David
as a 'second Moses' and this presentation owes a great deal to the
Priestly tradition of the Pentateuch. Just as Moses was presented by
God with a 'blueprint' (*tabnît*) of the Tabernacle and all its fittings
(Exod. 25.9, 40), so David passes on a 'blueprint' of the sanctuary and
all its arrangements to Solomon (1 Chron. 28.11, 12, 18, 19). Just as
Moses collected gifts from the people for the ornamentation of the
tabernacle (Exod. 35.4-29), so David does the same (1 Chron. 29.6-9).
In fact, the Chronicler's presentation of David is entirely that, not of
Temple-builder exactly, for Solomon builds it, but one mainly concerned with the Temple. David gathers all the materials and the plan
and passes on to Solomon a do-it-yourself kit which, as all the do-it-
yourself toys and models I ever bought for my children said in their
instructions, was 'so simple a child could do it'! It is not quite true to
say that the Chronicler passes over every fault of David which the
Deuteronomistic History recorded. He mentions David's sin in taking a
census of the people (1 Chron. 21), although its origin is in the incite-
ment of 'Satan', not Yahweh as in 2 Samuel 24, and it leads to an act of
sacrifice on the site of the future Temple. It is freely acknowledged that
David was a 'man of blood' and this is why he was forbidden to build
the Temple himself, as opposed to the Deuteronomistic History, which
says that he was too busy fighting his many battles to get around to it
(1 Chron. 22.8; cf. 1 Kgs 5.17, ET 3). Nevertheless, it is a sanitized
picture of David that is presented and far greater attention is given to
his actions in preparation for the building of the Temple and founding
all its orders of personnel and sacred festivals than to the historical
events which engaged the attention of the earlier work. The divine
choice of David and his line is given even greater emphasis by the
Chronicler (1 Chron. 28.4, 5; 2 Chron.13.5). The enormity of the sin of
schism by northern Israel under Jeroboam is stressed by Abijah: 'Should
you not know that Yahweh, the God of Israel, has given the kingdom
over Israel to David and his successors for ever by an immutable
covenant?' (2 Chron. 13.5). It is true that Jeroboam had been led astray
by worthless men, but he continues, 'Now you intend to fight against
the kingdom of Yahweh entrusted to David's descendants' (v. 8).

29. See H.G.M. Williamson, *Israel in the Books of Chronicles* (Cambridge:
Cambridge University Press, 1977), pp. 110-18.

Now it is just this emphasis on David and his dynasty and this stress on the immutability of the covenant made with him (the Chronicler retains the Nathan oracle of 2 Sam. 7 in 1 Chron. 17) which has led a number of commentators to see a real 'messianism' in the Chronicler's work. He could never have spoken like this had he not believed that it was God's purpose to restore the historic Davidic line. Indeed, there is a tantalizing hint in the speech of Shemaiah at the time of Shishak's invasion (2 Chron. 12.5-8). Shemaiah, announcing God's judgment against Jerusalem says, 'But they shall be subject to him so that they may experience both my service and service of kingdoms of this world' (my translation). Does that not suggest just the situation of Judah after the exile? They live within the tension of being both God's subjects and the subjects of their Persian overlords. Does the Chronicler mention this to say that it will be a permanent state of affairs, or does it carry a promise that ultimately God will restore their political freedom to them again? Why does the Chronicler contain references to the eternity of God's covenant with David which are peculiar to him (e.g. 2 Chron. 13.5)? All of this has led many to speak of the 'messianism' of the Chronicler.[30]

Nevertheless, exactly the same material has led others to deny any messianism in the books of Chronicles at all and to stress that the Chronicler's real purpose is to establish the divine foundation of the postexilic Temple theocracy as the true goal and heir of the historic Davidic line.[31] So, in David's speech in 1 Chron. 28.2-10 great stress is

---

30. The possible bibliography here is enormous, but see A.-M. Brunet, 'La théologie du Chroniste: Théocratie et Messianisme', in J. Coppens, A. Descamps and E. Massaux (eds.), *Sacra Pagina: Miscellanea Biblica Congressus Internationalis Catholici de Re Biblica*, I (BETL, 12–13; Paris, Duculot, 1959), pp. 384-97; D.N. Freedman, 'The Chronicler's Purpose', *CBQ* 23, (1961), pp. 436-42; W.F. Stinespring, 'Eschatology in Chronicles', JBL 80 (1961), pp. 209-19; R. North, 'Theology of the Chronicler', *JBL* 82 (1963), pp. 369-81; J.D. Newsome Jr, 'Towards a New Understanding of the Chronicler and His Purpose', *JBL* 94 (1975), pp. 201-17; Tae-Soo Im, *Das Davidbild in den Chronikbüchern: David als Idealbild theokratischen Messianismus für den Chronisten* (Europäische Hochschulschriften, 23.263; Frankfurt: Peter Lang, 1985); Brian E. Kelly, *Retribution and Eschatology in Chronicles* (JSOTSup, 211; Sheffield: Sheffield Academic Press; 1996).

31. Again, from a large bibliography see particularly André Caquot, 'Peut-on parler de messianisme dans l'oeuvre du Chroniste?', *RTP* 16 (1966), pp. 110-20; P.R. Ackroyd, 'History and Theology in the Writings of the Chronicler', in P.R.

laid on the divine choice of David, a choice running through the tribe of Judah, and his father's family to David himself. But that is not the goal of the process: 'And from all my sons (for Yahweh has given me many sons) he chose Solomon to sit on the throne of Yahweh's kingdom over Israel'. Why? '...for Yahweh has chosen you to build a Temple for him as a sanctuary'. That is the goal of the whole divine process of the choice of David and his descendants. Again, in David's charge to Solomon in 1 Chron. 28.20-21, he assures his son of Yahweh's presence with him. 'He will not let you down or desert you *until all the work in the service of Yahweh's sanctuary is complete*' (v. 20). Of course, that cannot be taken to mean that, once the Temple was completed, God would desert Solomon, but it does emphasize the goal of the divine choice.

Further, all those who are presented as faithful kings by the Chronicler are shown to be those who act in a 'David-like way' towards the Temple, rebuilding it, cleansing it, restoring its worship 'according to the order of David', as Jehoiada's action in cleansing the Temple is described (2 Chron. 23.18).

Again, the Chronicler's description of the rule of any Davidide should be noted, a description which we saw above in the words of David himself. It is always 'the throne of Yahweh's kingdom over Israel', not that of its human occupier (1 Chron. 28.5). And the divine choice extends to other Temple personnel besides the king, as Hezekiah reminds the Levites and priests: 'My children, do not be negligent now, for God has chosen you to stand in his presence, to lead worship to him and offer him worship and sacrifice' (2 Chron. 29.11).

Ackroyd, *The Chronicler in His Age* (JSOTSup, 101, Sheffield: Sheffield Academic Press; 1991), pp. 252-72, esp. pp. 268-69; J.Becker, *Messiaserwartung im Alten Testament* (SBS, 83; Stuttgart: Katholisches Bibelwerk, 1977), esp. pp. 75-77 (ET *Messianic Expectation in the Old Testament* [trans. D.E. Green; Fortress Press: Philadelphia, 1977], esp. pp. 80-82); R.A. Mason, *Preaching the Tradition: Homily and Hermeneutics after the Exile* (Cambridge: Cambridge University Press; 1990); W. Riley, *King and Cultus in Chronicles: Worship and the Reinterpretation of History* (JSOTSup, 160; Sheffield: Sheffield Academic Press, 1993). A mediating role between the two extreme views of total messianism or none is expressed by H.G.M. Williamson, 'Eshatology in Chronicles', *TynBul* 28 (1977), pp. 115-54. He summarizes his view by saying, '...it is by no means certain that Chr. is completely devoid of all messianism, even though it is clearly subordinated to other themes': *Israel in the Books of Chronicles*, p. 135.

Finally, we should note also that the Chronicler does not end his history where the Deuteronomistic historians ended theirs, with the restoration of the Davidic king to some kind of favour in Babylon. It ends with the decree of Cyrus which speaks of the restoration, not of the Davidic line, but of the Temple.

On this view, then, the Davidic dynasty for the Chronicler was not an end in itself but God's choice of agent to prepare for the postexilic Temple theocracy which has now replaced and fulfilled it. It is in this sense that the promises of an 'eternal' covenant with David find expression. Ackroyd speaks for this 'theocratic' position when he says, 'It [i.e. the postexilic Temple theocracy] is rather the embodiment of the David/Jerusalem theme no longer in political but in theological terms, in relation to the life and worship of the little Judaean community of his [i.e. the Chronicler's] own time'. Or, again, there is a 're-embodiment of the Davidic ideal in terms of what temple and cultus now mean'.[32] 'It is not a Davidic monarchy which the Chronicler hopes to see restored; it is the expression in the life of the community, particularly in its being gathered around the temple and its worship, of what David had established.'[33] (Of course, to take this view is not to deny that the Chronicler has an eschatological hope for the future. It is to deny that a restored Davidic dynasty has any significant part in it.)

Conclusion

If this is so then we have two major reinterpretations of the Davidic 'messianic' idea after 586 BCE. We have the 'democratization' of the concept in Isa. 55.3-5, an idea not without its echo, perhaps, in Joel and Zechariah 9–14.[34] In the Chronicler's writings we have what might be

32. Ackroyd, *The Chronicler in his Age*, p. 268.
33. Ackroyd, *The Chronicler in his Age*, p. 71.
34. Mowinckel's interpretation of Isa. 55.3-5 as still expressing a hope for a future Davidic messiah now seems very strange. He says, 'The future kingdom is founded on a renewal and fulfilment of precisely this concrete expression of the covenant, "the sure promises of the favour of David" (Isa. lv 3f.). The scion of David is so natural an element in the description of the future, that he is often not mentioned but tacitly assumed. That is so, for instance, in the passage in Deutero-Isaiah just referred to about the restoration of the Davidic covenant' (*He That Cometh*, p. 170). Much more general nowadays is the view expressed by R.N. Whybray: 'these verses contain no promise of the restoration of the Davidic monarchy in the person of one of David's descendants; rather what is stated here is that

termed a 'theocratization' of the idea.

In summary, then, we have to say how little influence the concept of a renewal of the Davidic line after the exile exercised in the extant post-exilic biblical literature. Apart from some possible hope of it expressed by Haggai, a hope somewhat diminished in the present form of Zechariah 1–8, it occurs, where it occurs at all, either to be reinterpreted and its fulfilment looked for in other ways, or to be severely modified, as in Zechariah 9–14. Otherwise it is ignored.

the covenant promises, originally made to David as the leader of the nation, are now transferred directly to the whole people' (*Isaiah 40–66* [NCB; London: Oliphants 1975], p.192).

THE MESSIAH IN OLD TESTAMENT THEOLOGY

John Barton

Our subject is the Messiah in Old Testament theology; but what is Old Testament theology? The very idea of such a discipline has come under fire in recent years, from two directions. First, there are those who say that writing a theology of the Old Testament is a Christian tendency, whose covert aim is to claim the Old Testament for Christianity and take it away from the Jews. There is no doubt that very few Jewish scholars have shown much interest in Old Testament theology, even when renamed Hebrew Bible theology. The case against it has been strongly argued by Jon D. Levenson, who tries to show that most Old Testament theologians have tried to unify the theological ideas of the Old Testament in such a way as to show that they contain a Christ-shaped hole, in other words that they require 'fulfilment' through the (alleged) Christian revelation.[1] I do not want to discuss this objection in detail, but note it here because I shall come back to it later, since it has a particular relevance to the question of the Messiah, the topic *par excellence* where Christian scholars may be expected to distort the natural contours of the Hebrew Scriptures.

The second objection to Old Testament theology has been advanced in the last few years above all by Rainer Albertz, in his two-volume work, *A History of Israelite Religion*.[2] Albertz shares the suspicion that Old Testament theology as traditionally conceived has had an inbuilt tendency to anti-Judaism or even to anti-Semitism, but this is not his main reason for rejecting it. Primarily he dislikes theologies of the Old

---

1. See J.D. Levenson, 'Why Jews are not Interested in Biblical Theology', in J. Neusner *et al.* (eds.), *Judaic Perspectives on Ancient Israel* (Philadelphia: Fortress Press 1987), pp. 281-307.

2. R. Albertz, *Religionsgeschichte Israels in alttestamentlicher Zeit* (Göttingen: Vandenhoek & Ruprecht, 1992) (ET *A History of Israelite Religion in Old Testament Times* [trans. J. Bowden; London: SCM Press, 1994]).

Testament as inappropriately systematizing data from different periods, different types of literature, different strata in society to make a fictitious theological unity, a creed, we might say, that no given historical person ever actually believed in. The more large-scale the theological scheme—and some, notably those of Eichrodt[3] and von Rad,[4] have been on a very large scale indeed—the less it does justice to the concrete reality of what people in ancient Israel in fact believed, and the more it becomes a kind of 'official' version of 'the faith of Israel' (to use Rowley's expression[5]). But the danger with this—and here Albertz's objection converges with the Jewish one—is that it is very likely to be shaped by the actual theological beliefs of the interpreter. Since the interpreter is likely to be Christian, almost inevitably the contours of the alleged 'faith of Israel' will be dictated by a Christian theological agenda. The Old Testament will be recognized as different from the New Testament, but the difference will be seen as a series of mortises into which the tenons of New Testament faith can be neatly fitted. The possibility that people in ancient Israel had, as people say nowadays, a different problematic from early (let alone modern) Christians will not be given a fair hearing, indeed will not even be noticed.

In Albertz's view, Old Testament theology should be replaced by the study of Israelite religion. At first glance one might think that this proposal goes too far in the opposite direction. If Old Testament theology concentrates too much on a supposed underlying structure of belief in ancient Israel, when in reality hardly anything can be known of what people actually *believed* in a spiritual or intellectual sense, one might object against Albertz that the study of the religion of Old Testament times ignores belief altogether in favour of concentrating on the external manifestations of religion: the cult, sacrifices, festivals, and so on. What becomes clear as one reads on in Albertz's work, however, is that he uses the term 'the religion of Israel' in a sufficiently broad way as to include quite a lot of what is commonly understood by Old Testament theology. His study is not a positivistic accumulation of

3. W. Eichrodt, *Theologie des Alten Testaments* (Stuttgart: Klotz, 6th edn, 1964 [5th edn, 1959]) (ET *Theology of the Old Testament* [trans. J.A. Baker; London: SCM Press, 1967 (1961)]).

4. G. von Rad, *Theologie des Alten Testaments* (Munich: Chr. Kaiser Verlag, 1957–60) (ET *Old Testament Theology* [trans. D.M.G. Stalker; Edinburgh: Oliver & Boyd, 1962–65]).

5. See H.H. Rowley, *The Faith of Israel* (London: SCM Press, 1956).

detailed facts about how many times people offered which sacrifices where and when. It also encompasses the question why they did so, what they thought they were up to; and that question inevitably involves matters that we should naturally call theological. Theology becomes a much less central concern for students of the Old Testament than it has been for much of the present century, but it does not fall out of the frame altogether, as one might imagine (or hope, or fear).

Albertz thus leaves open the possibility that one might write a theology of the Old Testament, not merely a phenomenology of the religion of ancient Israel, though he does not do much to illustrate the possibility. What should be noted, however, is that a theology in his sense would still have to be essentially historical, rather than a synthesis of what was believed in many periods or an analysis of some supposed essence of that belief. It would, that is to say, be a theology in the sense propounded by Gabler,[6] or in this century by Krister Stendahl: a statement of *what people believed*, not of what we should believe on account of having the Old Testament as our Scripture. The latter project, if legitimate at all, belongs to systematic theology, not to biblical studies. Where the Messiah is concerned, Old Testament theology in the sense allowed by Albertz could say what people at various times believed about the Messiah—a task to which other papers in this series have been contributing a lot—but not what the Messiah is 'really' like or whether Jesus of Nazareth fulfils the conditions necessary to confess him as that Messiah. The truth of Old Testament, of biblical theology is historical truth, the discipline is as Gabler insisted *e genere historico*: it is not the ultimate or metaphysical truth to which systematic theology aspires.

This still leaves an irreconcilable difference from Old Testament Theology as practised by, say, Gerhard von Rad. Von Rad, just as much as a canonical critic in our own day, approached the Old Testament as part of canonical Christian Scripture, and his understanding of what made it hang together was not driven by the empirical discovery of what various people in Israel believed from time to time, but by a quest for a theological shape that would enable it to flow into the New Testament. The Jewish suspicion of Christian Old Testament theology is justified to a great extent where von Rad is concerned, though we would do well to remember that in von Rad's own historical context

6.   J.P. Gabler, *Oratio de iusto discrimine theologiae biblicae et dogmaticae regundisque recte utriusque finibus* (Altdorf: n.p., 1787), in his *Kleinere theologische Schriften*, II (Ulm: Sumtibus Stettin, 1831), pp. 179-98.

any principled defence of the Old Testament was a stand against anti-Semitism—even if to our present eyes it looks as though the price he paid, by reading the Old Testament through New Testament eyes, was too high. The idea of *Heilsgeschichte* which dominates von Rad's conception of Old Testament faith is an idea that arises from a Christian sense of a divinely guided history in which the arrival of Jesus as Messiah is the final stage; it is not a central Jewish idea, not at least as Judaism has come to be in our times. If we want to say that it was normative before Judaism took its decisive 'rabbinic' turn, then we shall find ourselves having to declare that ancient Israel believed in something which Christianity built on, even though in the intervening period the Jews had lost sight of it: which leads to that emphasis on the pre-exilic period which until very recently was universal in Old Testament scholarship, and to that denigration of the Second Temple and all that went with it which is the heritage of Wellhausen, and which von Rad accepted as a matter of course. Since most of the 'messianic' texts in Scripture are probably postexilic, this would make a problem for our present concern. For von Rad, however, it is avoided because of his study of the Deuteronomistic History in his article 'The Deuteronomic Theology of History in I and II Kings',[7] where he seeks to show how central to the D History are the promises to David, which are bound to be fulfilled sooner or later. His immediate purpose is simply to argue that the History is hopeful, not (as Martin Noth maintained) pessimistic.[8] But I think it is not reading too much between the lines to detect a subtext or hidden agenda, which is to do with the fact that the Davidic promises never were fulfilled in the new dispensation after the exile. The restoration of the imprisoned Jehoiachin (2 Kgs 25.27-30) is a beginning, but there remains a great surplus of still unfulfilled Davidic prophecy. And just as, for the writer to the Hebrews, the original settlement of the Promised Land under Joshua was only a foretaste of the entry into the heavenly realm accomplished through the new Joshua,

---

7. G. von Rad, 'Die deuteronomistische Geschichtstheologie in den Königsbüchern', in *Gesammelte Studien zum Alten Testament* (TBü, 8; Munich: Chr. Kaiser Verlag, 1958), pp. 189-204 (ET 'The Deuteronomic Theology of History in I and II Kings', in *The Problem of the Hexateuch and Other Essays* [trans. E.W. Trueman Dicken; Edinburgh: Oliver & Boyd, 1966], pp. 205-21).

8. See M. Noth, *Überlieferungsgeschichtliche Studien*, in *Gesammelte Studien zum Alten Testamen* (Munich: Chr. Kaiser Verlag, 1958 [Tübingen: Niemeyer, 2nd edn, 1957]), pp. 1-110 (ET *The Deuteronomistic History* [trans. H.G.M. Williamson; JSOTSup, 15; Sheffield: JSOT Press, 1981]).

Jesus (Heb. 4.8-9), so for von Rad the rather pathetic 'restoration' of the last king of the Davidic line merely hinted at the coming of the true and final David. So, at least, it seems to me. There is more going on in von Rad's Old Testament theology than meets the eye.

So far I have talked about two options in the pursuit of Old Testament theology. There is a historical option, which is certainly theological in that it is concerned with the religious beliefs of the biblical writers and of the people who stand behind them: prophets, kings, officials, priests, landowners, peasants, and so on. The idea of the Messiah is a theological concept through and through, and any historical study of it is therefore bound to be also theological. But it is theological à la Gabler, not in the manner of a systematizing Old Testament theology. There is also the option pursued most clearly, as I would see it, by von Rad, which is systematizing. But the problem with this is that it so easily does less than justice to the historical variety and inconsistency lying behind our texts, and is so apt to import Christian ideas into the Old Testament. One might criticize von Rad, in effect, for bad faith: he claims to be writing an Old Testament theology which is historically rooted, but in practice he produces Christian theology loosely draped across a number of Old Testament pegs. Where the Messiah is concerned, he says little overtly, which is not surprising, given that the Old Testament for him hardly contains the postexilic texts where the Messiah is most (if indeed at all) to be encountered; but he smuggles a messianic interpretation into his Old Testament exegesis in a way that can only serve to show how threadbare the idea of a Christian Old Testament theology really is. The only solution to von Rad's difficulties, it seems to me, is to go more consistently down the road of integrating the two Testaments into a single canon, eschew historical concerns altogether, and practise a consistent canonical criticism.

For reasons which I cannot go into here, I am not personally convinced that the canonical approach will bring us into the Promised Land.[9] But if that is so, then the future for an Old Testament theology that is more than an empirical description of the realities of faith in Israel, that has something to say about the religious claims of the Old Testament text and its significance for either Jews or Christians, looks rather bleak. Aporia would seem to be the order of the day. Is there any way forward?

9. See my comments in *Reading the Old Testament: Method in Biblical Study* (London: Darton, Longman & Todd, 2nd edn, 1996 [1984]), pp. 77-103.

In 1994 I wrote a paper for a session at the International SBL meeting in Leuven dedicated to discussion of Albertz's work, and set out to ask whether there can be any Old Testament theology after Albertz.[10] I suggested that one might accept Albertz's argument that the history of Israelite religion is a more powerful tool than a traditionally conceived Old Testament theology for unifying the discipline of Old Testament studies around a theological centre, but might still wish to identify a space in the study of the Old Testament which the history of Israelite religion does not wholly fill—a kind of theology-shaped gap. The history of Israelite religion does not help with the task of connecting the theological concepts and insights of ancient Israel (as evidenced by the Old Testament) with the theological concerns of people in the later religious traditions that it nourishes. There needs to be some kind of interface between biblical study and systematic theology, for example, and it is not the task only of systematicians to investigate this; it is also the task of Old Testament specialists. 'Old Testament theology' might be an appropriate name for the enterprise, even if that is not exactly how the term has been used in the past.

I believe that the first aim of the scholar interested in theological aspects of the Old Testament must be historical and descriptive: we should not try to go back behind Gabler's formula *e genere historico* in the attempt to produce an account of what is in the Old Testament that is driven by a theological, *a priori* commitment to what we think ought to be in it. But description is not a purely factual, positivistic assembling of data. It already has an interpretative aspect too. How we describe the phenomena we have discovered inevitably involves using terms we ourselves can understand, which are not necessarily (and sometimes are necessarily not) terms that people in ancient Israel would have understood. It is therefore essential that we should compare their religious categories with ours, realizing that complete understanding is of course impossible, but not allowing this to produce a kind of nihilism in which ancient questions and modern questions are seen as so different that no kind of dialogue is possible. Somewhere the study of theology needs to have room for systematic theologians and biblical specialists to talk to each other about Old Testament texts. And anyone

10. J. Barton, 'Alttestamentliche Theologie nach Albertz? Religionsgeschichte oder Theologie des Alten Testaments', in B. Janowski, N. Lohfink *et al.* (eds.), *Religionsgeschichte oder Theologie des Alten Testaments* (Jahrbuch für Biblische Theologie, 10; Neukirchen–Vluyn: Neukirchener Verlag, 1995), pp. 25-34.

who helped to mediate in that discussion could reasonably be called an Old Testament theologian—though I have no commitment to that term in itself.

In effect, biblical theology as I am defining it is a critical analysis of the reception history of biblical texts, but one which compares that history carefully both with the original meaning of the texts and with the theological doctrine that has both resulted from and been read back into the texts in question.

In my article I illustrated this idea from the book of Ezekiel, which has often been taken to exemplify what might be called 'biblical monotheism', but which on a modern critical analysis is much nearer to the polytheism from which Judaeo-Christian monotheism emerged than a practitioner of Old Testament theology would probably want to think. I suggested, for example, that when Yahweh in Ezekiel acts 'for the sake of his holy name', that originally meant not 'out of his own sovereign freedom', but 'in order to protect his (fragile) reputation'; and that this concern for what the neighbours will say is in some ways the opposite of what the philosophical stream in Judaism or Christianity means by the omnipotence of the one and only God. But I also urged that that very philosophical tradition would not have come into being without texts such as Ezekiel, which laid the foundation for thinking about divine transcendence in such a way that something emerged which it is not unreasonable to call 'biblical' monotheism. We partly misread Ezekiel if we think it is about monotheism or divine omnipotence in our sense: yet the distorting lens through which we read the book is itself partly a result of the book's existence and contents. This is something like what in postmodernist theory is called a 'feedback loop', where information generated by a given system begins to scrutinize that system itself. Some such model seems to be required if we are to make any progress in understanding the relation of biblical texts to the theological concepts and systems which are partly their product but partly the framework through which we read them.

My question here is whether we could undertake a similar examination of the idea of the Messiah. Could we admit straightforwardly that the Messiah was not an important theme in most Old Testament books, and therefore probably not in the minds of most people in postexilic Israel, yet still see some lines of connection between the Old Testament texts that later messianism appealed to and the fully fledged messianic doctrine that, in different ways, has played an important role in both

Jewish and Christian belief? So far as I am aware comparatively little work has been done that would contribute to this possibility, unless perhaps by the Scandinavian critics to whom messianism was so much more interesting than it seems to have been to German or English-speaking scholars. I think of Mowinckel's great work, *He That Cometh*,[11] and of course of the book from which the present volume takes its title, Aage Bentzen's *King and Messiah*, originally published in German as *Messias–Moses redivivus–Menschensohn*,[12] a title which is a fairer pointer to its synthesizing and patternistic intention. These works attempted to trace the acorn in the oak: to show a certain appropriateness or inevitability in the way early Israelite conceptions of sacral kingship evolved into the idea of the Messiah. We might say that they illustrate the constructive, as well as the critical, function of Old Testament study within theology. They help to show that the job of the biblical critic is not merely to tell systematic theologians that the biblical texts do not mean what theology has thought they meant, but sometimes also to show how they are at least congruous with later developments. Reading Bentzen again to prepare this article, I was struck with a certain affinity to Brevard Childs, a concern for the wholeness of the Old Testament text as a witness to divine providence, which has not been common in studies of the Messiah by critical scholars in other traditions.[13] A less theological work, but one which is also interested in tracing the development of a messianic idea back to the ideology of kingship in Israel from Saul onwards, is the study by Tryggve Mettinger, also called *King and Messiah*.[14] In the Scandinavian tradition, as I see it, there is a concern not to lose sight of the wood by concentrating too much on the trees, to avoid the minimalism which might lead an English-speaking or German-speaking critic to note that the developed Messiah concept is not yet present in pre- and most post-exilic literature, and so to declare the idea simply post-biblical. Instead, scholars like Bentzen saw the development from king to Messiah as a

11. S. Mowinckel, *Han som kommer* (Copenhagen: G.E.C. Gad, 1951) (ET *He That Cometh* [trans. G.W. Anderson; Oxford: Basil Blackwell, 1956]).

12. A. Bentzen, *Messias–Moses redivivus–Menschensohn* (ATANT, 17; Zürich: Zwingli Verlag, 1948) (ET *King and Messiah* [trans. G.W. Anderson; London: Lutterworth Press, 1955]).

13. Cf. B.S. Childs, *Biblical Theology of the Old and New Testaments* (London: SCM Press, 1992).

14. T.N.D. Mettinger, *King and Messiah: The Civil and Sacral Legitimation of the Israelite Kings* (ConBOT, 8; Lund: C.W.K. Gleerup, 1976).

smooth and coherent one. The seeds of messianism were present in Israelite thought from very early times, although they did not sprout and blossom till the post-biblical period.

We might say that, despite this, Bentzen's concern remains primarily historical. He brings biblical texts into contact with post-biblical concepts, but he does not ask how they might relate to the concerns of modern systematic theology. This question could be asked, however, along the same lines as my brief discussion of Ezekiel, and in the remaining pages of this article I should like to sketch a possible discussion of it.

I began with a definition of Old Testament theology, but to say anything sensible about the Messiah within such a theology we also need a definition of the Messiah. The problem here is that it can be defined very narrowly or very broadly. A very narrow definition would make the link with the Israelite king explicit, and would regard any expected deliverer as the Messiah only if he was a new David, a descendant of the pre-exilic monarchs. This is how many Jews and Christians understood the 'messianic' prophecies in Jer. 23.5-6 or 33.14-18, and it is the reason why, in order to justify the claim of Jesus to be the Messiah, the New Testament writers had to show that he was of the line of David; if he were not, he could not be the Messiah. Hence the Matthaean and Lukan genealogies, the nativity in Bethlehem, and so on. A very broad definition of the Messiah would be that used by most sociologists, where the term is used by analogy with the Jewish and Christian tradition to apply to any charismatic leader, real or expected. Of course terms are ours to use, and there is no point in saying that one or other of these uses, or any other, is the 'true' meaning of the term 'Messiah' as it exists in modern English, as opposed to ancient Hebrew or Aramaic. But for the biblical scholar neither use is very helpful, because they filter out either too many texts or too few. I think a good definition is that provided by Jacob Neusner in the collection *Judaisms and their Messiahs at the Turn of the Christian Era*, which begins like this:

> A Judaism comprises a world view and a way of life that together comes to expression in the social world of a group of Jews. The 'Judaisms' of the title therefore constitute several such ways of life and world views addressed to groups of Jews. A Messiah in a Judaism is a man who at the end of history, at the eschaton, will bring salvation to the Israel conceived by the social group addressed by the way of life and world view of that Judaism. Judaisms and their Messiahs at the age of the beginning of Christianity therefore encompass a group of religious systems that

form a distinct family, all characterized by two traits: (1) address to
'Israel' and (2) reference to diverse passages of the single common holy
writing ('Old Testament', 'written Torah').[15]

This is narrow enough for our purposes, since it treats the Messiah as a
Jewish phenomenon and also limits its reference to an eschatological
context: not just any religious leader, but a Jewish one, and not at just
any time, but only in the last days. But it is also broad enough; it does
not, for example, run into difficulties when faced with the Messiah of
Judah and the Messiah of Aaron at Qumran on the grounds that one of
these is a royal figure and the other is not. It sees messianism as
squarely an aspect of Jewish eschatological expectations, but allows
that in different forms of Judaism, which includes early Christianity,
the Messiah may appear in different guises.

Now as with my discussion of Ezekiel, so here, it is plain that many
of the texts to which different 'Judaisms' have appealed for their idea
of the Messiah were not written in the context of such an eschatological
scheme. It is at least arguable that the prophecies of a new David in
Jeremiah are meant to refer, not to a figure of the end-time, but to a new
king who will be not the end of David's line but the beginning of a new
dynasty which will last for a very long time and make what we would
call an eschatological intervention by God unnecessary. In the case of
another important 'messianic' prophecy, Isa. 32.1 ('Behold, a king will
reign in righteousness'), it is entirely possible that the prophecy is not
predictive at all, but is a kind of wisdom saying, pointing out that it is
by righteousness that a king—any king—does or should reign. It is
equally plain that such texts, once read in the context of a prior commitment to the idea of an eschatological deliverer, can be made to yield
a 'messianic' sense; the history of reception of these texts makes that
obvious. I suppose that, still keeping to the model of my discussion of
Ezekiel, the question that concerns me is whether the messianic idea,
for all that it distorts the plain sense of these texts, is none the less also
in some way their source. And just as Ezekiel's concern for the honour
of Yahweh's name is recognizably an important source for Judaeo-
Christian monotheism, despite the fact that Ezekiel was not yet in that
sense monotheistic himself, so ancient Israel's thinking about the
monarchy can be seen to lie at the root of later messianism, despite the

15. J. Neusner, E.S. Frerichs, and W.S. Green (eds.), *Judaisms and their
Messiahs at the Turn of the Christian Era* (Cambridge: Cambridge University Press,
1987), p. ix.

great gulf between the two. Had there never been a monarchy in Israel, and had it not taken on the high ideological stance which the prophets often in fact criticized, messianism could hardly have taken root. That is where much of the Scandinavian work on kingship has been so important. When, as perhaps is the case with Bentzen, it tried to show that messianism is already latent in the kingship ideology of the Psalms, and even more, that people in Israel fused kingship with the image of Moses and with Deutero-Isaiah's suffering servant, it over-played its hand. But it could be said that it saw real, not illusory, lines of connection between ancient religio-political ideas and the messianic hopes of Jews and Christians. And this says something about the continuity of Judaism, helping us to see that—despite its enormous diversity—ancient Israel and the Judaism (or Judaisms) that succeeded it share certain ways of thinking and form a single religious tradition with certain common features. No-one in ancient Israel believed in the Messiah, and the texts they wrote which would later come to be taken as messianic were not so intended. Yet messianism was not simply an alien idea stuck unnaturally on to Judaism, but one which developed insights there from early times.

What are these insights? One is the intimate connection of God with political reality. Long before messianism appeared on the scene, writers in Israel were engaged in a violent dialogue about the legitimacy of kingship. Whatever the composition-history of the so-called Deuteronomistic History may have been, it can hardly be doubted that it bears witness to strongly opposed beliefs about the monarchy: whether it was divinely ordained, or evidence of rebellion against God. Even the notion that God himself is the true king of Israel does not settle this debate, because the kingship of God might be honoured through eschewing human kingship or, as in many human societies, by setting up a human king to be God's image on earth. Language about the making of human beings in God's image may indeed derive from what was sometimes said of ancient kings, and represent a 'democratizing' of such language. But what these fiercely opposed traditions had in common is just as important as what they quarrelled over. The common ground is a passionate belief that God cares how human society is ordered. The kind of 'indifferentism' that would characterize thinking about monarchy in some post-Reformation Christian traditions, notably Lutheran and Anglican, is hard to justify from the pages of the Old Testament, where it matters extremely how political affairs are organized, because

God has a clear view of his own about such matters which it behoves human beings to discover and to implement.

The idea of the Messiah is of a piece with this, because it presupposes that a day will come when God will find means of intervening to establish his own rule, and that he will do so through a human, and hence potentially political, agent. The Messiah is a human being among others: this is stressed even in the type of Judaism most inclined to believe in intervention through God in person, Christianity, which went through agonies to insist that the heavenly redeemer in whom it believed was nevertheless truly human. It is familiar ground that most Jewish eschatological predictions are, seen through later Christian eyes, rather strikingly realistic and this-worldly, and reflect a belief that God's blueprint for the future age still involves political realities, just as it still involves birth and death. The enormous gulf between, say, the royal Psalms on the one hand and the messianic hopes of late Jewish apocalyptic on the other should not be allowed to obscure the shared commitment to the belief that God is interested in the world order and has specific and detailed plans for it. Forms of Christianity that deny this are no longer in continuity with the tradition that runs through all the types of Judaism that were concerned either with kingship, pro or con, or with the Messiah, pro or con. I do not say they are wrong, only that they are out of step with biblical emphases; these two things for me are not analytically related.

Secondly, a point that perhaps may seem more negative: thinking about the Messiah, and thinking about the various political institutions such as kingship which were its forerunners and necessary preconditions, are characterized equally by extreme diversity. Some Jewish scholars (see for example William Scott Green in the volume mentioned earlier[16]) see the very interest in 'THE Messiah' in Judaism as already introducing a Christian bias into the discussion. One wonders whether it would have occurred to us to have a seminar series on the theme 'King and Messiah' if it had not been for Christian interest in the Messiah, which has kept the subject central when in a purely Jewish context it might have become little more than a footnote in religious history. Of course, there were and are many Jews for whom the concept of the Messiah is quite remote, and others for whom it makes sense to speak of a messianic *age* but not of the Messiah. Once again, we can

---

16. W.S. Green, 'Introduction: Messiah in Judaism: Rethinking the Question', in Neusner (ed.), *Judaisms and their Messiahs*, pp. 1-13.

say that this kind of diversity in expectations is matched by the diversity of political institutions which existed at various periods in Old Testament times. A characteristic feature of Judaism in all periods is the attempt to detect divine providence in whatever institutions there are, and to hope for deliverance either through or from these institutions. In many ways the book of Esther is one of the best illustrations of this, despite its reputation as a radically untheological work: Mordecai says to Esther, 'Who knows whether you have not come to the kingdom for such a time as this?' (Est. 4.14), surely an expression of faith in divine providence if ever there was one. Yet in the same breath he comments, 'If you keep silence at such a time as this, relief and deliverance will arise for the Jews from some other quarter'. The primary faith is in divine providence to use all circumstances to bring Israel deliverance, but at the same time there is a conviction that the present circumstances offer an opportunity of co-operating with these providential designs. Belief in the Messiah rests ultimately on the belief that God can be relied on to have the right people in place at the right time to save and deliver Israel, whether through the specific vehicle of a descendant of David or in some other way. The very diversity of the hope attests a belief in God's ingenuity and versatility in turning hopeless situations into occasions of salvation and deliverance.

Thirdly, the definition of the Messiah I quoted from Neusner specifies the deliverance of *Israel*—whether all Jews or the Jews who belong to the Judaism in question. It does not envisage the salvation of Gentiles, or any kind of universal deliverance involving also the natural world. In some ways this fails to do justice to some later apocalypses, and also to rabbinic thought, where the messianic age, whether or not it includes a Messiah, brings the gathering in of the Gentiles alongside the salvation of Israel. Here it is certainly possible to speak of a theological inheritance from the Old Testament, and not just from postbiblical books. Whether the term 'universalism' should be used of any biblical texts is disputed, though (as Anthony Gelston points out in his article 'Universalism in Deutero-Isaiah') it depends very much on our definition of universalism.[17] But at least we may say that the coming rule of the restored Israel (probably without a king at its head) over surrounding lands is thought of as a mild and beneficent rule, not as cruel domination. And in earlier texts the king who will exercise rightful dominion over all nations will be the king who attends to the needs

17. A. Gelston, 'Universalism in Second Isaiah', *JTS* NS 43 (1992), pp. 377-98.

of the poor and needy, no doubt abroad as well as at home—Psalm 72 perhaps exemplifies this.

This is part of the ideology of kingship outside, and indeed long before, Israel's monarchy, and is found in many ancient Near Eastern texts. Jewish belief that God would in the last days include the Gentiles in his blessings on Israel, and Christian belief that these last days had begun and that the conversion of Gentiles to the new faith was evidence of this, thus have roots that reach back well beyond the Exile, and they are bound up with kingship from early times. The underlying belief here is that the one God must have benign purposes for the whole world he has made, and that the election of Israel has to be understood within that context. We can see such a belief at work in most Old Testament texts, including those like Amos that go so far as to question the election of Israel on the basis of God's universal moral demands. Clearly it is possible to exaggerate the universalism of the Old Testament, and some, perhaps through a Christian commitment, have done so: I think, for example, that Zimmerli's insistence that the nations are to be saved in Ezekiel is probably a Christian exaggeration,[18] and the same could be said for von Rad's insistence on the traditional translation 'in you shall all the families of the earth be blessed' in Gen. 12.3 against the normal preference in modern scholarship for 'in you shall all the families of the earth bless themselves'.[19] Nevertheless the gathering in of the nations is an authentic Jewish theme, and also an authentic element in the theology of the Old Testament. Where it occurs in late messianic texts, it rests on something that is already present in earlier Israelite tradition, however differently conceptualized.

In this article I have tried to present a model for what might be meant by 'Old Testament theology' as a discipline that can be practised by theologians and by biblical specialists, in which a line is traced from the original Old Testament texts to the concepts in later Judaism and Christianity which both rest upon them and in some measure influence the way in which they are now read. I have applied this approach to the question of the Messiah, trying to show both how messianism departed

18. See W. Zimmerli, *Ezechiel* (BKAT, 13.2; Neukirchen–Vluyn: Neukirchener Verlag, 1969), pp. 877-78, 915 (ET *Ezekiel 25–48* [trans. J.D. Martin; Philadelphia: Fortress Press, 1979–83], pp. 248, 277).

19. See G. von Rad, *Das erste Buch Mose, Genesis* (ATD, 2.4; Göttingen: Vandenhoeck & Ruprecht, 1956) (ET *Genesis* [trans. J.A. Marks; OTL; London: SCM Press, 1961], *ad loc.*).

from the texts to which it appealed, but yet how it developed lines of thinking already present in those texts, in a manner sometimes now called a feedback loop. I hope thereby to have contributed something both to the question of messianism and to the theoretical basis of Old Testament theology as a discipline that may continue—despite the very proper criticisms of Albertz and others—to flourish in the world of biblical studies.

OLD TESTAMENT CHRISTOLOGY

David J. Reimer

1. *The Problem*

The purpose of this essay is to revisit and evaluate some of the more dramatic, important, or recent contributions on the subject of Old Testament Christology. I will not, however, be attending to the history of the subject for its own sake; the Christian inclination to find Christ in the Old Testament is deep-seated, stretching back to the New Testament itself. Nor will I be attending to the New Testament's use of the Old Testament to promote its christological portraits, although this is a subject of some interest.[1] Yet the relationship of Jesus to the Old Testament poses particular problems for the Christian student of the Hebrew Bible. This survey is an initial attempt to address these problems.

1.1. *Christ in the Old Testament*

As a child in Sunday School, I was taught that the man (*'îš*) who is called 'the commander of the Lord's army' (*śar-ṣᵉbā' yhwh*) whom Joshua worships was, in fact, Jesus Christ (Josh. 5.13-15). The learned E.W. Hengstenberg noticed that this mysterious figure makes two assumptions: he assumes divine status, and that his very presence ('I have now come', v. 14) assures the success of the mission laid on

---

1.   See, e.g., R.T. France, *Jesus and the Old Testament: His Application of Old Testament Passages to Himself and His Mission* (London: Tyndale Press, 1971), and Donald Juel, *Messianic Exegesis: Christological Intepretation of the Old Testament in Early Christianity* (Philadelphia: Fortress Press, 1988). More specialized studies are provided by K. Stendahl, *The School of St. Matthew and Its Use of the Old Testament* (Lund: C.W.K. Gleerup, 2nd edn, 1968), and Joel Marcus, *The Way of the Lord: Christological Exegesis of the Old Testament in Mark* (Edinburgh: T. &T. Clark, 1993).

Joshua.[2] What could be clearer, for the Christian, than that this mysterious 'commander' who is holy, accepts worship from Joshua, and assures his success, is the pre-existent Christ?

Certainly the New Testament itself urges us to find Christ in the Old Testament (a factor to be considered further below). Georges Barrois argues that if we only had three incidents in Luke, that would be enough to authorize the Christian discovery of Christ in the Old Testament.[3] When Jesus as a boy discussed questions with 'the teachers' (οἱ διδάσκαλοι) in the Temple, what else was he talking about but himself in the Scriptures (Lk. 2.46)? At the beginning of his teaching ministry, Jesus applies the words of Isaiah ('The Spirit of the Lord is upon me...', Lk. 4.18, cf. Isa. 61.1-2aα) to himself ('Today this Scripture has been fulfilled in your hearing', Lk. 4.21). Most important of all is the episode on the road to Emmaus, when two sorrowing disciples meet (unawares) the resurrected Jesus who explains to them things about 'the Christ': 'And beginning with Moses and all the prophets, he interpreted to them in all the scriptures the things concerning himself' (Lk. 24.27).[4] Barrois concludes, 'We should not need anything more than these three episodes to be convinced that we may confidently seek the face of our Christ in the Old Testament as in a magic mirror'.[5]

If Jesus Christ is the centre of the Christian faith, and if the Bible—which is comprised of the Old *and* New Testaments and which is Christianity's authoritative Scripture—is the product of timeless revelation,[6] then it must be the case that the Bible witnesses *in its entirety* to Jesus the Christ.

---

2. E.W. Hengstenberg, *Christologie des Alten Testamentes*, I (Berlin: L. Oehmigke, 2nd edn, 1854), pp. 140-41 (ET *Christology of the Old Testament*, I [trans. T. Meyer; Edinburgh: T. & T. Clark, 1854], p. 121).

3. G.A. Barrois, *The Face of Christ in the Old Testament* (New York: St Vladimir's Seminary Press, 1974), pp. 20-21.

4. Cf. Lk. 24.44: 'Then he said to them, "These are my words which I spoke to you, while I was still with you, that everything *written about me* in the law of Moses and the prophets and the psalms must be fulfilled"'.

5. Barrois, *The Face of Christ*, p. 21. Hermann Diem, *Theologie als kirchliche Wissenschaft*. II. *Dogmatik: Ihr Weg zwischen Historismus und Existenzialismus* (Munich: Chr. Kaiser Verlag, 3rd edn, 1960), pp. 132-44 (ET *Dogmatics* [Edinburgh: Oliver & Boyd, 1959], pp. 148-63), adopts a similar 'strategy of continuity' in his discussion of 'Jesus the Christ of the Old Testament', especially in debate with W.G. Kümmel and E. Käsemann.

6. D.L. Baker, *Two Testaments, One Bible: A Study of the Theological*

1.2. *Christ NOT in the Old Testament*

This view, however, is not without problems—even for Christians. One looks in vain among modern commentaries (of any kind!) for some mention of the christological option for 'commander of the Lord's army' in Joshua 5. Even Blaikie's commentary in the Expositor's Bible series is reticent about subscribing fully to the view that this is a pre-incarnational visit from the one who would be Jesus of Nazareth: 'There seems no good reason', he writes, 'to reject the view that these theophanies, though not incarnations, were yet foreshadows of the incarnation,—hints of the mystery afterwards to be realized when Jesus was born of Mary'.[7] Jewish commentators never identified this *śar* with Jesus, of course, but a similar dynamic can be discerned. The Targum already understood this figure as a *mal'āk*, thus easing the way for commentators such as Rashi and David Kimchi to equate this figure with the archangel Michael.[8] However, the notes to my Adi edition of the Tanak breathe not a word about the *śar*, although this pericope is headed (in Hebrew) by the words 'The commander of the Lord's army'.

Christian reluctance to find Christ in the Old Testament is no new development. Marcion is, of course, the obvious example of a Christian thinker who could not equate Christ with previous, Jewish, tradition nor tolerate the uniting of the two Testaments. Marcion, despite being branded a heretic, has had his disciples in the Church. In recent times these have included such scholars as Schleiermacher, Hirsch, Harnack, and Baumgärtel among others.[9] Baumgärtel,[10] a relatively cautious

Relationship Between the Old and New Testaments (Leicester: Apollos, 2nd rev. edn, 1991), pp. 103-104.

7. W.G. Blaikie, *The Book of Joshua* (The Expositor's Bible; London: Hodder & Stoughton, 1893), pp. 130-31.

8. The connection draws even closer in *2 Enoch*, which calls Michael 'the great captain' (33.10). Talmudic tradition identifies the 'messenger' figure consistently with Michael.

9. Cf. John Bright, *The Authority of the Old Testament* (London: SCM Press, 1967), pp. 60-79; F. Watson, *Text and Truth: Redefining Biblical Theology* (Edinburgh: T. & T. Clark, 1997), pp. 127-76; on Hirsch see E. Kraeling, *The Old Testament since the Reformation* (New York: Harper & Row, 1955), pp. 239-50. Individuals differ on whom to consign to the Marcionite following.

10. In an article based on a lecture delivered in 1954: 'Das hermeneutische Problem des Alten Testaments', in C. Westermann (ed.), *Probleme alttestament-licher Hermeneutik* (TBü, 11; Munich: Chr. Kaiser Verlag, 1960), pp. 114-39 (ET 'The Hermeneutical Problem of the Old Testament', in Claus Westermann [ed.],

proponent of such a view, provides one example. The Old Testament is a product of a particular history and religion which generates a 'self-understanding' which is not Christian: '... the Old Testament is a witness out of a non-Christian religion' (p. 115, ET p. 135); 'the Old Testament has its power ... in another religion' which is 'completely strange to the Christian faith' (p. 118, ET pp. 138-39). Baumgärtel recognizes that he 'has wandered along some precipices' (p. 137, ET p. 157), but there is no drawing back from the brink. Neither the prophecy–fulfilment schema nor typology—both utilized in the New Testament—are sufficient to bring the Old Testament within the Christian sphere, for from a modern perspective the Old Testament is 'a historically conditioned witness (today we cannot at all see it otherwise!)' (p. 124, ET p. 144). Although the New Testament writers understood it as 'the inspired Word of God', 'it can no longer be [such] for us today' (p. 124, ET p. 144). The Old Testament has claims to self-understanding, and these must be respected; they cannot be if it is christianized, and thus 'typological and christological understanding is excluded' (p. 132, ET p. 152). The Old Testament only retains value for Christians when they begin with gospel and use the Old Testament as a foil to see the religious distance Christianity has travelled.[11]

For Christian biblical scholars, the dilemma is acute. John Barton took up these issues in his Bampton Lectures when he pondered the nature of 'prophecy and fulfilment':[12]

> This is the clearest case of the imposition of a Christological perspective on the Old Testament... The old Scriptures remain in force only because they no longer speak with their own voice: they are turned into a collection of texts whose words express what is in reality a wholly new message... When people started to read the Old Testament on its own terms...then it became clear that by such arguments the Church had painted itself into a corner. For the Old Testament is of course not a Christian book in this direct sense at all. It is a Jewish book.

Essays on Old Testament Interpretation [trans. and ed. James Luther Mays; London: SCM Press, 1963], pp. 134-59).

11. Jon D. Levenson comments on this interpretative strategy in *The Hebrew Bible, the Old Testament, and Historical Criticism: Jews and Christians in Biblical Studies* (Louisville: Westminster/John Knox, 1993), pp. 9, 39.

12. John Barton, *People of the Book? The Authority of the Bible in Christianity* (London: SPCK, 1988), pp. 16-17.

1.3. *Necessity of Topic*

For the most part, however, the concern of Old Testament scholarship
(the label is deliberately chosen) has been quite consistently *historical*—a concern which resonates with Baumgärtel's conviction that
such a historicist perspective is inevitable for modern people. That is,
we agree that 'full blown messianism' (we all know intuitively what we
mean by that) is not to be found until very late in the day. Intimations
of 'messianism' are at best muted in the Old Testament itself, even in
its late stages. Even in the parts of the Old Testament most heavily
appealed to in Christian tradition as informing its understanding of
Jesus—the Psalms[13] and the latter prophets—nowhere have these semi-
nars discovered Jesus peeking out. The idea that Jesus of the New
Testament could be found in the writings of the Old Testament has not
been mooted, while the idea of 'Messiah' in the Old Testament has
often been rejected as simply 'not being there'.

Yet I doubt very much whether this lengthy and learned seminar
would have been embarked upon without Jesus lurking in the background. Big books have been written which, again, have their motive
force in the *Christian* development of messianic ideas.[14] It is clear
already that this subject brings us profoundly to the matter of Jewish–
Christian relations. As whole religious structures, Judaism and Christianity appear to be incompatible: the role accorded to Jesus in
Christianity excludes Jews, while the Jewish dismissal of Jesus as
'Messiah' denies to Christianity its *raison d'être*. While my primary
focus in this study is not to engage this important dialogue, it will ever
be whispering in the background.[15] Yet even in Christian terms, the

---

13. See the detailed studies of M. Hengel on Ps. 110.1 and other christological
psalms in M. Philonenko (ed.), *Le Trône de Dieu* (WUNT, 69; Tübingen: J.C.B.
Mohr [Paul Siebeck], 1993), pp. 108-94, and W. Baier *et al.* (eds.), *Weisheit
Gottes—Weisheit der Welt* (Festschrift J. Ratzinger; St Ottilien: EOS Verlag, 1988),
pp. 357-404 (reprinted in ET in M. Hengel, *Studies in Early Christology* [Edin-
burgh: T. & T. Clark, 1995], pp. 119-225, 227-91).

14. E.g. the 600 pages of the proceedings of the Princeton seminar which
appeared as J.H. Charlesworth (ed.), *The Messiah: Developments in Earliest
Judaism and Christianity* (Philadelphia: Fortress Press, 1992).

15. One attempt to grapple with 'Jesus between Jews and Christians' is offered
by Jürgen Moltmann in his little book, *Jesus Christus für uns heute* (Gütersloh:
Chr. Kaiser Verlag, 1994) (ET *Jesus Christ for Today's World* [trans. M. Kohl;
London: SCM Press, 1994]). From the Jewish side, see E. Borowitz, *Contemporary
Christologies: A Jewish Response* (Ramsey, NJ: Paulist Press, 1980). Note the care

relationship of Jesus to the Old Testament is enigmatic and poses particular problems for the Christian student of the Hebrew Bible in the modern climate. Such reflections supply an urgency that is much more than simply 'background'; with them in mind I now turn to survey some proposed solutions which may suggest strategies for the future.

2. *Prophecy and Fulfilment: Hengstenberg, Von Rad, Westermann*

Although the argument from Old Testament prophecy to fulfilment in Jesus was seen to be something like a combination of the blind alley and the garden path in Barton's comments (above), it has remained an attractive avenue for many to explore over many years. E.W. Hengstenberg's massive *Christologie des Alten Testamentes* (3 vols. in 4, 2nd edn, 1854–57), which went through successive German editions and appeared in English (also in successive editions) as *Christology of the Old Testament* (1854–58), gives evidence of this attraction, both by its size and its publishing history. Although Hengstenberg is of genuine interest,[16] it is not primarily for this work but rather for his place in the general conservative backlash to higher criticism in the nineteenth century.[17] Hengstenberg (1802–69), an interpreter of large talents and extensive influence, was part of a larger trend among confessional scholars who believed that 'the Bible was to be seen as a unity with the Old Testament pointing towards and being fulfilled in the New

taken over these issues by W. Brueggemann in his *magnum opus, Theology of the Old Testament: Testimony, Dispute, Advocacy* (Minneapolis: Fortress Press, 1997), pp. 311-12 (cf. his evaluation of Childs, p. 93).

16. Cf. J.H. Hayes and F.C. Prussner, *Old Testament Theology: Its History and Development* (London: SCM Press, 1985), pp. 80-84. He rates barely a mention in H.-J. Kraus's substantial work, *Die biblische Theologie: Ihre Geschichte und Problematik* (Neukirchen–Vluyn: Neukirchener Verlag, 1970), pp. 99, 101; E. Kraeling (*The Old Testament since the Reformation*) ignores him completely.

17. One element of Hengstenberg's work deserves further investigation—that is the frequency with which he draws on Johann Andreas Eisenmenger's *Entdecktes Judenthum* (2 vols.; Frankfurt am Main: n.p., 1700); the account below follows H.L. Strack and G. Stemberger, *Introduction to the Talmud and Midrash* (Edinburgh: T. & T. Clark, 1991), p. 24, a work which 'compiled all the references which were intended to prove Jewish errors or attacks on the Christian religion'. Eisenmenger's work was 'to become a veritable treasure trove of later anti-Jewish arguments', since the quotations, 'presented without their context, [were] open to every misinterpretation'. Despite being banned in 1701, it appeared in 1711 in a second edition, and was subsequently translated into English (1732–33).

Testament'.[18] Something of his approach has already been suggested in the glance at Joshua 5 above. Hengstenberg examines passages which have some intimation of deity in human form; these in turn point towards Christ who then fulfils the promise held out in temporary form in the Old Testament narratives, or promised in its predictive prophecies.

More recently, two of the major names in Old Testament scholarship in the twentieth century have adopted this schema: Gerhard von Rad in the final part of his magisterial *Old Testament Theology* ('The Old Testament and the New'), and Claus Westermann in a tiny work, *The Old Testament and Jesus Christ*.[19] For all that von Rad's work is on a grand scale while here, at least, Westermann works in miniature, they share the same approach. For both, prophecy and fulfilment provide the most useful way forward in attempting to relate the Old and New Testaments to each other through the figure of Jesus Christ. Westermann, in particular, seems most alive to the dangers of over-simplification in the use of this 'fundamentally correct description of the content of the Testaments', for it could leave the impression that 'the entire Old Testament consisted of "promise" and the entire New Testament of "fulfillment"' (p. 10, ET p. 14). Still, they insist that this scheme of future orientation has persuasive power. In von Rad's understanding, this is simply a logical extension of the way the Old Testament functions internally. The history of the relationship of God and people flows in a series of iterations (p. 329, ET p. 319: 'The history of Jahwism is thus characterised by repeated breaks'), as the understanding, and even designation, of God mutates and grows (pp. 337-38, ET p. 327). Similarly, for Westermann it is the 'main historical line' that runs between Israel and the church that carries 'the same structure of the salvation event' so that it is finally possible to say that 'Christ is the goal of the history of God's people' (pp. 25-26, ET pp. 39-40). It is, then, the *previous* transformations of faith observable within the Old Testament that validate the move which sees them

18. John Rogerson, *Old Testament Criticism in the Nineteenth Century: England and Germany* (London: SPCK, 1984), p. 80.

19. G. von Rad, *Theologie des Alten Testaments*, II (Munich: Chr. Kaiser Verlag, 1960), pp. 339-436 (ET *Old Testament Theology*, II [trans. D.M.G. Stalker; Edinburgh: Oliver & Boyd, 1965], pp. 319-429); C. Westermann, *Das Alte Testament und Jesus Christus* (Stuttgart: Calwer Verlag, 1968) (ET *The Old Testament and Jesus Christ* [trans. O. Kaste; Minneapolis: Augsburg Press, 1970]).

finally resolved in the revelation of Jesus Christ. Thus von Rad writes: 'Such a transformation of the traditional material in the light of a new saving event was as proper for early Christians as were many other such transformations which had already taken place in the Old Testament itself' (p. 353, ET p. 333).

How, though, to meet Barton's criticism cited above, namely, that to treat the Old Testament merely as prophecy which is fulfilled in the New is to deny it any independent status, to render it something which it is not? Both von Rad and Westermann argue that simply because 'fulfilment' has come, the 'promise' does not thereby lose its significance. 'To divorce promise as event, the living process by which the promise was given, from that which was promised, to insist on having the fulfillment without the promise—means that promise is no longer promise'.[20] The example is given of the promised land, a promise fulfilled, 'but that did not mean, however, that it stopped being the promised land. The promise did not lose its meaning because the fulfillment had come.'[21] Von Rad uses this same example (and adds others besides) and exploits the open-ended nature of fulfilment, for Christ, too, is both fulfilment and promise, so that 'Israel's experience is repeated in the Christian community'.[22]

Such a 'christological' approach is likely to remain a commonplace in Christian thinking for some time to come. It has the weight of many years behind it, and its simple structure, drawn from admittedly biblical patterns, is readily grasped. It needs little theological sleight of hand. As Moses was able to identify El-Shaddai with Yahweh (Exod. 6.2-3), so the Christian makes the analogous move, ending up with Jesus Christ. Thus the closing words of von Rad's *Old Testament Theology* point insistently to the New:[23]

> [O]nly when Old Testament theology takes this final step to the threshold
> of the New Testament, only when it makes the link with the witness of
> the Gospels and the Apostles perfectly openly, and when it is able to

20. Westermann, *Das Alte Testament und Jesus Christus*, p. 50 (ET *The Old Testament and Jesus Christ*, p. 77).

21. Westermann, *Das Alte Testament und Jesus Christus*, p. 50 (ET *The Old Testament and Jesus Christ*, p. 77).

22. Von Rad, *Theologie des Alten Testaments*, II, p. 408 (ET *Old Testament Theology*, II, p. 383).

23. Von Rad, *Old Testament Theology*, II, pp. 428-29 (not in German original).

make men believe that the two Testaments belong together, will it have
the right to term itself a theological undertaking, and therefore 'Biblical
theology'.

3. Neo-Pesherist Exegesis: Wilhelm Vischer

Hengstenberg's huge Christology was produced in the face of the threat
of higher criticism.[24] Wilhelm Vischer's interest in *The Witness of the
Old Testament to Christ* also has polemical origins. In spite of the
expectations aroused by their respective titles, so far as I know Vischer
makes no mention whatsoever of Hengstenberg. This immediately
suggests that, despite a superficial resemblance, the two were fighting
different battles. Hengstenberg was taking on liberal scholarship;
Vischer was confronting National Socialism. Two recent articles helpfully describe the impact Vischer's work had when it appeared.[25] In
spite of Vischer having such eminent and recent commentators, his
work continues to appear odd even if its strange contours are readily
explained. Thus, Vischer's programme demands some exposition and
quotation for, unlike von Rad, for example, his work remains relatively
unknown.[26]

24. Vischer lived from 1895–1988. All the citations from Vischer here are from
his work *Das Christuszeugnis des Alten Testaments*. I. *Das Gesetz* (Munich: Chr.
Kaiser Verlag, 2nd edn, 1935) (ET *The Witness of the Old Testament to Christ*. I.
The Pentateuch (trans A.B. Crabtree; London: Lutterworth Press, 1949). Volumes
II and III of the German work were never translated into English. The most recent
comprehensive study of Vischer's work, unavailable to me, is that of Brigitte
Schroven, *Theologie des Alten Testaments zwischen Anpassung und Widerspruch:
Christologische Exegese zwischen den Weltkriegen* (Neukirchen–Vluyn:
Neukirchener Verlag, 1995).

25. James Barr, 'Wilhelm Vischer and Allegory', in A. Graeme Auld (ed.),
Understanding Poets and Prophets: Essays in Honour of George Wishart Anderson
(JSOTSup, 152; Sheffield: JSOT Press, 1993), pp. 38-60; Rolf Rendtorff,
'Christologische Auslegung als "Rettung" des Alten Testaments? Wilhelm Vischer
und Gerhard von Rad', in R. Albertz, F.W. Golka, and J. Kegler (eds.), *Schöpfung
und Befreiung* (Stuttgart: Calwer Verlag, 1989), pp. 191-203 (ET 'Christological
Interpretation as a Way of "Salvaging" the Old Testament? Wilhelm Vischer and
Gerhard von Rad', in Rolf Rendtorff, *Canon and Theology: Overtures to an Old
Testament Theology* [trans. and ed. M. Kohl; Edinburgh: T. & T. Clark, 1994],
pp. 76-91).

26. Cf. '[A]lthough the book was enthusiastically received…it was just as swiftly forgotten…', Rendtorff, 'Christologische Auslegung', p. 198 (ET 'Christological
Interpretation', p. 87).

Vischer begins by thinking about the relationship of his task to history. He seems to concur with Wellhausen, who abandoned the search for Jesus of history:[27]

> [T]he effort to replace Christ Jesus by the historical Jesus remains, in view of the historical documents on which it must be based, a procedure which from a scientific standpoint is highly dubious... The Bible knows neither a historical Jesus nor a Christ-idea, but simply Jesus the Christ to whom it bears a double witness in the Old and New Testaments... That the concept of history is here transcended is obvious .

Such contentions might suggest that Vischer had no use for the standard range of critical exegetical tools, but this was not the case. 'If then we are really concerned to understand the Bible as God's Word, if we wish to read it as testimony to Christ, we cannot ignore what the historical and philological sciences have to say about the Old Testament'.[28] If the melting together of the Old and New Testaments in Vischer's thinking is already becoming apparent, he comes quickly to insist on the unity of the Testaments: 'The doctrine of the unity of the Bible establishes the genuine historicity of the incarnation...'[29] 'In any case, if the Testaments truly form a unity—and only if this is so, is Jesus the Christ—the men of faith under the old covenant were, through one and the same Mediator, partakers of the same salvation as the Christians' (p. 24, ET p. 20).

In this final quote, Vischer's concern for the place of Judaism in relation to Christianity begins to emerge. Rendtorff attends especially to this dimension, noting also Vischer's involvement with the 'Bethel Confession' for which he drafted a section on 'The Church and the Jews'.[30] Although it is not immediately apparent on reading through the *Christuszeugnis*, Rendtorff argues that Vischer was attempting 'to "salvage" the Old Testament from the attacks and persecutions of its

---

27 Vischer, *Das Christuszeugnis*, pp. 12-13, 15, ET pp. 12-13; cf. J. Wellhausen, *Einleitung in die drei ersten Evangelium* (Berlin: Georg Reimer, 2nd edn, 1911), pp. 104, 154.

28. Vischer, *Das Christuszeugnis*, p. 18, ET p. 16. There is some influence of Barth here; cf. p. 35, ET p. 29.

29. Vischer, *Das Christuszeugnis*, p. 24, ET p. 21; cf. his words, 'The Christian Church stands and falls with the recognition of the the unity of the two Testaments' (p. 32, ET p. 27).

30. Further on this, see Rendtorff, 'Christologische Auslegung', p. 199 (ET 'Christological Interpretation', p. 89).

opponents. Here ... was a clear counterposition to the contempt poured on the Old Testament as "Jewish".'[31] It is an irony (reflected on by Rendtorff at the conclusion of his article) that Vischer's 'salvaging' of the Old Testament would link pro-Jewish references to a thoroughly christological reading. Vischer thus robs Jews of their Bible through a desperate attempt to preserve it.

While Vischer thus sided with Barth in claiming that New Testament writers stand in continuity with Old Testament in writing of Christ, other comments go well beyond strict 'continuity' to something more like supersession:[32]

> With complete consistency the early Church took over Israel's entire scripture, since she maintained that 'We who believe that Jesus is the Son of God, we who believe His promise that we are His brothers, we— and not the synagogue which has rejected His messianic claims—are the legitimate heirs of the divine Testament.' By this appropriation the Church did not design to rob the Jews of the Old Testament.

One rarely comes up against a more blatant case of having one's cake and eating it too. Perhaps it is not surprising, then, to find ambiguous references to Buber (p. 39, ET pp. 32-33) regarding his persistence in Judaism. Vischer's interpretation is resonant with much of Buber's writing in *Königtum Gottes* and *Kampf um Israel*, though Vischer is at pains to point out that he is not *dependent* on Buber, had worked out his approach independently, and in any case gains only nuances at best from Buber's work! It seems clear that not only does Vischer's christological interpretation 'rob' Jews of their Scriptures, it ought also (in his opinion) to rob Jews of Judaism.

Two striking features emerge from a reading of Vischer's work: first, there is amazingly little about Christ; and secondly, there is nothing by way of method which attaches Old Testament text to christological interpretation.[33] Von Rad asked the questions, 'how far can Christ be a

---

31. Rendtorff, 'Christologische Auslegung', p. 192 (ET 'Christological interpretation', p. 79).

32. Vischer, *Christuszeugnis*, pp. 27-28, 31, ET pp. 23-24, 26. Vischer wonders 'whether in very truth when the Jews read [the Old Testament] even until this day the veil hangs over the Old Testament, and is only removed when Jesus is recognized as the Messiah' (p. 33, ET p. 27).

33. 'It seemed then as if he did not have a *method*, but rather a mixture of quite contradictory methods, held together by the fact that they appeared to produce a Reformational Christ'; Barr, 'Wilhelm Vischer and Allegory', p. 53.

help to the exegete in understanding the Old Testament, and how far can the Old Testament be a help...in understanding Christ?'[34] Vischer would, no doubt, vigorously claim that the *Christuszeugnis* and the exegeses it contains illumine both sides of this particular coin. Nonetheless, it remains difficult to see how Vischer's work helps the Christian to understand either Christ or the Old Testament. On the one hand, all that is said of Christ is already known from outside the Old Testament so that the Old Testament itself is left to play a supporting role only, while on the other hand, the Old Testament is so firmly subordinated to the christological agenda that it fails to speak with anything like an authentic voice of its own. For instance, having spent some time describing the process of creation in Genesis 1, Vischer declares that 'everything in the chapter proclaims the Christ' (p. 64, ET p. 51), whereupon he proceeds to string together a number of New Testament texts (under the presiding muse of Luther) which assert that the Christ is the root of creation, who is from eternity, who holds together all creation in himself (p. 65, ET pp. 51-52). This is not greatly different from his handling of the mark of Cain (Genesis 4) which is the sign of Ezekiel (9.4) which is the Christian sign of the cross (Rev. 7). 'The Christian amulet in the form of a cross thus probably had its origin not in the cross of Christ but in the sign which Jahweh set upon Cain, though it remains that it was filled with new meaning by the crucifixion of Christ...' (p. 94, ET p. 75).

Such examples suggest an interpretative 'method' for Vischer's work. Among the Dead Sea Scrolls are several commentaries which have been given the label of *pesharim* (singular, *pesher*). To the pesherists, those who wrote the Scriptures did not fully perceive the significance of what they wrote. The interpreter, however, is privy to more complete revelation so that the interpretation now unlocks the full message of the earlier text. The best known of the *pesharim*, that on the book of Habakkuk, declares that '...God told Habakkuk to write down that which would happen to the final generation, but He did not make known to him when time would come to an end. And as for that which He said, *That he who reads may read it speedily*: interpreted this concerns the Teacher of Righteousness, to whom God made known all the mysteries of the words of His servants the Prophets' (1QpHab,

---

34. G. von Rad, *Theologie des Alten Testaments*, II, p. 398 (ET *Old Testament Theology*, II, p. 374).

col. vii).[35] The 'oft-repeated features of revelatory fulfilment and actualization' can be seen in this example,[36] and these features, it seems to me, are also those which typify Vischer's exegeses. So Vischer, while admitting that his 'conjecture' concerning the sign of Cain may prove 'too audacious and untenable', persists in identifying these earlier 'signs' with the cross, just as the earlier pesherist did in equating certain references from the ancient prophets with figures known to him.

Although one is able to trace the leaps of interpretation made by the pesherist, few today would be willing to propose *pesher* exegesis as an appropriate means of solving the problem of whether or how to find Christ in the Old Testament. Its decidedly 'irrational' approach belongs to another day.

4. 'Real Presence': Anthony Tyrrell Hanson

This, at least, was the belief of Anthony Tyrrell Hanson who has pondered *pesher* exegesis as a possible way forward for Christian handling of the Old Testament: perhaps, he wondered, there is a useful precedent for the church in the practice of the sectarian exegetes of the Dead Sea Scrolls. Despite the fascination Hanson's work holds, it will be treated only briefly here. Basing his investigation on two passages (1 Cor. 10.4 and Jn 12.37-41), Hanson argues that New Testament writers believed that the pre-existent Jesus (the name is used deliberately) appeared in the Old Testament; he goes on to urge that 'all the consequences of this belief must be faced'.[37] As Hanson makes clear in this work, and more fully in his later work on New Testament exegesis of the Old Testament (1983),[38] this is not exactly *typology*. The centrality of Jesus Christ in the thinking and exegesis of the early Christians marks a decisive difference from the use of Scripture by the

35. Translation by G. Vermes, *The Complete Dead Sea Scrolls in English* (London: Allen Lane, 1997), p. 481.

36. T.H. Lim, *Holy Scripture in the Qumran Commentaries and Pauline Letters* (Oxford: Clarendon Press, 1997), p. 133. This generalized use of the term is not intended to deny the variety of pesherite exegesis for which Lim persuasively argues.

37. A.T. Hanson, *Jesus Christ in the Old Testament* (London: SPCK, 1965), p. 7.

38. A.T. Hanson, *The Living Utterances of God: The New Testament Exegesis of the Old* (London: Darton, Longman & Todd, 1983).

synagogue.[39] The attitude taken by Christian writers Hanson sums up in three observations:[40]

1. The end time has come, the time to which all Scripture is looking forward.
2. Scripture can therefore be freely applied to Jesus Christ and through him to the Christian church, which is the true inheritor of the promises made in Scripture to Israel.
3. From this it follows that the authors of scripture knew a great deal about Christ. Much information about Jesus may therefore be found by studying the Scriptures. Indeed it is no exaggeration to say that the Jewish Scriptures constituted the theological textbook of the New Testament church.

Hanson believes that this identification by the New Testament writers (of *Jesus* in the Old Testament) promotes greatly the sense of continuity between Jesus and Jewish history, and throughout—whether pre-incarnation or post—is one who 'inspires faith or is the occasion of unbelief'.[41] This continuity also informs what is new about the 'new dispensation', that it comes about through incarnation and not disembodied revelation.[42] On the other hand, there is a good deal of overlap with the 'promise and fulfilment' schema examined above. While the New Testament writers may have operated under the assumption that the Scriptures looked forward to Jesus, applied the Scriptures to him, and thus found information about him in the Scriptures, such assumptions do not control the modern reading of those Scriptures. Their proper referent is ancient Israel, not the person of Jesus. Of course, theological ideas discovered there may shape modern appropriations of Jesus' mission; they do not provide 'information' about Jesus in the way in which the first Christians found it.

Hanson's contribution has the great advantage of beginning with the structures of belief evidenced in a given time and place, and working from those structures back to the scriptural resources which nourished

39. Cf. the important contribution by Frances Young, whose nuanced argument reaches a similar conclusion by a different route: *Biblical Exegesis and the Formation of Christian Culture* (Cambridge: Cambridge University Press, 1997), pp. 122-30, and passim.
40. Hanson, *The Living Utterances of God*, pp. 41-42.
41. Hanson, *Jesus Christ in the Old Testament*, p. 168.
42. Hanson, *Jesus Christ in the Old Testament*, p. 170.

them. Here, Hanson anticipates a position staked by Jacob Neusner. Neusner argues with regard to the history of Judaism [*sic*] that 'a particular experience, transformed by a religious system into a paradigm of the life of the social group, became normative—and therefore generative'[43] so that 'the system comes before the texts and defines the canon. The exegesis of the canon then forms that on-going social action that sustains the whole... The whole works its way out through exegesis, and the history of any religious system... is the exegesis of its exegesis.'[44] This seems to me to be what Hanson is offering here. The structures of belief of the New Testament writers explain both their use of older Scripture as well as the nature of religious development that arose on that basis. In spite of the resistance of moderns to the notion that Jesus was present in the Old Testament, this idea is 'systemically active'[45] in the minds of those who framed the New Testament. Whether such a notion can control the modern Christian interpretation of the Old Testament is another question.

5. *Theological Exegesis: Bonhoeffer and Watson*

The name of Dietrich Bonhoeffer is one of the great names of twentieth-century Christendom. Although the name of Francis Watson is not as well known, they share much in terms of their approach to the Old Testament and its relation to Jesus Christ. This approach is neatly summed up in the study by Martin Kuske, *The Old Testament as the Book of Christ*.[46] In Bonhoeffer, attention is usually drawn to the infusion of Old Testament references in *Letters and Papers from Prison*,[47] as well

43. Jacob Neusner, 'Mr. Maccoby's Red Cow, Mr. Sanders's Pharisees—and Mine', *JSJ* 23 (1992), pp. 81-98 (84).

44. Jacob Neusner, 'Judaism and Christianity in the First Century: How Shall we Perceive their Relationship?', in P.R. Davies and R.T. White (eds.), *A Tribute to Geza Vermes: Essays on Jewish and Christian Literature and History* (JSOTSup, 100; Sheffield: JSOT Press, 1990), pp. 247-59 (255).

45. The terminology is Neusner's, 'Judaism and Christianity in the First Century', p. 257.

46. M. Kuske, *Das Alte Testament als Buch von Chrisus: Dietrich Bonhoeffers Wertung und Auslegung des Alten Testaments* (Berlin: Evangelische Verlagsanstalt, 1970) (ET *The Old Testament as the Book of Christ: An Appraisal of Bonhoeffer's Interpretation* [trans. S.T. Kimbrough, Jr; Philadelphia: Westminster Press, 1976]). I do not have access to the German original.

47. D. Bonhoeffer, *Widerstand und Ergebung: Briefe und Aufzeichnungen aus*

as the earlier and more programmatic *Creation and Fall*.[48] Watson's most important work in this regard is *Text and Truth* which has as its second part 'The Old Testament in Christological Perspective', this being in turn preceded by a chapter on 'Neo-Marcionism'.[49]

Watson's study—which is really about christological perspective, and not about Old Testament Christology per se—claims as fundamental two principles: first, he insists on the Old–New dichotomy for the Testaments of the Christian Bible (the old is old because it is not new, the new is new because it is not old [pp. 179-81]); and secondly, that 'the Old Testament comes to us with Jesus and from Jesus, and can never be understood in abstraction from him' (appears in italics in original) but this 'does not as yet imply any particular interpretative programme, except in the sense that it rejects all interpretative programmes that assume an autonomous Old Testament' (p. 182). Still, Watson distances himself from Vischer's contention that 'everywhere Scripture is about Christ alone' (p. 184), for scripture is not *only* about Jesus, 'it is about many things'. But, even so, 'Christian faith requires a *christocentric* reading of Christian scripture' (p. 185).

These words echo with those written much earlier by Bonhoeffer.[50] In the preface to *Creation and Fall*, Bonhoeffer declared that 'The Church of the Holy Scripture...lives from the end. Therefore it reads all Holy Scripture as the book of the end, of the new, of Christ' (p. 12). Genesis may refer to 'Yahweh' considered 'historically or psychologically', but 'theologically..., i.e., from the Church's point of view, it is speaking of God' (p. 12). Kuske's study identifies three points of view taken by Bonhoeffer on the Old Testament: first, there is a movement from Christ to the Old Testament; secondly, there is a reciprocal movement from the Old Testament to the New Testament; the third point of view 'consists no longer in a movement between Christ, the Old Testament, and the New Testament, but in Christ being found in

---

der Haft (Munich: Chr. Kaiser Verlag, 1952) (ET *Letters and Papers from Prison* [London: SCM Press, enlarged edn, 1971]).

48. D. Bonhoeffer, *Schöpfung und Fall* (Munich: Chr. Kaiser Verlag, 1937) (ET *Creation and Fall* [trans. John C. Fletcher *et al.*; London: SCM Press, 1959]).

49. F. Watson, *Text and Truth: Redefining Biblical Theology* (Edinburgh: T. & T. Clark, 1997).

50. Oddly, Bonhoeffer rates only two brief references in Watson's work: to *Christology* (p. 92), and to *Ethics* (p. 302). Most surprisingly, Watson's chapter on 'Creation in the Beginning' completely disregards Bonhoeffer's *Creation and Fall*!

the Old Testament'.[51] For Bonhoeffer, this 'theological' interpretation is a logical necessity 'if one adheres to the uniqueness of the revelation of God in Christ, and at the same time wants to interpret the Old Testament as the Word of One God through the entire Bible', and this is the case for the Christian.[52]

This might suggest that we are moving towards another sort of *pesher*-like relationship of Christianity to the Old Testament, but in Bonhoeffer this move is never made. 'Christological perspective' is, for him, exactly that: 'Christ stands between us and the Old Testament'.[53] The human condition as displayed in its multiplicity by the Old Testament is not submerged or resisted, but 'brought into the light' in order to understand 'how God has acted in the crucified and resurrected Lord'.[54] A letter written to Eberhard Bethge (20 May 1944) contains a poignant exemplar of this idea.[55]

> [I]n the Bible we have the Song of Songs; and really one can imagine no more ardent, passionate, sensual love than is portrayed there (see 7.6). It's a good thing that the book is in the Bible, in face of all those who believe that the restraint of passion is Christian... Where the *cantus firmus* is clear and plain, the counterpoint can be developed to its limits.... May not the attraction and importance of polyphony in music consist in its being a musical reflection of this Christological fact and therefore of our *vita christiana*?

On the other hand, Bonhoeffer was capable of quite different moves in which identification of moments or persons from the Old Testament with Christ (such as in his study 'Christ was in David')[56] have a heavy typological element to them. So marked is this in the exegetical work of the 1930s, that Kuske concurs with Baumgärtel's assessment that 'Bonhoeffer arbitrarily interpreted the Old Testament and therefore surrendered it when it concerned the exegetical-dogmatical question regarding the identity of the church at that time and today'.[57]

It is less easy to form an overarching impression of Watson's work,

---

51. Kuske, *The Old Testament as the Book of Christ*, p. 34.

52. Kuske, *The Old Testament as the Book of Christ*, pp. 56-57.

53. Kuske, *The Old Testament as the Book of Christ*, p. 47.

54. Kuske, *The Old Testament as the Book of Christ*, p. 57.

55. Bonhoeffer, *Widerstand und Ergebung*, pp. 192-93 (ET *Letters and Papers from Prison*, p. 303).

56. Cf. Kuske, *The Old Testament as the Book of Christ*, pp. 67-84.

57. Kuske, *The Old Testament as the Book of Christ*, p. 83.

perhaps because the chapters seem to some extent discrete rather than cumulative. It is not that they are incoherent; they hang together not least because of the theological ardour that Watson brings to his task. As in Bonhoeffer's work, it is the perspective which is vital. Thus, in reacting and responding to the biblical theology of Brevard Childs, Watson argues that

> It is not the case that the early church incorporated Jewish scripture unchanged into its authoritative canon. On the contrary, this incorporation only occurred on the basis of a reinterpretation of scripture in the light of the Christ-event...[T]he Christian Old Testament can only be understood as attesting and enacting the preparing of the way for Jesus. Old Testament exegesis can only be Christian in so far as it recognizes that this alone is the canonical role of the texts and learns to interpret them in the light of this role. It must recall that we receive the Old Testament only from Jesus and with Jesus.[58]

In other words, which Watson uses in evaluating von Rad's work, 'The goal of the Christian Old Testament must be the starting-point for interpretation' (p. 207).

As with Vischer's work, it is not always easy to see what we gain through Watson's readings. He has set his face like flint against the prevailing currents of the day, and one can at least admire his courage. Two examples serve to illustrate my unease with Watson's programme, both of which draw on creation themes. Watson links the days of creation from Genesis 1 with moments narrated in the Gospels. As light and darkness suggest the alternation of day and night, we are reminded that 'Jesus is subject to this same alternation' (p. 237). The second day brings the separation of the firmaments, and attention is drawn to the way Jesus had to sleep rough (pp. 237-38). The separation of sea and dry land on the third day prompts reflection on the fact that Jesus ministered mostly on dry land, although he also preached on a boat and travelled 'by way of the sea' (p. 238), and so on. What is the sum of these observations? 'Christologically', Watson concludes, 'we may say that these correlations *help to make visible Jesus' creatureliness*' (p. 239; italics in original). This strikes me as fairly optimistic. The correlations are minimal at best, fanciful at worst, and this case of intertextuality fails to illuminate; Jesus' 'creatureliness' is clear enough without the distraction of appeal to Genesis 1.

The other example comes from Watson's exploration of the problem

---

58. Watson, *Text and Truth*, p. 216.

of the divine image in humanity. Genesis itself is inadequate to formulate a solution to this problem, for 'it is impossible to explain how
humankind is created in the image of God without explaining how the
image of God is Christ' (p. 282). I remain puzzled by the logic of this
claim, but it propels Watson into a consideration of the thesis that 'we
learn from Jesus what it is to be human' (p. 283; italicized in original).
Watson argues that since Jesus bore God's image before he became
human, then we learn that 'what it is to be human is not in the first
instance a matter of gender, race or class. Jesus was a male, a Jew, and
an artisan, but to describe him as the image of God is to assert that his
humanity transcends his maleness, his Jewishness, and his artisan-
status... [W]e learn from Jesus that to be human precedes and transcends differences of ethnic origin and gender' (p. 286). In spite of an
admission to limitation by confining himself to the Genesis text (p. 300),
Watson seems to be missing something here. It strikes me that transcendence of gender, nationality and class all emerge nicely from
Genesis itself, and that the incarnation points in exactly the opposite
direction from that which Watson takes it here. Surely it is significant
that the incarnation is gendered, Jewish, and embodied in a particular
person's social situation. Watson's interpretation in christological perspective has the potential both to obscure the Hebrew scriptures and to
obliterate Jesus' true humanity.

6. *Concluding Reflections*

The approaches studied here suggest that a great deal of 'Old Testament
Christology' is engaged in a polemical exercise. For almost every
scholar mentioned, Old Testament Christology is a means of battling
some 'other'. This was most clearly the case with Hengstenberg
and Vischer, but it remains true of Watson and Bonhoeffer, and to
some extent of von Rad and Westermann (though quite muted in the
case of the latter). Usually, the 'enemy' is an internal one: the 'neo-
Marcionism' discussed by Watson is, it seems, an ever present threat.
This is not simply an 'academic' discussion, rather the polemics are
deeply embedded in *religious* commitment. Perhaps this seems less true
of the 'promise and fulfilment' strategy adopted by von Rad and
Westermann. But even here, it is the avowedly *Christian* starting point
in such a procedure—for without the New Testament it is unlikely that
one could plot a precise trajectory to it from the Old Testament—that is
so appealing to Francis Watson and yet is anathema to Jon Levenson.

Little wonder, then, that Levenson termed this move an 'anticritical act of faith'.[59]

Levenson's strictures point towards the essential confusion in most discussions of Christ and the Old Testament: the confusion between history and religion. The strains between these two forms of discourse begin to tear in the attempts of von Rad and Westermann to explain how it is that the 'promise' continues to have validity once 'fulfilment' has come. The affirmation of the continuing validity arises out of religious sensitivities; the prior intuition that fulfilment abrogates promise is the more natural judgment. The modern unease with *pesher* forms of exegesis arise out of the same tension. The 'real' referent is known by the interpreter only through religious insight which derives from circumstances unconnected with the original text. It is thus regarded today as 'irrational'; it offends our historical sensibilities. And yet there is a crucial difference between the 'prophecy and fulfilment' strategy, and the 'pesherist': unlike the former, the latter lays no claims to history—it is a wholly 'religious' interpretation. This makes the *pesher* approach an apt entry point for Hanson's considerations, even if he ultimately rejects the method himself.

The question, then, is not a new one. It is the old question about the proper referent of Scripture: to what (or to whom) does Scripture refer?[60] In the modern academic climate, this question tends to be posed in starkly historical terms: the more insistent are the demands of historicity, the shorter the answer becomes. But the question about Jesus' relation to the Old Testament is not, strictly speaking, a historical question at all. It is a religious question.

As long as Christianity has Christ at its centre (Christianity being the religion of a person not a book), then its Scriptures must in some sense witness to him, both Old Testament and New Testament. To this extent, Watson has a point: there is a sense in which Christian exegesis of the Old Testament inevitably has to do with being a disciple of Jesus. This is in the nature of things a question about religion rather than history or theology: it is about how belief is lived by the faithful community and

59. Levenson, *The Hebrew Bible, the Old Testament, and Historical Criticism*, p. 24.

60. For the ancients, 'the fundamental question for understanding meaning was discerning the reference'; Frances Young, *Biblical Exegesis and the Formation of Christian Culture*, p. 120.

how the community's expectations are formed, rather than about talk about God. Is it possible that just as Judaism can affirm about the Torah:

דברי תורה כולה אחת ויש בה מקרא ומשנה תלמוד הלכות והגדות:[61]

so Christianity can affirm that the Old Testament contains Christ? If the question is understood in 'historical-critical' terms, then Levenson is right and the answer is negative. But if religious structures provide the context for interpretation, then the Old Testament must nourish a Christian understanding of its Messiah.[62]

61. Sifre Deuteronomy 306. Text in L. Finkelstein, *Sifre on Deuteronomy* (New York: JTSA Reprint, 1969), p. 339. Reuven Hammer translates as '[W]ords of the Torah are all the same, yet they comprise Scripture, Mishnah, Talmud, Halakah, and Haggadah' (*Sifre: A Tannaitic Commentary on the Book of Deuteronomy* [Yale Judaica Series, 24; New Haven: Yale University Press, 1986], p. 306).

62. I wish to thank members of the Seminar for the stimulating discussion this paper received when it was originally presented; I was given much food for thought which I have not yet fully digested! I wish also to thank Dr Uwe Becker for his assistance with some details concerning Wilhelm Vischer, and especially Dr John Day whose contribution to this essay went well above and beyond the call of editorial duty.

Part III

THE MESSIAH IN POSTBIBLICAL JUDAISM
AND THE NEW TESTAMENT

MESSIANISM IN THE OLD TESTAMENT APOCRYPHA AND PSEUDEPIGRAPHA

William Horbury

Vocabulary and Scope

The advantage of the phrase 'Apocrypha and Pseudepigrapha' is that it points to the Old Testament background which is a vital but sometimes neglected aspect of these books. Broadly speaking, the Apocrypha are those writings associated with the Old Testament but outside the Hebrew canon which early Christian tradition approved; these books (Wisdom, Ecclesiasticus and others) were sometimes termed 'outside' or 'ecclesiastical' books, for they were 'outside' the canon, yet read in 'ecclesiastical' usage.[1] Jerome, like a number of his contemporaries and predecessors, especially in the Christian East, endorsed their use yet stressed their non-canonicity, saying that they should be 'set apart among the apocrypha'.[2] With emphasis, rather, on their acceptance in the church, a Western view advocated by Augustine and approved by two councils of Carthage (397, 419) and Pope Innocent I held them to be in principle (whatever might be the case in practice) fully as authoritative for Christians as the books of the Hebrew canon. The Pseudepigrapha, however, are those writings outside the Hebrew canon, but

---

1. So Origen, in Eusebius, *Hist. Eccles.* 6.25.2, quoting a Jewish book-list ('outside'); Rufinus, *Symb.* 36 ('there are other books which were called by our forbears not canonical but ecclesiastical').

2. Jerome, Prologues to the books of Kings and Solomon, in R. Weber (ed.), *Biblia Sacra iuxta Vulgatam Versionem* (2 vols.; Stuttgart: Württembergische Bibelanstalt, 2nd edn, 1975), I, p. 365 (original of the quotation here) and II, p. 957; comparably, a book-list in the Greek *Dialogue of Timothy and Aquila* lists Tobit, Wisdom, and Ecclesiasticus under the heading 'Apocrypha' (H.B. Swete, *An Introduction to the Old Testament in Greek* [Cambridge: Cambridge University Press, 1902], p. 206). On like-thinking predecessors and contemporaries of Jerome see W. Horbury, *Jews and Christians in Contact and Controversy* (Edinburgh: T. & T. Clark, 1998), pp. 208-10.

dubiously ascribed to or linked with biblical authors, which early Christian tradition generally doubted or disapproved; these books (*1 Enoch*, the *Assumption of Moses*, *2 Baruch* and many others) included several collectively called 'pseudepigrapha' in ancient book-lists, but they were often simply termed 'apocrypha' in a pejorative sense (so Athanasius, with allusion to pseudepigrapha of Enoch, Isaiah and Moses).[3]

The designation of the approved books not in the Hebrew canon as 'the Apocrypha', which is followed here, became familiar in the Middle Ages under the influence of Jerome, notably his 'helmeted preface' to Kings, *Prologus galeatus*, quoted above.[4] The currency of his terminology will have been enhanced by its entry into the mediaeval tradition of commentary both on Scripture and on canon law. Thus, according to the early mediaeval Gloss Ordinary on Scripture, 'the canonical books of the Old Testament are twenty-two in number ... any others...as Jerome says, must be placed among the apocrypha'; similarly, in the early thirteenth-century gloss on Gratian's *Decretum* by Johannes Teutonicus, the range of the word 'apocrypha' is illustrated from its customary application to Wisdom and the other approved Old Testament books not in the Hebrew canon: 'these are called apocryphal; yet they are read [*sc.* in the church], but perhaps not universally'.[5]

---

3. Swete, *Introduction*, p. 281; Coptic text of Athanasius, *Ep. Fest.* 39, discussed and translated in E. Junod, 'La formation et la composition de l'Ancien Testament dans l'Église grecque des quatre premiers siècles', in J.-D. Kaestli and O. Wermelinger (eds.), *Le Canon de l'Ancien Testament: Sa formation et son histoire* (Geneva: Labor et Fides, 1984), pp. 105-51, 124-25, 141-44.

4. Jerome's mediaeval influence was illustrated especially by J. Cosin, *A Scholastical History of the Canon of the Holy Scripture* (ed. J. Sansom; repr.; Oxford: Parker, 1849 [1657]). R. Rex, 'St John Fisher's Treatise on the Authority of the Septuagint', *JTS* NS 43 (1992), pp. 55-116 (p. 63 n. 23), suggests that Augustine's view was more prevalent in earlier mediaeval writing, Jerome's from about the twelfth century. It may be added that, throughout, the Old Testament was regularly divided between books of the Hebrew canon and other books, as in Isidore of Seville (*Etymol.* 6.1, 9, PL 82.228-29) and the ninth-century Latin version of the Stichometry of Nicephorus by the papal librarian Anastasius (in C. de Boor, *Theophanis Chronographia*, II [Leipzig: Teubner, 1885; repr.; Hildesheim: Georg Olms, 1963], pp. 57-59).

5. Gloss Ordinary, Preface 'on canonical and non-canonical books' (PL 113.21, from the edition of Douai, 1617); gloss on Gratian, *Decretum*, 1.16, interpreting 'apocrypha' in the passage of the Gelasian Decree which puts the Apostolic Canons 'among the apocrypha' (*Decretum Gratiani...una cum glossis* [Lyons,

Correspondingly, among a number of authors using this vocabulary, the fifteenth-century biblical commentator Alphonsus Tostatus of Avila wrote, with an appeal to Jerome, that Tobit, Judith, Wisdom and Ecclesiasticus 'are received in the church, and read, and copied in Bibles, and yet they are apocryphal'; and in 1540 a non-reformed Franciscan biblical expositor could still recommend to ordinands an answer to the question 'What are the books of the Old Testament?' which ended: 'All the books of the Old Testament are thirty-seven in number, twenty-eight canonical, nine apocryphal'.[6]

By 1540, however, Jerome's terminology had already been taken up in the reform party, notably through the work of Andreas von Karlstadt on the canon (1520). The designation of the relevant Old Testament books as apocryphal which had hitherto been widely current was now soon to be discouraged by the Council of Trent. In 1546 the Council reaffirmed the canonicity of most of these books, following Augustine, Innocent I, and subsequent conciliar lists including that of the Council of Florence.[7] In Luther's German Bible of 1534 and Coverdale's English Bible of 1535 these books had been set apart as 'Apocrypha', in accord with their separate registration in ancient and mediaeval lists, and under the name which could in the 1530s still be used irrespective of party; but in 1562 they were perhaps significantly listed in the Sixth of the Thirty-nine Articles simply as 'other books', not as 'Apocrypha'.[8]

1583], col. 60). Both are quoted by Cosin, *Scholastical History* (ed. Sansom), pp. 218, 224-25 (paras. 135, 140).

6.   Alphonsus Tostatus, *Opera*, VIII (Cologne, 1613), p. 12b (preface to Chronicles); Joannes Ferus, *Examen Ordinandorum*, in Ferus, *Opuscula Varia* (Lyons, 1567), pp. 900-26 (910). Compare Cosin, *Scholastical History* (ed. Sansom), pp. 248-49, para. 162 (similar remarks elsewhere in Tostatus's prefaces to Matthew and Chronicles); pp. 261-62, para. 176 (Ferus). The position of Luther's opponent, Cardinal Cajetan (Thomas de Vio), who also followed Jerome not long before the Council of Trent, seems therefore to have been rather less unusual than is suggested by G. Bedouelle, 'Le canon de l'Ancien Testament dans la perspective du Concile de Trente', in Kaestli and Wermelinger (eds.), *Le canon de l'Ancien Testament*, pp. 253-82 (257-60).

7.   Bedouelle, 'Le canon', pp. 262-69, describes the recurrence at Trent of arguments for expressing a distinction between the two classes of canonical books. Karlstadt's influence is noted without reference to the broad early sixteenth-century currency of the term 'apocrypha' by H.-P. Rüger, 'Le Siracide: Un livre à la frontière du canon', in Kaestli and Wermelinger (eds.), *Le Canon de l'Ancien Testament*, pp. 47-69 (58-59).

8.   The Sixth Article here followed the Württemberg Confession, marked by

The latter term was continued, however, in later English Bibles; in the Authorized Version of 1611 it appeared in the relatively cautious formula 'the books called Apocrypha'. The books of the Hebrew Bible and the Apocrypha therefore correspond, respectively, to the Old Testament books renamed after the Council of Trent by Sixtus Senensis in his *Bibliotheca Sancta* (1566) as 'protocanonical' and 'deutero-canonical'; the Pseudepigrapha correspond to those which he continued to call 'apocryphal'.[9] The frequently reprinted Clementine Vulgate of 1592 followed the practice of separating books separately registered in ancient lists, with regard to the Apocrypha which had not been recommended by Augustine and at Trent, 1–2 Esdras (*3–4 Ezra*) and the Prayer of Manasses; these were grouped in an appendix with one esteemed New Testament apocryphon, Laodicaeans.

Yet the beneficial association of the names Apocrypha and Pseudepigrapha with the Hebrew canon has a concomitant disadvantage. It may divert attention from other writings outside the Hebrew Bible which shed light on these books. In particular, the Apocrypha and Pseudepigrapha should be viewed together with the rich tradition of biblical interpretation attested in the Septuagint, Qumran exegesis, Philo, Josephus, the New Testament, the Targums and rabbinic literature. The books of the Apocrypha and Pseudepigrapha, then, are closely related to the Hebrew Bible, an important point which these two names attest; but these books are also to be set within the great stream of early biblical interpretation which was already moving in the Persian period.

In what follows there are some elements of a survey, but an attempt is also made to consider the Apocrypha and Pseudepigrapha as part of the evidence concerning messianism in the Second Temple period as a whole. The present writer has urged elsewhere that throughout this period, roughly from Haggai to Bar Kokhba, messianic hope was more pervasive than is usually allowed.[10] Here it is asked whether the relevant material in the Apocrypha and Pseudepigrapha, scattered chronologically over the years from Alexander the Great to Hadrian, is consistent with such a view. The Apocrypha, in which clear allusions to messianic hope are sparse, are reviewed with regard to the suggestion

Lutheran thought, which had been submitted at the Council of Trent in 1552.

9. On the new vocabulary sponsored by Sixtus (who notes the old terms which he is replacing) see Bedouelle, 'Le canon', pp. 268-74, 280-82.

10. W. Horbury, *Jewish Messianism and the Cult of Christ* (London: SCM Press, 1998).

that between the fifth and the second centuries there was a 'messianological vacuum'. The Pseudepigrapha, in which such allusions are more
plentiful, are considered in connection with the view that messianism
was predominantly diverse.

The Apocrypha and the Question of a Messianological Vacuum

The Apocrypha of the English Bible have for long been a centrepiece in
a regular manifestation of the study of messianism, which may be
called the 'no hope list'—the list of books wherein no messianic hope
is to be found. The books cited often come from the Hebrew Bible as
well as the Apocrypha; a representative list would include at least
Baruch, Tobit, Judith, 1–2 Maccabees, and the Wisdom of Solomon as
writings where mention of a Messiah might be expected, but is absent.[11]
The most obviously messianic book in the Apocrypha, 2 Esdras (*4 Ezra*
in the Vulgate), is also one of those which lacks strong support in
ecclesiastical tradition, as is evident from its fate at Trent and the loss
of its Greek text. The Apocrypha, therefore, the group among the books
of the Apocrypha and Pseudepigrapha which enjoyed more authority
among early Christians and probably also among Jews, seems almost to
suggest the unimportance rather than the importance of messianism.

Not all would accept that the distinction drawn by many patristic
authors between the groups of books which came to be known as the
Apocrypha and the Pseudepigrapha was already current among Jews at
the end of the Second Temple period. Some have regarded the two sets

---

11. For such lists see W.V. Hague, 'The Eschatology of the Apocryphal
Scriptures. I. The Messianic Hope', *JTS* 12 (1911), pp. 57-98 (64); A. von Gall,
*ΒΑΣΙΛΕΙΑ ΤΟΥ ΘΕΟΥ: Eine religionsgeschichtliche Studie zur vorkirchlichen
Eschatologie* (Heidelberg: Carl Winter, 1926), pp. 376-77; W. Bousset and
H. Gressmann, *Die Religion des Judentums im späthellenistischen Zeitalter*
(Tübingen: J.C.B. Mohr [Paul Siebeck], 3rd edn, 1926), p. 222; S.B. Frost, *Old
Testament Apocalyptic: Its Origins and Growth* (London: Epworth Press, 1952),
pp. 66-67; S. Mowinckel, *Han som kommer* (Copenhagen: G.E.C. Gad, 1951),
p.185 (ET *He That Cometh* [trans. G.W. Anderson, Oxford: Basil Blackwell, 1956],
p. 180); Morton Smith, 'What is Implied by the Variety of Messianic Figures?',
JBL 78 (1959), pp. 66-72 (reprinted in M. Smith, *Studies in the Cult of Yahweh* [ed.
S.J.D. Cohen; 2 vols, Leiden: E.J. Brill, 1996]), I, pp. 161-67 (163) (passing over
the Apocrypha); J. Becker, *Messiaserwartung im Alten Testament* (SBS, 83;
Stuttgart: Katholisches Bibelwerk, 1977), p. 74 (ET *Messianic Expectation in the
Old Testament* [trans. D.E. Green; Edinburgh: T. & T. Clark, 1980], p. 79).

of books as virtually indistinguishable in the pre-Christian and primitive Christian periods.[12] Many of the Pseudepigrapha were probably read as widely as many of the Apocrypha, as is suggested for the Judaean Jewish community by the Qumran finds and for early Christian Egypt by quotations and papyri; yet, on the other side, there is a case, accepted by the present writer, for holding that the Christian distinction between the authority to be attached to the two sets of writings probably has pre-Christian antecedents.[13] Hence in what follows it is presupposed that at the end of the Second Temple period, among Jews as well as Christians, most of the Apocrypha are likely to have been more widely acceptable than the Pseudepigrapha, even though they were not necessarily always more influential.

The Apocrypha and Pseudepigrapha overlap in date, but the Apocrypha include a far greater proportion of writings that can be securely assigned to the Greek period.[14] Thus pre-Maccabaean works in the Apocrypha include, together with Ecclesiasticus, probably also 1 Esdras, Tobit, Judith, the Greek adjuncts to Esther, and at least the first part of Baruch (1.1–3.8); coaeval with these books but within the Hebrew canon is the older part of Daniel, pre-Maccabaean work given its present form in the Maccabaean period. To return to the Apocrypha, a second-century date is likely for the Epistle of Jeremy (transmitted in the Vulgate as the sixth chapter of Baruch), the Greek adjuncts to

12. So Swete, *Introduction*, pp. 224-25; J. Barton, *Oracles of God* (London: Darton, Longman & Todd, 1986), pp. 35-81. R. Beckwith, *The Old Testament Canon of the New Testament Church and its Background in Early Judaism* (London: SPCK, 1985), pp. 406-408, similarly holds that the first Christians esteemed a number of books from the Apocrypha and Pseudepigrapha alike; but he suggests that Jewish groups valued various sets of books, including the Greek Apocrypha, as adjuncts to the canonical books.

13. W. Horbury, 'The Christian Use and the Jewish Origins of the Wisdom of Solomon', in J. Day, R.P. Gordon, and H.G.M. Williamson (eds.), *Wisdom in Ancient Israel: Essays in Honour of J.A. Emerton* (Cambridge: Cambridge University Press, 1995), pp. 182-96 (185-87); *idem, Jews and Christians in Contact and Controversy*, pp. 25-35, 206-15.

14. For discussion of date and attestation see especially E. Schürer, revised by G. Vermes and M.D. Goodman, in E. Schürer, *Geschichte des jüdischen Volkes im Zeitalter Jesu Christi* (Leipzig: J.C. Hinrichs, 3rd–4th edn, 1901–1909); ET (revised by G. Vermes, F. Millar, M. Black, M. Goodman and P. Vermes), *The History of the Jewish People in the Age of Jesus Christ* (3 vols.; Edinburgh: T. & T. Clark, 1973–87), III.1-2; on Wisdom, see also Horbury, 'Christian Use and Jewish Origins', pp. 183-85.

Daniel, and 2 Maccabees, while 1 Maccabees and probably also Wisdom can be assigned to the early years of the first century BCE. The short Prayer of Manasses, handed down in the LXX book of Odes, is probably pre-Christian. 2 Esdras, in which chs. 3–14 include material from the reign of Domitian, is probably the latest of all the books in the Apocrypha; but, as already noted, it teeters on the edge of the class of approved books because of its weak ecclesiastical support. The works from the Apocrypha represented in discoveries from the western shore of the Dead Sea are Tobit in Hebrew and Aramaic, the Epistle of Jeremy in Greek, and Ecclesiasticus in Hebrew. Also attested at Qumran in Hebrew is a pseudepigraph which through the LXX came near to gaining apocryphal status, Psalm 151. All four texts represented in Dead Sea discoveries are probably from the older material in the Apocrypha.

On these datings the relatively non-messianic Apocrypha are contemporary with other more strongly messianic texts in the LXX and the Pseudepigrapha. These include the LXX Pentateuch in the third century, the *Testaments of the Twelve Patriarchs* and the LXX Isaiah, Jeremiah, Ezekiel, Twelve Prophets and Psalms in the second, and the *Messianic Apocalypse* (4Q 521), the *Psalms of Solomon* and relevant parts of the Third Sibylline book in the first century BCE. Messianism is then important, from the time of Herod the Great onwards, in the series of apocalypses beginning with the Parables of Enoch (*1 Enoch* 37–71, not attested at Qumran) and including, after the destruction of Jerusalem by Titus, the apocalypses of Ezra (2 Esd. 3–14) and Baruch (*2 Baruch*, the Syriac *Apocalypse of Baruch*); the Fifth Sibylline book and the Christian Revelation of St John the Divine should be viewed together with this series.

The widespread silence of the Apocrypha on messianism, together with the ambiguity of Chronicles in this respect, has encouraged the view that a 'messianological vacuum' can be identified in Jewish literature between the fifth and the second centuries.[15] This view is already questioned by the third-century material noted in the preceding paragraph. The LXX Pentateuch in particular presents a messianic interpretation of the prophecies of Jacob and Balaam that is so strongly developed

---

15. Frost, *Old Testament Apocalyptic*, pp. 66-67; Becker, *Messiaserwartung*, pp. 74-77 (ET *Messianic Expectation*, pp. 79-82); J.J. Collins, *The Scepter and the Star: The Messiahs of the Dead Sea Scrolls and Other Ancient Literature* (Anchor Bible Reference Library; New York: Doubleday, 1995), pp. 31-38, 40 (with caution).

that it seems likely to be significant for the fourth century as well as the third, with regard to Chronicles and other possibly messianic material from the later Persian period.[16] Yet part of the strength of the 'vacuum' view lies in its association of silence on messianism, even if the extent of this silence is debatable, with a theocentric emphasis in postexilic Israelite religion.

This emphasis on 'God who lives for ever, and his kingdom' (Tob. 13.1) has sometimes been understood as involving an opposition to earthly Israelite monarchy that inspired the reapplication of messianic promises to the nation as a whole or to God himself, for instance in Deutero-Isaiah on the 'sure mercies of David' (Isa. 55.3-4) or Zech. 9.9-10 on the lowly king.[17] Despite the close links of kingship with Israel and the kingship of God, the reapplication envisaged by exegetes in instances such as these is not beyond question.[18] A more clearly marked aspect of theocentrism is the readiness to portray the deity himself as a warrior king, which is evident throughout the Second Temple period; the two Songs of Moses (Exod. 15; Deut. 32) evince this outlook in a manner which will have been particularly influential, as is illustrated below, given their incorporation into the Pentateuch.

Attention was drawn to the postexilic importance of this line of thought by H. Gressmann and A. von Gall, with reference to such passages as the enthronement psalms, Zechariah 14 and the Isaiah Apocalypse (Isa. 24–27). Its vitality throughout the later Second Temple period is confirmed by the hymns to the divine victor in the *War Scroll* (e.g. 1QM 12.11-12), by the development of the portrait of the divine warrior from Isa. 59.16-18 in Wis. 5.16-23, and by the bold anthropomorphism with which the Lord is envisaged as a man of war in some rabbinic tradition.[19] Gressmann justly called this hero–deity the double

---

16. Horbury, *Jewish Messianism and the Cult of Christ*, pp. 36-51.

17. So Becker, *Messiaserwartung*, pp. 63-64, 67-68 (ET *Messianic Expectation*, pp. 68-70 [Isa. 55], 72-73 [Zech. 9]); R. Albertz, *Religionsgeschichte Israels in alttestamentlicher Zeit*, II (Göttingen: Vandenhoeck & Ruprecht, 1992), p. 446 (ET *A History of Israelite Religion in the Old Testament Period*, II [trans. J. Bowden, London: SCM Press, 1992], p. 426 [Isa. 55]).

18. Thus C.R. North, who took Isa. 55 to speak of transference of the Davidic covenant to the community, specially noted the difficulty of deciding whether this or revival of monarchy is in view (C.R. North, *The Second Isaiah* [Oxford: Clarendon Press, 1964], p. 255); and Zech. 9.9 is taken by Albertz, *Religionsgeschichte*, II, p. 639 (ET *Religion*, II, p. 567) to envisage an earthly ruler.

19. See for example *Mekilta deRabbi Ishmael*, Beshallah, Shirata 4, on Exod.

of the Messiah.[20] For von Gall the Messiah played only a subordinate part in the eschatology of Judaism at the end of the Second-Temple period, partly because God himself was so vividly imagined as the coming king, and partly because only extreme nationalists went to the length of envisaging an earthly leader; that is why the Messiah is often unmentioned.[21] Thus in von Gall's reconstruction the Apocrypha and Pseudepigrapha, roughly speaking non-messianic and sometimes messianic respectively, would correspond to a dual Old Testament emphasis on the kingdom of God and the kingdom of the Messiah, respectively; and in the Greek and Roman periods, just as under the Persians, the theme of the kingdom of God would have been the more important.

As the reference to Wisdom has already suggested, in the Apocrypha a silence on messianism can indeed be accompanied by vivid portrayal of the God of Israel as a hero. Outside the Wisdom of Solomon this combination is especially noticeable in the substantial group of mainly prose and mainly narrative books: 1 Esdras, the Greek adjuncts to Esther and Daniel, Tobit, Judith, 1–2 Maccabees, and (with a smaller proportion of prose) Baruch and the Epistle of Jeremy. Assessment of their silence or near-silence on messianism is indeed affected by their narrative character. We should not expect messianic expectations to be straightforwardly mentioned in prose historical narrative following the biblical model; for in biblical prose directly messianic material is mainly found in prophecies or psalms inserted into the narrative, as is the case with the Song of Hannah or the Pentateuchal prophecies of Jacob and Balaam. It turns out, however, that even the poems and prayers in these narratives in the Apocrypha, although they do indeed express hopes for national redemption, regularly lay emphasis on the kingdom of God, not the kingdom of the Messiah.

The narrative books give occasion for the expression of redemptive hopes above all because their principal figures have prophetic and martyr-like characteristics. These characteristics are obvious in Daniel and the Three Children, and Eleazar the scribe and the seven brethren and their mother (2 Macc. 6–7); but they are there too in Tobit, who

---

15.3 (he appeared at the Red Sea like an armed warrior); *Pesiqta deRab Kahana* 22.5 (he puts on garments of vengeance and red apparel, as at Isa. 59.17, 63.2).

20. H. Gressmann, *Der Ursprung der israelitisch-jüdischen Eschatologie* (FRLANT, 6; Göttingen: Vandenhoeck & Ruprecht, 1905), pp. 294-301.

21. Von Gall, *ΒΑΣΙΛΕΙΑ*, pp. 214-57, 291, 374-77.

flees from persecution and suffers the loss of all his goods, but returns when times improve (1.19-20, 2.8), and before his death prophesies the glorification of Jerusalem. Baruch speaks prophetically of the consolation of Jerusalem at the ingathering. Mordecai and Esther can to some extent be associated with the martyrs, for in the Greek Esther his perilous refusal to bow to Haman is explained as a Zealot-like refusal to honour man rather than God (13.12-14), and she risks her life and endures a mortal agony of fear (14-15). Martyr-themes also appear in Judith, where the destruction of the Temple and the imposition of ruler-cult are feared (3.8, 6.2). To the martyr figures of the prose narratives there should of course be added, from a book which follows the verse tradition of the biblical wisdom literature, the righteous sufferer whose tribulation and vindication are vividly depicted in Wisdom 1–5.

The prophecies in these books are concerned above all with the ingathering and the divine vengeance, considered as a victory over idols and over earthly enemies. Thus in Esther, Judith, Tobit and 1–2 Maccabees stress is laid on the overthrow of Israel's enemies—Persian, Assyrian, or Greek. The prayers and prophecies in the narratives follow suit, often reflecting the influence of the depictions of a warrior-deity in the two Songs of Moses. In the Greek Esther, Mordecai and Esther pray to God as king and victor over idols, in words which echo the enthronement psalms and the greater song of Moses in Deuteronomy 32 (see 13.9, 15 [Lord, thou God, king, God of Abraham, cf. Ps. 47.7-10, ET 6-9], 14.3, 8-12 [king of the gods, cf. Ps. 95.3], 17 ['nor have I drunk the wine of the drink offerings', cf. Deut. 32.38]). Similarly, the prayer and thanksgiving of Judith (9.7, 16.3) echo Ps. 76.4 (ET 3) on the Lord who breaks the battle as a warrior king in Zion (compare also Ps. 46.10 [ET 9]); and in her thanksgiving (16.2-17) this thought leads to a passage echoing Psalm 96 and Exodus 15 which ends with a woe to the nations, for 'the Lord almighty will take vengeance on them in the day of judgment, to put fire and worms in their flesh' (compare Deut. 32.41-43; Isa. 66.14-16, 24). Judith's thanksgiving is immediately followed by a dedication of the spoils of Holofernes in Jerusalem (Jdt. 16.18-20), and this scene crowns an important series of allusions to the biblical Zion theme; Judith prays for the defence of the sanctuary (9.8, 13) and stands for 'the exaltation of Jerusalem' (10.8, 13.4, 15.9).

Tobit prophesies the ingathering and the end of idolatry (13–14), again with repeated emphasis on the kingdom of God in his prayer (13.1, 6, 7, 10, 11, 15), and now with an address to Jerusalem (13.9

onwards). Baruch 4–5 combines echoes of Deuteronomy 32, on Israel's idolatry and the coming punishment of the nations, with an apostrophe to Jerusalem on the ingathering, echoing Isaiah 60. Again, ingathering to the holy place (Exod. 15.17) and vengeance on the oppressor-nations are the main themes of the Jerusalem prayer in 2 Macc. 1.25-29, which reads like an antecedent of the Eighteen Benedictions. Lastly, divine vengeance on oppressors is envisaged in Wisdom 1–5 within the context of a hope of immortality (3.4). At Wis. 3.1-9 it includes the 'visitation' of righteous souls (compare Gen. 50.24-25; Isa. 10.3; Ps. 106.4-5 [LXX, 'visit us']; Ecclus 35.17-19; 1QS 3.14, 4.18-19; *Ass. Mos.* 1.18); and at Wis. 5.15-23 they are protected at the world-wide judgmental victory of the divine warrior (compare Isa. 59.16-19, as noted above).

Ingathering to Zion and vengeance on oppressors can of course involve a messianic leader, as in the explicitly messianic ingatherings depicted later on in *Pss. Sol.* 17.26, 42-44, and 2 Esd. 13.39-40, where in each case the event is still emphatically presented as the work of God. Is such a leader ruled out by the sole stress on the kingship of God in these passages from the Apocrypha, with their echoes of the enthronement psalms, Trito-Isaiah on Zion, and the two Songs of Moses?

The answer 'Yes' is not so clear as might perhaps be supposed. First, as already noted, the 'messianological vacuum' itself is by no means airtight. There is no question of centuries kept clear of any breath of messianic hope. The texts just considered from the Apocrypha are contemporary with others in which messianic hope is explicit, including the LXX Pentateuch and Prophets. Secondly, some of the theocentric biblical passages taken up in the Apocryphal texts were themselves interpreted in ways consonant with messianic hope. Thus the hymns to the divine warrior which were put in the mouth of Moses in Exodus 15 and Deuteronomy 32 had become part of an exodus narrative in which not only the divine king but also Israel's earthly ruler, Moses, was of great importance. Similarly, the Trito-Isaianic prophecies of Zion included during the Persian period the oracle of a redeemer for Zion, immediately following the description of the divine warrior taken up in Wisdom 5 (Isa. 59.20); by the second century they were also read as including another oracle of a saviour (Isa. 62.11 LXX).[22] Comparably,

22. On the 'redeemer' see A. Rofé, 'Isaiah 59:19 and Trito-Isaiah's Vision of Redemption', in J. Vermeylen (ed.), *The Book of Isaiah, le Livre d'Isaïe: Les*

the depiction of the divine avenger in Isa. 63.1-6 was immediately followed by a Zion-oriented prayer (63.7–64.11 [ET 12]) in which the thought of redemption by God alone once again came to be intensely expressed (Isa. 63.9 LXX, 'not an ambassador, nor an angel, but the Lord himself saved us', anticipating a rabbinic formula well known from the Passover Haggadah); but in this prayer the exodus, the paradigmatic redemption of old, also explicitly involves Moses, the 'shepherd' (Isa. 63.11). Thirdly, the occasions on which it is said that God himself fights Israel's battle do not exclude the figures of Moses and an angel, Joshua, the king, or Judas Maccabaeus and an angel (Exod. 14.14; Josh. 10.14; Ps. 20.7-10, ET 6–9; 2 Macc. 11.8-10). This is also true of the *War Scroll*, in a passage (1QM 11.1-7) which concludes, 'Truly the battle is thine and the power from thee. It is not ours. Our strength and the power of our hands accomplish no mighty deeds except by thy power and the might of thy great valour. This thou hast taught us from ancient times, saying, A star shall come out of Jacob...' Here God's own action is precisely the sending of the Messiah, the star from Jacob (Num. 24.17).

In sum, therefore, the prayers and predictions in the Apocrypha which have just been considered show that redemption and judgment could be satisfactorily imagined through concentration on the portrayal of God himself as the hero; but they hardly show that a messianic leader was ruled out. It seems indeed not unlikely that divine redemption could have been taken to involve human leadership of the kind which was archetypally depicted in the Pentateuchal narratives of the exodus.

The silence of the Apocrypha on messianism has claimed attention so far, with the theory of a 'messianological vacuum' in view. In at least three of these books, however, the silence is less than total. 2 Esdras will be considered below, with the Pseudepigrapha. The other two books in question are among the most influential of all the Apocrypha, Ecclesiasticus and 1 Maccabees. The relevant passages should be considered in the context of the exaltation of Jewish rulers in these and other books of the Apocrypha. Ben Sira himself of course glorifies Moses, Aaron, and Phinehas, without forgetting David, Solomon, the righteous kings, and Zerubbabel (45.1-26, 47.1-22, 48.17–49.4, 11), and Simon the high priest in his own days (50.1-21); but similarly,

oracles et leurs relectures, unité et complexité de l'ouvrage (BETL, 81; Leuven: Peeters, 1989), pp. 407-410.

1 Esdras honours Ezra 'the high priest' (9.40) as well as the Davidic Josiah and Zerubbabel (1.32, 4.13, 5.5-6); in Judith the high priest Joakim has a central place (4.6-15, 15.8), and in 2 Maccabees Onias the high priest has the attributes of a saint, represented in both legend and vision (3.1-36, 15.12-15). The encomia of the Maccabaean priestly rulers in 1 Maccabees are noted below. In Wisdom, high-priestly praise emerges again in the lines on Aaron, the blameless servant of God who stayed the plague, vested in cosmic glory, for 'in the long robe is the whole world' (18.20-25); and the presentation of King Solomon and a series of Israelite leaders as inspired by celestial wisdom (Wis. 7-10) is implicitly messianic, insofar as it suggests that Israel may still in the future be similarly blessed.

All these books reflect the glory of the high priest, as that was envisaged in the Second Temple period, but in Ecclesiasticus, 1 Esdras and Wisdom the éclat of the Davidic monarchy is also evident. It is therefore not surprising that David has a place in the Hymn of the Fathers in Ecclesiasticus; but it is striking, in view of the author's strong devotion to the high priest's honour, that David and his covenant are noticed three times.[23] First, Ben Sira proceeds as might be expected from Moses and Aaron to Phinehas; but then (45.25) he fits a reference to the covenant with David in after his reference to the covenant with Levi and Phinehas, and before he goes on to Joshua. The Hebrew text preserved in a Bodleian fragment of the Genizah MS B can be rendered on the following lines, in the light of the grandson's Greek:

> And there is also a covenant with David, son of Jesse, from the tribe of Judah;
> the inheritance of a Man [the king] is to his son alone, the inheritance of Aaron is also to his seed.[24]

23. On the context see J.D. Martin, 'Ben Sira's Hymn to the Fathers: a Messianic Perspective', in A.S. van der Woude (ed.), *Crises and Perspectives* (OTS, 24; Leiden: E.J. Brill, 1986], pp. 107-23. The line 'Praise him who makes a horn to flourish for the house of David' in the Hebrew psalm of fifteen verses found in two Cambridge leaves of the Genizah MS B after Ecclus. 51.12 (P.C. Beentjes, *The Book of Ben Sira in Hebrew* [VTSup, 58; Leiden: E.J. Brill, 1997], pp. 92-93) is not considered here; the case for the authenticity of these verses (M.Z. [H.] Segal, *Sepher Ben Sira ha-shalem* [Jerusalem: Bialik Institute, 2nd edn, 1958], p. 352) is outweighed for the present writer by their absence from the grandson's version.

24. Pointing *'iš* with R. Smend, and emending to *lbnw lbdw* with I. Lévi, both cited by Segal, *Ben Sira*, p. 316; for the text see A.E. Cowley and Ad. Neubauer (eds.), *The Original Hebrew of a Portion of Ecclesiasticus (xxxix. 15 to xlix. 11)*,

This abruptly expressed passage seems to praise the Levitical covenant of priestly descent though Phinehas by means of a comparison or contrast with the covenant of Davidic succession, as both the Greek and the Syriac versions suggest. Its placing and wording are probably influenced by Jer. 33.17-22, a comparison of the covenants of Levi and David, and one of the passages which promises that there should never be cut off a 'man' to sit on David's throne.[25] In any case, its presence when the context did not demand it suggests the abiding importance of the Davidic tradition and hope even when the high priest is the supreme contemporary figure; there would be no compliment to the priesthood in such a comparison or contrast if the Davidic covenant did not enjoy great prestige and expectation of continuity.

Comparably, the passage devoted to David separately in the praise of the fathers (47.1-11) dwells like Psalm 151 on the God-given strength of his youthful feats, and ends with a reference to his royal throne over Jerusalem; taking up an image with a firm place in Davidic dynastic oracles (1 Sam. 2.10, etc.), Ben Sira concludes that God 'exalted his horn for ever'.[26] In the light of the earlier passage there is no need to minimize this 'for ever', as is sometimes done; Ben Sira's great reverence for Simon the high priest need not imply that he thought the royal line was now subsumed in the high priesthood, never to revive independently.[27] On the contrary, after his ensuing account of Solomon

together with the Early Versions and an English Translation, followed by the Quotations from Ben Sira in Rabbinical Literature (Oxford: Clarendon Press, 1897), pp. 28-29, with English translation, or Beentjes, *Ben Sira*, p. 81.

25. On the royal 'man' in Ecclus 45.25 and other texts see W. Horbury, 'The Messianic Associations of "the Son of Man"', *JTS* NS 36 (1985), pp. 34-55 (51); for David and his seed as granted the covenant of kingship, see the interpretation of Gen. 49.10 in 4Q 252 (G. Vermes, *The Complete Dead Sea Scrolls in English* [London: Allen Lane, 1997], p. 463), quoted in n. 44, below.

26. On the horn in Davidic oracles and in this passage see D.C. Duling, 'The Promises to David and their Entrance into Christianity: Nailing down a Likely Hypothesis', *NTS* 20 (1973), pp. 55-77 (58, 62).

27. For minimizing interpretation on these lines see J.J. Collins, 'Messianism in the Maccabean Period', in J. Neusner, W.S. Green and E.S. Frerichs (eds.), *Judaisms and their Messiahs at the Turn of the Christian Era* (Cambridge: Cambridge University Press, 1987), pp. 97-109 (98); *idem*, *Scepter*, pp. 33-34; K.E. Pomykala, *The Davidic Dynasty Tradition in Early Judaism: Its History and Significance for Messianism* (Atlanta: Scholars Press, 1995), pp. 131-45. G.S. Oegema, *Der Gesalbte und sein Volk: Untersuchungen zum Konzeptualisierungsprozess der messianischen Erwartungen von den Makkabäern bis Bar Koziba* (Schriften des

he expresses at the end of 47.22, in a line of which only a few letters are preserved in Hebrew, the expectation that through God's mercy there will be a 'remnant' for Jacob, and a 'root' for David. M.H. Segal here identified an allusion to a prophecy quoted in Rom. 15.12 as a testimony to a messianic king of the Gentiles, Isa. 11.10 (cf. 1): 'And there shall be on that day a root of Jesse, who shall stand for an ensign of the peoples'.[28] This identification is strengthened by the fact that Isa. 11.1-10 continue the oracles of 10.20-34, which begin with the promise of the return of the 'remnant of Jacob' (10.20-21), which is also echoed in Ecclus 47.22, and themselves are in the sequel of the oracle of the prince of peace on David's throne (Isa. 9.6-7 [ET 5-6]). The comparable combination of 'the throne of David' (Isa. 9.7 [ET 6]) and 'the house of Jacob' (Isa. 10.20) occurs in the Davidic promise of Lk. 1.33. The association of the Davidic oracles of Isaiah 9 and 11 with the 'house' and 'remnant' of Jacob in Isaiah 10 will have been further assisted by the Davidic interpretation of the blessing of Jacob in Gen. 49.9-10. This was current before as well as after Ben Sira's time, as the LXX Pentateuch shows; compare 4Q 252 on Gen. 49.10 and the Davidic covenant of kingship (see n. 25, above) with Gen. 49.9 LXX, 'from the shoot, my son, you came up', alluding to Isa. 11.1.[29]

In the background of the Davidic passages in Ecclesiasticus there may then be envisaged the combination of the rich narrative material on David (including its development, outside the Hebrew canon, in Psalm 151) with prophetic Davidic oracles, notably those ascribed to Nathan and Isaiah, and probably also with a Davidic interpretation of Jacob's prophecy of kings descended from Judah. Ben Sira's threefold use of

Institutum Judaicum Delitzschianum, 2; Göttingen: Vandenhoeck & Ruprecht, 1994), pp. 50-56, without special discussion of the texts considered here, likewise judges that kings are solely past authorities for Ben Sira, who lacks messianic hope and tends rather to 'messianize' Simon the high priest. A. Laato, *A Star is Rising: The Historical Development of the Old Testament Royal Ideology and the Rise of the Jewish Messianic Expectations* (University of South Florida International Studies in Formative Christianity and Judaism, 5; Atlanta: Scholars Press, 1997), pp. 242-47, dissents from this view, on arguments overlapping with those presented above.

28. Segal, *Ben Sira*, p. 329; on this and other allusions to the Davidic promises in Ecclus 47.22 see also Duling, 'Promises', pp. 61-62. The Isaianic allusion is ignored by Pomykala, *The Davidic Dynasty Tradition*, pp. 145-47 (denying that 47.22 has any messianic aspect).

29. Horbury, *Jewish Messianism and the Cult of Christ*, p. 50.

this material, within a Levitical atmosphere which might have been expected to muffle Davidic allusion, has a sufficiently strong and consistent emphasis on succession and hope to merit the adjective 'messianic'.

One may compare these passages in Ecclesiasticus with the reference to David's throne for ever made perhaps nearly a century later in 1 Macc. 2.57. Once again the immediate setting of the reference is priestly, in this case the last words of Mattathias the priest, the patriarch of the Hasmonaean line. At the same time, therefore, the surrounding atmosphere is that of the court praise given to the ruling dynasty. In 1 Maccabees the Maccabaean house is 'the seed of those by whose hand salvation (σωτηρία) was given to Israel' (1 Macc. 5.62). Aretalogical poems honour Judas Maccabaeus as a veritable lion of Judah, 'saving Israel' (1 Macc. 3.3-9, 9.21), and Simon Maccabaeus in 'his authority and glory' (14.4-15). The rulers thus have some of the glamour of what could be called in a broad sense a fulfilled messianism; but future hopes probably remain important among Jews in general, as J.A. Goldstein has emphasized, and it seems possible that even in this court praise such hopes find rather more reflection than might be suggested by Goldstein's profile of Maccabaean propaganda.[30] Thus Judas Maccabaeus, 'saving Israel', still prays to God as saviour of Israel (1 Macc. 4.30), and the hymns in praise of Judas and Simon still leave room for divine deliverance to come. Similarly, the prayer of 2 Macc. 2.17-18, which takes it that through the Maccabees God has restored 'the heritage to all, and the kingdom, and the priesthood, and the hallowing', as promised in Exod. 19.6 LXX, still looks for a future ingathering into the holy place, and confirms that the Hasmonaean polity was not regarded as the total fulfilment of the divine promises.

In the last words of Mattathias (1 Macc. 2.49-70) his list of examples for his sons includes not only 'Phinehas our father', as might be expected of a priest, but also David, who 'by his mercy inherited a throne of kingdom for ever' (εἰς αἰῶνας, 2.57). 'Mercy' here seems to be David's own good deeds, as probably in the appeal to his 'mercies' at the end of Solomon's prayer in 2 Chronicles (6.42). The 'throne of

---

30. J.A. Goldstein, 'How the Authors of 1 and 2 Maccabees Treated the "Messianic" Promises', in Neusner, Green and Frerichs (eds.), *Judaisms and Their Messiahs*, 69-96, especially 69-81, followed in the main on 1 Macc. 2.57 by Pomykala, *The Davidic Dynasty Tradition*, pp. 152-59; for dissent, see Laato, *Star*, pp. 275-79.

kingdom for ever' echoes the promise of 2 Sam. 7.13, 'I will establish
the throne of his kingdom for ever' (compare 2 Sam. 7.16; 1 Chron.
17.12, 14; Isa. 9.7 [ET 6]). A similar echo of this promise and of Isa. 9.7
[ET 6]) can be heard at Lk. 1.33 (already noticed in connection with
Ecclus 47.22), 'the Lord God shall give him the throne of his father
David, and he shall reign over the house of Jacob for ever'. 'For ever'
need not be taken in its fullest sense in Mattathias's speech, as has
often been emphasized; but the presence of the phrase suggests that the
specifically messianic potential of the Davidic reference has not been
nullified by the author or redactor. Similarly, although the stress laid
here on David's good deeds fits the presentation in 1 Maccabees of
Hasmonaean achievements as Davidic, it also assimilates the past
David to the expected future son of David. Thus in the LXX Isaiah, perhaps also from the Maccabaean age, the Davidic Messiah's description
as a prince of peace is further underlined (Isa. 9.5-6 LXX); and in the
Psalms of Solomon, towards the end of the Hasmonaean period, the
virtue of the coming son of David is vividly portrayed (*Pss. Sol.* 17.32-
37, noticed further below).[31] In the context of the last words of
Mattathias, then, this sentence on David has no special messianic
emphasis; but its presence shows that a tradition with a clear messianic
aspect was current and could be used despite Maccabaean loyalties.

In Ecclesiasticus and 1 Maccabees alike, therefore, a writer who
appears to be a staunch upholder of the current authorities in Judaea
finds it natural to allude not just to David, but to the promises concerning his throne and line. These relatively slight references are therefore an impressive testimony to the strength of messianism as part of
the biblical tradition. A similar inference can be drawn from the
messianism of the LXX Pentateuch, a document used in settings where
Jews were profoundly conscious of the importance of loyalty to rulers.
In discussion of both Ecclesiasticus and 1 Maccabees by commentators
concerned with messianism, stress has naturally been laid, nevertheless,
on political circumstances which could have inhibited messianic interpretation of the references to David's throne and line; and Ecclesiasticus
and 1 Maccabees have sometimes been assigned accordingly to the
'messianological vacuum'. In the treatment offered above, by contrast,

---

31. The LXX form of Isa. 9.6-7 is associated with Maccabaean Davidic expectation by R. Hanhart, 'Die Septuaginta als Interpretation und Aktualisierung: Jesaja
9:1 (8:23)-7(6)', in A. Rofé and Y. Zakovitch (eds.), *Isac Leo Seeligmann Volume*,
III (Jerusalem: E. Rubinstein, 1983), pp. 331-46 (345-46).

an attempt has been made to show how much in both cases has been taken up from the messianic development of the biblical Davidic promises. Messianism involved an interaction between biblically-rooted tradition and the external political situation; but the roots of the tradition in the biblical books and their accepted interpretation were widespread and deep, as the LXX and later on the Targums show. Messianism therefore had a life in the common mind independently of the special circumstances which might encourage or discourage it. It is notable, finally, that Ecclesiasticus and 1 Maccabees, the books in which a reflection of messianic tradition has been traced, are unlikely to represent marginal opinion; these are the two books of the Apocrypha which have perhaps most clearly been esteemed among Jews as well as Christians in antiquity.[32]

The Pseudepigrapha and the Diversity of Messianism

The Pseudepigrapha, on the other hand, as noted already, are essentially the books connected with the Old Testament which Christian tradition doubted or disapproved. Disapproval implied interest rather than the lack of it, however, as has already been noted for Christian Egypt; a similar coexistence of disapproval and interest can be conjectured in earlier Jewish opinion, at the time of the copying of the texts of Pseudepigrapha deposited at Qumran. Modern usage has associated with these books some comparable Jewish works under Gentile pseudonyms, of which only the *Sibylline Oracles* are mentioned here, and some other books associated with Scripture which have been made known through discoveries of MSS, especially at Qumran.[33]

To note the earlier Pseudepigrapha roughly in chronological order, the pre-Maccabaean parts of the Third Sibylline book and of *1 Enoch* both include some possibly third-century material. The *Testament of*

---

32. On Jewish use of Ecclesiasticus in Hebrew see Cowley and Neubauer (eds.), *Portion*, pp. ix-xii, xix-xxx (collecting quotations); on 1 Maccabees in Hebrew, Origen in Eusebius, *Hist. Eccles.* 6.25.2, cited above (quoting a Jewish book-list in which 'the Maccabees' is an 'outside' book with a Semitic-language title); Jerome, in the Prologue to Kings cited above, 'I have found the first book of the Maccabees in Hebrew' (Weber, *Biblia Sacra*, I, p. 365).

33. On date and attestation of the books mentioned below see especially E. Schürer, revised by G. Vermes and M.D. Goodman, in Schürer, *Geschichte* (ET, revised by G. Vermes, Millar, Black, Goodman, and P. Vermes, *History*, III.1-2; Vermes, *Complete Dead Sea Scrolls*.

Kohath known fragmentarily from Qumran is third century or earlier, according to radiocarbon dating (1990).[34] This startling result supports other considerations suggesting that much of the expanded Bible attested in Qumran texts and in books like Baruch may come from early in the Greek period. Thus *Jubilees*, possibly also the *Genesis Apocryphon*, and the extra-canonical psalms—among which at least Psalm 151 attained near-canonical status—can be assigned to the second century, and this may be the case too with the *Temple Scroll* and the fragmentary Qumran *Second Ezekiel*, but still earlier dates are not impossible for all these sources. The *Testaments of the Twelve Patriarchs* are known in the main through Christian transmission, but their basis is probably of the second century BCE, for much in the work suits Hasmonaean circumstances. Then *3 Maccabees* is probably of the second century BCE, although it is often dated much later. The poem known as the *Messianic Apocalypse* (4Q 521) is at latest from the early part of the first century BCE, and the *Psalms of Solomon*, which also touch the messianic theme, are from the mid-first century BCE. The *Biblical Antiquities* of Pseudo-Philo have a kinship with Josephus's *Antiquities*, which is among the features suggesting a late Herodian date, but which might alternatively point to a common source in more ancient biblical paraphrase.

Among writings that enlarge on a particular biblical character or episode, *Joseph and Asenath* and *Jannes and Jambres* are probably both from Ptolemaic Egypt, and the *Prayer of Joseph* and the *Testament of Job* are usually dated about the time of Christian origins but may be older; *4 Maccabees* and the *Paralipomena of Jeremiah* are perhaps from about the end of the first century CE. Among works which can broadly be called prophecies, the Parables of Enoch (*1 En.* 37–71) are of disputed date, but can be ascribed to the Herodian period with fair probability (see ch. 56); the *Assumption of Moses* is Herodian but from some time after the death of Herod the Great, the fragmentarily attested *Eldad and Medad* is probably from before the time of Christian origins, and several writings reflect the impact of the destruction of Jerusalem by Titus—the Fourth and Fifth Sibylline books, the Syriac *Apocalypse of Baruch* (*2 Baruch*), and perhaps also the *Apocalypse of Abraham*, although it could be earlier. Outside the Pseudepigrapha category, 2 Esdras and the Revelation of St John the Divine should be viewed together with this group of apocalypses.

34. Vermes, *Complete Dead Sea Scrolls*, pp. 13, 532.

Finally, some more Christianized works like the *Life of Adam* and *Eve*, *2 Enoch* on Melchizedek, and the Greek *Apocalypse of Baruch* certainly include Jewish material coaeval with the writings mentioned so far. The Pseudepigraphic writings known through Christian transmission or quotation which are now also attested by Dead Sea discoveries include *1 Enoch*, apart from chs. 37–71 (Aramaic), *Jubilees* (Hebrew), *Second Ezekiel* (Hebrew), and fragments of the *Testaments of Levi* (Aramaic) and *Naphtali* (Hebrew) which are related to the *Testaments of the Twelve Patriarchs*. As with the Apocrypha, the books attested in these discoveries are all likely to be old, probably pre-Maccabaean.

Hence, the series of Pseudepigrapha begins at latest in the third century BCE, and is substantial in the second century, but it has more material from the Herodian period and from after the Roman destruction of Jerusalem than is the case with the Apocrypha. Nevertheless, the books from the Greek period in the Apocrypha are contemporary with a very considerable literature in the Pseudepigrapha which contributes to a rewritten and expanded Bible; indeed, the Bible assumed in the books of the Apocrypha will probably often have been understood on the lines attested in the Pseudepigrapha. The works classified as Pseudepigrapha because they did not win approval appear to be those which seemed to supplant the books of the Hebrew canon, either by rewriting the text, or by offering new revelations. Hence the Pseudepigrapha include *Jubilees* and its congeners, the apocryphal *Ezekiel*, and the whole series of Jewish apocalypses from *1 Enoch* onwards, with the half-exception of 2 Esdras; the relatively late date of many apocalypses has also probably worked against them.

The process of rejection seems already to be reflected in 2 Esdras. Here such books as the Pseudepigrapha are defended by what amounts to an attack on the prestige of the twenty-four 'public' books, through a theory of a double revelation to Moses like that later expressed in order to validate oral Torah; in the seventy additional books reserved for the wise is the true spring of understanding and knowledge (2 Esd. 14.45-48; cf. 14.5-6).[35] The serious use which could be made of Pseude-

---

35. Biblical and extra-biblical passages linked with or reflecting this theory, including Deut. 29.28, *2 Bar.* 59.4-11, and *Lev. R.* 26.7, are compared by M.E. Stone, *Fourth Ezra* (Hermeneia; Minneapolis: Fortress Press, 1990), pp. 418-19, 441; for specification of the Mishnah and other traditions as revealed to Moses at Sinai, see for example *Lev. R.* 22.1, quoting Joshua b. Levi on Deut. 9.10.

pigrapha by Christian readers, despite all disapproval, is illustrated by
Origen on the Prayer of Joseph (Origen, *Jo.* 2.186-92 [31], on Jn 1.6),
and by a probably early fourth-century request for a loan of 'Esdras'
(probably 2 Esdras) in exchange for a loan of *Jubilees*, now documented in a papyrus letter.[36]

The Pseudepigrapha which attest messianism in particular include, as
noted above, the *Testaments of the Twelve Patriarchs* in the second
century BCE, the *Psalms of Solomon* and relevant parts of the Third
Sibylline book in the first century BCE, and a series of apocalypses
extending throughout and beyond the Herodian period, notably the
Parables of Enoch, the apocalypses of Ezra (2 Esd. 3–14) and Baruch
(*2 Baruch*, the Syriac *Apocalypse of Baruch*), and the Fifth Sibylline
book.[37]

These books have been a focus of the widespread scholarly emphasis
on the diversity of messianic hope. Morton Smith drew attention, with
reference to Qumran texts and Pseudepigrapha, to the range of positions suggested by silence on messianism, dual messianism (as in the
Testaments of the Twelve Patriarchs), and concentration on a single
figure; he also noted what he described as an even greater range of
eschatological expectation in general, for example in the various sections of *1 Enoch*.[38] A. Hultgård, similarly, judges that diversity is so
great that the messianic conception of each document should be considered on its own; but he is also able to list some common features.[39]
Earlier, W. Bousset had separated and contrasted what he judged to be

---

36. E. Bammel, 'Die Zitate aus den Apokryphen bei Origenes', in E. Bammel
(ed. P. Pilhofer), *Judaica et Paulina: Kleine Schriften*, II (Tübingen: J.C.B. Mohr
[Paul Siebeck], 1997), pp. 161-67; (reprinted from R.J. Daly [ed.], *Origeniana
Quinta* [BETL, 105; Leuven: Peeters, 1991], pp. 131-36); D.A. Hagedorn, 'Die
"Kleine Genesis" in P. Oxy. LXIII 4365', *ZPE* 116 (1997), pp. 147-48.

37. For a survey of their messianism see especially Andrew Chester, 'Jewish
Messianic Expectations and Mediatorial Figures and Pauline Christology', in
M. Hengel and U. Heckel (eds.), *Paulus und das antike Judentum* (Tübingen: J.C.B.
Mohr [Paul Siebeck], 1991), pp. 17-89 (27-37), and 'The Parting of the Ways:
Eschatology and Messianic Hope', in J.D.G. Dunn (ed.), *Jews and Christians: The
Parting of the Ways AD 70 to 135* (Tübingen: J.C.B. Mohr [Paul Siebeck], 1992),
pp. 239-313 (239-52) (literature).

38. Smith, 'What is Implied?', pp. 162-66.

39. A. Hultgård, *L'eschatologie des Testaments des Douze Patriarches* (Acta
Universitatis Upsaliensis, Historia Religionum, 6; 2 vols.; Uppsala: Almqvist &
Wiksell, 1977, 1982), I, pp. 301, 323-35.

two very different messianic portraits: that of a human ruler, in the *Psalms of Solomon*, and that of a superhuman hero, in the apocalypses ascribed to Enoch, Ezra, and Baruch.[40] This separation exemplifies a distinction between human and superhuman messianic figures which is often drawn, although it can be added that the characteristics of the two figures merge in many sources.[41] A similar yet differently ordered separation is accordingly employed by J.J. Collins to describe the Davidic Messiah, with special reference to the *Psalms of Solomon*, on the one hand, and the heavenly saviour king with traits from Daniel 7 on the other; in contrast with Bousset's presentation, the Herodian apocalypses, indebted both to the Davidic tradition and to the Danielic Son of Man, are justly considered in both sections.[42]

Can any unity be detected in the messianic portraiture of the Pseudepigrapha? A living tradition of messianic biblical interpretation, such as was discerned above behind Ecclesiasticus and 1 Maccabees, can be expected to proliferate, but it will not lose all coherence. The biblical literary deposit of the circle of ideas surrounding the Davidic monarchy forms a background against which a considerable unity can in fact be perceived, as a number of students of messianism have pointed out.[43] Three points in support of this understanding can be briefly illustrated here.

First, a sharp division between Davidic and non-Davidic expectations is discouraged by the traces in the Pseudepigrapha of a habit of connecting the Messiah not just with David, but with the whole series of Jewish kings and rulers, including the judges. A particularly important antecedent is Gen. 49.10, cited already; Jacob, speaking of the latter days, foresees a succession of princes and rulers from Judah, who shall never fail until he comes, to whom the kingdom pertains.[44] Towards the

---

40. Bousset and Gressmann, *Religion*, pp. 228-30, 259-68.

41. So Mowinckel, *Han som kommer*, pp. 185-89 (ET *He That Cometh*, pp. 280-86).

42. Collins, *Scepter*, pp. 48-73, 173-94.

43. So, in different ways, H. Riesenfeld and M.A. Chevallier (see Horbury, *Jewish Messianism and the Cult of Christ*, p. 65), and Laato, *Star*.

44. For this interpretation see Peshiṭta ('whose it [fem.] is'), *Targum Onkelos* ('the Messiah, whose is the kingdom'), *Targum Neofiti* and *Fragment Targum* (both 'the king Messiah, whose is the kingdom'), part of the LXX tradition (ἕως ἐὰν ἔλθῃ ᾧ ἀπόκειται), perhaps followed by Symmachus, and 4Q252, cited in n. 25, above ('the Messiah of righteousness, the seed of David, for to him and to his seed was given the covenant of the kingdom of his people'); the emphasis of the main LXX

end of the first century CE the interpretation of the cloud vision in *2 Baruch* correspondingly makes the Messiah sit on the throne of his kingdom (chs. 70–73) at the climax of the series of good rulers— David, Solomon, Hezekiah and Josiah (61, 63, 66). The connection of the Messiah not just with David, but with the line of good kings, emerges in a different way in the perhaps roughly contemporary last words ascribed to Johanan b. Zaccai: 'Set a throne for Hezekiah, king of Judah, who is coming' (*Ber.* 28b); the Messiah can be envisaged not only as David, as in Ezek. 37.24-26, but also as one of David's great reforming heirs, the king in whose days Assyria was smitten.

The more straightforward presentation of a royal succession leading up to the Messiah, as in Gen. 49.10, reappears in Pseudo-Philo's *Biblical Antiquities*, a work which has a number of points of contact with *2 Baruch*.[45] Here Kenaz is presented as one of the kings and rulers mentioned in the prophecy of Jacob; at 21.5 Joshua quotes Gen. 49.10, 'a prince (*princeps*) shall not depart from Judah, nor a leader (*dux*) from between his thighs', and at 25.2 'the people said, Let us set up for ourselves a leader (*dux*)...and the lot fell upon Kenaz, and they set him up as a prince (*princeps*) in Israel'. This quotation and its development strengthen J. Klausner's messianic interpretation of the paraphrase of the Song of Hannah later in the *Biblical Antiquities* (51.5). Here (cf. 1 Sam. 2.9).

> the wicked [God] shall shut up in the shadows, for he keeps for the righteous his light.

> And when the wicked shall be dead, then shall they perish; and when the righteous shall sleep, then shall they be set free.

> Yet thus every judgment shall abide, until he who has possession (*qui tenet*) shall be revealed.

('until the things laid up for him come') is on the coming of the kingdom to Judah, and the following clause 'and he is the expectation of the nations' then refers back, without full clarity, to the never-failing ruler of the first half-verse in the LXX (M. Harl, *La Bible d'Alexandrie. I. La Genèse* [Paris: Cerf, 1986], *ad loc.*); the material is surveyed by S.R. Driver, *The Book of Genesis* (London: Methuen, 1904), pp. 410-415 and M. Pérez Fernández, *Tradiciones mesiánicas en el Targum Palestinense* (Valencia & Jerusalem: Institución San Jerónimo, 1981), pp. 127-35.

45. Stone, *Fourth Ezra*, pp. 39-40; K. Berger, with G. Fassbeck and H. Reinhard, *Synopse des Vierten Buches Esra und der Syrischen Baruch-Apokalypse* (Tübingen: Francke, 1992), pp. 4-5.

Klausner suggested that these last words allude to the 'Shiloh' oracle at the conclusion of Gen. 49.10, not quoted at 21.5, understood in the sense 'until he come, to whom it pertains', which was documented above.[46] The messianic king would then be 'revealed' (cf. 2 Esd. 7.28; *2 Bar.* 29.3) as judge, as in the Parables of Enoch (61.8-10) and elsewhere. This interpretation in turn fits Jonathan's words to David a little later in the *Biblical Antiquities* (62.9), 'Yours is the kingdom in this age, and from you shall be the beginning of the kingdom that is coming in due time'.[47] The messianic king, on this line of thought, is indeed Davidic, but he forms the climax of the whole line of good kings and rulers, including the judges, and can be envisaged not only as as David but also as Hezekiah come again.

Secondly, messianic expectation was linked with the royal line, the Jewish constitution, and the relevant biblical figures not as they *were* according to modern historical reconstruction, but as they were *envisaged* from time to time in the Graeco-Roman world. This means that material which now looks multifarious, for it includes messianic treatment of priests, judges and patriarchs, in the Greek and Roman periods would have naturally associated itself with the single succession of legitimate Jewish rulers. Thus the constitutional co-ordination of high-priest and king, as envisaged in the Pentateuchal portrait of Eleazar and Joshua (Num. 27.15-23), is reflected in the dual messianism of the *Testaments of the Twelve Patriarchs* and the Qumran texts, and, later on, the 'Simeon prince of Israel' and 'Eleazar the priest' coins of the Bar Kokhba revolt. This political theory could evidently cover what was noticed, in an oracular survey of history in a pseudepigraph known from a Qumran copy, as the change of government between the days of the kingdom of Israel and the (postexilic) time when 'the sons of Aaron shall rule over them' (4Q 390 [Pseudo-Moses Apocalypse[e]] fragment 1, lines 2-5).[48] Furthermore, the succession of rulers is traced back beyond

46. J. Klausner, *The Messianic Idea in Israel from Its Beginning to the Completion of the Mishnah* (three parts, 1902, 1909, 1921; ET of rev. edn, London: Allen & Unwin, 1956), p. 367.

47. Messianic interpretation of 51.4 and 62.9 is taken to be possible and probable, respectively, by H. Jacobson, *A Commentary on Pseudo-Philo's* Liber Antiquitatum Biblicarum (AGJU, 31; Leiden: E.J. Brill, 1996), I, p. 250; but he does not regard messianism as a strong concern of the author.

48. For text and translation see D. Dimant, 'The Seventy Weeks Chronology (Dan 9,24-27) in the Light of New Qumranic Texts', in A.S. van der Woude (ed.), *The Book of Daniel in the Light of New Findings* (BETL, 106; Leuven: Peeters,

David to the judges (Kenaz in Pseudo-Philo, as just noted) and Moses. So Moses is king, probably in the conception of the book of Deuteronomy (33.5), and certainly in the Pentateuch as understood by Ezekiel Tragicus and Philo and in the midrash;[49] Justus of Tiberias began his history of the Jewish kings with Moses.[50]

Similarly, some biblical redeemer-figures which are often reckoned as angelic rather than messianic in modern study were interpreted messianically in antiquity. This pre-eminently applies to the one like a Son of Man in Daniel, identified as an angelic figure by many modern interpreters,[51] but regularly understood as the messianic king at the end of the Second Temple period (in *1 Enoch*, 2 Esdras, and probably also *Sib. Or.* 5.414-33). This royal messianic exegesis seems to be related to the whole scene in Daniel 7 in the saying in the name of Akiba explaining the 'thrones' of v. 9 as two, 'one for him [the Almighty], and one for David' (baraitha in *Ḥag.* 14a, *Sanh.* 38b).[52] Secondly, Exod. 23.20-21, on the angel or messenger sent before Israel, was understood in rabbinic exegesis as referring to an angel, sometimes identified as Metatron (see *Exod. R.* 32.1-9, on 23.20; *3 En.* 12.5); but in probably earlier exegesis by Christians or preserved in Christian sources it was also applied to John the Baptist, perhaps in his capacity as Elijah (Mk 1.2), and to Joshua (Justin, *Dialogue*, 75.1-2), the latter being Moses's successor and a model of the royal deliverer. The indwelling of the spirit is prominent in the descriptions of both Joshua and John (Num. 27.16, 18; Lk. 1.15, 17), and it is likely that they were envisaged as embodied spirits, just as Moses is called 'holy and sacrosanct spirit' in the *Assumption of Moses* (11.16, quoted below); similarly, in the *Prayer of Joseph* noted above, Jacob embodies the archangel Israel, and

1993), pp. 57-76 (72-76).

49. *Ezekiel Tragicus* 36-41, 68-89; Philo, *Vit. Mos.* 1.148-62 (ὠνομάσθη γὰρ ὅλου τοῦ ἔθνους θεὸς καὶ βασιλεύς, 158); *Targum Ps.-Jonathan* on Deut. 33.5; see further J.R. Porter, *Moses and Monarchy* (Oxford: Basil Blackwell, 1963); L. Ginzberg, *The Legends of the Jews*, VI (Philadelphia: Jewish Publication Society of America, 1956), nn. 170, 918.

50. Photius, *Bibliotheca*, 33, cited and discussed by Schürer, *Geschichte* (ET *History*, revised by Vermes and Millar, I, pp. 35-37).

51. N. Schmidt, J.A. Emerton, C.C. Rowland and J. Day are among many noted by J.J. Collins, *Daniel* (Hermeneia; Minneapolis: Fortress Press, 1993), p. 310 nn. 288-94 as, like himself, representing this interpretative view.

52. The passages are discussed, together with the treatment of Dan. 7 in Justin, *Dialogue* 32, in Horbury, 'Messianic Associations', pp. 36, 40-48.

Origen judges accordingly that the Baptist was an angelic spirit. The applications of Exod. 23.20-21 to Joshua and John would then not be so far removed as might appear at first sight from the rabbinic applications of the passage to an angel.

Within the body of Pseudepigrapha, the same kind of ambiguity surrounds a heavenly emissary foretold in the *Assumption of Moses* (10.1-2):

> And then [God's] kingdom shall appear in all his creation. And then the devil shall have an end, and sadness shall be taken away with him. Then shall be filled the hands of the messenger (*nuntius*) who is appointed in the highest, who will at once avenge them of their enemies.

Here, then, the kingdom of God will appear, and the messenger will be consecrated (his hands will be 'filled', in a biblical phrase used of consecration to the priesthood, as at Exod. 28.41; Lev. 8.33); he is appointed in the highest to avenge the Israelites. This messenger has been interpreted as an angel, notably Michael, but there is a case for understanding him as a messianic figure.[53] He waits in heaven, as the Messiah does (2 Esd. 12.32; cf. 7.28, cited above; *1 En.* 46.1-4, 48.6). His hands 'shall be filled'; but although this term for consecration suits priests, and therefore angels, it was more broadly applied in later Hebrew, as appears in 1 Chron. 29.5 and 2 Chron. 29.31. He will avenge the Israelites, like a good king, and as the messianic king was expected to do (*1 En.* 48.7; cf. Isa. 11.4, 61.2; Ps. 2.9; *Pss. Sol.* 17.23-27; 2 Esd. 12.32-33, 13.37-38; *2 Bar.* 72.2-6). Similarly, 'Melchizedek will execute the vengeance of the judgements of G[od]', according to a Qumran text (11Q Melch 2.13). Moses himself in the *Assumption* is not only 'holy and sacrosanct spirit', *sanctus et sacer spiritus* but also 'great messenger', *magnus nuntius* (11.16-17). In 10.1-2, like a prophet–king, this 'great messenger' foretells another messenger who will vindicate Israel as soon as God's kingdom is revealed—not certainly, yet not improbably, the messianic king envisaged as a great pre-existent spirit.

These considerations underline the ambiguity of another figure sometimes described simply as angelic, Melchizedek in 11Q Melchizedek,

---

53. Collins, *Scepter*, p. 176 (an angel); T.W. Manson, 'Miscellanea Apocalyptica', *JTS* 46 (1945), pp. 41-45 (43-44) (Elijah); J. Tromp, *The Assumption of Moses: A Critical Edition with Commentary* (Studia in Veteris Testamenti Pseudepigrapha, 10; Leiden: E.J. Brill, 1993), pp. 228-31 (a human messenger, Taxo the Levite).

quoted above.[54] His initiation of the heavenly judgment and liberation, as it is represented in this fragmentary text, seems close to what is envisaged in the brief description of the messenger appointed in the highest in the *Assumption of Moses*. Melchizedek is mighty among the rebellious 'gods' (angels) of Psalm 82, but at the same time he is the ancient king of Salem and priestly forbear of David (Ps. 110.3). His messianic associations are borne out by the rabbinic tradition that Melchizedek is one of the four smiths of Zech. 2.3 (Elijah, the Messiah, Melchizedek, and the priest anointed for war, in the version in *Cant. R.* 2.13.4). In 11Q Melchizedek this departed royal figure is treated as a spirit who answers to what is envisaged in Isa. 61.1-2, when God's day is announced by one who is anointed and upon whom is the spirit of the Lord. He can be compared, however, not only with the angelic powers over whom he has the mastery, but also with great returning kings such as Hezekiah in the last words attributed to Johanan b. Zaccai. Although the fragmentary state of the text makes judgment tentative, it seems on balance likely that he is indeed a messianic figure, a king of old who has gained angelic status and will return as deliverer and judge, as could also be expected of Hezekiah or David.[55] In some important instances, therefore, the redeemer-figures classified as angelic could be interpreted as human deliverers linked with the line of Israelite kings and rulers.

Thirdly, the messianic portraiture in the Pseudepigrapha is not wholly suited to the distinctions which have often been drawn between human and superhuman figures. As noted above, a contrast between human and superhuman categories, sometimes identified especially with Davidic and Danielic tradition respectively, can be accompanied by the observation that the characteristics of each category often merge. Thus, strikingly, one of the few common features noted by A. Hultgård in messianic presentations of the Greek and Roman period is investiture by bestowal of the spirit (passages including *Pss. Sol.* 17.42 [37]; *1 En.* 49.1-3; 11Q Melch 18), under the influence of Isa. 11.1 and Isa.

---

54. Vermes, *Complete Dead Sea Scrolls*, pp. 500-502; Collins, *Scepter*, p. 176; É. Puech, *La croyance des Esséniens en la vie future: Immortalité, résurrection, vie éternelle?* (Paris: J. Gabalda, 1993), II, pp. 516-62.

55. So for example Hultgård, *L'eschatologie*, I, pp. 306-309; P.A. Rainbow, 'Melchizedek as a Messiah at Qumran', *Bulletin for Biblical Research* 7 (1997), pp. 179-94.

61.1-2;[56] this trait contributes to a conception of the messianic figure as above all the embodiment of an excellent spirit from above. There is in fact a case for seeing the 'superhuman' portrait as more widespread and more continuously attested than is commonly allowed, especially in the light of Septuagintal and rabbinic material.[57] Here attention is restricted to the Pseudepigrapha.

A 'superhuman' portrait has been widely recognized in the Herodian apocalypses. The apocalypses of Ezra and Baruch are roughly contemporary works which have much in common; they perhaps draw on shared traditions of prayer, hymnody, and instruction.[58] Comparable portraiture occurs in the Parables of Enoch preserved in Ethiopic (*1 En.* 37–71), and the Fifth Sibylline book, composed in Greek hexameters (see especially lines 414-33). In 2 Esdras, the Parables of Enoch, and probably also the Fifth Sibylline, traits of the Danielic Son of Man combine with those drawn from messianically interpreted passages in the Pentateuch, prophets and psalms.[59] The interpretation of these three texts as referring Danielic and other material to a single messianic figure seems preferable to K. Koch's suggestion that in 2 Esdras and elsewhere a 'two-stage messianology' is envisaged, turning first on the Messiah and then on the Son of Man.[60] Superhuman features in all these sources include pre-existence (2 Esd. 13.26; *1 En.* 48.3, 6; probably implied at *2 Bar.* 29.3; *Sib. Or.* 5.414), advent from heaven (2 Esd. 13.3 [from the sea, with the clouds], *Sib. Or.* 5.414; *1 En.* 48.4-7; probably implied at *2 Bar.* 29.3), and miraculous annihilation of foes and

---

56. Hultgård, *L'eschatologie*, I, pp. 281, 323-24.

57. Horbury, *Jewish Messianism and the Cult of Christ*, pp. 86-108.

58. Stone, *Fourth Ezra*, pp. 39-40; Berger, *Synopse*, pp. 8-9.

59. Horbury, 'Messianic Associations', pp. 36-48; J. VanderKam, 'Righteous One, Messiah, Chosen One, and Son of Man in I Enoch 37–71', in J.H. Charlesworth (ed.), *The Messiah: Developments in Earliest Judaism and Christianity* (Minneapolis: Fortress Press, 1992), pp. 169-91.

60. Within the longstanding and widespread tradition of messianic biblical interpretation vividly sketched by Koch, 'the Son of Man' would readily have been associated, in the present writer's view, with messianic interpretation of biblical words which can be rendered 'man'; see K. Koch, 'Messias und Menschensohn. Die zweistufige Messianologie der jüngeren Apokalyptik', in E. Dassmann, G. Stemberger *et al.* (eds.), *Der Messias* (Jahrbuch für Biblische Theologie, 8; Neukirchen–Vluyn: Neukirchener Verlag, 1993), pp. 73-102 (esp. 79-80, 85-97); Horbury, 'Messianic Associations', pp. 48-53.

establishment of kingdom (*1 En.* 49.2; *2 Esd.* 13.9-13; *2 Bar.* 29.3-5, 39.7–40.3; *Sib. Or.* 5.414-28).

Such features can also be perceived, however, in other messianic portraits in the Pseudepigrapha. Thus, advent from heaven is probably implied in *Sib. Or.* 3.652-56 on the 'king from the sun' sent by God.[61] It seems also, however, that in the seventeenth *Psalm of Solomon*, widely taken to represent a 'human' messianic figure, traces of a notion of pre-existence emerge in the lines on God's foreknowledge of the messianic king (*Pss. Sol.* 17.23 [21], 47 [42]):

> Behold, Lord, and raise up for them their king, the son of David
>   at the time which thou knowest, O God...
> This is the beauty of the king of Israel, of which God has knowledge,
>   to raise him up over Israel, to instruct him.

God knows the time when the king is to be raised up, as in *Pss. Sol.* 18.6 (5), where the time is the 'day of choice', the day chosen by God; God also knows the king's 'beauty' or 'majesty' (εὐπρέπεια). This noun is one of those used to describe the king's beauty in Greek versions of Ps. 45 (44).4, 'in your glory and beauty' (LXX variant recorded by Origen in the Hexapla) and 110 (109).3, 'in the beauty of the holy one' (Theodotion).[62] These textual witnesses both represent translations which could have come into being later than the *Psalms of Solomon*, although this is not necessarily so; attempts to revise LXX passages will have been made in the first century BCE, and some forms or antecedents of the version ascribed to Theodotion will certainly have circulated in the Herodian period.[63] In any case, however, the occurrence of εὐπρέπεια in Greek versions of these royal psalms is a pointer to contexts likely to be important for interpretation of the psalmodic portrait of a coming king in *Psalms of Solomon* 17. Both the passages concerned in the Psalms of David are exalted in style. Psalm 45 is a hymn to the king, and its lines on the king's beauty played an important part in second- and third-century Christian concepts of Christ.[64] In Ps. 110

---

61. Chester, 'Jewish Messianic Expectations', p. 35 and n. 50.

62. F. Field (ed.), *Origenis Hexaplorum quae supersunt*, II (Oxford: Clarendon Press, 1875), pp. 162, 266.

63. See E. Schürer, revised by M.D. Goodman, in Schürer, *Geschichte* (ET *History*, III.1, pp. 501-504).

64. Irenaeus, *Haer.* 3.19 (20), 2, cited with other passages by Horbury, 'Messianism among Jews and Christians in the Second Century', *Augustinianum* 28 (1988), pp. 71-88 (75 n. 16).

(109).3, according to Theodotion 'in the beauty of the holy one' imme-diately follows 'with you is the rule in the day of your power', and precedes 'from the womb before the daystar I have begotten you'; it is therefore associated both with the king's epiphany on the day of his power, and with his origin 'before the daystar'.

It seems likely, then, that in *Pss. Sol.* 17.47 (42) the king's beauty is considered to be known to God beforehand. It can have been envisaged as in heaven ready to be revealed, on the lines of the expectations about the revelation of the heavenly sanctuary—the 'ready dwelling' in the LXX at Exod. 15.17, 1 Kgs 8.39 and elsewhere—which are widely attested from the third century BCE onwards (for example, at Wis. 9.8; 2 Esd. 13.36; *2 Bar.* 4.1-6).[65] This way of thinking is applied to a messianic figure in passages including the Lukan canticle *Nunc Dimittis*: 'thy salvation, that which thou hast prepared' (Lk. 2.30-31), 2 Esd. 12.42, 'the Anointed whom thou hast kept' (compare 1 Pet. 1.4, 'kept in heaven'), and *2 Bar.* 29.3, 30.1 ('the Messiah shall begin to be revealed...shall return in glory').

Schürer and his revisers regarded the *Psalms of Solomon* as con-trasting with the Parables of Enoch and 2 Esdras precisely in the pre-sentation of a thoroughly human and non-pre-existent messianic figure.[66] Nevertheless, expectation of the kind just discerned in *Pss. Sol.* 17 is within the range of ideas independently suggested by *Pss. Sol.* 18.6 (5), cited above, on the day chosen by God for the 'raising up' or 'bringing back' (ἄναξις) of the Anointed.[67] It is consistent with this interpretation that the spiritual endowment of the king is emphasized; in a passage noted above with regard to investiture by bestowal of the spirit, he is pure from sin, and God has made him 'mighty in holy

65. W. Horbury, 'Land, Sanctuary and Worship', in J.M.G. Barclay and J.P.M. Sweet (eds.), *Early Christian Thought in its Jewish Context* (Cambridge: Cambridge University Press, 1996), pp. 207-24 (210-11).

66. Schürer, *Geschichte*, II, p. 616 (ET *History*, revised by Vermes, Millar and Black, II, p. 519).

67. H.E. Ryle and M.R. James (eds.), *Psalms of the Pharisees, commonly called the Psalms of Solomon* (Cambridge: Cambridge University Press, 1891), pp. 149-50, on 18.6, found pre-existence to be suggested by ἄναξις, but they rejected this interpretation because they could find no hint of it in *Pss. Sol.* 17; such hints seem to be given, however, by 17.23 and 42, as interpreted above. In 18.6 T.W. Manson's emendation ἀνάδειξις, 'showing' (Manson, 'Miscellanea Apocalyptica', pp. 41-42; cf. Lk. 1.80) would equally suggest a hidden period, on earth or in heaven; but the text, offering a word not familiar from the Gospels, seems preferable.

spirit' (*Pss. Sol.* 17.41-42 [36-37]; cf. Isa. 11.2, 61.1). In *Psalms of Solomon* 17–18, then, it seems likely that the glory and beauty of the Davidic king are known to God, waiting in heaven for the appointed time when the son of David is to be raised up.[68]

Against this background it seems likely that *Pseudo-Philo*, discussed above with reference to 2 Esdras and the Parables of Enoch, should also be taken to envisage the revelation of a Messiah who will be the heavenly judge. There is likewise a fair probability that the 'messenger' of *Ass. Mos.* 10.2, consecrated in heaven to avenge Israel, is a pre-existent messianic figure. Further, Bousset rightly associated with the 'transcendent Messiah' of the Herodian apocalypses the passages in the *Testaments of the Twelve Patriarchs* on the 'new priest' whose 'star shall rise in heaven, as a king' and on the 'star from Jacob', 'a man like a sun of righteousness', the 'shoot of God' to arise from Judah (*T. Levi* 18.2-3; *T. Jud.* 24.1, 4-6).[69] Particularly notable here are links with the star of Balaam (Num. 24.17) and, once more, with the oracle on Judah in the Blessing of Jacob (Gen. 49.10), here linked again with Isa. 11.1 (see above, with n. 29). The astral associations suggest that the priestly and royal messianic figures are being envisaged as embodied spirits, on the lines noted above with reference to *Ass. Mos.* 11.17.

In all the Pseudepigrapha noted at the beginning of this section as attesting the messianic theme, therefore, with the addition of *Pseudo-Philo* and perhaps also the *Assumption of Moses*, the messianic portraiture includes superhuman characteristics. These are not incompatible with the conception of the Messiah as a mortal king (2 Esd. 7.29), perhaps especially because emphasis is laid on his spiritual aspect. These features recall the superhuman glory of the king in such biblical passages as Isa. 9.5 (ET 6), Mic. 5.1 (ET 2), and Pss. 45.7 (ET 6), 110.3.

In conclusion, therefore, to summarize this short study, it may be said first of all that the name Apocrypha, inherited from mediaeval usage in its application to approved books outside the Hebrew canon, and the accompanying term Pseudepigrapha, recall an early Christian distinc-

---

68. The interpretation in the text above was formulated before I had seen Laato, *Star*, pp. 283-84, where it is rightly noted that the whole passage is not far from descriptions of 'transcendental divine agents', but the question of pre-existence is left open.

69. Bousset and Gressmann, *Religion*, p. 261 (suggesting links with the myth of a king of Paradise); Hultgård, *L'eschatologie*, especially I, pp. 203-13 (on *T. Jud.* 24), and pp. 300-26 (on *T. Levi* 18 in its Jewish setting).

tion that is not unlikely to have Jewish origins; some adjuncts to the canonical books were approved, others were disapproved. In the case of the Pseudepigrapha, the co-existence of disapproval with strong interest among early Christians probably replicates an earlier conjunction of contrasting Jewish attitudes to these books, as 2 Esd. 14.44-47 suggest.

The Apocrypha, although in many cases they exemplify silence on messianism and a theocentric concentration on divine deliverance, do not encourage the view that there was a 'messianological vacuum' in the late Persian and early Greek period. This notion is in any case implicitly questioned by the messianism of the LXX Pentateuch; but it is also questioned by the traces of messianic biblical interpretation in Ecclesiasticus and 1 Maccabees. These two influential Apocrypha show that authors who loyally upheld the Judaean authorities of their day were still affected by biblically-inspired messianic tradition, which had a life of its own in communal biblical interpretation independently of circumstances which might specially encourage its development.

The Pseudepigrapha at first glance seem to bear out the widespread view that the messianism of their period was predominantly diverse; but much of their material has an underlying unity arising from its roots in biblical tradition on the king. Modern distinctions between Davidic and non-Davidic expectations, or between angelic and human messianic figures, are overcome in ancient presentations. Thus in the Pseudepigrapha messianic figures can be connected with the whole line of Israelite rulers, from the patriarchs and Moses onwards, and it can be envisaged that past monarchs may attain angelic status as spirits in the hand of God.

Similarly, the widespread distinction between human and superhuman messianic portraits seems misplaced; superhuman traits can be detected throughout those Pseudepigrapha which are known for their messianic traditions, and also in material in which messianic expectation is less widely recognized (notably Pseudo-Philo's *Biblical Antiquities*, and perhaps also the *Assumption of Moses*). It is suggested here that these traits reflect above all the superhuman traits in biblical oracles on the present or future king. The oracular royal portraiture would have been developed in a continuous tradition of messianic biblical interpretation, which was always influenced by political circumstances, but retained its own independent life.

KINGSHIP AND MESSIANISM IN THE DEAD SEA SCROLLS

George J. Brooke

1. Introduction

Studies on the subject of messianism in the Dead Sea Scrolls are more than plentiful.[1] In one of the very first scrolls to come to light, the cave 1 version of the Community Rule (1QS), the phrase appeared, 'until

---

1. The most comprehensive early work was by A.S. van der Woude, *Die messianischen Vorstellungen der Gemeinde von Qumran* (Assen: van Gorcum, 1957); for other studies see the various bibliographies on the Dead Sea Scrolls, especially the list of studies in J.A. Fitzmyer, *The Dead Sea Scrolls: Major Publications and Tools for Study* (SBLRBS, 20; Atlanta: Scholars Press, rev edn, 1990), pp. 164-67; those indexed variously in F. García Martínez and D.W. Parry, *A Bibliography of the Finds in the Desert of Judah 1970–1995: Arranged by Author with Citation and Subject Indexes* (STDJ, 19; Leiden: E.J. Brill, 1996); and those highlighted in F. García Martínez, 'Two Messianic Figures in the Qumran Texts', in D.W. Parry and S.D. Ricks (eds.), *Current Research and Technological Developments on the Dead Sea Scrolls: Conference on the Texts from the Judean Desert, Jerusalem, 30 April 1995* (STDJ, 20; Leiden: E.J. Brill, 1996), pp. 14-40.

Among more recent studies, see especially, S. Talmon, 'Waiting for the Messiah: The Spiritual Universe of the Qumran Covenanters', in J. Neusner, W.S. Green, and E. Frerichs (eds.), *Judaisms and their Messiahs at the Turn of the Christian Era* (Cambridge: Cambridge University Press, 1987), pp. 111-37; L.H. Schiffman, 'Messianic Figures and Ideas in the Qumran Scrolls', in J.H. Charlesworth (ed.), *The Messiah: Developments in Earliest Judaism and Christianity* (The First Princeton Symposium on Judaism and Christian Origins; Minneapolis: Fortress Press, 1992), pp. 116-29; F. García Martínez, 'Messianische Erwartungen in den Qumranschriften', in E. Dassmann, G. Stemberger, *et al.* (eds.), *Der Messias* (Jahrbuch für Biblische Theologie, 8; Neukirchen–Vluyn: Neukirchener Verlag, 1993), pp. 171-208 (ET in F. García Martínez and J. Trebolle Barrera, *The People of the Dead Sea Scrolls: Their Writings, Beliefs and Practices* [Leiden: E.J. Brill, 1995], pp. 159-89); J.C. VanderKam, 'Messianism in the Scrolls', in E. Ulrich and J. VanderKam (eds.), *The Community of the Renewed Covenant: The Notre Dame Symposium on the Dead Sea Scrolls* (Christianity and Judaism in Antiquity Series,

there shall come the Prophet and the Messiahs of Aaron and Israel'.[2] Furthermore, spurred on by their interest to provide the background to early Christian reflections on the status of Jesus, many Christian scholars have stressed messianism more than any other aspect of the eschatological outlook of the sectarian scrolls. The aim of this study is to set the principal texts which are referred to in the debates on Qumran messianism within a slightly broader framework than is usual by also considering the whole concept of kingship in the scrolls; some of the main parameters in the debate concerning messianism in the scrolls will also be mentioned.

For the purposes of this study I consider that the scrolls found in the eleven caves at or near Qumran form some kind of coherent collection, though not all the caves may have served the same function for the community at any one time or over a period of time. The principal reasons for taking the collection as a whole are that it has a remarkable overall ideological consistency, especially with regard to the calendar, and that both the proportions of biblical, sectarian and non-biblical, non-sectarian documents are similar in the three principal caves (1, 4, and 11), and several distinctive compositions are found in more than one cave.[3] In addition, the principal reasons for linking the scrolls in the caves with the ruins at Qumran are, first, that the archaeological evidence suggests that the caves and the site were in use contemporaneously; secondly, that it is impossible to reach some of the caves

---

10; Notre Dame: University of Notre Dame Press, 1994), pp. 211-34; G.S. Oegema, *Der Gesalbte und sein Volk: Untersuchungen zum Konzeptualisierungsprozeß der messianischen Erwartungen von den Makkabäern bis Bar Koziba* (Schriften des Institutum Judaicum Delitzschianum, 2; Göttingen: Vandenhoeck & Ruprecht, 1994); J.J. Collins, *The Scepter and the Star: The Messiahs of the Dead Sea Scrolls and Other Ancient Literature* (Anchor Bible Reference Library; New York: Doubleday, 1995); K. Pomykala, *The Davidic Dynasty Tradition in Early Judaism: Its History and Significance for Messianism* (SBLEJL, 7; Atlanta: Scholars Press, 1995); and the thematic issue of *Dead Sea Discoveries* 2 (1995), pp. 125-216 (ed. J.C. VanderKam).

2. Though generally accepted as an expression of messianism, it could be argued that this is simply a reference to a future time when the priesthood and kingship would be properly restored.

3. E.g. the Community Rule (caves 1, 4 and 5; possibly also cave 11), the Damascus Document (caves 4, 5, and 6), the Temple Scroll (possibly caves 4 and 11), eschatological exegesis (caves 1, 4, and 11), the New Jerusalem text (caves 4, 5, and 11), the *Book of Jubilees* (caves 1, 2, 3, 4, and 11).

either without going through the site itself or without being seen from the site; and, thirdly, that there is a real chance that one of the ostraca recently discovered in the wall extending south from the principal Qumran ruins is a rough copy of a deed of gift, prepared as a new member joins the community as described in the Community Rule and the writings of Josephus.[4]

2. *Kings and Kingship in the Scrolls*

a. *The Terminology*

There is much on kings and kingship in the scrolls. One interesting fact can be noted at the outset of this more detailed discussion: in the fragmentary manuscripts that survive the term 'king' (*melek*) is never used of a Messiah and 'kingship' (*malkût*) features but twice in association with a royal eschatological person.[5] The terms are used in three principal ways: of non-Israelite kings, of Israelite kings, past, present or future, and of God. Related terms such as 'rule' (*mšl*) and 'take office' (*'md*) are, of course, found in texts which speak of the royal Messiah, but the paucity of those texts and the fact that a variety of epithets (especially 'prince of the congregation' and 'branch of David') are used of him leaves the indelible impression that the ideology of kingship in the scrolls was based in an overwhelming stress on theocracy, on divine sovereignty.

b. *The Biblical Evidence*

It is not uncommon for studies of anything thematic in the scrolls to forget entirely the biblical evidence from the caves. However, it is worth noting that something of the ideology of those responsible for gathering the collection of nearly nine hundred manuscripts together can be detected in the circumstantial evidence of what compositions, both biblical and non-biblical, have survived and in what quantities.

With regard to kings and kingship, it is perhaps significant that very few manuscripts of the historical books have survived. For 1 and

---

4. This observation holds good whether or not the ostracon concerned contains the word *yḥd*. The newly found ostraca have been published by F.M. Cross and E. Eshel, 'Ostraca from Khirbet Qumrân', *IEJ* 47 (1997), pp. 17-28; the texts in translation are now readily available in G. Vermes, *The Complete Dead Sea Scrolls in English* (London: Allen Lane, Penguin Press, 1997), pp. 596-97.

5. In 1QSb 5.21 and 4Q252 5.2, 4.

2 Kings we have remains of only three manuscripts.[6] For 1 and 2 Chronicles the number is even smaller: there is possibly only one surviving manuscript.[7] The implication of these statistics could be that accounts of the deeds or rather misdeeds of the kings of Israel and Judah were hardly considered to be popular or edifying reading by the occupants of Qumran. Some other matters support this view.[8]

The prominence of David in some scrolls does not seem to rest especially on his kingly status. Rather his position may be based on his role as a psalmist imbued with the spirit of prophecy (11QPs[a] 27.11). It is increasingly likely that it should be understood that there were two or more editions of the Psalter in circulation at the end of the Second Temple period.[9] One of these, as represented in 11QPs[a], was probably constructed as a Davidic collection. The other collection, largely as represented nowadays in the MT, differs from the 11QPs[a] Davidic collection most explicitly from Psalm 90 onwards. In this respect it should be noted that the kingship of God is a major feature of several of the psalms early in Book 4, especially Psalms 93, 95–99. Both forms of the emerging collection of Psalms can be understood as putting the earthly king in his place, either by emphasizing a non-kingly aspect of David's activity or by stressing the kingship of God.

Solomon, seldom mentioned in the scrolls, seems to be viewed as a figure of mixed blessings. According to MMT C 17–19 some of the blessings promised by Moses came to pass in the reigns of David and Solomon; thereafter it is curses that have been partially fulfilled.[10] And

---

6. 4Q54: J. Trebolle Barrera, '54. 4QKgs', in *Qumran Cave 4. IX. Deuteronomy, Joshua, Judges, Kings* (DJD, 14; Oxford: Clarendon Press, 1995), pp. 171-83; 5Q2: J.T. Milik, 'I Rois', in *Les 'Petites Grottes' de Qumrân* (ed. M. Baillet, J.T. Milik, and R. de Vaux; DJD, 3; Oxford: Clarendon Press, 1962), pp. 171-72; 6Q4: M. Baillet, 'Livre des Rois', in *Les 'Petites Grottes' de Qumrân* (ed. M. Baillet, J.T. Milik and R. de Vaux; DJD, 3; Oxford: Clarendon Press, 1962), pp. 107-12.

7. 4Q118: J. Trebolle Barrera, 'Édition préliminaire de 4QChroniques', *RevQ* 15 (1991–92), pp. 523-29.

8. Perhaps the books of Kings were read elsewhere for some kind of political reason; three fragments of the books of Kings in Nabataean script are assigned to 4Q235 (PAM 43.402).

9. See the detailed and convincing analysis of P.W. Flint, *The Dead Sea Psalms Scrolls and the Book of Psalms* (STDJ, 17; Leiden: E.J. Brill, 1997), esp. pp. 202-27.

10. See the composite text as proposed by E. Qimron and J. Strugnell, *Qumran*

in 11QPsAp[a] his name occurs but it is not possible to discern whether
the allusion puts him in a positive light. Other kings from the First
Temple period barely feature at all, though a fragment mentioning
Zedekiah (4Q470) may be understood as suggesting that king's
rehabilitation.[11]

c. The Parabiblical Evidence

The best known of the parabiblical scrolls from the Qumran caves is
the Temple Scroll. Columns 51–66 of 11QT[a] contain an abbreviated
rewrite of Deuteronomy 12–22 with an exceptional lengthening of
Deut. 17.14-20 in columns 56–59. This so-called king's law is
significant for the task of this study, because it must be noted immediately that it contains nothing messianic. Several scholars have observed
how it seems to stand as an overtly political tract and may well have
been written against a contemporary ruler.[12] It should be underlined
that the king envisaged in this legislation is not a high priest, since
according to 11QT[a] 58.18-19 the king, before he goes out to war, is
required to present himself before the high priest to consult him.

d. Other Compositions

In the non-sectarian compositions found at Qumran the title 'king' is
used of various figures: Pharaoh (1QapGen 20.8, 14), the kings of the
earth (1QapGen 20.15), a whole range of individual kings who have
dealings with Abram (1QapGen 21.23-33; 22.4, 12, 17), unspecified
kings (listed together with priests; 4Q213 2 12; 4Q385B 1 i 10), the
kings of the peoples (4Q243 24 4), an unnamed king of Babylon
(4Q244 1-3 1), another unnamed king (4Q246 1.2; 4Q318 2 ii 7), a king
of Judah (4Q247 4; 4Q381 31 4), king of the Kittim (4Q247 6), Darius

---

Cave 4. V. *Miqṣat Maʿaśe Ha-Torah* (DJD, 10; Oxford: Clarendon Press, 1994),
pp. 60-61.

11. See E. Larson, L.H. Schiffman and J. Strugnell, '470. 4QText Mentioning
Zedekiah', in *Qumran Cave 4. XIV. Parabiblical Texts, Part 2* (DJD, 19; Oxford:
Clarendon Press, 1995), pp. 235-44.

12. See, e.g., M. Hengel, J.H. Charlesworth and D. Mendels, 'The Polemical
Character of "On Kingship" in the Temple Scroll: An Attempt at Dating
11QTemple', *JJS* 37 (1986), pp. 28-38; E.-M. Laperrousaz, 'Does the Temple
Scroll Date from the First or Second Century BCE?', in G.J. Brooke (ed.), *Temple
Scroll Studies: Papers Presented at the International Symposium on the Temple
Scroll, Manchester, December 1987* (JSPSup, 7; Sheffield: JSOT Press, 1989),
pp. 91-97.

(4Q550), and an unnamed blasphemous king (4Q388 1 3). 4Q552 and 553, on the Four Kingdoms, speaks of the King Babel who rules over Persia. 4Q426 may contain some wisdom instruction addressed to kings, not unlike the Wisdom of Solomon (4Q426 1 i 13). Deliverance from the abuses of kings may be prayed for (4Q504 1-2 iii 15).

4Q448 contains the remains of three columns arranged stichometrically. At the top of the fragment is a poem, part of which contains a passage from Psalm 154. This may be important for how the other two columns on the fragment should be understood, since Psalm 154 is included in the collection of 11QPs[a] and is considered a Davidic composition. The other two columns may contain one or possibly two references to a King Jonathan. It seems as if the text is a prayer for the welfare of the king and the people of Israel.[13] The composition is not messianic.

As for God himself, several non-sectarian compositions refer to his kingship: for example, God is described as 'king of all the ages' (*melek kôl 'ōlāmîm*, 1QapGen 2.4, 7), and 'king of heaven' (1QapGen 2.14), 'king on Mount Zion' (4Q216; *Jub.* 1.28), and 'king for all of them' (4Q303 1 7). However, it is in the Songs of the Sabbath Sacrifice that the kingship of God himself comes to the fore most extensively.[14] It is of importance for our purposes to note that all the manuscripts of this composition are palaeographically late Hasmonaean or early Herodian.[15] Since typological dates correspond more or less with actual dates, the Songs thus become the exact contemporaries of those compositions in which there is a prominent role assigned to the lay, princely, kingly Davidic Messiah (4Q161; 4Q174; 4Q252; 4Q285 frg. 5). Whether or not this composition was narrowly sectarian in the strict

13. See E. Eshel, H. Eshel and A. Yardeni, 'A Qumran Composition Containing Part of Ps. 154 and a Prayer for the Welfare of King Jonathan and his Kingdom', *IEJ* 42 (1992), pp. 199-229; and note the comments of P.S. Alexander, 'A Note on the Syntax of 4Q448', *JJS* 44 (1993), pp. 301-302.

14. For a detailed analysis of divine kingship in the Sabbath Songs, see A.M. Schwemer, 'Gott als König und seine Königsherrschaft in den Sabbatliedern aus Qumran', in M. Hengel and A.M. Schwemer (eds.), *Königsherrschaft Gottes und himmlischer Kult im Judentum, Urchristentum und in der hellenistischen Welt* (WUNT, 55; Tübingen: J.C.B. Mohr [Paul Siebeck], 1991), pp. 45-118: she has concluded justifiably that the collection of Sabbath Songs is 'der wichtigste vorchristliche jüdische Text zum Thema "Gottes Königsherrschaft"'.

15. C. Newsom, *Songs of the Sabbath Sacrifice: A Critical Edition* (HSS, 27; Atlanta: Scholars Press, 1985), p. 1.

sense, or some part of a broader pattern of spirituality with which those at Qumran and in its wider movement were happy to live, makes no difference. The discovery of possibly eight copies of it in cave 4, another in cave 11, as well as another copy on Masada, suggest that it was a popular work.[16] It is not necessary here to distinguish between the various contexts in which God's kingship is stressed, nor to differentiate between the various referential nuances behind the terminology, since our purpose is to illustrate the frequency and force of the language of divine kingship. God is 'king of goodness' (MasShirShab 2.15; 4Q4031 i 5), 'king of holiness' (MasShirShab 2.18; 4Q403 1 i 7), 'king of holiest holiness' (4Q400 1 i 8), 'king of the heavenly [or godlike] beings' (*melek 'ᵉlôhîm*, 4Q400 1 ii 7; 2 5; 4Q401 1–2 5; 4Q402 3 ii 12; 4Q405 24 3), 'king of all' (4Q401 13 1; 4Q405 24 3; 11QShirShabb 1.1), 'king of the princes' (4Q400 1 ii 14), 'king of all' (*melek hakkôl*, 4Q403 1 i 28), 'king of majesty' (4Q403 1 i 38), 'king of truth and righteousness' (4Q403 1 i 46; 4Q404 5 6); he is 'king in the wonderful dwellings ... king in the assembly (*melek baqqāhāl*) ... king of glory ... king of purity' (4Q403 1 ii 23-26), 'king of glory' (4Q403 1 i 31; 4Q404 3 3), 'king of those who exalt' (4Q403 3 1; 4Q405 14-15 i 3) and undefined as king in fragmentary contexts (4Q401 5 7; 4Q404 6 2; 4Q405 56). He is envisaged as enthroned in the temple (earthly or heavenly): 'in the inner sanctuary of the king' (4Q402 2 4), 'in the inner sanctuaries of the king' (4Q405 14-15 i 7). He is 'the king exalted with seven words of his marvellous glory' (4Q403 1 i 13). He is the one who commands: 'at the utterance of the lips of the king' (4Q401 14 ii 8).

In the sectarian texts the following are called king: Nebuchadnezzar (CD 1.6), the kings of Israel (CD 3.9; 20.16; 1QM 11.3), the king of Babylon (4Q163 8-10 1; 4Q165 8 1), the assembly (CD 7.14), the kings of the peoples (CD 8.10; 19.23; 1Q27 9-10 3; 4Q299 57 4), kings of the Gentiles (1QM 12.14; 19.6), the kings of Greece (CD 8.11; 19.24), the kings of the North (1QM 1.4), kings of the East (4Q491 11 i 12), unspecified kings (1QM 12.7; 1QpPs 9–10 1), the king of the Kittim (1QM 15.2) and by implication the rulers of the Kittim (1QpHab 4.1-5 on Hab. 1.10). A King Hyrcanus (4Q322 2 6) is also mentioned. Furthermore, if MMT was composed as an open circular addressed to a leader outside the movement, then its appeal to the kings of Israel, from David to Zedekiah, king of Judah (4Q398) with respect to both their

---

16. Simply on the basis of this count, it comes close to the Community Rule and the Damascus Document in the popularity stakes.

bad and good acts is indicative of what a king or ruler should practise, namely 'whoever among them feared [the To]rah was delivered from troubles; and these were the seekers of the Torah whose transgressions were [for]given'.[17] Thus the model of kingship suggested in the scroll is one of obedience to the Torah, and not just the Torah in itself, but the Torah as interpreted by the community. When the Law is kept in a certain way, then God removes 'the plans of evil and the device of Belial'; the king or leader does little or nothing on his own.

In some of the sectarian compositions kingdom (*malkût*) is ascribed to earthly figures, such as Manasseh (4Q169 3-4 iv 3), but it is predominantly associated with divine sovereignty as in the Songs of the Sabbath Sacrifice, 4QMysteries (*hêkal malkûtô*, 4Q301 5 2), and the War Scroll (1QM 6.6; 12.7; 4Q491 15 3). Also, as in the Songs of the Sabbath Sacrifice, in the sectarian texts God is described as 'king of the glorious ones' (1QH 18.8), 'king of glory' (1QM 12.8; 19.1), and variously as king in 4Q471b.[18]

e. *Conclusion*

The field of terms associated with the root *mlk* are used in a variety of ways in the compositions found at Qumran. Overwhelmingly as positive terms they are used of God, and the manuscripts of the composition which speaks most explicitly of God's reign and kingship, the Songs of the Sabbath Sacrifice, are datable to the mid to end of the first century BCE. The exalted image of divine sovereignty is not restricted to the Songs of the Sabbath Sacrifice. It can also be found in compositions which are more clearly sectarian. So, for example, in the eschatologically oriented War Rule, there is a poetic acclamation of the sovereignty of God in which there is a marked contrast between God who is splendid in majesty and the kings of the earth who are to be treated with contempt. 'We will treat kings with contempt, the powerful with jeers and mockery, for the Lord is holy and the king of glory is with us' (1QM 12.7-8).[19]

'King' and 'kingship' are also used in relation to the kings of Israel,

17. Qimron and Strugnell, *Qumran Cave 4*, pp. 61-63.

18. On this text, see E. Eshel, '4Q471b: A Self-Glorification Hymn', forthcoming in the Proceedings of the 1996 International Conference on the Dead Sea Scrolls held at Brigham Young University, Utah.

19. It is noteworthy that the eschatological struggles depicted in 1QM barely refer to the prince of the whole congregation at all (1QM 5.1).

those in the past, the present and the future, though such use is hardly enthusiastic for the office. Most past Israelite kings have erred and in general kings need to be restrained, counselled, and taught obedience to the Law. The term 'kingship' (*malkût*) is also used in connection with the eschatological prince or lay leader who is described in various sectarian texts; to those compositions we now turn, though they will be set in the broad context of messianism in the scrolls.

3. *Messianism in the Scrolls*

a. *Messianism*

There have been two ways of focusing on the messianism of the scrolls, the one typological, the other historical. Some scholars have tried to describe and assess the full range of figures to be found in the scrolls who are associated with the last days in some way or other. This typological approach does not restrict its concern only to figures labelled *māšîaḥ*; it is interested in functions rather than titles. The most extensive recent analysis of messianism in the scrolls from the typological point of view is the study of J.J. Collins,[20] but such an approach can also be seen in the work of F. García Martínez, who has proposed that the term 'Messiah' should be used very loosely to cover even angelic figures who play a prominent part in end things.[21] On the other hand there are those scholars who have focused on the diachronic aspects of messianism in the scrolls; their work has tended to be based more narrowly on the term 'Messiah' itself as variously used to describe an office or offices in the end times of special significance for the community.[22] Because this study is concerned principally with the interplay of kingship and messianism in the scrolls, it too will take a narrower range of texts into consideration than those which the typological approach might advocate, and the goal will be to draw some broad historical conclusions.

Even a study like this, which is primarily diachronic and somewhat limited in its concerns, cannot ignore the wider aspects of the study of messianism that the typological approach has thrown into relief. Attention must first be paid to the term *māšîaḥ* itself. The term 'Messiah' is

20. Collins, *The Scepter and the Star*.

21. F. García Martínez, 'Messianische Erwartungen in den Qumranschriften'; *idem*, 'Two Messianic Figures in the Qumran Texts'.

22. The most recent exponent of this approach is Oegema, *Der Gesalbte und sein Volk*.

used in the plural of a priestly and of a kingly figure, 'the Messiahs of Aaron and Israel' (1QS 9.11). In the light of biblical texts like Zech. 4.14,[23] it is becoming increasingly common to read the scholarly opinion that a doctrine of two Messiahs is to be understood uniformly behind all the sectarian texts, even where the *nomen regens* is in the singular as in CD 12.23 (= 4Q266 10 i 2), 19.10, and probably 14.19.[24] This suggested uniformity has made the typological approach to the messianism of the scrolls all the more easy.[25]

However, before simply falling in line with the force of the argument that every messianic text from Qumran presupposes an understanding that there were two Messiahs, a priestly and a royal one,[26] it is important to take another look at the use of the term *māšîaḥ* itself. It is used as follows: (1) of prophets: 'your anointed ones, seers of decrees' (1QM 11.7); 'all his anointed ones' (4Q521 8 9); 'by the hand of the anointed ones through his holy spirit' (CD 2.12); 'by the hand of Moses and also of the holy anointed ones' (CD 6.1); 'the messenger is the anointed of the spirit' (11QMelch 18); 'concerning the anointed of his holy spirit' (4Q287 10 13); and probably 'the heavens and earth will listen to his Messiah' (4Q521 2+4 1);[27] (2) of a royal Messiah: 'when the Messiah is revealed with them' (1QSa 2.12);[28] 'afterwards, the Messiah of Israel

23. Now seen in 4Q254 4 2 and probably to be associated with the interpretation of the blessing of Judah in Genesis 49: G.J. Brooke, '254. 4Q Commentary on Genesis C', *Qumran Cave 4. XVII. Parabiblical Texts, Part 3* (DJD, 22; Oxford: Clarendon Press, 1996), pp. 223-24.

24. Cf. *māšîaḥ mē'ahʰrōn ûmiyyiśrā'ēl*, CD 20.1.

25. S. Talmon has been the major exponent of this uniform understanding; see esp. his study, 'Waiting for the Messiah'.

26. Argued most recently by F.M. Cross, 'Notes on the Doctrine of the Two Messiahs at Qumran and the Extracanonical Daniel Apocalypse (4Q246)', in Parry and Ricks (eds.), *Current Research and Technological Developments on the Dead Sea Scrolls*, pp. 1-13.

27. The prophetic understanding of the messianic figure in 4Q521 has been put forward most persuasively by J.J. Collins, 'The Works of the Messiah', *DSD* 1 (1994), pp. 98-112.

28. This translation of 1QSa 2.12 is based on the reading of E. Puech, 'Préséance sacerdotale et Messie-Roi dans la Règle de la Congrégation (1QSa ii 11-22)', *RevQ* 16 (1993-94), pp. 351-65. G. Vermes translates the same phrase as 'When God engenders (the Priest-)Messiah' and comments that the 'reading (*yolid*), which has been queried by many, including myself, seems to be confirmed by computer image enhancement' (*The Complete Dead Sea Scrolls in English*, p. 159, and n. 1)

shall enter' (1QSa 2.14); 'the Messiah of Israel shall stretch out his hand' (1QSa 2.20); 'until the coming of the Messiah of righteousness' (4Q252 5.3); (3) of a priest: 'the anointed priest' (4Q375 1 i 9; 4Q376 1 i 1); (4) of Moses: 'by the mouth of Moses his anointed' (4Q377 2 ii 5); (5) of a king: 'I, your anointed, have understood' (4Q381 15 7);[29] 'anointed with the oil of kingship' (4Q458 2 ii 6); (6) of an unspecified figure: 'the holy Messiah' (1Q30 1 2, a liturgical text). Three things are striking about this list. First, the term 'anointed' is used of a wide range of figures of the past, all of whom have their eschatological counterparts: prophets, priests, kings, the lawgiver. Secondly, since 1991, when all the unpublished fragments became generally available, the whole corpus has not thrown up a single extra reference in the strict sense to either an eschatological priest Messiah or king Messiah. Thirdly, the term *māšîaḥ*, however loosely applied, is never associated with an angel.[30]

b. *The Biblical Evidence*

Whilst the lack of manuscripts of the books of Kings and Chronicles amongst the scrolls may indicate something of a negative attitude towards kings and kingship, one can genuinely ask whether any of the other biblical manuscripts contain any evidence for the messianic adjustment of their texts.

The book of Isaiah has been considered most closely in relation to the adjustment of its text for eschatological and, more particularly, for messianic purposes.[31] W.H. Brownlee provoked a lively debate by claiming to discover a new messianic reading in Isa. 52.14-15 in 1QIsaᵃ.[32] P. Sacchi has been the most recent to discuss the *locus classicus*, Isa. 52.14, and has concluded that *māšaḥtî* must be accepted as a reading which makes the servant an individual messianic figure who

---

29. Probably a king, according to E.M. Schuller, *Non-Canonical Psalms from Qumran: A Pseudepigraphic Collection* (HSS, 28; Atlanta: Scholars Press, 1986), p. 101.

30. In particular this stands against the typological approach of F. García Martínez, 'Two Messianic Figures in the Qumran Texts', pp. 25-30.

31. See, most extensively, W.H. Brownlee, *The Meaning of the Qumrân Scrolls for the Bible with Special Attention to the Book of Isaiah* (New York: Oxford University Press, 1964), Part II.

32. W.H. Brownlee, 'The Servant of the Lord in the Qumran Scrolls I', *BASOR* 132 (1953), pp. 8-15; 'Certainly Mašaḥti!', *BASOR* 134 (1954), pp. 27-28; 'The Servant of the Lord in the Qumran Scrolls II', *BASOR* 135 (1954), pp. 33-38.

will know death and dishonour.[33] Perhaps the verse is then to be understood as describing not a marred figure but an anointed one, not overall a negative description in this instance, but a glorious one as Isa. 52.13 and 52.15 imply.

c. *Other Compositions*

ʾn the light of what will emerge as the overall thesis of this study, it is worth considering, albeit briefly, three compositions which have recently played a considerable part in the ongoing discussion of Qumran messianism. All three compositions could well be non-sectarian; two are in Aramaic, which may well indicate non-sectarian origin.[34]

The first composition to be considered is 4Q246, the so-called Son of God text.[35] The contents of the single piece of parchment assigned to this manuscript have given rise to a complicated debate. It is clear from what remains that a seer is interpreting a vision to a king, but the identification and status of the Son of God remains debatable. The first column is damaged on the right side, causing problems for modern interpreters, but the second column is more or less intact. Several theories about how best the text should be understood are in circulation and none has yet won the day. These need to be briefly outlined. (1) J.T. Milik suggested in his public presentation of the text in 1972 that the Son of God figure was a king, Alexander Balas, son of Antiochus Epiphanes.[36] He could be called Son of God because he is identified on coins as *theopator* or *Deo patre natus*. Though a messianic interpretation might seem more obvious, Milik has found partial support in the publication of the principal edition of the text by É. Puech, who allows

---

33. P. Sacchi, 'Ideologia e varianti della tradizione ebraica: Deut 27,4 e Is 52,14', in H. Merklein, K. Müller, and G. Stemberger (eds.), *Bibel in jüdischer und christlicher Tradition: Festschrift für Johann Maier zum 60. Geburtstag* (BBB, 88; Frankfurt am Main: Hain, 1993), pp. 26-32.

34. The only Aramaic composition which may be closely associated with the sectarian materials is 4Q548, 4QAmram[f], in which the 'sons of light' feature forcefully. I am grateful to Professor R.J. Bauckham for drawing this exception to my attention.

35. É. Puech, '246. 4QApocryphe de Daniel ar', in *Qumran Cave 4. XVII. Parabiblical Texts, Part 3* (DJD, 22; Oxford: Clarendon Press, 1996), pp. 165-84.

36. As reported by J.A. Fitzmyer, 'The Contribution of Qumran Aramaic to the Study of the New Testament', *NTS* 20 (1973–74), pp. 391-94 (reprinted with an addendum in *A Wandering Aramean: Collected Aramaic Essays* [SBLMS, 25; Missoula, MT: Scholars Press, 1979], pp. 90-94).

for the possibility that there is a reference to a Seleucid king, whether Alexander Balas or Antiochus Epiphanes himself.[37] (2) J.A. Fitzmyer himself sees no evidence of any connection between the title 'Son of God' and messianism. For him the king addressed in the text is on the Jewish side; the Son of God is a son or descendant of the enthroned king who will be supported by the great God, possibly an heir to the throne of David, 'a coming Jewish ruler, perhaps a member of the Hasmonaean dynasty, who may be a successor to the Davidic throne, but who is not envisaged as a Messiah'.[38] (3) For D. Flusser the spaces in the text should control its proper interpretation. Everything before the space in 4Q246 2.4 should be understood in terms of tribulations and afflictions. The figure is not a historical king, however, but the Antichrist. Flusser's key argument is based on the oracle of Hystaspes which describes 'a prophet of lies, and he will constitute and call himself God and will order himself to be worshipped as the Son of God'.[39] But Collins thinks this is almost certainly a Christian interpolation and that uniformly Jewish texts only ever speak of such eschatological adversaries in negative terms.[40] (4) F. García Martínez is convinced of the positive character of the Son of God figure and seeks to interpret it in the light of the other Qumran texts. He draws his parallels primarily from 11QMelch and concludes that the Son of God is another designation for Melchizedek, Michael or the Prince of Light.[41] (5) J.J. Collins himself has in several places advocated a messianic reading of the text, seeing 4Q246 as possibly the earliest interpretation of the Son of Man

37. Puech, '246. 4QApocryphe de Daniel ar', p. 181.

38. J.A. Fitzmyer, 'The Aramaic "Son of God" Text from Qumran Cave 4', in M. Wise, N. Golb, J.J. Collins, and D.G. Pardee (eds.), *Methods of Investigation of the Dead Sea Scrolls and the Khirbet Qumran Site: Present Realities and Future Prospects* (Annals of the New York Academy of Sciences, 722; New York: New York Academy of Sciences, 1994), pp. 163-75.

39. D. Flusser, 'The Hubris of the Antichrist in a Fragment from Qumran', *Immanuel* 10 (1980), pp. 31-37.

40. Collins, *The Scepter and the Star*, pp. 156-57.

41. F. García Martínez, '4Q246: Tipo del Anticristo o Libertador Escatologico?', in V. Collado and E. Zurro Rodriguez (eds.), *El Misterio de la Palabria: Homenaje a Luis Alonso Schökel* (Madrid: Ediciones Cristiandad, 1983), pp. 229-44 (reprinted as 'The eschatological figure of 4Q246', in *Qumran and Apocalyptic: Studies on the Aramaic Texts from Qumran* [STDJ, 9; Leiden: E.J. Brill, 1992], pp. 162-79).

in Daniel 7 as an individual figure.[42] É. Puech also allows that a messianic interpretation of the text is permissible.[43] (6) M. Hengel's hint that perhaps the figure should be seen corporately has recently been developed by A. Steudel.[44] She argues that the Son and the people are one and the same.

Can anything be made out of this great diversity of opinion? When faced with such problems in relation to a manuscript from Qumran, one should always begin by asking what date the manuscript was written, before attempting to jump to conclusions about the date of the composition itself. According to Puech, Milik has given the manuscript a date in the latter half of the first century BCE.[45] The text is thus being copied at a time when several compositions are implying an increased interest in the expectation of an eschatological king, specifically a Davidic figure (4Q161; 4Q174; 4Q252; 4Q285). Thus it seems to me likely that the scribe who copied the actual manuscript would have thought of the Son of God figure as referring to a Jewish king, but certain features need to be noticed which put this king firmly in his place. Perhaps some will think that he has taken the throne for himself, called himself 'Son of God' and 'Son of the Most High'; but that is of little matter, because the majority of the surviving column 2 can be interpreted as giving pride of place to the people of God and it is God himself who wages war for them.

Two New Testament texts can be used as hermeneutical devices to support such a reading. First, there is Lk. 1.32-35, in which the same pair of titles ('Son of God' and 'Son of the Most High') occurs, together with the phrase 'he will be great'. Collins comments that these correspondences are 'astonishing' and that 'it is difficult to avoid the conclusion that Luke is dependent in some way, whether directly or indirectly, on this long lost text from Qumran'.[46] Here then we would have an example of the messianic reading of the text or the tradition it represents, and a reading which takes the figure as an individual. The Lukan use of the tradition supposes a messianic figure without any

---

42. See esp. Collins, *The Scepter and the Star*, pp. 154-72.

43. Puech, '246. 4QApocryphe de Daniel ar', p. 181.

44. M. Hengel, *The Son of God* (Philadelphia: Fortress Press, 1976), p. 44; A. Steudel, 'The Eternal Reign of the People of God: Collective Expectations in Qumran Texts (4Q246 and 1QM)', *RevQ* 17 (1996), pp. 507-25.

45. Puech, '246. 4QApocryphe de Daniel ar', p. 166.

46. Collins, *The Scepter and the Star*, p. 155.

peer, and shows by contrast what cannot be denied the people and God himself in 4Q246. Secondly, there is Jn 10.22-39, in which the narrative and its dialogues are presented against the backdrop of the Feast of Dedication with its celebration of the removal of Antiochus IV;[47] Jesus walks in the Temple and the Jews demand that he tells them 'plainly' whether he is the Messiah. Jesus' answer is eventually clear: 'the father and I are one'. This causes an aggressive reaction as the Jews take up stones because they perceive Jesus, though only a human being, to be making himself God. Jesus disagrees that he makes himself anything but tacitly affirms that he has a distinct status, through his reply with Ps. 82.6,[48] showing that human beings can be called 'god'; and eventually he describes himself as Son of God. Thus, as with Lk. 1.32-35, Jn 10.22-39 contains mention of the Son of God, the implied mention of the Son(s) of the Most High and a debate about whether Jesus is making himself, we might say calling himself, God.[49] All these ingredients can be found in 4Q246, as I have mentioned. Whereas Lk. 1.32-35 highlights by contrast how the kingly figure of 4Q246 might be understood to refer to a Jewish eschatological king, Jn 10.22-39 suggests that

47. In the light of Antiochus IV being one of the contenders for the title of 'Son of God' in 4Q246, it is worth drawing out a little the significance of the Feast of Dedication in John 10. Amongst others J. VanderKam has brought out the parallels between Hanukkah and John 10 especially suitably. He writes: 'It should be recalled that Antiochus IV not only banned the practice of Judaism and the temple cult but that he also imposed new forms of worship which included veneration of himself as a god in Jerusalem's temple. Jesus' strong assertions that he and the father are one (10.30), that he was the Son of God (10.36), and that the father was in him as he was in the father were uttered at a time when the blasphemous pretensions of Antiochus IV to be a god would have been particularly fresh in the minds of Jewish people': 'John 10 and the Feast of Dedication', in H.W. Attridge, J.J. Collins, and T.H. Tobin (eds.), *Of Scribes and Scrolls: Studies on the Hebrew Bible, Intertestamental Judaism, and Christian Origins* (Resources in Religion, 5; Lanham, MD: University Press of America, 1990), p. 211. John 10 might confirm then that there was a way of reading the tradition as particularly about those who call themselves Son of God, or Son of the Most High, a tradition which was kept alive by the annual celebration of Hanukkah at which Antiochus's misappropriation of divine titles could have been recalled.

48. The whole of Ps. 82.6 reads 'I say, "You are Gods, sons of the Most High, all of you"'.

49. The difficult verse Jn 10.29, 'My father, as to what he has given me, is greater than all', may be a reflection of the use of 'great' at several points in the tradition of 4Q246.

there was ongoing lively debate about the identification of any 'Son of God'. If anyone, even a king, claimed such a title for themselves, they must be put in their place.

A second Aramaic text, 4Q541, the so-called Testament of Levi[d], is also worth a few comments.[50] It is likely that this composition describes the succession of priests from Levi to the end. What emerges as a possibility because of a few Hebrew loanwords in the text is that the language of the servant of Isaiah is applied to this priest. Fragment 24 seems to describe the death of one of these priests, perhaps the last one, since the fragment seems to contain the end of the text, so it would not be inappropriate for the language of the servant to be applied to this figure. Whatever the case, the manuscript conveying this composition is likely to be from the last third of the second century BCE and so it is to that time at least that we should date an overriding concern with the role of the priest at the eschaton.

Perhaps in the non-sectarian category should also be placed 4Q521,[51] the so-called 'messianic apocalypse'. As briefly mentioned above, this seems best understood as referring to the activity of the eschatological prophet. It is important to note that 4Q521 fragment 8 speaks of 'all his anointed ones', making the prophetic understanding of 'his anointed' in fragment 2 all the more likely. Puech has difficulty in determining a date for the manuscript copy of this text, since some letters have early forms, others late, but it belongs somewhere in the first quarter of the first century BCE, give or take a decade or two. A number of factors might make explicit consideration of the role of the eschatological prophet at such a time particularly pertinent.[52] Whatever the case, in

50. Text available in É. Puech, 'Fragments d'un apocryphe de Lévi et le personnage eschatologique: 4QTestLévi[c-d](?) et 4QAJa', in J. Trebolle Barrera and L. Vegas Montaner (eds.), *The Madrid Qumran Congress: Proceedings of the International Congress on the Dead Sea Scrolls, Madrid 18–21 March 1991* (2 vols.; STDJ, 11; Leiden: E.J. Brill; Madrid: Editorial Complutense, 1992), II, pp. 449-501. See my study on this text: '4QTestament of Levi[d](?) and the Messianic Servant High Priest', in M.C. de Boer (ed.), *From Jesus to John: Essays on Jesus and New Testament Christology in Honour of Marinus de Jonge* (JSNTSup, 84; Sheffield: Sheffield Academic Press, 1993), pp. 83-100.

51. É. Puech considers 4Q521 to be sectarian and its principal fragment to refer to the eschatological priest: 'Une apocalypse messianique (4Q521)', *RevQ* 15 (1991–92), pp. 475-522.

52. If the composition is non-sectarian, then thoughts about the prophet may relate to the view that John Hyrcanus had had prophetic powers; if sectarian, then

these three compositions we can see evidence for the expectation for eschatological prophet, priest and king. Because the focus of this study is on kingship, the way in which the figure in 4Q246 is kept in his place is to be particularly noticed.

For the clearly sectarian texts there is little that is new for messianism. Two fragments are worth mentioning explicitly before some overall comments are made. First, a clear reference to Zech. 4.14's 'two sons of oil' has now been published in the principal edition of 4Q254, Commentary on Genesis C.[53] If this belongs as a subsidiary quotation in an interpretation of Gen. 49.10, then we have the interesting possibility, in a mid-first century BCE manuscript, of the representation of dual messianism in what may have been the blessing of Judah. In other words, whilst the biblical starting point may have been concerned solely with the descendants of Judah, the commentator's interpretation has ensured that any future or eschatological kingly leader should at least be matched with a priestly counterpart, if not actually positioned as inferior to the priest.

A similar phenomenon can be observed in the much-disputed fragment 5 of 4Q285.[54] This contains an interpretation of Isa. 10.34–11.1. G. Vermes suitably translates the relevant lines of the interpretation as: 'the Branch of David and they will enter into judgement with [...] and the Prince of the Congregation, the Br[anch of David] will kill him [...by strok]es and by wounds. And a Priest [of renown (?)] will command.'[55] It seems clear that the prince of the congregation is involved in putting some enemy to death, a statement which makes his eschatological role as explicit and active as anywhere. However, it is also remarkable that even in the small amount of text that survives mention is made of the priest who will accompany the prince and who seems to be very much in command. Once again, even though the prince has a role to play, he is accompanied by or is subservient to a priest.

As already mentioned, the typological, synchronic approach to mes-

---

perhaps elaborate reflection on the eschatological prophet might come shortly after the death of the Teacher of Righteousness, whom some may have identified with such a prophet.

53. G.J. Brooke, '254. Commentary on Genesis C', p. 224.

54. See, *inter alia*, G. Vermes, 'The Oxford Forum for Qumran Research Seminar on the Rule of War (4Q285)', *JJS* 43 (1992), pp. 85-90; M.G. Abegg, 'Messianic Hope and 4Q285: A Reassessment', *JBL* 113 (1994), pp. 81-91.

55. Vermes, *The Complete Dead Sea Scrolls in English*, p. 189.

sianism in the Qumran texts has led to a widening of the discussion to include even the angels. From the comments made in this study on individual manuscripts it can be seen that a diachronic approach to messianism may still be suitable. Though it is evidently no longer possible to be as precise as J. Starcky in his landmark study,[56] nevertheless there does seem to be some development. Rather than the four stages proposed by Starcky, we may outline two more generally.[57]

In the sectarian material that stems from the end of the second century BCE and the start of the first century BCE there is a relatively balanced expectation of two messianic figures, sometimes preceded by or accompanied by a prophet. Amongst texts conveying this impression are the classic statement in 1QS 9.11, the likelihood that the first three quotations in 4Q175 refer primarily to eschatological prophet, king and priest respectively, and the statements about two Messiahs in the Damascus Document. In the later stage, the end of the first century BCE and later, or at least in compositions which only survive in later manuscripts, the royal figure, whether called Messiah, or prince of the congregation, or shoot of David, or even Son of God, comes to the fore, even though he is regularly accompanied by a guide of some sort, an Interpreter of the Law, who almost certainly was a priest (4Q161; 4Q174; 4Q252; 4Q285). This two-stage approach is supported variously by the work of G.S. Oegema and K. Pomykala.[58] Oegema is surprisingly uncritical of Starcky's over-precise model and reuses it without question, but his overall thesis is that the changing political circumstances after 63 BCE, and especially after the accession of Herod, resulted in messianic texts being far more overtly political by way of providing a religious counterbalance which embodied dissatisfaction with the political situation. Pomykala's work has focused on the explicit mention of David in relation to messianic expectation; he has concluded that Davidic messianism comes to the fore only in the later 'Herodian' texts at Qumran. But before we conclude that Qumran

---

56. J. Starcky, 'Les quatres étapes du messianisme à Qumrân', *RB* 70 (1963), pp. 481-505.

57. This outline of two stages does not preclude the need for attempting to say something about the earliest stages in the movement's thought: see, e.g., H. Stegemann, 'Some remarks to 1QSa, to 1QSb , and to Qumran Messianism', *RevQ* 17 (1996), pp. 479-505.

58. Oegema, *Der Gesalbte und sein Volk*; Pomykala, *The Davidic Dynasty Tradition in Early Judaism*.

messianism developed from an earlier well-balanced ideology of an anticipated double act of priest and king, towards being more militant and military, more overtly political, it is important to ask what the Messiahs do, especially the Davidic one.

The prophet and priest seem to have plenty to do. The anointed prophet performs deeds of local and national significance and in line with other prophetic figures has some role in interpretation. Perhaps the anointed Moses is recalled as the type of the prophet to come, as is made explicit in 4Q175.[59] The anointed eschatological priest atones for the people (4Q451 9 i 2) in a manner that reflects the worship of heaven, where Melchizedek has a similar function in order that divine judgment can proceed (11Q13 ii 5-9). The eschatological priest also seems to have a teaching role; if correctly identified as Interpreter of the Law, then clearly the interpretation is one of making the Law known for the messianic king (4Q174 3.10-11).

But it is remarkable that the anointed eschatological prince is something of a disappointment. He neither performs signs, nor knows the Law well enough to interpret it for himself. In some ways he is an individualistic projection of the king for whom there is legislation in the Temple Scroll. He can do nothing for himself or by himself, even though he arises to save Israel and to rule in Zion at the end of time (4Q174 3.10-11) and even though in one interpretation of Isa. 10.34–11.1 he has to kill an enemy (4Q285 5 3-4). Overall 4QpIsa[a] sums up his situation well: '[the interpretation of the matter (Isa. 11.1-5) concerns the branch of] David who will take his stand at the end of days ... enemies. And God will sustain him with a mighty spirit[and God will give him a th]rone of glory, a holy crown and garments of variegated stuff. And God will place a sceptre in his hand and over all the nations he will rule.' This perception of the prince of the congregation may be a consistent motif: it seems to be indicated in the necessity of prayer for the prince in 1QSb 5, an earlier text. Later it is indicated in the final form of the War Rule: in the scenarios depicted there the lay prince plays virtually no part at all. The victory is God's. Inasmuch as the kingly Messiah is also a projection of all true Israelites' aspirations for themselves the kingly Messiah is portrayed as one who obeys rather than commands, who is placed on the throne rather than wins his spurs, who acts as judge once all the important decisions have been made.

---

59. In the quotation of Exod. 20.21 according to the tradition as also represented in the Samaritan Pentateuch.

4. *Kingship and Messianism in the Scrolls*

Now, when the concepts of kingship and messianism in the scrolls are put side by side some further intriguing observations can be made about the two stages of messianism suggested here. As we have seen, there are several texts which speak in depth of the kingship of God, especially the Songs of the Sabbath Sacrifice, which is extant exclusively in manuscripts of the mid-first century BCE or later. Some of these compositions imply that God is king now, some that he will be recognized as such in the future. In none of them is there any mention of the kingly Messiah. God's sovereignty is known or to be known quite apart from any human intermediary who might represent his rule on earth.

There are a few compositions from the second half of the first century BCE or later in which the focus is indeed on the royal Messiah, but in these texts this messianism is commonly put into perspective through some recollection of the sovereignty of God himself or qualified by having the royal Messiah stand alongside some priestly counterpart. So, for example, in the most complete column of 4Q174 the kingship of God is declared through the explicit citation of Exod. 15.17-18 before the shoot of David is mentioned 'who will arise with the Interpreter of the Law'. Moreover, these compositions in which the kingly (and commonly Davidic) Messiah is to the fore, even though another eschatological figure is also often mentioned, all belong palaeographically to the Herodian period, that is to the last one hundred years of the existence of the Qumran community and the wider movement of which it was a part.

Two factors may have influenced the increasing stress on the Davidic Messiah in this later period. On the one hand, from 63 BCE onwards the political situation outside the community in Roman domination and in the rule of the Herodian house saw an emphasis on kingship predominantly apart from any temple setting. The aspiration for a Davidic Messiah was a natural compensatory counterpart to such foreign kings who had taken over the land. On the other hand, because the manuscript version of the Rule of the Community present in 4QS^d can be dated to the latter part of the first century BCE, it seems as if there was either a rediscovery of or a move towards increasing laicization within the community in the later period. This had two aspects to it. First, it meant that whilst purity remained a significant hallmark of the community member, it was no longer the priesthood that had sole jurisdiction in such matters; the priestliness of the community may have been some-what on the wane and thus it was natural for an increasingly lay com-munity to look primarily to a lay leader for the fulfilment of its hopes.[60] Secondly, the increasing laicization in the community meant that no living leader was the focus of community aspirations: those aspirations were focused primarily on a divinely chosen Davidic Messiah. But these factors, which were producing an interest in the Davidic Messiah, were also responsible for the stress on the overarching sovereignty of God himself. This explains the somewhat strange combination of ideas: that whilst several later compositions put forward the Davidic Messiah suitably accompanied by an advisor, his role always seems somewhat compromised by the very authority of God himself.

All this can be seen paradigmatically in 4Q174. The dominant posi-tion given to the sovereignty of God has already been mentioned in the way in which Exod. 15.17-18 is cited explicitly at the start of the interpretation of Nathan's oracle. After the interpretation of 2 Samuel 7 which has indeed eventually resulted in the mention of the shoot of David, there is an interpretation of Psalm 2. The manuscript is a little damaged at this point, but all scholars agree that the complete column contained the word *mᵉšîḥô* from Ps. 2.2. Thus the term *māšîaḥ* was explicitly there. But with whom is this Messiah to be identified? The *pesher* reaches the bottom of the column and mentions only the 'chosen ones of Israel in the last days'. Nor is there any room in what remains at the top of the next column to describe an individual messianic figure. The anointed one of the Psalm is the elect of Israel, the community itself. The sovereignty of God, the Davidic Messiah and the prominent place of the laicized community itself are all present in this one column of text in an 'Herodian' manuscript.

The Hasmonaeans as priest–kings may have stimulated the mes-sianism of the community in the earlier period as it pondered the duality

---

60. I have attempted elsewhere to explain the changes and developments in the messianism of the Damascus Document: G.J. Brooke, 'The Messiah of Aaron in the Damascus Document', *RevQ* 15 (1991–92), pp. 215-30. The waning of Zadokite priestly concerns may be represented there in the consistent motif that the 'king' of Amos 5.26-27 is the 'congregation', the 'star' is the Interpreter of the Law, and the 'sceptre' is the prince of the whole congregation; but also the continuing dominance of the priestly Messiah, if a single figure lies behind some of the phraseology of the text, reflects a possible Levitical (rather than Zadokite) concern which is not incompatible with a shift of power in the community and its wider movement away from the Zadokites.

of certain biblical texts, but it was the political circumstances of living under Herod and the Romans, together with the changing dynamics within the community which caused Davidic messianism to become prominent at the turn of the era, though always within the context of the forceful assertion of the kingship of God himself.

5. Conclusion

In many ways over the last fifty years, the Scrolls have put the 'mess' into 'messianism', making it difficult to be clear what constituted Jewish eschatological expectation at the time of Hillel and Jesus. But now that almost every fragment is in the public domain various conclusions can be stated relatively securely.

To begin with, in terms of the overall number of compositions found at Qumran, the number which contain explicit references to a Messiah or Messiahs is relatively few. Messianism does not seem to have been the major emphasis of the eschatological outlook of the Qumran community or the wider movement of which it was a part. Rather, the foundation seems to have been the belief that the community's experiences were to be understood as the fulfilment of prophecy.

Secondly, as it becomes easier to distinguish sectarian from non-sectarian compositions, it also becomes more important to recognize the way in which some of the elements in Qumran messianism were inherited not just from biblical texts, but also from biblical texts as mediated by other, especially Aramaic traditions (like 4Q541).

Thirdly, a typological reading of the messianism in the scrolls may be very suitable, but before every text is read as variously reflecting the same basic understanding, some recognition of developments over time should also be made; the diachronic must be set alongside the synchronic. Within the framework of dual messianism, in earlier texts, some of which persist into the later period, the priest Messiah is dominant alongside a royal figure, but in some later texts the king Messiah comes especially to the fore in an intriguing way. In those later texts the king Messiah is politically correct, but he is kept in his place both by the stress on the sovereignty of God and by the concern for the place of the community as God's elect. The consistent Qumran view in every generation seems to have been that nothing much of value could ever come from a palace, though a branch of David or princely leader could symbolize how God might represent some of his purposes at the end of time.

THE KING MESSIAH IN RABBINIC JUDAISM

Philip S. Alexander

My purpose in the present paper is to survey ideas regarding the king Messiah within the rabbinic tradition. Specifically I am interested in determining how central these ideas were to rabbinic Judaism and what role they played within it, in discovering what elements of rabbinic messianic doctrine have been taken over from Second Temple messianism and what have, apparently, been newly minted in the post-70 CE period. As evidence for rabbinic Judaism I confine myself strictly to the great classic rabbinic texts—the Mishnah, the Gemara and the Midrashim that were produced in the rabbinic Yeshivot. There were other texts which circulated within the rabbinic milieu—prayers such as the Amidah, and mystical literature such as the Books of Heikhalot—which contain messianic material, but they are either not rabbinic in origin, as in the case of the Amidah (though the Amidah was modified under rabbinic influence), or do not belong to the canon of rabbinic literature, as in the case of the Books of Heikhalot. I have resisted the temptation to produce a composite picture that synthesizes all the Talmudic period sources. My approach is analytical, and central to my argument is the perception of a certain tension between the ideas of the major rabbinic texts and ideas that may have been more widely and popularly held within rabbinically dominated society.

I begin in the post-Talmudic era with the Eighth Treatise of Saadia Gaon's theological masterpiece, *The Book of Beliefs and Opinions*.[1] The reasons for starting here, so late in the history of Rabbanism, are to my mind compelling. Saadia marks the first clear, full and coherent statement of messianism strictly within the rabbinic tradition. Messianic ideas can be found at a much earlier period both in Talmudic literature

---

1. Saadia, *Kitab al-Amanat wa-'l'tiqadat* (ed. J. Kafiḥ; Jerusalem: Mossad Harav Kook, 1970), pp. 237-60 (ET in S. Rosenblatt, *The Book of Beliefs and Opinions* [New Haven: Yale University Press, 1948], pp. 290-319).

and, as we have noted, in liturgical and apocalyptic texts known to the Rabbis, but it is hard to say how these ideas relate to the rabbinic world-view or what part they play in the rabbinic system of thought. The Talmudic material is especially problematic. There is a considerable corpus of messianic midrashim and aggadot in Talmud, but it is scattered here and there in highly allusive form; it is hard to see how it all fits together, to work out the Rabbis' attitude towards it and to integrate it with their thought. Take one instructive example. As early as *m. Sanh.* 10.1 we read: 'These are they who have no share in the world to come: he that says there is no resurrection of the dead prescribed in the Torah, and he that says that the Torah is not from heaven, and an Epicurean'. This well-known text is intended, however obscurely, to indicate some of the fundamental beliefs of rabbinic Judaism, but what is meant here by the resurrection of the dead? The resurrection of the dead in certain texts is part of a comprehensive scenario of the end which includes the coming of the king Messiah. Does the reference here to resurrection allude to this larger scenario, and does it automatically draw in messianism as a basic tenet of the rabbinic system of thought? This was certainly the view taken by Maimonides when he came to write his commentary on this passage in the Mishnah, from which are derived the famous thirteen principles of the faith.[2] But the doctrine of the resurrection of the dead does not necessarily imply the doctrine of the Messiah. One can envisage a resurrection at the end of history simply for judgment, to reward the righteous and to punish the wicked in a final balancing of the moral ledger, without implying the coming of a Messiah or of the restoration of the Jewish state. With Saadia, however, for the first time in a *rabbinic* text all the pieces of the jigsaw are fitted into a coherent picture and stated authoritatively as a central rabbinic belief. Saadia (882–942), who ended his life as the head of the Suran academy in Baghdad, was one of the most important rabbinic scholars of the middle ages, and he wrote his *Book of Beliefs and Opinions* precisely to define and to defend the essential tenets of

---

2.   Maimonides, *Commentary on the Mishnah* (ed. J. Kafiḥ; Jerusalem: Mossad Harav Kook, 1963–68), *Neziqin*, pp. 210-217 (ET in P.S. Alexander, *Textual Sources for the Study of Judaism* [Manchester: Manchester University Press, 1984], pp. 111-16). On the rabbinic doctrine of the resurrection of the dead see H. Sysling, *Teḥiyyat Ha-Metim: The Resurrection of the Dead in the Palestinian Targums of the Pentateuch and Parallel Traditions in Classical Rabbinic Literature* (Tübingen: J.C.B. Mohr [Paul Siebeck], 1996).

Rabbanism against the attacks of the Qaraites. Not only was his *Beliefs and Opinions* as a whole widely read in both its Arabic and its Hebrew versions, but a Hebrew adaptation of his Eighth Treatise circulated as an independent apocalyptic tract.[3] He is the first clearly datable authority to make messianism a dogma of rabbinic Judaism, and his influence in this, as in other areas, was decisive. Later writers, when expounding Jewish messianic ideas, are usually directly or indirectly indebted to him, and some mention him by name.[4]

What, then, is Saadia's messianic scenario? For Saadia the coming of the Messiah is most decidedly a real historical event. There is not a trace of mysticism in his account. He envisages a political process strictly on the terrestrial plane. This is reinforced by the fact that, despite a Talmudic warning to the contrary, he makes a serious attempt to calculate the date of the Messiah's coming.[5] He produces from Scripture three different computations of the end, but argues that the existence of these different dates can no more be used to question the ending of the present exile than the different figures in Scripture for the duration of the Babylonian and Egyptian exiles can be used to deny that those exiles came to an end. God in his wisdom knows how the dates are to be reconciled.

For Saadia the present exile has an absolutely foreordained fixed term, a point in time beyond which God will not allow it to run. The coming of the Messiah can be hastened, if Israel repents of her sins, but if the term is reached before Israel repents, then God will bring upon her misfortunes and disasters which will compel her to resolve upon repentance, so that she should be worthy of redemption.

The first stage of these messianic woes will be the appearance in Upper Galilee of the Messiah the son of Joseph. He will gather around himself individuals from the Jewish nation and go up and seize Jeru-

3. For an edition see Yehudah Even Shemuel, *Midreshei Ge'ullah* (Jerusalem: Mosad Bialik, 2nd edn, 1954), pp. 117-28.

4. Note, e.g., Maimonides' reference to Saadia in his *Epistle to the Yemen*, section III (ed. J. Kafiḥ), *Rabbi Mosheh ben Maimon: Iggerot* (Jerusalem: Mossad Harav Kook, 1972) (ET by A. Halkin in A. Halkin and D. Hartman, *Epistles of Maimonides: Crisis and Leadership* [Philadelphia and Jerusalem: Jewish Publication Society, 1993]). Maimonides' own scenario of the messianic era may be found in his *Mishneh Torah*, Shofetim XI.

5. For a discussion see H. Malter, 'Saadia Gaon's Messianic Computation', *Journal of Jewish Lore and Philosophy* 1 (1919), pp. 45-59. The Talmudic injunction against calculating the end is found in *b. Sanh.* 97b.

salem back from the Romans. The Messiah ben Joseph will reign in Jerusalem for a certain unspecified period of time, but Jerusalem will then be recaptured in a surprise attack by the Romans under the leadership of the anti-Messiah Armilus, who will 'subject its inhabitants to massacre, captivity, and disgrace'. And included among those that will be slain will be the Messiah ben Joseph. Then the tribulations of Israel will truly begin. 'There will come upon the Jewish nation at that time great misfortunes, the most difficult to endure being the deterioration of their relationship with the governments of the world, who will drive them into the wilderness to let them starve and be miserable. As a result of what has happened to them, many of them will desert their faith, only those purified remaining.' The period of woes will be brought to an end by the appearance of Elijah the prophet, who will complete the work of purification begun by the Messiah ben Joseph and herald the coming of the Messiah ben David.

Whether or not he is preceded by Elijah, the Messiah ben Joseph and the period of tribulation, or he comes suddenly and unheralded because Israel has repented of her own accord, the Messiah ben David will assuredly come. He will gather about him his retinue and go and occupy Jerusalem, and if Armilus is there he will kill him. He will inaugurate a period of rebuilding and prosperity in the land of Israel. However, Gog and Magog, having heard of the prosperity of Israel will marshal their hosts and go up to attack the Messiah ben David. The hosts of Gog and Magog will comprise two categories: first, notorious sinners marked out for perdition, and secondly, 'people who have mended their ways in order to enter the faith'. There will then ensue the last great battle between Israel and the nations in the Valley of Jehoshaphat, which will result in the destruction of Gog and Magog and of the sinners in their host. Their followers who have mended their ways will be absorbed into Israel, apparently as converts or as righteous Gentiles, though in a subordinate role. Some will serve as domestics in the homes of the Israelites, some will serve in cities and villages, some will serve in the fields, and the remainder will return to their own countries and be submissive to Israel, making pilgrimage to Jerusalem each year on the Feast of Tabernacles.

Then will follow the ingathering of the exiles. In order to ingratiate themselves with the Messiah the nations will expedite the sending of the exiles to the Holy Land, transporting them on 'horses and mules, in litters and on dromedaries', in ships and boats, and, if need be, even carrying them on their own backs, and heaping upon them gifts as they depart. Those Jews who will remain in the desert or who have no one of the nations to bring them to Jerusalem, will be brought swiftly to Israel by divine agency, as though a cloud had lifted them up and carried them.

The ingathering of the exiles will be followed by the resurrection of the dead, which will encompass only Israelites, so that they may unite with the Jews who are still alive to enjoy the messianic kingdom. The Holy City will be renewed and the Temple which Ezekiel saw in his vision established. The Shekhinah will reappear 'shining upon the Temple with such brilliance that all lights will become faint or dim in comparison to it'. Various natural marvels will occur. The Mount of Olives will be split in two, and a river will issue from the Temple, on the banks of which will grow marvellous trees. And prophecy will be restored to Israel, and be so widespread that even children and slaves will be endowed with the gift. 'This will, then', says Saadia, 'be the position that will be held by the believers as long as the world exists, without change, as it has been said in Scripture: "O Israel, you are saved by the Lord with an everlasting salvation; you shall not be ashamed nor confounded world without end" (Isa. 45.17).' In other words, Israel will rebel against God no more; the messianic kingdom will endure to the end of the world.

Saadia rounds off his account of the redemption by polemicizing against two groups. The first is a Jewish group which claims that all the messianic prophecies in the Bible were actually fulfilled in the time of the Second Temple. Who this group was it is now hard to say, but it is clear from Saadia's detailed refutation that they had a well worked out position. Such historicizing attitudes towards apocalyptic are attested in both Judaism and Christianity. The second group against whom he polemicizes are clearly the Christians, who had, of course, a vested interest in messianic prophecy and who advocated a split fulfilment of the end of history, with a first and a second coming of Christ.

Here, then, we have most of the elements of the classic rabbinic messianic agenda set out clearly for the first time. The major motifs are: (1) the importance of Israel's repentance in hastening the coming of the Messiah; (2) the role of the slain Messiah ben Joseph and of Elijah in preparing the way for the coming of the Messiah ben David; (3) the messianic woes and the figure of Armilus, the anti-Messiah; (4) the Messiah ben David; (5) the wars of Gog and Magog and the battle of

Armageddon; (6) the 'conversion' of the Gentiles; (7) the ingathering of the Jewish exiles; (8) the resurrection of the dead; (9) the rebuilding of Jerusalem and of the Temple, with the reappearance of the Shekhinah and of prophecy; (10) the consolations of the messianic age—the wonderful fertility of the Land, and the absence of pestilence and disease. What is not here, or deliberately fudged, is as significant as what is here and clearly expressed. There is no mention of divine judgment in the messianic age. The resurrection is partial and affects only Israelites, and its purpose is to allow those who have died to enjoy the messianic blessings. For Saadia the judgment takes place in the spiritual world after death and results either in the destruction of the soul, or in its purification and its entry into Gan Eden. There is also no doctrine of the immortality of the body. Saadia clearly implies that those who are alive in the messianic age, though they will enjoy uncommon felicity, will in the course of nature die. He is somewhat unclear as to what will happen to them then. Presumably they enter directly into Gan Eden. Saadia is also noticeably vague about the ultimate fate of the physical world. It is unclear whether he thinks that the physical world will endure for ever, or whether it will come to an end, and if so, what will happen then.[6]

What are the sources of Saadia's messianic doctrine? Saadia carefully grounds his ideas in Scripture and some of the refinements of his messianic scenario may result from his close exegesis of the Bible. However, he makes it quite clear that he is relying also on tradition, and, in fact, most of the elements of his picture can be found individually much earlier in non-biblical texts. A possible source for his ideas may have been the Hebrew apocalyptic writings of the seventh and eighth centuries. There seems to have been a major revival of apocalyptic in Palestine at this time, which produced a considerable body of literature.[7] The most important of these late apocalypses is *Sefer*

6. Joseph Klausner, *The Messianic Idea in Israel: From its Beginning to the Completion of the Mishnah* (trans. W.F. Stinespring; London: Allen & Unwin, 1956), pp. 408-19, claims that some rabbinic traditions distinguish between 'the days of the Messiah' and the 'world to come', the latter referring to the condition of the world *after* the Messiah's reign, which will be of limited duration. But this distinction is less clear-cut than he implies.

7. See P.S. Alexander, 'Late Hebrew Apocalyptic: A Preliminary Survey', in P. Geoltrain, J.-C. Picard and A. Desremaux (eds.), *La Fable Apocryphe*, I (Turnhout: Brepols, 1990), pp. 197-217. A useful collection in English of late Hebrew apocalyptic texts may be found in G.W. Buchanan, *Revelation and*

Zerubbavel—an important text which has not received the attention it deserves, and which lacks to this day an adequate edition and commentary. Its textual transmission is very confused. In the important Bodleian manuscript it is clearly a composite work made up of different recensions of the same basic text.[8] Its scenario of the end combines the elements into broadly the same pattern as Saadia. However, since the origins of the work are obscure we should not jump to the conclusion that it originated in a rabbinic milieu and can be classified as 'rabbinic'. It contains colourful and significant details which are not in Saadia. Thus in *Sefer Zerubbavel* Armilus is born of Satan and a statue of the Virgin Mary. Metatron/Michael, the *angelus interpres* of the book, seizes hold of Zerubbavel and takes him to 'a house of disgrace and merrymaking', namely a church in Rome the Great (i.e. Byzantium), and shows him there a marble stone in the shape of a virgin, the beauty of whose appearance is wonderful to behold. He says: 'This statue is the wife of Belial. Satan will come and lie with her, and she will bear a son named Armilus, who will destroy the people.' This interest in the cult of the Virgin also comes out indirectly in *Sefer Zerubbavel* in the figure of Hephzibah. She is the mother of the Messiah ben David, who is called Menahem ben Amiel in *Sefer Zerubbavel*, and she plays a significant role in the scenario of the end; for example she protects Jerusalem with her staff after the defeat and death of the Messiah ben Joseph, here called Nehemiah ben Hushiel. As Martha Himmelfarb plausibly suggests, there is an allusion here to the use by the Byzantines

Redemption: Jewish Documents of Deliverance from the Fall of Jerusalem to the Death of Nahmanides (Dillsboro, NC: Western North Carolina Press, 1978). However, Buchanan's translations are unreliable and his notes hasty and sporadic.

8.   The textual confusion of the *Sefer Zerubbavel* attests its popularity. The most adequate edition is still that by I. Lévi, *Revue des Études Juives* 68 (1914), pp. 108-21; 71 (1920), pp. 57-65. There is also an edition in Even Shemuel, *Midreshei Ge'ullah*, pp. 55-88; cf. pp. 379-89 (ET by Martha Himmelfarb in D. Stern and M.J. Mirsky [eds.], *Rabbinic Fantasies: Imaginative Narratives from Classical Hebrew Literature* [Philadelphia/New York: Jewish Publication Society, 1990], pp. 67-90). That this work was still influential as late as the seventeenth century is shown by the Shabbataean version of it published by S.A. Wertheimer as *Pirqei Heikhalot Rabbati (Batei Midrashot)* (Jerusalem: Mossad Harav Kook, 2nd edn, 1968) , I, pp. 118-34; cf. Yehudah Even Shemuel, *Midreshei Ge'ullah*, pp. 352-70. See further, G. Scholem, *Sabbatai Sevi: The Mystical Messiah 1626–1676* (Princeton: Princeton University Press, 1973), pp. 737-40.

of images of the Virgin to protect cities under siege or armies in battle.[9] Hephzibah, the mother of the Messiah ben David is the Jewish answer to Mary the mother of Jesus. Interestingly, Hephzibah occurs in Jewish tradition only in the Book of Zerubbavel. All later Jewish scenarios of the end, not just Saadia's, ignore her. Perhaps her Christian pedigree was too obvious. Also present in *Sefer Zerubbavel*, but absent from Saadia, is the idea of the hidden Messiah, who is already here, living incognito, despised, lowly and unprepossessing, in the wicked city of Rome itself. This notion of the despised and hidden Messiah, which has antecedents in Talmud and Midrash, seems to me also to have a strong Christian colouring: he is the Jewish answer to the despised and lowly Galilaean who is finally to triumph in his second coming. Again, Saadia may have perceived and been uncomfortable with the Christian parallels.

There seems to be little doubt that the background to *Sefer Zerubbavel* lies in the wars between Byzantium and Persia in the years 604–30. The Persian campaigns in the West appear to have produced an upsurge of messianic fervour among the Jews. After all, was not there a tradition that one should expect the redemption when one sees a Persian horse tethered to a grave in the land of Israel?[10] The image of Persia is clearly present in the *Book of Zerubbavel* and it is not entirely positive. It is Shiroi, king of Persia, who in the fifth year of Nehemiah son of Hushiel, after the ingathering of the exiles, goes up against Nehemiah and causes great trouble for Israel, but it is Armilus, probably the Emperor Heraclius, who actually kills Nehemiah. The *Book of Zerubbavel* marks a revival of Hebrew apocalyptic which seems to have lasted for the rest of the seventh and into the eighth century. It was further fuelled by the arrival of Islam on the political stage of the middle east in the 630s. The tract known as the *Secrets of Rabbi Shim'on ben Yohai* appears to have reworked some of the *Sefer Zerubbavel* material in the light of the Islamic conquest of the Fertile Crescent.[11] A number of the

9. Himmelfarb in Stern and Mirsky (eds), *Rabbinic Fantasies*, p. 69.

10. *Cant. R.* 8.9.3; cf. *b. Sanh.* 98a-98b.

11. Bernard Lewis, 'An Apocalyptic Vision of Islamic History', in B. Lewis, *Studies in Classical and Ottoman Islam (7th–16th Centuries)* (London: Variorum Reprints, 1976), no. V (= *BSOAS* 13 [1950], pp. 308-38). Note also B. Lewis, 'On That Day: A Jewish Apocalyptic Poem on the Arab Conquests', no. VI in the same volume (= *Mélanges d'Islamologie: Volume dédié à la mémoire de Arnauld Abel* [Leiden: E.J. Brill, 1974], pp. 197-200).

other texts published by Yehudah Even Shemuel in *Midreshei Ge'ullah* also belong to this period. There seems to have been a revival of apocalyptic in the Christian world round about the same time—both in Greek and in Syriac—the literature of which is often associated with the biblical figure of Daniel and the four world empires of the biblical book of Daniel.[12] That there are links between the Christian and the Jewish apocalypses, and that both are responding to the same political circumstances, is a highly plausible hypothesis.[13]

Many of the ideas contained in *Sefer Zerubbavel* and the other seventh and eighth century Hebrew apocalypses can be paralleled in earlier rabbinic texts, but some seem to reach back over the Talmudic period into Second Temple times. How can this be explained? I think it unlikely that Second Temple apocalyptic literature had survived as a living transmission within Jewish circles right through the Talmudic period to the days of the Geonim. There is really no trace of this literature in the rabbinic texts of the Talmudic period. Rather, what we may have in post-Talmudic times is a rediscovery by Jewish scholars of literature that had been lost to them for some five or six hundred years. How could this have happened? I think the key to this rediscovery probably lies in a contemporary revival of the apocalyptic genre in Christianity. Somehow Jewish scholars were influenced by this revival and through it became aware again of certain Jewish texts of the Second

---

12. The most important of these was the Syriac *Apocalypse of Pseudo-Methodius* (Cod. Vat. Syrus 58), composed around the mid-seventh century CE. See P.J. Alexander, *The Byzantine Apocalyptic Tradition* (Berkeley: University of California Press, 1985), especially pp. 13-51; G.T. Zervos, 'Apocalypse of Daniel', in *OTP*, I, pp. 755-70.

13. The apocalyptic and messianic mood of the post-Islamic era affected not only Jews and Christians, but Zoroastrians and, finally, Muslims as well, as Bernard Lewis notes: 'During the first four centuries of Islamic rule Messianic hopes ran high among the peoples of the Caliphate. Christians, Jews and Zoroastrians, subjected to the rule of a new and alien religion, cherished and embellished their traditions of a Messiah or *Saoshyant* of God-chosen line who, in God's time, would come or return to the world, end the sufferings of the faithful and the dominion of their opponents, and establish the kingdom of God upon earth. Before very long Islam itself was affected. First in the heresies of the newly-converted, dissatisfied with the status assigned to them in what was still an Arab kingdom, grafting their old beliefs on their new faith; then in the orthodoxy of all Islam, the belief arose in a *Mahdi*, a "divinely guided one" who, in the words of the tradition, would "fill the earth with justice and equity as it is now filled with tyranny and oppression"' ('An Apocalyptic Vision of Islamic History', p. 308).

Temple Period. Recognizing that, although they were now being transmitted by Christians, these texts actually belonged to the Jewish literary heritage, they were ready to exploit them for their own ends. A similar rediscovery of 'lost' early Jewish literature seems to have led to the creation of the *Sefer Yosippon* and to the Hebrew Judith literature.[14] A rediscovery of Second Temple apocalyptic in the seventh to eighth centuries may be reflected also in works such as *Pirqei deRabbi Eli'ezer*. *Pirqei deRabbi Eli'ezer* has long been recognized as one of the most puzzling Jewish texts of the early middle ages. It seems to contain a large number of ideas which are not found anywhere in the rabbinic aggadot of the preceding centuries, but which can be paralleled much further back in the Enochic literature of the Second Temple period.[15] There are grounds for thinking that round about this time Syriac Christian scholars may have been rediscovering the books of *Enoch* and the book of *Jubilees*, as well as other Second Temple Jewish literature. This would explain the strong allusions to these texts in works such the Cave of Treasures, which is commonly dated to the late sixth century CE.[16]

Three other unusual Jewish texts, probably from the same period, should be mentioned in this connection. (1) The first is the so-called *Targum Pseudo-Jonathan* to the Pentateuch. It has long been noticed

14. The *Sefer Yosippon* was probably composed in southern Italy in the ninth century. See D. Flusser, *The Josippon [Joseph Gerionides]: Edited with an Introduction, Commentary and Notes* (2 vols.; Jerusalem: Mosad Bialik, 1980–81) (Hebrew). For the Judith literature see A. Jellinek, *Bet ha-Midrasch* (repr.; Jerusalem: Wahrmann Books, 1967), I, pp. 130-31; II, pp. 12-22; J.D. Eisenstein, *Ozar Midrashim* (New York: Bibliotheca Midrashica, 1915), I, pp. 203-209.

15. See the notes in G. Friedlander, *Pirke de Rabbi Eliezer* (repr.; New York: Sepher-Hermon Press, 1981), and in Miguel Pérez Fernández, *Los Capítulos de Rabbi Eliezer: Versión crítica, introducción y notas* (Valencia: Institución San Jerónimo, 1984). The date of *Pirqei deRabbi Eliezer* is discussed in G. Stemberger, *Introduction to Talmud and Midrash* (trans. M. Bockmuehl; Edinburgh: T. & T. Clark, 2nd edn, 1996), pp. 328-30.

16. See C. Bezold, *Die Schatzhöhle* (Leipzig: J.C. Hinrichs, 1988); E.A. Wallis Budge, *The Book of the Cave of Treasures* (London: Religious Tract Society, 1927). It should be borne in mind that there is little evidence of the influence of *Enoch* or *Jubilees* in earlier Syriac literature, nor is there evidence that either of these works was translated into Syriac. Both *Jubilees* and *1 Enoch* were preserved by the Ethiopian church, which had strong links with Syriac Christianity. Just how or when *Jubilees* and *Enoch* reached Ethiopia is unclear. Could they have come in the sixth century from Syria, where Syriac scholars were developing an interest in this literature?

that this peculiar Targum has a curious mixture of both very late and very early traditions: it cannot in its present form have been finally redacted before the seventh century and yet it contains elements which are very old and apparently go back to Second Temple times. It has also been noticed that it shows significant parallels to *Pirqei deRabbi Eli'ezer*. It is probably a literary Targum which arose in the same milieu in which *Pirqei deRabbi Eli'ezer* was compiled, and, like *Pirqei deRabbi Eli'ezer* one of its sources was Second Temple Jewish literature.[17] (2) The second text which should be mentioned is the *Targum of Shir ha-Shirim*. This highly paraphrastic Targum, which was probably composed in the seventh or eighth century CE, offers a historical reading of the Song of Songs which correlates the text of the Song with the history of Israel from the first Exodus from Egypt to the final Exodus from exile in the messianic age. The section of the Targum which covers the Maccabaean period is unusually well informed and positive in its evaluation of the Hasmonaeans. And its scenario of the end shows significant parallels to *Sefer Zerubbavel* and to Saadia.[18] (3) The third text is *Sefer Heikhalot*, dubbed by Hugo Odeberg *3 Enoch*, because of the central role played in it by Enoch-Metatron and because of its many and detailed parallels to the first and second books of *Enoch*. *3 Enoch* is probably to be dated in its present form to the seventh century CE.[19] Its interest in, and positive evaluation of, the figure of

17. Miguel Pérez Fernández, 'Sobre los textos mesiánicos del targum Pseudo-Jonatán y el Midrás Pirqé de Rabbi Eliezer', *EstBíb* 45 (1987), pp. 39-55; C.T.R. Hayward, 'The Date of Targum Pseudo-Jonathan: Some Comments', *JJS* 40 (1989), pp. 7-30 (Hayward disputes the links with *Pirqei deRabbi Eli'ezer*); A. Shinan, 'Dating Targum Pseudo-Jonathan: Some More Comments', *JJS* 41 (1990), pp. 56-61; A. Shinan, *The Embroidered Targum* (Jerusalem: Magnes Press, 1992), pp. 176-85 (Hebrew).

18. See especially *Targum Shir ha-Shirim* from 7.12 onwards. For the Maccabaean period in *Targum Shir ha-Shirim*, see 6.8-12. On *Targum Shir ha-Shirim* see P.S. Alexander, 'The Aramaic Version of the Song of Songs', in Geneviève Contamine (ed.), *Traduction et traducteurs au moyen âge: Colloque international du CNRS, IHRT, 26-28 mai 1986* (Paris: Éditions du CNRS, 1989), pp. 119-31; *idem*, 'Tradition and originality in the Targum of the Song of Songs', in M. McNamara and D.R.G. Beattie (eds.), *The Aramaic Bible: Targums in their Historical Context* (Sheffield: Sheffield Academic Press, 1994), pp. 318-39; *idem*, *Targum Canticles*, in *The Aramaic Bible*, XVII (Liturgical Press, forthcoming).

19. See P.S. Alexander, '3 Enoch', in *OTP*, I, pp. 223-316. There I dated *3 Enoch* to the fifth to sixth centuries. I am now inclined to put it a little later, possibly in the seventh century.

Enoch contrasts with the general lack of reference to, and sharply negative evaluation of, this patriarch in classic rabbinic literature.[20] A reasonable case can, therefore, be made out for a rediscovery by Jewish scholars of Second Temple apocalyptic in the seventh to eighth centuries CE. In this context the possibility that the author of *Sefer Zerubbavel* might have known some Second Temple traditions or literature seems less implausible than one might at first sight suppose.[21]

The most obvious source of Saadia's traditions about the Messiah is classic rabbinic literature, especially the Babylonian Talmud, of which Saadia was an unquestioned master. Certainly most of the individual elements of Saadia's messianic scenario are attested in classic rabbinic texts, but they are scattered over a very wide area and there is nowhere in Talmud and related literature from which he could have taken the overall story.[22]

20. See P.S. Alexander, 'From Son of Adam to Second God: Transformations of the Biblical Enoch', in M.E. Stone and T.A. Bergren (eds.), *Biblical Figures outside the Bible* (Trinity Press International, forthcoming).

21. One hesitates to introduce further speculation into an already speculative argument by invoking the story of the early mediaeval discovery of the Dead Sea Scrolls. This discovery, which seems to have been a genuine event that occurred around 800 CE and which has left its mark on Qaraite literature, as well as two copies of the Damascus Document in the Cairo Genizah, illustrates how Jewish scholars of the early middle ages might have reacted positively to Second Temple texts. See A. Paul, *Écrits de Qumran et sectes juives aux premiers siècles de l'Islam* (Paris: Letouzey & Ané, 1969); M. Gil, *A History of Palestine* (Cambridge: Cambridge University Press, 1992), pp. 785-87.

22. The nearest we get to such a scenario is in *b. Sanh.* 96b-99a. This *sugya*, despite its numerous baraitot, is probably late Amoraic in redaction. The relationship of Saadia to the extensive messianic material in *Pes. R.* 34–37 is unclear. These *pisqas* are generally regarded as being late. J. Mann argued that they were composed in the first half of the ninth century by an Italian aggadist who had joined the penitential group in Jerusalem known as the 'Mourners for Zion', in which case the chances of Saadia knowing this text are probably not high, though it would attest a strong messianic interest at this time (see J. Mann, *The Jews in Egypt and Palestine under the Fatimid Caliphs*, I [Oxford: Oxford University Press, 1920], pp. 47-49). But this proposal has been disputed: see A. Goldberg, *Erlösung durch Leiden: Drei rabbinische Homilien über die trauernden Zions und den leidenden Messias Efraim (PesR 34. 36. 37)* (Frankfurt am Main: Gesellschaft zur Förderung Judaistischer Studien, 1978). The tradition of mourning for Zion is attested much earlier: see *t. Soṭ.* 15.11; *b. B. Bat* 60b. It is unclear whether the mediaeval 'Mourners for Zion' were Rabbanite or Qaraite or from both these parties. See Gil, *A History of Palestine 634–1099*, pp. 617-622; H. Ben-Shammai, in S. Elizur *et al.*

The attitude towards the Messiah in Mishnah and Talmud is the subject of intense debate. The lack of messianic references in the Mishnah is well known. By way of contrast messianic pericopae in the Babylonian Talmud are rich and plentiful, albeit scattered throughout the corpus. Jacob Neusner has argued in *Messiah in Context* [23] that the Messiah plays no part in the Mishnah's world-view; indeed the Mishnah is anti-messianic. The Mishnah 'presented a system of Judaism aimed at the sanctification of Israel and bore a teleology lacking an eschatological dimension'. There are, of course, some elements of messianism in the Mishnah,[24] but they are residual, the heritage of a messianic past; they serve no real purpose but are 'left like rubble after a building has been completed: stones that might have been used, but were not'. By late Amoraic times, however, a 'remessianization' of rabbinic Judaism has taken place, the reintroduction of 'the eschatologically oriented teleology of the Messiah and his salvation that the Mishnah's framers had rejected'. 'The Talmuds and (in lesser measure) the collections of scriptural exegeses presented a system of Judaism focused upon salvation and which promised to carry Israel to the age that was to bring the Messiah and the end of history'. But this reinstated messianism was reshaped so that it conformed to the Mishnah's world-view and reinforced the central tenet of rabbinic Judaism, namely, obedience to the Torah of Moses, at least as this was understood by the Rabbis. The Amoraic Rabbis used popular messianic yearning to serve the halakhic imperative: if all Israel were to repent and to observe the Torah they would hasten the coming of the Messiah. The Messiah in the Talmud

> emerged as a figure meant to encourage and foster a view of life above time and beyond history, a life lived in full acceptance of God's rule in eternity, a life that rejected man's rule in history. The Mishnah had originally made that life the foundation of its system. Accordingly, when

(eds.), *Knesset Ezra: Studies Presented to Ezra Fleischer* (Jerusalem: Yad Ben-Zvi and Ben Zvi Institute, 1994), pp. 191-234.

23. J. Neusner, *Messiah in Context: Israel's History and Destiny in Formative Judaism* (Philadelphia: Fortess Press, 1984).

24. E.g. 'the footprints of the Messiah' and the messianic woes (*m. Soṭ.* 9.15); 'the days of the Messiah' (*m. Ber.* 1.5); Elijah as the forerunner (*m. Šeq.* 2.5; *m. B. Meṣ.* 1.8; 2.8; 3.4-5); the resurrection of the dead (*m. Sanh.* 10.1). It has also been suggested that the detailed discussion of the Temple service in Qodashim was intended to preserve the details of the cult so that it could be restored in the messianic age, but this is far from certain. There are other reasons why the Rabbis may have been interested in this material.

the canon of Judaism reached the end of its formative period, it presented a version of the Messiah myth entirely congruent with the character of the foundation document, the Mishnah. The Judaism emerging from late antiquity would then deliver to Israel an enduring message of timeless sanctification, in the guise of historical, and hence eschatological, salvation.[25]

Neusner's view is somewhat startling, but I believe that it is fundamentally correct, both in point of method and in point of interpretation. It stands in stark contrast to the account of messianism in the Mishnaic period presented by Joseph Klausner in his classic study, *The Messianic Idea in Israel*.[26] The reader of Klausner gets the strong impression that messianism was fundamental to Tannaitic Judaism, and that there is an abundance of Tannaitic messianic material. However, closer inspection of his evidence reveals that it overwhelmingly consists of baraitot, that is to say of supposedly Tannaitic material quoted in the Gemara, but not actually recorded in the Mishnah. Even if *all* these baraitot are genuine (a highly debatable assumption), the question can still be raised why, if it was so important, this material was not included in the Mishnah. The fact is that messianism does not sit easily with Mishnaic Judaism. Messianic Judaism and Mishnaic Judaism are pulling in opposite directions. There were very good political reasons why the Rabbis would have attempted to suppress messianism. The Talmudic period opens with two bitter and disastrous wars, both of which took on a messianic tinge. I have little doubt that Bar Kokhba did proclaim himself as Messiah and that Rabbi Aqiva endorsed that claim. The

25. The quotations are all on pp. ix-xi of Neusner, *Messiah in Context*.

26. Klausner, *The Messianic Idea in Israel* (see above, n. 6). The third part of this volume, covering the messianic idea in the period of the Tannaim, is based on Klausner's Heidelberg doctorate, which was published in Berlin in 1903–1904 under the title *Die messianischen Vorstellungen des jüdischen Volkes im Zeitalter der Tannaiten*. That Klausner has read the classic rabbinic sources through the spectacles of Zionist ideology seems to me beyond reasonable doubt, and as a result he has overemphasized the centrality of messianism to Judaism. Messianim has been important to both secular and religious Zionism in legitimating the State of Israel. It is hard now for any present-day writer on Jewish messianism not to be influenced by his own attitude towards the State of Israel. Another classic essay on messianism which, in a more subtle way, shows the influence of Zionist thought is Gershom Scholem's 'Towards an Understanding of the Messianic Idea in Judaism', in G. Scholem, *The Messianic Idea in Judaism and other Essays on Jewish Spirituality* (London: Allen & Unwin, 1971), pp. 1-36.

rabbinic innovation of the slain Messiah ben Joseph, who heralds the coming of the Messiah ben David, probably arose in a desperate attempt to salvage faith after the debacle of Betar.[27] The Rabbis were level-headed enough to realize that messianism spelt trouble.

Moreover, with the gradual triumph of Rabbanism and the maturing of Jewish political institutions from the late second century CE onwards, the need for messianism sharply decreased. The rabbinic communities both of Palestine and Babylonia enjoyed a great deal of prosperity and autonomy under the Romans, the Parthians and the Sassanians. Each community had its political leader—in Palestine, the Patriarch (Nasi), in Babylonia the Exilarch (Resh Galuta)—for whom Davidic descent was claimed.[28] If rabbinic Jews were in effect already ruled by Davidic rulers, the need for a Davidic Messiah is less obvious, and those Davidic rulers would doubtless have been loath to foster yearnings for the end of their own hegemony.[29]

But the profoundest reason for the Mishnah's lack of interest in messianism is the fact, as Neusner saw, that there is little need, indeed no place, for the Messiah in the Mishnaic world-view. It can be argued that it is hardly surprising that the Mishnah says nothing about the Messiah. After all, it is simply not talking about such matters. But this argument misses the point. The Mishnah is the manifesto of the rabbinic party. It is intended, surely, to present a *comprehensive* religious world-view. The fact, therefore, that the Messiah plays no part in that world-view *is* highly significant. The Mishnah's dominant perspective is this-worldly. It is concerned with defining and achieving piety and a civic society here and now. And it marks a strong universalizing

27. The rabbinic references to the messianic claims of Bar Kokhba are supported by Christian sources such as the *Apocalypse of Peter*. See P. Schäfer, *Der Bar Kokhba-Aufstand* (Tübingen: J.C.B. Mohr [Paul Siebeck], 1981), pp. 59-62; R.J. Bauckham, 'The Two Fig Tree Parables in the Apocalypse of Peter', *JBL* 104 (1985), pp. 269-87; D.D. Bucholz, *Your Eyes will be Opened: A Study of the Greek (Ethiopic) Apocalypse of Peter* (Atlanta: Scholars Press, 1988), pp. 408-12. On the Messiah ben Joseph, see J. Heinemann, 'The Messiah of Ephraim and the Premature Exodus of the Tribe of Ephraim', *HTR* 68 (1975), pp. 1-16.

28. According to one formulation Rabbi Judah ha-Nasi was descended by the female line from David, and Rav Huna, the Resh Galuta, from David by the male line. See J. Neusner, 'Exilarch' in *EncJud*, VI, cols. 1023–27 (1025).

29. Note the opposition in some rabbinic traditions to the Patriarchate and the Exilarchate, and the claim that the Messiah will only come when they have disappeared (*b. Sanh.* 38a; further, Klausner, *Messianic Idea*, pp. 435-37).

trend within post-70 Judaism. Rabbinic Judaism retained, probably in part as a reaction against emergent Christianity, a particularist doctrine of the election of Israel and an exclusivist definition of who was a Jew, but it regarded a fully halakhic existence for a Jew as liveable anywhere in the world. There is little hint till late in the Amoraic period that Jewish existence outside of the land of Israel is somehow impaired or deficient. It should be borne in mind that there were large Jewish communities living in the diaspora, which grew increasingly self-confident, and in the end eclipsed in intellectual endeavour and authority the communities of the old homeland. The Babylonian communities, surely, felt no inferiority towards the land of Israel: quite the reverse. Talmudic Judaism, then, it can be argued, was largely anti-nationalistic, and showed little interest in the re-establishment of a Jewish state. The stress on the centrality of the land of Israel to Jewish life that creeps into the rabbinic tradition in the later Amoraic period has probably little to do with a resurgence of Jewish nationalism. Rather it reflects the growing political rivalry between the rabbinic schools of the land of Israel and of Babylonia.[30]

What helped to keep messianism alive in the rabbinic communities was the fact that it was embedded in the liturgy, particularly in the Amidah. Five or six of the nineteen benedictions of the Amidah are messianic in content, and pray for the comprehensive restoration of the Jewish state—its king and his counsellors, its judges, its Temple and priesthood, together with the overthrow of Israel's political foes. The origins of the Amidah are puzzling. It is not a rabbinic composition,

---

30. The rise of Zionism and the re-establishment of a Jewish state in 1948 has led to a renewed understanding of the importance of the land of Israel in Jewish tradition, but it has also engendered the rather unquestioning assumption that the land has always been central to Judaism. This over-emphasis on the centrality of the land is found in W.D. Davies, *The Gospel and the Land: Early Christianity and Jewish Territorial Doctrine* (Berkeley: University of California Press, 1974); *idem*, *The Territorial Dimension of Judaism* (Berkeley: University of California Press, 1982). For the beginnings of an attempt to create a more nuanced view see P.S. Alexander, 'Jerusalem as the *Omphalos* of the World: On the History of a Geographical Concept', *Judaism* 46 (1997), pp. 147-59, especially pp. 155-57. Other useful studies of the subject are: L.A. Hoffman (ed.), *The Land of Israel: Jewish Perspectives* (Notre Dame: University of Notre Dame Press, 1986); Katherine Elena Wolff, *'Geh in das Land, das ich Dir zeigen werde...': Das Land Israel in der frühen rabbinischen Tradition und im Neuen Testament* (Frankfurt am Main: Peter Lang, 1989).

though some attempts were made to rabbanize it. A form of it probably goes back to Second Temple times, but its wording at that period, and its *Sitz im Leben*, are problematic. It reads like a great national liturgy: it is concerned with great public issues; but it is political dynamite. Who would have stood up on any public occasion and openly prayed for the overthrow of the arrogant kingdom and the establishment of the messianic state? One thing seems reasonably certain: by the early second century CE the Amidah was so deeply entrenched in the synagogue liturgy that the Rabbis could do little about it, even though in some ways the ethos of the prayer went against the grain of the halakhic world-view which they were promoting.

The Targum also, though to a lesser degree, may have helped to keep messianism alive. Throughout the Talmudic period the Targum appears to have been regularly recited in synagogue to accompany the reading of the Torah, both in Palestine and in Babylonia. Like the Amidah, the Targum is not a rabbinic institution, though attempts were made to bring it under rabbinic control. There is a great deal of messianism in the Targumim, particularly in the Targumim to the Prophets and the Writings.[31] The Targum's messianic motifs are not original, but are all paralleled elsewhere.

To sum up what has, of necessity, been a sketchy, and rather speculative, survey:

1. Messianism, when it does occur in classic rabbinic literature, is fundamentally a this-worldy political process. The miraculous and supernatural are played down. What is in view is the establishment of a real Jewish state, in real historical time. There are hints here and there in the vast rabbinic corpus of a superhuman, mystical Messiah, and of the messianic redemption as a cosmic event. These ideas were to bear fruit in the mediaeval Qabbalah, but they are peripheral to the rabbinic tradition.

31. See the useful collection of texts in S.H. Levey, *The Messiah: An Aramaic Interpretation. The Messianic Exegesis of the Targum* (Cincinnati: HUC-JIR, 1974). Piyyut, which originated in Palestine in the fourth century, may also have helped to foster messianic hopes. There are certainly powerful messianic piyyutim, but it is not always certain what can be attributed to the early paytanim such as Yose ben Yose, Yannai amd Qillir. See L. J. Weinberger, *Jewish Hymnography: A Literary History* (London: Littman Library of Jewish Civilization, 1998), pp. 28-49.

2. Rabbinic tradition inherited a considerable baggage of messianic speculation from the Second Temple period, a baggage which was largely carried within the rabbinic communities by the liturgy and the Targum, though oral folk tradition, often reflected in popular funerary art,[32] may also have played a part.

3. The rabbinic attitude towards this inheritance was initially negative. Messianism was not only politically dangerous and disruptive, but out of joint with the halakhic world-view promoted by the Rabbis. They seem to have actively discouraged messianic speculation. However, the folk tradition proved too strong, and by the late Amoraic period they were beginning to integrate elements of messianism—suitably rabbinized—into their world-view.

4. The seventh century was critical in the development of messianism within rabbinic Judaism. The struggle between Byzantium and Persia for control of the Middle East, and the rise of Islam, prompted an outburst of apocalyptic and eschatological speculation, not only among Christians but also among Jews, which led to a rediscovery and reuse of Second Temple apocalyptic. The key Jewish text of this apocalyptic revival was the *Book of Zerubbavel*.

5. Saadia's incorporation of messianism into his great definition and defence of rabbinic Judaism in his *Book of Beliefs and Opinions* marks the decisive moment in the domestication of messianism within the *rabbinic* tradition. After Saadia messianism becomes one of the fundamentals of the rabbinic credo.

6. Finally, though full of new colourful detail, the post-70 messianic tradition was, on the whole, not innovative. The vast majority of its themes and motifs can be paralleled before 70 CE. However, the ideas of the slain Messiah ben Joseph and of the Messiah living incognito are hard to parallel in earlier literature.

---

32. Thus the ubiquitous shofar in Jewish funerary art of late antiquity probably has messianic reference. On this whole subject see E.R. Goodenough, *Jewish Symbols in the Greco-Roman Period* (ed. and abr. J. Neusner; Princeton, NJ: Princeton University Press, 1988), index *sub* 'Messianism'. Though he overstates the case, Goodenough is probably basically correct in claiming that Jewish art in late antiquity gives us access to a popular, non-rabbinic form of Judaism.

CHRIST IN THE NEW TESTAMENT

FOR CHARLIE MOULE ON HIS NINETIETH BIRTHDAY

Christopher Rowland

As Christianity focuses on the coming of the Messiah and the relationship of the Messiah to the world, our subject could cover all aspects of the experience of early Christians as reflected in the pages of the New Testament.[1] Much early Christian experience, and the language Christians chose to use to express their convictions and practice, are affected by messianism. If one looks at some of the key concepts in the New Testament—kingdom of God, resurrection, heaven on earth, the conquest of the earthly and heavenly powers, cross/exaltation—they all seem to have a messianic/eschatological dimension. The repeated reference to the Spirit and prophecy also corresponds with some contemporary Jewish views on the return of the prophetic era and the foretaste of the new age (Rom. 8.23; 2 Cor. 1.22; Lk. 1.67; Jn 16.13; Acts 2.17; Rev. 19.10, 22.6; cf. *t. Soṭ.* 13.20). The individual eschatological details are not, on the whole, peculiar to the Christian texts, and parallels may be found in many contemporary texts. There is one exception,

---

1. Surveys in E. Schürer revised and edited by G. Vermes, F. Millar and M. Black, *The History of the Jewish People in the Age of Jesus Christ*, II (Edinburgh: T. & T. Clark, 1979), pp. 488-554; J. Neusner, W.S. Green and E. Frerichs (eds.), *Judaisms and their Messiahs at the Turn of the Christian Era* (Cambridge: Cambridge University Press, 1987); J.H. Charlesworth, *The Messiah: Developments in Earliest Judaism and Christianity* (Minneapolis: Fortress Press, 1992); J.J. Collins, *The Scepter and the Star: The Messiahs of the Dead Sea Scrolls and Other Ancient Literature* (New York: Doubleday, 1995); J.C. O'Neill, *Who Did Jesus Think He Was?* (Biblical Interpretation Series, 11; Leiden: E.J. Brill, 1995); W. Grundmann, 'Χριστός', in G. Friedrich (ed.), *Theologisches Wörterbuch zum Neuen Testament*, IX (Stuttgart: W. Kohlhammer, 1973), pp. 518-570 (ET *Theological Dictionary of the New Testament*, IX [trans. G.W. Bromiley; Grand Rapids: Eerdmans, 1974], pp. 527-73); J.D.G. Dunn, *The Origin of Christology* (London: SCM Press, 1980).

however. What does distinguish early Christian literature is the repeated emphasis on a hope already being realized, though still to be fulfilled (e.g. Lk. 11.20; Jn 5.24; Acts 2.17; Rom. 8.18-25; 1 Cor. 10.11; 2 Cor. 6.2; Col. 3.1; 1 Pet. 1.3-11; 1 Jn 3.2), and the notion that both realized and future hope focus on the figure of Jesus as Messiah. There is little to parallel this in the extant Jewish sources, with the possible exception of hints in the prophetic movements described by Josephus.

What I propose to do in this essay is to concentrate on the material in the New Testament where Christ/Messiah is mentioned. Even that would be a daunting task given the extent of the use of Χριστός in the Pauline corpus.[2] So, I shall look in more detail at particular books (Matthew, John and the Apocalypse will be singled out for particular attention). I have adopted a variety of interpretative approaches, more because they happen to reflect particular interests rather than any commitment to hermeneutical eclecticism or carefully honed methodology. In the case of Matthew's Gospel, I shall consider the way in which the titles merge with the rest of the narrative; I shall use the Johannine corpus to reflect on the role of messianism in the development of Johannine Christianity and the reasons for a continued attachment to it; with regard to the Apocalypse, I will suggest that the visionary form and the abrupt transitions, so typical of prophetic literature, have made possible the subversion of a, possibly dominant, form of messianism; and, finally, I shall offer some reflections on the historical and theological significance of messianism in Christianity. I shall content myself with some general comments on the New Testament epistles, exploring a particular feature of Pauline theology, namely, the way in which Christology and ecclesiology overlap in the confusion between the identity of Christ and his apostle.

The Gospels and Acts

The kingship of God plays an important part in the Gospels as the key component of Jesus' message. The meaning of the kingship, or reign,

---

2.   Survey in M. Hengel, 'Erwägungen zum Sprachgebrauch von Χριστός bei Paulus und in der "vorpaulinischen Überlieferung"', in M.D. Hooker and S.G. Wilson (eds.), *Paul and Paulinism: Essays in Honour of C.K. Barrett* (London: SPCK, 1982), pp. 135-59 (ET '"Christos" in Paul', in *Between Jesus and Paul* [trans. J. Bowden; London: SCM Press, 1983], pp. 65-77).

of God in the Gospels is much disputed.[3] A resort to the contemporary material yields little information, and the frequent juxtaposition of the kingship of God or heaven with parables only heightens the enigma. Hints of a sphere of divine influence in the world may be detected in passages like Mk 1.15, 9.1, and 14.25; compare 10.25 and Col. 1.13, though odd references like Lk. 23.2 and Acts 17.6-7 (cf. Jn 6.15) may indicate attempts to distance Christianity from *revolutionary* politics. Outside the synoptic Gospels the phrase 'kingdom of God' largely disappears, though Rom. 14.17, 1 Cor. 6.9 and 15.50 and Gal. 5.21 are odd exceptions. The reign of God seems to be a sphere to be entered into by those whose practice conforms to the standards of the divine reign. Christ as king is particularly prominent in Rev. 1.5 and 19.16, for example, and the messianic reign on earth has a central place in the vision of the eschatological future in that book, something which may be hinted at elsewhere in 1 Cor. 15.24. It became a feature of early Christian eschatology, for example, Justin, *Dial.* 113, 139; Tertullian, *Adv. Marcionem* 3. 24; Irenaeus, *Adv. Haer.* 5. 33.3-4; Eusebius, *Hist. Eccles.* 3. 28; Epiphanius, *Pan.* 49; Hippolytus, *Comm. on Dan.* 4.23-24; Lactantius, *Institutes* 7.14; compare *4 Ezra* 7.26; *2 (Syriac) Baruch* 25.[4] By the beginning of the third century the Alexandrians, like Origen, were challenging the hope for a this-worldly reign of God, and it disappeared from Christian theology with the solution that Augustine offered in Book 20.7-8 of *The City of God*, only to return in a rather different form in the later Middle Ages with Joachim of Fiore and his successors.

That there is a messianic dimension to Matthew's Christology is evident from the opening verses. The Davidic messianism parallels Jn 7.25-44, 10.24-25, and 12.34-35, where the identity of the Messiah is also an issue. For Matthew, more than Mark, Jesus as Son of David plays a more prominent role (1.1; cf. Mk 10.47-48 and 12.35), and, unlike Mark, there is a less obvious contrast between Messiah and Son of Man. In 11.2 the Matthaean addition τὰ ἔργα τοῦ Χριστοῦ suggests that the mighty acts of Jesus are the signs of the Messiah's appearing. Throughout the Gospel Jesus engages in acts of compassion and healing (4.23-24, 9.35) which affect primarily the crowds (9.36, 14.14,

---

3.   Survey in N. Perrin, *The Kingdom of God in the Teaching of Jesus* (London: SCM Press, 1963).

4.   See B. Daley, *The Hope of the Early Church: A Handbook of Patristic Eschatology* (Cambridge: Cambridge University Press, 1991).

15.32) rather than leaders, and, among the former, the blind, lepers, and the lame (9.27, 11.5, 20.29-30, 21.14), tax collectors (11.19, 21.31-32), and children (18.1, 19.14), who, according to Matthew's version of the scene in the Temple, respond to the humble king (21.5) with a cry of 'Hosanna' (21.15). Although by ch. 27 the crowds have forsaken Jesus, earlier they follow (4.25, 12.15, 19.1, 20.29) and see him as prophet (21.11, 21.46) or Son of David (12.23, 21.9; cf. 9.27, 20.31, 15.22, 21.15), whereas the Pharisees and other leaders express suspicion or hostility (9.34, 12.14, 21.23, 21.46). Jesus teaches as Messiah (23.10), perhaps a hint here of messianic Torah? As in Mark there is the redefinition of the Davidic link with the Messiah, and a subtle exposition of the nature of the messianic expectation and its Christian presentation (2.4, 16.16, 20-21, 22.42). There is a striking juxtaposition of messianism and the death of Jesus in 27.17 and 22 (cf. 20.28 and 26.28). The charge put over Jesus' head (27.37; cf. 27.17) leads to a succession of taunts of 'the king of Israel' (27.42; cf. Jn 19.19). Not surprisingly, in the light of this, messianic kingship in Matthew does not involve force of arms (26.52-53; cf. Jn 18.36). Jesus's kingship is most evident at the time of greatest humiliation and dissonance with a conventional understanding of kingship, for example, in Jn 18.33 and Mt. 27.29 and parallels.

Jesus is the humble king (21.5; cf. Isa. 62.11; Zech. 9.9), though one who brings division (21.14-15; cf. 10.34 and 12.23-24). His kingship is hidden in this age and will only be manifest when the king sits on the throne of judgment at the Last Assize (Mt. 25.31-46). Then, to the surprise of righteous and unrighteous alike, he will have been found already among the hungry, the thirsty, the strangers, the naked, the sick and the imprisoned. Final judgment is based on response to the king in the destitute situation of his brethren as they meet the members of the nations in this age. The destiny of humankind is based on the present response to those who, like the humble king, have nowhere to lay their heads (8.20).

The humble king of Matthew's gospel parallels the formation of the understanding of kingship and lordship in John's Gospel. In the confrontation between the representatives of God and Caesar in the discussion with Pilate in Jn 18.33-38, for example, true kingship is manifested in Jesus' words and demeanour.[5] This human dialogue between the representative of Rome and the Messiah reflects a much larger drama,

---

5. D. Rensberger, *Overcoming the World* (London: SPCK, 1988).

which is played out in a cosmic, apocalyptic struggle in which the prince of this world is judged and cast out (Jn 12.27-33), just as the persecutor of the Messiah and his followers is ejected from heaven in Rev. 12.7.

This mix of humility and power is evident also in the use of other titles in Matthew, like 'Son of Man', by which Jesus speaks of his homelessness (8.20), authority (9.6, 12.8), death (17.22, 20.18-19, 26.2 and 24), vindication (24.64; cf. 28.18) and kingship in the new age (25.31-46, 19.28; cf. 13.41). Similarly, the title 'Son of God', which has overlaps with 'Messiah' in some contemporary Jewish texts like *4 Ezra*, is used at the baptism, where Jesus demonstrates his humility (3.14-15), which, together with his marginal status, is predicted in Scripture (2.15, 4.13-16). Knowledge of his divine sonship comes, appropriately enough, through extraordinary means (3.17, 4.3, 8.29, 11.27, 14.33, 16.16, 17.5) and is usually confined to persons who find themselves on the fringes of society. Matthew, like Luke, includes references to Jesus' prophetic vocation (13.57, 21.11, 21.46, 23.37; cf. 10.41, 11.9, 11.13, 14.5, 16.14, 21.26, 23.29-30, 23.35; also John the Baptist in 21.32), though Jesus is no ordinary prophet but the last in the line. Indeed, he is the one who sends the prophets (23.34).

There is some affinity with some recently published Scrolls material, such as 4Q521, where the particular concern with the poor and oppressed is alluded to in this fragmentary messianic prophecy. That should not surprise us given biblical texts like Isaiah 11 and 61. Matthew's account of Jesus' activity, the persons to whom he ministered and the commentary on that activity in the discourses, offers an extended narrative version of the brief comments about the Messiah contained in 4Q521. Matthew's Gospel could be said to present a story of God's Messiah, whose coming, from the very start, is greeted with suspicion, dismay and persecution by those in positions of power. Born in an apparently insignificant place, identifying with those regarded as sinners, taking children as examples of the attitude of humility appropriate for the kingdom, Jesus' message is exemplified in the character of those who are blessed at the beginning of the Sermon on the Mount. In the new age, the Son of Man will reign as the humble king. That rule will be according to criteria very different from those of the kings of the nations (20.26-27), and this forms the heart of what the nations need to be taught (28.20, 7.21-22, 10.42-43, 25.40). Matthew's Gospel is a story where the reversal of values and priorities and the undermining of conventions are central. It is the rulers who misunderstand and mislead the crowd, and it is the demon-possessed and outsiders, rather than the 'normal', who glimpse Jesus' true character. Of the four canonical Gospels Matthew seems to offer most sympathy to messianism and offers us a text in which are integrated titles, discourse and narrative in the exposition of Βίβλος γενέσεως Ἰησοῦ Χριστοῦ υἱοῦ Δαυὶδ υἱοῦ Ἀβραάμ.

The situation is somewhat different in Mark, however, not least because the title Χριστός is used only seven times, and 'Son of David' significantly less. In modern New Testament scholarship messianism in Mark has been closely tied with the theme of secrecy.[5] The paucity of references to Messiah has lent weight to the belief that there has been a deliberate attempt, for apologetic reasons, to explain Jesus' reluctance to claim the messianic title. There is no doubt that secrecy is a significant strand within Mark's presentation, though commentators will differ on the extent to which it is the result of the evangelist's own editorial hand, not least because secrecy is a motif which looms large in Jewish teaching, particularly concerning the most profound of divine mysteries, eschatological and theological.[6]

The opening of the Gospel includes a clear assertion that the Gospel concerns Jesus Christ (1.1), though the juxtaposition with 'Son of God' prefigures the importance of the latter title at key junctures (e.g. 1.11, 9.7, 15.38-39, as well as on the lips of demons in 5.7). In 9.41 ('whoever gives you a cup of cold water to drink ὅτι Χριστοῦ ἐστε will by no means lose their reward'), we have a saying which is found in slightly different form in Mt. 10.42. A comparison of these two passages suggests that Mark may have a later version than Matthew's because there is identification of the recipients with the disciples around Jesus. The subordination of David to the Messiah in Mk 12.35 suggests a separation of messianism from the Davidic tradition. Jesus' response to christological confession often involves a command to secrecy (1.34), or teaching about the Son of Man who must suffer. In 8.29-33 Jesus' response to Peter is widely interpreted as a correction of Peter's sentiments, or, at least, an exposition of the true nature of messianism. Other references concern the meaning of Christ. There is a similar

5. The subject is surveyed in C.M. Tuckett (ed.), *The Messianic Secret in Mark's Gospel* (London: SPCK, 1983).

6. See G.A. Wewers, *Geheimnis und Geheimhaltung im rabbinischen Judentum* (Berlin: W. de Gruyter, 1975).

(though not as explicit) emphasis to Matthew's picture of Jesus entering Jerusalem as the humble king (11.10). In the eschatological discourse (13.21-22; cf. Mt. 24.5, 23) there is the possibility of the emergence of false Christs, something which the early Christian communities had to deal with, as 1 Jn 2.19 indicates.

Mark sets the pattern followed by the other Gospels in including the repeated prediction that the Son of Man must suffer before he will be vindicated, a pattern familiar from Wisdom 2–3 and Isaiah 53. There may be an implicit reference to kingship in the anointing at Bethany (cf. 1 Sam. 16.13), where suffering is juxtaposed with kingship as in John 19. It is in the Markan Passion Narrative that 'Christ' and king of 'Israel' are juxtaposed in 15.32 (cf. 15.26), the moment when conventional regal status seems most lacking. The prominence given to the phrase 'Son of Man' rather than 'king' or 'Messiah' in Mark's Gospel is only superficially less political. After all, in Daniel 7 the triumph of the Human Figure and the destruction of the beasts, which represent the empires of the world, offer a vision of the ultimate triumph of the divine polity, which, according to Mark, is based on service (10.42-45). At the climax of Mark's story the apparent defeat of Jesus turns out to be the moment of his triumph and the destruction of the symbolic focus of the old order, the Temple. The juxtaposition of the account of Jesus's death and the rending of the veil of the Temple signifies both the triumph of the executed king and the moment of judgment upon a great, but obsolescent, institution.

There are several distinctive uses of 'Christ' in Luke–Acts. First, we find the phrase 'Messiah of God' (Lk. 9.20, 23.35; cf. 'Lord's Messiah' in 2.26 and Acts 4.26). The proof of Jesus as Messiah is found in some examples of early Christian preaching (e.g. Acts 5.42, 17.3, 18.5, 28). Secondly, in the important manifesto in Lk. 4.18-19 (cf. Lk. 7.22 and 4Q521) it is the prophetic messianism which is to the fore, based on Isa. 61.1-2,[8] a text which is referred to in the fragmentary description of the angelic redeemer in 11QMelch. The conclusion to that chapter (4.40) suggests that the healing ministry which had already begun demonstrated Jesus' messiahship. Thirdly, in Lk. 23.2 there is a list of the charges brought by the hierarchy against Jesus, one of which includes a reference to his claim to be Christ the king, a claim which

---

8. See the interesting reflections on this in A.E. Harvey, *Jesus and the Constraints of History* (London: Gerald Duckworth, 1982). See also M. Prior, *Jesus the Liberator* (The Biblical Seminar, 26; Sheffield: Sheffield Academic Press, 1995).

anticipates charges of subversion which were to be levelled against Christians (Acts 17.6-7). The importance of the Davidic background to messianism is stressed in Lk. 1.32 and 2.11, where it is specifically linked with the idea of salvation. In Acts 3.19-21 there is a relic of what may be a very early Christology (or, if not, one which has few parallels in the New Testament). Here repentance is a condition of the coming of the Messiah, contrasting with the dominant Parousia doctrine in which the coming of Christ is viewed as inevitable and, ultimately, independent of human response. This view has its parallel in debates found in some Jewish texts over whether the condition of the Messiah's coming is Israel's repentance and obedience.[9] As in Mt. 25.31-46, there is a link between the Christ and judgment (Acts 10.42, 17.31). In parallel to the theme of the necessity of the suffering of the Son of Man, which Luke shares with the other Gospels, we have the exposition in the post-resurrection appearances of the necessity of the Christ's suffering as the solution of Scripture's messianic riddles (Lk. 24.26, 46; cf. Acts 3.18, 17.3, 26.23), which function as a privileged time of sharing of information by the now glorified Saviour, much as, in the Enochic tradition, Enoch returns from heaven, temporarily, to share the divine wisdom with his children (e.g. 2 [*Slavonic*] *Enoch* 13). In Luke 24 the clue to the meaning of the Scriptures, and an exposition of their true importance are offered, parallel in some ways to 1 Pet. 1.11-12.

What is striking about the Gospel of John is how much belief that Jesus is Christ still matters in this sophisticated christological narrative. We can see this in the summary of the purpose of the Gospel in Jn 20.31. There is evidence that the messiahship of Jesus was a live issue in the Gospel of John, especially 7.25-27, where contemporary expectations lead to a negative evaluation of Jesus' claim to authority. Nevertheless, alongside this, the complex of christological titles at the end of John 1 also suggests that the climax of an appropriate confession is not 'Messiah' but 'Son of Man' (1.51). Indeed, the blind man, the typical convert, confesses Jesus as Son of Man in 9.35-36.

Messianism has been widely acknowledged as a key element in the development of Johannine Christianity. Often it has been located at an earlier stage in the formation of the community when relations with the Jewish synagogue were still close. It thus precedes the more developed Christology of the divine emissary and the ascending and descending Son of Man that dominate the Gospel. Messianism *is* important in John,

9. See E.E. Urbach, *The Sages* (Jerusalem: Magnes Press, 1975), pp. 669-71.

however, as is evident in the editorial addition in 9.20. But in contrast to what is often assumed, I think it is not just a hangover from the story of the community's past life but continues as a present means of ensuring the uniqueness of the revelation in Christ. That concentration on more exalted Christologies assumes an importance in the text as we now have it cannot be doubted, nor can the possibility be excluded that it might have loomed too large in the minds of some of the evangelist's readers, but in the Fourth Gospel these sophisticated ideas do not displace the central affirmation of Jesus's messiahship, which became a point of conflict between Church and Synagogue.[10]

Messiahship also comes up in the related 1 John.[11] It would appear that a schism had taken place within the community (2.19), which had led to a complete separation between the opponents, denounced so vehemently in 1 John, and those who agree with the author. The first letter was written to those who were left, to persuade them of the truth of the position of the author, and to warn them against following their former colleagues, whose schismatic action and wayward belief had demonstrated their diabolical character (2.18-19 and 3.10). *One* of the issues which split the community seems to have been the question of Christology (1 Jn 2.22-23, 4.3, 5.6, to which could also be added 5.9-11). In 2.22-23 (cf. 5.12) there seem to have been those who, apparently, denied that Jesus was the Messiah, and thought that it was possible to have a relationship with God without any intermediary activity of Jesus: 'Who is the liar but the one who denies that Jesus is the Christ? This is the Antichrist, the one who denies the Father and the Son. No one who denies the Son has the Father; everyone who confesses the Son has the Father also' (2.22-23).

One way in which people who denied the messiahship of Jesus but who were aligned with the church (suggested by the opening words of 1 Jn 2.19), and who might also have wanted to retain connections with the synagogue, might have been by denying the messiahship of Jesus while affirming a role for Jesus in the divine economy. This last could have been managed by accepting Jesus as an angelic intermediary[12] but

---

10. Survey in J. Ashton, *Understanding the Fourth Gospel* (Oxford: Oxford University Press, 1991), pp. 381-405.

11. See A. Wurm, *Die Irrlehrer im ersten Johannesbrief* (Freiburg: Herder, 1903).

12. There is some evidence to suggest that Jewish-Christian thought did make extensive use of angelomorphic categories; see, e.g., the quotation from the Gospel

not the final, eschatological, agent of salvation, the messianic king. That angel Christology played a larger part in early Christian doctrinal discussions than is usually supposed is now being recognized, and it is one possible way of understanding the Johannine traditions, where Jesus is the one sent by God from heaven to speak God's will and do the will of the God above (7.16). He was the one, like the angel of God in the Old Testament, whose task it was to be the emissary of God and who was 'no longer clearly distinguishable from his master but in his appearing and speaking clothes himself with Yahweh's own appearance and speech'.[13] To regard Jesus as an angelic envoy rather than the Messiah of Jewish expectation, however, *may* have meant denying his humanity, an issue possibly alluded to in 1 Jn 5.6 (angel Christology could lead to docetism as the Christology of the *Ascension of Isaiah* suggests). Angels often can be said to have human appearance (e.g. Dan. 8.16).[14] The lack of emphasis in 1 John on Jesus as the emissary from above, the stress on his messiahship and humanity, and the unique significance of his saving death of Jesus (2.1-2), suggest that there could be no compromise over the ultimate significance of these doctrines. Either the believer accepts the unique messianic role of Jesus or forfeits a relationship with God (2.23, 5.12). To deny Jesus' messiahship and his humanity, with the assertion that he is one of a number of angelic

of the Hebrews in E. Hennecke, *Neutestamentliche Apokryphen*, I (Tübingen: J.C.B. Mohr [Paul Siebeck], 3rd edn, 1959), p. 107 (ET *New Testament Apocrypha*, I [trans. R. McL. Wilson *et al.*; London: Lutterworth, 1963], p.163) and further J. Daniélou, *Théologie du judéo-christianisme* (Paris: Desclée de Brouwer and Cerf, 1958) (ET *The Theology of Jewish Christianity* [trans. J.A. Baker; London: Darton, Longman & Todd, 1964]); A.F.J. Klijn and G.S. Reinink, *Patristic Evidence for Jewish Christian Sects* (Leiden: E.J. Brill, 1973); J. Fossum *The Name of God and the Angel of the Lord* (Tübingen: J.C.B. Mohr [Paul Siebeck], 1985); L. Stuckenbruck, *Angel Veneration and Christology* (Tübingen: J.C.B. Mohr [Paul Siebeck], 1995); C.H.T. Fletcher-Louis, *Luke–Acts: Angels, Christology and Soteriology* (Tübingen: J.C.B. Mohr [Paul Siebeck], 1997).

13. W. Eichrodt, *Theologie des Alten Testaments*, II (Stuttgart: Klotz, 4th edn, 1961), pp. 7-11 (ET *The Theology of the Old Testament* [trans. J.A. Baker; London: SCM Press, 1967], pp. 23-29), and J. Ashton's essay on the importance of Jewish angelology for Johannine Christology, 'Bridging Ambiguities', in *idem, Studying John* (Oxford: Oxford University Press, 1994), pp. 71-89.

14. For other passages which suggest that some compared Jesus with an angel, see the Slavonic Josephus (*War* 2.174, Loeb edn, III, p. 649) and *Gospel of Thomas* logion 13.

emissaries, however exalted, undermines the eschatological thrust of the early Christian message.

In the Gospel of John messiahship and kingship sit alongside the dominant theme of Christ as the revealer of the divine glory who is sent from the Father. At the heart of the Johannine Christology is the conviction that Jesus is the one who makes God's person and will known (1.18 and 14.6). Acceptance of this is not by itself adequate for the author of the Fourth Gospel, however, who offers the collection and redaction of the Johannine traditions to enable readers to accept Jesus as Messiah, and, as such, also a man and not merely a celestial envoy (Jn 20.31). With the possible exception of 11QMelch, in contemporary Jewish sources the anointed one is a human, even if occasionally exalted to angelic status. In the Gospel of John the disciple of Jesus has to accept the unique role of Jesus as the agent of God's saving purposes. He cannot be placed alongside other heavenly messengers: he is the Messiah. He is not just one in a succession of divine envoys but the ultimate manifestation of God. What the messianic belief does is guarantee this note of finality.[15] With the coming of the Messiah there could be no eschatological figure of significance to follow. His is the decisive revelation. So in the teaching on the Spirit–Paraclete in John 14–17 the other figure who comes is one who continues to point back to Jesus's words, though, occasionally, this mysterious figure too can be a bringer of new revelation (Jn 16.13).

The issue of succession to the Messiah is a theme explored in different ways in several places in the New Testament. Paul writes of the apostle and the Christian ecclesia as an embodiment of Christ. In Matthew's judgment scene in Mt. 25.31-46, for example, there is an affinity between the heavenly Son of Man and a human group, whether that be Christ's disciples only or all the poor and neglected (cf. Mt. 18.20, 28.20). Luke's Gospel is to be read with the Acts of the Apostles, and this is, in some sense, a continuation of the work of Jesus through the Spirit (Acts 1.1). In the Fourth Gospel the relationship between Jesus and the disciples is articulated in the Farewell Discourses. Even if the activity of the Spirit–Paraclete is not ultimately dependent on faithful disciples as an environment in which to work, their witness is

---

15. Cf. the *Gospel of the Hebrews* where the prophet Christology incorporates the element of finality by describing Jesus as the one in whom the divine Spirit achieves its ultimate resting place.

parallel to that of the Paraclete continuing the witness to the Messiah (Jn 15.27).

Let me conclude this section with some (all too brief) comments on the vexed question of the evidence for the historical Jesus's acceptance of the messianic office. The evidence for Jesus claiming messianic status is small and probably only indirect at best.[16] There are good reasons for supposing that the eschatological character of Jesus's life and work is not a secondary accretion but goes back to the historical Jesus. It seems unlikely that the early Christians would have so consistently claimed the messianic office for him if there had been no warrant for that in the memories of his life. In the light of the eschatological character of Jesus's message, it seems unlikely that the messianic issue would not have come up, either for him or his contemporaries, for Jesus's claim to be the agent of the kingdom of God placed him in a similar category to the Messiah. His apparent reluctance to accept the title 'Son of David', or to use the title 'Messiah' of himself, may lie with its bellicose connotations and may suggest that Jesus thought of himself as a (or *the*) prophet rather than the Davidic Messiah. The direct revelation as the basis of authority, the tradition of rejection and suffering, and the eschatological character of both the Spirit and prophecy may all indicate how many themes of central importance are covered by the term prophet and its messianic character in parts of Second Temple Judaism.[17] Yet an emphasis on the prophetic Messiah does not entirely explain passages like the triumphal entry, where the king Messiah, however humble, seems to be suggested. So, while the accounts of Jesus's life suggest a reticence on his part to claim messiahship, there are many indications that his life should be understood within the wide parameters of ancient Jewish messianism.

The closest parallels to Jesus are to be found in the passages where Josephus describes the crushing of popular prophetic movements, though even here there is no record of their having been led by someone

16. The literature on this is immense. Surveys may be found in J. Meier, *A Marginal Jew* (New York: Doubleday, 1991), and M. Borg, *Jesus in Contemporary Scholarship* (Valley Forge, PA: Trinity Press International, 1994).

17. Harvey, *Constraints of History*, p. 140; N.T. Wright, *Jesus and the Victory of God* (London: SPCK, 1995), pp. 147-96; C. Rowland, *Christian Origins* (London: SPCK, 1985), pp. 178 and 182, and C.F.D. Moule, *The Origin of Christology* (Cambridge: Cambridge University Press, 1977), pp. 31-35.

who claimed to be Messiah.[18] From the brief comments made about their actions the leaders seem to have been claiming to repeat some of the distinctive actions which marked the formation and liberation of the people of God in the past: the crossing of the Jordan, the miraculous destruction of the city walls of Jerusalem, the desert experience, and so on. Here are the hallmarks of hope rooted in traditions of deliverance which have ceased to be mere items of faith and have become instruments of eschatological action.

Such a brief reference to the historical Jesus, a matter which has been the subject of intense (and ongoing) debate, where opinions are frequently polarized, cannot do justice to the complexity of the subject and the sophistication of the methods needed to embark on it. The debate about the historical Jesus and the relationship between his messianism and that of the first Christians is bound to be inconclusive when sources are sparse and the methods are so contested.[19]

Epistles and Apocalypse

According to Acts Paul preached Jesus as the Messiah (Acts 9.22, 17.3, 18.5) and also that he must suffer (cf. Acts 8.37). A passage like Gal. 3.13 suggests that the problem of the crucified Messiah may have remained an issue for Paul, though there is surprisingly little apologetic on this subject elsewhere in the letters. For Paul the basic confession is 'Jesus is Lord' (1 Cor. 12.3; Rom. 10.9) rather than 'Jesus is Christ'. Κύριος is used when referring to the Parousia (though note Phil 1.10, 2.16), probably linked with the early *maranatha* formula (1 Cor. 16.22), and as the source of the ethical tradition (1 Cor. 7.10). The replacement of 'Jesus is Christ' by 'Jesus is Lord' need not represent a retreat from the political and may reflect the need for a clearer means of sociopolitical delineation of what was involved in membership of the Christian community in the Graeco-Roman environment. The significance of the

18. Josephus, *War* 6. 281 and 301; *Ant.* 20. 97, 167, 185, on which see R. Gray, *Prophetic Figures in Late Second Temple Jewish Palestine* (Oxford: Oxford University Press, 1993).

19. R.H. Lightfoot's tantalizing words are a salutary reminder of the formidable barriers which stand in the way of those who would search for the Jesus of history: 'For all the inestimable value of the gospels they yield us little more than a whisper of his voice; we trace in them but the outskirts of his ways' (R.H. Lightfoot, *History and Interpretation in the Gospels* [London: Hodder & Stoughton, 1935], p. 225).

messianic confession would not be so clear to Greek speakers. Philippians 2.9-11 would be a good example of this political dimension, drawing on Isa. 45.23, paralleling Rev. 19.16.[20] Paul offers no proof of Jesus's messiahship, though he presupposes that Jesus is the descendant of David (Rom. 1.3). Christ is an anointed one who anoints others (2 Cor. 1.21), and, in Rom. 15.12, the messianic hope is alluded to in the quotation of Isaiah 11. The frequency of usage of Χριστός in the Pauline corpus has suggested to most commentators that Christ is often little more than a way of referring to Jesus in which specifically messianic connotations are excluded. Its ubiquitous presence reminds us of how deeply rooted it had become in early Christian discourse, that, at least as far as Paul is concerned, it needed no explanation or apology. But, the eschatological dimension of Paul's usage must not be so quickly discarded. Charlie Moule has pointed out that 'Christ' is often found together with verbs in the indicative mood and statements about the fact of salvation, while he tends to be spoken of as 'Lord' when it is a matter of exhortations or commands, in the subjunctive or imperative.[21] Examples of the use of Χριστός in statements in which he is the subject of sentences dealing with the saving/eschatological act of God include Rom. 5.6 ('for while we were still weak, at the right time, Christ died for the ungodly'), Rom. 5.8, 6.3-4, 8.9-10, 10.4, 14.9, 14.15, 15.3 (with definite article), 15.8;1 Cor. 8.11, 15.3,12; Gal. 3.13. Salvation involves an identification on the part of Christ with sinful humanity in order that the latter might share his glory (e.g. 2 Cor. 5.14,21).[22]

One of the most perplexing aspects of the discussion of Messiah/Christ in the Pauline corpus is the phrase 'in Christ'. There is no consensus about its meaning: is it merely an instrumental preposition meaning 'by means of' or 'through', does it indicate representation, or does it indicate something altogether more spatial whereby the believer

20. An issue which is explored by P. Oakes, 'From People to Letter' (DPhil thesis, University of Oxford, 1995).

21. Moule, *The Origin of Christology*, pp. 59: '...broadly speaking, Jesus tends to be spoken of as "Christ" in the context of verbs in the indicative mood and of statements, while he tends to be spoken of as "Lord" when it is a matter of exhortations or commands, in the subjunctive or the imperative. Roughly speaking, "Christ" is associated with the *fait accompli* of God's saving *work*, and the "Lord" with its implementation and its working out in human conduct.'

22. M.D. Hooker, 'Interchange in Christ', *JTS* 22 (1971), pp. 349-61.

becomes part of a 'Christ environment'?[23] Perhaps an analogy would be
with that holy space into which community members entered and then
shared the inheritance of the angels in their common life according to
certain passages from the Dead Sea Scrolls (1QS 11.7; 1 QH 3.20)? 'In
Christ' might then refer to that sphere of influence into which, as the
result of baptism, the believer enters (cf. Phil. 3.9, which implies place).
In a passage like 1 Cor. 6.15 there is a real sense of identification
between the believer and Christ and thence with fellow-Christians:

> Do you not know that your bodies are members of Christ ? Should I take
> the members of Christ and make them members of a prostitute ? Never.
> Do you not know that whoever is united with a prostitute becomes one
> body with her? For it is said the two shall be one flesh. But any one
> united with the Lord becomes one spirit with him (1 Cor. 6.15-16).[24]

There is a parallel to this change in the way in which Paul describes
the change of dominion which is the consequence of baptism and life in
the Spirit in Rom. 6.11-14, a passage full of the dualism characteristic
of apocalyptic eschatology. 'Baptism into Christ' means stripping off
the old person and putting on the new, like a garment (cf. Gal. 3.27;
Col. 2.11, 3.9; Eph. 4.22-24). Present identification with Christ points
to a future hope of resurrection and a present demand to walk in
newness of life.

On rare occasions Paul could describe himself (Gal. 2.20; cf. Gal.
1.16) and Christians (Rom. 8.10) as being indwelt by Christ rather than
the Spirit.[25] It is as if the Messiah/Son of God now permeates the being
of his apostle, so closely is he identified with the crucified Christ. So
much so that he can write of bearing his death in his body (2 Cor. 4.10;
cf. Gal. 6.14). In Col. 1.24 (if authentically Pauline) the tribulations of
Christ (possibly a reference to the messianic woes) are something which
the apostle shares and fills up what is lacking, a statement which is not
entirely without parallel elsewhere in the Pauline corpus, as 2 Cor. 1.4-
5 indicate. That vocation of suffering and tribulation is not the sole
prerogative of the apostle, however. Responsive churches are described

---

23. Moule, *The Origin of Christology*, p. 62: 'For my part, I still find it difficult
to escape the conclusion that a (metaphorically) locative sense is involved in at
least a limited number of occurrences' (of ἐν Χριστῷ).

24. See Moule, *The Origin of Christology*, p. 73.

25. See Moule, *The Origin of Christology*, pp. 56-69, where the contrast between Pauline and Johannine indwelling language is explored.

by Paul as sharing the sufferings of the apostle of Christ (Phil. 1.29) as they emulate him (1 Cor. 11.1).

There is a particularly close relationship between the Christ and his apostle. Whether in the person of the apostle, one of his co-workers, or through letter, the presence of Christ confronts the congregations (Rom. 15.14-29; especially 1 Cor. 4.14-21, 5.3-5; Phil. 2.12). Paul is the imitator of Christ (11.1) and, more than that, an embodiment of the Messiah (Gal. 2.20; cf. 2 Cor. 4.10). His coming to the churches, like the apocalypse of Jesus Christ (1 Cor. 1.7), will be with power (cf. 1 Cor. 4.20) and will bring blessing (Rom. 15.29).[26] Even his absence will not diminish the force of his influence (1 Cor. 5.4). So, one could say, that like the Risen Christ who stands in the midst of his churches in Rev. 1.13-17, the apostle of Christ comes as a threat and a promise: a threat to those who have lost their first love or exclude the Messiah and his apostle, and a promise of blessing at his coming for those who 'conquer'.

This dimension is a reminder that treatment of messianism in early Christianity must extend to a consideration of what is written about the community and its leaders. The apostle embodies Christ in a special way, but the communities are the body of Christ and share that special relationship with God which was the prerogative of Christ (Rom. 8.15-16; Gal. 4.6; cf. Mk 14.36). This sharing of the messianic privilege of 2 Sam 7.14-15 is anticipated in the eschatology of a Second Temple Jewish text like *Jub.* 1.24-25:

> And I will create in them a Holy Spirit, and I will cleanse them so that they shall not turn away from me again, from that day till eternity. And they will hold fast to me and all my commandments, and fulfil my commandments, and I will be their father, and they shall be my children. And they shall all be called children of the living God, and every angel and spirit shall know that these are my children, and that I am truly and genuinely their father, and that I love them.

Similar sentiments are also apparent in the eschatological climax of John's vision of the New Jerusalem in Rev. 21.7, where 2 Sam. 7.14 (cf. Ps. 89.27-28, ET 26-27) is applied to all the inhabitants of the eschatological city.

Reference to Revelation brings us to the Apocalypse of Jesus Christ.

---

26. On this theme see R. Funk, 'The Apostolic Parousia: Form and Significance', in W.R. Farmer, C.F.D. Moule and R.R. Niebuhr (eds.), *Christian History and Interpretation: Studies Presented to John Knox* (Cambridge: Cambridge University Press, 1967), pp. 249-68.

The fulcrum of this visionary narrative hinges on the demonstration in history of the messianic reign. In 11.14 after the second eschatological woe there is a significant moment, underlined in the following verse when the series of trumpet blasts reaches its climax. The seventh trumpet is accompanied by great shouts in heaven: 'the kingdom of this world has become the kingdom of our Lord and of his Messiah, and he will reign for ever and ever'. The heavenly voices assert the transfer of kingship to God. Although Revelation never denies that the kingdom of this world has belonged to any other than God (cf. Ps. 10.16), there has been a temporary usurpation of possession, authority and administration, which is now ending. The heavenly voice is asserting what always has been the case (cf. Rev. 19.6), perhaps reclaiming possession from those who had trespassed on the divine domain (cf. Zech. 14.9). The shout in heaven is an 'illocutionary act' in which the words bring about the reality on earth which John has already seen to be the case in heaven in ch. 4. Parallel to this in 12.10 a voice is heard in heaven. An emphatic 'now' stresses the significance of the moment when the kingdom is seen to belong to God and the rule to God's Messiah, both of which are closely related to Satan's ejection from heaven.

But the most important passage of all is Revelation 5. Christ, having appeared as one like a son of man in 1.13-17, for the rest of the book appears as a Lamb (6.1, 7.9, 12.11, 13.8, 14.1, 22.3).[27] The lack of specifically 'Christian' elements in connection with the Lamb have occasionally raised questions about an identification between Jesus and the Lamb, but reference to the fact that the Lamb 'as if it had been slaughtered' and 'the blood of the Lamb' in 5.6, 7.14 and 12.11 offer sufficient indication of their 'Christian' content. The Lamb's slaughter is shared by saints and prophets (6.9; 18.24). The Lamb's is redemptive (5.9; cf. 1.5). It is no random event but one whose significance lies deep within the mists of time (13.8). Σφάζω, employed of the Lamb in 5.6, is the word used by 1 Jn 3.12 of the 'primal' killing, the original sin of fratricide (cf. Mt. 23.35 and Heb. 11.37; Isa. 53.7), and, later in John's vision, the beast in 13.3 'seemed to have received a mortal death-blow' (ὡς ἐσφαγμένην). The inspiration for the passages about both the Lamb and the Beast appears to be the fourth beast of Dan. 7.7 ('I saw in the visions by night a fourth beast, terrifying and dreadful and exceedingly strong... It was different from all the beasts that preceded it, and had

---

27. See R. Bauckham, *The Theology of the Book of Revelation* (Cambridge: Cambridge University Press, 1993), pp. 54-65.

ten horns'). The close parallels between the Lamb and the Beast is an important feature of the dualistic contrast, with a clear choice presented to the readers throughout the Apocalypse which comes to a climax in chs. 13–14.

In ch. 5 John at first reacts to the vision of the sealed scroll by weeping (v. 4). One of the elders commands him not to weep because 'the Lion from the tribe of Judah, the Root of David, has conquered'. The Davidic origin of the messianic belief, well-documented in the Old Testament (Gen. 49.9; Isa. 11.1; cf. Rom. 15.12; Heb. 7.14; Rev. 22.16) is, if you will, the 'standard' messianic hope, represented in contemporary Jewish texts like the *Pss. Sol.* 17.25-26. Revelation, like *Psalms of Solomon* and texts like *4 Ezra* 13.9-10, is indebted to the language of Isaiah 11, a chapter which may lie behind several other passages in the New Testament also (e.g. Mt. 3.16 and parallels; Eph. 1.17; 1 Pet. 4.14; Rom. 15.14; 2 Thess. 2.8; Rev. 19.15). The words about Davidic messianism in Rev. 5.5 are immediately followed by the appearance of a 'Lamb standing as if it had been slaughtered'. Despite the fact that John hears the voice cry out that no one is able to open the book and loose the seals, John *sees* a Lamb. In the middle of the throne and of the four creatures and in the middle of the elders, there emerges one who has the right to do just that. Here, the Lamb stands for the only time in Revelation as a suppliant (in 14.1 the Lamb stands on Mount Zion with its armies like the Messiah in *4 Ezra* 13.6). The Lamb's position at this point is ambiguous, being related in some way to the creatures and elders as well as to the throne and so not yet identified with either. In other words, it is at that point in a liminal, intermediary position. That position changes by the time John speaks of the Lamb and the throne in 7.17, however, where the Lamb is in the midst of the throne.

In the vision of Revelation 5, as elsewhere in the Apocalypse, what is heard contrasts with what is seen, with the latter offering the authentic meaning of that which is heard. The juxtaposition we find of Lion and Lamb is parallel in some ways with the juxtaposition of Christ and Son of Man in the Gospel of Mark (8.29-31 and 14.61-62; cf. 12.35-37). On two occasions where Christ is mentioned, in Mk 8.29 and 14.61, the references are both followed by sayings which include the phrase Son of Man. In the juxtaposition the interpretation of the meaning of messiahship is offered in the second antithetical statement, much as the ascending and descending Son of Man saying in Jn 3.13 is illuminated by v. 14. Antithetic discourses put in the starkest possible form the contrast and challenge of the new and old ways of looking at things. So, the response of Peter in Mk 8.29 is answered by Jesus in alternative terms, then repeated in the succeeding narrative (9.31, 10.33). The alternative discourse in Mark, which, if as seems likely, is based on Daniel 7, concerns the faithfulness and resistance of a group in the face of an overwhelming political threat and a promise of the ultimate vindication of an alternative way over against the political powers of the day. In Mark's Gospel the language of king, Davidic dynasty, political domination and the centrality of Jerusalem are contrasted with the new way, the polity of servanthood:

> You know that among the gentiles those whom they recognize as their rulers lord it over them, and their great ones are tyrants over them. But it is not so among you; but whoever wishes to become great among you must be your servant, and whoever wishes to be first among you must be slave of all (Mk 10.42-43).[28]

Such a contrast is typical of the apocalyptic genre of Revelation, where rival patterns of dominion are set up in the visions, in an apocalyptic form of the Two Ways doctrine familiar to us from the Bible (Deut. 30.15) and other early Christian texts (e.g. *Didache*).

Elsewhere in the New Testament references in Hebrews and 1 Peter call for comment. Of the references to Christ in Hebrews (3.6, 5.5, 6.1, 9.11, 14, 24, 28, 10.10, 11.26, 13.8, 21) I would like to focus on two, 11.26 and 13.13. Readers are summoned to share with Christ a place of shame 'outside the camp' (13.13). In this they share the lot of Moses who rejected his status as a member of Pharaoh's court, preferring to share the suffering and oppression of the slaves (11.25-26). He shared the reproach of Christ (τὸν ὀνειδισμὸν τοῦ Χριστοῦ, cf. 1 Pet. 4.14), sentiments which mirror those in the Pauline corpus, especially Col. 1.24 and other texts which may hint at present experience of the messianic tribulations.[29] Similar too are the references in 1 Peter (1.11, 19, 2.21, 3.18, 4.13, 14, 5.1, 10), where the link between Christ and suffering is evident. 1 Peter 2.22-23 offers one of the most explicit links

---

28. See K. Wengst, *Pax Romana. Anspruch und Wirklichkeit: Erfahrungen und Wahrnehmungen des Friedens bei Jesus und im Urchristentum* (Munich: Chr. Kaiser Verlag, 1986) (ET *Pax Romana and the Peace of Jesus Christ* [trans. J. Bowden; London: SCM Press, 1987] pp. 55-56). The German original is inaccessable to me

29. D. Allison, *The End of the Ages Has Come* (Philadelphia: Fortress Press, 1985).

with Isaiah 53 in the New Testament. Suffering is something which may be expected to be shared by followers of Christ (1 Pet. 4.13, 5.1). The most intriguing reference in this epistle is found in 1.11, however, where the work of the revelatory spirit is said to be the action of 'Christ's spirit', which enabled the secrets of the messianic suffering and subsequent glorification to be predicted (cf. Lk. 10.23, 24.26), messianic mysteries which even the angels longed to have a glimpse of (1 Pet. 1.12; cf. Eph. 3.3-7). This is a reminder that throughout the New Testament there is an insistence on the unpreparedness and novelty of the messianic revelation, which is only very partially hinted at in the scriptures (cf. Rom. 3.21).

Concluding Historical and Theological Reflections

This survey of New Testament material concerning king and Messiah is not easily reduced to neat conclusions. Two issues have emerged, however. First of all, there is evidence of attempts to reinterpret the meaning of kingship and Messiah. This may have been in large part a reaction to the circumstances of Jesus' death. In any case it led to a more sharply demarcated focus on biblical passages concerning the Messiah's humility and advocacy for the poor and outcast. Secondly, the element of finality, which is a consequence of messianic conviction, seems to have led many of the major New Testament writers to explore how the past earthly presence of Jesus the Messiah related to the present situation, and, indeed, the future eschatological consummation. The messianic presence is not simply equated with a past earthly life or with a future coming, but in their ecclesiology and pneumatology we find early Christian writers exploring how the unique event of the Messiah's coming persisted in its effects and continued in the persons of others.

The main difference about early Christianity as compared with what we now know of other movements for change in the Second Temple period is that this was a messianic movement which survived. The hopes surrounding other groups mentioned by Josephus were, in all likelihood, short-lived. With Christianity we are dealing with a much more complicated phenomenon: an example of, what seems to have been from the very start, a self-consciously messianic group which had managed to survive (in whatever way) the trauma of the death of its leader and the rejection of his message by the dominant culture, to become a widely-spread group within the last decades of Second Temple Judaism. There is little in the extant literature that resembles the peculiar features that characterize the emergence and development of Christianity. That is something that needs to be borne in mind as we compare the New Testament with the contemporary Jewish texts. Differences between the Jewish and Christian sources may often better be explained by the latter being messianic (in the sense that they were written by those who believed that the messianic age had in some sense already arrived) and the former non-messianic (in the sense that hopes for the future of the world remained mere hopes and were still, in the main, a matter for speculation). The fact that the Christians believed that the Messiah had come involved them in dealing with a range of issues which would hardly have affected those Jews who did not share their convictions: the character of life in the messianic age, the continued relevance of the Torah, the order of the fulfilment of eschatological events and the timetable for the consummation of all things. For most other Jews such issues would have remained, at most, a matter of theoretical interest only. For the first Christians they had become a matter of decisive importance as a necessary corollary of their belief in the coming of the messianic kingdom.

Early Christian writings never abandoned the messianic hope for the future transformation of the world.[30] It may have gradually diminished in importance, as greater concern was expressed with the individual struggle against the flesh, in the face of the limited possibilities for change in a world where societal change seemed to be difficult, if not impossible. The quest for personal perfection and the struggle in the human person became a means of giving effect to a realized messianism when hopes for global transformation seemed remote. The tension between old and new could focus primarily on the individual overcoming the passions of the flesh rather than the, apparently unrealistic, preoccupation with the breaking in of the new order in the wider world. Early Christian writings present us with a classic example of a radical movement engaging in that process of accommodation with the wider world leading to the channelling of the charismatic vision in a way which would guarantee preservation. The hope for the transformation of the world was kept alive, though Christians were increasingly accepting of many of the institutions of society while they enjoyed, and looked forward to, the messianic kingdom. The early Christians did not reject Jewish political messianism, therefore, by replacing it with a doctrine of a spiritual Messiah, at least immediately. The typical

30. On the importance of eschatology see Rowland, *Christian Origins*.

features of a Jewish this-worldly eschatology, remained an important component of belief until at least the end of the second century.[31] So I disagree with Gershom Scholem,[32] at least as far as the earliest period of the church is concerned, that there is a clear difference between messianism in Judaism and Christianity, the former being centred on this world and its transformation, the latter being of a more spiritual kind. The continuous emergence of chiliastic movements indebted to messianism throughout Christian history is testimony to the resilience of this dimension of Christianity's messianic heritage.[33] It is in the elucidation of the phenomenon of the rise and fall and the mutation, of a radical religion that the investigation of millennial and apocalyptic movements is so important and may, in fact, offer just as important insights into the character and development of earliest Christianity and its theology as sources which come from the Second Temple period.[34]

It is a feature of radical movements in Christian history, where the barrier between divine and human is broken down, that an individual or group becomes the bearer of the divine nature. The divine can then be apprehended by those who are spiritually sensitive to its working within the human person, who are not dependent for that insight solely on specialized knowledge of the Scriptures or conventional wisdom, however authoritative. For them God speaks directly, and Scripture and

31. Daley, *The Hope of the Early Church*.

32. G. Scholem, *The Messianic Idea in Judaism and other Essays on Jewish Spirituality* (New York: Allen & Unwin, 1971), pp. 1-2: 'A totally different concept of redemption determines the attitude to messianism in Judaism and Christianity. What appears to the one as a proud indication of its understanding and positive achievement of its message is most unequivocally belittled and disputed by the other. Judaism, in all its forms and manifestations, has always maintained a concept of redemption as an event which takes place publicly, on the stage of history and within the community... In contrast, Christianity conceives of redemption as an event in the spiritual and unseen realm, in the private world of each individual, and which effects an inner transformation which need not correspond to anything outside... The Church was convinced that...it had overcome an external conception that was bound to the material world...the reinterpretation of the prophetic promises of the Bible to refer to a realm of inwardness'. Also M. Walzer, *Exodus and Revolution* (New York: HarperCollins, 1985), pp. 122-23.

33. N. Cohn, *The Pursuit of the Millennium* (London: Secker & Warburg 1957).

34. See W.D. Davies, 'From Schweitzer to Scholem', in W. D Davies, *Jewish and Pauline Studies* (London: SPCK 1984), pp. 257-77, and J. Taubes, 'The Price of Messianism', in *JJS* 33 (1982) (*Essays in Honour of Yigael Yadin*), pp. 595-600.

tradition provide a secondary support for insight obtained by other means. The important thing is to respond to the prompting of the Spirit and subordinate the letter to the Spirit, a view outlined by Paul in 1 Cor. 2.10-16. But as later chapters of 1 Corinthians indicate such devotion to the Spirit required the complementary restraint of the practical wisdom of the apostolic teaching.

Many examples could be offered of later Christians who attached great weight to this doctrine. I mention one, from the Radical Reformation, who would not normally feature in discussions of New Testament theology: Thomas Muentzer, who perished in the Peasants' War in 1525. His spirituality was imbued with the outlook of late mediaeval mysticism. The Elect know, by the prompting of the Holy Spirit within, the mind of God: 'We fleshly, earthly men shall become gods through the incarnation of Christ, and at the same time God's scholars, taught and made god-like by himself, utterly and completely transformed into him, so that our earthly life is taken into the heavenlies' (echoes of Ephesians here).[35] For Muentzer the whole process of becoming a disciple involved a period of trial and identification with the sufferings of Christ, sentiments which echo Paul's language in 2 Corinthians. It is only through the period of spiritual turmoil that true faith can come. Paul wrote that the mark of the spirit of the Messiah was to bear the same kind of reproach as the Messiah.

A similar story can be found in succeeding centuries. In the seventeenth century, for example, radicals in Judaism and Christianity, Sabbatai Sevi (who himself claimed to be Messiah), Gerrard Winstanley and the Diggers, the radicals who were the forerunners of Quakerism, and later William Blake and his antinomian contemporaries all provide a rich source for the kind of comparative study which may be a suggestive guide to understanding the dynamics of the messianism of early Christianity. Perhaps they glimpsed something of that transgression of the bounds of normality which has often characterized outbursts of messianic enthusiasm, and so they may have been able to empathize with what made Paul and other early Christians tick in ways which our balanced rationalism and suspicion of enthusiasm often prevent us from seeing. But that is another story.

35. Discussed briefly in C. Rowland, *Radical Christianity* (Oxford: Polity Press, 1988), pp. 89-101; C. Hill, *The World Turned Upside Down* (Harmondsworth: Penguin Books, 1972); and A. Bradstock, *Faith in the Revolution* (London: SPCK, 1997).

INDEXES

INDEX OF REFERENCES

OLD TESTAMENT

Please note that where Hebrew and English verse numbers differ,
the Index refers to the Hebrew numbering

10.16	359	2.2	341	6.15	347
10.18	359	2.4	201	9–14	351, 353,
		2.20-23	305		363, 364
Hosea		2.21-23	343	9	352, 354,
2.16-17	326	2.21	341		409
7.7	72	2.23	340, 342	9.1–11.3	352
8.4	280			9.1-8	353
10.3-4	280	*Zechariah*		9.7	356
11.1	276	1–8	340, 343,	9.8	355, 356
			347, 349,	9.9-10	351, 353,
Joel			351, 358,		354, 356,
3.1-5	357		364		357, 409
3.1-2	350	2.3	428	9.9	355, 409,
		2.15	343		477
Amos		3.1	201	9.10	354, 357
1.5	137	3.6-10	347	9.11	354
1.8	137	3.8	201, 305,	9.13	354
2.3	72		344, 347	9.16	123, 125
5.26-27	453	4	343	9.25	358
7–8	249	4.6-10	305, 342,	10.1-3	352, 353
7	247		343, 347,	10.11	137
7.9-17	250		348	11.4-17	353
7.15	341	4.6	343, 344	11.22	358
8.2	250	4.7-10	344	12.1–13.6	352
9.11	263	4.10	343	12.1	352, 353
		4.14	348, 443,	12.7–13.1	351, 356
Micah			450	12.7	356
3.11	253	5	345	12.8	356, 357
4.8	339	6	121, 122,	12.10	357
5.1-3	339		129	13.1	357
5.1	432	6.9-15	346, 347	13.7-9	353
		6.11	121, 122,	14	228, 352,
Habakkuk			129, 201,		353, 409
1.10	440		305	14.9	490
1.12	201	6.12-13	305		
		6.12	344	*Malachi*	
Haggai		6.13	344, 347,	3.1	350
1.1	201, 341		348	3.5	350
1.12	201	6.14	121, 346,	3.23-24	350
1.14	201, 341		347		

APOCRYPHA

1 Esdras		9.40	414	3–4	408
1.32	414	15.8	414	7.28	425, 427
4.6-15	414			7.29	432
4.13	414	*2 Esdras*		12.32-33	427
5.5-6	414	3–14	408, 422	12.32	427

OTHER ANCIENT WORKS

INDEX OF AUTHORS

JOURNAL FOR THE STUDY OF THE OLD TESTAMENT
SUPPLEMENT SERIES

Lightning Source UK Ltd.
Milton Keynes UK
UKOW04f1238190114

224825UK00002B/22/P

9 780567 574343